Lecture Notes in Computer Science 6544

Commenced Publication in 1973
Founding and Former Series Editors:
Gerhard Goos, Juris Hartmanis, and Jan van Leeuwen

Alex Biryukov Guang Gong
Douglas R. Stinson (Eds.)

Selected Areas in Cryptography

17th International Workshop, SAC 2010
Waterloo, Ontario, Canada, August 12-13, 2010
Revised Selected Papers

Springer

Volume Editors

Alex Biryukov
University of Luxembourg, FSTC
6, rue Richard Coudenhove-Kalergi, 1359 Luxembourg-Kirchberg, Luxembourg
E-mail: alex.biryukov@uni.lu

Guang Gong
University of Waterloo, Department of Electrical and Computer Engineering
Waterloo, Ontario, Canada, N2L 3G1
E-mail: ggong@uwaterloo.ca

Douglas R. Stinson
University of Waterloo, David R. Cheriton School of Computer Science
Waterloo, Ontario, N2L 3G1, Canada
E-mail: dstinson@uwaterloo.ca

ISSN 0302-9743
e-ISSN 1611-3349
ISBN 978-3-642-19573-0
ISBN 978-3-642-19574-7 (eBook)
DOI 10.1007/978-3-642-19574-7
Springer Heidelberg Dordrecht London New York

Library of Congress Control Number: 2011922161

CR Subject Classification (1998): E.3, D.4.6, K.6.5, F.2.1-2, C.2, H.4.3

LNCS Sublibrary: SL 4 – Security and Cryptology

Typesetting: Camera-ready by author, data conversion by Scientific Publishing Services, Chennai, India

Printed on acid-free paper

Springer is part of Springer Science+Business Media (www.springer.com)

Preface

The book in front of you contains the proceedings of SAC 2010, the 17th Annual Workshop on Selected Areas in Cryptography. SAC 2010 took place on the campus of the University of Waterloo, Ontario, Canada, during August 12–13. There were 78 participants from 16 countries. Previous workshops in this series were held at Queen's University in Kingston (1994, 1996, 1998, 1999, and 2005), Carleton University in Ottawa (1995, 1997, and 2003), the University of Waterloo (2000, 2004), the Fields Institute in Toronto (2001), the Memorial University of Newfoundland in St. John's (2002), Concordia University in Montréal (2006), the University of Ottawa (2007), Mount Allison University in Sackville (2008), and the University of Calgary (2009).

The objective of the workshop is to present cutting-edge research in the designated areas of cryptography and to facilitate future research through an informal and friendly workshop setting. Now in its 17th year, the SAC workshop series has established itself as a premier international forum for information, discussion and exchange of ideas in cryptographic research.

Starting in 2008, SAC has been organized in cooperation with the International Association for Cryptologic Research (IACR). The themes for SAC 2010 were:

- Design and analysis of symmetric key primitives and cryptosystems, including block and stream ciphers, hash functions and MAC algorithms
- Efficient implementations of symmetric and public key algorithms
- Mathematical and algorithmic aspects of applied cryptology
- Applications of coding theory and combinatorics in cryptography

The workshop attracted 90 submissions and the paper review was double-blind. Each paper was reviewed by three members of the Program Committee and submissions that were co-authored by a member of Program Committee received two additional reviews. In all, 24 papers were accepted for presentation at the workshop. The accepted papers covered a wide range of topics in cryptography, including hash functions, stream ciphers, efficient implementations, coding and combinatorics, block ciphers, side channel attacks and mathematical aspects. In addition to these 24 presentations, two invited talked completed the technical program:

- Keith Martin gave the Stafford Tavares Lecture on "The Rise and Fall and Rise of Combinatorial Key Predistribution."
- Alexandra Boldyreva gave a lecture dealing with "Search on Encrypted Data in the Symmetric-Key Setting."

We are grateful to the authors of all the submitted papers. We also would like to thank the Program Committee and the many external reviewers for their hard work and expertise in selecting the high-quality research papers for presentation at the conference. A list of all external referees appears here.

We would like to thank Philip Regier and Fernando Rivero Hernandez for technical support, and Lisa Szepaniak for her constant support. Our special thanks go to Chris Schroeder for her endless efforts that ensured the smooth running of the workshop, to Xinxin Fan for his tremendous help in compiling the proceedings, and to Qi Chai for the design and host of the website of SAC 2010.

Finally, we gratefully acknowledge the Department of Electrical and Computer Engineering and the David R. Cheriton School of Computer Science of the University of Waterloo, and the Fields Institute for Research in Mathematical Science (Toronto) for their enthusiastic and generous financial support.

December 2010

Alex Biryukov
Guang Gong
Douglas Stinson

Organization

The SAC workshop series is managed by the SAC Organizing Board, in cooperation with the International Association for Cryptologic Research (IACR).

SAC Organizing Board

Carlisle Adams (Chair)	University of Ottawa, Canada
Roberto Avanzi	Ruhr University Bochum, Germany
Orr Dunkelman	Weizmann Institute of Science, Israel
Francesco Sica	Mount Allison University, Canada
Doug Stinson	University of Waterloo, Canada
Nicolas Theriault	Universidad de Talca, Chile
Mike Jacobson	University of Calgary, Canada
Vincent Rijmen	Graz University of Technology, Austria
Amr Youssef	Concordia University, Canada

SAC 2010 Organizing Committee

Alex Biryukov	University of Luxembourg, Luxembourg
Guang Gong	University of Waterloo, Canada
Douglas Stinson	University of Waterloo, Canada

Program Committee

Roberto Avanzi	Ruhr University Bochum, Germany
Paulo Barreto	University of Sao Paulo, Brazil
Simon Blackburn	Royal Holloway, University of London, UK
Christophe De Cannière	Katholieke Universiteit Leuven, Belgium
Anne Canteaut	INRIA, France
Joan Daemen,	ST Microelectronics, Belgium
Orr Dunkelman	Weizmann Institute of Science, Israel
Henri Gilbert	Orange Labs, France
Helena Handschuh	Katholieke Universiteit Leuven, Belgium and Intrinsic-ID Inc., USA
Martin Hell	Lund University, Sweden
Howard Heys	Memorial University, Canada
Tetsu Iwata	Nagoya University, Japan
Mike Jacobson	University of Calgary, Canada
David Jao	University of Waterloo, Canada
Marc Joye	Technicolor, France

Tanja Lange	Technische Universiteit Eindhoven, The Netherlands
Barbara Masucci	Università di Salerno, Italy
Ali Miri	Ryerson University and University of Ottawa, Canada
Ilya Mironov	Microsoft Research, USA
David Naccache	ENS, France
Kaisa Nyberg	Helsinki University of Technology and NOKIA, Finland
Carles Padró	Universitat Politecnica de Catalunya, Spain
Maura Paterson	Birkbeck University of London, UK
Svetla Petkova-Nikova	K.U. Leuven Belgium and University of Twente, The Netherlands
Bart Preneel	Katholieke Universiteit Leuven, Belgium
Christian Rechberger	Katholieke Universiteit Leuven, Belgium
Thomas Ristenpart	UC San Diego, USA
Rei Safavi-Naini	University of Calgary, Canada
Yu Sasaki	NTT, Japan
Martijn Stam	EPFL, Switzerland
François-Xavier Standaert	Université Catholique de Louvain, Belgium
Tamir Tassa	The Open University, Israel
Nicolas Theriault	Universidad de Talca, Chile
Serge Vaudenay	EPFL, Switzerland
Ruizhong Wei	Lakehead University, Canada
Amr Youssef	Concordia University, Canada
Gilles Zemor	Université Bordeaux, France

External Reviewers

Martin Ågren
Hadi Ahmadi
Toru Akishita
Elena Andreeva
Paolo D'Arco
Gilles Van Assche
Jean-Philippe Aumasson
Balasingham Balamohan
Lejla Batina
Daniel J. Bernstein
Guido Bertoni
Olivier Billet
Joppe Bos
Julien Bringer
Billy Brumley
David Cash
Guilhem Castagnos
Hervé Chabanne
Chen-Mou Cheng
Sarah Chisholm
Stelvio Cimato
Baudoin Collard
Thomas Eisenbarth
Junfeng Fan
Anna Lisa Ferrara
Felix Fontein
Kris Gaj
Clemente Galdi
Nicolas Gama
Benedikt Gierlichs
Matthew Green
Risto M. Hakala

Jens Hermans
Miia Hermelin
Javier Herranz
Naofumi Homma
Sebastiaan Indesteege
Kimmo Järvinen
Jorge Nakahara Jr
Marcos Antonio Simplicio Junior
Dina Kamel
Shahram Khazaei
Chong Hee Kim
Aleksandar Kircanski
Thorsten Kleinjung
Miroslav Knezevic
Yang Li
Richard Lindner
Julio Lopez
Behzad Malek
Mark Manulis
Sarah Meiklejohn
Florian Mendel
Rafael Misoczki
Petros Mol
Nicky Mouha
Elke De Mulder
Yoni De Mulder
Kris Narayan
Maria Naya-Plasencia
Monica Nevins
Ventzislav Nikov
Dag Arne Osvik
Ayoub Otmani
Onur Özen
Francesco Palmieri
Goutam Paul
Chris Peikert
Thomas Peyrin
Hoi Ting Poon
Carla Rafols
Francesco Regazzoni
Oded Regev
Jean-René Reinhard
Mathieu Renauld
Vincent Rijmen
Andrea Röck
Markku-Juhani O. Saarinen
Juraj Šarinay
Martin Schläffer Arthur Schmidt
Peter Schwabe
Michael Scott
Pouyan Sepehrdad
Francesco Sica
Jamshid Shokrollahi
Claudio Soriente
Paul Stankovski
John Steinberger
Hung-Min Sun
Petr Sušil
Robert Szerwinski
Adrian Tang
Jean-Pierre Tillich
Deniz Toz
Ashraful Tuhin
Antonino Tumeo
Vesselin Velichkov
Damien Vergnaud
Nicolas Veyrat-Charvillon
Marion Videau
Panagiotis Voulgaris
Lei Wang
Pengwei Wang
Ralf-Philipp Weinmann
Kjell Wooding
Kan Yasuda
Sung-Ming Yen
Hirotaka Yoshida
Gregory Zaverucha

Sponsoring Institutions

Department of Electrical and Computer Engineering, University of Waterloo
David R. Cheriton School of Computer Science, University of Waterloo
Fields Institute for Research in Mathematical Science, Toronto, Canada

Table of Contents

Hash Functions I

Stream Ciphers

The Stafford Tavares Lecture

Efficient Implementations

Coding and Combinatorics

Block Ciphers

Side Channel Attacks

Invited Talk

Mathematical Aspects

Hash Functions II

Zero-Sum Distinguishers for Iterated Permutations and Application to KECCAK-f and Hamsi-256*

Christina Boura[1,2] and Anne Canteaut[1]

[1] SECRET Project-Team - INRIA Paris-Rocquencourt - B.P. 105
78153 Le Chesnay Cedex - France
[2] Gemalto - 6, rue de la Verrerie - 92447 Meudon sur Seine - France
{Christina.Boura,Anne.Canteaut}@inria.fr

Abstract. The zero-sum distinguishers introduced by Aumasson and Meier are investigated. First, the minimal size of a zero-sum is established. Then, we analyze the impacts of the linear and the nonlinear layers in an iterated permutation on the construction of zero-sum partitions. Finally, these techniques are applied to the KECCAK-f permutation and to Hamsi-256. We exhibit several zero-sum partitions for 20 rounds (out of 24) of KECCAK-f and some zero-sum partitions of size 2^{19} and 2^{10} for the finalization permutation in Hamsi-256.

Keywords: Hash functions, integral properties, zero-sums, SHA-3.

1 Introduction

The existence of zero-sum structures is a new distinguishing property which has been recently investigated by Aumasson and Meier [2], and by Knudsen and Rijmen [14]. For a given function F, a *zero-sum* is a set of inputs which sum to zero, and whose images by F also sum to zero. Such zero-sum properties can be seen as a generalization of multiset properties (a.k.a. integral properties) [10,15]. Classical integral attacks for block ciphers include higher-order differential attacks and saturation attacks. Similarly, zero-sum structures may exploit either the fact that the permutation or its inverse after a certain number of rounds has a low degree, or some saturation properties due to a low diffusion. The keypoint is that the first type of weakness arises from the nonlinear part of the function whereas the second type arises from its linear part. The first direction has been investigated in [2] for three SHA-3 candidates, Luffa, Hamsi and KECCAK. Here, we show that, when the nonlinear part of the round transformation consists of several parallel applications of a smaller Sbox, an improved bound on the degree of the iterated function can be deduced, leading to zero-sums with a smaller size. Moreover, we investigate the impact of the linear part of the inner round permutation on the construction of zero-sums. Then, combining both types of

* Partially supported by the French Agence Nationale de la Recherche through the SAPHIR2 project under Contract ANR-08-VERS-014.

A. Biryukov, G. Gong, and D.R. Stinson (Eds.): SAC 2010, LNCS 6544, pp. 1–17, 2011.

properties enables us to find zero-sum partitions for the inner permutations of two SHA-3 Round-2 candidates, KECCAK [4] and Hamsi-256 [16]. More precisely, we exhibit several zero-sum partitions up to 20 (out of 24) rounds of the inner permutation in KECCAK and we improve the zero-sum partitions found in [1] for the finalization permutation of Hamsi-256. Even if our results do not seem to affect the security of KECCAK and Hamsi-256, they point out that the involved inner permutation of Hamsi-256 and 20 rounds of the inner permutation of KECCAK do not have an ideal behavior.

The rest of the paper is organized as follows. Section 2 defines the notions of zero-sum and of zero-sum partition, and it also establishes the minimal size for a zero-sum. Section 3 analyzes how a low degree of the nonlinear part of the round transformation and of its inverse can be exploited for constructing zero-sum partitions. It also applies a result from [8], and shows that the size of the previously obtained zero-sum partitions can be improved when the nonlinear layer in the round transformation consists of several applications of a small Sbox. The role of the linear layer in the construction of zero-sum partitions is investigated in Section 4. Finally some applications to the inner permutation of KECCAK and to the finalization permutation of Hamsi-256 are presented in Sections 5 and 6.

2 Zero-Sum Structures and Distinguishing Properties

In the whole paper, the addition in $\mathbb{F}_2^n$, *i.e.* the bitwise exclusive-or will be denoted by $+$, while $\oplus$ will be used for denoting the direct sum of subspaces of $\mathbb{F}_2^n$.

Zero-sum distinguishers were firstly introduced by J.-P. Aumasson and W. Meier in [2].

Definition 1. *Let F be a function from $\mathbb{F}_2^n$ into $\mathbb{F}_2^m$. A* zero-sum *for F of size K is a subset $\{x_1, \ldots, x_K\} \subset \mathbb{F}_2^n$ of elements which sum to zero and for which the corresponding images by F also sum to zero,* i.e.,

$$\sum_{i=1}^{K} x_i = \sum_{i=1}^{K} F(x_i) = 0 .$$

2.1 Zero-Sums and Codewords in a Linear Code

We use standard notation of the algebraic coding theory (see [18]). A binary linear code of length n and dimension k, denoted by $[n, k]$, is a k-dimensional subspace of $\mathbb{F}_2^n$. It can then be defined by a $k \times n$ binary matrix G, named generator matrix for $\mathcal{C}$: $\mathcal{C} = \{xG, x \in \mathbb{F}_2^k\}$. Any $[n, k]$-linear code $\mathcal{C}$ is associated with its dual $[n, n-k]$-code, denoted by $\mathcal{C}^\perp$ and defined by $\mathcal{C}^\perp = \{x \in \mathbb{F}_2^n, \ x \cdot c = 0 \text{ for all } c \in \mathcal{C}\}$.

Let $(x_i, 0 \leq i < 2^n)$ denote the set of all elements in $\mathbb{F}_2^n$. To any function $F : \mathbb{F}_2^n \rightarrow \mathbb{F}_2^m$, we associate the linear code $\mathcal{C}_F$ of length 2^n and dimension $n+m$ defined by the generator matrix

$$G_F = \begin{pmatrix} x_0 & x_1 & x_2 & x_3 & \dots & x_{2^n-1} \\ F(x_0) & F(x_1) & F(x_2) & F(x_3) & \dots & F(x_{2^n-1}) \end{pmatrix},$$

where each entry is viewed as a binary column vector. Then, we get the following result.

Proposition 1. *Let F be a function from $\mathbb{F}_2^n$ into $\mathbb{F}_2^m$.*
The set of inputs $\{x_{i_1}, \dots, x_{i_K}\} \subset \mathbb{F}_2^n$ is a zero-sum *for F if and only if the codeword of Hamming weight K with support $\{i_1, \dots, i_K\}$ belongs to the dual code $\mathcal{C}_F^\perp$. Most notably, when $m = n$, we deduce that*

- *there exists at least one zero-sum of size 5 for F;*
- *F has no zero-sum of size less than or equal to 4 if and only if F is an almost perfect nonlinear permutation,* i.e., *if $\max_{a,b \neq 0} \#\{x \in \mathbb{F}_2^n,\ F(x+a)+F(x) = b\} = 2$.*

Proof. Clearly, a binary vector $(c_0, \dots, c_{2^n-1})$ belongs to $\mathcal{C}_F^\perp$ if and only if

$$\sum_{i=0}^{2^n-1} c_i x_i = 0 \text{ and } \sum_{i=0}^{2^n-1} c_i F(x_i) = 0 .$$

This equivalently means that the support of c, *i.e.*, $\{i, c_i = 1\}$, defines a zero-sum for F. Moreover, the size of the zero-sum corresponds to the Hamming weight of the codeword. For $m = n$, $\mathcal{C}_F^\perp$ is a linear code of length 2^n and dimension $2^n - 2n$. It is known that the minimum distance for such a linear code with these parameters cannot exceed 5 [6,11], implying that F has some zero-sums of size 5. The correspondence between the APN property and the fact that $\mathcal{C}_F^\perp$ has minimum distance 5 has been established in [9]. Since the smallest possible size for a non-trivial zero-sum is 3, F has some zero-sums of size 3 or 4 if and only if F is not APN. □

When F is a randomly chosen function from $\mathbb{F}_2^n$ into $\mathbb{F}_2^n$, it is clear that any subset of size K is a zero-sum with probability 2^{-2n}. Therefore, random functions have many zero-sums of size $K \geq 5$ and there exist efficient generic algorithms for finding zero-sums. For instance, the generalized birthday algorithm [19] finds a zero-sum of size 2^κ with complexity

$$\mathcal{O}\left(2^{\frac{2n}{\kappa+1}+\kappa}\right),$$

which corresponds to the $2^{\frac{2n}{\kappa+1}+\kappa}$ evaluations of F required for building the 2^κ initial lists of size $2^{\frac{2n}{\kappa+1}}$. When the size of the zero-sum, K, is larger than $2n$, the previous generic algorithm can be improved by the XHASH attack [3], as pointed out in [5,1]: the complexity of this improved algorithm essentially corresponds to K evaluations of F, while the generalized birthday algorithm behaves similarly only for $K \geq 2^{\sqrt{2n}}$. It is worth noticing that the information set decoding algorithm (and its variants [7]) can also be used for solving this problem and improve the previous algorithm when the size of the zero-sum is very small [12], but all these methods take as input a generator matrix for the code and then require a complete evaluation of F.

There is a trivial case where zero-sums can be easily found: any affine subspace of dimension $\deg(F)+1$ is a zero-sum for F, leading to a distinguishing property when $\deg(F) \leq n-1$ (resp. $\deg(F) \leq n-2$ if F is a permutation)[1]. These zero-sums exactly correspond to the minimum-weight codewords of $R(n, n-\deg(F)-1) \subset \mathcal{C}_F^{\perp}$, where $R(n,r)$ denotes the Reed-Muller code of length 2^n and order r, *i.e.*, the set of all Boolean functions of n variables and degree at most r. This is because $\mathcal{C}_F \subset R(n, \deg(F))$ and the dual of $R(n,r)$ is $R(n, n-r-1)$.

2.2 Zero-Sum Partitions

However, in the case where F is a permutation over $\mathbb{F}_2^n$, the minimum-weight codewords of $R(n, n-\deg(F)-1)$ correspond to zero-sums with an additional property: any coset of such a zero-sum is still a zero-sum. This leads to a much stronger property, named *zero-sum partition.*

Definition 2. *Let P be a permutation from $\mathbb{F}_2^n$ into $\mathbb{F}_2^n$. A* zero-sum partition *for P of size $K = 2^k$ is a collection of 2^{n-k} disjoint zero-sums $X_i = \{x_{i,1}, \ldots, x_{i,2^k}\} \subset \mathbb{F}_2^n$,* i.e.,

$$\bigcup_{i=1}^{2^{n-k}} X_i = \mathbb{F}_2^n \text{ and } \sum_{j=1}^{2^k} x_{i,j} = \sum_{j=1}^{2^k} P(x_{i,j}) = 0, \ \forall 1 \leq i \leq 2^{n-k} .$$

A generic algorithm for finding a zero-sum partition of size 2^κ, with $2^\kappa \geq 2n$, consists in iteratively applying the XHASH attack as follows: we first apply this method for finding a zero-sum of size 2^{n-1}, which defines a zero-sum partition of $\mathbb{F}_2^n$. Then, within both resulting sets of size 2^{n-1}, the same technique is applied for finding a zero-sum of size 2^{n-2}. And the algorithm is iterated until a decomposition into zero-sums of size 2^κ is found. With this algorithm, we need to evaluate the permutation at all points except the last $2^\kappa - 2n$ points. Besides these evaluations of the permutation, the complexity of the algorithm can be approximated by $\left((2n)^3(2^{n-\kappa}-1)\right)$, leading to an overall complexity of roughly $\left(2^n + 2^{n-\kappa}(2n)^3 - 2^\kappa\right)$.

It clearly appears that, for a randomly chosen permutation, the description of the zero-sums found by such a generic algorithm requires the evaluation of the permutation at almost all points since the searching technique is not deterministic. This makes a huge difference with zero-sum partitions coming from

[1] In this paper, the *degree* of a Boolean function corresponds to the degree of its algebraic normal form. Moreover, the *degree* of a vectorial function $F : \mathbb{F}_2^n \to \mathbb{F}_2^m$ is defined as the highest degree of its coordinates.

a structural property of the permutation, which can be described by means of some close formula. Note that, structural zero-sums like those described in this paper can be used for proving that some given permutations do not satisfy the expected property, and this may only require the evaluation of the permutation on a few sets X_i.

3 Exploiting the Degree of the Nonlinear Part

In the rest of the paper we focus on the search for zero-sum partitions coming from structural properties of the permutation P, when P is an iterated permutation of the form

$$P = R_r \circ \ldots \circ R_1,$$

where all R_i are simpler permutations over $\mathbb{F}_2^n$, named the *round permutations*. In most practical cases, all R_i are derived from a unique keyed permutation for r different choices of the parameter. The first weakness which has been exploited in [2] for constructing zero-sum partitions for some iterated permutations is the low algebraic degrees of the round permutation and of its inverse.

3.1 Zero-Sum Partitions from Higher-Order Derivatives

As previously mentioned, the algebraic degree of a permutation F provides some particular zero-sums, which correspond to all affine subspaces of $\mathbb{F}_2^n$ with dimension $(\deg(F)+1)$. This result comes from the following property of higher-order derivatives of a function.

Definition 3. *[17] Let F be a function from $\mathbb{F}_2^n$ into $\mathbb{F}_2^m$. For any $a \in \mathbb{F}_2^n$ the* derivative *of F with respect to a is the function $D_aF(x) = F(x+a)+F(x)$. For any k-dimensional subspace V of $\mathbb{F}_2^n$, the k-th order derivative of F with respect to V is the function defined by*

$$D_VF(x) = D_{a_1}D_{a_2}\ldots D_{a_k}F(x) = \sum_{v\in V} F(x+v), \forall x \in \mathbb{F}_2^n .$$

It is well-known that the degree of any first-order derivative of a function is strictly less than the degree of the function. This simple remark, which is also exploited in higher-order differential attacks [13], implies that for every subspace V of dimension $(\deg F + 1)$,

$$D_VF(x) = \sum_{v\in V} F(x+v) = 0, \quad \text{for every} \quad x \in \mathbb{F}_2^n.$$

The fact that the permutation used in a hash function does not depend on any secret parameter allows to exploit the previous property starting from the middle, *i.e.*, from an intermediate internal state. This property was used by Aumasson and Meier [2] and also by Knudsen and Rijmen in the case of a known-key property of a block cipher [14]. The only information needed for finding such zero-sums on the iterated permutation using this first approach is an upper bound on the algebraic degrees of both the round transformation and its inverse.

More precisely, we consider $P = R_r \circ \ldots \circ R_1$, and we choose some integer t, $1 \leq t \leq r$. We define the following functions involved in the decomposition of P: F_{r-t} consists of the last $(r-t)$ round transformations, *i.e.*, $F_{r-t} = R_r \circ \ldots \circ R_{t+1}$ and G_t consists of the inverse of the first t round transformations, *i.e.*, $G_t = R_1^{-1} \circ \ldots \circ R_t^{-1}$. Then, we can find many zero-sum partitions for P by the technique introduced in [2] and described in the following proposition.

Proposition 2. *Let d_1 and d_2 be such that* $\deg(F_{r-t}) \leq d_1$ *and* $\deg(G_t) \leq d_2$. *Let V be any subspace of $\mathbb{F}_2^n$ of dimension $d+1$ where* $d = \max(d_1, d_2)$, *and let W denote the complement of V,* i.e., $V \oplus W = \mathbb{F}_2^n$. *Then, the sets*

$$X_a = \{G_t(a+z),\ z \in V\},\quad a \in W$$

form a zero-sum partition of $\mathbb{F}_2^n$ of size 2^{d+1} for the r-round permutation P.

Proof. Let a be any element in W. First, we prove that all input states $x \in X_a$ sum to zero:

$$\sum_{x \in X_a} x = \sum_{z \in V} G_t(a+z) = D_V G_t(a)$$

which is the value of a derivative of order $(d+1)$ of a function with degree $d_2 \leq d$ and thus it vanishes. Now, the images of these input states under P correspond to the images of the intermediate states z under F_{r-t}. Similarly, we have

$$\sum_{x \in X_a} P(x) = \sum_{z \in V} F_{r-t}(a+z) = D_V F_{r-t}(a)$$

which is the value of a derivative of order $(d+1)$ of a function of degree less than d. Thus, this sum vanishes, implying that each X_a is a zero-sum. Since all X_a are the images of disjoint sets by the permutation G_t, they are all disjoint and then they form a partition of $\mathbb{F}_2^n$. □

The permutations studied in [2] consist in iterating a low-degree round transformation. Then, the zero-sum partitions described in [2] are obtained by choosing for V a subspace spanned by $(d+1)$ elements of the canonical basis, where $d = \max(\deg(F_{r-t}), \deg(G_t))$.

3.2 An Improved Bound on the Degree Based on the Walsh Spectrum

It clearly appears from the description of the previous method that we are interested in estimating the degree of a composed permutation and of its inverse. If F and G are two mappings from $\mathbb{F}_2^n$ into $\mathbb{F}_2^n$, we can bound the degree of the composition $G \circ F$ by $\deg(G \circ F) \leq \deg(G)\deg(F)$. Though, this trivial bound is often very little representative of the real degree of the permutation, in particular if we are trying to estimate the degree after a high number of rounds. In some special cases, exploring the spectral properties of the permutation can lead to a better upper bound. In particular, it was shown by Canteaut and Videau [8] that the trivial bound can be improved when the values occurring in the Walsh spectrum of F are divisible by a high power of 2.

The Walsh spectrum of a vectorial function $F : \mathbb{F}_2^n \to \mathbb{F}_2^n$ consists of the Walsh spectra of all nonzero linear combinations of its coordinates:

$$\left\{ \sum_{x \in \mathbb{F}_2^n} (-1)^{b \cdot F(x) + a \cdot x}, b \in \mathbb{F}_2^n \setminus \{0\}, a \in \mathbb{F}_2^n \right\},$$

where $x \cdot y$ denotes the dot product between two vectors x and y. The divisibility by a large power of 2 of all elements in the Walsh spectrum of F may provide an upper bound on the degree of $G \circ F$.

Theorem 1. *[8] Let F be a function from $\mathbb{F}_2^n$ into $\mathbb{F}_2^n$ such that all values in its Walsh spectrum are divisible by 2^ℓ, for some integer ℓ. Then, for any $G : \mathbb{F}_2^n \to \mathbb{F}_2^n$, we have*

$$\deg(G \circ F) \leq n - \ell + \deg(G).$$

From now on, we focus on a very common case where the Walsh spectrum of the round permutation is divisible by a large power of 2 and when its nonlinear part, denoted by χ, consists of n/n_0 parallel applications of a small permutation χ_0 over $\mathbb{F}_2^{n_0}$. In this situation, any n-bit vector is seen as a collection of $n_r = n/n_0$ rows, where each row is an element in $\mathbb{F}_2^{n_0}$. Then, χ applies on each row separately. For implementation reasons, this situation occurs for many iterated permutations used in cryptography. Then, since the Walsh spectrum is invariant under composition with a linear transformation, for any $\alpha \in \mathbb{F}_2^n$, there exists some β such that

$$\mathcal{F}(R + \varphi_\alpha) = \mathcal{F}(\chi + \varphi_\beta) = \prod_{i=1}^{n_r} \mathcal{F}(\chi_0 + \varphi_{\beta_i}) . \quad (1)$$

Then, if all elements in the Walsh spectrum of χ_0 are divisible by 2^{ℓ_0}, we deduce that the Walsh spectrum of the round transformation is divisible by $2^{n_r \ell_0}$.

4 Exploiting the Structure of the Diffusion Part

Besides the degree of the round transformation, a second element can be exploited for constructing zero-sum partitions, similarly to the techniques used for mounting saturation attacks. Indeed, the fact that χ consists of many parallel applications of a smaller function can be used for extending the previously described zero-sum partitions to one additional round. Moreover, we can also exploit the fact that a few iterations of the round permutation R are not enough for providing full diffusion. This leads to some *multiset* properties for a small number of rounds.

In the following, we denote by B_i, $0 \leq i < n_r$, the n_0-dimensional subspaces corresponding to the rows, *i.e.*,

$$B_i = \langle e_{n_0 i}, \ldots, e_{n_0 i + n_0 - 1} \rangle$$

where $e_0, \ldots, e_{n-1}$ denotes the canonical basis of $\mathbb{F}_2^n$ and where the positions of the n bits in the internal state are numbered such that the n_0-bit rows correspond to n_0 consecutive bits.

4.1 One-Round Multiset Property

First, we show how to extend a number of zero-sum partitions that have been found for t rounds, to $t+1$ rounds, without increasing the complexity. The idea is the following: the zero-sum partition described in Proposition 2 is obtained from a set of intermediate states after t rounds, which is a coset of a $(d+1)$-dimensional subspace V. Moreover, such a zero-sum partition is obtained for any choice of V. However, we now focus on those subspaces V which correspond to a collection of any $\lceil (d+1)/n_0 \rceil$ rows: $V = \bigoplus_{i \in \mathcal{I}} B_i$, for some set $\mathcal{I} \subset \{0, \ldots, n_r\}$ of size $\lceil (d+1)/n_0 \rceil$. Since χ applies to the rows separately, variables from different rows are not mixed after the application of χ. This implies that $\chi(a+V) = b+V$, for some b. Then, we can find some zero-sum partitions of size 2^{d+1} for the r-round permutation P as follows.

Proposition 3. *Let d_1 and d_2 be such that $\deg(F_{r-t-1}) \leq d_1$ and $\deg(G_t) \leq d_2$. Let us decompose the round transformation after t rounds into $R_{t+1} = A_2 \circ \chi \circ A_1$ where both A_1 and A_2 have degree 1. Let $\mathcal{I}$ be any subset of $\{0, \ldots, n_r - 1\}$ of size $\lceil (d+1)/n_0 \rceil$,*

$$V = \bigoplus_{i \in \mathcal{I}} B_i$$

and W be its complement. Then, the sets

$$X_a = \{(G_t \circ A_1^{-1})(a+z),\ z \in V\},\quad a \in W$$

form a zero-sum partition of $\mathbb{F}_2^n$ of size 2^k, with $k = n_0 \lceil \frac{d+1}{n_0} \rceil$, for the r-round permutation P.

Proof. For any a, the sum of all input states in X_a is given by

$$\sum_{x \in X_a} x = \sum_{z \in V} G_t \circ A_1^{-1}(a+z) = D_V(G_t \circ A_1^{-1})(a) = 0$$

since $\deg(G_t \circ A_1^{-1}) = \deg(G_t) \leq d$. Using that $\chi(a+V) = b+V$, we obtain that the sum of the corresponding outputs satisfies

$$\sum_{x \in X_a} P(x) = \sum_{z \in V} F_{r-t-1} \circ A_2 \circ \chi(a+z) = \sum_{z \in V} F_{r-t-1} \circ A_2(b+z)$$
$$= D_V(F_{r-t-1} \circ A_2)(b) = 0$$

since $\deg(F_{r-t-1} \circ A_2) = \deg(F_{r-t-1}) \leq d$. □

4.2 Multiset Property on Several Rounds

Now, we consider some multiset properties on several rounds which arise both from the particular structure of the round transformation and from the linear part, and we show how they can be exploited to further extend the already known zero-sum partitions to more rounds. For the sake of clarity, we first describe a 2-round multiset property for Rounds $(t+1)$ and $(t+2)$. We decompose those two rounds into

$$R_{t+2} \circ R_{t+1} = A_2 \circ \chi \circ A \circ \chi \circ A_1$$

where A_1, A_2 and A have degree 1.

Theorem 2. *Let d_1 and d_2 be such that $\deg(F_{r-t-2}) \leq d_1$ and $\deg(G_t) \leq d_2$. Let L denote the linear part of the affine permutation A. Let W be a k-dimensional subspace of $\mathbb{F}_2^n$ satisfying both following conditions*

(i) *there exists a set $\mathcal{I} \subset \{0, \ldots, n_r - 1\}$ such that*

$$W \subset \bigoplus_{i \in \mathcal{I}} B_i \text{ and } |\mathcal{I}| \leq n_r - \left\lceil \frac{d_2 + 1}{n_0} \right\rceil .$$

(ii) *there exists a set $\mathcal{J} \subset \{0, \ldots, n_r - 1\}$ such that*

$$L(W) \subset \bigoplus_{j \in \mathcal{J}} B_j \text{ and } |\mathcal{J}| \leq n_r - \left\lceil \frac{d_1 + 1}{n_0} \right\rceil .$$

Let V denote the complement of W. Then, the sets

$$X_a = \{(G_t \circ A_1^{-1} \circ \chi^{-1})(a + z),\ z \in V\},\quad a \in W$$

form a zero-sum partition of $\mathbb{F}_2^n$ of size 2^{n-k} for the r-round permutation P.

Proof. The definition of the sets X_a means that we choose the intermediate states z after the nonlinear layer in R_{t+1} in a coset of V. The required properties on W imply that there exist two subspaces B_b and B_f such that

$$B_b = \bigoplus_{i \in \overline{\mathcal{I}}} B_i \subset V \text{ and } B_f = \bigoplus_{j \in \overline{\mathcal{J}}} B_j \subset L(V)$$

with $\overline{\mathcal{I}} = \{0, \ldots, n_r - 1\} \setminus \mathcal{I}$ and $\overline{\mathcal{J}} = \{0, \ldots, n_r - 1\} \setminus \mathcal{J}$, where the last relation comes from the fact that $L(V)$ and $L(W)$ are complementary. From the second property, we deduce that $A(V)$ can be seen as a union of cosets of B_f:

$$A(V) = \bigcup_{b \in \mathcal{E}} (b + B_f) ,$$

where $\mathcal{E}$ is a subset of $\mathbb{F}_2^n$. Moreover, the same property holds for the image by A of any coset of V. Then, since χ applies to the rows separately, variables from different rows are not mixed after the application of χ. This implies that

$$\chi(A(V)) = \bigcup_{b \in \mathcal{E}'} (b + B_f) ,$$

where $\mathcal{E}'$ is another subset of $\mathbb{F}_2^n$. By definition, the images by P of all elements in X_a correspond to the images of $a+z$, $z \in V$, by $F_{r-t-2} \circ A_2 \circ \chi \circ A$. It follows that their sum is given by

$$\sum_{z \in V} F_{r-t-2} \circ A_2 \circ \chi \circ A(a+z) = \sum_{b \in \mathcal{E}'} \sum_{x \in B_f} (F_{r-t-2} \circ A_2)(b+x)$$
$$= \sum_{b \in \mathcal{E}'} D_{B_f}(F_{r-t-2} \circ A_2)(b) = 0 .$$

Actually, this derivative vanishes since

$$\dim B_f \geq n - n_0 |\mathcal{J}| > d_1 .$$

Now, we compute backwards the images of $a+V$ by $G_t \circ A_1^{-1} \circ \chi^{-1}$. Since V satisfies $B_b \subset V$, it can be written as a union of cosets of B_b. As χ^{-1} does not mix the rows, we deduce that

$$\chi^{-1}(a+V) = \bigcup_{b \in \mathcal{E}''} (b + B_b) ,$$

for some set $\mathcal{E}'' \subset \mathbb{F}_2^n$. Then, the sum of the corresponding input states $x \in X_a$ is given by

$$\sum_{x \in X_a} x = \sum_{z \in V} (G_t \circ A_1^{-1} \circ \chi^{-1})(a+z) = \sum_{b \in \mathcal{E}''} \sum_{x \in B_b} (G_t \circ A_1^{-1})(b+x)$$
$$= \sum_{b \in \mathcal{E}''} D_{B_b}(G_t \circ A_1^{-1})(b) = 0 .$$

Actually, this derivative vanishes since

$$\dim B_b \geq n - n_0 |\mathcal{I}| > d_2 .$$

□

Figure 1 summarizes the steps of our method.

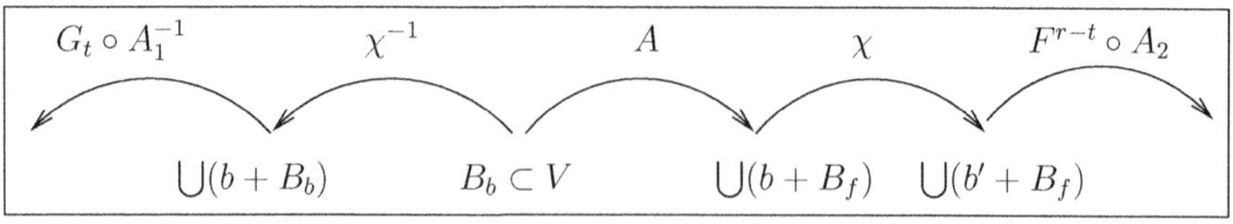

Fig. 1. General method with a 2-round multiset property

Remark 1. There is a simple necessary condition on the existence of some W as in the previous theorem. We define the weight of any $x \in \mathbb{F}_2^n$ with respect to the decomposition into rows, $H_w(x)$, as the number of rows on which x does not vanish. Then, a subspace W defined as in the previous theorem satisfies

$$\forall x \in W,\ H_w(x) \leq n_r - \left\lceil \frac{d_2+1}{n_0} \right\rceil \text{ and } H_w(L(x)) \leq n_r - \left\lceil \frac{d_1+1}{n_0} \right\rceil . \quad (2)$$

Obviously, this condition is also sufficient when $\dim W = 1$. In particular, the search for zero-sum partitions by the method described in Theorem 2 can be avoided by choosing for the linear part of the round transformation a function L such that

$$\min_{x \neq 0} \left(H_w(x) + H_w(L(x)) \right) > 2n_r - \left\lceil \frac{d_1+1}{n_0} \right\rceil - \left\lceil \frac{d_2+1}{n_0} \right\rceil .$$

Now, we can obviously use a similar property of the diffusion not only for 2 rounds of the round transformation, but for a higher number of rounds.

Theorem 3. *Let d_1 and d_2 be such that $\deg(F_{r-t-2}) \leq d_1$ and $\deg(G_t) \leq d_2$. Let L denote the linear part of the affine permutation A. Let W be a k-dimensional subspace of $\mathbb{F}_2^n$ satisfying all following conditions for two nonzero integers s_b and s_f:*

(i) *there exists a set $\mathcal{I}_1 \subset \{0, \ldots, n_r - 1\}$ such that*

$$W \subset \bigoplus_{i \in \mathcal{I}_1} B_i \text{ and } |\mathcal{I}_1| \leq n_r - \left\lceil \frac{d_2+1}{n_0} \right\rceil .$$

(ii) *there exists a set $\mathcal{J}_1 \subset \{0, \ldots, n_r - 1\}$ such that*

$$L(W) \subset \bigoplus_{j \in \mathcal{J}_1} B_j \text{ and } |\mathcal{J}_1| \leq n_r - \left\lceil \frac{d_1+1}{n_0} \right\rceil .$$

(iii) *for all s, $1 \leq s < s_f$, there exists a set $\mathcal{J}_{s+1} \subset \{0, \ldots, n_r - 1\}$ such that*

$$L\left(\bigoplus_{j \in \mathcal{J}_s} B_j \right) \subset \bigoplus_{j \in \mathcal{J}_{s+1}} B_j \text{ and } |\mathcal{J}_{s_f}| \leq n_r - \left\lceil \frac{d_1+1}{n_0} \right\rceil .$$

(iv) *for all s, $1 \leq s < s_b$, there exists a set $\mathcal{I}_{s+1} \subset \{0, \ldots, n_r - 1\}$ such that*

$$L^{-1}\left(\bigoplus_{j \in \mathcal{I}_s} B_j \right) \subset \bigoplus_{j \in \mathcal{I}_{s+1}} B_j \text{ and } |\mathcal{I}_{s_b}| \leq n_r - \left\lceil \frac{d_2+1}{n_0} \right\rceil .$$

Let V denote the complement of W. Then, the sets

$$X_a = \{(G_t \circ A_1^{-1} \circ (\chi^{-1} \circ A^{-1})^{s_b - 1} \circ \chi^{-1})(a + z),\ z \in V\},\ \ a \in W$$

form a zero-sum partition of $\mathbb{F}_2^n$ of size 2^{n-k} for the $(r + s_b + s_f - 2)$-round permutation P.

It is worth noticing that there is no requirement on the sizes of the intermediate states $\mathcal{I}_2, \ldots, \mathcal{I}_{s_b-1}$ and $\mathcal{J}_2, \ldots, \mathcal{J}_{f_b-1}$. However, by definition, the conditions on the sizes of $\mathcal{I}_{s_b}$ and $\mathcal{I}_{s_f}$ obviously imply that the same bounds hold for the corresponding intermediate sets.

5 Application to the KECCAK-*f* Permutation

5.1 The KECCAK-*f* Permutation

KECCAK [4] is one of the fourteen hash functions selected for the second round of the SHA-3 competition. Its mode of operation is the sponge construction. The inner primitive in KECCAK is a permutation, composed of several iterations of very similar round transformations. Within the KECCAK-family, the SHA-3 candidate operates on a 1600-bit state, which is represented by a 3-dimensional binary matrix of size $5 \times 5 \times 64$. Then, the state can be seen as 64 parallel slices, each one containing 5 rows and 5 columns. The permutation in KECCAK is denoted by KECCAK-$f[b]$, where b is the size of the state. So, for the SHA-3 candidate, $b = 1600$.

The number of rounds in KECCAK-$f[1600]$ was 18 in the original submission, and it has been updated to 24 for the second round. Every round R consists of a sequence of 5 permutations modifying the state:

$$R = \iota \circ \chi \circ \pi \circ \rho \circ \theta.$$

The functions θ, ρ, π, ι are transformations of degree 1 providing diffusion in all directions of the 3-dimensional state. Then, keeping the same notation as in the previous section, we have $A_1 = \pi \circ \rho \circ \theta$, which is linear and $A_2 = \iota$, which corresponds to the addition of a constant value. Therefore, the linear part of $A = A_1 \circ A_2$ corresponds to $L = \pi \circ \rho \circ \theta$. The nonlinear layer, χ, is a quadratic permutation which is applied to each row of the 1600-bit state. In other words, 320 parallel applications of χ_0 are implemented in order to provide confusion. The inverse permutation, denoted by χ^{-1}, is a permutation of degree 3.

We need to define a numbering for the $n = 1600$ bits of the internal state of KECCAK-f. We associate to the bit of the state positioned at the intersection of the i-th row and the j-th column of the k-th slice, *i.e.*, to the element (i, j, k), $0 \leq i \leq 4$, $0 \leq j \leq 4$, $0 \leq k \leq 63$, the number $25k + 5j + i$. We recall that the elements of the form $(0, 0, z)$ are found in the center of each slice. Then, the 5-dimensional subspace corresponding to the j-th row in the k-th slice, $0 \leq j \leq 4$, $0 \leq k \leq 63$, is defined by

$$B_{5k+j} = \langle e_{25k+5j}, e_{25k+5j+1}, e_{25k+5j+2}, e_{25k+5j+3}, e_{25k+5j+4} \rangle.$$

Aumasson and Meier [2] used the trivial bound on the degree of a composed function in order to find many zero-sum partitions for 16 rounds of the KECCAK-f permutation. Actually, the degree of the permutation after 10 rounds is at most $2^{10} = 1024$ and the degree of the inverse after 6 rounds is at most $3^6 = 729$. Thus, they choose the intermediate states after $t = 6$ rounds in a coset of a subspace V of dimension 1025 and compute 6 rounds backwards. This method leads to many zero-sum partitions of size 2^{1025}.

5.2 Zero-Sum Partitions for 18 Rounds of Keccak-*f*

We first show that the degree of 7 rounds of the inverse Keccak-f permutation cannot exceed 1369 and thus is much lower than the estimation given by the trivial bound $\min(3^7 = 2187, 1599)$. Actually, all elements in the Walsh spectrum of the nonlinear permutation χ_0 are divisible by 2^3. Since the Walsh spectra of a permutation and of its inverse are the same, we deduce that the Walsh spectrum of χ_0^{-1} is also divisible by 2^3. It is worth noticing that $2^{\frac{n+1}{2}}$ is the lowest possible divisibility for the Walsh spectrum of a quadratic permutation of $\mathbb{F}_2^n$, n odd. Then, the fact that the Walsh spectrum of χ_0^{-1} is divisible by 2^3 holds for any other choice for the quadratic permutation χ_0 over $\mathbb{F}_2^5$. There are $n_r = 320$ parallel applications of χ_0. Then, we deduce from (1) that the Walsh spectra of R and R^{-1} applied on the whole 1600-bit state are divisible by $2^{3\times 320} = 2^{960}$. Using that 6 rounds of the inverse of the round permutation have degree at most $3^6 = 729$, Theorem 1 leads to

$$\deg(R^{-7}) = \deg(R^{-6} \circ R^{-1}) \leq 1600 - 960 + \deg(R^{-6}) \leq 1369 \,.$$

This new bound allows us to find zero-sum partitions for 17 rounds of the permutation, by choosing the intermediate states after $t = 7$ rounds in the cosets of a subspace V of dimension 1370 and by computing 7 rounds backwards. Moreover, we can apply Proposition 3 with $t = 7$: by choosing $V = \bigoplus_{i\in\mathcal{I}} B_i$ where $\mathcal{I}$ is any collection of 274 rows, we can find some zero-sum partitions of size 2^{1370} for 18 rounds of Keccak-f.

5.3 Zero-Sum Partitions for 19 Rounds of Keccak-*f*

Now, we apply Theorem 2 with $t = 7$ to 19 rounds of Keccak-f. As previously explained, $F_{r-t-2} = F_{10}$ has degree at most 1024 and $G_t = G_7$ has degree at most 1369. We then need to find a subspace W such that there exist two sets of rows, $\mathcal{I}, \mathcal{J} \subset \{0, \ldots, n_r - 1\}$ satisfying

$$W \subset \bigoplus_{i\in\mathcal{I}} B_i \text{ with } |\mathcal{I}| \leq 46 \text{ and } L(W) \subset \bigoplus_{j\in\mathcal{J}} B_j \text{ with } |\mathcal{J}| \leq 115 \,.$$

Here, we take for W the subspace spanned by the first 4 slices, *i.e.*, $W = \bigoplus_{i=0}^{19} B_i$. Then, we can check that there exists a subset $\mathcal{J}$ of size 114 such that $L(W) \subset \bigoplus_{j\in\mathcal{J}} B_j$, implying that the second condition is satisfied. The first condition obviously holds by definition of W. Since $\dim W = 5 \times 20 = 100$, we deduce from Theorem 2 that we have found a zero-sum partition of size 2^{1500} for 19 rounds of Keccak-f. It is worth noticing that the previous situation occurs when W is the subspace spanned by any 4 consecutive slices. Actually, all the step-mappings in the Keccak-f round permutation except ι are translation invariant in the z axis direction. Therefore, we obtain 64 zero-sum partitions of this type for the 19-round Keccak-f.

Though, we can further improve the complexity of the 19-round distinguisher by increasing the dimension of W, without at the same time increasing the cardinality of $\mathcal{J}$, where $L(W) \subset \bigoplus_{j\in\mathcal{J}} B_j$. In order to achieve this, we add to W a number of linearly independent vectors whose images by L lie in $\bigoplus_{j\in\mathcal{J}} B_j$ for the set $\mathcal{J}$ as before. The new considered subspace W is generated by the rows $0, \ldots, 19$ and by the following 39 linearly independent vectors.

$$\begin{array}{lllll}
e_{450} \oplus e_{460}, & e_{450} \oplus e_{465}, & e_{451} \oplus e_{461}, & e_{451} \oplus e_{466}, & e_{464} \oplus e_{469}, \\
e_{475} \oplus e_{485}, & e_{475} \oplus e_{490}, & e_{476} \oplus e_{486}, & e_{476} \oplus e_{491}, & e_{478} \oplus e_{498}, \\
e_{489} \oplus e_{494}, & e_{650} \oplus e_{660}, & e_{650} \oplus e_{665}, & e_{651} \oplus e_{666}, & e_{652} \oplus e_{662}, \\
e_{659} \oplus e_{664}, & e_{662} \oplus e_{672}, & e_{667} \oplus e_{672}, & e_{668} \oplus e_{673}, & e_{1100} \oplus e_{1110}, \\
e_{1102} \oplus e_{1112}, & e_{1102} \oplus e_{1117}, & e_{1103} \oplus e_{1113}, & e_{1103} \oplus e_{1118}, & e_{1105} \oplus e_{1110}, \\
e_{1106} \oplus e_{1116}, & e_{1125} \oplus e_{1135}, & e_{1127} \oplus e_{1137}, & e_{1127} \oplus e_{1142}, & e_{1138} \oplus e_{1143}, \\
e_{1150} \oplus e_{1160}, & e_{1152} \oplus e_{1162}, & e_{1162} \oplus e_{1167}, & e_{1163} \oplus e_{1168}, & e_{1175} \oplus e_{1180}, \\
e_{1175} \oplus e_{1185}, & e_{1175} \oplus e_{1190}, & e_{1177} \oplus e_{1187}, & e_{1188} \oplus e_{1193}. &
\end{array}$$

These 39 elements correspond to words whose support belongs to a single column and that have a Hamming weight of 2. Actually, any word X with support belonging to a single column and having even weight satisfies $\theta(X) = X$. Then, if X is a word of this type, the weight of $L(X)$, with respect to our definition in Remark 1, is exactly 2. One can easily check that $W \subset \bigoplus_{i\in\mathcal{I}} B_i$, with $|\mathcal{I}| = 46$ and $L(W) \subset \bigoplus_{j\in\mathcal{J}} B_j$, with $|\mathcal{J}| = 115$. Since $\dim W = 5 \times 20 + 39 = 139$, Theorem 2 leads to 64 new zero-sum partitions of size 2^{1461} for 19 rounds of KECCAK-f.

5.4 Zero-Sum Partitions for 20 Rounds of KECCAK-*f*

For finding a zero-sum partition for 20 rounds of KECCAK-f, we now apply Theorem 3 with $s_f = 2$, *i.e.*, we compute one additional step forwards. Then, we need to find a subspace W such that there exist some sets of rows, $\mathcal{I}$, $\mathcal{J}_1$ and $\mathcal{J}_2$ with $|\mathcal{I}| \leq 46$ and $|\mathcal{J}_2| \leq 115$ satisfying

$$W \subset \bigoplus_{i\in\mathcal{I}} B_i, \;\; L(W) \subset \bigoplus_{j\in\mathcal{J}_1} B_j \text{ and } L\left(\bigoplus_{j\in\mathcal{J}_1} B_j\right) \subset \bigoplus_{j\in\mathcal{J}_2} B_j .$$

As previously mentioned, the image by L of 4 consecutive slices involves 114 rows only. Then, we only have to find a subspace W such that the first condition holds and that $L(W)$ belongs to the union of 4 consecutive slices, namely slices s to $s+3$. For this search, we concentrate as before on the words with Hamming weight 2 whose support belongs to a single column. We want to find all words X of this form such that the two rows that are affected by $L(X)$ are positioned in at most two out of the four consecutive slices s to $s+3$, for a fixed s. For this, we need to look at the translation offsets of ρ, which is the function translating the bits in the z-direction. These offsets are given in Table 1(a). Let (x, y, z) and (x, y', z) be the coordinates of the two bits in the support of X. Let c_1 and c_2 be the offsets corresponding to the positions (x, y) and (x, y'). Then the image of X by L will affect two slices at distance $|c_1 - c_2|$.

Suppose that we can find two translation offsets in the same column of Table 1(a) having a difference smaller than or equal to 3, namely $c_1 = \text{Offset}(x_0, y_1)$, and $c_2 = \text{Offset}(x_0, y_2)$ with $0 \leq (c_2 - c_1) \leq 3$. Then, the word in the slice $z_0 = s - c_1 \bmod 64$ with support $\{(x_0, y_1, z_0), (x_0, y_2, z_0)\}$ will have an image belonging to the slices s and $s + (c_2 - c_1)$. The appropriate pairs of translation constants derived from Table 1(a) are given in Table 1(b).

Table 1. Finding appropriate pairs of translation constants

(a) The translation offsets of ρ for the SHA-3 candidates.

	$x=3$	$x=4$	$x=0$	$x=1$	$x=2$
$y=2$	25	39	3	10	43
$y=1$	55	20	36	44	6
$y=0$	28	27	0	1	62
$y=4$	56	14	18	2	61
$y=3$	21	8	41	45	15

(b) Appropriate pairs of offsets.

	(y_1, y_2)	(c_1, c_2)	$c_2 - c_1$
$x=0$	$(0,2)$	$(0,3)$	3
$x=1$	$(0,4)$	$(1,2)$	1
	$(1,3)$	$(44,45)$	1
$x=2$	$(0,4)$	$(62,61)$	1
$x=3$	$(1,4)$	$(55,56)$	1
	$(0,2)$	$(28,25)$	3

By using this technique, we find the following subspace W of dimension 14:

$$W = \langle\, e_1 \oplus e_{21},\quad e_{25} \oplus e_{35},\quad e_{26} \oplus e_{46},\quad e_{51} \oplus e_{71},\quad e_{102} \oplus e_{122},\\ e_{127} \oplus e_{147},\ e_{152} \oplus e_{172},\ e_{258} \oplus e_{273},\ e_{283} \oplus e_{298},\ e_{308} \oplus e_{323},\\ e_{531} \oplus e_{541},\ e_{556} \oplus e_{566},\ e_{581} \oplus e_{591},\ e_{1003} \oplus e_{1013} \rangle.$$

Clearly $W \subset \bigoplus_{i \in \mathcal{I}} B_i$ with $|I| < 114$ and we have computed that $L(W)$ belongs to the union of the slices 1, 2, 3 and 4. Since $\dim W = 14$ we deduce from Theorem 2 that we have found a zero-sum partition of size 2^{1586} for 20 rounds of Keccak-f. As previously explained, there are 64 such zero-sum partitions, obtained by translating the previous W in the z-direction.

6 Application to the Hamsi-256 Finalization Permutation

Hamsi [16] is another candidate among the fourteen functions selected for the second round of the SHA-3 competition. It is based on a Davies-Meyer construction. It uses a finalization permutation P_f which operates on a 512-bit internal state corresponding to the concatenation of the 256-bit chaining value and of a 256-bit codeword resulting from the expansion of the last 32-bit message block. In Hamsi-256, P_f consists of 6 rounds of a round transformation $R = L \circ S$, where S corresponds to 128 parallel applications of a 4×4 Sbox of degree 3. Using that three iterations of the round transformation have degree at most $3^3 = 27$, Proposition 2 leads to zero-sum partitions of size 2^{28}, as reported in [1]. However, our techniques can be used for exhibiting zero-sum partitions of smaller size.

First, we define a numbering for the bits of the internal state. The j-th bit in the word which lies in the k-th column and i-th row is numbered by $128k+4j+i$, where $0 \leq j \leq 31$, $0 \leq i \leq 3$ and $0 \leq k \leq 3$. We also define the subspace B_i, $0 \leq i < 128$ spanned by a column of the internal state: $B_i = \langle e_{4i}, e_{4i+1}, e_{4i+2}, e_{4i+3} \rangle$ (the columns of the internal state play the same role as the rows in KECCAK).

Here, we choose the intermediate state after $t = 3$ rounds of P_f into the 19-dimensional subspace

$$V = \bigoplus_{i=14}^{16} B_i \oplus \langle e_{68}, e_{237}, e_{241}, e_{245}, e_{249}, e_{507}, e_{511} \rangle \ .$$

Then, we consider the sets $X_a = \{((R^{-1})^2 \circ S^{-1})(a+z),\ z \in V\}$. Actually, we apply the same technique as in Theorem 2. Both V and $S^{-1}(V)$ can be seen as the union of some cosets of $B_{14} \oplus B_{15} \oplus B_{16}$. Since two iterations of R^{-1} have degree at most 9, all elements in X_a sum to zero because $\dim(\bigoplus_{i=14}^{16} B_i) > 9$. Moreover, $\langle e_0, e_4, e_8, e_{12} \rangle \subset L(V)$ and it has been observed in [1] that 3 rounds of R have degree 3 with respect to the first four lsbs of the first word of the internal state. Therefore, since $L(V)$ can be seen as a union of cosets of $B_f = \langle e_0, e_4, e_8, e_{12} \rangle$, and $D_{B_f} R^3(x) = 0$ for all x, we deduce that the images of all elements in X_a under six rounds of R sum to zero. Many zero-sum partitions of size 2^{19} can be constructed by this method, since we only need that $L(V)$ contains the subspace spanned by the first four consecutive bits of any word in the internal state.

Also, zero-sum partitions of size 2^{10} can be easily found for P_f. Consider any 10 elements in a 32-bit word of the state matrix after 3 rounds of the permutation and fix the other bits of the state to an arbitrary value. Then 3 rounds of the permutation applied to this state have degree at most 9. This is because there is only one variable per active Sbox, so every bit after the first round will be a linear function in the variables considered. But 3 rounds of the inverse permutation applied to the state have also degree at most 9, as after the application of L^{-1} there will be variables only in one word per column, implying again at most one active bit per Sbox.

7 Conclusions

We have found zero-sum distinguishers for the finalization permutation of Hamsi-256 and for 20 rounds of KECCAK-f, pointing out that these permutations do not behave like random permutations. For Hamsi-256, this property does not seem to lead to an attack on the hash function since the finalization permutation only applies to the 2^{288} internal states, which can be obtained from the message expansion. For KECCAK reduced to 20 rounds (out of 24), even if the security of the hash function is not affected, our results contradict the so-called hermetic sponge strategy.

Acknowledgments. We would like to thank Christophe De Cannière for his valuable comments and especially for the indication of a better bound on the degree of iterated permutations. This new bound improves in part the results on the KECCAK hash function, presented in this paper.

References

1. Aumasson, J.-P., Käsper, E., Knudsen, L.R., Matusiewicz, K., Ødegård, R., Peyrin, T., Schläffer, M.: Distinguishers for the compression function and output transformation of Hamsi-256. In: Steinfeld, R., Hawkes, P. (eds.) ACISP 2010. LNCS, vol. 6168, pp. 87–103. Springer, Heidelberg (2010)
2. Aumasson, J.-P., Meier, W.: Zero-sum distinguishers for reduced KECCAK-f and for the core functions of Luffa and Hamsi. Presented at the rump session of Cryptographic Hardware and Embedded Systems - CHES 2009 (2009)
3. Bellare, M., Micciancio, D.: A new paradigm for collision-free hashing: Incrementality at reduced cost. In: Fumy, W. (ed.) EUROCRYPT 1997. LNCS, vol. 1233, pp. 163–192. Springer, Heidelberg (1997)
4. Bertoni, G., Daemen, J., Peeters, M., Van Assche, G.: KECCAK sponge function family main document. Submission to NIST (Round 2) (2009)
5. Bertoni, G., Daemen, J., Peeters, M., Van Assche, G.: Note on zero-sum distinguishers of KECCAK-f. Public comment on the NIST Hash competition (2010), `http://keccak.noekeon.org/NoteZeroSum.pdf`
6. Brouwer, A.E., Tolhuizen, L.M.G.M.: A sharpening of the Johnsson bound for binary linear codes and the nonexistence of linear codes with Preparata parameters. Designs, Codes and Cryptography 3(2), 95–98 (1993)
7. Canteaut, A., Chabaud, F.: A new algorithm for finding minimum-weight words in a linear code: application to primitive narrow-sense BCH codes of length 511. IEEE Transactions on Information Theory 44(1), 367–378 (1998)
8. Canteaut, A., Videau, M.: Degree of composition of highly nonlinear functions and applications to higher order differential cryptanalysis. In: Knudsen, L.R. (ed.) EUROCRYPT 2002. LNCS, vol. 2332, pp. 518–533. Springer, Heidelberg (2002)
9. Carlet, C., Charpin, P., Zinoviev, V.: Codes, bent functions and permutations suitable for DES-like cryptosystems. Designs, Codes and Cryptography 15(2), 125–156 (1998)
10. Daemen, J., Knudsen, L.R., Rijmen, V.: The block cipher Square. In: Biham, E. (ed.) FSE 1997. LNCS, vol. 1267, pp. 149–165. Springer, Heidelberg (1997)
11. Dodunekov, S.M., Zinoviev, V.: A note on Preparata codes. In: Proceedings of the 6th Intern. Symp. on Information Theory, Moscow-Tashkent Part 2, pp. 78–80 (1984)
12. Finiasz, M., Sendrier, N.: Security bounds for the design of code-based cryptosystems. In: Matsui, M. (ed.) ASIACRYPT 2009. LNCS, vol. 5912, pp. 88–105. Springer, Heidelberg (2009)
13. Knudsen, L.R.: Truncated and higher order differentials. In: Preneel, B. (ed.) FSE 1994. LNCS, vol. 1008, pp. 196–211. Springer, Heidelberg (1995)
14. Knudsen, L.R., Rijmen, V.: Known-key distinguishers for some block ciphers. In: Kurosawa, K. (ed.) ASIACRYPT 2007. LNCS, vol. 4833, pp. 315–324. Springer, Heidelberg (2007)
15. Knudsen, L.R., Wagner, D.: Integral cryptanalysis. In: Daemen, J., Rijmen, V. (eds.) FSE 2002. LNCS, vol. 2365, pp. 112–127. Springer, Heidelberg (2002)
16. Küçük, O.: The Hash Function Hamsi. Submission to NIST (Round 2) (2009)
17. Lai, X.: Higher order derivatives and differential cryptanalysis. In: Proc. Symposium on Communication, Coding and Cryptography, in honor of J. L. Massey on the occasion of his 60'th birthday, Kluwer Academic Publishers, Dordrecht (1994)
18. MacWilliams, F.J., Sloane, N.J.A.: The theory of error-correcting codes. North-Holland, Amsterdam (1977)
19. Wagner, D.: A generalized birthday problem. In: Yung, M. (ed.) CRYPTO 2002. LNCS, vol. 2442, pp. 288–303. Springer, Heidelberg (2002)

Attacks on Hash Functions Based on Generalized Feistel: Application to Reduced-Round *Lesamnta* and *SHAvite-3*$_{512}$*

Charles Bouillaguet[1], Orr Dunkelman[2],
Gaëan Leurent[1], and Pierre-Alain Fouque[1]

[1] École normale supérieure
{charles.bouillaguet,gaetan.leurent,pierre-alain.fouque}@ens.fr
[2] Weizmann Institute of Science
orr.dunkelman@weizmann.ac.il

Abstract. In this paper we study the strength of two hash functions which are based on Generalized Feistels. We describe a new kind of attack based on a cancellation property in the round function. This new technique allows to efficiently use the degrees of freedom available to attack a hash function. Using the cancellation property, we can avoid the non-linear parts of the round function, at the expense of some freedom degrees.

Our attacks are mostly independent of the round function in use, and can be applied to similar hash functions which share the same structure but have different round functions. We start with a 22-round generic attack on the structure of *Lesamnta*, and adapt it to the actual round function to attack 24-round *Lesamnta* (the full function has 32 rounds). We follow with an attack on 9-round *SHAvite-3*$_{512}$ which also works for the tweaked version of *SHAvite-3*$_{512}$.

1 Introduction

Many block ciphers and hash functions are based on generalized Feistel constructions. In this paper we treat such generalized Feistel constructions and especially concentrate on the case where an n-bit round function is used in a $4n$-bit structure. Two of these constructions, shown at Figure 1,[1] used in the *Lesamnta* and the *SHAvite-3*$_{512}$ hash functions, are the main focus of this paper.

While in the ideal Luby-Rackoff case, the round functions are independent random functions, in practice, most round functions $F(k, x)$ are usually defined as $P(k \oplus x)$, where P is a fixed permutation (or function). Hence, we introduce several attacks which are based on *cancellation property*: if the fixed function P accepts twice the same input, it produces twice the same output. In a hash

* The full version of this paper appears as IACR ePrint report 2009/634 [3].
[1] Note that the direction of the rotation in the Feistel structure is not really important: changing the rotation is equivalent to considering decryption instead of encryption.

A. Biryukov, G. Gong, and D.R. Stinson (Eds.): SAC 2010, LNCS 6544, pp. 18–35, 2011.

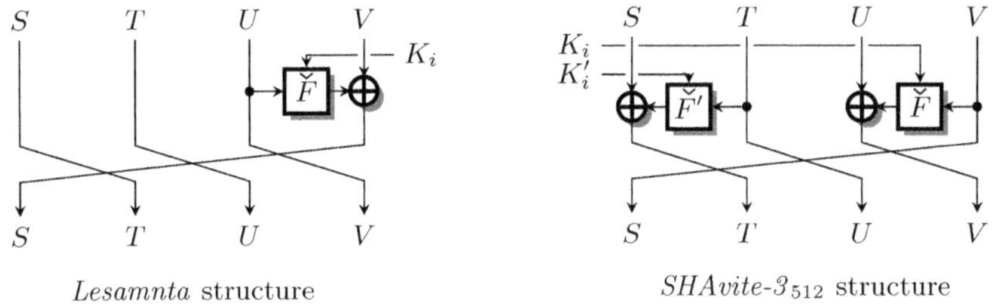

Fig. 1. The Generalized Feistel Constructions Studied in this paper

function setting, as there is no secret key, the adversary may actually make sure that the inputs are the same.

For *Lesamnta* we start with generic attacks that work independent of the actual P in use, but then use the specific properties of *Lesamnta*'s round functions to offer better attacks. The attack on *SHAvite-3*$_{512}$ is a more complicated one, following the more complex round functions (and the structure which uses two functions in each round), but at the same time, is of more interest as *SHAvite-3*$_{512}$ is still a SHA3 candidate.

1.1 Overview of the Attacks

Our attacks are based on a partial preimage attack, *i.e.* we can construct specific inputs where part of the output H is equal to a target value $\overline{H}$. To achieve such a partial preimage attack, we use truncated differentials built with the cancellation property, and we express the constraints needed on the state of the Feistel network in order to have the cancellation with probability one. We use degrees of freedom in the inputs of the compression function to satisfy those constraints. Then, we can compute some part of the output as a function of some of the remaining degrees of freedom, and try to invert the equation. The main idea is to obtain a simple equation that can be easily inverted using cancellations to limit the diffusion.

A partial preimage attack on the compression function allows to choose k bits of the output for a cost of 2^t (with $t < k$), while the remaining $n - k$ bits are random. We can use such an attack on the compression function to target the hash function itself, in several scenarios.

Preimage Attacks. By repeating such an attack 2^{n-k} times, we can obtain a full preimage attack on the compression function, with complexity 2^{n+t-k}. This preimage attack on the compression function can be used for a second preimage attack on the hash function with complexity $2^{n+(t-k)/2}$ using a standard unbalanced meet-in-the middle [8]. Note that $2^{n+(t-k)/2} < 2^n$ if $t < k$.

Moreover, we point out that *Lesamnta* is built following the Matyas-Meyer-Oseas construction, *i.e.* the chaining value is used as a key, and the message enters the Feistel rounds. Since our partial preimage attack does not use degrees of freedom in the key (we only need the key to be known, not chosen), we can use a chaining value reached from the IV as the key. We have to repeat the partial preimage attack with many different keys in order to build a full preimage, but we can use a first message block to randomize the key. This gives a second preimage attack on the hash function with complexity 2^{t+n-k}.

Collision Attacks. The partial preimage attack can also be used to find collisions in the compression function. By generating $2^{(n-k)/2}$ inputs where k bits of the output are fixed to a common value, we expect a collision thanks to the birthday paradox. This collision attack on the compression function costs $2^{t+(n-k)/2}$. If $t < k/2$, this is more efficient than a generic birthday attack on the compression function.

If the compression function is built with the Matyas-Meyer-Oseas mode, like *Lesamnta*, this attack translates to a collision attack on the hash function with the same complexity. However, if the compression function follows the Davies-Meyer mode, like *SHAvite-3*, this does not translate to an attack on the hash function.

1.2 Our Results

The first candidate for the technique is the *Lesamnta* hash function. The best known generic attack against this structure is a 16-round attack by Mendel described in the submission document of *Lesamnta* [6]. Using a cancellation property, we extend this attack to a generic attacks on 22-round *Lesamnta*. The attack allows to fix one of the output words for an amortized cost of 1, which gives collisions in time $2^{3n/8}$ and second preimages in time $2^{3n/4}$ for *Lesamnta-n*. Moreover, the preimage attack can be extended to 24 rounds using $2^{n/4}$ memory. We follow with adaptations of the 24-round attacks without memory using specific properties of *Lesamnta*'s round function.

The second target for our technique is the hash function *SHAvite-3*$_{512}$. We show a 9-round attack using a cancellation property on the generalized Feistel structure of *SHAvite-3*$_{512}$. The attack also works for the tweaked version of *SHAvite-3*$_{512}$, and allows fixing one out of the four output words. This allows a second preimage attack on 9-round *SHAvite-3*$_{512}$ that takes about 2^{448} time. Note that this attack has recently been improved in a follow-up work [5]. First a new technique was used to add one extra round at the beginning, leading to attacks on 10 rounds of the compression function. Second, a pseudo-attack against the full *SHAvite-3*$_{512}$ is described, using additional degrees of freedom in the salt input. The follow-up work has been published first because of calendar issues, but it is heavily based on this work which was available as a preprint to the authors of [5]. Moreover, in this paper, we describe a more efficient way to find a suitable key for the attack, which improves the 10-round attack of [5].

In the full version of this paper, we also show some applications to block ciphers, with an integral attack on 21 rounds of the inner block cipher of *Lesamnta*, and a new truncated differential for *SMS4*.

Table 1. Cancellation property on *Lesamnta*
On the left side, we have full diffusion after 9 rounds. On the right side, we use the cancellation property to control the diffusion of the differences.

i	S_i	T_i	U_i	V_i	
0	x	-	-	-	
1	-	x	-	-	
2	-	-	x	-	
3	y_1	-	-	x	$x \to y_1$
4	x	y_1	-	-	
5	-	x	y_1	-	
6	z	-	x	y_1	$y_1 \to z$
7	y'	z	-	x	$x \to y_2,\ y' = y_1 \oplus y_2$
8	x	y'	z	-	
9	w	x	y'	z	$z \to w$

S_i	T_i	U_i	V_i	
x	-	-	-	
-	x	-	-	
-	-	x	-	
y	-	-	x	$\underline{x \to y}$
x	y	-	-	
-	x	y	-	
z	-	x	y	$y \to z$
$\underline{-}$	z	-	x	$\underline{x \to y}$
x	$\underline{-}$	z	-	
w	x	$\underline{-}$	z	$z \to w$

The paper is organized as follows. Section 2 explains the basic idea of our cancellation attacks. Our results on *Lesamnta* are presented in Section 3, while application to *SHAvite-3*$_{512}$ is discussed in Section 4. These results are summarized in Tables 9 and 10.

2 The Cancellation Property

In this paper we apply cancellation cryptanalysis to generalized Feistel schemes. The main idea of this technique is to impose constraints on the values of the state in order to limit the diffusion in the Feistel structure. When attacking a hash function, we have many degrees of freedom from the message and the chaining value, and it is important to find efficient ways to use those degrees of freedom.

Table 1 shows the diffusion of a single difference in *Lesamnta*. After 9 rounds, all the state words are active. However, we note that if the transitions $x \to y_1$ at rounds 3 and $x \to y_2$ at round 7 actually go to the *same* y, *i.e.* $y_1 = y_2$, this limits the diffusion. In the ideal case, the round functions are all independent, and the probability of getting the same output difference is very small. However, in practice, the round functions are usually all derived from a single fixed permutation (or function). Therefore, if we add some constraints so that the input *values* of the fixed permutation at round 3 and 7 are the same, then we have the same output values, and therefore the same output difference with probability one. This is the *cancellation property*. A similar property can be used in *SHAvite-3*$_{512}$.

Our attacks use an important property of the Feistel schemes of *Lesamnta* and *SHAvite-3*$_{512}$: the diffusion is relatively slow. When a difference is introduced in the state, it takes several rounds to affect the full state and two different round functions can receive the same input difference x. Note that the slow diffusion of *Lesamnta* is the basis of a 16-round attack in [6] (recalled in Section 3.1), and the slow diffusion of *SHAvite-3*$_{512}$ gives a similar 8-round attack [4]. Our new attacks can be seen as extensions of those.

We now describe how to enforce conditions of the state so as to have this cancellation with probability 1. Our attacks are independent of the round function, as long as all the round functions are derived from a single function as $F_i(X_i) \triangleq F(K_i \oplus X_i)$.

2.1 Generic Properties of $F_i(X_i) = F(K_i \oplus X_i)$

We assume that the round functions F_i are built by applying a fixed permutation (or function) F to $K_i \oplus X_i$, where K_i is a round key and X_i is the state input. This practice is common in many primitives like DES, *SMS4*, GOST, or *Lesamnta*.

This implies the followings, for all i, j, k:

(i) $\exists c_{i,j} : \forall x,\ F_i(x \oplus c_{i,j}) = F_j(x)$.
(ii) $\forall \alpha,\ \#\{x : F_i(x) \oplus F_j(x) = \alpha\}$ is even.
(iii) $\bigoplus_x F_k(F_i(x) \oplus F_j(x)) = 0$.

Property (i) is the basis of our cancellation attack. We refer to it as the *cancellation property*. It states that if the inputs of two round functions are related by a specific fixed difference, then the outputs of both rounds are equal. The reminder of the paper is exploring this property.

Properties (ii) and (iii) can be used in an integral attack, as shown in the full version [3]. Note that Property (ii) is a well known fact from differential cryptanalysis.

Proof. (i) Set $c_{ij} = K_i \oplus K_j$.

(ii) If $K_i = K_j$, then $\forall x,\ F_i(x) \oplus F_j(x) = 0$. Otherwise, let x be such that $F_i(x) \oplus F_j(x) = \alpha$. Then $F_i(x \oplus K_i \oplus K_j) \oplus F_j(x \oplus K_i \oplus K_j) = F_j(x) \oplus F_i(x) = \alpha$. Therefore x is in the set if and only if $x \oplus K_i \oplus K_j$ is in the set, and all the elements can be grouped in pairs.

(iii) Each term $F_k(\alpha)$ in the sum appears an even number of times, by (ii). □

2.2 Using the Cancellation Property

To better explain the cancellation property, we describe how to use it with the truncated differential of Table 1. In Table 2, we show the *values* of the registers during the computation of the truncated differential, starting at round 2 with $(S_2, T_2, U_2, V_2) = (a, b, c, d)$. To use the cancellation property, we want to make S_7 independent of c. Since we have $S_7 = F_6(F_3(b) \oplus \underline{c}) \oplus F_2(\underline{c}) \oplus d$, we can cancel the highlighted terms using property (i). The dependency of S_7 on c disappears if $F_3(b) = K_2 \oplus K_6$, *i.e.* if $b = F_3^{-1}(K_2 \oplus K_6)$:

$$S_7 = F_6(F_3(b) \oplus c) \oplus F_2(c) \oplus d = F(K_6 \oplus K_2 \oplus K_6 \oplus c) \oplus F(K_2 \oplus c) \oplus d = d.$$

Therefore, we can put any value c in U_2, and it does not affect S_7 as long as we fix the value of T_2 to be $F^{-1}(K_2 \oplus K_6) \oplus K_3$. Note that in a hash function, we

Table 2. Values of the Registers for Five Rounds of *Lesamnta*

i	S_i	T_i	U_i	V_i
2	a	b	c	d
3	$F_2(c) \oplus d$	a	b	c
4	$F_3(b) \oplus c$	$F_2(c) \oplus d$	a	b
5	$F_4(a) \oplus b$	$F_3(b) \oplus c$	$F_2(c) \oplus d$	a
6	$F_5(F_2(c) \oplus d) \oplus a$	$F_4(a) \oplus b$	$F_3(b) \oplus c$	$F_2(c) \oplus d$
7	$F_6(F_3(b) \oplus c) \oplus F_2(c) \oplus d$	$F_5(F_2(c) \oplus d) \oplus a$	$F_4(a) \oplus b$	$F_3(b) \oplus c$

can compute $F^{-1}(K_2 \oplus K_6) \oplus K_3$ since the keys are known to the adversary (or controlled by him), and we can choose to have this value in T_2.

This shows the three main requirements of our cancellation attacks:

- The generalized Feistel structures we study have a relatively slow diffusion. Therefore, the same difference can be used as the input difference of two different round functions.
- The round functions are built from a fixed permutation (or a fixed function), using a small round key. This differs from the ideal Luby-Rackoff case where all round functions are chosen independently at random.
- In a hash function setting the key is known to the adversary, and he can control some of the inner values.

Note that some of these requirements are not strictly necessary. For example, we show a 21-round integral attack on *Lesamnta*, without knowing the keys in the full version. Moreover, in Section 4 we show attacks on 9-round *SHAvite-3*$_{512}$, where the round functions use more keying material.

3 Application to *Lesamnta*

Lesamnta is a hash function proposal by Hirose, Kuwakado, and Yoshida as a candidate in the SHA-3 competition [6]. It is based on a 32-round unbalanced Feistel scheme with four registers used in MMO mode. The key schedule is also based on a similar Feistel scheme. The round function can be written as:

$$S_{i+1} = V_i \oplus F(U_i \oplus K_i) \qquad T_{i+1} = S_i \qquad U_{i+1} = T_i \qquad V_{i+1} = U_i$$

3.1 Previous Results on *Lesamnta*

The best known attack on *Lesamnta* is the self-similarity attack of [2]. Following this attack, the designers have tweaked *Lesamnta* by changing the round constants [10]. In this paper we consider attacks that work with any round constants, and thus are applicable to the tweaked version as well.

Several attacks on reduced-round *Lesamnta* are presented in the submission document [6]. A series of 16-round attacks for collisions and (second) preimage attacks are presented, all of which are based on a 16-round truncated differential with probability 1.

In the next sections we show new attacks using the cancellation property. We first show some attacks that are generic in F, as long as the round functions are defined as $F_i(X_i) = F(K_i \oplus X_i)$, and then improved attacks using specific properties of the round functions of *Lesamnta*.

3.2 Generic Attacks

Our attacks are based on the differential of Table 3, which is an extension of the differential of Table 1. In this differential we use the cancellation property three times to control the diffusion. Note that we do not have to specify the values of y, z, w, r and t. This specifies a truncated differential for *Lesamnta*: starting from a difference $(x, -, -, -)$, we reach a difference $(?, ?, ?, x_1)$ after 22 rounds. In order to use this truncated differential in our cancellation attack, we use two important properties: first, by adding constraints on the state, the truncated differential is followed with probability 1; second, the transition $x \to x_1$ is known because the key and values are known. Therefore, we can actually adjust the value of the last output word.

Table 3. Cancellation Property on 22 Rounds of *Lesamnta*

i	S_i	T_i	U_i	V_i	
0	x	-	-	-	
1	-	x	-	-	
2	-	-	x	-	
3	y	-	-	x	$x \to y$
4	x	y	-	-	
5	-	x	y	-	
6	z	-	x	y	$y \to z$
7	-	z	-	x	$x \to y$
8	x	-	z	-	
9	w	x	-	z	$z \to w$
10	z	w	x	-	
11	x_1	z	w	x	$x \to x_1$
12	r	x_1	z	w	$w \to x \oplus r$
13	-	r	x_1	z	$z \to w$
14	?	-	r	x_1	
15	$x_1 + t$	?	-	r	$r \to t$
16	r	$x_1 + t$	?	-	
17	?	r	$x_1 + t$	?	
18	?	?	r	$x_1 + t$	
19	x_1	?	?	r	$r \to t$
20	?	x_1	?	?	
21	?	?	x_1	?	
22	?	?	?	x_1	
FF	?	?	?	x_1	

In order to express the constraints that we need for the cancellation properties, we look at the *values* of the registers for this truncated differential. In Table 4, we begin at round 2 with $(S_2, T_2, U_2, V_2) = (a, b, c, d)$, and we compute the state values up to round 19. This is an extension of the values computed in Table 2.

We can see that we have $S_{19} = F(c \oplus \alpha) \oplus \beta$, where $\alpha = K_{10} \oplus F_7(F_4(a) \oplus b) \oplus F_3(b)$ and $\beta = d$ provided that (a, b, d) is the unique triplet satisfying the following cancellation conditions:

Round 7: we have $F_6(F_3(b) \oplus c) \oplus F_2(c)$. They cancel if:
$F_3(b) = c_{2,6} = K_2 \oplus K_6$ $\quad$ *i.e.* $b = F_3^{-1}(K_2 \oplus K_6)$
Round 13: we have $F_{12}(F_9(d) \oplus F_5(F_2(c) \oplus d) \oplus a) \oplus F_8(F_5(F_2(c) \oplus d) \oplus a)$.
They cancel if:
$F_9(d) = c_{8,12} = K_8 \oplus K_{12}$ $\quad$ *i.e.* $d = F_9^{-1}(K_8 \oplus K_{12})$
Round 19: we have $F_{18}(F_{15}(F_4(a) \oplus b) \oplus S_{12}) \oplus F_{14}(S_{12})$. They cancel if:
$F_{15}(F_4(a) \oplus b) = c_{14,18} = K_{14} \oplus K_{18}$ $\quad$ *i.e.* $a = F_4^{-1}(F_{15}^{-1}(K_{14} \oplus K_{18}) \oplus b)$

Note that a, b, d and α, β are uniquely determined from the subkeys. Hence, one can set S_{19} to any desired value S_{19}^* by setting $c = F^{-1}(S_{19}^* \oplus \beta) \oplus \alpha$.

Table 4. Values of the Register for the 22-round Cancellation Property of *Lesamnta*. Steps −5 to −2 will be used for the 24-round attacks.

i	S_i
−5	$d \oplus F_0(c \oplus F_1(b \oplus F_2(a \oplus F_3(d))))$
−4	$c \oplus F_1(b \oplus F_2(a \oplus F_3(d)))$
−3	$b \oplus F_2(a \oplus F_3(d))$
−2	$a \oplus F_3(d)$
−1	d
0	c
1	b
2	a
3	$F_2(c) \oplus d$
4	$F_3(b) \oplus c$
5	$F_4(a) \oplus b$
6	$F_5(F_2(c) \oplus d) \oplus a$
7	$F_6(F_3(b) \oplus c) \oplus F_2(c) \oplus d$
8	$F_7(F_4(a) \oplus b) \oplus F_3(b) \oplus c$
9	$F_8(F_5(F_2(c) \oplus d) \oplus a) \oplus F_4(a) \oplus b$
10	$F_9(d) \oplus F_5(F_2(c) \oplus d) \oplus a$
11	$F_{10}(F_7(F_4(a) \oplus b) \oplus F_3(b) \oplus c) \oplus d$
12	$F_{11}(F_8(F_5(F_2(c) \oplus d) \oplus a) \oplus F_4(a) \oplus b) \oplus F_7(F_4(a) \oplus b) \oplus F_3(b) \oplus c$
13	$F_{12}(F_9(d) \oplus F_5(F_2(c) \oplus d) \oplus a) \oplus F_8(F_5(F_2(c) \oplus d) \oplus a) \oplus F_4(a) \oplus b$
15	$F_{14}(S_{12}) \oplus F_{10}(F_7(F_4(a) \oplus b) \oplus F_3(b) \oplus c) \oplus d$
16	$F_{15}(F_4(a) \oplus b) \oplus S_{12}$
19	$F_{18}(F_{15}(F_4(a) \oplus b) \oplus S_{12}) \oplus F_{14}(S_{12}) \oplus F_{10}(F_7(F_4(a) \oplus b) \oplus F_3(b) \oplus c) \oplus d$

22-Round Attacks. The truncated differential of Table 3 can be used to attack 22-round *Lesamnta*. We start with the state at round 2 $(S_2, T_2, U_2, V_2) = (a, b, c, d)$ satisfying the cancellation properties, and we can compute how the various states depend on c, as shown in Table 5. A dash (-) is used to denote a value that is independent of c. We know exactly how c affects the last output word, and we can select c in order to get a specific value at the output. Suppose we are given a set of subkeys, and a target value $\overline{H}$ for the fourth output word. Then the attack proceeds as follows:

Table 5. Collision and Preimage Characteristic for the 22-Round Attack

i	S_i	T_i	U_i	V_i
0	c	-	-	η
1	-	c	-	-
2	-	-	c	-
2–19	Repeated Cancellation Property: Table 4			
19	$F(c \oplus \alpha) \oplus \beta$	?	?	?
20	?	$F(c \oplus \alpha) \oplus \beta$	?	?
21	?	?	$F(c \oplus \alpha) \oplus \beta$	?
22	?	?	?	$F(c \oplus \alpha) \oplus \beta$
FF	?	?	?	$\eta \oplus F(c \oplus \alpha) \oplus \beta$

η, α and β can be computed from a, b, d and the key:
$\eta = b \oplus F_0(a \oplus F_3(d))$, $\alpha = K_{11} \oplus F_8(F_5(a) \oplus b) \oplus F_4(b)$, $\beta = d$.

1. Set a, b, and d to the values that allow the cancellation property. Then we have $V_0 \oplus V_{22} = \eta \oplus F(c \oplus \alpha) \oplus \beta$, as shown in Table 5.
2. Compute c as $F^{-1}(\overline{H} \oplus \eta \oplus \beta) \oplus \alpha$.
3. This sets the state at round 2: $(S_2, T_2, U_2, V_2) \triangleq (a, b, c, d)$. With this state, we have $V_0 \oplus V_{22} = \overline{H}$.
4. Compute the round function backwards up to round 0, to get the input.

This costs less than one compression function call, and does not require any memory.

For a given chaining value (*i.e.* a set of subkeys), this algorithm can only output one message. To build a full preimage attack or a collision attack on the compression function, this has to be repeated with random chaining values. Since the attack works for any chaining value, we can build attacks on the hash function using a prefix block to randomize the chaining value. This gives a collision attack with complexity 2^{96} (2^{192} for *Lesamnta*-512), and a second-preimage attack with complexity 2^{192} (2^{384} for *Lesamnta*-512).

24-Round Attacks. We can add two rounds at the beginning of the truncated differential at the cost of some memory. The resulting 24-round differential is given in Table 6. The output word we try to control is equal to $F(c \oplus \gamma) \oplus F(c \oplus \alpha)$, for some constants α, and γ that depend on the chaining value (note that $\beta = \lambda$ in Table 6). We define a family of functions $h_\mu(x) = F(x) \oplus F(x \oplus \mu)$, and for a given target value $\overline{H}$, we tabulate $\varphi_{\overline{H}}(\mu) = h_\mu^{-1}(\overline{H})$. For each μ, $\varphi_{\overline{H}}(\mu)$ is a possibly empty set, but the average size is one (the non-empty values form a partition of the input space). In the special case where $\overline{H} = 0$, $\varphi_0(\mu)$ is empty for all $\mu \neq 0$, and $\varphi_0(0)$ is the full space.

Table 6. Collision and Preimage Path for the 24-round Attack

i	S_i	T_i	U_i	V_i
0	-	-	$c \oplus \gamma$	$F(c \oplus \gamma) \oplus \lambda$
1	-	-	-	$c \oplus \gamma$
2	c	-	-	-
3	-	c	-	-
4	-	-	c	-
4–21	Repeated Cancellation Property: Table 4			
21	$F(c \oplus \alpha) \oplus \beta$	?	?	?
22	?	$F(c \oplus \alpha) \oplus \beta$	?	?
23	?	?	$F(c \oplus \alpha) \oplus \beta$	?
24	?	?	?	$F(c \oplus \alpha) \oplus \beta$

α, β, γ and λ can be computed from a, b, d and the key by:
$\alpha = K_{13} \oplus F_{10}(F_7(a) \oplus b) \oplus F_6(b)$, $\beta = d$ and
$\gamma = F_1(b \oplus F_2(a \oplus F_3(d)))$, $\lambda = d$

We store $\varphi_{\overline{H}}$ in a table of size $2^{n/4}$, and we can compute it in time $2^{n/4}$ by looking for values such that $F(x) \oplus F(y) = \overline{H}$ (this gives $\varphi_{\overline{H}}(x \oplus y) = x$). Using this table, we are able to choose one output word just like in the 22-round attack.

We start with a state $(S_4, T_4, U_4, V_4) = (a, b, c, d)$ such that a, b, d satisfy the cancellation conditions, and we compute α, β, γ, λ. If we use $c = u \oplus \alpha$, where $u \in \varphi_{\overline{H}}(\alpha \oplus \gamma) = h^{-1}_{\alpha \oplus \gamma}(\overline{H})$, we have:

$$V_0 \oplus V_{24} = F(c \oplus \gamma) \oplus F(c \oplus \alpha) = F(u \oplus \alpha \oplus \gamma) \oplus F(u) = h_{\alpha \oplus \gamma}(u) = \overline{H}$$

On average this costs one compression function evaluation to find a $n/4$-bit partial preimage. If the target value is 0, this only succeeds if $\alpha \oplus \gamma = 0$, but in this case it gives $2^{n/4}$ solutions. This gives a preimage attack with complexity $2^{3n/4}$ using $2^{n/4}$ memory.

Note that it is possible to make a time-memory trade-off with complexity 2^{n-k} using 2^k memory for $k < n/4$.

3.3 Dedicated 24-Round Attacks on *Lesamnta*

We now describe how to use specific properties of the round functions of *Lesamnta* to remove the memory requirement of our 24-round attacks.

Slow Diffusion in F_{256}. The AES-like round function of *Lesamnta*-256 achieves full diffusion of the values after its four rounds, but some linear combinations of the output are not affected. Starting from a single active diagonal, we have:

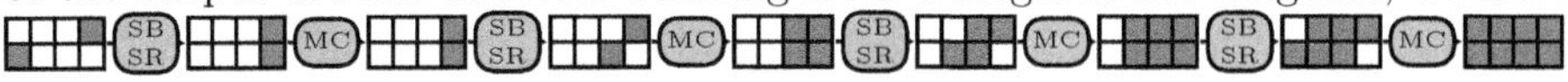

All the output bytes are active, but there are some linear relations between them. More precisely, the inverse MixColumns operation leads to a difference with two inactive bytes.

This gives two linear subspaces Γ and Λ for which $x \oplus x' \in \Gamma \Rightarrow F(x) \oplus F(x') \in \Lambda$. The subspaces Γ and Λ have dimensions of 16 and 48, respectively.

Collision and Second Preimage Attacks on Lesamnta-256. Using this property, we can choose 16 linear relations of the output of the family of function h_μ, or equivalently, choose 16 linear relations of the output of the compression function.

Let $\bar{\Lambda}$ be a supplementary subspace of Λ. Any 64-bit value x can be written as $x = x_\Lambda + x_{\bar{\Lambda}}$, where $x_\Lambda \in \Lambda$ and $x_{\bar{\Lambda}} \in \bar{\Lambda}$. We can find values x such that $h_\mu(x)_{\bar{\Lambda}} = \overline{H}_{\bar{\Lambda}}$ for an amortized cost of one, without memory:

1. Compute $h_\mu(u)$ for random u's until $h_\mu(u)_{\bar{\Lambda}} = \overline{H}_{\bar{\Lambda}}$
2. Far all v in Γ, we have $h_\mu(u+v)_{\bar{\Lambda}} = \overline{H}_{\bar{\Lambda}}$

This gives 2^{16} messages with 16 chosen relations for a cost of 2^{16}. It allows a second-preimage attack on 24-round *Lesamnta*-256 with complexity 2^{240}, and a collision attack with complexity 2^{120}, both memoryless.

Symmetries in F_{256} and F_{512}. The AES round function has strong symmetry properties, as studied in [9]. The round function F of *Lesamnta* is heavily inspired by the AES round, and has similar symmetry properties. More specifically, if an AES state is such that the left half is equal to the right half, then this property still holds after any number of SubBytes, ShiftRows, and MixColumns operations.

When we consider the F functions of *Lesamnta*, we have that: *if $x \oplus K_i$ is symmetric, then $F_i(x) = F(x \oplus K_i)$ is also symmetric.*

Collision Attacks on Lesamnta-256 and Lesamnta-512. This property can be used for an improved collision attack. As seen earlier we have $V_0 \oplus V_{24} = F(c \oplus \gamma) \oplus F(c \oplus \alpha)$. In order to use the symmetry property, we first select random chaining values, and we compute the value of α and γ until $\alpha \oplus \gamma$ is symmetric. Then, if we select c such that $c \oplus \gamma$ is symmetric, we have that $V_0 \oplus V_{24}$ is symmetric.

This leads to a collision attack with complexity 2^{112} for *Lesamnta*-256, and 2^{224} for *Lesamnta*-512.

4 Application to *SHAvite-3*$_{512}$

SHAvite-3 is a hash function designed by Biham and Dunkelman for the SHA-3 competition [1]. It is based on a generalized Feistel construction with an AES-based round function, used in Davies-Meyer mode. In this section we study *SHAvite-3*$_{512}$, the version of *SHAvite-3* designed for output size of 257 to 512 bits. The cancellation property can not be used on *SHAvite-3*$_{256}$ because the Feistel structure is different and has a faster diffusion. We describe an attack on the *SHAvite-3*$_{512}$ hash function reduced to 9 rounds out of 14. An earlier variant of our attack was later extended in [5] to a 10-round attack. We note that our improved 9-round attack can be used to offer an improved 10-round attack.

4.1 A Short Description of *SHAvite-3*$_{512}$

The compression function of *SHAvite-3*$_{512}$ accepts a chaining value of 512 bits, a message block of 1024 bits, a salt of 512 bits, and a bit counter of 128 bits. As this is a Davies-Meyer construction, the message block, the salt, and the bit counter enter the key schedule algorithm of the underlying block cipher. The key schedule algorithm transforms them into 112 subkeys of 128 bits each. The chaining value is then divided into four 128-bit words, and at each round two words enter the nonlinear round functions and affect the other two:

$$S_{i+1} = V_i \qquad T_{i+1} = S_i \oplus F'_i(T_i) \qquad U_{i+1} = T_i \qquad V_{i+1} = U_i \oplus F_i(V_i)$$

The nonlinear function F and F' are composed of four full rounds of AES, with 4 subkeys from the message expansion:

$$F_i(x) = P(k^3_{0,i} \oplus P(k^2_{0,i} \oplus P(k^1_{0,i} \oplus P(k^0_{0,i} \oplus x))))$$
$$F'_i(x) = P(k^3_{1,i} \oplus P(k^2_{1,i} \oplus P(k^1_{1,i} \oplus P(k^0_{1,i} \oplus x))))$$

where P is one AES round (without the AddRoundKey operation).

In this section we use an alternative description of *SHAvite-3*$_{512}$ with only two variables per round. We have

$$S_i = Y_{i-1} \qquad T_i = X_i \qquad U_i = X_{i-1} \qquad V_i = Y_i$$

The message expansion generates an array $rk[\cdot]$ of 448 32-bit words by alternating linear steps and AES rounds:

Using the counter: the counter is used at 4 specific positions.
In order to simplify the description, we define a new table holding the preprocessed counter:
$ck[\ 32] = cnt[0]$, $ck[\ 33] = cnt[1]$, $ck[\ 34] = cnt[2]$, $ck[\ 35] = \overline{cnt[3]}$
$ck[164] = cnt[3]$, $ck[165] = cnt[2]$, $ck[166] = cnt[1]$, $ck[167] = \overline{cnt[0]}$
$ck[440] = cnt[1]$, $ck[441] = cnt[0]$, $ck[442] = cnt[3]$, $ck[443] = \overline{cnt[2]}$
$ck[316] = cnt[2]$, $ck[317] = cnt[3]$, $ck[318] = cnt[0]$, $ck[319] = \overline{cnt[1]}$
For all the other values, $ck[i] = 0$.

AES rounds: for $i \in \{0, 64, 128, 192, 256, 320, 384\} + \{0, 4, 8, 12, 16, 20, 24, 28\}$:
$tk[(i, i+1, i+2, i+3)] = \mathrm{AESR}(rk[(i+1, i+2, i+3, i)] \oplus salt[(i, i+1, i+2, i+3) \bmod 16])$

Linear Step 1: for $i \in \{32, 96, 160, 224, 288, 352, 416\} + \{0, \ldots, 31\}$:
$rk[i] = tk[i-32] \oplus rk[i-4] \oplus ck[i]$

Linear Step 2: for $i \in \{64, 128, 192, 256, 320, 384\} + \{0, \ldots, 31\}$:
$rk[i] = rk[i-32] \oplus rk[i-7]$

Table 7. Cancellation Property on 9 Rounds of *SHAvite-3*$_{512}$

i	S_i	T_i	U_i	V_i	
0	?	x_2	?	x	
1	x	-	x_2	x_1	
2	x_1	x	-	-	$x_1 \to x_2$
3	-	-	x	-	$x \to x_1$
4	-	-	-	x	
5	x	-	-	y	$x \to y$
6	y	x	-	z	$y \to z$
7	z	-	x	w	$x \to y$, $z \to w$
8	w	z	-	?	
9	?	-	z	?	$z \to w$
FF	?	x_2	?	?	

Table 8. Values of the Registers for the 9-round Cancellation Property of *SHAvite-3*$_{512}$

i	X_i	Y_i
0	$b \oplus F_3(c) \oplus F'_1(c \oplus F_2(d \oplus F'_3(a)))$	$d \oplus F'_3(a) \oplus F_1(a \oplus F'_2(b \oplus F_3(c)))$
1	$a \oplus F'_2(b \oplus F_3(c))$	$c \oplus F_2(d \oplus F'_3(a))$
2	$d \oplus F'_3(a)$	$b \oplus F_3(c)$
3	c	a
4	b	d
5	$a \oplus F_4(b)$	$c \oplus F'_4(d)$
6	$d \oplus F_5(a \oplus F_4(b))$	$b \oplus F'_5(c \oplus F'_4(d))$
7	$c \oplus F'_4(d) \oplus F_6(d \oplus F_5(a \oplus F_4(b)))$	$a \oplus F_4(b) \oplus F'_6(b \oplus F'_5(c \oplus F'_4(d)))$
8	$b \oplus F'_5(c \oplus F'_4(d)) \oplus F_7(c)$	?
9	$a \oplus F_4(b) \oplus F'_6(b \oplus F'_5(c \oplus F'_4(d))) \oplus F_8(b \oplus F'_5(c \oplus F'_4(d)) \oplus F_7(c))$	

4.2 Cancellation Attacks on *SHAvite-3*$_{512}$

The cancellation path is described in Table 7. We use the cancellation property twice to control the diffusion. Note that we do not have to specify the values of y, z, and w. Like in the *Lesamnta* attack, this path is a truncated differential, and we use constraints on the state to enforce that it is followed. Moreover, the transitions $x \to x_1$ and $x_1 \to x_2$ are known because the key is known.

Note that the round functions of *SHAvite-3*$_{512}$ are not defined as $F(k, x) = P(k \oplus x)$ for a fixed permutation P. Instead, each function takes 4 keys and it is defined as:

$$F(k_i^0, k_i^1, k_i^2, k_i^3, x) = P(k_i^3 \oplus P(k_i^2 \oplus P(k_i^1 \oplus P(k_i^0 \oplus x))))$$

where P is one AES round. In order to apply the cancellation property to *SHAvite-3*$_{512}$, we need that the subkeys k^1, k^2, k^3 of two functions be equal, so that $F_i(x)$ collapses to $P'(k_i^0 \oplus x)$ and F_j to $P'(k_j^0 \oplus x)$, where $P'(x) \triangleq P(k_i^3 \oplus P(k_i^2 \oplus P(k_i^1 \oplus P(x)))) = P(k_j^3 \oplus P(k_j^2 \oplus P(k_j^1 \oplus P(x))))$.

In order to express the constraints needed for the cancellation properties, we look at the *values* of the registers for this truncated differential. In Table 8, we begin at round 4 with $(S_4, T_4, U_4, V_4) = (Y_3, X_4, X_3, Y_4) = (a, b, c, d)$, and we compute up to round 9.

We have a cancellation property on 9 rounds under the following conditions:

Round 7. We have $\underline{F_4'(d)} \oplus F_6(\underline{d} \oplus F_5(a \oplus F_4(b)))$. They cancel if: $F_5(a \oplus F_4(b)) = k_{1,4}^0 \oplus k_{0,6}^0$ and $(k_{1,4}^1, k_{1,4}^2, k_{1,4}^3) = (k_{0,6}^1, k_{0,6}^2, k_{0,6}^3)$.

Round 9. We have $F_6'(\underline{b \oplus F_5'(c \oplus F_4'(d))}) \oplus F_8(\underline{b \oplus F_5'(c \oplus F_4'(d))} \oplus F_7(c))$. They cancel if: $F_7(c) = k_{1,6}^0 \oplus k_{0,8}^0$ and $(k_{1,6}^1, k_{1,6}^2, k_{1,6}^3) = (k_{0,8}^1, k_{0,8}^2, k_{0,8}^3)$.

Therefore, the truncated differential is followed if:

$$F_5(a \oplus F_4(b)) = k_{1,4}^0 \oplus k_{0,6}^0 \qquad F_7(c) = k_{1,6}^0 \oplus k_{0,8}^0 \qquad \text{(C0)}$$

$$(k_{1,4}^1, k_{1,4}^2, k_{1,4}^3) = (k_{0,6}^1, k_{0,6}^2, k_{0,6}^3) \qquad (k_{1,6}^1, k_{1,6}^2, k_{1,6}^3) = (k_{0,8}^1, k_{0,8}^2, k_{0,8}^3) \qquad \text{(C1)}$$

The constraints for the cancellation at round 7 are easy to satisfy and allow a 7-round attack on *SHAvite-3*$_{512}$. However, for a 9-round attack we have more constraints on the subkeys, and this requires special attention.

4.3 Dealing with the Key Expansion

Let us outline an algorithm to find a suitable message (recall that *SHAvite-3*$_{512}$ is used in a Davies-Meyer mode) for a given salt and counter value. We have to solve a system involving linear and non-linear equations, and we use the fact that the system is almost triangular. We note that it might be possible to improve our results using the technique of Khovratovich, Biryukov and Nikolic [7] to find a good message efficiently.

For the cancellation attack on 9-round *SHAvite-3*$_{512}$, we need to satisfy a 768-bit condition on the subkeys, *i.e.*:

$$(k_{1,4}^1, k_{1,4}^2, k_{1,4}^3) = (k_{0,6}^1, k_{0,6}^2, k_{0,6}^3) \qquad (k_{1,6}^1, k_{1,6}^2, k_{1,6}^3) = (k_{0,8}^1, k_{0,8}^2, k_{0,8}^3) \qquad \text{(C1)}$$

Or in $rk[\cdot]$ terms:

$$rk[148, \ldots, 159] = rk[196, \ldots, 207] \qquad rk[212, \ldots, 223] = rk[260, \ldots, 271]$$

We are actually trying to solve a system of equation with:

- 224 variables: $tk[128..159]$, $tk[192..223]$ and $rk[128..287]$
- 192 equations from the key schedule (64 non-linear and 128 linear)
- 24 constraints

Therefore we have 8 degrees of freedom. The relations between the variables are shown in Figure 2, while the full key expansion of *SHAvite-3*$_{512}$ is described in Appendix.

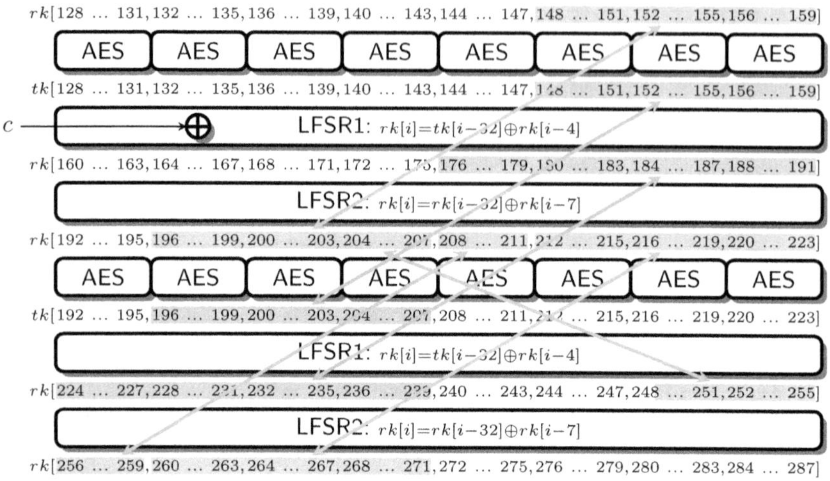

Fig. 2. Constraints in the Key Expansion of $SHAvite\text{-}3_{512}$
Initial constraints in pink, constraints from steps 1 to 3 in yellow, constraints from step 4 in green

Propagation of the Constraints. First, we propagate the constraints and deduce new equalities between the variables. Figure 2 shows the initial constraints and the propagated constraints.

1. The non-linear equations of the key-schedule give:

$$tk[156..159] = AESR\Big((rk[157, 158, 159, 156]) \oplus (salt[12..15])\Big)$$

$$tk[204..207] = AESR\Big((rk[205, 206, 207, 204]) \oplus (salt[12..15])\Big)$$

   since $rk[156..159] = rk[204..207]$, we know that $tk[156..159] = tk[204..207]$. Similarly, we get $tk[148..159] = tk[196..207]$
2. From the key expansion, we have $rk[191] = rk[223] \oplus rk[216]$, and $rk[239] = rk[271] \oplus rk[264]$. Since we have the constraints $rk[223] = rk[271]$ and $rk[216] = rk[264]$, we can deduce that $rk[191] = rk[239]$ Similarly, we get $rk[187..191] = rk[235..239]$.
3. From the linear part of the expansion, we have $rk[186] = rk[190] \oplus tk[158]$ and $rk[234] = rk[238] \oplus tk[206]$. We have seen that $rk[190] = rk[238]$ at step 2 and $tk[158] = tk[206]$ at step 1, therefore $rk[186] = rk[234]$ Similarly, we get $rk[176..186] = rk[224..234]$.
4. Again, from the linear part of the key expansion, we have $rk[211] = rk[218] \oplus rk[186]$ and $rk[259] = rk[266] \oplus rk[234]$. We have seen that $rk[186] = rk[234]$ at step 3 and we have $rk[218] = rk[266]$ as a constraint, thus $rk[211] = rk[259]$ Similarly, we obtain $rk[201..211] = rk[249..259]$ Note that we have $rk[201..207] = rk[153..159]$ as a constraint, so we must have $rk[249..255] = rk[153..159]$.

Finding a Solution. To find a solution to the system, we use a guess and determine technique. We guess 11 state variables, and we show how to compute the rest of the state and check for consistency. Since we have only 8 degrees of freedom, we expect the random initial choice to be valid once out of $2^{32\times 3} = 2^{96}$ times. This gives a complexity of 2^{96} to find a good message.

- Choose random values for $rk[200], rk[204..207], rk[215..216], rk[220..223]$
- Compute $tk[220..223]$ from $rk[220..223]$
- Compute $rk[248..251]$ from $tk[220..223]$ and $rk[252..255]$ $(= rk[204..207])$
- Deduce $rk[201..203] = rk[249..251]$, so $rk[200..207]$ is known
- Compute $tk[152..159]$ from $rk[152..159]$ $(= rk[200..207])$
- Compute $rk[190..191]$ from $rk[215..216]$ and $rk[222..223]$
- Compute $rk[186..187]$ from $rk[190..191]$ and $rk[158..159]$
- Compute $rk[182..183]$ from $rk[186..187]$ and $rk[154..155]$
- Compute $rk[214]$ from $rk[207]$ and $rk[182]$
- Compute $rk[189]$ from $rk[214]$ and $rk[219]$; then $rk[185]$ and $rk[181]$
- Compute $rk[213]$ from $rk[206]$ and $rk[181]$
- Compute $rk[188]$ from $rk[213]$ and $rk[220]$, then $rk[184]$ and $rk[180]$
- Compute $rk[212]$ from $rk[205]$ and $rk[180]$
- Compute $rk[219]$ from $rk[212]$ and $rk[187]$
- Compute $rk[208, 209]$ from $rk[215, 216]$ and $rk[183, 184]$
- We have $tk[216..219] = AESR\big((rk[216..219])\big)$ with a known key. Since $rk[216]$ and $rk[219]$ are known, we know that $tk[216..219]$ is a linear subspace of dimension 64 over $\mathbb{F}_2$.
- Similarly, $tk[208..211]$ is in a linear subspace of dimension 64 ($rk[208]$ and $rk[209]$ are known).
- Moreover, there are linear relations between $tk[216..219]$ and $tk[208..211]$: we can compute $rk[240..243]$ from $tk[208..211]$ and $rk[236..239]$; $rk[244..247]$ from $rk[240..243]$ and $tk[212..215]$; $tk[216..219]$ from $rk[244..247]$ and $rk[248..251]$.
- On average, we expect one solution for $tk[216..219]$ and $tk[208..211]$.
- At this point we have computed the values of $rk[200..223]$. We can compute $tk[200.223]$ and $rk[228..255]$.
- Compute $rk[176..179]$ from $rk[201..204]$ and $rk[208..211]$
- Since $rk[224..227] = rk[176..179]$, we have a full state $rk[224..255]$. We can check consistency of the initial guess.

4.4 9-Round Attacks

The cancellation property allows to find a key/message pair with a given value on the last 128 bits. The attack is the following: first find a message that fulfills the conditions on the subkeys, and set a, b and c at round 4 satisfying the cancellation conditions (C0). Then the second output word is:

$$T_9 \oplus T_0 = X_9 \oplus X_0 = a \oplus F_4(b) \oplus b \oplus F_3(c) \oplus F_1'\big(c \oplus F_2(d \oplus F_3'(a))\big)$$

Table 9. Summary of the Attacks on the *Lesamnta* Hash Function

	Attack		Rnds	*Lesamnta*-256 Time	*Lesamnta*-256 Mem.	*Lesamnta*-512 Time	*Lesamnta*-512 Mem.
Generic	Collision	[6]	16	2^{97}	-	2^{193}	-
	2nd Preimage	[6]	16	2^{193}	-	2^{385}	-
	Collision	(Sect. 3.2)	22	2^{96}	-	2^{192}	-
	2nd Preimage	(Sect. 3.2)	22	2^{192}	-	2^{384}	-
	Collision	(Sect. 3.2)	24	2^{96}	2^{64}	2^{192}	2^{128}
	2nd Preimage	(Sect. 3.2)	24	2^{192}	2^{64}	2^{384}	2^{128}
Specific	Collision	(Sect. 3.3)	24	2^{112}	-	2^{224}	-
	2nd Preimage	(Sect. 3.3)	24	2^{240}	-	*N/A*	

If we set

$$d = F_2^{-1}\Big(F_1'^{-1}(\overline{H} \oplus a \oplus F_4(b) \oplus b \oplus F_3(c)) \oplus c\Big) \oplus F_3'(a)$$

we have $X_9 \oplus X_0 = \overline{H}$. Each key (message) can be used with 2^{128} different a,b,c, and the cost of finding a suitable key is 2^{96}. Hence, the amortized cost for finding a 128-bit partial preimage is one compression function evaluation. The cost of finding a full preimage for the compression function is 2^{384}.

Second Preimage Attack on the Hash Function. We can use the preimage attack on the compression function to build a second preimage attack on the hash function reduced to 9 rounds. Using a generic unbalanced meet-in-the-middle attack the complexity is about 2^{448} compression function evaluations and 2^{64} memory. Note that we cannot find preimages for the hash function because we cannot find correctly padded message blocks.

Table 10. Summary of the Attacks on *SHAvite-3*$_{512}$

Attack		Rnds	Comp. Fun. Time	Comp. Fun. Mem.	Hash Fun. Time	Hash Fun. Mem.
2nd Preimage	[4]	8	2^{384}	-	2^{448}	2^{64}
2nd Preimage	(Sect. 4.4)	9	2^{384}	-	2^{448}	2^{64}
2nd Preimage	(extension of this work) [5]	10	2^{480}	-	2^{496}	2^{16}
2nd Preimage	(improving [5] w/ Sect. 4.3)	10	2^{448}	-	2^{480}	2^{32}
2nd Preimage	(improving [5] w/ Sect. 4.3)	10	2^{416}	2^{64}	2^{464}	2^{64}
2nd Preimage	(improving [5] w/ Sect. 4.3)	10	2^{384}	2^{128}	2^{448}	2^{128}
Collision[1]	(extension of this work) [5]	14	2^{192}	2^{128}	*N/A*	
Preimage[1]	(extension of this work) [5]	14	2^{384}	2^{128}	*N/A*	
Preimage[1]	(extension of this work) [5]	14	2^{448}	-	*N/A*	

[1] Chosen salt attacks

Acknowledgements

We would like to thank the members of the Graz ECRYPT meeting. Especially, we would like to express our gratitude to Emilia Käsper, Christian Rechberger, Søren S. Thomsen, and Ralf-Philipp Weinmann for the inspiring discussions. We are grateful to the *Lesamnta* team, and especially to Hirotaka Yoshida, for helping us with this research. We would also like to thank the anonymous referees for their comments.

References

1. Biham, E., Dunkelman, O.: The SHAvite-3 Hash Function. Submission to NIST (2008)
2. Bouillaguet, C., Dunkelman, O., Fouque, P.A., Leurent, G.: Another Look at Complementation Properties. In: Hong, S., Iwata, T. (eds.) FSE 2010. LNCS, vol. 6147, pp. 347–364. Springer, Heidelberg (2010)
3. Bouillaguet, C., Dunkelman, O., Leurent, G., Fouque, P.A.: Attacks on Hash Functions based on Generalized Feistel - Application to Reduced-Round Lesamnta and SHAvite-3_{512}. Cryptology ePrint Archive, Report 2009/634 (2009), `http://eprint.iacr.org/`
4. Mendel, F., et al.: A preimage attack on 8-round SHAvite-3-512. Graz ECRYPT meeting (May 2009)
5. Gauravaram, P., Leurent, G., Mendel, F., Naya-Plasencia, M., Peyrin, T., Rechberger, C., Schläffer, M.: Cryptanalysis of the 10-Round Hash and Full Compression Function of SHAvite-3-512. In: Bernstein, D.J., Lange, T. (eds.) AFRICACRYPT 2010. LNCS, vol. 6055, pp. 419–436. Springer, Heidelberg (2010)
6. Hirose, S., Kuwakado, H., Yoshida, H.: SHA-3 Proposal: Lesamnta. Submission to NIST (2008)
7. Khovratovich, D., Biryukov, A., Nikolic, I.: Speeding up Collision Search for Byte-Oriented Hash Functions. In: Fischlin, M. (ed.) CT-RSA 2009. LNCS, vol. 5473, pp. 164–181. Springer, Heidelberg (2009)
8. Lai, X., Massey, J.L.: Hash Functions Based on Block Ciphers. In: Rueppel, R.A. (ed.) EUROCRYPT 1992. LNCS, vol. 658, pp. 55–70. Springer, Heidelberg (1993)
9. Van Le, T., Sparr, R., Wernsdorf, R., Desmedt, Y.: Complementation-Like and Cyclic Properties of AES Round Functions. In: Dobbertin, H., Rijmen, V., Sowa, A. (eds.) AES 2005. LNCS, vol. 3373, pp. 128–141. Springer, Heidelberg (2005)
10. Hirose, S., Kuwakado, H., Yoshida, H.: Security Analysis of the Compression Function of Lesamnta and its Impact (2009) (available online)

The Differential Analysis of S-Functions*,**

Nicky Mouha[1,2,***], Vesselin Velichkov[1,2,†],
Christophe De Cannière[1,2,‡], and Bart Preneel[1,2]

[1] Department of Electrical Engineering ESAT/SCD-COSIC,
Katholieke Universiteit Leuven, Kasteelpark Arenberg 10, B-3001 Heverlee, Belgium
[2] Interdisciplinary Institute for BroadBand Technology (IBBT), Belgium
{Nicky.Mouha,Vesselin.Velichkov,Christophe.DeCanniere}@esat.kuleuven.be

Abstract. An increasing number of cryptographic primitives use operations such as addition modulo 2^n, multiplication by a constant and bitwise Boolean functions as a source of non-linearity. In NIST's SHA-3 competition, this applies to 6 out of the 14 second-round candidates. In this paper, we generalize such constructions by introducing the concept of S-functions. An S-function is a function that calculates the i-th output bit using only the inputs of the i-th bit position and a finite state $S[i]$. Although S-functions have been analyzed before, this paper is the first to present a fully general and efficient framework to determine their differential properties. A precursor of this framework was used in the cryptanalysis of SHA-1. We show how to calculate the probability that given input differences lead to given output differences, as well as how to count the number of output differences with non-zero probability. Our methods are rooted in graph theory, and the calculations can be efficiently performed using matrix multiplications.

Keywords: Differential cryptanalysis, S-function, xdp^{+}, $\text{xdp}^{\times C}$, $\text{adp}^{\oplus}$, counting possible output differences, ARX.

1 Introduction

Since their introduction to cryptography, differential cryptanalysis [7] and linear cryptanalysis [26] have shown to be two of the most important techniques in both the design and cryptanalysis of symmetric-key cryptographic primitives.

Differential cryptanalysis was introduced by Biham and Shamir in [7]. For block ciphers, it is used to analyze how input differences in the plaintext lead to

* The framework proposed in this paper is accompanied by a software toolkit, available at `http://www.ecrypt.eu.org/tools/s-function-toolkit`

** This work was supported in part by the IAP Program P6/26 BCRYPT of the Belgian State (Belgian Science Policy), and in part by the European Commission through the ICT program under contract ICT-2007-216676 ECRYPT II.

*** This author is funded by a research grant of the Institute for the Promotion of Innovation through Science and Technology in Flanders (IWT-Vlaanderen).

† DBOF Doctoral Fellow, K.U. Leuven, Belgium.

‡ Postdoctoral Fellow of the Research Foundation – Flanders (FWO).

A. Biryukov, G. Gong, and D.R. Stinson (Eds.): SAC 2010, LNCS 6544, pp. 36–56, 2011.

output differences in the ciphertext. If this happens in a non-random way, this can be used to build a distinguisher or even a key-recovery attack.

The analysis of how differences propagate through elementary components of cryptographic designs is therefore essential to differential cryptanalysis. As typical S-boxes are no larger than 8×8, this analysis can be done by building a difference distribution table. Such a difference distribution table lists the number of occurrences of every combination of input and output differences.

The combination of S-box layers and permutation layers with good cryptographic properties, are at the basis of the wide-trail design. The wide-trail design technique is used in AES [10] to provide provable resistance against both linear and differential cryptanalysis attacks.

However, not all cryptographic primitives are based on S-boxes. Another option is to use only operations such as addition modulo 2^n, exclusive or (xor), Boolean functions, bit shifts and bit rotations. For Boolean functions, we assume that the same Boolean function is used for each bit position i of the n-bit input words.

Each of these operations is very well suited for implementation in software, but building a difference distribution table becomes impractical for commonly used primitives where $n = 32$ or $n = 64$. Examples using such constructions include the XTEA block cipher [32], the Salsa20 stream cipher family [5], as well as the hash functions MD5, SHA-1, and 6 out of 14 second-round candidates[1] of NIST's SHA-3 hash function competition [31].

In this paper, we present the first known fully general framework to analyze these constructions efficiently. It is inspired by the cryptanalysis techniques for SHA-1 by De Cannière and Rechberger [12] (clarified in [30]), and by methods introduced by Lipmaa, Wallén and Dumas [23]. The framework is used to calculate the probability that given input differences lead to given output differences, as well as to count the number of output differences with non-zero probability. Our methods are based on graph theory, and the calculations can be efficiently performed using matrix multiplications. We show how the framework can be used to analyze several commonly used constructions.

Notation is defined in Table 1. Section 2 defines the concept of an S-function. This type of function can be analyzed using the framework of this paper. The differential probability xdp^+ of addition modulo 2^n, when differences are expressed using xor, is analyzed in Sect. 3. We show how to calculate xdp^+ with an arbitrary number of inputs. In Sect 4, we study the differential probability $\mathrm{adp}^\oplus$ of xor when differences are expressed using addition modulo 2^n. Counting the number of output differences with non-zero probability is the subject of Sect. 5. We conclude in Sect. 6. The matrices obtained for xdp^+ are listed in Appendix A. We show all possible subgraphs for xdp^+ in Appendix B. In Appendix C, we extend xdp^+ to an arbitrary number of inputs. The computation of $\mathrm{xdp}^{\times C}$ is explained in Appendix D.

[1] The hash functions BLAKE [4], Blue Midnight Wish [14], CubeHash [6], Shabal [8], SIMD [20] and Skein [13] can be analyzed using the general framework that is introduced in this paper.

Table 1. Notation

Notation	Description
$x \parallel y$	concatenation of the strings x and y
$\|A\|$	number of elements of set A
$x \ll s$	shift of x to the left by s positions
$x \gg s$	shift of x to the right by s positions
$x \lll s$	rotation of x to the left by s positions
$x \ggg s$	rotation of x to the right by s positions
$x + y$	addition of x and y modulo 2^n (in text)
$x \boxplus y$	addition of x and y modulo 2^n (in figures)
$x[i]$	selection: bit (or element) at position i of word x, where $i = 0$ is the least significant bit (element)

2 S-Functions

In this section, we define S-functions, the type of functions that can be analyzed using our framework. In order to show the broad range of applicability of the proposed technique, we give several examples of functions that follow our definition.

An S-function (short for "state function") accepts n-bit words $a_1, a_2, \ldots, a_k$ and a list of states $S[i]$ (for $0 \leq i < n$) as input, and produces an n-bit output word b in the following way:

$$(b[i], S[i+1]) = f(a_1[i], a_2[i], \ldots, a_k[i], S[i]), \qquad 0 \leq i < n \ . \qquad (1)$$

Initially, we set $S[0] = 0$. Note that f can be any arbitrary function that can be computed using only input bits $a_1[i], a_2[i], \ldots, a_k[i]$ and state $S[i]$. For conciseness, the same function f is used for every bit $0 \leq i < n$. Our analysis, however, does not require functions f to be the same, and not even to have the same number of inputs. A schematic representation of an S-function is given in Fig. 1.

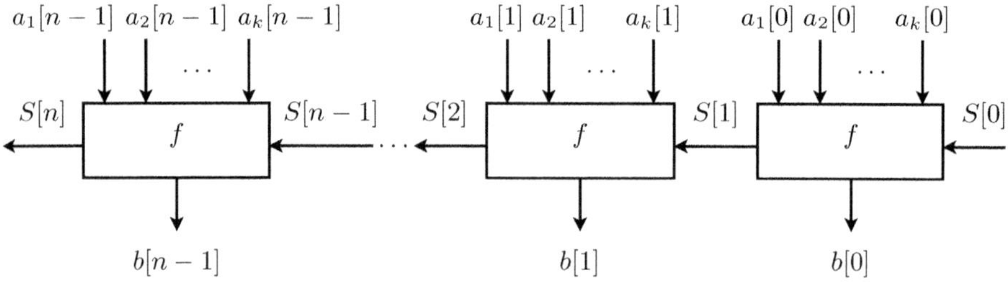

Fig. 1. Representation of an S-function

Examples of S-functions include addition, subtraction and multiplication by a constant (all modulo 2^n), exclusive-or (xor) and bitwise Boolean functions. Although this paper only analyzes constructions with one output b, the extension to multiple outputs is straightforward. Our technique therefore also applies to larger constructions, such as the Pseudo-Hadamard Transform used in SAFER [1] and Twofish [34], and first analyzed in [21].

With a minor modification, the concept of S-functions allows the inputs $a_1, a_2, \ldots, a_k$ and the output b to be rotated (or reordered) as well. This corresponds to rotating (or reordering) the bits of the input and output of f. This results in exactly the same S-function, but the input and output variables are relabeled accordingly. An entire step of SHA-1 as well as the `MIX` primitive of the block cipher RC2 can therefore be seen as an S-function. If the extension to multiple output bits is made, this applies as well to an entire step of SHA-2: for every step of SHA-2, two 32-bit registers are updated.

Every S-function is also a *T-function*, but the reverse is not always true. Proposed by Klimov and Shamir [19], a T-function is a mapping in which the i-th bit of the output depends only on bits $0, 1, \ldots, i$ of the input. Unlike a T-function, the definition of an S-function requires that the dependence on bits $0, 1, \ldots, i-1$ of the input can be described by a finite number of states. Therefore, squaring modulo 2^n is a T-function, but not an S-function.

In [11], Daum introduced the concept of a *narrow T-function*. A w-narrow T-function computes the i-th output bit based on some information of length w bits computed from all previous input bits. An S-function, however, requires only the i-th input bit and a state $S[i]$ to calculate the i-th output bit and the next state $S[i+1]$. There is a subtle difference between narrow T-functions and S-functions. If the number of states is finite and not dependent on the word length n, it may not always be possible for a narrow T-function to compute $S[i+1]$ from the previous state $S[i]$ and the i-th input bit.

It is possible to simulate every S-function using a *finite-state machine* (FSM), also known as a finite-state automaton (FSA). This finite-state machine has k inputs $a_1[i], a_2[i], \ldots, a_k[i]$, and one state for every value of $S[i]$. The output is $b[i]$. The FSM is clocked n times, for $0 \leq i < n$. From (1), we see that the output depends on both the current state and the input. The type of FSM we use is therefore a Mealy machine [27].

The straightforward hardware implementation of an S-function corresponds to a *bit-serial* design. Introduced by Lyon in [24,25], a bit-serial hardware architecture treats all n bits in sequence on a single hardware unit. Every bit requires one clock cycle to be processed.

The S-function framework can also be used in differential cryptanalysis, when the inputs and outputs are xor- or additive differences. Assume that every input pair (x_1, x_2) satisfies a difference $\Delta^{\bullet} x$, using some group operator $\bullet$. Then, if both x_1 and $\Delta^{\bullet} x$ are given, we can calculate $x_2 = x_1 \bullet \Delta^{\bullet} x$. It is then straightforward to define a function to calculate the output values and the output difference as well.This approach will become clear in the following sections, when we calculate the differential probabilities xdp^{+} and $\mathrm{adp}^{\oplus}$ of modular addition and xor respectively.

3 Computation of xdp^{+}

3.1 Introduction

In this section, we study the differential probability xdp^{+} of addition modulo 2^n, when differences are expressed using xor. Until [22], no algorithm was published to compute xdp^{+} faster than exhaustive search over all inputs. In [22], the first algorithm with a linear time in the word length n was proposed. If n-bit computations can be performed, the time complexity of this algorithm becomes sublinear in n.

In [23], xdp^{+} is expressed using the mathematical concept of rational series. It is shown that this technique is more general, and can also be used to calculate the differential probability $\mathrm{adp}^{\oplus}$ of xor, when differences are expressed using addition modulo 2^n.

In this paper, we present a new technique for the computation of xdp^{+}, using graph theory. The main advantage of the proposed method over existing techniques, is that it is not only more general, but also allows results to be obtained in a fully automated way. The only requirement is that both the operations and the input and output differences of the cryptographic component can be written as the S-function of Sect. 2. In the next section, we introduce this technique to calculate the probability xdp^{+}.

3.2 Defining the Probability xdp^{+}

Given n-bit words $x_1, y_1, \Delta^{\oplus}x, \Delta^{\oplus}y$, we calculate $\Delta^{\oplus}z$ using

$$x_2 \leftarrow x_1 \oplus \Delta^{\oplus}x \ , \tag{2}$$

$$y_2 \leftarrow y_1 \oplus \Delta^{\oplus}y \ , \tag{3}$$

$$z_1 \leftarrow x_1 + y_1 \ , \tag{4}$$

$$z_2 \leftarrow x_2 + y_2 \ , \tag{5}$$

$$\Delta^{\oplus}z \leftarrow z_2 \oplus z_1 \ . \tag{6}$$

We then define $\mathrm{xdp}^{+}(\alpha, \beta \to \gamma)$ as

$$\mathrm{xdp}^{+}(\alpha, \beta \to \gamma) = \frac{|\{(x_1, y_1) : \Delta^{\oplus}x = \alpha, \Delta^{\oplus}y = \beta, \Delta^{\oplus}z = \gamma\}|}{|\{(x_1, y_1) : \Delta^{\oplus}x = \alpha, \Delta^{\oplus}y = \beta\}|} \ , \tag{7}$$

$$= 4^{-n}|\{(x_1, y_1) : \Delta^{\oplus}x = \alpha, \Delta^{\oplus}y = \beta, \Delta^{\oplus}z = \gamma\}| \ , \tag{8}$$

as there are $2^n \cdot 2^n = 4^n$ combinations for the two n-bit words (x_1, y_1).

3.3 Constructing the S-Function for xdp^+

We rewrite (2)-(6) on a bit level, using the formulas for multiple-precision addition in radix 2 [28, §14.2.2]:

$$x_2[i] \leftarrow x_1[i] \oplus \Delta^{\oplus}x[i] \ , \tag{9}$$

$$y_2[i] \leftarrow y_1[i] \oplus \Delta^{\oplus}y[i] \ , \tag{10}$$

$$z_1[i] \leftarrow x_1[i] \oplus y_1[i] \oplus c_1[i] \ , \tag{11}$$

$$c_1[i+1] \leftarrow (x_1[i] + y_1[i] + c_1[i]) \gg 1 \ , \tag{12}$$

$$z_2[i] \leftarrow x_2[i] \oplus y_2[i] \oplus c_2[i] \ , \tag{13}$$

$$c_2[i+1] \leftarrow (x_2[i] + y_2[i] + c_2[i]) \gg 1 \ , \tag{14}$$

$$\Delta^{\oplus}z[i] \leftarrow z_2[i] \oplus z_1[i] \ , \tag{15}$$

where carries $c_1[0] = c_2[0] = 0$. Let us define

$$S[i] \leftarrow (c_1[i], c_2[i]) \ , \tag{16}$$

$$S[i+1] \leftarrow (c_1[i+1], c_2[i+1]) \ . \tag{17}$$

Then, (9)-(15) correspond to the S-function

$$(\Delta^{\oplus}z[i], S[i+1]) = f(x_1[i], y_1[i], \Delta^{\oplus}x[i], \Delta^{\oplus}y[i], S[i]), \qquad 0 \le i < n \ . \tag{18}$$

Because we are adding two words in binary, both carries $c_1[i]$ and $c_2[i]$ can be either 0 or 1.

3.4 Computing the Probability xdp^+

In this section, we use the S-function (18), defined by (9)-(15), to compute xdp^+. We explain how this probability can be derived from the number of paths in a graph, and then show how to calculate xdp^+ using matrix multiplications.

Graph Representation. For $0 \le i \le n$, we will represent every state $S[i]$ as a vertex in a graph (Fig. 2). This graph consists of several subgraphs, containing only vertices $S[i]$ and $S[i+1]$ for some bit position i. We repeat the following for all combinations of $(\alpha[i], \beta[i], \gamma[i])$:

Set $\alpha[i] \leftarrow \Delta^{\oplus}x[i]$ and $\beta[i] \leftarrow \Delta^{\oplus}y[i]$. Then, we loop over all values of $(x_1[i], y_1[i], S[i])$. For each combination, $\Delta^{\oplus}z[i]$ and $S[i]$ are uniquely determined by (18). We draw an edge between $S[i]$ and $S[i+1]$ in the subgraph, if and only if $\Delta^{\oplus}z[i] = \gamma[i]$. Note that several edges may have the same set of endpoints.

For completeness, all subgraphs for xdp^+ are given in Appendix B. Let α, β, γ be given. As shown in Fig. 2, we construct a full graph containing all vertices $S[i]$ for $0 \le i \le n$, where the edges between these vertices correspond to those of the subgraphs for $\alpha[i], \beta[i], \gamma[i]$.

Theorem 1. *Let P be the set of all paths from $(c_1[0], c_2[0]) = (0,0)$ to any of the four vertices $(c_1[n], c_2[n]) \in \{(0,0),(0,1),(1,0),(1,1)\}$ (see Fig. 2). Then, there is exactly one path in P for every pair (x_1, y_1) of the set in the definition of* xdp^+, *given by (8).*

Proof. Given $x_1[i]$, $y_1[i]$, $\Delta^{\oplus}x[i]$, $\Delta^{\oplus}y[i]$, $c_1[i]$ and $c_2[i]$, the values of $\Delta^{\oplus}z[i]$, $c_1[i+1]$ and $c_2[i+1]$ are uniquely determined by (9)-(15). All paths in P start at $(c_1[0], c_2[0]) = (0,0)$, and only consist of vertices $(c_1[i], c_2[i])$ for $0 \leq i \leq n$ that satisfy (9)-(15). Furthermore, edges for which $\Delta^{\oplus}z[i] \neq \gamma[i]$ are not in the graph, and therefore not part of any path P. Thus by construction, P contains every pair (x_1, y_1) of the set in (8) exactly once. □

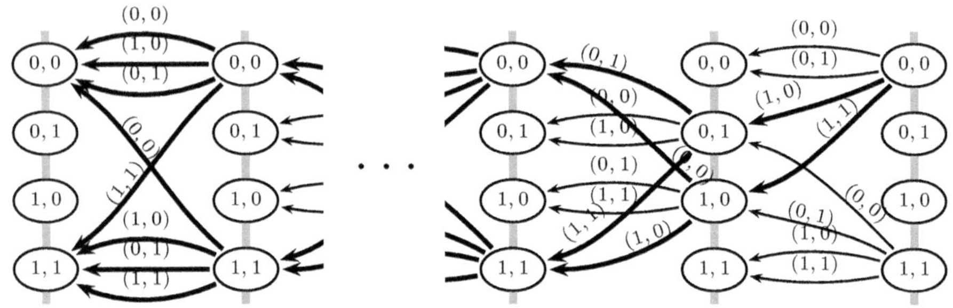

Fig. 2. An example of a full graph for xdp^+. Vertices $(c_1[i], c_2[i]) \in \{(0,0),(0,1),(1,0),(1,1)\}$ correspond to states $S[i]$. There is one edge for every input pair (x_1, y_1). All paths that satisfy input differences α, β and output difference γ are shown in bold. They define the set of paths P of Theorem 1.

Multiplication of Matrices. The differential $(\alpha[i], \beta[i] \rightarrow \gamma[i])$ at bit position i is written as a bit string $w[i] \leftarrow \alpha[i] \parallel \beta[i] \parallel \gamma[i]$. Each $w[i]$ corresponds to a subgraph of Appendix B. As this subgraph is a bipartite graph, we can construct its biadjacency matrix $A_{w[i]} = [x_{kj}]$, where x_{kj} is the number of edges that connect vertices $j = S[i]$ and $k = S[i+1]$. These matrices are given in Appendix A.

Let the number of states $S[i]$ be N. Define $1 \times N$ matrix $L = [1\,1 \cdots 1]$ and $N \times 1$ matrix $C = [1\,0 \cdots 0]^T$. For any directed acyclic graph, the number of paths between two vertices can be calculated as a matrix multiplication [9]. We can therefore calculate the number of paths P as

$$|P| = LA_{w[n-1]} \cdots A_{w[1]}A_{w[0]}C \ . \tag{19}$$

Using (8), we find that $\text{xdp}^+(\alpha, \beta \rightarrow \gamma) = 4^{-n}|P|$. Therefore, we can define $A^*_{w[i]} = A_{w[i]}/4$, and obtain

$$\text{xdp}^+(\alpha, \beta \rightarrow \gamma) = LA^*_{w[n-1]} \cdots A^*_{w[1]}A^*_{w[0]}C \ . \tag{20}$$

As such, we obtain a similar expression as in [23], where the xdp^+ was calculated using the concept of rational series. Our matrices $A^*_{w[i]}$ are of size 4×4 instead of 2×2, however. We now give a simple algorithm to reduce the size of our matrices.

3.5 Minimizing the Size of the Matrices for xdp^+

Corresponding to (20), we can define a non-deterministic finite-state automaton (NFA) with states $S[i]$ and inputs $w[i]$. Compared to a deterministic finite-state automaton, the transition *function* is replaced by a transition *relation*. There are several choices for the next state, each with a certain probability. This NFA can be minimized as follows.

First, we remove non-accessible states. A state is said to be non-accessible, if it can never be reached from the initial state $S[0] = 0$. This can be done using a simple algorithm to check for connectivity, with a time complexity that is linear in the number of edges.

Secondly, we merge indistinguishable states. The method we propose, is similar to the FSM reduction algorithms found independently by [17] and [29]. Initially, we assign all states $S[i]$ to one equivalence class $T[i] = 0$. We try to partition this equivalence class into smaller classes, by repeating the following steps:

- We iterate over all states $S[i]$.
- For every input $w[i]$ and every equivalence class $T[i]$, we sum the transition probabilities to every state $S[i]$ of this equivalence class.
- If these sums are different for two particular states $S[i]$, we partition them into different equivalence classes $T[i]$.

The algorithm stops when the equivalence classes $T[i]$ cannot be partitioned further.

In the case of xdp^+, we find that all states are accessible. However, there are only two indistinguishable states: $T[i] = 0$ and $T[i] = 1$ when $(c_1[i], c_2[i])$ are elements of the sets $\{(0,0),(1,1)\}$ and $\{(0,1),(1,0)\}$ respectively. Our algorithm shows how matrices $A^*_{w[i]}$ of (20) can be reduced to matrices $A'_{w[i]}$ of size 2×2. These matrices are the same as in [23], but they have now been obtained in an automated way. For completeness, they are given again in Appendix A. Our approach also allows a new interpretation of matrices $A'_{w[i]}$ in the context of S-functions (18): every matrix entry defines the transition probability between two sets of states, where all states of one set were shown to be equivalent by the minimization algorithm.

3.6 Extensions of xdp^+

In this section, we show how S-functions not only lead to expressions to calculate $\mathrm{xdp}^+(\alpha, \beta \to \gamma)$, but can be applied to related constructions as well.

Multiple Inputs $\mathrm{xdp}^+(\alpha, \beta, \ldots \to \gamma)$. Using the framework of this paper, we can easily calculate xdp^+ for more than two (independent) inputs. This calculation can be used, for example, in the differential cryptanalysis of XTEA [32] using xor differences. In [15], a 3-round iterative characteristic $(\alpha, 0) \to (\alpha, 0)$ is used, where $\alpha =$ `0x80402010`. In the third round of the characteristic, there are two consecutive applications of addition modulo 2^n. Separately, these result in probabilities $\text{xdp}^+(\alpha, 0 \to \alpha) = 2^{-3}$ and $\text{xdp}^+(\alpha, \alpha \to 0) = 2^{-3}$. It is shown in [15] that the joint probability $\text{xdp}^+(\alpha, 0, \alpha \to 0)$ is higher than the product of the probabilities $2^{-3} \cdot 2^{-3} = 2^{-6}$, and is estimated to be $2^{-4.755}$. Using the techniques presented in this paper, we evaluate the exact joint probability to be 2^{-3}. We also verified this experimentally. The calculations are detailed in Appendix C. This result can be trivially confirmed using the commutativity property of addition: $\text{xdp}^+(\alpha, \alpha \to 0) \cdot \text{xdp}^+(0, 0 \to 0) = \text{xdp}^+(\alpha, \alpha \to 0) = 2^{-3}$. Nevertheless, our method is more general and can be used for any input difference.

Multiplication by a Constant $\text{xdp}^{\times C}$. A problem related to xdp^+, is the differential probability of multiplication by a constant C where differences are expressed by xor. We denote this probability by $\text{xdp}^{\times C}$. In the hash function Shabal [8], multiplications by 3 and 5 occur. EnRUPT [33] uses a multiplication by 9. In the cryptanalysis of EnRUPT [18], a technique is described to calculate $\text{xdp}^{\times 9}$. This technique is based on a precursor of the framework in this paper. In Appendix D, we show how each of these probabilities can be calculated efficiently, using the framework of this paper. The example of $\text{xdp}^{\times 3}$ is fully worked out.

Pseudo-Hadamard Transform xdp^{PHT}. The Pseudo-Hadamard Transform (PHT) is defined as $\text{PHT}(x_1, x_2) = (2x_1 + x_2, x_1 + x_2)$. It is a reversible operation, used to provide diffusion in several cryptographic primitives, including block ciphers SAFER [1] and Twofish [34]. Its differential properties were first studied in [21]. If we allow an S-function to be constructed with two outputs b_1 and b_2, the analysis of this construction becomes straightforward using the techniques of this paper.

Step Functions of the MD4 Family. The MD4 family consists of several hash functions, including MD4, MD5, SHA-1, SHA-2 and HAS-160. Currently, the most commonly used hash functions worldwide are MD5 and SHA-1. The step functions of MD4, HAS-160 and SHA-1 can each be represented as an S-function. This applies as well to the `MIX` primitive of the block cipher RC2. They can therefore also be analyzed using our framework. The calculation of the uncontrolled probability $P_u(i)$ in the cryptanalysis of SHA-1 [12,30] uses a precursor of the techniques in this paper. By making the extension to multiple outputs, the same analysis can be made as well for the step function of SHA-2.

4 Computation of $\text{adp}^{\oplus}$

4.1 Introduction

In this section, we study the differential probability $\text{adp}^{\oplus}$ of xor when differences are expressed using addition modulo 2^n. The best known algorithm to compute $\text{adp}^{\oplus}$ was exhaustive search over all inputs, until an algorithm with a linear time in n was proposed in [23].

We show how the technique introduced in Sect. 3 for xdp^+ can also be applied to $\text{adp}^{\oplus}$. Using this, we confirm the results of [23]. The approach we introduced in this section is conceptually much easier than [23], and can easily be generalized to other constructions with additive differences.

4.2 Defining the Probability adp$^{\oplus}$

Given n-bit words $x_1, y_1, \Delta^+x, \Delta^+y$, we calculate Δ^+z using

$$x_2 \leftarrow x_1 + \Delta^+x \ , \tag{21}$$

$$y_2 \leftarrow y_1 + \Delta^+y \ , \tag{22}$$

$$z_1 \leftarrow x_1 \oplus y_1 \ , \tag{23}$$

$$z_2 \leftarrow x_2 \oplus y_2 \ , \tag{24}$$

$$\Delta^+z \leftarrow z_2 - z_1 \ . \tag{25}$$

Similar to (8), we define $\mathrm{adp}^{\oplus}(\alpha, \beta \to \gamma)$ as

$$\mathrm{adp}^{\oplus}(\alpha, \beta \to \gamma) = \frac{|\{(x_1, y_1) : \Delta^+x = \alpha, \Delta^+y = \beta, \Delta^+z = \gamma\}|}{|\{(x_1, y_1) : \Delta^+x = \alpha, \Delta^+y = \beta\}|} \ , \tag{26}$$

$$= 4^{-n}|\{(x_1, y_1) : \Delta^+x = \alpha, \Delta^+y = \beta, \Delta^+z = \gamma\}| \ , \tag{27}$$

as there are $2^n \cdot 2^n = 4^n$ combinations for the two n-bit words (x_1, y_1).

4.3 Constructing the S-Function for adp$^{\oplus}$

We rewrite (21)-(25) on a bit level, again using the formulas for multiple-precision addition and subtraction in radix 2 [28, §14.2.2]:

$$x_2[i] \leftarrow x_1[i] \oplus \Delta^+x[i] \oplus c_1[i] \ , \tag{28}$$

$$c_1[i+1] \leftarrow (x_1[i] + \Delta^+x[i] + c_1[i]) \gg 1 \ , \tag{29}$$

$$y_2[i] \leftarrow y_1[i] \oplus \Delta^+y[i] \oplus c_2[i] \ , \tag{30}$$

$$c_2[i+1] \leftarrow (y_1[i] + \Delta^+y[i] + c_2[i]) \gg 1 \ , \tag{31}$$

$$z_1[i] \leftarrow x_1[i] \oplus y_1[i] \ , \tag{32}$$

$$z_2[i] \leftarrow x_2[i] \oplus y_2[i] \ , \tag{33}$$

$$\Delta^+z[i] \leftarrow (z_2[i] \oplus z_1[i] \oplus c_3[i])[0] \ , \tag{34}$$

$$c_3[i+1] \leftarrow (z_2[i] - z_1[i] + c_3[i]) \gg 1 \ , \tag{35}$$

where carries $c_1[0] = c_2[0] = 0$ and borrow $c_3[0] = 0$. We assume all variables to be integers in two's complement notation, all shifts are signed shifts. Let us define

$$S[i] \leftarrow (c_1[i], c_2[i], c_3[i]) \ , \tag{36}$$

$$S[i+1] \leftarrow (c_1[i+1], c_2[i+1], c_3[i+1]) \ . \tag{37}$$

Then (28)-(35) correspond to the S-function

$$(\Delta^+z[i], S[i+1]) = f(x_1[i], y_1[i], \Delta^+x[i], \Delta^+y[i], S[i]), \quad 0 \le i < n \ . \tag{38}$$

Both carries $c_1[i]$ and $c_2[i]$ can be either 0 or 1; borrow $c_3[i]$ can be either 0 or -1.

4.4 Computing the Probability $\text{adp}^{\oplus}$

Using the description of the S-function (38), the calculation of $\text{adp}^{\oplus}$ follows directly from Sect. 3.4. We obtain eight matrices $A_{w[i]}$ of size 8×8. After applying the minimization algorithm of Sect. 3.5, the size of the matrices remains unchanged. Here, we use the expression $-4 \cdot c_3[i] + 2 \cdot c_2[i] + c_1[i]$ as an index to order the states $S[i]$. The matrices we obtain are then permutation similar to those of [23]; their states $S'[i]$ can be related to our states $S[i]$ by permutation σ:

$$\sigma = \begin{pmatrix} 0 & 1 & 2 & 3 & 4 & 5 & 6 & 7 \\ 0 & 4 & 2 & 6 & 1 & 5 & 3 & 7 \end{pmatrix} . \tag{39}$$

We calculate the number of paths using (19). From (27), we get $\text{adp}^{\oplus}(\alpha, \beta \to \gamma) = 4^{-n}|P|$. Therefore, we can define $A^*_{w[i]} = A_{w[i]}/4$, and obtain

$$\text{adp}^{\oplus}(\alpha, \beta \to \gamma) = L A^*_{w[n-1]} \cdots A^*_{w[1]} A^*_{w[0]} C . \tag{40}$$

5 Counting Possible Output Differences

5.1 Introduction

In the previous sections, we showed for several constructions how to calculate the probability that given input differences lead to a given output difference. A related problem is to calculate the number of *possible* output differences, when the input differences are given. We say that an output difference is possible, if it occurs with a non-zero probability.

First, we describe a naive algorithm to count the number of output differences. It has a time complexity that is exponential in the word length n. We investigate both improvements in existing literature, as well as cryptanalysis results where such a calculation is necessary.

Then, we introduce a new algorithm. We found it to be the first in existing literature with a time complexity that is linear in n. We show that our algorithm can be used for all constructions based on S-functions.

5.2 Algorithm with a Exponential Time in n

Generic Exponential-in-n Time Algorithm. A naive, but straightforward algorithm works as follows. All output differences with non-zero probability can be represented in a search tree. Every level in this tree contains nodes of one particular bit position, with the least significant bit at the top level. This tree is traversed using depth-first search. For each output difference with non-zero probability that is found, we increment a counter for the number of output differences by one. When all nodes are traversed, this counter contains the total number of possible output differences. The time complexity of this algorithm is exponential in n, the memory complexity is linear in n.

Improvement for $\text{xdc}^+(\alpha, \beta)$. We introduce the notation $\text{xdc}^+(\alpha, \beta)$ for the number of output xor-differences of addition modulo 2^n, given input xor-differences α and β. In [3], xdc^+ was used to build a key-recovery attack on top of a boomerang distinguisher for 32-round Threefish-512 [13]. They introduced a new algorithm to calculate xdc^+. The correctness of this algorithm is proven in the full version of [3], i.e. [2]. The algorithm, however, only works if one of the inputs contains either no difference, or a difference only in the most significant bit. Also, it does not generalize to other types of differences. The time complexity of this algorithm is exponential in the number of non-zero input bits, and the memory complexity is linear in the number of non-zero input bits. As a result, it is only usable in practice for sparse input differences. We were unable to find any other work on this problem in existing literature.

5.3 Algorithm with a Linear Time in n

In Sect. 3 and 4, we showed how to calculate the probability of an output difference using both graph theory and matrix multiplications. We now present a similar method to calculate the number of possible output differences. First, the general algorithm is explained. It is applicable to any type of construction based on S-functions. Then, we illustrate how the matrices for xdp^+ can be turned into matrices for xdc^+. This paper is the first to present an algorithm for this problem with a linear-in-n time complexity. We also extend the results to $\text{adp}^\oplus$. Our strategy is similar to the calculation of the controlled probability $P_c(i)$, used in the cryptanalysis of SHA-1 [12,30].

Graph Representation. As in Sect. 3.4, we will again construct a graph. Let N be the number of states $|T[i]|$ that we obtained in Sect. 3.5. For xdp^+, we found $N = 2$. We will now construct larger subgraphs, where the nodes do not represent states $T[i]$, but elements of its power set $\mathcal{P}(T[i])$. This power set $\mathcal{P}(T[i])$ contains 2^N elements, ranging from the empty set $\varnothing$ to set of all states $\{0, 1, \ldots, N-1\}$. In automata theory, this technique is known as the subset construction [16, §2.3.5]. It converts the non-deterministic finite-state automaton (NFA) of Sect. 3.5 into a deterministic finite-state automaton (DFA).

For every subgraph, the input difference bits $\alpha[i]$ and $\beta[i]$ are fixed. We then define exactly one edge for every output bit $\gamma[i]$ from every set in $\mathcal{P}(T[i])$ to the corresponding set of next states in $\mathcal{P}(T[i+1])$. The example in the next section will clarify this step.

Theorem 2. *Let P be the set of all paths that start in $\{0\}$ at position $i = 0$ and end in a non-empty set at position $i = n$. Then, the number of paths $|P|$ corresponds to the number of possible output differences.*

Proof. All paths P start in $\{0\}$ at $i = 0$, and end in a non-empty set at $i = n$. For a given output difference bit, there is exactly one edge leaving from a non-empty set of states to another non-empty set of states. Therefore by construction, every possible output difference corresponds to exactly one path in P. □

Multiplication of Matrices. The differential $(\alpha[i], \beta[i])$ at bit position i is written as a bit string $w[i] \leftarrow \alpha[i] \parallel \beta[i]$. As in Sect. 3.4, we construct the biadjacency matrices of these subgraphs. They will be of size $2^N \times 2^N$. As we are only interested in possible output differences, these matrices can be reduced to matrices $B_{w[i]}$ of size $(2^N - 1) \times (2^N - 1)$ by removing the empty set $\varnothing$.

Define $1{\times}(2^N{-}1)$ matrix $L = [\,1\,1 \cdots 1\,]$ and $(2^N-1){\times}1$ matrix $C = [\,1\;0 \;\cdots\; 0\,]^T$. Similar to (19), we obtain the number of possible output differences as

$$|P| = LB_{w[n-1]} \cdots B_{w[1]} B_{w[0]} C \ . \tag{41}$$

The time complexity of (41) is linear in the word length n.

We note that these matrices can have large dimensions. However, this is often not a problem in practice, as they are typically very sparse. If we keep track of only non-zero elements, there is little memory required to store vectors, and fast algorithms exist for sparse matrix-vector multiplications. Also, the size of the matrices can be minimized using Sect. 3.5.

5.4 Computing the Number of Output Differences xdc^+

In the minimized matrices for xdp^+ (given in [23] and again in Appendix A), we refer to the states corresponding to the first and the second column as $S[i] = 0$ and $S[i] = 1$ respectively. Then, the subgraphs for xdc^+ can be constructed as in Fig. 3. Regardless of the value of the output bit, edges leaving from the empty set $\varnothing$ at i will always arrive at the empty set at $i+1$. Assume that the input differences are $\alpha[i] = \beta[i] = 0$, and that we are in state $S[i] = 1$, represented in Fig. 3 as $\{1\}$. Recall that the matrices for xdp^+ are

$$A'_{000} = \begin{bmatrix} 1 & 0 \\ 0 & 0 \end{bmatrix}, \quad A'_{001} = \frac{1}{2} \begin{bmatrix} 0 & 1 \\ 0 & 1 \end{bmatrix}, \tag{42}$$

for output differences $\gamma[i] = 0$ and $\gamma[i] = 1$ respectively. To find out which states can be reached from state $S[i] = 1$, we multiply both matrices to the right by $\begin{bmatrix} 0 & 1 \end{bmatrix}^T$. We obtain

$$A'_{000} \begin{bmatrix} 0 \\ 1 \end{bmatrix} = \begin{bmatrix} 0 \\ 0 \end{bmatrix}, \quad A'_{001} \begin{bmatrix} 0 \\ 1 \end{bmatrix} = \frac{1}{2} \begin{bmatrix} 1 \\ 1 \end{bmatrix}. \tag{43}$$

We see that we cannot reach a valid next state if $\gamma[i] = 0$, so there is an edge between $\{1\}$ at i and $\varnothing$ at $i+1$ for $\gamma[i] = 0$. If $\gamma[i] = 1$, both states can be reached. Therefore, we draw an edge between $\{1\}$ at i and $\{0, 1\}$ at $i+1$ for $\gamma[i] = 1$. The other edges of Fig. 3 can be derived in a similar way.

Matrices $B_{00}, B_{01}, B_{10}, B_{11}$ of (41) can be derived from Fig. 3 as

$$B_{00} = \begin{bmatrix} 1 & 0 & 1 \\ 0 & 0 & 0 \\ 0 & 1 & 1 \end{bmatrix}, \quad B_{01} = B_{10} = \begin{bmatrix} 0 & 0 & 0 \\ 0 & 0 & 0 \\ 1 & 1 & 2 \end{bmatrix}, \quad B_{11} = \begin{bmatrix} 0 & 0 & 0 \\ 0 & 1 & 1 \\ 1 & 0 & 1 \end{bmatrix} \ . \tag{44}$$

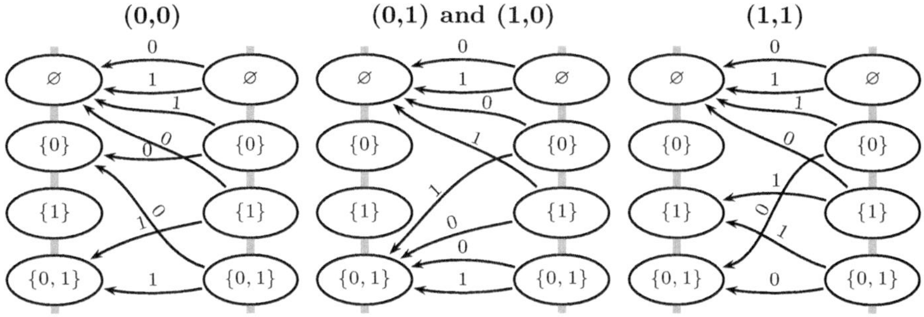

Fig. 3. All possible subgraphs for xdc^+. Vertices correspond to valid sets of states $S[i]$. There is one edge for every output difference bit $\gamma[i]$. Above each subgraph, the value of $(\alpha[i], \beta[i])$ is given in bold.

If the input differences are very sparse or very dense, (41) can be sped up by using the following expressions for the powers of matrices:

$$B_{00}^k = \begin{bmatrix} 1 & k-1 & k \\ 0 & 0 & 0 \\ 0 & 1 & 1 \end{bmatrix}, \quad B_{01}^k = B_{10}^k = \begin{bmatrix} 0 & 0 & 0 \\ 0 & 0 & 0 \\ 2^{k-1} & 2^{k-1} & 2^k \end{bmatrix}, B_{11}^k = \begin{bmatrix} 0 & 0 & 0 \\ k-1 & 1 & k \\ 1 & 0 & 1 \end{bmatrix} . \tag{45}$$

This way, we obtain an algorithm with a time complexity that is linear in the number of non-zero input bits. As such, our algorithm always outperforms the naive exponential time algorithm, as well as the exponential time algorithm of [3] that only works for some input differences.

Let $L = [1\ 1]$ and $C = [1\ 0]^T$. We illustrate our method by recalculating the example given in [3]:

$$\mathrm{xdc}^+(\mathtt{0x1000010402000000}, \mathtt{0x0000000000000000}) \tag{46}$$
$$= L \cdot B_{00}^3 \cdot B_{10} \cdot B_{00}^{19} \cdot B_{10} \cdot B_{00}^5 \cdot B_{10} \cdot B_{00}^8 \cdot B_{10} \cdot B_{00}^{25} \cdot C \tag{47}$$
$$= 5880 \tag{48}$$

5.5 Calculation of $\mathrm{adc}^\oplus$

We can also calculate $\mathrm{adc}^\oplus$, which is the number of output differences for xor, when all differences are expressed using addition modulo 2^n. As the matrices $A_{w[i]}^*$ for $\mathrm{adp}^\oplus$ are of dimension 8×8, the matrices $B_{w[i]}$ of $\mathrm{adc}^\oplus$ would be of dimension $(2^8 - 1) \times (2^8 - 1) = 255 \times 255$. However, we find that only 24 out of 255 states are accessible. Furthermore, we find that all 24 accessible states are equivalent to 2 states. In the end, we obtain the following 2×2 matrices:

$$B_{00} = \begin{bmatrix} 1 & 0 \\ 0 & 2 \end{bmatrix}, \quad B_{01} = B_{10} = B_{11} = \begin{bmatrix} 0 & 0 \\ 1 & 2 \end{bmatrix} . \tag{49}$$

These matrices $B_{w[i]}$ are consistent with Theorem 2 of [23]. Although the end result is simple, this example encompasses many of the techniques presented in this paper.

6 Conclusion

In Sect. 2, we introduced the concept of an S-function, for which we build a framework in this paper. In Sect. 3, we analyzed the differential probability xdp^+ of addition modulo 2^n, when differences are expressed using xor. This probability was derived using graph theory, and calculated using matrix multiplications. We showed not only how to derive the matrices in an automated way, but also give an algorithm to minimize their size. The results are consistent with [23]. This technique was extended to an arbitrary number of inputs and to several related constructions, including an entire step of SHA-1. A precursor of the methods in this section was already used for the cryptanalysis of SHA-1 [12,30]. We are unaware of any other fully systematic and efficient framework for the differential cryptanalysis of S-functions using xor differences.

Using the proposed framework, we studied the differential probability $\text{adp}^{\oplus}$ of xor when differences are expressed using addition modulo 2^n in Sect 4. To the best of our knowledge, this paper is the first to obtain this result in a constructive way. We verified that our matrices correspond to those obtained in [23]. As these techniques can easily be generalized, this paper provides the first known systematic treatment of the differential cryptanalysis of S-functions using additive differences.

Finally, in Sect. 5, we showed how the number of output differences with non-zero probability can be calculated. An exponential-in-n algorithm was already used for this problem in the cryptanalysis of Threefish [3]. As far as we know, this paper is the first to present an algorithm for this with a time complexity that is linear in the number of non-zero bits.

Acknowledgments. The authors would like to thank their colleagues at COSIC, and Vincent Rijmen in particular, for the fruitful discussions, as well as the anonymous reviewers for their detailed comments and suggestions. Thanks to James Quah for pointing out an error in one of the matrices of Appendix A, and for several suggestions on how to improve the text.

References

1. Anderson, R.J. (ed.): FSE 1993. LNCS, vol. 809. Springer, Heidelberg (1994)
2. Aumasson, J.-P., Calik, C., Meier, W., Ozen, O., Phan, R.C.-W., Varıcı, K.: Improved Cryptanalysis of Skein. Cryptology ePrint Archive, Report 2009/438 (2009), `http://eprint.iacr.org/`
3. Aumasson, J.-P., Calik, C., Meier, W., Özen, O., Phan, R.C.-W., Varıcı, K.: Improved Cryptanalysis of Skein. In: Matsui, M. (ed.) ASIACRYPT 2009. LNCS, vol. 5912, pp. 542–559. Springer, Heidelberg (2009)

4. Aumasson, J.-P., Henzen, L., Meier, W., Phan, R.C.-W.: SHA-3 proposal BLAKE. Submission to the NIST SHA-3 Competition (Round 2) (2008)
5. Bernstein, D.J.: The Salsa20 Family of Stream Ciphers. In: Robshaw, M.J.B., Billet, O. (eds.) New Stream Cipher Designs. LNCS, vol. 4986, pp. 84–97. Springer, Heidelberg (2008)
6. Bernstein, D.J.: CubeHash specification (2.B.1). Submission to the NIST SHA-3 Competition (Round 2) (2009)
7. Biham, E., Shamir, A.: Differential Cryptanalysis of DES-like Cryptosystems. J. Cryptology 4(1), 3–72 (1991)
8. Bresson, E., Canteaut, A., Chevallier-Mames, B., Clavier, C., Fuhr, T., Gouget, A., Icart, T., Misarsky, J.-F., Naya-Plasencia, M., Paillier, P., Pornin, T., Reinhard, J.-R., Thuillet, C., Videau, M.: Shabal, a Submission to NIST's Cryptographic Hash Algorithm Competition. Submission to the NIST SHA-3 Competition (Round 2) (2008)
9. Chittenden, E.W.: On the number of paths in a finite partially ordered set. The American Mathematical Monthly 54(7), 404–405 (1947)
10. Daemen, J., Rijmen, V.: The Design of Rijndael: AES - The Advanced Encryption Standard. Springer, Heidelberg (2002)
11. Daum, M.: Narrow T-Functions. In: Gilbert, H., Handschuh, H. (eds.) FSE 2005. LNCS, vol. 3557, pp. 50–67. Springer, Heidelberg (2005)
12. De Cannière, C., Rechberger, C.: Finding SHA-1 Characteristics: General Results and Applications. In: Lai, X., Chen, K. (eds.) ASIACRYPT 2006. LNCS, vol. 4284, pp. 1–20. Springer, Heidelberg (2006)
13. Ferguson, N., Lucks, S., Schneier, B., Whiting, D., Bellare, M., Kohno, T., Callas, J., Walker, J.: The Skein Hash Function Family. Submission to the NIST SHA-3 Competition (Round 2) (2009)
14. Gligoroski, D., Klima, V., Knapskog, S.J., El-Hadedy, M., Amundsen, J., Mjølsnes, S.F.: Cryptographic Hash Function BLUE MIDNIGHT WISH. Submission to the NIST SHA-3 Competition (Round 2) (2009)
15. Hong, S., Hong, D., Ko, Y., Chang, D., Lee, W., Lee, S.: Differential Cryptanalysis of TEA and XTEA. In: Lim, J.I., Lee, D.H. (eds.) ICISC 2003. LNCS, vol. 2971, pp. 402–417. Springer, Heidelberg (2004)
16. Hopcroft, J.E., Ullman, J.D.: Introduction to Automata Theory, Languages, and Computation, 3rd edn. Addison-Wesley, Reading (2006)
17. Huffman, D.: The synthesis of sequential switching circuits. Journal of the Franklin Institute 257(3), 161–190 (1954)
18. Indesteege, S., Preneel, B.: Practical Collisions for EnRUPT. Journal of Cryptology 23(3) (2010) (to appear)
19. Klimov, A., Shamir, A.: Cryptographic Applications of T-Functions. In: Matsui, M., Zuccherato, R.J. (eds.) SAC 2003. LNCS, vol. 3006, pp. 248–261. Springer, Heidelberg (2004)
20. Leurent, G., Bouillaguet, C., Fouque, P.-A.: SIMD Is a Message Digest. Submission to the NIST SHA-3 Competition (Round 2) (2009)
21. Lipmaa, H.: On Differential Properties of Pseudo-Hadamard Transform and Related Mappings. In: Menezes, A., Sarkar, P. (eds.) INDOCRYPT 2002. LNCS, vol. 2551, pp. 48–61. Springer, Heidelberg (2002)
22. Lipmaa, H., Moriai, S.: Efficient Algorithms for Computing Differential Properties of Addition. In: Matsui, M. (ed.) FSE 2001. LNCS, vol. 2355, pp. 336–350. Springer, Heidelberg (2002)

23. Lipmaa, H., Wallén, J., Dumas, P.: On the Additive Differential Probability of Exclusive-Or. In: Roy, B.K., Meier, W. (eds.) FSE 2004. LNCS, vol. 3017, pp. 317–331. Springer, Heidelberg (2004)
24. Lyon, R.F.: Two's Complement Pipeline Multipliers. IEEE Transactions on Communications 24(4), 418–425 (1976)
25. Lyon, R.F.: A bit-serial architectural methodology for signal processing. In: Gray, J.P. (ed.) VLSI 1981, pp. 131–140. Academic Press, London (1981)
26. Matsui, M., Yamagishi, A.: A New Method for Known Plaintext Attack of FEAL Cipher. In: Rueppel, R.A. (ed.) EUROCRYPT 1992. LNCS, vol. 658, pp. 81–91. Springer, Heidelberg (1993)
27. Mealy, G.H.: A method for synthesizing sequential circuits. Bell Systems Technical Journal 34, 1045–1079 (1955)
28. Menezes, A., van Oorschot, P.C., Vanstone, S.A.: Handbook of Applied Cryptography. CRC Press, Boca Raton (1996)
29. Moore, E.F.: Gedanken experiments on sequential machines. Automata Studies, 129–153 (1956)
30. Mouha, N., De Cannière, C., Indesteege, S., Preneel, B.: Finding Collisions for a 45-Step Simplified HAS-V. In: Youm, H.Y., Yung, M. (eds.) WISA 2009. LNCS, vol. 5932, pp. 206–225. Springer, Heidelberg (2009)
31. National Institute of Standards and Technology. Announcing Request for Candidate Algorithm Nominations for a New Cryptographic Hash Algorithm (SHA-3) Family. Federal Register 27(212), 62212–62220 (2007), `http://csrc.nist.gov/groups/ST/hash/documents/FR_Notice_Nov07.pdf` (October 17, 2008)
32. Needham, R.M., Wheeler, D.J.: Tea extensions. Computer Laboratory, Cambridge University, England (1997), `http://www.movable-type.co.uk/scripts/xtea.pdf`
33. O'Neil, S., Nohl, K., Henzen, L.: EnRUPT Hash Function Specification. Submission to the NIST SHA-3 Competition (Round 1) (2008)
34. Schneier, B., Kelsey, J., Whiting, D., Wagner, D., Hall, C., Ferguson, N.: The Twofish encryption algorithm: a 128-bit block cipher. John Wiley & Sons, Inc., New York (1999)

A Matrices for xdp^+

The four distinct matrices $A_{w[i]}$ obtained for xdp^+ in Sect. 3.4 are given in (50). The remaining matrices can be derived using $A_{001} = A_{010} = A_{100}$ and $A_{011} = A_{101} = A_{110}$.

$$A_{000} = \begin{bmatrix} 3&0&0&1 \\ 0&0&0&0 \\ 0&0&0&0 \\ 1&0&0&3 \end{bmatrix}, \quad A_{001} = \begin{bmatrix} 0&1&1&0 \\ 0&2&0&0 \\ 0&0&2&0 \\ 0&1&1&0 \end{bmatrix}, \quad A_{011} = \begin{bmatrix} 2&0&0&0 \\ 1&0&0&1 \\ 1&0&0&1 \\ 0&0&0&2 \end{bmatrix}, \quad A_{111} = \begin{bmatrix} 0&0&0&0 \\ 0&1&3&0 \\ 0&3&1&0 \\ 0&0&0&0 \end{bmatrix}. \tag{50}$$

Similarly, we give the four distinct matrices $A'_{w[i]}$ of Sect. 3.4 in (51). The remaining matrices satisfy $A'_{001} = A'_{010} = A'_{100}$ and $A'_{011} = A'_{101} = A'_{110}$.

$$A'_{000} = \begin{bmatrix} 1&0 \\ 0&0 \end{bmatrix}, \quad A'_{001} = \frac{1}{2}\begin{bmatrix} 0&1 \\ 0&1 \end{bmatrix}, \quad A'_{011} = \frac{1}{2}\begin{bmatrix} 1&0 \\ 1&0 \end{bmatrix}, \quad A'_{111} = \begin{bmatrix} 0&0 \\ 0&1 \end{bmatrix}. \tag{51}$$

B All Possible Subgraphs for xdp$^+$

All possible subgraphs for xdp$^+$ are given in Fig. 4.

C Computation of xdp$^+$ with Multiple Inputs

In Sect. 3, we showed how to compute the probability $\text{xdp}^+(\alpha, \beta \rightarrow \gamma)$, by introducing S-functions and using techniques based on graph theory and matrix multiplications. In the same way, we can also evaluate the probability $\text{xdp}^+(\alpha[i], \beta[i], \zeta[i], \ldots \rightarrow \gamma[i])$ for multiple inputs. We illustrate this for the simplest case of three inputs. We follow the same basic steps from Sect. 3 and Sect. 4: construct the S-function, construct the graph and derive the matrices, minimize the matrices, and multiply them to compute the probability.

Let us define

$$S[i] \leftarrow (c_1[i], c_2[i]) \ , \tag{52}$$

$$S[i+1] \leftarrow (c_1[i+1], c_2[i+1]) \ . \tag{53}$$

Then, the S-function corresponding to the case of three inputs x, y, q and output z is:

$$(\Delta^{\oplus} z[i], S[i+1]) = f(x_1[i], y_1[i], q_1[i], \Delta^{\oplus} x[i], \Delta^{\oplus} y[i], \Delta^{\oplus} q[i], S[i]). \quad 0 \leq i < n \ . \tag{54}$$

Because we are adding three words in binary, the values for the carries $c_1[i]$ and $c_2[i]$ are both in the set $\{0, 1, 2\}$. The differential $(\alpha[i], \beta[i], \zeta[i] \rightarrow \gamma[i])$ at bit position i is written as a bit string $w[i] \leftarrow \alpha[i] \parallel \beta[i] \parallel \zeta[i] \parallel \gamma[i]$. Using this S-function and the corresponding graph, we build the matrices $A_{w[i]}$. After we apply the minimization algorithm (removing inaccessible states and combining equivalent states) we obtain the following minimized matrices. The remaining matrices satisfy $A_{0001} = A_{0010} = A_{0100} = A_{1000}$, $A_{0011} = A_{0101} = A_{0110} = A_{1001} = A_{1010} = A_{1100}$ and $A_{0111} = A_{1011} = A_{1101} = A_{1110}$.

$$A_{0000} = \begin{bmatrix} 4 & 0 & 0 & 2 \\ 0 & 0 & 8 & 0 \\ 0 & 0 & 0 & 0 \\ 4 & 0 & 0 & 6 \end{bmatrix}, \quad A_{0001} = \begin{bmatrix} 0 & 1 & 0 & 0 \\ 0 & 4 & 0 & 0 \\ 0 & 0 & 0 & 0 \\ 0 & 3 & 0 & 0 \end{bmatrix}, \quad A_{0011} = \begin{bmatrix} 2 & 0 & 0 & 0 \\ 4 & 0 & 4 & 4 \\ 0 & 0 & 2 & 0 \\ 2 & 0 & 2 & 4 \end{bmatrix},$$

$$A_{0111} = \begin{bmatrix} 0 & 0 & 0 & 0 \\ 0 & 4 & 0 & 0 \\ 0 & 1 & 0 & 0 \\ 0 & 3 & 0 & 0 \end{bmatrix}, \quad A_{1111} = \begin{bmatrix} 0 & 0 & 0 & 0 \\ 8 & 0 & 0 & 0 \\ 0 & 0 & 4 & 2 \\ 0 & 0 & 4 & 6 \end{bmatrix}.$$

D Computation of $\text{xdp}^{\times 3}$

Given n-bit words $x_1, \Delta^{\oplus} x$, we can calculate $\Delta^{\oplus} z$ using

$$x_2 \leftarrow x_1 \oplus \Delta^{\oplus} x \ , \tag{55}$$

$$z_1 \leftarrow x_1 \cdot 3 = (x_1 \ll 1) + x_1 \ , \tag{56}$$

$$z_2 \leftarrow x_2 \cdot 3 = (x_2 \ll 1) + x_2 \ , \tag{57}$$

$$\Delta^{\oplus} z \leftarrow z_2 \oplus z_1 \ . \tag{58}$$

We then define $\text{xdp}^{\times 3}(\alpha \rightarrow \gamma)$ as

$$\text{xdp}^{\times 3}(\alpha \rightarrow \gamma) = \frac{|\{x_1 : \Delta^{\oplus} x = \alpha, \Delta^{\oplus} z = \gamma\}|}{|\{x_1 : \Delta^{\oplus} x = \alpha\}|} \ , \tag{59}$$

$$= 2^{-n} |\{x_1 : \Delta^{\oplus} x = \alpha, \Delta^{\oplus} z = \gamma\}| \ , \tag{60}$$

as there are 2^n values for the n-bit word x_1.

The left shift by one requires one bit of both $x_1[i]$ and $x_2[i]$ to be stored for the calculation of the next output bit. For this, we will use $d_1[i]$ and $d_2[i]$. In general, shifting to the left by i positions requires the i previous inputs to be stored. Therefore, (55)-(58) correspond to the following bit level expressions:

$$x_2[i] \leftarrow x_1[i] \oplus \Delta^{\oplus} x[i] \ , \tag{61}$$

$$z_1[i] \leftarrow x_1[i] \oplus d_1[i] \oplus c_1[i] \ , \tag{62}$$

$$c_1[i+1] \leftarrow (x_1[i] + d_1[i] + c_1[i]) \gg 1 \ , \tag{63}$$

$$d_1[i+1] \leftarrow x_1[i] \ , \tag{64}$$

$$z_2[i] \leftarrow x_2[i] \oplus d_2[i] \oplus c_2[i] \ , \tag{65}$$

$$c_2[i+1] \leftarrow (x_2[i] + d_2[i] + c_2[i]) \gg 1 \ , \tag{66}$$

$$d_2[i+1] \leftarrow x_2[i] \ , \tag{67}$$

$$\Delta^{\oplus} z[i] \leftarrow z_2[i] \oplus z_1[i] \ , \tag{68}$$

where $c_1[0] = c_2[0] = d_1[0] = d_2[0] = 0$. Let us define

$$S[i] \leftarrow (c_1[i], c_2[i], d_1[i], d_2[i]) \ , \tag{69}$$

$$S[i+1] \leftarrow (c_1[i+1], c_2[i+1], d_1[i+1], d_2[i+1]) \ . \tag{70}$$

Then (61)-(68) correspond to the S-function

$$(\Delta^{\oplus} z[i], S[i+1]) = f(x_1[i], \Delta^{\oplus} x[i], S[i]), \qquad 0 \leq i < n \ . \tag{71}$$

Each of $c_1[i]$, $c_2[i]$, $d_1[i]$, $d_2[i]$ can be either 0 or 1. After minimizing the 16 states $S[i]$, we obtain only 4 indistinguishable states. Define again 1×4 matrix $L = [1\ 1\ 1\ 1]$ and 4×1 matrix $C = [1\ 0\ 0\ 0]^T$. The differential $(\alpha[i] \rightarrow \gamma[i])$ at bit position i is written as a bit string $w[i] \leftarrow \alpha[i] \parallel \gamma[i]$. Then $\text{xdp}^{\times 3}$ is equal to

$$\text{xdp}^{\times 3}(\alpha \rightarrow \gamma) = L A^*_{w[n-1]} \cdots A^*_{w[1]} A^*_{w[0]} C \ , \tag{72}$$

where

$$A^*_{00} = \frac{1}{2}\begin{bmatrix}1&0&2&0\\0&0&0&2\\1&0&0&0\\0&0&0&0\end{bmatrix},\ A^*_{01} = \frac{1}{2}\begin{bmatrix}0&1&0&0\\0&1&0&0\\0&0&0&0\\0&0&0&0\end{bmatrix},\ A^*_{10} = \frac{1}{2}\begin{bmatrix}0&0&0&0\\0&1&0&0\\0&0&0&0\\0&1&0&0\end{bmatrix},\ A^*_{11} = \frac{1}{2}\begin{bmatrix}0&0&0&0\\2&0&0&0\\0&0&0&1\\0&0&2&1\end{bmatrix}.$$

We now illustrate this calculation by example. Let $\alpha = \texttt{0x12492489}$ and $\gamma = \texttt{0x3AEBAEAB}$. Then $\mathrm{xdp}^{\times 3}(\alpha \to \gamma) = 2^{-15}$, whereas $\mathrm{xdp}^{+}(\alpha, \alpha \ll 1 \to \gamma) = 2^{-25}$. From this example, we see that approximating the probability calculation of multiplication by a constant using xdp^{+}, can give a result that is completely different from the actual probability. This motivates the need for the technique that we present in this section. We note there is no loss in generality when we analyze $\mathrm{xdp}^{\times 3}$: the same technique can be automatically applied for $\mathrm{xdp}^{\times \mathrm{C}}$, where C is an arbitrary constant.

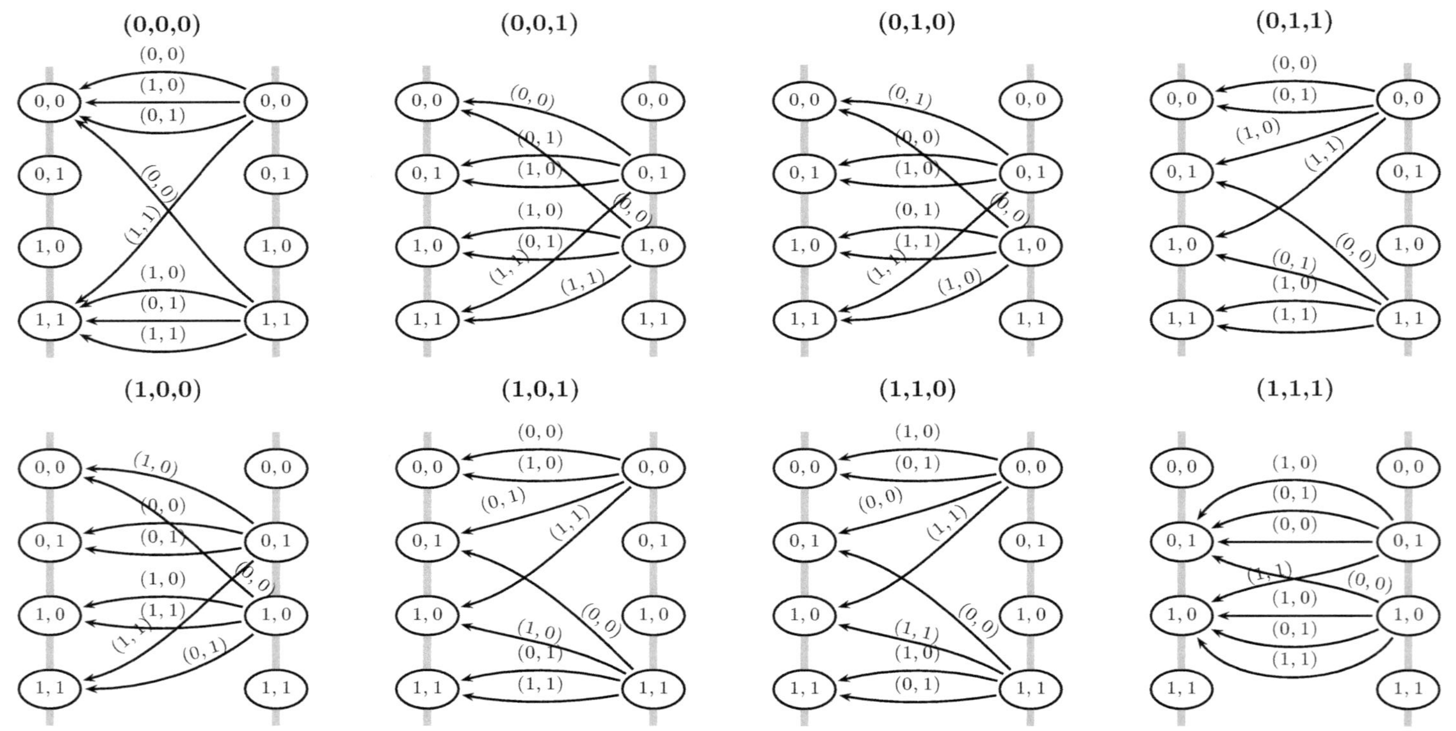

Fig. 4. All possible subgraphs for xdp^+. Vertices $(c_1[i], c_2[i])$ correspond to states $S[i]$. There is one edge for every input pair (x_1, y_1). Above each subgraph, the value of $(\alpha[i], \beta[i], \gamma[i])$ is given in bold.

Hill Climbing Algorithms and Trivium

Julia Borghoff[1], Lars R. Knudsen[1], and Krystian Matusiewicz[2]

[1] Department of Mathematics, Technical University of Denmark
{J.Borghoff,Lars.R.Knudsen}@mat.dtu.dk
[2] Institute of Mathematics and Computer Science, Wroclaw University of Technology
Krystian.Matusiewicz@pwr.wroc.pl

Abstract. This paper proposes a new method to solve certain classes of systems of multivariate equations over the binary field and its cryptanalytical applications. We show how heuristic optimization methods such as hill climbing algorithms can be relevant to solving systems of multivariate equations. A characteristic of equation systems that may be efficiently solvable by the means of such algorithms is provided. As an example, we investigate equation systems induced by the problem of recovering the internal state of the stream cipher Trivium. We propose an improved variant of the simulated annealing method that seems to be well-suited for this type of system and provide some experimental results.

Keywords: simulated annealing, cryptanalysis, Trivium.

1 Introduction

Cryptanalysis focuses on efficient ways of exploiting, perhaps unexpected, structure of cryptographic problems. It could be a difference which propagates with a high probability through the cipher as used in differential cryptanalysis [6,2] or a linear approximation of the non-linear parts of a cipher that holds for many of the possible inputs as is the case in linear cryptanalysis [20]. More recently, the so-called algebraic attacks have received much attention. They exploit the fact that many cryptographic primitives can be described by sparse multivariate non-linear equations over the binary field in such a way that solving these equations recovers the secret key or the initial state in the case of stream ciphers. In general, solving random systems of multivariate non-linear Boolean equations is an NP-hard problem [12]. However, when the system has a specific structure, we can hope that more efficient methods may exist.

One technique to tackle such equation systems is linearisation, where each non-linear term is replaced by an independent linear variable. It works only if there are enough linear independent equations in the resulting system. The XL algorithm [7] increases the number of equations by multiplying them with all monomials of a certain degree. It has been refined to the XSL algorithm [9], which, when applied to the AES, exploits the special structure of the equation

A. Biryukov, G. Gong, and D.R. Stinson (Eds.): SAC 2010, LNCS 6544, pp. 57–73, 2011.

system. Neither the XL nor the XSL algorithm have been able to break AES but algebraic attacks were successful in breaking a number of stream cipher designs [1,8].

In this paper we also investigate systems of sparse multivariate equations. The important additional requirement we make is that each variable appears only in a very limited number of equations. The equation system generated by the keystream generation algorithm of the stream cipher Trivium [10] satisfies those properties and will be examined in this paper as our main example. The fully determined Trivium system consists of 954 equations in 954 variables. Solving this system allows us to recover the 288-bit initial state.

Our approach considers the problem of finding a solution for the system as an optimization problem and then applies an improved variant of simulated annealing to it. As opposed to the XL and XSL algorithms, the simulated annealing algorithm does not increase the size of the problem, it does not generate more nor change the existing equations. The only additional requirement is an objective function, called the cost function, that should be minimized.

Simulated annealing has been studied in the context of cryptography before. An attack on an identification scheme based on the permuted perceptron problem (PPP) [19] was presented. An appropriate cost function was found which made it possible to solve the simpler perceptron problem as well as the PPP using a simulated annealing search. The attack showed that the recommended smallest parameters for the identification scheme are not secure. The same identification scheme was later a subject to an improved attack [5]. Simulated annealing was used to solve a related problem that had solutions highly correlated with the solution of the actual problem. Furthermore, timing analysis was applied where the search process is monitored and one can observe that some variables are stuck at correct values at an early state and never change again.

With the current experiments, we are not able to break Trivium in the cryptographic sense which means with a complexity equivalent to less than 2^{80} key setups and the true complexity of our method against Trivium is unknown. However, if one considers the Trivium system purely as a multivariate quadratic Boolean system in 954 variables this system can be solved significantly faster than exhaustive search, namely by around 2^{210} bit flips which is roughly equivalent to 2^{203} evaluations of the system. This shows that this variant of simulated annealing seems to be a promising tool for solving non-linear Boolean equation systems with certain properties.

2 Hill Climbing Algorithms

Hill climbing algorithms are a general class of heuristic optimization algorithms that deal with the following optimization problem. There is a finite set X of possible configurations. Each configuration is assigned a non-negative, real number called cost, or, in other words, a cost function is defined as $f : X \to \mathbb{R}$. For each configuration $x \in X$ a set of neighbours $\eta(x) \subset X$ is defined. The aim of the search is to find $x_{min} \in X$ minimizing the cost function $f(x)$,

$f(x_{min}) = \min\{f(x) : x \in X\}$, by moving from neighbour to neighbour depending on the cost difference between the neighbouring configurations.

Johnson and Jacobsen [15] presented a unified view of many hill climbing algorithms by describing conditions on accepting a move from one configuration to another. The transition probability $p_k(x, y)$ of accepting a move from x to $y \in \eta(x)$ is defined as the product of a configuration generation probability $g_i(x, y)$ and a configuration acceptance probability $\Pr[R_k(x, y) \geq f(y) - f(x)]$, where $R_k(x, y)$ is a random variable and k is an iteration index that is increased by one after a fixed number of moves. Algorithm 1 presents a general form of a hill climbing algorithm.

Algorithm 1. General formulation of hill climbing algorithms

```
x_best ← x
while stopping criterion not met do
    k ← 0                                              ▷ set the outer loop counter
    while k < K do
        for m = 0, ..., M − 1 do
            generate a neighbour y ∈ η(x) with probability g_k(x, y)
            compute the cost function f(y) of the candidate
            if R_k(x, y) ≥ f(y) − f(x) then
                x ← y                                  ▷ accept the move
                if f(x) < f(x_best) then
                    x_best ← x                         ▷ store the best configuration
                end if
            end if
        end for
        k ← k + 1
    end while
end while
```

Note that when $R_k(x, y) = 0$, we obtain a local search algorithm as only moves that decrease the cost are accepted.

Simulated Annealing. The classical simulated annealing algorithm [18] is a special case of the general hill climbing algorithm presented above with a particular definition of the transition probability.

The simulated annealing algorithm uses a key parameter called the temperature t. The configuration generation probability is taken to be uniform, i.e., each neighbour is equally likely to be picked from each state. The acceptance probability depends on the difference $f(y) - f(x)$ in the cost function between the current state x and the selected neighbour y and the current temperature t_k. The move is always accepted when it decreases the cost and with probability $e^{-(f(y)-f(x))/t_k}$ when the cost increases. In terms of the general formulation presented above, we get this behaviour when we define $R_k(x, y) = -t_k \ln(U)$, where U is a uniform random variable on $[0, 1]$.

Note that when the temperature t_k is high, many cost-increasing moves are accepted. When the temperature is lower, worsening moves are less and less likely to be accepted.

The way the "temperature" t_k of the system decreases over time (k) is called the cooling schedule. The condition necessary for the global convergence of the method is that $t_k \geq 0$ and $\lim_{k\to\infty} t_k = 0$. In practice, two most commonly used cooling schedules are the exponential cooling schedule $t_k = \alpha \cdot \beta^k$ for some parameter $0 < \beta < 1$ and the logarithmic cooling schedule $t_k = \alpha / \log_2(k+1)$ proposed in [13], where α is a constant corresponding to the starting temperature.

3 Trivium System as an Optimization Problem

Trivium [10] is an extremely simple and elegant stream cipher that was submitted to the ECRYPT eStream project. It successfully withstood significant cryptanalytical attention [21,22,23,24,3] and became part of the portfolio of the eStream finalists.

To our knowledge, there is no attack on Trivium faster than the exhaustive key search so far. However, several attacks have been proposed which are faster than the naive guess-and-determine attack with complexity 2^{195} which was considered by the designers [10]. A more intelligent guess-and-determine attack with complexity 2^{135} using a reformulation of Trivium has been sketched in [17]. Furthermore, Maximov and Biryukov [21] described an attack with complexity $2^{85.5}$ and Raddum proposed a new algorithm for solving non-linear Boolean equations and applied it to Trivium in [23]. The attack complexity was 2^{164}. McDonald at al [22] considered Trivium as a Boolean satisfiability problem and used the SAT-solver MiniSAT in order to solve it. This approach was faster than exhaustive key search for small scale variants of Trivium called Bivium. However, for the full Trivium the estimated complexity is about $2^{159.9}$ seconds and is therefore worse than exhaustive search.

Trivium has an 80-bit key, an 80-bit IV and 288 bits of the internal state $(s_1, \ldots, s_{288})$. At each clock cycle it updates only three bits of the state and produces one bit of the keystream using the following procedure.

for $i = 1, 2, \ldots$ **do**
  $z_i \leftarrow s_{66} + s_{93} + s_{162} + s_{177} + s_{243} + s_{288}$ ▷ Generate output bit z_i
  $t_{i,1} \leftarrow s_{66} + s_{93} + s_{91} \cdot s_{92} + s_{171}$
  $t_{i,2} \leftarrow s_{162} + s_{177} + s_{175} \cdot s_{176} + s_{264}$
  $t_{i,3} \leftarrow s_{243} + s_{288} + s_{286} \cdot s_{287} + s_{69}$
  $(s_1, s_2, \ldots, s_{93}) \leftarrow (t_{i,3}, s_1, \ldots, s_{92})$
  $(s_{94}, s_{95}, \ldots, s_{177}) \leftarrow (t_{i,1}, s_{94}, \ldots, s_{176})$
  $(s_{178}, s_{179}, \ldots, s_{288}) \leftarrow (t_{i,2}, s_{178}, \ldots, s_{287})$
end for

During the key setup phase, the key is loaded into the first 80 bits of the state, followed by 13 zero bits, then the IV is loaded into the next 80 bits of the state and the remaining bits are filled with constant values. Then $4 \cdot 288$ clockings are computed without producing any keystream bits. Our results do not depend on this procedure.

The initial state which is the state of the registers at the time when the key generation starts can be expressed as system of sparse linear and quadratic Boolean equations [23]. We consider the initial state bits as variables and label them with $s_1 \ldots, s_{288}$. In each clocking of the Trivium algorithm three state bits are updated. The update function is a quadratic Boolean function of the state bits. In order to keep the degree low and the equations sparse we introduce new variables for each updated state bit $t_{i,1}$, $t_{i,2}$, $t_{i,3}$. We get the following equations from the first clocking

$$\begin{aligned} s_{66} \oplus s_{93} \oplus s_{91} \cdot s_{92} \oplus s_{171} &= s_{289} \\ s_{162} \oplus s_{177} \oplus s_{175} \cdot s_{176} \oplus s_{264} &= s_{290} \\ s_{243} \oplus s_{288} \oplus s_{286} \cdot s_{287} \oplus s_{69} &= s_{291} \\ s_{66} \oplus s_{93} \oplus s_{162} \oplus s_{177} \oplus s_{243} \oplus s_{288} &= z \end{aligned} \tag{1}$$

where the last equation is the keystream equation with z being the known keystream bit.

After observing 288 keystream bits we can set up a fully determined system of 954 Boolean equations in 954 unknowns [23]. We only need to consider 954 equations and unknowns instead of $4 \cdot 288$ since we do not care about the last 66 state updates for each register. These variables will not be used in the keystream equation because the new bits are not used for the keystream generation before 66 further clockings of the cipher. By clocking the algorithm more than 288 times we can easily obtain an overdetermined system. We know that the initial state together with the corresponding updated state bits satisfies all the generated equations (1). On the other hand, for a random point each equation is satisfied with probability $\frac{1}{2}$. It is obvious that a random point satisfies the linear equation with probability $\frac{1}{2}$. A quadratic equation is satisfied if the quadratic term and the linear part have the same value. In the Trivium system each variable appears at most once per equation. Therefore the probabilities for the quadratic term and the linear part of the equation are independent. Hence the probability that a random point fulfills a quadratic equation of the Trivium system is $\Pr[\text{quadratic term} = 0] \cdot \Pr[\text{linear part} = 0] + \Pr[\text{quadratic term} = 1] \cdot \Pr[\text{linear part} = 1] = \frac{1}{2} \cdot \frac{3}{4} + \frac{1}{2} \cdot \frac{1}{4} = \frac{1}{2}$.

If we consider the problem of solving the Trivium equation system as an optimization problem which is suitable for hill climbing algorithms (cf. Section 2) $X = \{0,1\}^{954}$ is the set of possible configurations. As a cost function $f : X \to \mathbb{R}$ we count the number of not satisfied equations in the system. We know that the minimum of the cost function is 0 and that the initial state of the Trivium system is a configuration for which the cost function is minimal. There might be other optimal solutions, however, it is easy to check if the solution we found is the desired one. If a configuration is an optimal solution for the discrete optimization problem, it generates the same first 288 bits of keystream as the initial state we are looking for. But it is unlikely that the keystream will be the same for the following keystream bits. Therefore we can check if a solution is the desired one by observing a few more keystream bits and comparing them to the keystream generated by the solution. In our experiments it is unlikely that multiple solutions occur because we set some of the variables to their correct values and therefore consider a highly overdetermined equation system.

4 Properties of Trivium Landscapes

Hill climbing algorithms are sensitive to the way in which the cost function changes when moving between configurations. The best results are obtained when a move from a configuration $x \in X$ to one of the neighbours $\eta(x)$ does not change the value of the cost function too much.

In our case we move from one configuration to another by flipping the value of a single variable. Each variable appears in at most 8 equations and in 6 equations on average, so when moving to a neighbour of the current configuration the cost function will change by at most 8. Furthermore, each variable appears only once in an equation. Therefore changing the value of a single variable will change the value of the equation with probability 1 if the variable appears in a linear term and with probability $\frac{1}{2}$ if the variable appears in a quadratic term. In the latter case flipping the value of a variable will just change the outcome of the equation if the other variable in the quadratic term is assigned to '1'. If a variable appears in the maximum of eight equations it appears in two equations in the quadratic term only. The expected number of equations which change their outcome is 7. Additionally it is unlikely that flipping the value of a variable changes the outcome of all equations which contain this variable in the same direction or respectively it is unlikely that all equations which contain the variable have the same outcome for the configuration before the flip. (The case that a lot or even all equations have the same outcome will appear with higher probability the closer we are to the minimum.)

From these observations we infer that even if we move from a configuration x to one of its neighbours by flipping the value of a variable which appears in 8 equations we do not expect that the value of the cost function changes by 8 in almost all of the cases.

We confirmed this by the following experiment. We generated a Trivium system for a random key and calculated the cost function for a random starting point. Then we chose a neighbour configuration of our starting point and recorded the absolute value of the change in the cost function. To simulate being close to the minimum we set a number of bits to the correct solution but we allowed those bits to be flipped to move to a neighbouring configuration. The results are summarized in Table 5.

These properties of Trivium cost landscapes can be captured more formally using the notion of NK-landscapes and landscape auto-correlation as follows.

4.1 Trivium Systems and NK-Landscapes

NK-landscapes were introduced by Kaufmann [16] to model fitness landscapes with tunable "ruggedness". An NK-landscape is a set of configurations $X = \{0,1\}^n$ together with the cost function defined as

$$f(x) = \sum_{i=1}^{n} f_i(x_i; x_{\pi_{i,1}}, \ldots, x_{\pi_{i,k}}) \ ,$$

where each π_i is a tuple of k distinct elements from the set $\{1, \ldots, n\} \setminus \{i\}$. In other words, the cost function of an NK-landscape is a sum of n local cost functions f_i, each one of them depending on the main variable x_i and a set of k other variables. In a random neighbourhood model, the k indices are selected randomly and uniformly for each f_i. Depending on the value of k, we get either smooth landscapes with relatively few local minima when k is small and rugged landscapes for large values of k.

The Trivium optimization problem can be seen as a particular instance of such a combinatorial landscape. Consider the basic system of equations. We define each f_i as the contribution of i-th equation (either 0 or 1 depending on whether it is satisfied). Each equation depends on six distinct variables, we verified by a computer program that indeed we can always pick one of them as the main variable leaving exactly five other ones for each equation. Trivium optimization problem can thus be seen as an instance of NK-landscape with $n = 954$ and $k = 5$, a rather small value hinting at a certain smoothness of this landscape.

4.2 Landscape Auto-correlation

Another measure of landscape ruggedness is the notion of landscape correlation introduced by Weinberger [25]. We will follow the exposition by Hordijk [14]. The main idea is to perform a random walk on the landscape via neighbouring points. At each step, the cost function y_t is recorded. In this way a sequence $(y_t)_{t=1\ldots T}$ is obtained and we compute its auto-correlation coefficients.

The auto-correlation of a sequence (y_t) for the time lag i is defined as $\rho_i = Corr(y_t, y_{t+i}) = \frac{E[y_t \cdot y_{t+i}] - E[y_t]E[y_{t+i}]}{Var[y_t]}$ where E means the expected value and Var variance of a random variable. Estimates r_i of these auto-correlations ρ_i are $r_i = \frac{\sum_{t=1}^{T-i}(y_t - \bar{y})(y_{t+i} - \bar{y})}{\sum_{t=1}^{T}(y_t - \bar{y})^2}$ where $\bar{y}$ means the mean value of the sample $y_1, \ldots, y_t$. Here a large auto-correlation coefficient corresponds to a smooth landscape. An important assumption that has to be made for such analysis to be meaningful is that the landscape is statistically isotropic. This means that the statistics of the time series generated by a random walk are the same, regardless of the starting point. Only then a random walk is "representative" of the entire landscape. By computing correlation coefficients for many random walks starting at different points we experimentally verified that the Trivium landscape can be seen as isotropic.

Selected correlation coefficients computed for a basic version of Trivium system and overdefined versions are presented in Table 1. We used sequences of length 1000000 and averaged results over 100 runs with different keys, IVs and starting points of the walks. Clearly, generating the overdefined system makes the landscape smoother.

Table 1. Correlation coefficients for landscapes generated by Trivium systems of different sizes. n denotes the number of variables in the system.

keystream length	n	$r(1)$	$r(10)$	$r(20)$	$r(30)$	$r(40)$	$r(50)$
288	954	0.987	0.892	0.798	0.713	0.638	0.570
576	1818	0.993	0.942	0.889	0.839	0.791	0.747
1152	3546	0.997	0.970	0.942	0.914	0.886	0.862

5 Solving Trivium Systems with Modified Simulated Annealing

The properties of landscapes generated by the Trivium system of equations suggest that it might be possible to employ stochastic search methods such as simulated annealing to try to find a global optimum and thus recover the secret state of the cipher. In this section we report the results of our experiments in this direction.

Initial experiments with standard simulated annealing were not very encouraging. To be able to solve the Trivium system in reasonable time, we needed to simplify the initial system by setting around 600 out of 954 variables to their correct values throughout the search.

We experimented with the algorithm and its various modifications and found one that yielded a significant improvements over the standard algorithm. The algorithm works as follows. As with standard simulated annealing, we randomly generate a neighbour. If the cost decreases, we accept this move. If not, instead of accepting with probability related to the current temperature, we pick another neighbour and test that one. If after testing a certain number of neighbours we cannot find any cost decreasing move, we accept the increasing move with some probability, just as in the plain simulated annealing. The parameter of this procedure is the number of additional candidates to test before accepting cost increase.

If the parameter is zero, we get plain simulated annealing. On the other end of the spectrum, if we test all possible neighbours, it is easy to see that we get an algorithm that is equivalent to local search, we look for any possible decreasing move and we follow it. When we are in a local minimum, we enter a loop, we finally accept one of the cost increasing candidates but in the next move we always go back to the local optimum we found. Setting the parameter between those extremes yields an intermediate algorithm.

In practice, we used a probabilistic variant of this approach that randomly selects neighbours until it finds one with smaller cost or it exceeds the number of tests defined as a parameter nochangebound. This algorithm is presented in Alg. 2.

Algorithm 2. Modified version of simulated annealing

```
x_best ← x
T ← α                                      ▷ initial temperature parameter is α
k ← 0                                      ▷ set the outer loop counter
while T > 1 do
    for m = 0, ..., M − 1 do               ▷ parameter M is the number of inner runs
        generate a neighbour y ∈ η(x) uniformly
        if f(y) < f(x) then                ▷ if cost decreased
            x ← y                          ▷ accept the move
            if f(x) < f(x_best) then       ▷ found a new best value
                x_best ← x                 ▷ store the best configuration
                nc ← 0                     ▷ reset the neighbor counter
                if f(x_best) = 0 then      ▷ if we found a solution
                    return x_best          ▷ finish and return it
                end if
            end if
        else                               ▷ the candidate cost is higher
            nc ← nc + 1
            if (nc > nochangebound) ∧ (exp((f(y) − f(x))/T > rnd[0, 1]) then
                x ← y                      ▷ accept the move
                nc ← 0                     ▷ reset the counter of tested neighbours
            end if
        end if
    end for
    k ← k + 1
    T = α/ log_2(k · M)                    ▷ Logarithmic cooling schedule
end while
```

The relationship between the number of neighbours tested and the time it took to find a solution (measured in the number of neighbours tested) is presented in Fig 1. Values of nochangebound below 25 result in running times exceeding 2^{40} flips. It suggests that the proper choice of nochangebound is critical for the efficiency of the simulated annealing, in particular, it cannot be too small.

6 Experimental Results

In this section we report results of our computational experiments with the basic equation system generated by the problem of recovering internal state of Trivium. We took the fully determined system with 954 equations and variables obtained after observing 288 bits of the keystream.

We made some comparisons between exponential and logarithmic cooling schedules and from our limited experience the logarithmic cooling schedule performed better in more cases, so we decided to pick that one for our further tests.

The values of α were picked based on empirical observations. Too large α resulted in prolonged periods of almost-random walks where there was no clear sign that any optimization might occur. Too small values gave the behavior

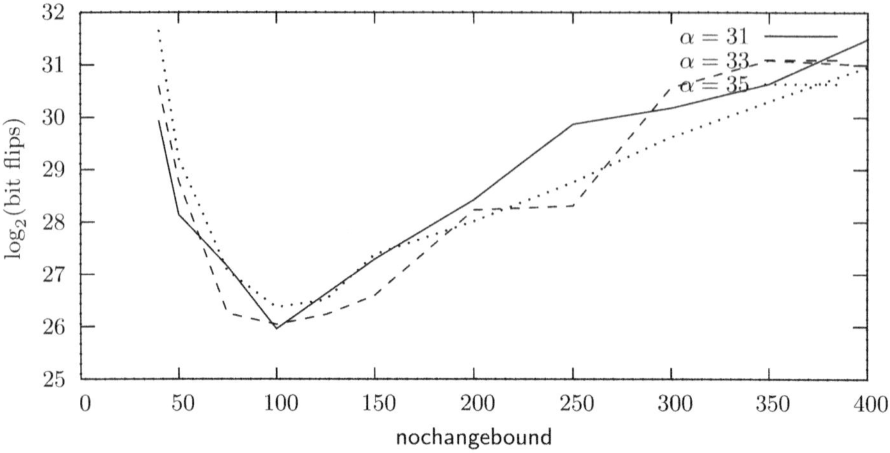

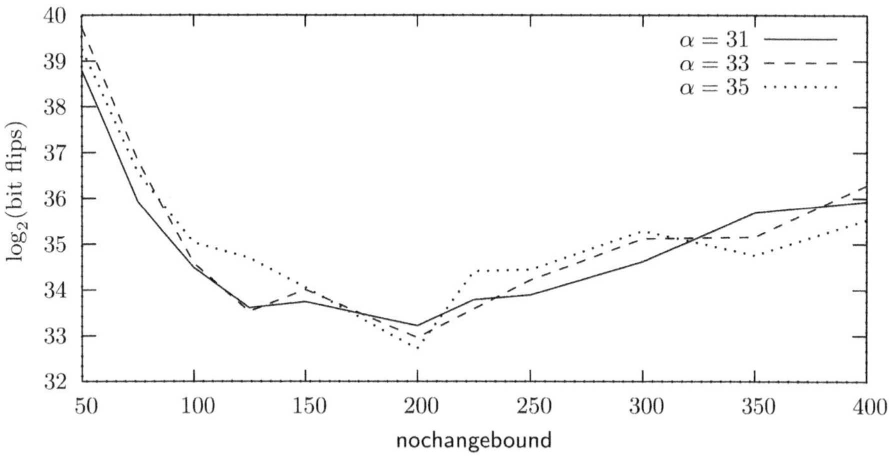

Fig. 1. Influence of nochangebound parameter on the efficiency of simulated annealing applied to basic Trivium system for three values of initial temperature α. Other parameters are $M = 1024$ (cf. Alg. 2), averages are over 10 tests. In the top figure we guessed 200 first bits of the state, in the bottom one 180 bits.

similar to a simple local search when the process was getting stuck in some shallow local optima. After a few trials we decided to use the initial temperature parameter $\alpha = 35$.

For each number of bits of the state fixed to their correct values (preassigned) we ran ten identical tests with different random seeds testing various values of nochangebound parameter (from the set 100, 150, 175, 200, 250, 300). After the test batch finished, we picked that value of nochangebound that yielded lowest search time. We managed to obtain optimal values for nochangebound for 200, 195, 190, 185, 180, 175 and 170 preassigned bits where we set the values of the first bits of the internal state. We use this optimal nochangebound to estimate the total complexity of the attack. The graph is presented in Fig. 2.

The total complexity is the product of the number of guesses we would need to make ($2^{preassigned}$) multiplied by the experimentally obtained running time of the search for the solution. We take the complexity for the correct guess. For a wrong guess the algorithm will not find a solution with costs 0 and terminate.

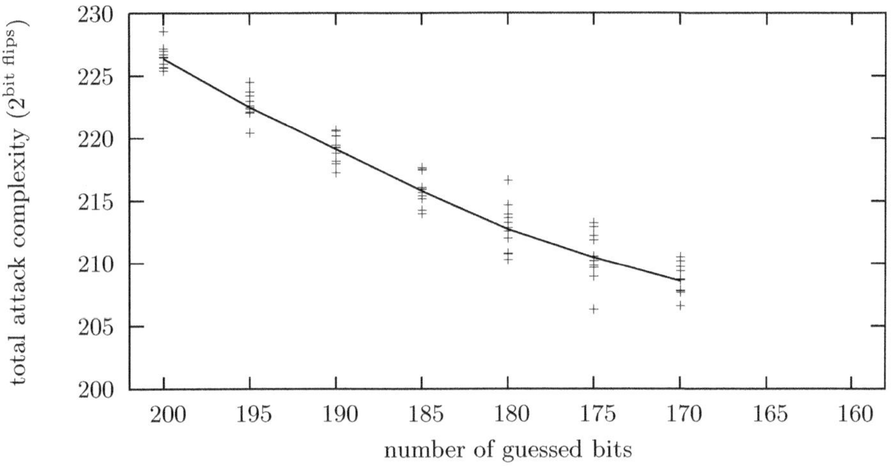

Fig. 2. Running times of the attack based on modified simulated annealing depending on the number of guessed bits. The numbers on the vertical axis are base two logarithms of the total number of moves necessary to find the solution. Crosses represent results of single experiments, the line connects averages.

The results show that the running time of the attack decreases with the smaller number of guessed bits since the increase in time of the search procedure is smaller than the decrease due to the smaller number of bits we have to guess. If the curve goes down below the complexity level corresponding to 2^{80} key setups of Trivium, it would constitute a state-recovery attack. However, the problem is that due to limited computational power we were not able to gather enough results for values of *preassigned* smaller than 170. Our program running on 1.1GHz AMD Opteron 2354 was able to compute 2^{35} bit flips per hour and tests with $preassigned = 170$ required around $2^{38} \sim 2^{39}$ bit flips.

It seems that trying to extrapolate the running times is rather risky, since we do not have any analytical explanation of the complexities we get as often is the case with heuristic search methods. Therefore we do not claim anything about the feasibility of such an attack on full Trivium. We can only conjecture that there might be a set of parameters for which such attack may become possible.

Due to the computational complexity, our experimental results are so far based on only rather small samples of runs for the fixed set of parameters. Therefore, they cannot be taken as a rigorous statisticial analysis but rather as a reconnaissance of the feasibility of this approach. However, we have noticed that for overwhelming fraction of all the experiments, the running times for different runs with the same set of parameters do not deviate from the average exponent of the bit flips by more than ±2, i.e. most of the experiments have the number of flips between 2^{avg-2} and 2^{avg+2}. Therefore, we believe that the results give some reasonable impression of the actual situation.

7 Some Variations

The previous section presented the set of our basic experiments. However, there is a multitude of possible variations of the basic setup which could possibly lead to better results. We report on some variations of the search problem we considered while looking for possible optimizations in the Appendix.

8 Conclusions and Future Directions

We presented a new way of approaching the problem of solving systems of sparse, multivariate equations over the binary field. We represent them as combinatorial optimization problems with the cost function being the number of not satisfied equations and then we apply some heuristic search methods, such as simulated annealing to solve them.

We showed that such systems may be relevant in cryptography by giving an example of the system generated by the problem of recovering the internal state of the stream cipher Trivium.

Our experimental results were focused on the Trivium system and they seem to be promising but for now they do not seem to pose any real threat to the security of this algorithm.

We hope that this paper will serve as a starting point for further research in this direction. There are many open problems in this area, the most obvious ones are the selection of better parameters of the search procedures and analytically estimating the possible complexity of such algorithms.

The other interesting direction seems to be the investigation of alternative cost functions. In all our experiments we use the simplest measure counting the number of not satisfied equations. However, many results in heuristic search literature suggest that the selection of a suitable cost function may dramatically change the efficiency of a search. The question of determining whether in our case there exist measures better than the ones we used is still open.

Acknowledgements. We would like to thank the anonymous reviewers of SAC 2010 and Tools for Cryptanalysis 2010 for their comments that helped to improve this paper.

References

1. Armknecht, F., Krause, M.: Algebraic attacks on combiners with memory. In: Boneh, D. (ed.) CRYPTO 2003. LNCS, vol. 2729, pp. 162–175. Springer, Heidelberg (2003)
2. Biham, E., Shamir, A.: Differential Cryptanalysis of the Data Encryption Standard. Springer, Heidelberg (1993)

3. Borghoff, J., Knudsen, L.R., Stolpe, M.: Bivium as a mixed-integer linear programming problem. In: Parker, M.G. (ed.) Cryptography and Coding 2009. LNCS, vol. 5921, pp. 133–152. Springer, Heidelberg (2009)
4. Chardaire, P., Lutton, J.L., Sutter, A.: Thermostatistical persistency: A powerful improving concept for simulated annealing algorithms. European Journal of Operational Research 86(3), 565–579 (1995)
5. Clark, J.A., Jacob, J.L.: Fault injection and a timing channel on an analysis technique. In: Knudsen, L.R. (ed.) EUROCRYPT 2002. LNCS, vol. 2332, pp. 181–196. Springer, Heidelberg (2002)
6. Coppersmith, D.: The data encryption standard (DES) and its strength against attacks. IBM Journal of Research and Development 38(3), 243–250 (1994)
7. Courtois, N., Klimov, A., Patarin, J., Shamir, A.: Efficient algorithms for solving overdefined systems of multivariate polynomial equations. In: Preneel, B. (ed.) EUROCRYPT 2000. LNCS, vol. 1807, pp. 392–407. Springer, Heidelberg (2000)
8. Courtois, N., Meier, W.: Algebraic attacks on stream ciphers with linear feedback. In: Biham, E. (ed.) EUROCRYPT 2003. LNCS, vol. 2656, pp. 644–644. Springer, Heidelberg (2003)
9. Courtois, N.T., Pieprzyk, J.: Cryptanalysis of block ciphers with overdefined systems of equations. In: Zheng, Y. (ed.) ASIACRYPT 2002. LNCS, vol. 2501, pp. 267–287. Springer, Heidelberg (2002)
10. De Cannière, C., Preneel, B.: Trivium – a stream cipher construction inspired by block cipher design principles. eSTREAM, ECRYPT Stream Cipher Project, Report 2005/030 (2005), `http://www.ecrypt.eu.org/stream/papers.html` (April 29, 2005)
11. Eibach, T., Pilz, E., Steck, S.: Comparing and optismising two generic attacks on Bivium. In: Preproceedings of SASC 2008, pp. 57–68 (2008)
12. Fraenkel, A.S., Yesha, Y.: Complexity of solving algebraic equations. Information Processing Letters 10(4/5), 178–179 (1980)
13. Geman, S., Geman, D.: Stochastic relaxation, Gibbs distributions, and the bayesian restoration of images. IEEE Transactions on Pattern Analysis and Machine Intelligence 6(6), 721–741 (1984)
14. Hordijk, W.: A measure of landscapes. Evolutionary Computation 4(4), 335–360 (1996)
15. Johnson, A.W., Jacobson, S.H.: A class of convergent generalized hill climbing algorithms. Applied Mathematics and Computation 125(2-3), 359–373 (2002)
16. Kauffmann, S.A.: The Origins of Order: Self-Organization and Selection in Evolution. Oxford University Press, Oxford (1993)
17. Khazaei, S.: Re: A reformuation of TRIVIUM. Posted on the eSTREAM Forum (2006), `http://www.ecrypt.eu.org/stream/phorum/read.php?1,448`
18. Kirkpatrick, S., Gelatt Jr., C.D., Vecchi, M.P.: Optimization by Simulated Annealing. Science 220(4598), 671–680 (1983)
19. Knudsen, L.R., Meier, W.: Cryptanalysis of an identification scheme based on the permuted perceptron problem. In: Stern, J. (ed.) EUROCRYPT 1999. LNCS, vol. 1592, pp. 363–374. Springer, Heidelberg (1999)
20. Matsui, M.: Linear cryptanalysis method for DES cipher. In: Helleseth, T. (ed.) EUROCRYPT 1993. LNCS, vol. 765, pp. 386–397. Springer, Heidelberg (1994)
21. Maximov, A., Biryukov, A.: Two trivial attacks on TRIVIUM. In: Adams, C., Miri, A., Wiener, M. (eds.) SAC 2007. LNCS, vol. 4876, pp. 36–55. Springer, Heidelberg (2007)

22. McDonald, C., Charnes, C., Pieprzyk, J.: An algebraic analysis of trivium ciphers based on the boolean satisfiability problem. Cryptology ePrint Archive, Report 2007/129 (2007), http://eprint.iacr.org/2007/129
23. Raddum, H.: Cryptanalytic results on Trivium. eStream (March 2006), http://www.ecrypt.eu.org/stream/papersdir/2006/039.ps
24. Turan, M.S., Kara, O.: Linear approximations for 2-round Trivium. In: Security of Information and Networks – SIN 2007, pp. 96–105. Trafford Publishing (2007)
25. Weinberger, E.: Correlated and uncorrelated fitness landscapes and how to tell the difference. Biological Cybernetics 63(5), 325–336 (1990)

A Variants of the Optimization Problem

In this appendix we present results of our experiments with different variations of the basic search problem.

A.1 Guessing Strategy

In order to lower the complexity of solving the equation system we set some of the variables to their correct values. However, the search complexity depends on which variables we choose.

We used different guessing strategies for pre-assigning variables and compared the influence on the running time of our algorithm. We used the following strategies to guess subsets of the state bits:

1. Select the first variables of the initial state.
2. Select the first variables of each register of the initial state.
3. Select the last variables of the initial state.
4. Select the last variables of the each register of the initial state.
5. Select the most frequent variables. These are the variables which are introduced by the update function at the beginning of the keystream generation. We guess values for variable s_{289} and the consecutive ones in this case.
6. An adaptive pre-assignment strategy which is similar to the ThreeFour strategy in [11] (see Subsection A.1).
7. Select the variables in such a way that the equation interdependence measure is minimal. (see Subsection A.1).

It turns out that the best guessing strategy of the ones we tested is to guess the first bits of the initial state. In addition to a pre-assignment of variables we can determine the value of further variables by considering the linear and quadratic equations (see below). We use this technique in the adaptive pre-assignment strategy.

Table 2. Running time for different pre-assignment strategies. nochangebound=110, 190 bits are preassigned, average taken over ten runs.

	first bits of the initial state	most frequent bits	first bit of every register	last bit of the initial state	last bit of each register
average	**29.5**	33.0	34.5	31.2	36.4

Adaptive Pre-Assignment Strategy. In this pre-assignment strategy we use the fact that assigning 5 of the variables in a linear equation will uniquely determine the 6th variable. Starting with an arbitrary linear equation we guess and pre-assign 5 of the 6 variables, determine the value of the remaining variable and assign this to its value. We know that a large fraction of the variables appear in two linear equations. So in the next round of pre-assignment we pick an equation in which at least one variable is already assigned. That means we only have to guess at most 4 variable to get one for free. We continue until we have made the maximum number of guesses or we cannot find an equation in which one variable is already assigned. In the latter case we just have to pick an equation without preassigned variables and run the algorithm again until we made the maximum number of guesses.

Additionally we also use the quadratic equations to determine the value of variables.

The advantage of this pre-assignment strategy is that we can assign many more variables than we actually have to guess. Table 3 gives us an impression of this advantage.

Table 3. The table shows how many bits additional to the guessed bits can be assigned using the adaptive pre-assignment strategy

# guessed bits	# assigned bits	additional assigned bits in %
5	6	20%
50	66	32%
100	135	35%
200	281	40.5%

The disadvantage is that we instead of making the equations sparser we fix some equations to be zero. That means that there are less equations left which contain free variables but the maximum number of equations in which a variables appears is still 8. Therefore a variable influences a higher percentage of equations.

Minimizing Equation Interdependency. If all the equations used different sets of variables, it would be trivial to solve the system by a simple local search. However, variables appear in many equations and changing the value of one of them influences other equations at the same time. This suggests the idea of

Table 4. Running times and landscape auto-correlation coefficients ξ for bit pre-assignment strategies minimizing equation interdependence. Experiments used $\alpha = 33$, $M = 1024$, $\mathsf{nochangebound} = 110$.

strategy:	reference	Case 1	Case 2
avg:	29.34	38.9	28.72
ξ	90.1	97.4	96.1

guessing (pre-assigning) bits to minimize the number of variables shared by many equations and thus reduce the degree of mutual relationships between equations.

Capturing this intuition more formally, let E_i be an equation and let $\mathcal{V}(E_i)$ denote the set of *not preassigned* variables that appear in the equation. We can define the measure of interdependence of two equations E_i, E_j as $IntrDep(E_i, E_j) = |\mathcal{V}(E_i) \cap \mathcal{V}(E_j)|$. If the measure is zero, equations use different variables and we can call them separated. Note that pre-assigning any bit that is used by both equations decreases the value of interdependence.

To capture the notion of equations interdependence in the whole system of Trivium equations E, the following measure could be used

$$\sum_{e,g \in E, e \neq g} |\mathcal{V}(e) \cap \mathcal{V}(g)|^2 \ . \tag{2}$$

We used the sum of squares to prefer systems with more equations with only few active (non-preassigned) variables over less equations that have more active variables, but it is possible to use an alternative measure without the squares,

$$\sum_{e,g \in E, e \neq g} |\mathcal{V}(e) \cap \mathcal{V}(g)| \ . \tag{3}$$

The algorithm for pre-assigning bits to minimize the above measure is rather simple. We start with computing the initial interdependence of the system. Then, we temporarily pick a free variable and assign it to compute the new interdependence of the system. If this value is smaller than the current record, we remember it as a new record. After we test all possible candidates, we pick the record one and assign it for good. We repeat this procedure until we get the required number of preassigned bits.

We performed an experiment that compared the results of the reference pre-assignment strategy fixing the first 190 bits of the state with two variants minimizing (2) and (3). Results presented in Table 4 are interesting. It seems that in spite of significant smoothening of the landscape indicated by higher values of the coefficient ξ the first strategy minimizing (2) significantly worsens the running time. A possible explanation may be that the landscape became more like "golf-course" with large areas without any direction and only very small attraction basins leading to global solution(s). Another possibility is that for such systems, different parameter of `nochangebound` is preferred. The second variant minimizing (3) seems to be only slightly better than setting the first bits, but more tests would be needed for more parameters to decide any definite advantage.

A.2 Using Overdefined Systems

Results on landscape auto-correlation suggest that using overdefined systems may yield landscape with better structural properties. However, this happens at the expense of a larger set of variables and equations we have to deal with. Our experimental results on overdefined systems suggest that the gain we get from a better landscape is offset by the larger system size so search times are actually not better.

A.3 Variable Persistence

According to [4,5] while using simulated annealing to some optimization problems, one can observe a bias in the frequency of assigning values to variables during the simulated annealing procedure. This bias is related to the solution of the system and observing it can give some information on the solution we are looking for.

We made some experiments that investigated if configurations of local minima (states we run into after a long cooling run) have variables correlated with the global minimum state. In our limited experiments with the basic Trivium system we did not observe any such correlations.

Furthermore, we could see from our preliminary experiments that for a local minimum with a cost value around 40 the current solution still had a large hamming distance to the known optimal solution.

B Cost Change Statistics

Table 5. Change of the cost function when moving to a neighbour configuration: The first row denotes the number of preassigned bits we use to simulate different distances from the minimum. We count how often out of 10000 trials the cost function changes by 0 to 8 units. The last row gives us the average change of the cost function.

i	0	100	200	300	400	500	600	700	800	900	954
0	1714	1702	1685	1560	1309	1052	944	767	601	264	0
1	3253	3246	3297	3158	2641	2143	1856	1550	1120	389	34
2	2248	2235	2240	2241	1930	1720	1385	1172	937	1001	1062
3	1557	1571	1550	1659	1821	1757	1488	1278	1258	1515	1537
4	675	665	668	754	1024	1020	911	810	741	596	648
5	386	400	380	409	691	940	1088	1078	1024	1068	1160
6	127	128	130	164	409	916	1372	1630	1866	2002	2049
7	32	44	41	46	165	439	837	1352	1854	2297	2534
8	8	9	9	9	10	13	119	363	599	868	976
average change	1.81	1.824	1.814	1.9	2.32	2.83	3.32	3.85	4.38	4.97	5.3

Discovery and Exploitation of New Biases in RC4

Pouyan Sepehrdad, Serge Vaudenay, and Martin Vuagnoux

EPFL
CH–1015 Lausanne, Switzerland
http://lasecwww.epfl.ch

Abstract. In this paper, we present several weaknesses in the stream cipher RC4. First, we present a technique to automatically reveal linear correlations in the PRGA of RC4. With this method, 48 new exploitable correlations have been discovered. Then we bind these new biases in the PRGA with known KSA weaknesses to provide practical key recovery attacks. Henceforth, we apply a similar technique on RC4 as a black box, i.e. the secret key words as input and the keystream words as output. Our objective is to exhaustively find linear correlations between these elements. Thanks to this technique, 9 new exploitable correlations have been revealed. Finally, we exploit these weaknesses on RC4 to some practical examples, such as the WEP protocol. We show that these correlations lead to a key recovery attack on WEP with only 9 800 encrypted packets (less than 20 seconds), instead of 24 200 for the best previous attack.

1 Introduction

RC4 is a stream cipher designed by Ronald Rivest in 1987. It had initially been a trade secret until the algorithm was anonymously posted to the Cypherpunks mailing list in September 1994. Nowadays, RC4 is still widely used: it is the default cipher of the SSL/TLS protocol and a cryptographic primitive of the WEP (Wired Equivalent Privacy) and WPA (Wi-Fi Protected Access) protocols. Its popularity probably comes from its simplicity and the low computational cost of the encryption and decryption operations. Due to its straightforwardness, RC4 sparked extensive research, revealing weaknesses in case of misuse. The most famous example is the attack on the WEP protocol used in IEEE 802.11.

WEP was designed to provide confidentiality on wireless communications by using RC4. In order to simplify the key set up, WEP uses fixed keys. In wireless communications, packets may be easily lost. Because of the lack of transport control at the link level, IEEE 802.11 designers chose to encrypt each packet independently. However, RC4 is a stream cipher: the same secret key must never be used twice. To prevent any key repetition, WEP concatenates an initialization vector (IV) to the key, where the IV is a 24-bit value which is publicly disclosed in the header of the protocol. This particular use of RC4 is subject to many weaknesses. However, RC4 is not generally used with an IV and almost all the attacks concerning WEP cannot be applied to the plain RC4. Thus, RC4 is still believed to be secure, even if many weaknesses have been explored.

A. Biryukov, G. Gong, and D.R. Stinson (Eds.): SAC 2010, LNCS 6544, pp. 74–91, 2011.

1.1 Description of RC4

The stream cipher RC4 consists of two algorithms: the Key Scheduling Algorithm (KSA) and the Pseudo Random Generator Algorithm (PRGA). The KSA generates an initial state from a random key K of ℓ words of n bits as described in Algorithm 1. It starts with an array $\{0,1,\ldots,N-1\}$, where $N = 2^n$ and swaps N pairs, depending on the value of the secret key K. At the end, we obtain the initial state S_{N-1}.

Algorithm 1. RC4 Key Scheduling Algorithm (KSA)

for $i = 0$ to $N-1$ **do**
  $S[i] \leftarrow i$
end for
$j \leftarrow 0$
for $i = 0$ to $N-1$ **do**
  $j \leftarrow j + S[i] + K[i \bmod \ell] \bmod N$
  swap($S[i]$,$S[j]$)
end for

Algorithm 2. RC4 Pseudo Random Generator Algorithm (PRGA)

$i \leftarrow 0$
$j \leftarrow 0$
loop
  $i \leftarrow i+1 \bmod N$
  $j \leftarrow j + S[i] \bmod N$
  swap($S[i]$,$S[j]$)
  keystream word $z_i = S[S[i] + S[j] \bmod N]$
end loop

Once the initial state S_{N-1} is created, it is used by the second algorithm of RC4, the PRGA. Its role is to generate a keystream of words of n bits, which will be XORed with the plaintext to obtain the ciphertext. Thus, RC4 computes the loop of the PRGA each time a new keystream word z_i is needed, according to Algorithm 2. Note that each time a word of the keystream is generated the internal state of RC4 is updated.

Notation. In this paper, we define all the operators such as addition, subtraction and multiplication in the group $\mathbf{Z}/N\mathbf{Z}$. Thus, $x+y$ should be read as $(x+y) \bmod N$. The indices of the table respect the C-style programming reference. This means that the first entry of the table has the index 0. Let $S_i[k]$ denote the value of the array S at index k, after round i in KSA. S_{-1} denotes the array where $S[i] = i$, where $i = 0,1,\ldots,N-1$. Let $S_i^{-1}[p]$ be the index of the value p in the array S after round i in KSA. For example, $S_i^{-1}[S_i[k]] = k$ and $S_i[S_i^{-1}[p]] = p$. Let j_i (resp. j'_i) be the value of j during the round i of KSA (resp. PRGA) where the rounds are indexed with respect to i. Thus, the KSA has rounds $0,1,\ldots,N-1$ and the PRGA has rounds $1,2,\ldots$. Let S'_i denote the array S after the ith round of the PRGA (i.e. S'_1 is equal to S_{N-1} with $S_{N-1}[1]$ and $S_{N-1}[S_{N-1}[1]]$ swapped). We also denote $S_{N-1} = S'_0$. In this paper, RC4 is always used with $N = 256$.

Thus, instead of words we may use bytes, which are equivalent. The keystream z_i is defined by

$$z_i = S'_i[S'_i[i] + S'_i[j'_i] \bmod N] = S'_i[S'_{i-1}[j'_i] + S'_{i-1}[i] \bmod N] \tag{1}$$

Let p be an integer and $\theta = e^{\frac{2i\pi}{p}}$. Unless otherwise mentioned, $\mathbf{G}$ denotes the $\mathbf{Z}_p$ group. The Discrete Fourier transform (DFT) of a function f over $\mathbf{G}^s$ is defined as

$$\hat{f}(c) = \sum_{x \in \mathbf{G}^s} f(x)\theta^{-c \bullet x}$$

where $\bullet$ is the dot product.

Previous Work. There are two approaches in the study of cryptanalysis of RC4: attacks based on the weaknesses of the KSA and attacks based on the weaknesses of the PRGA. Concerning the KSA, one of the first weakness published on RC4 was discovered by Roos [28] in 1995. This correlation binds the secret key bytes to the initial state S'_0. Roos [28] and Wagner [34] identified classes of weak keys which reveal the secret key if the first key bytes are known. This property has been largely exploited against WEP (see [5,9,2,15,16,32,30,29]). Another study of cryptanalysis of the KSA is the secret key recovery when the initial state S'_0 is known [25,1]. On the PRGA, The analysis has been largely motivated by distinguishing attacks [7,6,19,21] or initial state reconstruction from the keystream bytes [8,31,14,22] with complexity of 2^{241} for the best state recovery attack. Relevant studies of the PRGA reveal biases in the keystream output bytes in [20,27]. Mironov in [23] recommends that the first 512 initial keystream bytes must be discarded to avoid these weaknesses. Jenkins published in 1996 on his website [11] two biases in the PRGA of RC4. These biases have been generalized by Mantin in his Master Thesis [18] as *useful states*. Paul, Rathi and Maitra [26] discovered in 2008 a biased output index of the first keystream word generated by the PRGA. Ultimately, the last bias on the PRGA has been experimentally discovered by Maitra and Paul [17]. In practice, key recovery attacks on RC4 must bind KSA and PRGA weaknesses to correlate secret key words to keystream words. Some biases on the PRGA [13,26,17] have been successfully bound to the Roos correlation [28] to provide known plaintext attacks.

Our Contributions. Since, almost all known PRGA correlations have been experimentally found, we propose a method to exhaustively reveal new weaknesses in the PRGA. From 4 known biases in the PRGA, we have found 48 additional new exploitable correlations thanks to this technique. To provide key recovery attacks on RC4, we must bind KSA and PRGA weaknesses, we show that some of these new correlations can be bound to KSA vulnerabilities and lead to new key recovery attacks. Subsequently, we present another technique which does not consider the KSA and the PRGA, but only RC4 as a black box with the secret key words as input and the keystream words as output. Similar to the previous technique, we exhaustively search for correlations to rediscover the 3 known biases. Thanks to this technique, we have discovered 9 additional exploitable correlations between the secret key and the keystream words. Then, we exploit the known and new weaknesses against plain RC4 (with 48 first keystream words known by the attacker) and we obtain a key recovery attack with a complexity of $2^{122.06}$ instead of 2^{128} for RC4 with $N = 256$ and a key length of 16 bytes.

We also show that some of these correlations can be applied to WEP, decreasing the number of required encrypted packets to 9 800. The best previous key recovery attacks on WEP needed 24 200 encrypted packets [32,29] for the same success probability. This permits to recover a WEP key of 104 bits with a passive ciphertext only attack in less than 20 seconds in practice. This new attack is the best key recovery on WEP to our knowledge.

Structure of the Paper. In Section 2 we briefly explore known correlations in the PRGA of RC4. Section 3 details the technique used to visually represent correlations in the PRGA. Then, we describe the new biases discovered with our technique. In Section 4 we bind some of these new PRGA correlations with known KSA weaknesses to provide practical attacks on RC4. In Section 5 we detail another kind of exhaustive search where RC4 is a black box with the secret key words as input and the keystream words as output. Then, we present the new correlations found with this technique. Section 6 briefly describes a practical application of these biases to RC4 and RC4 with an IV such as used by WEP and WPA. Finally, we conclude.

2 Known Correlations in the PRGA of RC4

Jenkins Correlation. In 1996, Robert Jenkins described in his website [11] two biased correlations experimentally found on the PRGA of RC4. The first correlation considers the case where $S'_i[i] + S'_i[j'_i] = j'_i$. Thus, the ith keystream byte given by Equation (1) becomes

$$z_i = S'_i[S'_i[i] + S'_i[j'_i]] = S'_i[j'_i] = j'_i - S'_i[i] \tag{2}$$

which holds with probability of $2/N$ instead of $1/N$ with $i = 1, 2, \ldots$. The second correlation appears when $S'_i[i] + S'_i[j'_i] = i$. In this case, the ith byte of the keystream is given by

$$z_i = S'_i[S'_i[i] + S'_i[j'_i]] = S'_i[i] = i - S'_i[j'_i] \tag{3}$$

which holds with probability of $2/N$.

Mantin and Shamir Correlation. Mantin and Shamir [20] discovered a biased distribution for the second keystream word.

Theorem 1. *Assume an initial state S'_0 is chosen randomly. The probability that the second keystream word z_2 of RC4 is 0 is approximately $2/N$ instead of $1/N$.*

Paul, Rathi and Maitra Correlation. In 2008, Paul, Rathi and Maitra [26] described a biased correlation between the three first words of the secret key and the first keystream word z_1 of RC4.

Theorem 2. *Assume that the initial state S'_0 is chosen uniformly at random from the set of all possible permutations of the set $\{0, 1, \ldots, N-1\}$. Then the probability distribution* *of the output index* $S_1'[1] + S_1'[S_0'[1]] = S_1'^{-1}[z_1]$ *that selects the first byte of the keystream output is given by*

$$P\left(S_1'[1] + S_1'[j_i'] = x\right) = \begin{cases} \frac{1}{N} & \text{for odd } x \\ \frac{1}{N} - \frac{2}{N(N-1)} & \text{for even } x \neq 2 \\ \frac{2}{N} - \frac{1}{N(N-1)} & \text{for even } x = 2 \end{cases}$$

3 Visual Representation of Correlations in the PRGA

In general, the methods used to find correlations in RC4 are either opportunistic or not given. Papers tend to describe the characteristics of the biases without revealing the techniques used to discover them. We propose to describe some simple but efficient techniques to highlight weaknesses in the PRGA through exhaustive search on a subset of elements.

We define a set of linear equations which contains all the known biased correlations of the PRGA described in the previous section. Our objective is to highlight linear correlations between the internal values of a round of the PRGA and the keystream word generated by this round i.e. the subset of elements $\{i, j_i', S_i'[i], S_i'[j_i'], z_i\}$. The correlations previously discovered by Jenkins, Mantin and Shamir and Paul, Rathi and Maitra must be rediscovered with this method. Surprisingly, some new biases are found as well. We define the linear equations as

$$(a_0 \cdot i + a_1 \cdot j_i' + a_2 \cdot S_i'[i] + a_3 \cdot S_i'[j_i'] + a_4 \cdot z_i) \bmod N = b \tag{4}$$

where the a_i's are elements of $\mathbf{Z}/256\mathbf{Z}$ and b is a fixed value in $\mathbf{Z}/256\mathbf{Z}$. This defines 2^{48} linear equations. To reduce this number, we decompose these equations into 256 subgroups. Each of them corresponds to a specific round (i.e. i is fixed). Thus, both $a_0 \cdot i$ and b can be merged into one value and Equation (4) becomes

$$(c_0 \cdot j_i' + c_1 \cdot S_i'[i] + c_2 \cdot S_i'[j_i'] + c_3 \cdot z_i) \bmod N = C \tag{5}$$

where $C = (b - a_0 \cdot i) \bmod 256$ and c_i's are elements of $\mathbf{Z}/256\mathbf{Z}$. Since the number of linear equations is still too large, we limit the coefficients set of the c_i's to $\{-1, 0, 1\}$. Indeed, this set is enough to include all the previously known biased correlation in the PRGA. We obtain 256 graphs of 81 linear equations. We compute 256 first rounds of the PRGA with 10^9 randomly chosen RC4 secret keys of 16 bytes and we verify all the linear equations described by Equation 5. For every equation, a counter is incremented when it holds. Subsequently, we represent these counters as a graph to visually illustrate potential biases. Human brains are very efficient to visually detect anomalies in uniform distributions (see Figure 1). Below we give the biased correlations found for the 256 first keystream bytes (from z_1 to z_{256}) generated by the PRGA. Every coefficient c_i has been replaced by the corresponding element to provide an easier reading of the table (i.e. j_i' must be read as c_0, $S_i'[i]$ as c_1, etc.). Correlations with z_i (i.e. $c_3 \neq 0$) are called New_XXX and biases without z_i (i.e. $c_3 = 0$) are named New_noz_XXX.

In Figure 2, we confirm the presence of known biases such as the Jenkins correlations. More interestingly, new biases in the PRGA appear. Some of them have a probability of success which depends on the value of i.

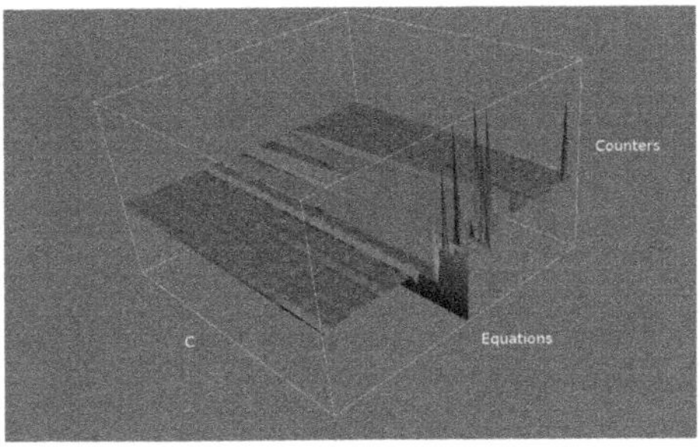

Fig. 1. 3D representation of the equations of the second round of the PRGA according to C and the counters of the equations. The objective of this graph is to visually detect biased.

Some rounds of the PRGA provide additional biased correlations. In Figure 3, we give extra biases which appear in round 1. Figure 4 depicts the additional correlations in the second round of the PRGA. Finally, Figure 5 describes further biased correlations in rounds 0 mod 16 of the PRGA. The probability of the biased correlations New_001 and New_002 depends on the round of the PRGA and the value C. In Figure 6 we show the success probability of New_001 according to C and the rounds 1, 16, 32, 64, 128, 192 and 256 of the PRGA. Similarly, we compute the evolution of the success probability of the biased correlations New_002 in Figure 8. Figure 7 gives the 3D representation of the same bias. Figure 9 depicts the same bias for all the first 256 rounds of the PRGA using a 3D representation.

3.1 Spectral Approach to Derive New Biases

Another systematic method to derive linear relations is to use Fourier transform of the type f of the distribution that some state bits of RC4 is following. We can use exactly the same approach to derive a linear relation between the main key bits and the key stream. Deploying this method over $\mathbf{Z}_{256}^{s}$, we can derive some *good* linear relations. We call a linear relation good if the probability of Equation (4) occurring is much higher than expected ($\gg \frac{1}{N}$). We use the 4-tuple defined above as an example. In fact, we can use exactly the same method to derive biases for linear relations in Section 5.2 between the secret key and keystream. To deal with this problem, we assume $\mathbf{G} = \mathbf{Z}_{256}$ and we query RC4 for $\mathcal{N}$ vectors $\mathcal{V}_t \in (j_i', S_i'[i], S_i'[j_i'], z_i)_t \in \mathbf{G}^4$ for $1 \leq t \leq \mathcal{N}$ and we define a function f as follows.

$$f(x) = \text{counter}(x) = \frac{1}{\mathcal{N}} \sum_{t=1}^{\mathcal{N}} \mathbf{1}_{\mathcal{V}_t = x}$$

where $x \in \mathbf{G}^4$. In fact, f is the *type* of the distribution the 4-tuples are following. Deploying DFT on f, we have

$$\hat{f}(c) = \sum_{x} \theta^{-c.x} f(x) = \sum_{C} \sum_{x:c.x=C} \theta^{-C} f(x) = \sum_{C} \theta^{-C}.\ \Pr[c\ .\ v = C]$$

Then, we follow this approach: we compute $|\hat{f}(c)|^2$ for c's such that this norm is high. Filtering those c's yields "good" c's.

j'_i	$S'_i[i]$	$S'_i[j'_i]$	z_i	C	Probability	Remark
1	-1	0	-1	0	$2/N$	Jenkins Equation (2)
0	0	1	1	i	$2/N$	Jenkins Equation (3)
0	1	1	-1	0	$1.9/N$	New_000
0	1	1	-1	1	$0.89/N$	New_001
⋮	⋮	⋮	⋮	⋮	⋮	⋮
0	1	1	-1	255	$1.25/N$	New_001
0	1	1	1	0	$0.95/N$	New_002
⋮	⋮	⋮	⋮	⋮	⋮	⋮
0	1	1	1	255	$0.95/N$	New_002
1	1	0	0	0	$0.95/N$	New_noz_000
⋮	⋮	⋮	⋮	⋮	⋮	⋮
1	1	0	0	255	$0.95/N$	New_noz_000
1	1	-1	0	i	$2/N$	New_noz_001
1	-1	1	0	i	$2/N$	New_noz_002
1	-1	0	0	1	$0.9/N$	New_noz_003
⋮	⋮	⋮	⋮	⋮	⋮	⋮
1	-1	0	0	255	$1.25/N$	New_noz_003
1	-1	0	0	0	$1.9/N$	New_noz_004
0	0	1	0	$i+1$	$1.36/N$	New_noz_005
⋮	⋮	⋮	⋮	⋮	⋮	⋮
0	0	1	0	255	$0.9/N$	New_noz_005
0	0	1	0	i	$2.34/N$	New_noz_006

Fig. 2. Correlations experimentally observed for rounds $1, 2, 3, \ldots, 256$ of the PRGA. Note that probability of biases New_000, New_noz_005 and New_noz_006 decrease according to i. The probabilities given in this table correspond to round 3 (i.e. $i = 3$). New_noz_004 and New_noz_006 are not biased when $i = 1$.

j'_i	$S'_i[i]$	$S'_i[j'_i]$	z_i	C	Probability	Remark
0	1	0	-1	0	$0.95/N$	New_003
0	1	1	0	2	$1.95/N$	Paul, Rathi and Maitra
1	1	0	0	2	$1.94/N$	New_noz_014

Fig. 3. Additional biased correlations experimentally observed using Equation (5) in the first round of the PRGA (i.e. $i = 1$)

We construct the table $|\hat{f}(c)|^2$ of all linear masks and filter out c's that leads to small value for $|\hat{f}(c)|^2$. This remains us some c's. Then, we can exhaustively search in the c's left and find the good $c's$. This method is much faster than exhaustive search. Assume we consider the linear relation between the elements of the vector $(j'_i, S'_i[j'_i], z_i)$ instead of $(j'_i, S'_i[i], S'_i[j'_i], z_i)$. This already gives us all biases quite fast. This method can be easily generalized to the case when $S'_i[i]$ is also involved and it is dramatically faster than exhaustive search.

j'_i	$S'_i[i]$	$S'_i[j'_i]$	z_i	C	Probability	Remark
0	0	0	1	0	$2/N$	Mantin and Shamir [20]
1	-1	1	-1	0	$2/N$	New_004
1	1	0	-1	even	$1.0183/N$	New_005
1	1	0	-1	odd	$1.0316/N$	New_006
1	0	1	0	6	$2.37/N$	New_noz_007
1	0	-1	0	255	$0.75/N$	New_noz_008
1	-1	1	0	0	$2/N$	New_noz_009
0	-1	1	0	0	$0.95/N$	New_noz_010

Fig. 4. Additional biased correlations experimentally observed using Equation (5) in the second round of the PRGA ($i = 2$). Note that the probability of success of correlations New_005 and New_006 decreases according to the value C.

j'_i	$S'_i[i]$	$S'_i[j'_i]$	z_i	C	Probability	Remark
0	0	0	1	-i	$1.0411/N$	New_007
0	0	1	-1	i	$1.0500/N$	New_008
0	0	1	1	-i	$1.0338/N$	New_009
0	1	1	0	-i	$1.1107/N$	New_noz_011
0	1	0	0	-i	$1.1276/N$	New_noz_012
0	1	-1	0	-i	$1.1067/N$	New_noz_013

Fig. 5. Additional biased correlations experimentally observed using Equation (5) in rounds 0 mod 16 of the PRGA. Note that the probability of success of these correlations decreases according to the value i and become barely exploitable when $i > 48$. Probabilities given in this table come from round 16.

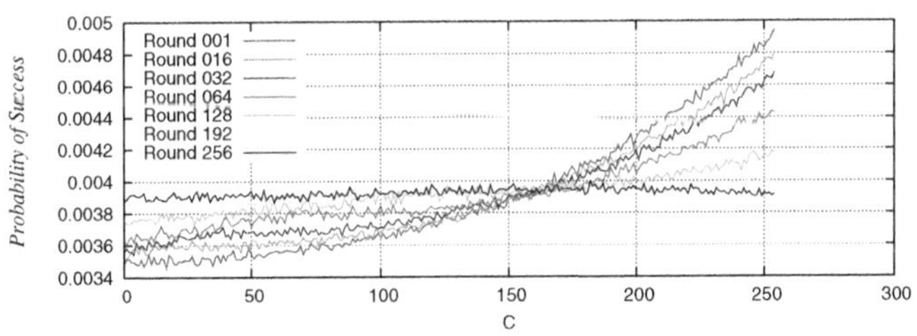

Fig. 6. Probability of success of biased correlation New_001, according the value C for some rounds of the PRGA

The complexity of this method for the triplet case is 3.2^{32}, while for exhaustive search the complexity reaches to 2^{47} if $N = 10^7$, which is a reasonable number of samples we found out experimentally. This will gain us all the biases for the triplet over $\mathbf{Z}^3_{256}$. Using this method, we found out some new biases. We only list those which are not artifact of known biases and which can be bound with biases of KSA. They are listed in Fig 10. Any time the coefficient of $S'_i[j'_i]$ is one in the table, we can use that equation to bind it like what would be explained in the next section for binding New_008 and New_009 biases.

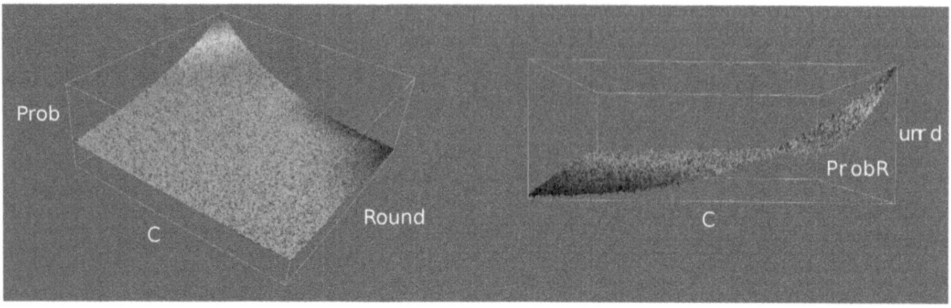

Fig. 7. Probability of biased correlation New_001, according the value C for the first 256 rounds of the PRGA, using a 3D representation

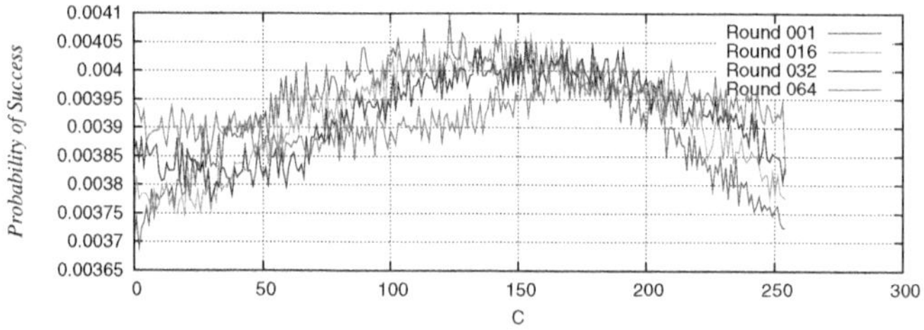

Fig. 8. Probability of success of biased correlation New_002, according the value C for some rounds of the PRGA

Fig. 9. Probability of biased correlation New_002, according the value C for the first 256 rounds of the PRGA, using a 3D representation

This method removes the restriction on coefficients to be only in the set $\{-1,0,1\}$. Using these technique, we can recover all biases in $\mathbf{Z}_{256}^4$ in a reasonable time.

After investigation, it seems that all the listed biases are artifact of a new conditional bias which is

$$\Pr[S'_{16}[j'_{16}] = 0 | z_{16} = -16] = 0.038488$$

So far, we have no explanation about this new bias.

j'_i	$S'_i[i]$	$S'_i[j'_i]$	z_i	C	i	Probability	Remark
0	0	1	1	240	16	$1.04/N$	New_010
0	0	1	50	224	16	$1.04/N$	New_011
0	0	1	68	192	16	$1.05/N$	New_012
0	0	1	98	224	16	$1.04/N$	New_013
0	0	1	148	192	16	$1.05/N$	New_014
0	0	1	162	224	16	$1.05/N$	New_015
0	0	1	186	96	16	$1.03/N$	New_016
0	0	1	187	80	16	$1.04/N$	New_017
0	0	1	251	80	16	$1.04/N$	New_018
0	0	2	19	208	16	$1.04/N$	New_019
0	0	2	127	16	16	$1.04/N$	New_020
0	0	2	147	208	16	$1.04/N$	New_021
0	0	2	255	16	16	$1.04/N$	New_022
0	0	4	59	80	16	$1.04/N$	New_023
0	0	4	123	80	16	$1.04/N$	New_024
0	0	8	19	208	16	$1.04/N$	New_025
0	0	8	55	144	16	$1.03/N$	New_026
0	0	8	81	240	16	$1.03/N$	New_027
0	0	8	215	144	16	$1.03/N$	New_028
0	0	8	241	48	16	$1.03/N$	New_029
0	0	8	243	208	16	$1.04/N$	New_030
0	0	32	39	144	16	$1.04/N$	New_031
0	0	32	191	16	16	$1.04/N$	New_032

Fig. 10. Correlations in PRGA derived using DFT. If coefficient of $S'_i[j'_i]$ is one, that equation can be bound with KSA biases

4 Binding PRGA and KSA Weaknesses

Since we have new PRGA biased correlations, we have to bind them with KSA weaknesses to provide key recovery attacks.

4.1 Known Binding between KSA and PRGA Weaknesses

Already known bindings between KSA and PRGA have been exploited. In 2006, Klein [12,13] demonstrated that the Jenkins correlation of the PRGA and some weaknesses in the KSA can be combined.

$$S'_i[j'_i] \overset{P_j}{=} i - z_i \qquad \text{from Equation (3) with } P_j = 2/N \qquad (6)$$

$$S'_i[j'_i] = S'_{i-1}[i] \qquad \text{step 6 of the PRGA} \qquad (7)$$

$$S'_{i-1}[i] \overset{P'}{=} S_i[i] \qquad P' = ((N-1)/N)^{N-2} \qquad (8)$$

$$S_i[i] = S_{i-1}[j_i] \qquad \text{KSA} \qquad (9)$$

$$j_i = S_{i-1}[i] + j_{i-1} + K[i] \qquad \text{step 6 of the KSA} \qquad (10)$$

From (6) with respectively (7), (8), (9) and (10) we have

$$K[i] \overset{P_{\mathsf{Klein}}}{=} S_{i-1}^{-1}[i - z_i \bmod N] - S_{i-1}[i] - j_{i-1} \bmod N \tag{11}$$

which holds with probability

$$P_{\mathsf{Klein}} = \frac{2}{N} \cdot \left(\frac{N-1}{N}\right)^{N-2} + \frac{N-2}{N(N-1)} \cdot \left(1 - \left(\frac{N-1}{N}\right)^{N-2}\right) \approx \frac{1.36}{N} \tag{12}$$

In 2007, Vaudenay and Vuagnoux [32] improved this attack by using the Roos correlation and the repetition of the secret key modulo ℓ. Thus, the sum of the secret key bytes can be recovered with

$$\sum_{y=0}^{i} K[y] \overset{P_{\mathsf{KleinImproved}}}{=} i - z_i - \frac{i \cdot (i+1)}{2} \bmod N \tag{13}$$

with success probability of $P_{\mathsf{KleinImproved}}(i)$ defined by

$$\begin{aligned} P_{\mathsf{C}}(i) &= \left(\tfrac{N-1}{N}\right)^{i} \cdot \prod_{k=1}^{i} \left(\tfrac{N-k}{N}\right) \cdot \left(\tfrac{N-1}{N}\right)^{N-2} \\ P_{\mathsf{KleinImproved}}(i) &= \tfrac{2}{N} \cdot P_{\mathsf{C}}(i) + \tfrac{N-2}{N(N-1)} \cdot (1 - P_{\mathsf{C}}(i)) \end{aligned} \tag{14}$$

for any $i - z_i \mod N \neq \{0, 1, \ldots, i-1\}$.

4.2 Binding New PRGA Bias Where $S'_i[j'_i]$ Is Involved

Interestingly, from the Jenkins correlation described by $S'_i[j'_i] = i - z_i$ and Equation (13) we have

$$S'_i[j'_i] \overset{P_{\mathsf{KleinImproved}}}{=} \frac{i \cdot (i+1)}{2} + \sum_{y=0}^{i} K[y] \bmod N \tag{15}$$

for the same success probability. Hence, every new biased equation containing $S'_i[j'_i]$ and public values such as i and z_i can be exploited as key recovery attack.

New_009 ($-i - S_i[j'_i] = z_i$). This biased correlation concerns rounds 0 mod 16 of the PRGA. The success probability is $1.0338/N$ for round 16. Using the same technique described above, we can exploit this bias to recover the secret key sum

$$\sum_{y=0}^{i} K[y] \overset{P_0}{=} -i - z_i - \frac{i \cdot (i+1)}{2} \bmod N$$

with a success probability equal to

$$P_0(i) = \frac{1.0338}{N} \cdot P_{\mathsf{C}}(i) + \frac{N - 1.0338}{N(N-1)} \cdot (1 - P_{\mathsf{C}}(i))$$

for any $-i - z_i \mod N \neq \{0, 1, \ldots, i-1\}$ and $i = 16$.

New_008 ($-i + S_i[j'_i] = z_i$). Similarly, we can exploit this biased equation using the same technique

$$\sum_{y=0}^{i} K[y] \overset{P_1}{=} -i + z_i - \frac{i \cdot (i+1)}{2} \mod N$$

with a success probability equal to

$$P_1(i) = \frac{1.05}{N} \cdot P_C(i) + \frac{N - 1.05}{N(N-1)} \cdot (1 - P_C(i))$$

for any $-i + z_i \mod N \neq \{0, 1, \ldots, i-1\}$ and $i = 16$.

4.3 Exploiting Additional Biased Linear Correlations in the PRGA

The binding between KSA weakness and PRGA biases presented above is an example of a practical application of the correlations discovered in the previous section. We did not find a way to exploit biases where $S'_i[i]$ or j'_i are involved. However, these correlations could be exploited in future work.

5 RC4 as a Black Box

In Section 4 we have seen that secret key words and keystream words may be correlated if weaknesses in the KSA and PRGA can be bound. However, from an attacker's point of view there is no reason to determine weaknesses in the KSA or the PRGA. The objective is to find correlations between known values and the secret key words. Moreover, the biased correlations previously found concern only elements inside a round of the PRGA. Correlations between elements from different rounds cannot be highlighted.

In this section, we present another way to attack RC4. We consider RC4 as a black box. The objective is to discover linear correlations between the input (the secret key words) and the output (the keystream words), since we consider known keystream attacks. First, we study known RC4 correlations between the keystream words and the secret key words. Then, we propose a method to highlight new biases. Finally, we list new discovered biases in RC4.

5.1 Maitra and Paul Correlation

In 2008, Maitra and Paul [17] discovered a new experimental observation on RC4 which holds with probability of $\approx 1.10/N$ for $i = 0$.

$$z_{i+1} \overset{P_{\text{Maitra}}}{=} \frac{i \cdot (i+1)}{2} + \sum_{y=0}^{i} K[y] \tag{16}$$

Maitra and Paul did not find any practical application for this bias in protocols using or based on RC4. However, from Equation 15 we can rewrite Equation (16) as

$$z_{i+1} \overset{P_{\text{Maitra}}}{=} S'_i[j'_i]$$

This bias has not been found with our previous technique, since these elements are not in the same round of the PRGA. However, with the black box technique we are able to rediscover this bias and new ones.

5.2 Discovering New Linear Correlations in RC4

We define a linear equation containing input and output elements.

$$(a_0 \cdot K[0] + \ldots + a_{\ell-1} \cdot K[\ell-1] + a_\ell \cdot z_1 + \ldots + a_{N+\ell-1} \cdot z_N) \bmod N = b \qquad (17)$$

This kind of exhaustive search is identical to those presented in Section 3. First, we consider the subset of all a_i's defined by $A = \{-1, 0, 1\}$ and $b \in \mathbf{Z}/N\mathbf{Z}$. The number of equation is $N \cdot 3^{\ell+N} = 2^{439.11}$ for $N = 256$ and $\ell = 16$, which is obviously too large for an exhaustive search.

Based on the pseudo T-function's behavior of the KSA (i.e. $S_{N-1}[i]$ depends only on $K[i-1], K[i-2], \ldots, K[0]$ with a non negligible probability) and the Roos correlation, we can reduce the size of the equation by considering only the first ℓ keystream words. Equation (17) becomes

$$(a_0 \cdot K[0] + \ldots + a_{\ell-1} \cdot K[\ell-1] + a_\ell \cdot z_1 + \ldots + a_{2\ell-1} \cdot z_\ell) \bmod N = b \qquad (18)$$

Thus, we obtain a number of equations equals to $N \cdot 3^{2\ell} = 2^{58.7}$ which is still too large for an exhaustive search. Thus, we reduced the secret keys length to $\ell = 5$ bytes to obtain $2^{23.8496}$ equations. Indeed, based on the pseudo T-function behavior's of the KSA, we suppose that the correlations found with a RC4 key length of 5 bytes can be generalized to RC4 with a secret key of 16 bytes. Then, the supposed biased correlation are tested experimentally. After a few computation, we remarked that the constant value represented by b can be reduced to the subset generated by $i \cdot (i+1)/2$ with $i = 0, 1, 2 \ldots, 22$,

Equation	Probability	Remarks
$z_1 + K[0] + K[1] = 0$	1.35779/N	Klein Improved
$z_1 - K[0] = 0$	1.11784/N	Maitra and Paul
$z_2 = 0$	2.01825/N	Mantin and Shamir
$z_2 + K[0] + K[1] + K[2] = -1$	1.36095/N	Klein Improved
$z_1 - K[0] - K[1] = 1$	1.04237/N	New_bb_000
$z_1 - K[0] + K[1] = -1$	1.04969/N	New_bb_001
$z_3 + K[0] + K[1] + K[2] + K[3] = -3$	1.35362/N	Klein Improved
$z_3 - K[0] + K[3] = -3$	1.04620/N	New_bb_002
$z_1 - K[0] - K[1] - K[2] = 3$	1.33474/N	Roos/Paul et al.
$z_2 - K[0] - K[1] - K[2] = 3$	0.64300/N	New_bb_003
$z_3 - K[0] - K[1] - K[2] = 3$	1.13555/N	Maitra and Paul
$z_2 + K[1] + K[2] = -3$	1.36897/N	New_bb_004
$z_2 - K[1] - K[2] = 3$	1.36733/N	New_bb_005
$z_1 - K[2] = 3$	1.14193/N	New_bb_006
$z_1 + K[0] + K[1] - K[2] = 3$	1.14116/N	New_bb_007
$z_4 - K[0] + K[4] = 4$	1.04463/N	New_bb_008
$z_4 + K[0] + K[1] + K[2] + K[3] + K[4] = -6$	1.35275/N	Klein Improved
$z_4 - K[0] - K[1] - K[2] - K[3] = 10$	1.11432/N	Maitra and Paul

Fig. 11. Biased correlations experimentally observed with the black box technique with $\ell = 5$ in Equation 18. Note that these biases are exploitable in RC4 with a secret key of 16 bytes as well.

since only the Roos correlation seems to be exploited in the KSA. Thus, the number of equations decreases to $23 \cdot 3^{10} = 2^{20.373}$. Figure 11 gives the correlations found in RC4 with a secret key of 5 bytes which are experimentally confirmed on RC4 with a key length of 16 bytes.

For every index i corresponding to the index of a key byte, let d_i the number of biased equations we have for $\bar{K}[i] = K[0] + \cdots + K[i]$. Let $p_{i,j}$ be the probability of the j_{th} equation for this byte. The list of biases we use is depicted in Fig 12.

If the key has size ℓ, indices $i = k.\ell - 1$ correspond to the same byte, so we can merge the associated list of biases. Similarly, if $\bar{K}[\ell - 1]$ is known, indices which are equal modulo ℓ correspond to the same byte, so we can merge these lists as well. Let $p'_{i,j}$ be the table of merged lists and d'_i be the length of list $p'_{i,j}$.

Equation	Probability	Remarks
$\bar{K}[0] - z_1 = 0$	1.10873/N	Maitra and Paul
$\bar{K}[1] + z_1 = 0$	1.36467/N	Klein Improved
$\bar{K}[1] - z_1 = 255$	1.04237/N	New_bb_000
$\bar{K}[2] - z_2 = 253$	0.64300/N	New_bb_003
$\bar{K}[2] + z_2 = 255$	1.36036/N	Klein Improved
$\bar{K}[2] - z_3 = 253$	1.12742/N	Maitra and Paul
$\vdots$	$\vdots$	$\vdots$
$\bar{K}[14] + z_{14} = 165$	1.22758/N	Klein Improved
$\bar{K}[14] - z_{15} = 151$	1.06444/N	Maitra and Paul
$\bar{K}[15] + z_{15} = 151$	1.21317/N	Klein Improved
$\bar{K}[15] - z_{16} = 136$	1.07519/N	Maitra and Paul
$\bar{K}[15] + \bar{K}[0] - z_{16} = 104$	1.01838/N	New_008
$\bar{K}[15] + \bar{K}[0] + z_{16} = 104$	1.01242/N	New_009
$\bar{K}[15] + \bar{K}[0] + z_{16} = 136$	1.19880/N	Klein Improved
$\bar{K}[15] + \bar{K}[0] - z_{17} = 136$	1.05983/N	Maitra and Paul
$\vdots$	$\vdots$	$\vdots$
$\bar{K}[15] + \bar{K}[14] + z_{30} = 77$	1.04582/N	Klein Improved
$\bar{K}[15] + \bar{K}[14] - z_{31} = 47$	1.02118/N	Maitra and Paul
$2\bar{K}[15] + z_{31} = 47$	1.03963/N	Klein Improved
$2\bar{K}[15] - z_{32} = 16$	1.03833/N	Maitra and Paul
$2\bar{K}[15] + \bar{K}[0] - z_{32} = 208$	1.009/N	New_008
$2\bar{K}[15] + \bar{K}[0] + z_{32} = 208$	1.0062/N	New_009
$2\bar{K}[15] + \bar{K}[0] + z_{32} = 16$	1.03403/N	Klein Improved
$\vdots$	$\vdots$	$\vdots$
$2\bar{K}[15] + \bar{K}[14] + z_{46} = 57$	1.00027/N	Klein Improved
$3\bar{K}[15] + z_{47} = 199$	0.99951/N	Klein Improved

Fig. 12. Useful biases in key recovery attack on RC4 for $\ell = 16$

6 Key Recovery Attacks

6.1 Theoretical Key Recovery Attack on Plain RC4

We consider RC4 with $N = 256$ and a secret key length $\ell = 16$ bytes. Thus, the exhaustive search has complexity of 2^{128}. Using all the exploitable biased correlations presented in this paper and the previously known biases in RC4 and considering that they are independent, we are able to recover the RC4 secret key words from the 48 first keystream words (known keystream attack) with a complexity of $2^{122.06}$. In fact, the probability that all key bytes are expressed by at least one bias is

$$p \approx \prod_{i=0}^{\ell-1} \left(1 - \prod_{j=1}^{d'_i} (1 - p'_{i,j}) \right)$$

and the number of combination of biases is $k = \prod_{i=0}^{\ell-1} d'_i$. So the average complexity is $\frac{k}{2}$ with success probability p. The average complexity by iterating is $\frac{k}{p}$. With our table, we compute $p \approx 2^{-87.90}$ and $k \approx 2^{38.09}$. Thus, the complexity of attacking plain RC4 would be $2^{125.99}$.

Note that p is optimized this way, but not $\frac{k}{p}$. By taking only the largest bias for each byte, we obtain $\frac{k}{p} = 2^{122.06}$ with $k = 1$.

6.2 Practical Key Recovery Attack on WEP

To provide a practical use of these attacks, we tried to deploy them on RC4 with an IV such as used by the protocol WEP or WPA. For some people, attacking WEP is like beating a dead horse, since it has been already badly broken [5,9,2,15,16,32,30,29]. First, the new biases presented in this paper are related to the stream cipher RC4. WEP is an example of a practical exploitation of these biases. Moreover, the cryptanalysis of WEP is one of the most applied cryptographic attack in practice. Indeed, tools such as *Aircrack* [4] are massively downloaded to provide a good example of weaknesses in cryptography.

In the case of WEP and WPA, the first 3 bytes are known and the key is a repetition of $\ell = 16$ bytes. So, we can remove the $P_{0,j}, P_{1,j}, P_{2,j}$ lists, redo the merge operation, then merge the lists for $i' = 3, 4, \ldots, 15$. In practice, this gives $k \approx 2^{31.77}$ biases and results in $p = 2^{-70.57}$. So, we have a complexity of $\frac{k}{p} \approx 2^{102.34}$ to recover the full key K with a single packet.

We picked the same key recovery algorithm described in [32], but we added known and new correlation presented in this paper. We also include all conditional biases from the Korek attacks [15,16,3] with the improvement described in [32,33]. The complexity of the key recovery attacks on WEP depends on the number of encrypted packets captured. For every captured packet, we sort the list of potential secret keys given by the key recovery attacks and we test the first 10^6 keys according to this list. See [32] for more details. The previous best key recovery attack described in [32] and better implemented in [29] needs 24 200 packets to recover a secret key of 104 bits with a success probability

$> 1/2$. With the new key recovery described in this paper, we are able to recover the secret key with an average of 9 800 encrypted packets for the same success probability. This complexity of 9 800 packets was measured experimentally by running the attacks on 10^6 random secret keys. This represents the best key recovery attack on WEP to our knowledge.

6.3 Theoretical Key Recovery Attacks on WPA

In order to correct the weaknesses on WEP discovered before 2004, the Wi-Fi Alliance proposed a WEP improved protocol called WPA [10]. It has been established that WPA must be hardware compatible with existing WEP capable devices to be deployed as a software patch. Basically, WPA is a WEP wrapper which contains anti-replay protections and a key management scheme to avoid key reuse. In 2004, Moen, Raddum and Hole [24] discovered that the recovery of at least two RC4 packet keys in WPA leads to a full recovery of the temporal key and the message integrity check key. The complexity of this attack is defined by the exhaustive search of two 104-bit long keys, i.e. 2^{104}.

Almost all known and new key recovery attacks on WEP can be applied to WPA. Only the Fluhrer, Mantin and Shamir attack [5] is filtered. Indeed, WPA encryption is similar to WEP, using RC4 with an IV. But, WPA uses a different secret key for every encrypted packet. Once from the same segment of 2^{16} consequetive packets, two keys are successfully recovered, the Moen, Raddum and Hole attack can be applied. However, the attack in Section 6.2 has a success probability p too low to recover two keys. The actual application to attacking WPA is left for future work.

7 Conclusion

In this paper, we have seen some techniques to exhaustively highlight linear correlations in RC4. First, we have considered only the elements inside a round of the PRGA. Then, we have generalized this method to the whole RC4 as a black box with the secret key words as input and the keystream words as output. These techniques led to the discovery of 57 new correlations in RC4. Some of them can be directly applied to existing key recovery attacks on RC4, WEP and WPA. For example, a WEP secret key of 128 bits (104 unknown bits) can be recovered in less than 20 seconds, the time to eavesdrop at least 9 800 encrypted packets. This is the best attack on WEP to our knowledge.

However, the main interest of this paper is the application of an automated discovery of weaknesses in ciphers. Similar to fuzzing techniques used to highlight security vulnerabilities in computer systems, these methods, although relatively simple, reveal an impressive number of new weaknesses in a intensively analyzed stream cipher such as RC4. This may suggest a new kind of automated tools for cryptanalysts. Indeed, weaknesses in network protocol or computer systems are largely found by automated tools such as fuzzers, negative testers or black box analyzers. With the results presented in this paper, it may be interesting to adapt these tools for cryptanalysis.

References

1. Biham, E., Carmeli, Y.: Efficient Reconstruction of RC4 Keys from Internal States. In: Nyberg, K. (ed.) FSE 2008. LNCS, vol. 5086, pp. 270–288. Springer, Heidelberg (2008)
2. Bittau, A.: Additional Weak IV Classes for the FMS Attack (2003), http://www.cs.ucl.ac.uk/staff/a.bittau/sorwep.txt
3. Chaabouni, R.: Breaking WEP Faster with Statistical Analysis. Ecole Polytechnique Fédérale de Lausanne, LASEC, Semester Project (2006)
4. Devine, C., Otreppe, T.: Aircrack, http://www.aircrack-ng.org/
5. Fluhrer, S.R., Mantin, I., Shamir, A.: Weaknesses in the Key Scheduling Algorithm of RC4. In: Vaudenay, S., Youssef, A.M. (eds.) SAC 2001. LNCS, vol. 2259, pp. 1–24. Springer, Heidelberg (2001)
6. Fluhrer, S.R., McGrew, D.A.: Statistical Analysis of the Alleged RC4 Keystream Generator. In: Schneier, B. (ed.) FSE 2000. LNCS, vol. 1978, pp. 19–30. Springer, Heidelberg (2001)
7. Golic, J.D.: Linear statistical weakness of alleged RC4 keystream generator. In: Fumy, W. (ed.) EUROCRYPT 1997. LNCS, vol. 1233, pp. 226–238. Springer, Heidelberg (1997)
8. Golic, J.D.: Iterative Probabilistic Cryptanalysis of RC4 Keystream Generator. In: Dawson, E., Clark, A., Boyd, C. (eds.) ACISP 2000. LNCS, vol. 1841, pp. 220–233. Springer, Heidelberg (2000)
9. Hulton, D.: Practical Exploitation of RC4 Weaknesses in WEP Environments (2001), http://www.dachb0den.com/projects/bsd-airtools/wepexp.txt
10. IEEE. ANSI/IEEE standard 802.11i: Amendment 6 Wireless LAN Medium Access Control (MAC) and Physical Layer (phy) Specifications, Draft 3 (2003)
11. Jenkins, R.: ISAAC and RC4, http://burtleburtle.net/bob/rand/isaac.html
12. Klein, A.: Attacks on the RC4 Stream Cipher. Personal Andreas Klein website (2006), http://cage.ugent.be/~klein/RC4/RC4-en.ps
13. Klein, A.: Attacks on the RC4 Stream Cipher. Des. Codes Cryptography 48(3), 269–286 (2008)
14. Knudsen, L.R., Meier, W., Preneel, B., Rijmen, V., Verdoolaege, S.: Analysis Methods for (Alleged) RC4. In: Ohta, K., Pei, D. (eds.) ASIACRYPT 1998. LNCS, vol. 1514, pp. 327–341. Springer, Heidelberg (1998)
15. KoreK. Need Security Pointers (2004), http://www.netstumbler.org/showthread.php?postid=89036#post89036
16. KoreK. Next Generation of WEP Attacks? (2004), http://www.netstumbler.org/showpost.php?p=93942&postcount=35
17. Maitra, S., Paul, G.: New Form of Permutation Bias and Secret Key Leakage in Keystream Bytes of RC4. In: Nyberg, K. (ed.) FSE 2008. LNCS, vol. 5086, pp. 253–269. Springer, Heidelberg (2008)
18. Mantin, I.: Analysis of the Stream Cipher RC4, http://www.wisdom.weizmann.ac.il/~itsik/RC4/rc4.html
19. Mantin, I.: Predicting and Distinguishing Attacks on RC4 Keystream Generator. In: Cramer, R. (ed.) EUROCRYPT 2005. LNCS, vol. 3494, pp. 491–506. Springer, Heidelberg (2005)
20. Mantin, I., Shamir, A.: A Practical Attack on Broadcast RC4. In: Matsui, M. (ed.) FSE 2001. LNCS, vol. 2355, pp. 152–164. Springer, Heidelberg (2002)
21. Maximov, A.: Two Linear Distinguishing Attacks on VMPC and RC4A and Weakness of RC4 Family of Stream Ciphers. In: Gilbert, H., Handschuh, H. (eds.) FSE 2005. LNCS, vol. 3557, pp. 342–358. Springer, Heidelberg (2005)
22. Maximov, A., Khovratovich, D.: New State Recovery Attack on RC4. In: Wagner, D. (ed.) CRYPTO 2008. LNCS, vol. 5157, pp. 297–316. Springer, Heidelberg (2008)

23. Mironov, I.: (Not So) Random Shuffles of RC4. In: Yung, M. (ed.) CRYPTO 2002. LNCS, vol. 2442, pp. 304–319. Springer, Heidelberg (2002)
24. Moen, V., Raddum, H., Hole, K.J.: Weaknesses in the Temporal Key Hash of WPA. Mobile Computing and Communications Review 8(2), 76–83 (2004)
25. Paul, G., Maitra, S.: Permutation After RC4 Key Scheduling Reveals the Secret Key. In: Adams, C., Miri, A., Wiener, M. (eds.) SAC 2007. LNCS, vol. 4876, pp. 360–377. Springer, Heidelberg (2007)
26. Paul, G., Rathi, S., Maitra, S.: On Non-negligible Bias of the First Output Bytes of RC4 towards the First Three Bytes of the Secret Key. In: WCC 2007 - International Workshop on Coding and Cryptography, pp. 285–294 (2007)
27. Paul, S., Preneel, B.: A New Weakness in the RC4 Keystream Generator and an Approach to Improve the Security of the Cipher. In: Roy, B., Meier, W. (eds.) FSE 2004. LNCS, vol. 3017, pp. 245–259. Springer, Heidelberg (2004)
28. Roos, A.: A Class of Weak Keys in RC4 Stream Cipher (sci.crypt) (1995), http://groups.google.com/group/sci.crypt.research/msg/078aa9249d76eacc?dmode=source
29. Tews, E., Beck, M.: Practical attacks against WEP and WPA. In: Basin, D.A., Capkun, S., Lee, W. (eds.) WISEC, pp. 79–86. ACM, New York (2009)
30. Tews, E., Weinmann, R.-P., Pyshkin, A.: Breaking 104 Bit WEP in Less Than 60 Seconds. In: Kim, S., Yung, M., Lee, H.-W. (eds.) WISA 2007. LNCS, vol. 4867, pp. 188–202. Springer, Heidelberg (2008)
31. Tomasevic, V., Bojanic, S., Nieto-Taladriz, O.: Finding an internal state of RC4 stream cipher. Finding an internal state of RC4 stream cipher 177(7), 1715–1727 (2007)
32. Vaudenay, S., Vuagnoux, M.: Passive–Only Key Recovery Attacks on RC4. In: Adams, C., Miri, A., Wiener, M. (eds.) SAC 2007. LNCS, vol. 4876, pp. 344–359. Springer, Heidelberg (2007)
33. Vuagnoux, M.: Computer Aided Cryptanalysis from Ciphers to Side channels. PhD thesis, Ecole Polytechnique Fédérale de Lausanne — EPFL (2010)
34. Wagner, D.: Weak Keys in RC4 (sci.crypt) (1995), http://www.cs.berkeley.edu/~daw/my-posts/my-rc4-weak-keys

The Rise and Fall and Rise of Combinatorial Key Predistribution

Keith M. Martin

Information Security Group
Royal Holloway, University of London
Egham, Surrey TW20 0EX, U.K.
keith.martin@rhul.ac.uk

Abstract. There are many applications of symmetric cryptography where the only realistic option is to predistribute key material in advance of deployment, rather than provide online key distribution. The problem of how most effectively to predistribute keys is inherently combinatorial. We revisit some early combinatorial key predistribution shemes and discuss their limitations. We then explain why this problem is back "in fashion" after a period of limited attention by the research community. We consider the appropriateness of combinatorial techniques for key distribution and identify potential areas of further research.

Keywords: Key predistribution, combinatorial designs, sensor networks.

1 Introduction

Key management is a vital, and often overlooked, component of any cryptosystem. One of the most challenging phases of the cryptographic key life cycle is key establishment. This is particularly so in symmetric cryptosystems, where keys need to be established using some form of secure channel prior to use. In the following discussion we will only consider fully symmetric cryptosystems.

One of the main options for conducting symmetric key establishment is for one entity, which could be a trusted third party, to generate a key and then distribute it to those entities that require it. This process is often referred to as *key distribution*. Many application environments in which symmetric cryptography is deployed cannot rely on a key distribution service being regularly available whenever keys are required. Indeed in many applications such a service is impossible to provide after the network entities (which we will refer to as *nodes*) have been deployed. In such cases the only realistic option is for a trusted third party (which we will subsequently refer to as a *key centre*) to *predistribute* keys prior to deployment as part of a secure initialisation process. After deployment of the network, the key centre plays no further role in key establishment. Two nodes who require a common key must now try to derive one from the keys that they were each equipped with by the key centre prior to deployment. For this approach to be effective, the precise allocation of keys to nodes during initialisation is critical. This allocation is often termed a *key predistribution scheme*.

A. Biryukov, G. Gong, and D.R. Stinson (Eds.): SAC 2010, LNCS 6544, pp. 92–98, 2011.

A potential advantage of key predistribution is that the establishment of keys must happen at the key centre, which should be a controlled environment. However a significant disadvantage is that later stages of the key life cycle become more challenging to manage. Nonetheless, key predistribution is a popular approach to key establishment in real applications, especially those whose network topology is essentially "star-shaped", in the sense that communication only takes place between node and a central authority (*hub*) of some sort. In such cases it generally suffices to predistribute a unique key to each node, which its shares with the hub.

2 The Rise and Fall of Combinatorial Key Predistribution

A more interesting question is how to design a predistribution scheme for more general network topologies. Early research on key predistribution schemes focussed on the case where the network topology is the complete graph. The goal of such a key predistribution scheme is thus to enable any pair of nodes to share a predistributed key. One trivial solution is to predistribute a single key to all nodes, which results in minimal storage requirements for each node but has severe consequences if any node is compromised. At the other extreme, predistributing a unique key to every pair of nodes results in optimal resilience against node compromise but results in excessive storage requirements ($n - 1$ keys for each node in a network of size n).

An interesting compromise between these two trivial solutions is the idea of a *w-key distribution pattern* (*KDP*) [12]. A w-KDP is an allocation of keys to nodes with the property that:

1. any pair of nodes (N_1, N_2) have some keys in common;
2. any w nodes other than N_1 and N_2 do not collectively have all the keys that are shared by N_1 and N_2.

Thus if a w-KDP is used as the basis for a key predistribution scheme, any pair of nodes have at least one predistributed key that is not known by an adversary who has compromised up to w other nodes in the network. Some (or all) of these keys than then be used to derive a key that N_1 and N_2 can use to secure their communication. We describe the resulting key predistribution schemes as *combinatorial* because most of the known techniques for constructing w-KDPs rely on combinatorial mathematics. Various generalisations of the idea of a w-KDP are possible and have been studied.

An alternative approach to designing a key predistribution scheme for networks based on the complete graph is to use symmetric polynomials. In *Blom's* key predistribution scheme [2] a polynomial $P(x, y) \in \mathrm{GF}(q)[x, y]$ with the property that $P(i, j) = P(j, i)$ for all $i, j \in \mathrm{GF}(q)$. The elegantly simple idea is that:

- Node N_i stores the univariate polynomial $f_i(y) = P(N_i, y)$;
- In order to establish a common key with N_j, node N_i computes $K_{ij} = f_i(N_j) = f_j(N_i)$.

Similarly to a w-KDP, this scheme is secure against an adversary who can compromise at most w nodes. A significant advantage is that each node is only required to store $w + 1$ polynomial coefficients, which is less information than most w-KDPs. The main related cost is that each node is not actually storing predistributed keys, but rather information that can be used to derive them. For many applications this tradeoff is likely to favour the Blom scheme.

The Blom key predistribution scheme easily generalises to key predistribution applications where groups of t nodes require common keys [3]. It was further shown that this approach is optimal with respect to node key storage. These observations lie behind my assertion that research combinatorial key predistribution underwent a rise and fall. The "rise" was the discovery of some very elegant key predistribution schemes based on combinatorial mathematics. The "fall" was a period of inactivity in this area, perhaps due to an impression that that the interesting questions had all been answered.

3 Evolving Network Security

There has been a significant increase in interest in key predistribution schemes in recent years. The main motivation is evolution of networking technology, with a trend towards distributed, dynamic, wireless networks consisting of lightweight devices of limited capability. These can manifest themselves in various different guises, including examples of mobile ad-hoc networks, tactical networks, ambient networks, vehicular networks and sensor networks. What is of most interest for a key management perspective is the following two common properties of such networks:

1. a lack of centralised post-deployment infrastructure;
2. the reliance on *hop-based* communication between nodes, where nodes are expected to act both as end points and routers of communication.

The first of these properties favours the use of key predistribution for key establishment. The second of these implies that it is not necessary for *every* pair of nodes to share a predistributed key, thus motivating the study of key predistribution schemes for more "relaxed" network topologies than the complete graph. Indeed, in many cases it suffices that nodes share keys with a small number of immediate neighbour nodes.

The lightweight nature of nodes in such networks has additional implications for key predistribution scheme design:

- limited memory may constrain the number of key that a node can store;
- limited power may constrain the computations and communications that a node can perform;
- fragility of nodes increase the risk of node compromise.

Thus the requirements for a particular application will almost always necessitate a tradeoff between contradictory requirements. For example it may be desirable to predistribute a large number of keys to each node from a connectivity perspective, since it increases the chances of two nodes sharing a key. However, it may also be desirable to limit the number of keys that each node stores due to memory constraints and a desire to reduce the impact of node compromise.

4 A Key Establishment Framework

In order to capture the different requirements placed on a key predistribution scheme by a potential application, a basic framework was proposed in [9]. The significant factors that influence the design of a key predistribution scheme are:

- *Homogeneity of nodes.* This determines whether all the nodes in the network have the same capabilities. The most common assumptions are that a network is either *homogeneous* (all nodes have the same capabilities) or *hierarchical* (there exists a hierarchy of capabilities, with nodes at higher levels having increased capabilities).
- *Deployment location control.* This categorises the extent to which the location of a node within the network is known prior to deployment, at the time that the key centre initalises it with predistributed keys. Clearly, location information is likely to help in the design of a suitable key distribution scheme. One extreme is *full location control*, where the precise location is known prior to deployment. In particular this means that the network neighbours of a node are predetermined. At the other extreme is *no location control*, where there is no information about the node location prior to deployment. Interestingly, there is potential for *partial location control*, where some location information may be known, for example that a certain group of nodes will be deployed in close proximity. Also of relevance is whether nodes are *static* or *mobile*.
- *Communication structure.* This determines what the desired communication structure of the network is. For example, are all nodes expected to directly communicate with one another, if possible, or are they only expected to communicate with near neighbours? Are group keys required as well as pairwise keys?

A particular key distribution scheme designed for a specific set of requirements within this framework can then be assessed in terms of the relevant metrics, for example storage requirements, energy requirements, efficiency of secure path establishment, etc.

5 The Second Rise of Combinatorial Key Predistribution

There has been a resurgence of interest in key predistribution schemes since Eschenauer and Gligor proposed the *random key predistribution scheme* [5], in which the key centre allocates keys to a node uniformly without replacement from a finite pool of keys. Schemes with different properties can be designed based on the size of the key pool and the number of keys allocated to each node, but they are all probabilistic, since it can no longer be guaranteed that a specific pair of nodes share a key.

This idea has been the basis for a large number of key predistribution scheme proposals, not all of which have been well motivated or analysed. While a substantial number of these proposals have been extensions of the random key predistribution scheme, one interesting avenue of research has focussed on the design of deterministic key predistribution schemes. These have certain potential advantages:

- by being deterministic, certain properties are guaranteed;
- analysis of deterministic key predistribution schemes is often simpler;
- an amount of established research has already been conducted on deterministic key predistribution schemes (the "first rise");
- some deterministic key predistribution schemes have useful algebraic structure (for example, they allow efficient shared key discovery).

A natural place to look for ideas for constructing deterministic key predistribution schemes is combinatorial mathematics. The focus of the earliest research in this "second rise" was to look at classical combinatorial structures, such as *projective planes*, most of which still provided full connectivity, in the sense that they were designed to facilitate a shared key between any pair of nodes. While some of these schemes offer interesting tradeoffs between the important parameters, they tend to be too restrictive and have high storage and resilience costs. More flexibility can be obtained by basing key predistribution schemes on combinatorial structures that are not fully connected. Indeed, several entirely new combinatorial structures of this type, for example *common intersection designs* [7], have been proposed and investigated specifically for adoption as key predistribution schemes for evolving networks.

However, given that design requirements of a key predistribution scheme often involve tradeoffs between competing parameters, a more natural role for combinatorial structures is to provide components from which more complex key predistribution scheme scan be built (for example [6]). A range of techniques for building key predistribution schemes in this way has been explored. Some of these build deterministic key predistribution schemes from deterministic components, while others use both deterministic and probabilistic components (for example. There would seem potential for further development of these *combinatorial engineering* approaches.

6 Research Directions

There have been a large number of recent proposals for key predistribution schemes, mostly explicitly targeted at wireless sensor network applications ([4] provides a good survey from 2005, but much has happened since). A substantial number of these consider the case of homogeneous, static nodes which are deployed with no location control. Many proposals seem rather ad hoc and are only compared against a limited number of previous proposals, largely using simulations to support claims about their worth. It is far from clear that such ad hoc proposals necessarily add much to the knowledge base concerning the design of key predistribution schemes. That said, there has also been some very interesting research conducted in this area and there is plenty more to do. We suggest the following guidance on future research direction:

1. *Deeper exploration of construction techniques.* It is relatively easy to propose a new construction technique for a key predistribution scheme. What is sometime harder, but is equally important, is to explore why the resulting properties arise. Simply showing that something works can suffice in some engineering disciplines, but we should be aiming higher in the study of key predistribution schemes.
2. *Better understanding of tradeoffs.* The tradeoffs between the desirable properties of a key predistribution scheme mean that, in theory, there are many different notions of "desirable tradeoff" amongst the potential properties of a key predistribution scheme. While this does suggest that there is a need for different design approaches, it is important to also develop a better general understanding of how different properties trade off against one another. In particular, the tradeoff between notions of connectivity and resilience seems deep and intriguing.
3. *Meaningful and well-motivated scenarios.* The diversity of potential evolving network application scenarios have the potential to motivate a number of quite distinct types of key predistribution scheme. In particular, consideration of degrees of location control present interesting variations of the more established problem (existing work on this includes our own treatment of linear networks [10], grids [1] and group-based deployment [11]). What is important is that particular application models are well-motivated and assessed in a meaningful way.
4. *Greater consideration of the key lifecycle.* Key establishment is just one phase of the wider key lifecycle. The use of key predistribution is mainly due to an assumption that the key centre is not generally available to maintain keys after deployment. However, this does not prevent the nodes in the network from jointly conducting some key management activities, such as network optimisation, key refreshment and key change, perhaps with occasional external assistance. Further research on post-deployment key management issues is merited.

The supporting theory behind combinatorial techniques has already played a significant role in helping to form the basis for a deeper understanding of how to build desirable key predistribution schemes for a wide range of different types of application (a survey of the role of combinatorics in key predistribution scheme design can be found in [8]). While not all of the above research will rely entirely on combinatorial approaches to key predistribution, there is no doubt that such approaches have a significant role to play.

References

1. Blackburn, S.R., Etzion, T., Martin, K.M., Paterson, M.B.: Distinct-Difference Configurations: Multihop Paths and Key Predistribution in Sensor Networks. IEEE Transactions in Information Theory 56(8), 3961–3972 (2010)
2. Blom, R.: An optimal class of symmetric key generation systems. In: Beth, T., Cot, N., Ingemarsson, I. (eds.) EUROCRYPT 1984. LNCS, vol. 209, pp. 335–338. Springer, Heidelberg (1985)
3. Blundo, C., De Santis, A., Herzberg, A., Kutten, S., Vaccaro, U., Yung, M.: Perfectly-secure key distribution for dynamic conferences. In: Brickell, E.F. (ed.) CRYPTO 1992. LNCS, vol. 740, pp. 471–486. Springer, Heidelberg (1993)
4. Çamtepe, S.A., Yener, B.: Key distribution mechanisms for wireless sensor networks: a survey. Rensselaer Polytechnic Institute, Computer Science Department, Technical Report TR-05-07 (March 2005)
5. Eschenauer, L., Gligor, V.: A key management scheme for distributed sensor networks. In: Proceedings of 9th ACM Conference on Computer and Communication Security (November 2002)
6. Lee, J., Stinson, D.R.: Deterministic key predistribution schemes for distributed sensor networks. In: Handschuh, H., Hasan, M.A. (eds.) SAC 2004. LNCS, vol. 3357, pp. 294–307. Springer, Heidelberg (2004)
7. Lee, J., Stinson, D.R.: Common intersection designs. Journal of Combinatorial Designs 14(4), 251–269 (2009)
8. Martin, K.M.: On the applicability of combinatorial designs to key predistribution for wireless sensor networks. In: Chee, Y.M., Li, C., Ling, S., Wang, H., Xing, C. (eds.) IWCC 2009. LNCS, vol. 5557, pp. 124–145. Springer, Heidelberg (2009)
9. Martin, K.M., Paterson, M.B.: An application-oriented framework for wireless sensor network key establishment. Electron. Notes Theor. Comput. Sci. 192(2), 31–41 (2008)
10. Martin, K.M., Paterson, M.B.: Ultra-lightweight key predistribution in wireless sensor networks for monitoring linear infrastructure. In: Markowitch, O., Bilas, A., Hoepman, J.-H., Mitchell, C.J., Quisquater, J.-J. (eds.) Information Security Theory and Practice. LNCS, vol. 5746, pp. 143–152. Springer, Heidelberg (2009)
11. Martin, K.M., Paterson, M.B., Stinson, D.R.: Key predistribution for homogeneous wireless sensor networks with group deployment of nodes. ACM Transactions in Sensor Networks, 7(2), article No. 11 (2010)
12. Mitchell, C.J., Piper, F.C.: Key storage in secure networks. Discrete Applied Mathematics 21, 215–228 (1988)

A Low-Area Yet Performant FPGA Implementation of Shabal

Jérémie Detrey[1], Pierrick Gaudry[1], and Karim Khalfallah[2]

[1] CARAMEL project-team, LORIA, INRIA / CNRS / Nancy Université, Campus Scientifique, BP 239, 54506 Vandœuvre-lès-Nancy Cedex, France
[2] Laboratoire de cryptographie et composants, SGDSN / ANSSI, 51 boulevard de la Tour-Maubourg, 75700 Paris 07 SP, France

Abstract. In this paper, we present an efficient FPGA implementation of the SHA-3 hash function candidate Shabal [7]. Targeted at the recent Xilinx Virtex-5 FPGA family, our design achieves a relatively high throughput of 2 Gbit/s at a cost of only 153 slices, yielding a throughput-*vs.*-area ratio of 13.4 Mbit/s per slice. Our work can also be ported to Xilinx Spartan-3 FPGAs, on which it supports a throughput of 800 Mbit/s for only 499 slices, or equivalently 1.6 Mbit/s per slice.

According to the SHA-3 Zoo website [1], this work is among the smallest reported FPGA implementations of SHA-3 candidates, and ranks first in terms of throughput per area.

Keywords: SHA-3, Shabal, low area, FPGA implementation.

1 Introduction

Following the completion of the first round of the NIST SHA-3 hash algorithm competition in September 2009, fourteen candidates [16] have been selected to participate in the second round [18]. As such, developing and benchmarking software and hardware implementations of these remaining hash functions is key to assess their practicality on various platforms and environments.

Building toward that objective, this paper presents an area-efficient implementation of the SHA-3 candidate Shabal, submitted by Bresson *et al.* [7], on Xilinx Virtex-5 and Spartan-3 FPGAs [20,23]. Even though the core contribution of this work is to demonstrate that Shabal can be brought to area-constrained devices such as smart cards or RFID tags, it also appears from the benchmark results that our design also performs extremely well in terms of throughput per area, ranking first among the other published implementations of SHA-3 candidates.

Roadmap. After a brief description of the Shabal hash function, we explain in Section 2 how this algorithm can be adapted to make full use of the shift register primitives embedded in some FPGA families. A detailed description of our design is given in Section 3, along with implementation results and comparisons in Section 4.

A. Biryukov, G. Gong, and D.R. Stinson (Eds.): SAC 2010, LNCS 6544, pp. 99–113, 2011.

Notations. In the following, unless specified otherwise, all words are 32 bits long and are to be interpreted as unsigned integers. Given two such words X and Y along with an integer k, we write the rotation of X by k bits to the left as $X \lll k$; the bitwise exclusive disjunction (XOR) of X and Y as $X \oplus Y$; the bitwise conjunction (AND) of X and Y as $X \wedge Y$; the bitwise negation (NOT) of X as $\overline{X}$; the sum and difference of X and Y modulo 2^{32} as $X \boxplus Y$ and $X \boxminus Y$, respectively; and the product of X by k modulo 2^{32} as $X \boxtimes k$. We also denote by $X \leftarrow Y$ the assignment of the value of Y to the variable X.

Furthermore, given an n-stage-long shift register R, we denote its elements by $R[0]$, $R[1]$, and so on up to $R[n-1]$. Inserting a word X into $R[n-1]$ while shifting the other elements by one position to the left (*i.e.*, $R[i] \leftarrow R[i+1]$ for $0 \leqslant i < n-1$) is denoted by $R \twoheadleftarrow X$, whereas $X \twoheadrightarrow R$ indicates the insertion of X into $R[0]$ while the rest of the register is shifted by one step to the right (*i.e.*, $R[i] \leftarrow R[i-1]$ for $n-1 \geqslant i > 0$).

2 Shabal and Shift Registers

2.1 The Shabal Hash Algorithm

For a complete description of the Shabal hash function, please refer to [7, Ch. 2].

The internal state of Shabal consists of three 32-bit-wide shift registers, A, B, and C, of length 12, 16, and 16, respectively, along with a 64-bit counter W. Shabal splits a message in 512-bit blocks, which are stored into another 16-stage-long and 32-bit-wide shift register called M.

Processing a block M in Shabal involves the following sequence of operations:

1. XOR the counter into the first two words of A: $A[i] \leftarrow A[i] \oplus W[i]$, $i = 0, 1$.
2. Add the message to B: $B[i] \leftarrow B[i] \boxplus M[i]$, for $0 \leqslant i < 16$.
3. Rotate each word of B by 17 bits: $B[i] \leftarrow B[i] \lll 17$, for $0 \leqslant i < 16$.
4. Apply the keyed permutation, as depicted in Fig. 1, for 48 iterations:
   - compute the two 32-bit words P and Q as

$$V \leftarrow (A[11] \lll 15) \boxtimes 5, \qquad U \leftarrow (V \oplus A[0] \oplus C[8]) \boxtimes 3,$$
$$P \leftarrow U \oplus M[0] \oplus (\overline{B[6]} \wedge B[9]) \oplus B[13], \quad Q \leftarrow \overline{P} \oplus (B[0] \lll 1);$$

   - shift the four registers: $A \twoheadleftarrow P$, $B \twoheadleftarrow Q$, $C[15] \twoheadrightarrow C$, and $M \twoheadleftarrow M[0]$.
5. Add three words of C to each word of A: for $0 \leqslant i < 12$,

$$A[i] \leftarrow A[i] \boxplus C[(i+3) \bmod 16] \boxplus C[(i+15) \bmod 16] \boxplus C[(i+11) \bmod 16].$$

6. Subtract the message from C: $C[i] \leftarrow C[i] \boxminus M[i]$, for $0 \leqslant i < 16$.
7. Swap the contents of shift registers B and C: $(B, C) \leftarrow (C, B)$.
8. Increment the counter: $W \leftarrow (W + 1) \bmod 2^{64}$.

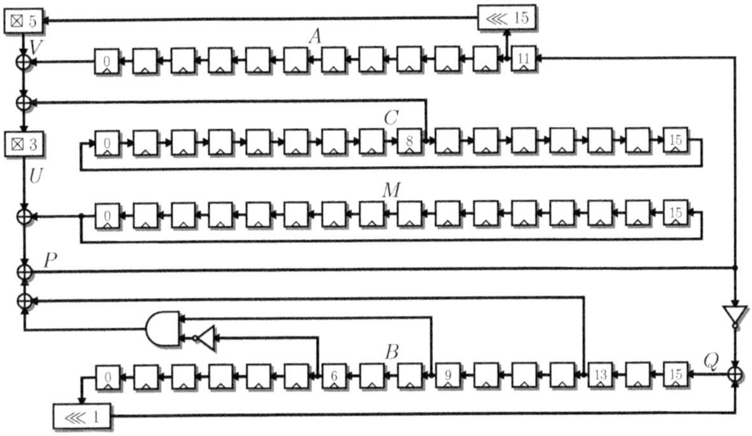

Fig. 1. Main structure of the keyed permutation [7, Fig. 2.4]

2.2 The Xilinx SRL16 Shift Register Primitive

As described in Section 2.1, the internal state of Shabal involves 46 32-bit words of storage and the message block M requires another 16 words. A naive implementation, using one FPGA flip-flop resource for each of these 1 984 bits of storage, would then result in a relatively large circuit.

However, it is important to note here that only a small fraction of the internal state is actually used at any step of the execution of Shabal. For instance, only $A[0]$, $A[11]$, $B[0]$, $B[6]$, $B[9]$, $B[13]$, $C[8]$, and $M[0]$ are required to compute P and Q when applying the keyed permutation (see Fig. 1), the other words simply being stepped through their respective shift registers. We can therefore exploit this fact and take advantage of the dedicated shift register resources offered by some FPGA families in order to minimize the overall area of the circuit.

This is the case in the recent Xilinx FPGAs—such as the high-end Virtex-5 and -6 families, or the low-cost Spartan-3's and -6's—which all support the SRL16 primitive [20,21,23,24]. As depicted in Fig. 2, this primitive implements a 16-stage-long and 1-bit-wide addressable shift register in a single 4-to-1-bit look-up table (LUT), as it is in fact nothing but a 16-bit memory. A dedicated input `DIN` is used to shift the data in, whereas the regular 4-bit input `A` addresses which bit is driven to the LUT output `D` [20, Ch. 7]. It is therefore possible to implement variable-size shift registers with this primitive. For instance, fixing the address `A` to `0000`, `0011`, or `1111` results in 1-, 4-, and 16-stage-long shift registers, respectively. Note that this idea has already been successfully exploited for linear- and non-linear-feedback-shift-register-based stream ciphers such as Grain or Trivium [8].

Furthermore, since the most recent Virtex-5, -6, and Spartan-6 FPGA families are based on 64-bit LUTs—supporting either 6-to-1-bit or 5-to-2-bit modes of operation—it is possible to pack two SRL16 instances in a single LUT, thus implementing a 16-stage-long and 2-bit-wide addressable shift register (see for instance [23, Fig. 5-17]).

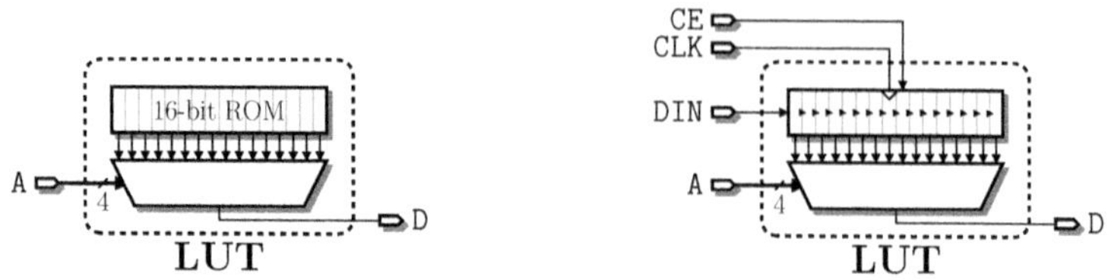

Fig. 2. Xilinx LUT as a look-up table (left) and as an SRL16 shift register (right)

2.3 Adapting Shabal to Use Shift Registers

Since we want to benefit as much as possible from the low area requirements of the SRL16 primitive, we need to implement the full Shabal algorithm using only shift registers. In other words, all the parallel register-wide operations—such as the $B \leftarrow B \boxplus M$ affectation in step 2—should be serialized in a word-by-word fashion.

From the algorithm given in Section 2.1, all steps but steps 4 and 8 should therefore be serialized in such a way. This is a rather simple task for steps 2, 3, 6, and 7, but special care needs to be paid to the other two.

Accumulating C into A. The first non-trivial serialization to address is that of step 5, which requires the accumulation of three words of the shift register C into each word of A. From the original specification of Shabal [7], we can remark that the indices of the three words of C are actually separated by exactly 12 positions each:

$$\begin{aligned} C[(i+\ \ 3) \bmod 16] &= C[(i+3+0\times 12) \bmod 16], \\ C[(i+15) \bmod 16] &= C[(i+3+1\times 12) \bmod 16], \text{ and} \\ C[(i+11) \bmod 16] &= C[(i+3+2\times 12) \bmod 16]. \end{aligned}$$

We therefore choose to accumulate those words of C in a disctinct shift register of length 12, denoted by D, by executing the iteration $D \twoheadleftarrow D[0] \boxplus C[3]$ and $C \twoheadleftarrow C[0]$ for 36 consecutive cycles (assuming that every word of D was initialized to 0 beforehand).

Once each word $D[i]$ contains $C[(i+3) \bmod 16] \boxplus C[(i+15) \bmod 16] \boxplus C[(i+11) \bmod 16]$, the contents of D are accumulated into A in 12 cycles, both 12-stage-long shift registers A and D stepping simultaneously.

Shifting C both left and right. Note that, in the previous situation, the shift register C is rotated by one position to the left at each step (*i.e.*, $C \twoheadleftarrow C[0]$), whereas the keyed permutation (step 4 of the algorithm) requires C to rotate to the right (*i.e.*, $C[15] \twoheadrightarrow C$). In order to solve this issue, we duplicate the shift register C into two separate shift registers C and C', both stepping to the left—so as to match the direction of the other shift registers A, B, D, and M.

- The first shift register, C, is then responsible for delivering the words $C[3]$ in the proper order to accumulate them into D.

– The second one, C', is loaded simultaneously with C—and therefore contains the same data—and is addressed by a 4-bit counter k fed to the A port of the SRL16s. So as to constantly point to the word $C[8]$ required by the keyed permutation, k has to be decremented by 2 at each cycle to compensate for C' stepping to the left.

The 64-bit counter *W*. Looking at step 1 of the Shabal algorithm, it seems natural to consider the 64-bit counter W as a 2-word shift register, synchronized with A, so that we can execute step 1 in two consecutive cycles.

Additionally, this has the interesting side-effect of splitting in half the 64-bit-long carry propagation required for incrementing W in step 8 and which might have been on the critical path. The incrementation of W is then performed word by word, storing the carry output in a separate 1-bit register W_{cy} before reinjecting it as carry-in for the next word of W.

Finally, since implementing 2- or 16-stage-long shift registers requires exactly the same amount of SRL16 primitives—it consists only in changing the A input from 0001 to 1111—we choose to use also a 16-word shift register for W, words $W[2]$ to $W[15]$ set to 0, so as to match the 16-cycle period of registers B, C, C', and M, and thus simplifying the control.

2.4 Scheduling of a Shabal Message Round

From the Shabal algorithm in Section 2.1, it appears that several steps can be merged or performed in parallel. We first present the justification and validity of such merges before giving the resulting scheduling of the algorithm, as implemented in our circuit.

Merging and parallelizing steps in the algorithm. First of all, assuming that the shift register D contains the sums $C[(i+3) \bmod 16] \boxplus C[(i+15) \bmod 16] \boxplus C[(i+11) \bmod 16]$ from the step 5 of the previous round, we can postpone the 12-cycle accumulation of D into A of that previous round to the beginning of the current round, effectively combining it with the XORing of W into A (step 1). During that time, since only the shifted-out value $D[0]$ is required, we can also reset D to 0 by shifting-in 12 successive 0 words.

Additionally, we can merge the 16-cycle steps 2 and 3 by directly rotating $B[i] \boxplus M[i]$ by 17 bits to the left. This can further be combined with the word-by-word loading of the current message block into the shift register M, along with the swapping of B and C (step 7) from the previous round—thus postponed to the current stage—by shifting $B[0]$ into C and C' while simultaneously shifting the newly received message word M_{in} into M and $(C[0] \boxplus M_{\mathrm{in}}) \lll 17$ into B. Finally, as all the registers involved are independent of A and D, this can be performed in parallel with their previously discussed initialization.

We can also accumulate the words of C into D—which takes 36 iterations—while executing the 48 iterations of the keyed permutation in parallel. Furthermore, during the last 16 cycles of those 48, notice that only the shifted-out value $M[0]$ is necessary to the permutation. We can then use the shift register M to temporarily store the difference $C \boxminus M$ before shifting it again to B in the next round. To that intent, $C[0] \boxminus M[0]$ is then shifted into M during those last 16 cycles. Finally, the incrementation of W can also be performed in parallel during those 16 cycles.

All in all, we end up with a 64-cycle round comprising two main steps:

- a 16-cycle step, during which the shift registers A, B, C, C', D, and M are initialized before performing the keyed permutation; followed by
- a 48-cycle step, actually computing the permutation, while preparing the shift registers D, M, and W for the next round.

Detailed scheduling. As discussed in the previous paragraphs, postponing steps of the Shabal algorithm from one round to the next changed the preconditions on the internal state of Shabal at the beginning of the round, with respect to what was presented as a round in Section 2.1. Therefore, for the scheduling detailed here, we assume (a) that each word $D[i]$ contains $C[(i+3) \bmod 16] \boxplus C[(i+15) \bmod 16] \boxplus C[(i+11) \bmod 16]$, (b) that these sums have not yet been accumulated into A, (c) that the shift register M contains $C \boxminus M$, and (d) that the shift registers B and C have not yet been swapped.

The scheduling of the 64-cycle round then breaks down as follows (where the current cycle is denoted by c, and where all the shifts and assignments are performed synchronously):

<table>
<tr><td>c</td><td>$=$</td><td>$0,\ldots,11$</td><td>$12,\ldots,15$</td><td>$16,\ldots,47$</td><td>$48,\ldots,51$</td><td>$52,\ldots,63$</td></tr>
<tr><td>A</td><td>$\twoheadleftarrow$</td><td>A_{in}</td><td>—</td><td colspan="3">P</td></tr>
<tr><td>B</td><td>$\twoheadleftarrow$</td><td colspan="2">B_{in}</td><td colspan="3">Q</td></tr>
<tr><td>C</td><td>$\twoheadleftarrow$</td><td colspan="2">$B[0]$</td><td colspan="3">$C[0]$</td></tr>
<tr><td>C'</td><td>$\twoheadleftarrow$</td><td colspan="2">$B[0]$</td><td colspan="3">—</td></tr>
<tr><td>D</td><td>$\twoheadleftarrow$</td><td colspan="2">0</td><td colspan="2">$D[0] \boxplus C[3]$</td><td>—</td></tr>
<tr><td>M</td><td>$\twoheadleftarrow$</td><td colspan="2">M_{in}</td><td>$M[0]$</td><td colspan="2">$C[0] \boxminus M[0]$</td></tr>
<tr><td>W</td><td>$\twoheadleftarrow$</td><td colspan="5">$W[0] \boxplus W_{\mathrm{cy}}$</td></tr>
<tr><td>W_{cy}</td><td>$\leftarrow$</td><td colspan="5">Output carry of $W[0] + W_{\mathrm{cy}}$</td></tr>
<tr><td>k</td><td>$\leftarrow$</td><td colspan="5">$(k+14) \bmod 16$</td></tr>
</table>

In this scheduling, at each cycle, the two words P and Q are computed as

$$V \leftarrow (A[11] \lll 15) \boxtimes 5, \qquad U \leftarrow (V \oplus A[0] \oplus C'[k]) \boxtimes 3,$$
$$P \leftarrow U \oplus M[0] \oplus (\overline{B[6]} \wedge B[9]) \oplus B[13], \text{ and} \quad Q \leftarrow \overline{P} \oplus (B[0] \lll 1).$$

Furthermore, A_{in} designates $(A[0] \boxplus D[0]) \oplus W[0]$, B_{in} is $(M[0] \boxplus M_{\mathrm{in}}) \lll 17$, and the input carry W_{cy} is forced to 1 at cycle $c = 48$.

3 FPGA Implementation

3.1 Overall Architecture

The main architecture of our FPGA implementation of Shabal is given in Fig. 3, where the control logic is omitted for clarity's sake. The small rounded boxes indicate control bits such as the *clock enable* signals for the various shift registers, whereas the light-gray rounded boxes identify how this circuit is mapped onto basic Virtex-5 primitives. Further details about this mapping are given in Section 3.3.

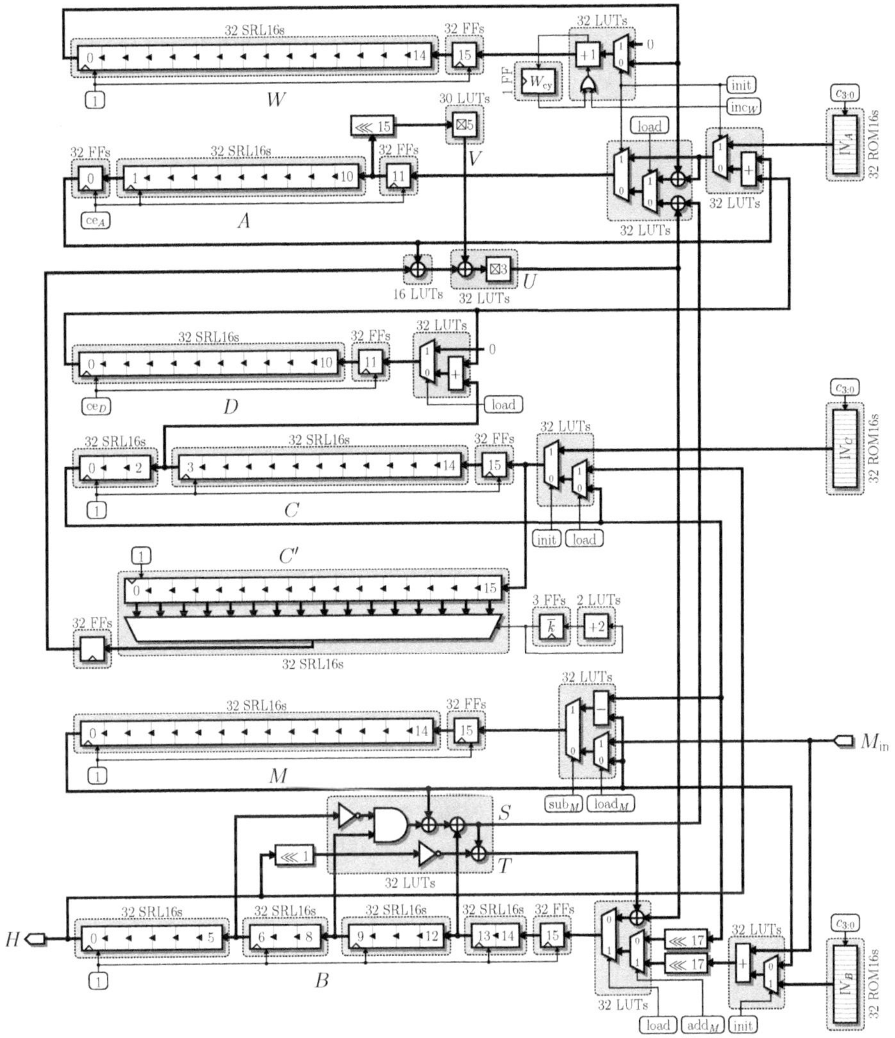

Fig. 3. Main architecture of our Shabal design mapped onto Virtex-5 primitives

Up to now, we have not discussed the initialization of Shabal. According to [7], this can be achieved by setting the registers A, B, and C to specific initialization vectors, denoted here by IV_A, IV_B, and IV_C, respectively. In our architecture, these initialization vectors are stored into small 12- and 16-word

ROMs, addressed by the four least significant bits of c and implemented by means of 16-by-1-bit ROM16 primitives. During the first 16 cycles of the first round of Shabal, the initialization words are then shifted into the corresponding registers. In the meantime, the register W is initialized to 0, except for $W[0]$ which is set to 1.

When addressing an SRL16 primitive such as C', using the address `0000` gives the contents of the first stage of the register (*i.e.*, $C'[15]$) whereas `1111` addresses the last stage (*i.e.*, $C'[0]$). Consequently, as we want to retrieve $C'[k]$ at each clock cycle, we need to address the corresponding shift register with $\overline{k} = 15 - k$ instead of k. We therefore directly store and update $\overline{k}$ by means of a 4-bit up counter. Additionally, since $\overline{k}$ is always incremented by 2, its least significant bit is constant and need not be stored.

So as to shorten the critical path of the circuit, we also use the associativity of the XOR operation to extract some parallelism out of the main feedback loop which computes P and Q. Indeed, while computing V then U as before, we also compute in parallel the two words S and T as

$$S \leftarrow M[0] \oplus (\overline{B[6]} \wedge B[9]) \oplus B[13] \qquad \text{and} \qquad T \leftarrow S \oplus \overline{(B[0] \lll 1)}.$$

We then immediately have P as $U \oplus S$ and Q as $U \oplus T$.

3.2 Control Logic

Although not depicted in Fig. 3, we claim that the logic required to generate the control bits of our architecture entails but a small overhead. This is achieved by restricting the number of control bits to a bare minimum:

- First of all, since the shift registers B, C, C', M, and W are always stepping, according to our scheduling, we fix their *clock enable* signal to 1. Only A and D have distinct signals—ce_A and ce_D, respectively—as they sometimes have to be stalled for a few cycles due to their shorter length.
- The *load* signal, which identifies the first 16 cycles of each round, is also shared by most shift registers. Only M is controlled by load_M, as no message block M_{in} should be loaded during the three final rounds of Shabal [7].
- An *init* signal also controls whether we are in the first round and therefore should load the initialization values for registers A, B, C, C', and W.
- Finally, the signals sub_M, add_M, and inc_W indicate when to subtract or add the message to C and B, or when to increment W, respectively. Note that these three signals are disabled during the three final rounds of Shabal.

A waveform of those signals during a message round of Shabal is given Fig. 4. Not represented on this waveform, the init signal is high only during the first 16 cycles of the first round, and the load_M signal is identical to the load signal during message rounds. As for the three final rounds, the control bits are the same, except for load_M, sub_M, add_M, and inc_W which are driven low.

The reader should note at this point that we opted for keeping the I/O interface of our circuit as simple as possible, since the choice of which interface

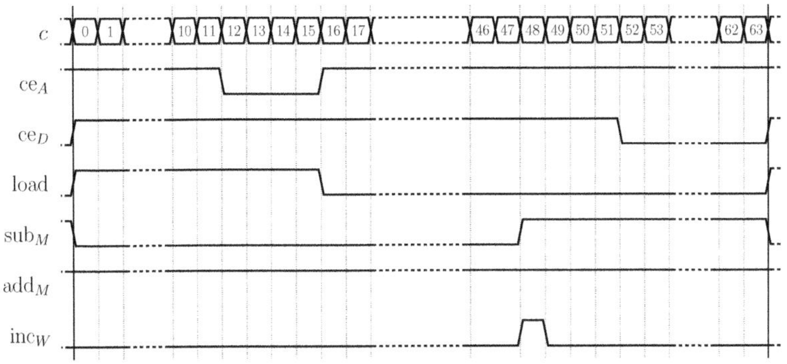

Fig. 4. Waveform of the control signals during a message round

to actually use heavily depends on the usage of the hash function and on the environment in which it will run. Therefore, no message padding mechanism was implemented here, and our circuit assumes that the message blocks are always available and fed to the hash function during the 16 first cycles of each message round. However, disabling the clock signal for the shift registers and the control logic via a circuit-wide clock enable signal would allow the hash function to be interrupted in order to wait for message words, for but a moderate overhead.

3.3 Technology Mapping

As previously mentioned, the light-gray rounded boxes in Fig. 3 refer to the mapping of our Shabal circuit onto basic Virtex-5 primitives.[1] In the figure, next to the boxes, we also indicate the count and type of required primitives, where LUT refers to a Virtex-5 look-up table—in either 6-to-1-bit or 5-to-2-bit mode of operation—FF to a 1-bit flip-flop, SRL16 to an addressable shift register as described in Section 2.2, and ROM16 to a 16-by-1-bit ROM. Note that the fixed-length rotations ($\lll$) involve only wires and do not require any logic resource.

In order to reduce the critical path of the circuit, we choose to implement the first stage of each shift register—except for C'—using flip-flops instead of merging them into the SRL16 primitives. Indeed, this saves the routing delay between the LUT-based multiplexers feeding the registers and the SRL16 primitives, and entails no resource overhead as each Virtex-5 LUT is natively paired with a matching flip-flop on the FPGA.

Furthermore, the clock-to-ouput delay of the SRL16 primitives being quite high [22, Tab. 67], we also use flip-flops to implement the last stage of shift register A which lies on the critical path.

Finally, it is worth noting that, on Virtex-5 FPGAs, two SRL16 or two ROM16 primitives can fit on a single LUT. Since a large part of our implementation is

[1] A similar mapping was made for the Spartan-3 technology, but is not included in this paper for the sake of concision.

Table 1. Resource count of the main architecture as mapped on Virtex-5 (excluding the control logic)

Component	High-level mapping				Actual mapping	
	LUTs	FFs	SRL16s	ROM16s	LUTs	FFs
Register A	64	64	32	32	96	64
Register B	64	32	128	32	144	32
Registers C and C'	34	67	96	32	98	67
Register D	32	32	32	0	48	32
Register M	32	32	32	0	48	32
Register W	32	33	32	0	48	33
Feedback loop	110	0	0	0	110	0
Total	368	260	352	96	592	260

based on these primitives, this reduces ever further the overall area of the design. To illustrate this, we present in Table 1 a complete breakdown of the resource requirements of our circuit, both in terms of high-level primitives—*i.e.*, LUTs, FFs, SRL16s, and ROM16s—and in terms of actually mapped primitives—*i.e.*, LUTs and FFs only.

4 Benchmarks and Comparisons

4.1 Place-and-Route Results

We have implemented the fully autonomous Shabal circuit presented in this paper in VHDL.[2] We have placed-and-routed it using the Xilinx ISE 10.1 toolchain, targeting a Xilinx Virtex-5 LX 30 FPGA with average speed grade (xc5vlx30-2ff324), along with a low-cost Xilinx Spartan-3 200 with highest speed grade (xc3s200-5ft256).

On the Virtex-5, the whole circuit occupies only 153 slices, that is, more precisely, 605 LUTs and 274 flip-flops. Interestingly enough, these figures are very close to the technology mapping estimations from Table 1: the control logic overhead, totaling to 13 LUTs and 14 flip-flops, is quite small, as expected. This design supports a clock period of 3.9 ns—*i.e.*, a frequency of 256 MHz—and since it processes a 512-bit message block in 64 clock cycles, it delivers a total throughput of 2.05 Gbit/s and thus a throughput-*vs.*-area ratio of 13.41 Mbit/s per slice.

On the Spartan-3 target, our Shabal architecture uses 499 slices and can be clocked at 100 MHz. This yields a throughput of 800 Mbit/s, which corresponds to 1.6 Mbit/s per slice.

Note that these results are given for the Shabal-512 flavor, even though changing the digest length does not affect the circuit performance in any way.

[2] This VHDL code is available at `http://hwshabal.gforge.inria.fr/` under the terms of the GNU Lesser General Public License.

4.2 Against Other Shabal Implementations

A comparison between our circuit and previously published implementations is given in Table 2. Since all state-of-the-art papers present benchmarks on Virtex-5 or Spartan-3, we believe this comparison to be quite fair. It is to be noted that, if our Shabal circuit does not deliver the highest throughput, it is by far the smallest implementation in the literature, and also the most efficient in terms of throughput per area.

Table 2. FPGA implementations of Shabal on Virtex-5 and Spartan-3

FPGA	Implementation	Area [slices]	Freq. [MHz]	Cycles / round	TP [Mbps]	TP / area [kbps/slice]
Virtex-5	Baldwin *et al.* [3]*	2 307	222	85	1 330	577
		2 768	139	49	1 450	524
	Kobayashi *et al.* [13]	1 251	214	63	1 739	1 390
	Feron and Francq [9]	1 171	126	25	**2 588**	2 210
		596†	109	49	1 142	1 916
	This work	**153**	256	64	2 051	**13 407**
Spartan-3	Baldwin *et al.* [3]*	1 933	90	85	540	279
		2 223	71	49	740	333
	This work	**499**	100	64	**800**	**1 603**

*Only the core functionality was implemented. †This design requires 40 additional DSP blocks.

Also note that Namin and Hasan published another FPGA implementation of Shabal [17]. However, not only do they present benchmarks on Altera Stratix-III FPGAs—against which it becomes difficult to compare Virtex-5 or Spartan-3 results in a fair way—but it also seems from their paper that they only implement part of the Shabal compression function. We therefore deliberately choose not to compare our work to theirs.

4.3 Against Implementations of the Other SHA-3 Candidates

Since Shabal is but one hash function among the fourteen remaining SHA-3 candidates, we also provide the reader with a compilation of the Virtex-5 and Spartan-3 implementation results for the other hash functions as gathered on the SHA-3 Zoo website [1] in Tables 3 and 4, respectively.

Comparing our Shabal circuit with these other designs, it is clear that, in terms of raw speed, we cannot compete against the high-throughput implementations of ECHO [15] or Grøstl [10] which all exceed the 10 Gbit/s mark on Virtex-5. However, it appears that our implementation ranks among the smallest SHA-3 designs, third only to the low-area implementations of BLAKE and ECHO by Beuchat *et al.* [6,5]. Therefore, if a high throughput is the objective, one can replicate our circuit several times in order to increase the overall throughput by the same factor: for instance, eight instances of our implementation running in parallel would yield a total of 16.4 Gbit/s for a mere 1 224 slices on Virtex-5, thus more than four times smaller than the 5 419 slices of the 15.4-Gbit/s

Table 3. FPGA implementations of SHA-3 candidates on Virtex-5

Hash function	Digest length	Implementation	Area [slices]	Freq. [MHz]	TP [Mbps]	TP / area [kbps/slice]
BLAKE	256	Submission doc. [2]*	1 694	67	3 103	1 832
			1 217	100	2 438	2 003
			390	91	575	1 474
		Kobayashi *et al.* [13]	1 660	115	2 676	1 612
		Beuchat *et al.* [6]	**56**	372	225	4 018
	512	Submission doc. [2]*	4 329	35	2 389	552
			2 389	50	1 766	739
			939	59	533	568
		Beuchat *et al.* [6]	108	358	314	2 907
CubeHash	all	Baldwin *et al.* [3]*	1 178	167	160	136
			1 440	55	110	76
		Kobayashi *et al.* [13]	590	185	2 960	5 017
ECHO	224/256	Lu *et al.* [15]	9 333	87	14 860	1 592
		Kobayashi *et al.* [13]	3 556	104	1 614	454
		Beuchat *et al.* [5]	127	352	72	567
	384/512	Lu *et al.* [15]	9 097	84	7 810	859
Grøstl	224/256	Submission doc. [10]	1 722	201	10 276	5 967
		Baldwin *et al.* [3]*	3 184†	250	6 410	2 013
			4 516†	143	7 310	1 619
			5 878	128	3 280	558
			8 196	102	5 210	636
		Kobayashi *et al.* [13]	4 057	101	5 171	1 275
	384/512	Submission doc. [10]	5 419	211	**15 395**	2 841
		Baldwin *et al.* [3]*	6 368†	144	5 260	826
			10 848	111	4 060	374
			19 161	83	6 090	318
Hamsi	256	Kobayashi *et al.* [13]	718	210	1 680	2 340
Keccak	all	Updated submission [4]	1 412	122	6 900	4 887
			444¶	265	70	158
Luffa	256	Kobayashi *et al.* [13]	1 048	223	6 343	6 052
Shabal	all	Baldwin *et al.* [3]*	2 307	222	1 330	577
			2 768	139	1 450	524
		Kobayashi *et al.* [13]	1 251	214	1 739	1 390
		Feron and Francq [9]	1 171	126	2 588	2 210
			596‡	109	1 142	1 916
		This work	153	256	2 051	**13 407**
Skein	256	Long [14]*	1 001	115	409	409
		Tillich [19]	937	68	1 751	1 869
		Kobayashi *et al.* [13]	854	115	1 482	1 735
	512	Long [14]*	1 877	115	817	435
		Tillich [19]	1 632	69	3 535	2 166

*Only the core functionality was implemented. ‡This design requires 40 additional DSP blocks.
†This design uses several additional RAM blocks. ¶This design uses an additional external memory.

Table 4. FPGA implementations of SHA-3 candidates on Spartan-3

Hash function	Digest length	Implementation	Area [slices]	Freq. [MHz]	TP [Mbps]	TP / area [kbps/slice]
BLAKE	256	Beuchat *et al.* [6]	**124**	190	115	927
	512	Beuchat *et al.* [6]	229	158	138	603
CubeHash	all	Baldwin *et al.* [3]*	2 883	59	50	17
			3 268	38	70	21
Grøstl	224/256	Submission doc. [10]	6 582	87	4 439	674
		Jungk *et al.* [12]	6 136	88	4 520	737
			2 486	63	404	163
		Baldwin *et al.* [3]*	3 183†	91	2 330	732
			4 827†	72	3 660	758
			5 508	60	1 540	280
			8 470	50	2 560	302
		Jungk *et al.* [11]	1 276	60	192	150
			1 672	38	243	145
			4 491†	100	2 560	570
			5 693†	54	2 764	486
	384/512	Submission doc. [10]	20 233	81	**5 901**	292
		Baldwin *et al.* [3]*	6 313†	80	2 910	461
			10 293	50	1 830	178
			17 452	43	3 180	182
		Jungk *et al.* [11]	2 110	63	144	68
			2 463	36	164	66
			8 308†	95	3 474	418
Shabal	all	Baldwin *et al.* [3]*	1 933	90	540	279
			2 223	71	740	333
		This work	499	100	800	**1 603**
Skein	256	Tillich [19]	2 421	26	669	276
	512	Tillich [19]	4 273	27	1 365	319

*Only the core functionality was implemented. †This design uses several additional RAM blocks.

implementation of Grøstl-512 [10]. Of course, this reasoning solely applies when hashing distinct messages in parallel, and not one single large message—in which case only the raw throughput matters.

Consequently, we also detail this throughput per area ratio in the last column of Tables 3 and 4. Reaching 13.4 Mbit/s per slice on Virtex-5, and 1.6 Mbit/s/slice on Spartan-3, our design is the best of the literature according to this metric.

5 Conclusion

We have described an FPGA implementation of the SHA-3 candidate Shabal that provides a decent 2 Gbit/s throughput using as few as 153 slices of a Virtex-5. Obtaining this tiny size was made possible by taking advantage of the specificity of the design of Shabal where only a small percentage of the large internal state of the compression function is active at a given time, thus allowing us to use the builtin SRL16 shift registers of Xilinx FPGAs. This very good tradeoff between size and speed yields the best throughput per area ratio of all SHA-3 implementations published so far. It demonstrates that Shabal is very well suited for hardware implementations, even in constrained environments.

These results should nevertheless be taken with some caution, as our implementation strongly depends on the underlying FPGA technology and architecture, which in our case allows us to benefit from the cheap shift register primitives. However, Altera FPGAs for instance do not support SRL16-like primitives, but shift-register-capable memory blocks. Porting our circuit to such targets might have an important impact on the overall performance. Similarly, an ASIC implementation of our Shabal circuit might not perform as well against other candidates as our Xilinx implementations do. However, the control simplification and scheduling tricks described in this paper are still applicable independently of the considered targets, and should Shabal be selected for the final round of the SHA-3 contest, we plan to investigate these issues further.

Acknowledgements

The authors would like to thank the anonymous reviewers for their insightful and encouraging comments.

We would also like to express our gratitude to the whole Shabal team for coming up with such a nice hash function to implement in hardware, and more especially Marion Videau who came to us with this funny challenge in the first place!

References

1. The SHA-3 zoo, `http://ehash.iaik.tugraz.at/wiki/The_SHA-3_Zoo`
2. Aumasson, J.P., Henzen, L., Meier, W., Phan, R.C.W.: SHA-3 proposal BLAKE (October 2008), `http://131002.net/blake/`
3. Baldwin, B., Byrne, A., Mark, H., Hanley, N., McEvoy, R.P., Pan, W., Marnane, W.P.: FPGA implementations of SHA-3 candidates: CubeHash, Grøstl, LANE, Shabal and Spectral Hash. In: 12th Euromicro Conference on Digital Systems Design, Architectures, Methods and Tools (DSD 2009), pp. 783–790. IEEE Computer Society, Patras (August 2009)
4. Bertoni, G., Daemen, J., Peeters, M., Van Assche, G.: The Keccak sponge function family (April 2009), `http://keccak.noekeon.org/`
5. Beuchat, J.L., Okamoto, E., Yamazaki, T.: A compact FPGA implementation of the SHA-3 candidate ECHO. Report 2010/364, Cryptology ePrint Archive (June 2010), `http://eprint.iacr.org/2010/364`
6. Beuchat, J.L., Okamoto, E., Yamazaki, T.: Compact implementations of BLAKE-32 and BLAKE-64 on FPGA. Report 2010/173, Cryptology ePrint Archive (April 2010), `http://eprint.iacr.org/2010/173`
7. Bresson, E., Canteaut, A., Chevallier-Mames, B., Clavier, C., Fuhr, T., Gouget, A., Icart, T., Misarsky, J.F., Naya-Plasencia, M., Paillier, P., Pornin, T., Reinhard, J.R., Thuillet, C., Videau, M.: Shabal, a submission to NIST's cryptographic hash algorithm competition (October 2008), `http://www.shabal.com/?page_id=38`

8. Bulens, P., Kalach, K., Standaert, F.X., Quisquater, J.J.: FPGA implementations of eSTREAM phase-2 focus candidates with hardware profile. Report 2007/024, eSTREAM, ECRYPT Stream Cipher Project (January 2007), http://www.ecrypt.eu.org/stream/papersdir/2007/024.pdf
9. Feron, R., Francq, J.: FPGA implementation of Shabal: Our first results (February 2010), http://www.shabal.com/?page_id=38
10. Gauravaram, P., Knudsen, L.R., Matusiewicz, K., Mendel, F., Rechberger, C., Schläffer, M., Thomsen, S.S.: Grøstl: A SHA-3 candidate (October 2008), http://www.groestl.info/
11. Jungk, B., Reith, S.: On FPGA-based implementations of Grøstl. Report 2010/260, Cryptology ePrint Archive (May 2010), http://eprint.iacr.org/2010/260
12. Jungk, B., Reith, S., Apfelbeck, J.: On optimized FPGA implementations of the SHA-3 candidate Grøstl. Report 2009/206, Cryptology ePrint Archive (May 2009), http://eprint.iacr.org/2009/206
13. Kobayashi, K., Ikegami, J., Matsuo, S., Sakiyama, K., Ohta, K.: Evaluation of hardware performance for the SHA-3 candidates using SASEBO-GII. Report 2010/010, Cryptology ePrint Archive (January 2010), http://eprint.iacr.org/2010/010
14. Long, M.: Implementing Skein hash function on Xilinx Virtex-5 FPGA platform (February 2009), http://www.skein-hash.info/downloads/
15. Lu, L., O'Neill, M., Swartzlander, E.: Hardware evaluation of SHA-3 hash function candidate ECHO (May 2009), http://www.ucc.ie/en/crypto/CodingandCryptographyWorkshop/TheClaudeShannonWorkshoponCodingCryptograpy2009/
16. Naehrig, M., Peters, C., Schwabe, P.: SHA-2 will soon retire: The SHA-3 song. Journal of Craptology 7 (February 2010)
17. Namin, A.H., Hasan, M.A.: Hardware implementation of the compression function for selected SHA-3 candidates. Tech. Rep. 2009-28, Centre for Applied Cryptographic Research, University of Waterloo (July 2009), http://www.cacr.math.uwaterloo.ca/techreports/2009/tech_reports2009.html
18. Regenscheid, A., Perlner, R., Chang, S., Kelsey, J., Nandi, M., Paulu, S.: Status report on the first round of the SHA-3 cryptographic hash algorithm competition. Report NISTIR 7620, National Institute of Standards and Technology (September 2009), http://csrc.nist.gov/groups/ST/hash/sha-3/Round1/documents/sha3_NISTIR7620.pdf
19. Tillich, S.: Hardware implementation of the SHA-3 candidate Skein. Report 2009/159, Cryptology ePrint Archive (April 2009), http://eprint.iacr.org/2009/159
20. Xilinx: Spartan-3 generation FPGA user guide, http://www.xilinx.com/support/documentation/user_guides/ug331.pdf
21. Xilinx: Spartan-6 FPGA Configurable Logic Block user guide, http://www.xilinx.com/support/documentation/user_guides/ug384.pdf
22. Xilinx: Virtex-5 FPGA data sheet: DC and switching characteristics, http://www.xilinx.com/support/documentation/data_sheets/ds202.pdf
23. Xilinx: Virtex-5 FPGA user guide, http://www.xilinx.com/support/documentation/user_guides/ug190.pdf
24. Xilinx: Virtex-6 FPGA Configurable Logic Block user guide, http://www.xilinx.com/support/documentation/user_guides/ug364.pdf

Implementation of Symmetric Algorithms on a Synthesizable 8-Bit Microcontroller Targeting Passive RFID Tags

Thomas Plos, Hannes Groß, and Martin Feldhofer

Institute for Applied Information Processing and Communications (IAIK), Graz University of Technology, Inffeldgasse 16a, 8010 Graz, Austria
{Thomas.Plos,Martin.Feldhofer}@iaik.tugraz.at,
Hannes.Gross@student.tugraz.at

Abstract. The vision of the secure Internet-of-Things is based on the use of security-enhanced RFID technology. In this paper, we describe the implementation of symmetric-key primitives on passive RFID tags. Our approach uses a fully synthesizable 8-bit microcontroller that executes, in addition to the communication protocol, also various cryptographic algorithms. The microcontroller was designed to fulfill the fierce constraints concerning chip area and power consumption in passive RFID tags. The architecture is flexible in terms of used program size and the number of used registers which allows an evaluation of various algorithms concerning their required resources. We analyzed the block ciphers AES, SEA, Present and XTEA as well as the stream cipher Trivium. The achieved results show that our approach is more efficient than other dedicated microcontrollers and even better as optimized hardware modules when considering the combination of controlling tasks on the tag and executing cryptographic algorithms.

Keywords: passive RFID tags, 8-bit microcontroller, symmetric-key algorithms, low-resource hardware implementation.

1 Introduction

Radio frequency identification (RFID) is the enabler technology for the future Internet-of-Things (IoT), which allows objects to communicate with each other. The ability to uniquely identify objects opens the door for a variety of new applications. Some of these applications like proof-of-origin of goods or privacy protection require the use of cryptographic algorithms for authentication or confidentiality.

An RFID system typically comprises three components: an RFID reader, a back-end database, and one or more RFID tags. The reader is connected to the back-end database and communicates with the tag contactless by means of an RF field. The so-called tag is a small microchip attached to an antenna that receives the data and probably the clock signal from the RF field. Passive tags also receive their power supply from the RF field. Supplying the tag from the RF

A. Biryukov, G. Gong, and D.R. Stinson (Eds.): SAC 2010, LNCS 6544, pp. 114–129, 2011.

field strongly limits the power consumption of the tag (typically, around 30 µW are available). Moreover, passive RFID tags are produced in high volume and need to be cheap in price. In order to keep the price of the tag low, its microchip must not exceed a certain size in terms of silicon area (typically, a whole tag has a size of 20000 gate equivalents). These two constraints make it a challenging task to implement cryptographic security on passive RFID tags.

For a secure system, not only the reader and the back-end database need to provide cryptographic security, but also the tags have to perform cryptographic operations. During the last years, a lot of effort was made by the research community to bring cryptographic security to RFID tags. The most prominent attempts among others are for example symmetric schemes like the Advanced Encryption Standard (AES) [11, 15], or asymmetric schemes like Elliptic Curve Cryptography (ECC) [2, 27]. All these attempts use dedicated hardware modules that are highly optimized for a specific cryptographic algorithm. Moreover, they do not consider the increased controlling effort that comes along with adding security to RFID tags. Even without adding security, a substantial part of the chip size is consumed by the controlling unit of the tag that handles the communication protocol. The work of Yu *et al.* [29] states that about 7500 gate equivalents (GEs) (one GE is the silicon area required by a NAND gate) are consumed for only handling the protocol.

Several tasks have to be accomplished by the control unit of a tag when using a simple challenge-response protocol to verify the authenticity of the tag. First, the control unit of the tag needs to generate random data and combine it with the challenge from the RFID reader. Second, random data and challenge need to be provided to the cryptographic hardware module and processing of data has to be started. Finally, the processed data needs to be transferred to the RFID reader. Other security services like mutual authentication or secure key update are even more demanding in terms of controlling effort.

Today's RFID tags have their control unit implemented as a finite-state machine (FSM) in hardware. However, increased controlling effort is easier to handle with a simple microcontroller. Particularly, microcontrollers are more flexible and allow faster integration of new functionalities, which reduces the time to market. Moreover, when using the microcontroller for control tasks, it seems reasonable to reuse it also for computing cryptographic algorithms. This reuse enables a better utilization of resources like the memory, which can help to reduce the chip size of the tag and in turn also the costs.

In this work, we present a synthesizable hardware implementation of a simple 8-bit microcontroller that is suitable to handle complex control tasks. The microcontroller fulfills the fierce requirements of passive RFID tags regarding power consumption and chip size. Five symmetric-key algorithms are implemented on this microcontroller, which are: the Advanced Encryption Standard (AES), the Scalable Encryption Algorithm (SEA), Present, the Extended Tiny Encryption Algorithm (XTEA), and Trivium. The performance of our implementations is evaluated and compared with results from implementations on other dedicated microcontroller platforms. Finally, the hardware costs that are added due to the implementation of the cryptographic algorithms are compared with the costs of stand-alone hardware modules. The results clearly show that the implementations on our microcontroller have lower costs than the dedicated hardware modules. For example, AES encryption and decryption comes at cost of less than 3000 GEs on our microcontroller.

The remainder of this paper is organized as follows. Section 2 describes the synthesizable 8-bit microcontroller that is used for implementing the cryptographic algorithms. In Section 3, a short overview of the selected algorithms is given, followed by the implementation results of the algorithms in Section 4. Discussion of the results with respect to passive RFID tags is done in Section 5. Conclusions are drawn in Section 6.

2 Description of the Synthesizable 8-Bit Microcontroller

The overhead that comes along with adding security to RFID tags in terms of controlling effort is often underestimated. Increased controlling effort is easier to accomplish with a simple microcontroller than with dedicated finite-state machines. In the following, we present a simple 8-bit microcontroller that is suitable to handle such complex control tasks. Moreover, it is a fully synthesizable microcontroller (available in VHDL) and it fulfills the fierce requirements of passive RFID tags.

Our 8-bit microcontroller uses a Harvard architecture with separated program memory and data memory. Such an architecture has the advantage that the program memory can have a different word size (16-bit) than the data memory (8-bit). The microcontroller supports 36 instructions and is a so-called Reduced Instruction Set Computer (RISC). The instructions have a width of 16 bits and can mainly be divided into three groups: logical operations like AND or XOR, arithmetic operations like addition (ADD) and subtraction (SUB), and control-flow operations like GOTO, CALL, and branching.

The main components of the microcontroller are the read-only memory (ROM), the register file, the program counter, the instruction decode unit, and the arithmetic-logic unit (ALU). An overview of the microcontroller is presented in Figure 1. The ROM contains the program of up to 4096 instructions and is realized as look-up table in hardware. It gets mapped to an unstructured mass of standard cells by the synthesis tool. Unused program space reduces the chip size of the microcontroller which makes our approach flexible and efficient. The register file is the data memory of the microcontroller and consists of at most 64 8-bit registers. If not all registers are needed by an application (during protocol execution and cryptographic calculations), unused registers can be omitted reducing the overall size of the microcontroller. This flexibility is only possible with a customizable processor architecture. Instructions are executed within a two-stage pipeline that consists of a fetch and a decode/execute step. In the first stage, the instruction that is addressed by the 12-bit program counter is loaded from the ROM into the instruction decode unit. In the second stage, the instruction is decoded by the instruction decode unit and executed by the ALU. Afterwards, the program counter

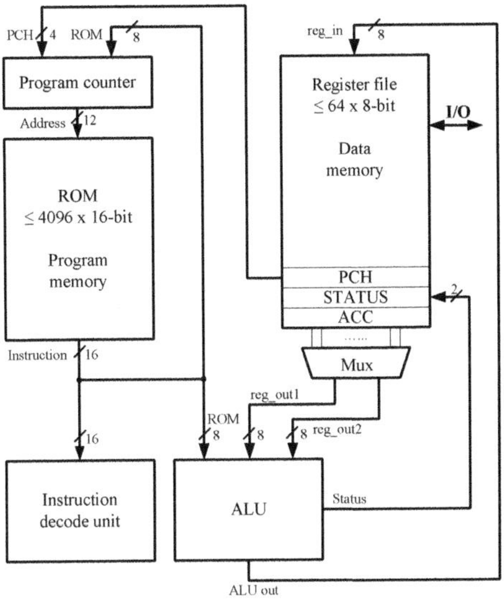

Fig. 1. Overview of the 8-bit microcontroller

is updated. The program counter contains a call stack that allows up to three recursive subroutine calls. All instructions are executed within a single clock cycle, except control-flow operations which require two clock cycles.

There are two types of registers in the register file of the microcontroller: special-purpose registers and general-purpose registers. The special-purpose registers involve an accumulator register (ACC) for advanced data manipulation, a status register (STATUS) that gives information about the status of the ALU (*e.g.* carry bit after addition), a program-counter register (PCH) for addressing the higher 4 bits of the program counter, and input/output (I/O) registers. The I/O registers are used for accessing external devices. In case of RFID tags, external devices can be the digital front-end for sending and receiving byte streams or the EEPROM. The I/O registers are also used for reacting on external events via busy waiting, since interrupts are not supported by the microcontroller. General-purpose registers are used for arbitrary data manipulations and temporarily storing data.

We have developed a self-written instruction-set simulator and an assembler for implementing the microcontroller program that is stored in the ROM. Both programs are written in JAVA and allow a fast and easy way of program development. The simulator supports a single-step mode and gives access to the internal state of the microcontroller. This makes debugging and testing of the program very convenient. After simulation, the assembler is used to generate a file with the content of the ROM. Figure 2 presents a code snippet of a microcontroller program written in JAVA with resulting ROM content after applying the assembler. The file with the ROM content is directly integrated into the hardware-description language (HDL) model of the microcontroller. This HDL

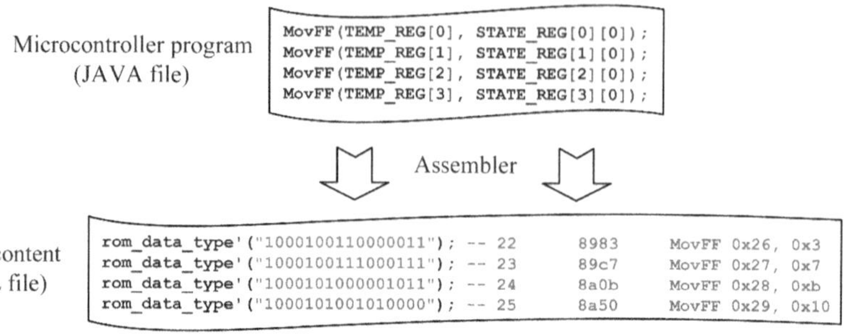

Fig. 2. Code snippet of a microcontroller program written in JAVA with resulting ROM content after applying the assembler

model is then synthesized with Cadence RTL Compiler for a 0.35 µm CMOS technology using a semi-custom design flow. The synthesis results in Table 1 show that the microcontroller can be implemented within less than 5600 gate equivalents (GEs), excluding the ROM. The by far largest part is the register file (for 64 x 8-bit) with 4582 GEs. As already mentioned, our approach allows to flexibly reduce the instantiated number of registers. Moreover, we performed power simulations with Synopsys Nanosim. The simulations show a mean power consumption of 10.3 µA for the microcontroller when operating at 100 kHz clock frequency and 3 V supply voltage. The power consumption can be further reduced by switching to a more recent CMOS technology or by reducing the supply voltage.

Both chip area and power consumption of the microcontroller fulfill the requirements of passive RFID tags. Hence, when using the microcontroller for handling the control tasks of the tag, it seems reasonable to reuse it also for computing the cryptographic algorithms. In order to address this issue, different cryptographic algorithms are implemented on the microcontroller. The following sections contain a short description of the selected cryptographic algorithms and evaluate their implementations with respect to execution time and code size.

Table 1. Synthesis results of the microcontroller excluding the ROM

Component	**Chip area**	
	[GEs]	[%]
Program counter with call stack	463	8.3
ALU	265	4.7
Register file (64 x 8 bit)	4582	81.9
Instruction decode unit	284	5.1
Total	**5594**	**100.0**

3 Overview of the Selected Cryptographic Algorithms

Several cryptographic algorithms that could be interesting for RFID applications were selected for implementation on the microcontroller. Main selection criteria were adequate security of the algorithm and moderate resource usage. We selected four block ciphers and one stream cipher for evaluation. The block ciphers are: AES, XTEA, Present, and SEA. The stream cipher is Trivium. Table 2 provides an overview of the selected algorithms and compares some of their properties like key size, block size, and number of rounds.

Table 2. Comparison of the selected cryptographic algorithms

Algorithm	**Key size** [bits]	**Block size** [bits]	**Number of rounds** per block
	Block ciphers		
AES-128	128	128	10
$SEA_{96,8}$	96	96	93
Present-80	80	64	31
XTEA	128	64	64
	Stream ciphers		/128 bits
Trivium	80	-	128

The Advanced Encryption Standard (AES) is the successor of the Data Encryption Standard (DES) and was introduced by the National Institute of Standards and Technology (NIST) in 2001 [21]. AES uses a so-called substitution-permutation network (SPN) and works on a fixed block size of 128 bits. We selected AES-128 for our implementations, which has a key length of 128 bits and uses 10 rounds. AES-128 is treated as very secure since it is widely deployed and well researched. The best known attack on AES-128 applies on 8 out of 10 rounds and was published in 2009 [14].

SEA stands for Scalable Encryption Algorithm and was developed by Standaert *et al.* in 2006 [25]. The algorithm is a so-called Feistel block cipher and was designed for resource-constrained devices such as microcontrollers that have only a limited instruction set and little memory available. As the name implies, SEA is scalable. This means that parameters like the word size b, the width n of the key and the plaintext, and the number of rounds n_r can be adjusted for the requirements of the target device. As suggested by the designers, we selected for implementation on our 8-bit microcontroller (word size b=8) n=96 bits and n_r=93 rounds ($SEA_{96,8}$). SEA is a rather new algorithm and not as well researched as other block ciphers. Hence, further analysis of its security is still necessary.

Present is another lightweight block cipher suitable for implementation on constrained devices. It uses a substitution-permutation network (SPN) like AES and was introduced by Bogdanov *et al.* in 2007 [3]. Present operates on 64-bit data blocks and supports key lengths of 80 bits (Present-80) and 128 bits (Present-128). In our implementations we selected Present-80 since it is most interesting for low-resource implementations. Present-80 uses 31 rounds. The best known attack on Present-80 applies on 26 out of the 31 rounds and was recently published by Cho in [6].

The Extended Tiny Encryption Algorithm (XTEA) was published in 1997 [22] and is the successor of the Tiny Encryption Algorithm (TEA). XTEA is a 64-bit block cipher with a Feistel structure that iterates a simple round function over a number of 64 rounds. The key used by XTEA has a length of 128 bits. Encryption and decryption operation of XTEA have a similar structure allowing a rather compact implementation of the block cipher. The best known attack on XTEA is a so-called related-key rectangle attack that addresses 36 rounds out of the 64 rounds [16].

Trivium is a hardware-oriented stream cipher developed by De Cannière *et al.* [4]. Although the stream cipher is optimized for hardware designs, it provides also low-resource usage in software implementations. Trivium follows a very simple design strategy and allows to generate up to 2^{64} bits of key stream from an 80-bit initial value (IV) and an 80-bit secret key. Trivium operates on a 288-bit internal state, which needs to be initialized first before generation of the key stream is started. There exist several attacks on reduced variants of Trivium as described in [8] and [28]. However, there is no successful attack against the full version of Trivium.

Implementation results of the five selected algorithms are presented in the next section, followed by comparing the results with implementations on other microcontroller platforms.

4 Implementation Results

This section presents the implementation results of the cryptographic algorithms on our microcontroller. All implementations were done in our own assembler environment and optimized towards three targets: execution time, code size, and efficiency. In order to determine the efficiency of an implementation, a scaling factor $s = 10^8$ is divided by the product of execution time in clock cycles and code size in bytes (s is used to obtain easier-manageable values). As mentioned in the previous section, we selected four block ciphers and one stream cipher for implementation. For the block ciphers both encryption and decryption were implemented. When the block ciphers need to compute round keys this is done on-the-fly during the encryption or the decryption routine. Moreover, we compare our results with implementations on other platforms like AVR microcontrollers from Atmel, PIC microcontrollers from Microchip, 68HC08 microcontrollers from Motorola, or 8051 microcontrollers from various manufacturers. The latter are based on a so-called Complex Instruction-Set Computer (CISC) architecture where the execution of a single instruction (a machine cycle) typically requires several clock cycles. This makes a comparison with 8051 microcontrollers difficult, since depending on the manufacturer, the number of clock cycles per instruction can vary. An overview of our implementation results is given in Table 3, which contains also results from implementations on the other microcontroller platforms.

4.1 AES-128

AES-128 was the first cryptographic algorithm implemented on our microcontroller. Round keys are computed on-the-fly. Encryption and decryption operation were implemented. Decryption consumes significantly more execution time than encryption, since the last round key need to be computed at the beginning. S-box operation and inverse S-box operation are realized as look-up tables with 256 entries each. The AES implementation with the best efficiency requires only 3304 clock cycles for encryption and only 5037 clock cycles for decryption (both values already include the key schedule). Code size of this version is 1940 bytes. A more compact implementation that extensively uses function calls saves 200 bytes of code, which comes at the prize of a significantly longer execution time, 5064 clock cycles for encryption and 8226 clock cycles for decryption. The speed-optimized version of AES uses code duplication and requires only 3084 clock cycles for encrypting a data block and 4505 clock cycles for decrypting a data block. This moderate speed up causes the code-size to increase to 2158 bytes. Regardless of the optimization target, 39 registers are used by our implementations.

AES-128 is widely deployed and many implementations of this algorithm for various microcontroller platforms are available. In Table 3 we list some of them, and compare them with our results. We also added two encryption-only versions of our implementations, one optimized for speed and one optimized for code size, to provide better comparability with related work where the decryption operation is omitted. When comparing with implementations on AVR or PIC microcontrollers, our versions are not only faster but also more compact in code size, leading to a much better efficiency. At first glance, the situation looks different for our encryption-only versions. There, the AES implementations on the 8051 microcontrollers seem to provide better efficiency. However, it has to be noted that the performance numbers of the 8051 microcontrollers are related to machine cycles (a machine cycle requires typically several clock cycles).

4.2 SEA

The simple structure of SEA allows a rather straight-forward implementation on the microcontroller. Encryption and decryption operation of SEA are quite similar and can efficiently be combined in a single function. In that way, a very compact implementation of SEA is obtained that requires only 332 bytes of code. Encryption or decryption of a 96-bit data block lasts 14723 clock cycles each with this version. When optimizing the implementation towards efficiency, execution time is reduced to 8597 clock cycles, by using 488 bytes of code. The speed-optimized implementation of SEA is only about 500 clock cycles faster and uses separate functions for encryption and decryption. However, this minor speed up increases the code size by nearly 300 bytes. All implementations of SEA utilize 12 registers each.

Table 3 gives an overview of the results and compares them with implementations on other microcontroller platforms. Our implementations have a

Table 3. Implementation results of the cryptographic algorithms and comparison with related work

Algorithm	Platform	Target	Code size [bytes]	Encryption clock cycles	Encryption efficiency	Decryption clock cycles	Decryption efficiency
			Block ciphers				
AES-128	**This work**	**size**	**1704**	**5064**	**11.6**	**8226**	**7.1**
	This work	**eff.**	**1940**	**3304**	**15.6**	**5037**	**10.2**
	This work	**speed**	**2158**	**3084**	**15.0**	**4505**	**10.3**
	AVR [24]	-	3410	3766	7.8	4558	6.4
	AVR [10]	-	2606	6637	5.8	7429	5.2
	PIC [19]	-	2478	5273	7.7	7041	5.7
AES-128 (encr. only)	**This work**	**size**	**918**	**4192**	**26.0**	-	-
	This work	**speed**	**1110**	**3004**	**30.0**	-	-
	8051 [7]	-	1016	3168[1]	31.1[1]	-	-
	8051 [7]	-	826	3744[1]	32.3[1]	-	-
	8051 [7]	-	768	4065[1]	32.0[1]	-	-
	68HC98 [7]	-	919	8390	13.0	-	-
$SEA_{96,8}$	**This work**	**size**	**332**	**14723**	**20.5**	**14723**	**20.5**
	This work	**eff.**	**488**	**8597**	**23.8**	**8597**	**23.8**
	This work	**speed**	**786**	**8053**	**15.8**	**8053**	**15.8**
	AVR [24]	-	2132	9654	4.9	9654	4.9
	AVR [25]	-	386	17745	14.6	17745	14.6
	AVR [9]	-	834	9658	12.4	9658	12.4
	8051 [9]	-	604	8250[1]	20.1[1]	8250[1]	20.1[1]
Present-80	**This work**	**size**	**920**	**28062**	**3.9**	**60427**	**1.8**
	This work	**eff.**	**1148**	**15042**	**5.8**	**17677**	**4.9**
	This work	**speed**	**2146**	**8958**	**5.2**	**11592**	**4.0**
	AVR [23]	-	2398	9595	4.3	9820	4.2
	AVR [23]	-	1474	646166	0.1	634614	0.1
	AVR [10]	-	936	10723	10.0	11239	9.5
XTEA	**This work**	**size**	**504**	**17514**	**11.3**	**19936**	**10.0**
	This work	**eff.**	**820**	**7786**	**15.7**	**8928**	**13.7**
	This work	**speed**	**1246**	**7595**	**10.6**	**8735**	**9.2**
	AVR [24]	-	1160	6718	12.8	6718	12.8
	8051 [18]	-	542	6954[1]	26.5[1]	7053[1]	26.2[1]
	PIC [20]	-	962	7408	14.0	7408	14.0
	Stream ciphers			Initialization		/128 bits	
Trivium	**This work**	**size**	**332**	**85697**	**3.5**	**9488**	**31.7**
	This work	**eff.**	**726**	**40337**	**3.4**	**4448**	**31.0**
	This work	**speed**	**1226**	**39833**	**2.0**	**4112**	**19.8**
	AVR [1]	-	424	775726	0.3	85120	2.8

good efficiency, which is even better than on the 8051 microcontroller, whose execution time is indicated in machine cycles.

[1] The values for the 8051 microcontrollers refer to machine cycles. Typically, a machine cycle requires several clock cycles.

4.3 Present-80

Both encryption and decryption operation of Present-80 were implemented. Round keys are computed on-the-fly. As in case of AES-128, decryption operation requires significantly longer than encryption operation since the last round key needs to be computed at the beginning. The most compact implementation of Present-80 uses two look-up tables with 16 entries each, one for the S-box operation and one for the inverse S-box operation. This results in a code size of 920 bytes, allowing encryption of data within 28062 clock cycles, and decryption of data within 60427 clock cycles. A more efficient implementation uses two additional look-up tables with 16 entries each to speed-up the S-box and inverse S-box operation. This implementation requires 15042 clock cycles for encryption and 17677 clock cycles for decryption. Code size increases to 1148 bytes. The fastest version of Present-80 uses two big look-up tables with 256 entries each, performing the S-box operation on a whole byte. In that way, execution time reduces to 8958 clock cycles for encryption and 11592 clock cycles for decryption. Code size significantly increases to 2146 bytes. All versions of Present-80 require a total number of 30 registers each.

An overview of the implementation results of Present-80 is provided in Table 3. A comparison with implementation results on AVR devices shows that our speed-optimized version allows encryption within less clock cycles and that our code-size optimized version is even more compact. However, the implementation of [10] provides better efficiency.

4.4 XTEA

XTEA has a Feistel structure just like SEA. Thus, similar optimization strategies can be applied. Again, we implemented both encryption and decryption operation of the cipher. The most compact version needs 504 bytes of code and requires 17514 clock cycles for encryption and 19936 clock cycles for decryption. The efficiency-optimized version reduces the execution time to 7786 clock cycles for encryption and 8928 clock cycles for decryption. Code size is nearly doubled and increases to 820 bytes. The fastest version of XTEA uses code duplication and provides only a minor speed-up of about 200 clock cycles, while spending more than 400 bytes of additional code. The register usage of the XTEA implementations is between 23 registers for the most compact version, and 27 registers for the fastest version. This low values result from the simple structure of the key schedule.

Table 3 compares our results of XTEA with implementations on other 8-bit microcontroller platforms. The implementations on the AVR microcontroller and on the PIC microcontroller are a bit faster than our speed-optimized version. This is a consequence of the limited instruction set of our microcontroller, which prevents from efficiently adding 32-bit words. Nevertheless, our microcontroller achieves compact code size with slightly better efficiency for encryption.

4.5 Trivium

Trivium is the last algorithm that was implemented on the microcontroller. Although Trivium is a hardware-oriented design, it can be implemented in a very compact way in software. The code-size optimized version of Trivium generates on key-stream bit per iteration and requires only 332 bytes of code. Execution time results in 85697 clock cycles for initialization and 9488 clock cycles for generating 128 bits of key stream. The efficiency-optimized version generates 8 key-stream bits per iteration. This noticeably reduces execution time by doubling the code size. The speed-optimized version of Trivium generates 16 key-stream bits per iteration. Such an approach only slightly improves execution time by significantly increasing code size. All our versions of Trivium require 39 registers.

The results of Trivium are listed in Table 3 together with an implementation on an AVR microcontroller. The implementation of Trivium on the AVR microcontroller is done in C, leading to poor performance values compared to our versions.

4.6 Summary of Implementation Results

The results above clarify that our microcontroller allows implementing the selected cryptographic algorithms in a very compact and efficient way. Our implementations of AES-128, SEA, Present-80, and Trivium are faster than on the other compared 8-bit microcontroller platforms. Except in the case of AES, our implementations are also the most compact ones.

Comparing the performance numbers of the cryptographic algorithms shows that AES has by far the shortest execution time, but also requires most code size. When looking at code size, SEA and Trivium are the algorithms that can be implemented with minimum number of bytes. However, the initialization phase of Trivium takes exceptionally long. All these results are used in the next section to give actual values for the hardware costs that arise from implementing the algorithms on the microcontroller.

5 Discussing the Costs of Integrating the Implemented Algorithms on Passive RFID Tags

Two important constraints need to be considered when implementing cryptographic algorithms on passive RFID tags: power consumption and chip size. Power consumption affects the read range of the tag while chip size affects the costs of the tag. First, the power consumption of our microcontroller is more or less independent of the number of instructions present in the synthesized ROM. Thus, increasing the number of instructions by implementing cryptographic algorithms will not increase the power consumption. Second, the chip size of our microcontroller is not fixed, rather it is mainly defined by the size of the register file and by the size of the synthesized ROM. Depending on the application, the register file can contain up to 64 8-bit registers. These registers are already used by the microcontroller for handling the control tasks. Reusing them for computing cryptographic algorithms introduces no additional hardware costs. Hence, the only factor that influences the chip size of the microcontroller when implementing cryptographic algorithms is the code size. For this reason, we only consider the code size of the implemented algorithms as cost factor. Less attention is drawn on the execution speed of the algorithms, since RFID tags typically have enough time for the computations and only need to handle little data.

Actual values for chip-size increase were determined by implementing the cryptographic algorithms on our microcontroller platform. These values are obtained by synthesizing the program code of the implementations described in the previous section. Synthesis was done for a 0.35 µm CMOS technology using a semi-custom design flow with Cadence RTL Compiler. Table 4 presents the synthesis results, by bringing code size of each implementation in relation with chip area. Code size is given in terms of bytes and chip area is given in terms of gate equivalents (GEs). The chip area of the implementations ranges from 745 GEs for the code-size optimized version of Trivium to 3273 GEs for the speed-optimized version of AES.

Looking at the synthesis results brings up an interesting observation that concerns the area efficiency of the implemented algorithms. The area efficiency in terms of bits per GE is not constant but strongly varies and mainly depends on two factors. First, the area efficiency is improved when the code size of an implementation increases. For example, the speed-optimized version of AES with 2158 bytes of code has an area efficiency of 5.3 bits/GE, but the code-size optimized version of Trivium with 332 bytes of code has only 3.6 bits/GE. This varying area efficiency is caused by the synthesis tool, which can better optimize larger look-up tables. However, it is not intended that the algorithm implementations are used on their own, but together with the implementation of the communication protocol. This leads to a larger overall code size, which finally improves the area efficiency. Second, implementations with a lot of redundancy in the code reach even a much better area efficiency. An example for such an implementation is the speed-optimized version of Present which reaches 8.0 bits/GE. In this version, the 4-bit S-box is replicated 16 times to achieve faster execution of the algorithm (code duplication). Although this replication significantly increases code size, the chip area is only moderately increased since the synthesis tool removes redundancies in the resulting look-up table.

Table 4 gives not only an overview of the synthesis results, but also compares them with the area requirements of stand-alone hardware modules. In almost all cases, the hardware modules require more chip area than the implementations on our microcontroller (only code size is treated as cost factor since the register file is reused). Even the speed-optimized versions, which have the highest area requirements are smaller. The hardware implementation of Present-80 is the only exception. It consumes about 300 GEs less than the most compact version on the microcontroller. Looking at the results of AES shows that an implementation on the microcontroller supporting encryption and decryption can be realized within

Table 4. Synthesis results of the algorithm implementations on the microcontroller and comparison with dedicated hardware modules

Algorithm	Platform	Target	Code size [bytes]	Area [GEs]	Area efficiency [bits/GE]
		Block ciphers			
AES-128	**This work**	**size**	**1704**	**2911**	**4.7**
	This work	**efficiency**	**1940**	**3130**	**5.0**
	This work	**speed**	**2158**	**3273**	**5.3**
	Feldhofer [13]	-	-	3400	-
AES-128 (encr. only)	**This work**	**size**	**918**	**1755**	**4.2**
	This work	**speed**	**1110**	**1871**	**4.7**
	Hämäläinen [15]	-	-	3100	-
$SEA_{96,8}$	**This work**	**size**	**332**	**786**	**3.4**
	This work	**efficiency**	**488**	**1083**	**3.6**
	This work	**speed**	**786**	**1619**	**3.9**
	Mace [17]	-	-	3758	-
Present-80	**This work**	**size**	**920**	**1399**	**5.3**
	This work	**efficiency**	**1148**	**1763**	**5.2**
	This work	**speed**	**2146**	**2139**	**8.0**
	Poschmann [23]	-	-	1075	-
XTEA	**This work**	**size**	**504**	**1230**	**3.3**
	This work	**efficiency**	**820**	**1718**	**3.8**
	This work	**speed**	**1246**	**2507**	**4.0**
	Feldhofer [12]	-	-	2636	-
		Stream ciphers			
Trivium	**This work**	**size**	**332**	**745**	**3.6**
	This work	**efficiency**	**726**	**1476**	**3.9**
	This work	**speed**	**1226**	**2228**	**4.4**
	Feldhofer [12]	-	-	2390	-

less than 3000 GEs. This is even less area than the smallest encryption-only AES hardware module consumes.

Particularly for AES there exist several other approaches that try to minimize the costs of implementing the algorithm on a microcontroller. For example, microcontrollers with AES-specific design like the AESMPU [5] or microcontrollers with instruction-set extensions (ISE) [26]. Although both examples only need about half the code size of our AES implementations they are less flexible. The lack of flexibility comes from the AES-specific hardware parts that are used by both approaches. These parts need to be removed (redesign of the microcontroller on HDL level necessary) when implementing other cryptographic algorithms. Otherwise, the AES-specific parts will unnecessarily increase the chips size of the microcontroller. Moreover, the AESMPU is not designed for low-resource usage since it precomputes all round keys and stores them in its internal memory (176 8-bit registers required). This enormous memory usage makes the AESMPU inapplicable for passive RFID tags. ISE are more attractive than the AESMPU in terms of resource usage.

The ISE consume about 1100 GEs for the AES-specific hardware parts and require 840 bytes of code for implementing encryption and decryption. When assuming an area efficiency of 3.7 bits/GE (realistic for 840 bytes), the ISE will end up with roughly the same hardware costs as our most compact AES implementation. When using a more optimistic value of 4.8 bits/GE, the size of the ISE approach will be about 400 GEs smaller. This is not that much compared to the overall size of the AES implementation, but comes at cost of less flexibility. Moreover, the AES-specific hardware parts will slightly increase the overall power consumption of the microcontroller. Nevertheless, ISE are much faster. They allow to encrypt or decrypt a block of data within less than 1500 clock cycles. Thus, when the execution time is an important factor for an application, using ISE is beneficial. Due to the flexibility of our synthesizable microcontroller, it should not be too much effort to integrate also ISE if required in order to achieve an additional speed up.

The results of our algorithm implementations let us come to two important conclusions. First, our microcontroller platform that is mainly intended for simple control tasks on RFID tags, allows also to efficiently implement cryptographic algorithms like AES, Present, or XTEA. Second, the additional hardware costs that are introduced by implementing cryptographic algorithms on our synthesizable microcontroller are in almost all cases lower (except in case of Present) than by using stand-alone hardware modules. The additional hardware costs are only affected by the code size of the algorithm. The data memory in the register file is already used by the microcontroller for handling control tasks and will not result in additional hardware costs (Note that this statement is only correct in an environment where the microcontroller is used anyway and the question how much does security cost arises). This makes our synthesizable microcontroller a resource saving and flexible concept to bring cryptographic security to passive RFID tags.

6 Conclusion

In our work, we showed a very efficient concept of reusing a dedicated 8-bit microcontroller for the implementation of symmetric-key algorithms. The microcontroller, which is highly optimized for controlling tasks like protocol execution, is synthesizable and optimized concerning low chip area and low power consumption. It is also flexible concerning the program-memory size and the number of used registers. We evaluated the block ciphers AES, SEA, Present and XTEA as well as the stream cipher Trivium with respect to program size and required number of clock cycles. Our findings clearly show that the implemented microcontroller is more efficient than other dedicated microcontrollers and outperforms even optimized hardware modules when considering the reuse of the microcontroller for protocol execution tasks.

Acknowledgements

This work has been supported by the Austrian Government through the research program FIT-IT Trust in IT Systems under the Project Number 820843 (Project CRYPTA) and by the IAP Programme P6/26 BCRYPT of the Belgian State (Belgian Science Policy).

References

[1] AVR-Crypto-Lib, http://www.das-labor.org/wiki/AVR-Crypto-Lib/en
[2] Batina, L., Guajardo, J., Kerins, T., Mentens, N., Tuyls, P., Verbauwhede, I.: Public-Key Cryptography for RFID-Tags. In: Workshop on RFID Security 2006 (RFIDSec 2006), July 12-14, Graz, Austria (2006)
[3] Bogdanov, A., Knudsen, L.R., Leander, G., Paar, C., Poschmann, A., Robshaw, M.J.B., Seurinand, Y., Vikkelsoe, C.: PRESENT: An Ultra-Lightweight Block Cipher. In: Paillier, P., Verbauwhede, I. (eds.) CHES 2007. LNCS, vol. 4727, pp. 450–466. Springer, Heidelberg (2007) ISBN 978-3-540-74734-5
[4] Canniére, C.D., Preneel, B.: TRIVIUM Specifications. eSTREAM, ECRYPT Stream Cipher Project, Report 2005/030 (April 2005), http://www.ecrypt.eu.org/stream
[5] Chia, C.-C., Wang, S.-S.: Efficient Design of an Embedded Microcontroller for Advanced Encryption Standard. In: Proceedings of the 2005, Workshop on Consumer Electronics and Signal Processing, WCEsp 2005 (2005), http://www.mee.chu.edu.tw/labweb/WCEsp2005/96.pdf
[6] Cho, J.Y.: Linear cryptanalysis of reduced-round PRESENT. In: Pieprzyk, J. (ed.) CT-RSA 2010. LNCS, vol. 5985, pp. 302–317. Springer, Heidelberg (2010)
[7] Daemen, J., Rijmen, V.: AES proposal: Rijndael. First AES Conference (August 1998)
[8] Dinur, I., Shamir, A.: Cube attacks on tweakable black box polynomials. In: Joux, A. (ed.) EUROCRYPT 2009. LNCS, vol. 5479, pp. 278–299. Springer, Heidelberg (2009)
[9] EFTON s.r.o. Implementing SEA on x51 and AVR, http://www.efton.sk/crypt/sea.htm
[10] Eisenbarth, T., Kumar, S., Paar, C., Poschmann, A., Uhsadel, L.: A Survey of Lightweight-Cryptography Implementations. IEEE Design & Test of Computers - Design and Test of ICs for Secure Embedded Computing 24(6), 522–533 (2007) ISSN 0740-7475
[11] Feldhofer, M., Dominikus, S., Wolkerstorfer, J.: Strong Authentication for RFID Systems using the AES Algorithm. In: Joye, M., Quisquater, J.-J. (eds.) CHES 2004. LNCS, vol. 3156, pp. 357–370. Springer, Heidelberg (2004)
[12] Feldhofer, M., Wolkerstorfer, J.: Hardware Implementation of Symmetric Algorithms for RFID Security. In: RFID Security: Techniques, Protocols and System-On-Chip Design, pp. 373–415. Springer, Heidelberg (2008)
[13] Feldhofer, M., Wolkerstorfer, J., Rijmen, V.: AES Implementation on a Grain of Sand. IEE Proceedings on Information Security 152(1), 13–20 (2005)
[14] Gilbert, H., Peyrin, T.: Super-sbox cryptanalysis: Improved attacks for aes-like permutations. Cryptology ePrint Archive, Report 2009/531 (2009), http://eprint.iacr.org/

[15] Hämäläinen, P., Alho, T., Hännikäinen, M., Hämäläinen, T.D.: Design and Implementation of Low-Area and Low-Power AES Encryption Hardware Core. In: 9th EUROMICRO Conference on Digital System Design: Architectures, Methods and Tools (DSD 2006), Dubrovnik, Croatia, August 30-September 1, pp. 577–583. IEEE Computer Society, Los Alamitos (2006)
[16] Lu, J.: Related-key rectangle attack on 36 rounds of the XTEA block cipher. International Journal of Information Security 8, 1–11 (2009)
[17] Mace, F., Standaert, F.-X., Quisquater, J.-J.: ASIC Implementations of the Block Cipher SEA for Constrained Applications. In: Munilla, J., Peinado, A., Rijmen, V. (eds.) Workshop on RFID Security 2007 (RFIDSec 2007), Malaga, Spain, July 11-13, 2007, pp. 103–114 (2007)
[18] Pavlin, M.: Encription Using Low Cost Microcontrollers, http://citeseerx.ist.psu.edu/viewdoc/download?doi=10.1.1.61.5755/&rep=rep1&type=pdf
[19] Microchip Technology Inc. AN821: Advanced Encryption Standard Using the PIC16XXX (June 2002), http://ww1.microchip.com/downloads/en/AppNotes/00821a.pdf
[20] Microchip Technology Inc. AN953: Data Encryption Routines for PIC18 Microcontrollers (January 2005), http://ww1.microchip.com/downloads/en/AppNotes/00953a.pdf
[21] National Institute of Standards and Technology (NIST). FIPS-197: Advanced Encryption Standard (November 2001), http://www.itl.nist.gov/fipspubs/
[22] Needham, R.M., Wheeler, D.J.: Tea extensions. Technical report, Computer Laboratory, University of Cambridge (October 1997)
[23] Poschmann, A.Y.: Lightweight Cryptography - Cryptographic Engineering for a Pervasive World. PhD thesis, Faculty of Electrical Engineering and Information Technology, Ruhr-University Bochum,Germany (Februrary 2009)
[24] Rinne, S., Eisenbarth, T., Paar, C.: Performance Analysis of Contemporary Light-Weight Block Ciphers on 8-bit Microcontrollers (June 2007), http://www.crypto.ruhr-uni-bochum.de/imperia/md/content/texte/publications/conferences/lw_speed2007.pdf
[25] Standaert, F.-X., Piret, G., Gershenfeld, N., Quisquater, J.-J.: SEA: a Scalable Encryption Algorithm for Small Embedded Applications. In: Domingo-Ferrer, J., Posegga, J., Schreckling, D. (eds.) CARDIS 2006. LNCS, vol. 3928, pp. 222–236. Springer, Heidelberg (2006)
[26] Tillich, S., Herbst, C.: Boosting AES Performance on a Tiny Processor Core. In: Malkin, T. (ed.) CT-RSA 2008. LNCS, vol. 4964, pp. 170–186. Springer, Heidelberg (2008)
[27] Tuyls, P., Batina, L.: RFID-Tags for Anti-counterfeiting. In: Pointcheval, D. (ed.) CT-RSA 2006. LNCS, vol. 3860, pp. 115–131. Springer, Heidelberg (2006)
[28] Vielhaber, M.: Breaking one.fivium by aida an algebraic iv differential attack. Cryptology ePrint Archive, Report 2007/413 (2007), http://eprint.iacr.org/, http://eprint.iacr.org/
[29] Yu, Y., Yang, Y., Yan, N., Min, H.: A Novel Design of Secure RFID Tag Baseband. In: RFID Convocation, Brussels, Belgium (March 14, 2007)

Batch Computations Revisited: Combining Key Computations and Batch Verifications

René Struik

723 Carlaw Ave, Toronto ON M4K 3K8, Canada
rstruik.ext@gmail.com

Abstract. We consider the effect of combining the key computation step in particular key agreement protocols, such as ECMQV and static-DH, with verifying particular elliptic curve equations, such as those related to ECDSA signature verification. In particular, we show that one can securely combine ECDSA signature verification and ECMQV and static-ECDH key computations, resulting in significant performance improvements, due to saving on doubling operations and exploiting multiple point multiplication strategies. Rough estimates (for non-Koblitz curves) suggest that the incremental cost of ECDSA signature verification, when combined with ECDH key agreement, improves by a factor 2.3× compared to performing the ECDSA signature verification separately and by a factor 1.7×, when the latter is computed using the accelerated ECDSA signature verification technique described in [3]. Moreover, the total cost of combined ECDSA signature verification and ECDH key agreement improves by 1.4×, when compared to performing these computations separately (and by 1.2×, if accelerated ECDSA signature verification techniques are used). This challenges the conventional wisdom that with ECC-based signature schemes, signature verification is always considerably slower than signature generation and slower than RSA signature verification. These results suggest that the efficiency advantage one once enjoyed using RSA-based certificates with ECC-based key agreement schemes may be no more: one might as well use an ECC-only scheme using ECDSA-based certificates. Results apply to all prime curves standardized by NIST, the NSA 'Suite B' curves, and the so-called Brainpool curves.

Keywords: elliptic curve, authenticated key agreement, key computation, certificate verification, ECDSA, efficient computations.

1 Introduction

Discrete logarithm based authenticated public-key key agreement protocols typically include the following steps:

- *Key contributions.* Each party randomly generates a short-term (ephemeral) public key pair and communicates the ephemeral public key to the other party (but not the private key). In addition, it may communicate its long-term static public key.

A. Biryukov, G. Gong, and D.R. Stinson (Eds.): SAC 2010, LNCS 6544, pp. 130–142, 2011.

- *Key establishment.* Each party computes the shared key based on the static and ephemeral public keys it obtained from the other party and based on the static and ephemeral private keys it generated itself. The key computation is such that either party indeed arrives at the same shared key.
- *Key authentication.* Each party verifies the authenticity of the long-term static key of the other party, to obtain evidence that the only party that may have been capable of computing the shared key is, indeed, its perceived communicating party.
- *Key confirmation.* Each party evidences possession of the shared key to the other party, usually by communicating a message authentication check value over the strings corresponding to the key contributions communicated by either party using a key derived from the shared key. This confirms to each party the true identity of the other party and proves that that party successfully computed the shared key.

The key authentication step is typically carried out separately from the other protocol steps described above and usually involves checking the validity of a certificate that vouches for the authenticity of the binding between a party and its private key (by means of the corresponding public key). While separating the key authentication step from the remaining protocol steps allows more flexibility (e.g., in use of certificates), it may present a significant computational burden, since the online computational cost of the key agreement protocol – and thereby its running time – is dominated by the cost of the key authentication step and that of the key computation performed during the key establishment step. Here, we assume key authentication has to be performed at each instantiation of the protocol.

In this paper, we consider a method for securely combining the key authentication and the key computation steps, rather than carrying these out separately, thus realizing a significant reduction of the online computational cost of the resulting protocol and, thereby, of its running time. While this approach leads to some loss of flexibility (since one has to carry out computations on similar mathematical objects), quite remarkable efficiency gains seem possible.

The remainder of the paper is organized as follows. In §2, we provide some preliminaries that facilitate the main exposition of the paper, while §3 gives applications that illustrate the performance advantages that can be reaped when applying joint computations in the context of some well-known authenticated key agreement schemes. Summary conclusions appear in §4.

2 Preliminaries

In this section, we introduce some simple notions that facilitate the exposition in the remainder of the paper. §2.1 introduces some probability results, which we apply in §2.2 to key establishment schemes. §2.3 summarizes some properties of ECDSA and the related signature scheme ECDSA*.

The exposition below is relative to a group $\mathbb{E}$ with (cyclic) subgroup $\mathbb{G}$ of prime order n generated by some point G and with identity element $\mathcal{O}$.

2.1 Probabilities

Let f be a function defined on $\mathbb{E}$. For each $z \in \mathrm{Im}(f)$, define $f^{-1}(z) := \{X \in \mathbb{E} \mid f(X) = z\}$ and define $d_\infty(f^{-1}) := \max\{|f^{-1}(z)| \mid z \in \mathrm{Im}(f)\}$.

Lemma 1. *Let $K_A \in \mathbb{E}$, let $\Delta \in \mathbb{G}$, and let $\lambda \in_R \Omega$, where $\Omega \subset \mathbb{Z}_n{}^*$. Let $K'_A := K_A + \lambda \cdot \Delta$. Then*

$$\max_{K \in \mathbb{E}} \Pr\{K'_A = K\} = \begin{cases} 1 & \text{if } \Delta = \mathcal{O}; \\ |\Omega|^{-1} & \text{otherwise.} \end{cases}$$

Proof. Trivial. □

Lemma 2. *Let $K_A \in \mathbb{E}$, let $\Delta \in \mathbb{G}$, and let $\lambda \in_R \Omega$, where $\Omega \subset \mathbb{Z}_n{}^*$. Let $K'_A := K_A + \lambda \cdot \Delta$. Then*

$$\max_{\tau \in \mathrm{Im}(f)} \Pr\{f(K'_A) = \tau\} = \begin{cases} 1 & \text{if } \Delta = \mathcal{O}; \\ \leq d_\infty(f^{-1}) \cdot |\Omega|^{-1} & \text{otherwise.} \end{cases}$$

Proof. This follows from Lemma 1 and the observation that for $\Delta \neq \mathcal{O}$ and for any $z \in \mathrm{Im}(f)$, the maximum in Lemma 1 may not be realized for all $K \in f^{-1}(z)$ simultaneously (hence, the inequality for $\Delta \neq \mathcal{O}$). □

Note 3. Lemma 2 reduces to Lemma 1 if one takes f to be the identity function.

2.2 Key Establishment Schemes

In this section, we apply the results of the previous subsection (§2.1) towards scenarios where a party executes a key agreement scheme resulting in a key in group $\mathbb{E}$ and where it also may verify a set of equations in $\mathbb{G}$ (such as those arising from checking ECDSA*certificate verification equations – to be discussed in §2.3). We also consider the scenario where the shared key is mapped from $\mathbb{E}$ towards another group (such as is the case when mapping a computed elliptic curve point to its x-coordinate, which then forms the real shared key (cf., e.g., [2,15])).

Lemma 4. *Consider a key agreement scheme $\mathcal{C}$ between two parties A and B resulting in the establishment of a shared key in group $\mathbb{E}$. Let K_A be the shared key computed by A by executing this key agreement scheme. Let $\Delta_1, \ldots, \Delta_t \in \mathbb{G}$. Let $\Omega_1, \ldots, \Omega_t$ be non-empty subsets of $\mathbb{Z}_n{}^*$, each with cardinality M. Consider the modified key agreement scheme $\mathcal{C}'$ that differs from $\mathcal{C}$ solely in that A generates random secret values $\lambda_i \in_R \Omega_i$ for all $1 \leq i \leq t$ and uses the value $K'_A := K_A + \lambda_1 \Delta_1 + \cdots + \lambda_t \Delta_t$ (rather than K_A) as the shared key in protocol $\mathcal{C}$ instead. We assume these random values are kept secret and are not reused. Then the following holds:*

1. *If $\Delta_1 = \cdots = \Delta_t = \mathcal{O}$, then protocols $\mathcal{C}$ and $\mathcal{C}'$ have the same outcome.*
2. *Otherwise, the probability that A and B establish a shared key K is at most $1/M$.*

Proof. This follows directly from Lemma 1. □

Lemma 5. *Consider a key agreement scheme $\mathcal{C}$ between two parties A and B resulting in the establishment of a shared key in group $\mathbb{E}$, which is mapped to a derived key using a fixed function f defined on $\mathbb{E}$. Let K_A be the shared key computed by A by executing this key agreement scheme. Let $\Delta_1, \ldots, \Delta_t \in \mathbb{G}$. Let $\Omega_1, \ldots, \Omega_t$ be non-empty subsets of ${\mathbb{Z}_n}^*$, each with cardinality M. Consider the modified key agreement scheme $\mathcal{C}'$ that differs from $\mathcal{C}$ solely in that A generates random secret values $\lambda_i \in_R \Omega_i$ for all $1 \leq i \leq t$ and uses the value $K'_A := K_A + \lambda_1\Delta_1 + \cdots + \lambda_t\Delta_t$ (rather than K_A) as the shared key in protocol $\mathcal{C}$ instead. We assume these random values are kept secret and are not reused. Then the following holds:*

1. *If $\Delta_1 = \cdots = \Delta_t = \mathcal{O}$, then protocols $\mathcal{C}$ and $\mathcal{C}'$ have the same outcome.*
2. *Otherwise, the probability that A and B establish the same derived key k is at most $d_\infty(f^{-1})/M$.*

Proof. This follows directly from Lemma 4, using Lemma 2. □

2.3 ECDSA and the Modified Signature Scheme ECDSA*

In this section, we briefly summarize those properties of the signature scheme ECDSA [1,9,11] and the modified signature scheme ECDSA*presented in [3] that are relevant to the remainder of the exposition of this paper. For all other details, we refer to the referenced papers themselves.

The ECDSA and ECDSA signature schemes*
With the ECDSA signature scheme, the signature is a pair (r, s) of integers in ${\mathbb{Z}_n}^*$, where the value r is derived from an ephemeral public key R generated by the signer during signature generation via a fixed public function. The ECDSA*signature scheme is the same as ECDSA, except that it outputs the signature (R, s), rather than (r, s).

With the ECDSA*signature scheme, the signature (R, s) over some message m produced by some entity with signature verification key Q may only be valid if $R \in \mathbb{G}$ and if $\Delta := \mathcal{O}$, where

$$\Delta := s^{-1}(eG + rQ) - R, \tag{1}$$

and where e and r are derived from message m and from elliptic curve point R, respectively, via some fixed public functions. For future reference, we mention that the mapping from R to r is such that both R and $-R$ map to the same value. Valid signatures also require the check that $r, s \in {\mathbb{Z}_n}^*$.

One can show that a valid ECDSA*signature (R, s) gives rise to a valid ECDSA signature (r, s) and that, conversely, any valid ECDSA signature (r, s) corresponds to some ECDSA*signature (R, s) with the property that the elliptic curve point $R \in \mathbb{G}$ maps to r via the fixed public function referred to above.

Conversion between ECDSA and ECDSA signatures*
ECDSA has the well-known property that (r, s) is a valid ECDSA signature only if $(r, -s)$ is, i.e., the validity of some ECDSA signature (r, s) does not depend on the 'sign' of signature component s. Similarly, (R, s) is a valid ECDSA*signature only if $(-R, -s)$ is. Both results follow from the observation that the elliptic curve point R and its inverse $-R$ map to the same integer r. Another consequence of this observation is that, while an ECDSA*signature corresponds to a unique ECDSA signature, the converse process generally yields *two* candidate solutions, viz. (R, s) and $(-R, s)$, and uniqueness can only be established by ruling out one of these candidate solutions based on some side information available to the verifier. For a detailed discussion of explicit and implicit side information that realizes this 1-1 mapping, we refer to §4.2 of [3].

3 Accelerated Authenticated Key Agreement

In this section, we introduce a method for securely combining the key authentication step and the key computation step of particular public-key key agreement schemes, rather than carrying these out separately, as is heretofore typically the case. Since the online computational cost of a key agreement protocol - and thereby its running time - are dominated by the computational burden of these two steps, one may anticipate that carrying out these steps in one single computation, rather than carrying these out separately, would result in significant efficiency gains. We show that this is indeed the case. Although the main idea applies more broadly, we are mainly interested in scenarios involving elliptic curves.

In what follows, the exposition is relative to a fixed elliptic curve $\mathbb{E}$, with (cyclic) subgroup $\mathbb{G}$ of prime order n generated by some base point G and with identity element $\mathcal{O}$. In particular, we assume that key computations involve operations on this elliptic curve.

We consider a scenario where two parties execute an elliptic curve key agreement scheme that involves computing a shared key $K \in \mathbb{E}$ and mapping this to a derived key k. Depending on the details of the scheme in question, this derived key is further processed (e.g., passed through a key derivation function) or used in a subsequent key confirmation step. Examples of such protocols include the elliptic curve variant of the original Diffie-Hellman scheme [8], ECMQV [14], and all elliptic curve key agreement schemes specified by NIST [15] and ANSI [2]. With all these schemes, the mapping f from a shared key $K \in \mathbb{E}$ to a derived key k is the projective map, which maps an elliptic curve point that is represented in affine coordinates to its x-coordinate. So, in the notation of §2.1, one has $d_\infty(f^{-1}) = 2$ (since an elliptic curve point and its inverse have the same x-coordinate).

Execution of an authenticated key agreement protocol typically involves checking a public key certificate, to vouch for the binding between the long-term key of the communicating party and its private key (via the corresponding public key). In our exposition, we restrict ourselves to ECDSA*certificates (although our techniques may also be used with, e.g., ephemeral Diffie-Hellman with signed exponents). Verification of such an ECDSA*certificate involves checking the equation $\Delta = \mathcal{O}$, where the signature verification expression Δ is defined by Equation (1) in §2.3. Notice that $\Delta \in \mathbb{G}$ (since one checks that $R \in \mathbb{G}$).

It now follows from Lemma 4 that one can securely combine the computation of a shared key K_A with verifying a number of ECDSA*signature verification equations $\Delta_1 = \mathcal{O}, \ldots, \Delta_t = \mathcal{O}$ (e.g., those arising from checking a certificate chain) by computing

$$K'_A := K_A + \lambda_1 \Delta_1 + \cdots + \lambda_t \Delta_t,$$

since any non-verifying equation would result in a very small probability that a shared key is indeed established (with proper setting of the size M of the randomness source for integers $\lambda_1, \ldots, \lambda_t$). The same result holds if the shared key is subsequently mapped to a derived key (cf. Lemma 5), where the probability increases by at most a factor $d_\infty(f^{-1}) = 2$, and if the derived key k is subsequently used in a key confirmation step between both communicating parties. (The latter relies on scheme-specific cryptographic details regarding the public functions $g_A : k \to g_A(k)$, resp. $g_B : k \to g_B(k)$ that implement the key confirmation mechanisms – generally, second-preimage resistance of these functions should suffice to carry forward the properties of Lemma 5.)

3.1 Static-ECDH with ECDSA*Signatures

In this section, we illustrate how combining the key computation step in the elliptic curve authenticated public-key key agreement protocol Static-ECDH with the ECDSA*signature verification step may result in significant overall efficiency improvements.

Static-ECDH is an authenticated elliptic curve version of the basic Diffie-Hellman protocol [8], where two parties A and B exchange certified long-term public keys and verify these upon receipt prior to computing a shared Diffie-Hellman key. We assume that the public keys are certified by a CA via an ECDSA*certificate and that these public keys and the CA's public signature verification key are on the same elliptic curve.

In what follows, we analyze the cost of carrying out the ECDH key computation step and the ECDSA*certificate verification step separately and compare this with the cost of combining both steps in one single computation.

A precise analysis is difficult to give, due to the large number of methods available and implementation-specific trade-offs that favor one method over another. We use multiple-point multiplication and use the Non-Adjacent Form (NAF) and Joint Sparse Form (JSF) representations; for details, see [18], [10, Chapter 3, §3.3.3].

We adopt the following notation: By A and D, we denote the cost of a single point addition and point doubling operation, respectively. By m, we denote the bit-length of finite field elements in $\mathbb{F}_q$, i.e., $m := \lceil \log_2 q \rceil$. We assume the elliptic curve $\mathbb{E} := E(\mathbb{F}_q)$ to have a small co-factor h, so that $m \approx \lceil \log_2 n \rceil$.

With static-DH, the key computation for A involves computing the shared key

$$K_A := aQ_B, \tag{2}$$

where Q_B is B's long-term public key extracted from its public key certificate (and checked to be on the curve $\mathbb{E}$) and where a is A's private key. Key authentication for A involves verifying B's ECDSA*certificate with signature (R, s) and includes checking that $R \in \mathbb{G}$, evaluating the expression

$$\Delta := s^{-1}(eG + rQ) - R, \tag{3}$$

where e is derived from the to-be-signed certificate information (including B's public key Q_B and B's unique name), where r is derived from signature component R via some fixed public function, and where Q is CA's public key, and checking that $\Delta = \mathcal{O}$ (and that $r, s \in \mathbb{Z}_n{}^*$).

With static-DH, A can combine the key computation (2) and the evaluation of expression (3) and instead compute the expression

$$K'_A := K_A + \lambda\Delta = (aQ_B - \lambda R) + ((\lambda e s^{-1})G + (\lambda r s^{-1})Q), \tag{4}$$

where λ is a suitably chosen random element of $\mathbb{Z}_n{}^*$, after first having checked that $R \in \mathbb{G}$ and $Q_B \in \mathbb{E}$.

We now compare the cost of computing expressions (2) and (3) and compare this with the cost of computing expression (4) instead.

When representing scalar a in (2) in NAF format, the expected running time of computing the key K_A is approximately $(m/3)A + mD$ operations. Similarly, when representing the scalars es^{-1} and rs^{-1} in (3) in JSF, the expected running time of evaluating the ECDSA*signature verification equation is approximately $(m/2+2)A+mD$ operations. (Here, 2 point additions account for pre-computing $G \pm Q$, which is necessary for using JSF.) As a result, computing the key K_A and checking the signature verification equation $\Delta = \mathcal{O}$ separately has total running time of approximately $(5m/6 + 2)A + 2 \cdot mD$ operations.

When computing the key K'_A in Equation (4) via multiple-point multiplication and representing both the rightmost two scalars $\lambda \cdot es^{-1}$ and $\lambda \cdot rs^{-1}$ and the leftmost two scalars a and $-\lambda$ in JSF, one obtains a total running time of approximately $2 \cdot (m/2 + 2)A + mD = (m + 4)A + mD$ operations. Thus, combining the key computation step and the signature verification step in one single computation results in a reduction of half of the point doubling operations (at the expense of a small increase of approximately $m/6 + 2$ point addition operations). In fact, one can show that one can do even better and avoid this small increase of point additions altogether, by computing $aQ_B - \lambda R$ differently, by choosing λ suitably, as follows. Recall that λ should be picked at random from a set $\Omega \subset \mathbb{Z}_n{}^*$ of size $|\Omega| \approx \sqrt{n}$. Let I be the set of non-zero coordinates of scalar a, when represented in NAF format. Now, let Ω be the set of all integers in $\mathbb{Z}_n{}^*$ with a representation in NAF format that is zero outside this set I. Since all integers in NAF format are unique and since one can expect the NAF weight of a to be approximately $m/3$ ([10, Theorem 3.29]), one has $|\Omega| = 3^{|I|} \approx 3^{m/3} > \sqrt{n}$. As a result, for $\lambda \in_R \Omega$, one might write

$$aQ_B - \lambda R = (a - \lambda^+ + \lambda^-)Q_B - \lambda^+(R - Q_B) - \lambda^-(R + Q_B), \tag{5}$$

where $\lambda = \lambda^+ + \lambda^-$ and where λ^+ and λ^- denote those components of λ with the same, respectively different, sign as the corresponding components of a. Since for any coordinate, at most one of the scalars in NAF format on the right-hand side of Equation (5) is nonzero, one can compute this expression using the same number of point additions involved in computing just aQ_B with a in NAF format (after pre-computing $R \pm Q_B$). With this modification, the total running time of computing K'_A becomes $(m/2+2)A + (m/3+2)A + mD = (5m/6+4)A + mD$ operations, i.e., using only half of the point doubling operations required with the separate computations (and just 2 additional point additions).

This result could be interpreted as reducing the incremental running time of ECDSA*signature verification to approximately $(m/2+4)A$ operations, from the approximately $(m/2+2)A + mD$ operations that would have been required if ECDSA*signature verification would have been carried out separately using the traditional approach (or roughly $(m/2+4)A+(m/2)D$ operations using the accelerated verification technique of [3]). In other words: the new method effectively removes *all* point doubling operations from the incremental cost of ECDSA*signature verification compared to previously known techniques (in all contexts where this can be combined with key computations).

Rough analysis for P-384 curve
We provide a rough analysis of the relative efficiency of combining the key computation step of the elliptic curve based authenticated key agreement schemes static-DH and ECMQV with the verification of ECDSA*signatures, as proposed in this paper, compared to the traditional method of carrying out both steps separately. Our analysis is based on the elliptic curve curve P-384 defined over a 384-bit prime field, as specified by NIST [9]. All NIST prime curves have co-factor $h = 1$, so by Hasse's theorem, the bit-size of the order of the cyclic group $\mathbb{G}$ is approximately $m = 384$. We consider the cost of public-key operations only (and ignore, e.g., hash function evaluations). Moreover, we ignore the cost of converting the computed shared key to a representation using affine coordinates, as required by most standards (cf., eg., [2,15]).

We assume points to be represented using Jacobian coordinates and that the cost S of a squaring in $\mathbb{Z}_q$ is slightly less than the cost M of a multiplication (we take $S \approx 0.8M$). With Jacobian coordinates, one has $A \approx 8M + 3S$ and $D \approx 4M + 4S$ (see [10, Table 3.3]). Substitution of $S \approx 0.8M$ now yields $A \approx 10.4M$ and $D \approx 7.2M$ and, hence, $D/A \approx 0.69$.

With Static-ECDH, the running time of the key computation is roughly $128A+384D \approx 393A$ operations. With ECDSA*signature verification, the running time using the traditional method is roughly $194A + 384D \approx 459A$ operations and roughly $196A + 192D \approx 328A$ operations with the accelerated method described in [3]. However, if the key computation step of Static-ECDH and the step of checking the ECDSA*signature verification equation are combined, the incremental running time of signature verification becomes roughly only $196A$ operations. As a result, the new method yields a speed-up of the incremental cost of signature verification of roughly 2.3× compared to the separate method (and roughly 1.7×

P-384 curve	ECDH	ECDSA*(incremental cost)		
		Separately		Combined
ECC operations	key	Ordinary	Fast	with ECDH
– Add	128	194	196	196
– Double	384	384	192	–
– Total (normalized)	393	459	328	196

Fig. 1. Comparison of incremental signature verification cost of ECDSA*, when carried out separately from, resp. combined with, the key computation step of Static-ECDH. Total cost is normalized, using Double/Add cost ratio $D/A = 0.69$.

when compared with the accelerated method of [3]). These results are summarized in Figure 1.

One can perform a similar analysis for the authenticated key agreement scheme ECMQV. With ECMQV, the running time of the key computation is roughly $194A+384D \approx 459A$ operations. If the key computation step of ECMQV and the step of checking the ECDSA*signature verification equation are combined, the incremental running time of signature verification becomes roughly only $196A$ operations, as was also the case with Static-ECDH. As a result, the new method again yields a speed-up of the incremental cost of signature verification of roughly $2.3\times$ compared to the separate method (and roughly $1.7\times$ when compared with the accelerated method of [3]). These results are summarized in Figure 2.

P-384 curve	ECMQV	ECDSA*(incremental cost)		
		Separately		Combined
ECC operations	key	Ordinary	Fast	with ECMQV
– Add	194	194	196	196
– Double	384	384	192	–
– Total (normalized)	459	459	328	196

Fig. 2. Comparison of incremental signature verification cost of ECDSA*, when carried out separately from, resp. combined with, the key computation step of ECMQV. Total cost is normalized, using Double/Add cost ratio $D/A = 0.69$.

A summary of the total normalized cost of various methods is shown in Figure 3.

P-384 curve		Key computation + ECDSA*(total cost)		
Total ECC	Key	ECDSA*separately		ECDSA*
operations	computation	Ordinary	Fast	combined
ECDH	393	852	721	588
ECMQV	459	918	787	655

Fig. 3. Comparison of total normalized combined cost of the key computation step of Static-ECDH and ECMQV and that of ECDSA*signature verification. Normalized cost uses Double/Add cost ratio $D/A = 0.69$.

Experimental results on HP iPAQ 3950 platform
The rough analysis above suggests a significant improvement of the incremental cost of ECDSA*signature verification, when combined with the key computation step of elliptic curve based key agreements schemes over the same curve. This begs the question as to whether the perceived efficiency advantage of using RSA certificates with elliptic curve based key agreement schemes still holds, or whether one might as well use elliptic curve based certificates instead, using our new method. To test this hypothesis, we implemented the various incremental methods of verifying ECDSA*signatures discussed in this paper on an HP iPAQ 3950, Intel PXA250 processor running at a 400MHz clock rate and compared the computational cost hereof with that of RSA signature verification. We compared implementation cost for various cryptographic bit strengths, using the guidance for cryptographic algorithm and key size selection provided by NIST [16]. Our analysis was based on the elliptic curves defined over a prime field for these bit strengths, as specified by NIST [9]. Since these NIST curves all have co-factor $h = 1$, the bit-size of the order of the cyclic group $\mathbb{G}$ and that of the elliptic curve $\mathbb{E}$ are the same. The obtained data is shown in Figure 4.

Crypto strength (bits)	Certificate size[1] (bytes)		Ratio ECC/RSA certificates	Verify – incremental cost (ms)			Ratio ECDSA*verify vs. RSA verify
	ECDSA*	RSA		RSA[2]	ECDSA* ordinary[2]	ECDSA* combined[3]	
80	72	256	4x smaller	1.4	4.0	1.7	0.8x faster
112	84	512	6x smaller	5.2	7.7	3.2	1.6x faster
128	96	768	8x smaller	11.0	11.8	4.9	2.2x faster
192	144	1920	13x smaller	65.8	32.9	13.7	4.8x faster
256	198	3840	19x smaller	285.0	73.2	30.5	9.3x faster

Fig. 4. Comparison of (incremental) cost of verifying ECDSA*and RSA certificates, when carried out during the execution of an elliptic curve based authenticated key agreement scheme, for various cryptographic bit strengths and using NIST curves over a prime field. Computational cost considers public-key operations only (and ignores, e.g., hash function evaluation). [1]Excludes non-cryptographic overhead (e.g., identification data) [2]Benchmark Certicom Security Builder™ [3]Estimate.

The implementation benchmarks of Figure 4 suggest a shift of the cross-over point where verification of ECDSA*certificates becomes more efficient than that of RSA certificates, from 128-bit cryptographic bit strength (without the new method) towards roughly 80-bit cryptographic bit-strength (with the new method). Thus, the efficiency advantage one once enjoyed using RSA-based certificates with discrete logarithm based key agreement schemes is no more: one might as well use an 'elliptic curve only' scheme using ECDSA-based certificates instead.

While we did not conduct experiments with ordinary discrete logarithm based key agreement schemes and DSA-based certificates, we speculate one can draw similar conclusions here.

3.2 Extension of Results to ECDSA

The acceleration techniques in this paper depend on signature schemes for which verification can be described as verifying an algebraic equation. An example hereof is ECDSA*, for which verification requires checking Equation (1). The results do not directly apply to ECDSA – a much more widely used signature scheme. To make our efficiency improvements applicable to ECDSA as well, one could map an ECDSA signature (r, s) to an ECDSA*signature (R, s). As explained in §2.3, this mapping is generally a 2-to-1 mapping (since R and $-R$ map to the same integer r). However, there are techniques to eliminate all but one candidate points R that map to the integer r, thus realizing the required 1-1 mapping. Below, we describe various techniques for doing so.

This side information may be appended explicitly to the communicated signature or may be established implicitly, e.g., by generating ECDSA signatures so as to allow unique recovery of the ephemeral point R corresponding to signature component r and used during signing (in particular, it may be realized by changing the sign of signature component s based on inspection of the ephemeral point R used during signing). Since *any* party can change the sign of signature component s of the ECDSA signature without impacting the validity hereof, this procedure can be implemented as post-processing operation by any party and does not necessarily have to be part of the signing process (in particular, this can be done to all legacy ECDSA signatures, to ensure unique conversion hereof into ECDSA*signatures, so as to make the efficiency improvements discussed in this paper and in [3] directly applicable). More specifically, any party who wishes to engage in an authenticated key agreement protocol can bring his public-key certificate into the required format first (as a one-time pre-processing step). While explicitly added side information changes the format of ECDSA, use of implicit side information does not and, therefore, can be used without requiring changes to standardized specifications of ECDSA.

4 Conclusions

We presented a simple technique for combining the key computation step of elliptic curve based key agreement schemes, such as static-ECDH, with the step of verifying particular digital signatures, such as ECDSA*. We demonstrated that the technique easily extends to most standardized elliptic curve based schemes [2,15] using ECDSA, a much more widely used scheme. We demonstrated that this extremely simple technique may result in spectacular computational improvements of overall protocols in which both key computations and, e.g., signature verifications play a role.

We illustrated that the combined key computation and key authentication technique, while exemplified in terms of a single elliptic curve key computation and a single ECDSA signature verification, can be easily generalized towards combined key computations and batch verifications: rather than computing a key K and verifying each of a set of t elliptic curve equations $\Delta_1 = O, \ldots, \Delta_t = O$ separately, simply compute the quantity $K' := K + \lambda_1\Delta_1 + \cdots \lambda_t\Delta_t$ instead, where each of $\lambda_1, \ldots, \lambda_t$ is drawn at random from a suitably chosen subset of $\mathbb{Z}_n{}^*$ of size roughly $M \approx \sqrt{n}$. This generalizes the batch verification technique discussed in, e.g., [4,6,7] and covers, e.g., scenarios where one wishes to verify multiple ECDSA signatures (as with certificate chains) or, more generally, any set of elliptic curve equations (batch verification). Moreover, the technique obviously generalizes to settings where one wishes to combine verifications with the computation of a non-secret value (rather than a key), as long as the correctness hereof can be checked.

The approach is not restricted to combining key authentication and key establishment steps during the execution of a key agreement protocol; it can be applied to any setting where one has to compute some keys and verify some elliptic curve equations (provided computations take place on the same curve). This being said, the approach is most useful in settings where one can verify whether the computed key is correct (since this would yield a verdict on whether the homogeneous elliptic curve equation $\Delta = \mathcal{O}$ holds). Thus, the approach works effectively in all settings where one indeed evidences knowledge of the computed key.

As a final note, we would like to emphasize that the presented efficiency improvements do depend on the Double/Add cost ratio D/A of the underlying curve in question. Our analysis in §3.1 used NIST curves defined over a prime field and Jacobian coordinates. Careful analysis is needed before one were to apply results directly to, e.g., binary non-Koblitz curves, curves using different coordinate systems, or, e.g, (twisted) Edwards curves [5]. As an example, for twisted curves, Table 1 of [13] suggests one has $A \approx 7M$ and $D \approx 4M + 3S$. Substitution of $S \approx 0.8M$ now yields $A \approx 7M$ and $D \approx 6.4M$ and, hence, $D/A \approx 0.91$. If so, the new method of this paper become more pronounced and would yield a 2.85× efficiency improvement of the incremental ECDSA*verification cost compared to the traditional ECDSA signature verification approach, whereas the acceleration technique in [3] yields a 1.75× efficiency improvement hereto. Since, to our knowledge, this is still very much a nascent research area, this seems to be a promising area of future research.

References

1. ANSI X9.62-1998. Public Key Cryptography for the Financial Services Industry: The Elliptic Curve Digital Signature Algorithm (ECDSA). American National Standard for Financial Services. American Bankers Association (January 7, 1999)
2. ANSI X9.63-2001. Public Key Cryptography for the Financial Services Industry: Key Agreement and Key Transport Using Elliptic Curve Cryptography. American National Standard for Financial Services. American Bankers Association (November 20, 2001)
3. Antipa, A., Brown, D.R., Gallant, R., Lambert, R., Struik, R., Vanstone, S.A.: Accelerated Verification of ECDSA Signatures. In: Preneel, B., Tavares, S. (eds.) SAC 2005. LNCS, vol. 3897, pp. 307–318. Springer, Heidelberg (2006)
4. Bellare, M., Garay, J.A., Rabin, T.: Fast Batch Verification for Modular Exponentiation and Digital Signatures. In: Nyberg, K. (ed.) EUROCRYPT 1998. LNCS, vol. 1403, pp. 236–250. Springer, Heidelberg (1998)

5. Bernstein, D.J., Birkner, P., Lange, T., Peters, C.: Twisted Edwards Curves. International Association for Cryptologic Research, IACR e/Print 2008-013
6. Cao, T., Lin, D., Xue, R.: Security Analysis of Some Batch Verifying Signatures from Pairings. International Journal of Network Security 3(2), 138–143 (2006)
7. Cheon, J.H., Lee, D.H.: Use of Sparse and/or Complex Exponents in Batch Verification of Exponentiations. International Association for Cryptologic Research, ePrint 2005/276 (2005)
8. Diffie, W., Hellmann, M.E.: New Directions in Cryptography. IEEE. Trans. Inform. Theory IT-22, 644–654 (1976)
9. FIPS Pub 186-3. Digital Signature Standard (DSS). Federal Information Processing Standards Publication 186-3. US Department of Commerce/National Institute of Standards and Technology, Gaithersburg, Maryland, USA (February 2009), Includes change notice (October 5, 2001)
10. Hankerson, D.R., Menezes, A.J., Vanstone, S.A.: Guide to Elliptic Curve Cryptography. Springer, New York (2003)
11. Johnson, D.J., Menezes, A.J., Vanstone, S.A.: The Elliptic Curve Digital Signature Algorithm (ECDSA). International Journal of Information Security 1, 36–63 (2001)
12. LaMacchia, B., Lauter, K., Mityagin, A.: Stronger Security for Authenticated Key Exchange. International Association for Cryptologic Research, ePrint 2006/073 (2006)
13. Longa, P., Gebotys, C.: Efficient Techniques for High-Speed Elliptic Curve Cryptography. International Association for Cryptologic Research, IACR e/Print 2010-315
14. Law, L., Menezes, A., Qu, M., Solinas, J., Vanstone, S.: An Efficient Protocol for Authenticated Key Agreement. Centre for Applied Cryptographic Research, Corr 1998-05, University of Waterloo, Ontario, Canada (1998)
15. NIST Pub 800-56a. Recommendation for Pair-Wise Key Establishment Schemes Using Discrete Logarithm Cryptography (Revised). NIST Special Publication 800-56A. US Department of Commerce/National Institute of Standards and Technology, Springfield, Virginia (March 8, 2007)
16. NIST Pub 800-57. Recommendation for Key Management – Part 1: General (Revised), NIST Special Publication 800-57. US Department of Commerce/National Institute of Standards and Technology, Springfield, Virginia (March 8, 2007)
17. Proos, J.: Joint Sparse Forms and Generating Zero Columns when Combing. Centre for Applied Cryptographic Research, Corr 2003-23, University of Waterloo, Ontario, Canada (2003)
18. Solinas, J.: Low-Weight Binary Representations for Pairs of Integers. Centre for Applied Cryptographic Research, Corr 2001-41, University of Waterloo, Ontario, Canada (2001)

Wild McEliece

Daniel J. Bernstein[1], Tanja Lange[2], and Christiane Peters[2]

[1] Department of Computer Science
University of Illinois at Chicago, Chicago, IL 60607–7045, USA
djb@cr.yp.to
[2] Department of Mathematics and Computer Science
Technische Universiteit Eindhoven, P.O. Box 513, 5600 MB Eindhoven, Netherlands
tanja@hyperelliptic.org, c.p.peters@tue.nl

Abstract. The original McEliece cryptosystem uses length-n codes over $\mathbf{F}_2$ with dimension $\geq n - mt$ efficiently correcting t errors where $2^m \geq n$. This paper presents a generalized cryptosystem that uses length-n codes over small finite fields $\mathbf{F}_q$ with dimension $\geq n - m(q-1)t$ efficiently correcting $\lfloor qt/2 \rfloor$ errors where $q^m \geq n$. Previously proposed cryptosystems with the same length and dimension corrected only $\lfloor (q-1)t/2 \rfloor$ errors for $q \geq 3$. This paper also presents list-decoding algorithms that efficiently correct even more errors for the same codes over $\mathbf{F}_q$. Finally, this paper shows that the increase from $\lfloor (q-1)t/2 \rfloor$ errors to more than $\lfloor qt/2 \rfloor$ errors allows considerably smaller keys to achieve the same security level against all known attacks.

Keywords: McEliece cryptosystem, Niederreiter cryptosystem, Goppa codes, wild Goppa codes, list decoding.

1 Introduction

Code-based cryptography was proposed in 1978 by McEliece [28] and is one of the oldest public-key cryptosystems. Code-based cryptography has lately received a lot of attention because it is a good candidate for public-key cryptography that remains secure against attacks by a quantum computer. See Overbeck and Sendrier [32] for a detailed overview of the state of the art; see also Bernstein [3] for the fastest known quantum attack.

Encryption in McEliece's system is very efficient (a matrix-vector multiplication) and thanks to Patterson's algorithm [33] decryption is also efficient. However, this system is rarely used in implementations. The main complaint is that the public key is too large.

Obviously, in the post-quantum setting, some secure public-key cryptosystem is better than none, and so one can tolerate the large key sizes. However,

* This work was supported in part by the Cisco University Research Program, in part by the Fields Institute, and in part by the European Commission under Contract ICT-2007-216646 ECRYPT II. Permanent ID of this document: 69b9a7e1df30d1cd1aaade333b873601. Date: 2010.10.06.

A. Biryukov, G. Gong, and D.R. Stinson (Eds.): SAC 2010, LNCS 6544, pp. 143–158, 2011.

convincing users to already now switch over to code-based systems requires shorter keys.

McEliece's original system uses binary Goppa codes. Several smaller-key variants have been proposed using other codes, such as Reed–Solomon codes [31], generalized Reed–Solomon codes [38], quasi-dyadic codes [30] or geometric Goppa codes [22]. Unfortunately, many specific proposals turned out to be breakable.

The most confidence-inspiring proposal is still McEliece's original proposal to use binary Goppa codes. For these only information-set-decoding attacks apply; these are generic attacks that work against any code-based cryptosystem. In 2008, Bernstein, Lange, and Peters [7] ran a highly optimized information-set-decoding attack to break the specific parameters proposed by McEliece in 1978. After 30 years the system had lost little of its strength; the break would not have been possible with the computation power available in 1978.

The best defense against this attack is to use codes with a larger error-correcting capability. Slightly larger binary Goppa codes are still unbreakable by any algorithm known today.

The disadvantage of binary Goppa codes is that they have a comparably large key size. The construction of the code is over $\mathbf{F}_{2^m}$ but then only codewords with entries in $\mathbf{F}_2$ are considered. Doing a similar construction with $\mathbf{F}_q$, for a prime power $q > 2$, as base field decreases the key size at the same security level against information-set decoding, as shown by Peters [34]. However, this effect appears only with sufficiently big base fields such as $\mathbf{F}_{31}$; codes over $\mathbf{F}_3$ and $\mathbf{F}_4$ look worse than those over $\mathbf{F}_2$. The main reason making $\mathbf{F}_2$ better is that for binary Goppa codes it is well known that the subfield construction almost doubles the error-correcting capability of the code (more precisely, of known fast decoding algorithms), improving the security of the resulting scheme. For codes over other fields no increase in the error-correcting capability was used in the estimates.

In this paper we propose using "wild Goppa codes". These are subfield codes over small $\mathbf{F}_q$ that have an increase in error-correcting capability by a factor of about $q/(q-1)$. McEliece's construction using binary Goppa codes is the special case $q = 2$ of our construction.

These codes were analyzed in 1976 by Sugiyama, Kasahara, Hirasawa, and Namekawa [41] but have not been used in code-based cryptography so far. We explain how to use these codes in the McEliece cryptosystem and how to correct $\lfloor qt/2 \rfloor$ errors where previous proposals corrected only $\lfloor (q-1)t/2 \rfloor$ errors. We also present a list-decoding algorithm that allows even more errors.

In the following sections we give the mathematical background of our proposal and explain where the increase in error-correcting capability comes from. After reviewing structural attacks and their applicability to our proposal we present parameters for different base fields that achieve 128-bit security against information-set-decoding attacks. These show that base fields $\mathbf{F}_q$ with $q \leq 32$ are interesting alternatives to $\mathbf{F}_2$. For $\mathbf{F}_{32}$ the increase factor $q/(q-1)$ is close to 1 and so our results are close to the results of Peters; but for $q = 3, 4$, or 5 the change is significant. Using list decoding further decreases the size of the key and leads to the smallest public keys proposed for subfield Goppa codes.

2 The McEliece Cryptosystem

This section gives background on the McEliece cryptosystem in two variants: the classical setup by McEliece as in [28] and Niederreiter's variant [31].

Codes. A linear code of length n and dimension k over $\mathbf{F}_q$ is a k-dimensional subspace of $\mathbf{F}_q^n$. Such a code C can be represented (usually in many ways) by a *generator matrix*, a $k \times n$ matrix G such that $C = \{mG : m \in \mathbf{F}_q^k\}$; or by a *parity-check matrix*, an $(n-k) \times n$ matrix H such that $C = \{c \in \mathbf{F}_q^n : Hc^t = 0\}$.

Given a generator matrix G for a linear code C one can easily determine a parity-check matrix H for C by linear transformations. In particular, if G has *systematic form*, i.e., $G = (I_k|Q)$ where Q is a $k \times (n-k)$ matrix, then $H = (-Q^t|I_{n-k})$ is a parity-check matrix for the code $\mathbf{F}_q^k G$.

The *Hamming distance* between two words in $\mathbf{F}_q^n$ is the number of coordinates where they differ. The *Hamming weight* of a word is the number of nonzero coordinates in the word. The *minimum distance* of a nonzero linear code C is the smallest Hamming weight of a nonzero codeword in C.

A *decoding algorithm* for C receives a vector y in $\mathbf{F}_q^n$ and a positive integer w as inputs. The output is a codeword c in C at distance at most w from y if such c exists. The linear codes that are interesting candidates for the McEliece cryptosystem are codes allowing fast error correction, i.e. fast computation of an error vector e of weight $\leq w$ such that $y - e$ lies in C.

The McEliece public-key cryptosystem. Choose a linear code C over $\mathbf{F}_q$ of length n and dimension k which can correct w errors. Take a generator matrix G for C. Also choose uniformly at random an $n \times n$ permutation matrix P and an invertible $k \times k$ matrix S. Compute the matrix $\hat{G} = SGP$ and publish $\hat{G}$ together with the parameters n, k, and w. Make sure to keep G, P, and S as well as C secret.

Messages suitable for encryption are messages $m \in \mathbf{F}_q^k$. Encryption works as follows: Compute $m\hat{G}$. Compute a random error vector e of weight w. Send $y = m\hat{G} + e$.

Decryption: Compute $yP^{-1} = mSG + eP^{-1}$. Apply C's decoding algorithm to find mSG which is a codeword in C from which one obtains the original message m.

The Niederreiter public-key cryptosystem. Choose C as above. Take a parity-check matrix H of C. Choose a random $n \times n$ permutation matrix P and a random invertible $(n-k) \times (n-k)$ matrix M. Publish the matrix $\hat{H} = MHP$ and the error weight w. Again keep the code and the matrices H, P, and M secret.

Messages suitable for encryption are vectors $u \in \mathbf{F}_q^n$ of Hamming weight w. Encryption works as follows: Encrypt u by multiplication with $\hat{H}$. Send $y = \hat{H}u^t$.

Decryption: Compute v in $\mathbf{F}_q^n$ with $M^{-1}y = Hv^t$ by linear algebra. Note that $v^t - Pu^t$ lies in the kernel of H, i.e. is a codeword in C. Use the decoding algorithm to retrieve $v^t - Pu^t$, and since v is known get Pu^t. Inverting P yields u.

Choice of codes. Niederreiter proposed his system using generalized Reed–Solomon codes (GRS codes) whereas McEliece proposed to use classical binary

Goppa codes. The use of GRS codes was proven to be insecure in [38]. However, Niederreiter's system with binary Goppa codes has the same security as the McEliece cryptosystem as shown in [26].

3 Goppa Codes

This section gives an introduction to classical Goppa codes over $\mathbf{F}_q$.

Fix a prime power q; a positive integer m; a positive integer $n \leq q^m$; an integer $t < n/m$; distinct elements $a_1, \ldots, a_n$ in $\mathbf{F}_{q^m}$; and a polynomial $g(x)$ in $\mathbf{F}_{q^m}[x]$ of degree t such that $g(a_i) \neq 0$ for all i.

The words $c = (c_1, \ldots, c_n)$ in $\mathbf{F}_{q^m}^n$ with

$$\sum_{i=1}^{n} \frac{c_i}{x - a_i} \equiv 0 \pmod{g(x)} \tag{3.1}$$

form a linear code $\Gamma_{q^m}(a_1, \ldots, a_n, g)$ of length n and dimension $n - t$ over $\mathbf{F}_{q^m}$. The *Goppa code* $\Gamma_q(a_1, \ldots, a_n, g)$ with *Goppa polynomial* $g(x)$ and *support* $a_1, \ldots, a_n$ is the restriction of $\Gamma_{q^m}(a_1, \ldots, a_n, g)$ to the field $\mathbf{F}_q$, i.e., the set of elements $(c_1, \ldots, c_n)$ in $\mathbf{F}_q^n$ that satisfy (3.1). As a subfield subcode of $\Gamma_{q^m}(a_1, \ldots, a_n, g)$ the code $\Gamma_q(a_1, \ldots, a_n, g)$ has dimension $\geq n - mt$. Beware that there is a conflicting definition of "support" elsewhere in coding theory.

Let $\Gamma_q(a_1, \ldots, a_n, g)$ be a Goppa code of length n, support $a_1, \ldots, a_n$, and Goppa polynomial g of degree t. Assume that $\Gamma_q(a_1, \ldots, a_n, g)$ has dimension exactly $n - mt$. Fix a basis of $\mathbf{F}_{q^m}$ over $\mathbf{F}_q$ and write each element of $\mathbf{F}_{q^m}$ with respect to that basis. Then a parity-check matrix for $\Gamma_q(a_1, \ldots, a_n, g)$ is given by the $mt \times n$ matrix

$$H = \begin{pmatrix} \frac{1}{g(a_1)} & \frac{1}{g(a_2)} & \cdots & \frac{1}{g(a_n)} \\ \frac{a_1}{g(a_1)} & \frac{a_2}{g(a_2)} & \cdots & \frac{a_n}{g(a_n)} \\ \vdots & \vdots & \ddots & \vdots \\ \frac{a_1^{t-1}}{g(a_1)} & \frac{a_2^{t-1}}{g(a_2)} & \cdots & \frac{a_n^{t-1}}{g(a_n)} \end{pmatrix},$$

over $\mathbf{F}_q$ where each entry is actually a column vector written in the chosen $\mathbf{F}_q$-basis of $\mathbf{F}_{q^m}$.

The code $\Gamma_q(a_1, \ldots, a_n, g)$ is often referred to as a "classical" Goppa code since it is the basic construction of a genus-0 geometric Goppa code which Goppa later generalized for higher-genus varieties.

For the decoding algorithm in Section 5 it is useful to recall that the codewords in $\Gamma_{q^m}(a_1, \ldots, a_n, g)$ can be constructed by evaluating certain functions at $a_1, \ldots, a_n$. Specifically: Define $h(x) = \prod_i (x - a_i)$. Note that $g(x)$ and $h(x)$ are coprime. For each $f \in g\mathbf{F}_{q^m}[x]$ define

$$\mathrm{ev}(f) = \left(\frac{f(a_1)}{h'(a_1)}, \frac{f(a_2)}{h'(a_2)}, \ldots, \frac{f(a_n)}{h'(a_n)} \right),$$

where h' denotes the derivative of h.

If f has degree less than n then one can recover it from the the entries of $\text{ev}(f)$ by Lagrange interpolation: namely, $f/h = \sum_i (f(a_i)/h'(a_i))/(x-a_i)$. Consequently $\sum_i (\text{ev}(f))_i/(x-a_i)$ is 0 in $\mathbf{F}_{q^m}[x]/g$, where $(\text{ev}(f))_i$ denotes the i-th entry of $\text{ev}(f)$.

Let $(c_1,\ldots,c_n)$ in $\mathbf{F}_{q^m}^n$ be such that $\sum_i c_i/(x-a_i) \equiv 0 \pmod{g(x)}$. Define $f = \sum_i c_i h/(x-a_i)$ in $\mathbf{F}_{q^m}[x]$. Then $f \in g\mathbf{F}_{q^m}[x]$. Since the polynomial $\sum_i c_i h/(x-a_i)$ has degree less than n, also f has degree less than n. Moreover, $c_j = f(a_j)/h'(a_j) = \text{ev}(f)_j$.

Therefore $\Gamma_{q^m}(a_1,\ldots,a_n,g) = \{\text{ev}(f) : f \in g\mathbf{F}_{q^m}[x],\ \deg(f) < n\} = \{(f(a_1)/h'(a_1),\ldots,f(a_n)/h'(a_n)) : f \in g\mathbf{F}_{q^m}[x],\ \deg(f) < n\}$.

4 Wild McEliece

We propose using the McEliece cryptosystem, the Niederreiter cryptosystem, etc. with Goppa codes of the form $\Gamma_q(a_1,\ldots,a_n,g^{q-1})$ where g is an irreducible monic polynomial in $\mathbf{F}_{q^m}[x]$ of degree t. Note the exponent $q-1$ in g^{q-1}. We refer to these codes as "wild Goppa codes" for reasons explained later in this section.

We further propose to use error vectors of weight $\lfloor qt/2 \rfloor$. The advantage of wild Goppa codes is that they allow us to efficiently correct $\lfloor qt/2 \rfloor$ errors (or slightly more with the help of list decoding). For $q \in \{3,4,\ldots\}$ this is strikingly better than the performance of an irreducible polynomial of the same degree $(q-1)t$, namely correcting $\lfloor (q-1)t/2 \rfloor$ errors. This change does not hurt the code dimension: polynomials of the form g^{q-1} produce codes of dimension at least $n - m(q-1)t$ (and usually exactly $n - m(q-1)t$), just like irreducible polynomials of degree $(q-1)t$.

Comparison to previous proposals. For $q = 2$ this proposal is not new: it is exactly McEliece's original proposal to use a binary Goppa code $\Gamma_2(a_1,\ldots,a_n,g)$, where g is an irreducible polynomial of degree t, and to use error vectors of weight t. McEliece used Patterson's algorithm to efficiently decode t errors.

We also do not claim credit for considering Goppa codes over slightly larger fields $\mathbf{F}_3$, $\mathbf{F}_4$, etc. Peters in [34, Section 8] pointed out that switching from binary Goppa codes to codes of the form $\Gamma_{31}(a_1,\ldots,a_n,g)$, with $t/2$ errors, reduces the key size by a factor of more than 2 while preserving security against all known attacks.

What is new in our cryptosystem is the use of Goppa polynomials of the form g^{q-1} for $q \geq 3$, allowing us to correct more errors for the same field size, the same code length, and the same code dimension.

Minimum distance of wild Goppa codes. The following theorem is the main theorem of the 1976 paper [41] by Sugiyama, Kasahara, Hirasawa, and Namekawa. What the theorem states is that, for any monic squarefree polynomial g in $\mathbf{F}_{q^m}[x]$, the code $\Gamma_q(a_1,\ldots,a_n,g^{q-1})$ is the same as $\Gamma_q(a_1,\ldots,a_n,g^q)$. The code therefore has minimum distance at least $qt+1$. Efficient decoding of $\lfloor qt/2 \rfloor$ errors requires more effort and is discussed in the next section.

The case $q = 2$ of this theorem is due to Goppa, using a different proof that can be found in many textbooks. The case $q \geq 3$ has received less attention. We include a streamlined proof to keep this paper self-contained.

The proof immediately generalizes from the pair (g^{q-1}, g^q) to the pair (g^{rq-1}, g^{rq}), and to coprime products of such pairs. These generalizations also appear in [41]. Wirtz in [44], and independently Katsman and Tsfasman in [23], further generalized the results of [41] to geometric Goppa codes. See Janwa and Moreno [22] for discussion of the possibility of using geometric Goppa codes in the McEliece cryptosystem but also Minder's thesis [29] and the paper by Faure and Minder [15] for attacks on the elliptic-curve version and the genus-2 version. We do not consider this possibility further in this paper.

Theorem 4.1 *Let q be a prime power. Let m be a positive integer. Let n be an integer with $1 \leq n \leq q^m$. Let $a_1, a_2, \ldots, a_n$ be distinct elements of $\mathbf{F}_{q^m}$. Let g be a monic squarefree polynomial in $\mathbf{F}_{q^m}[x]$ coprime to $(x - a_1) \cdots (x - a_n)$. Then $\Gamma_q(a_1, a_2, \ldots, a_n, g^{q-1}) = \Gamma_q(a_1, a_2, \ldots, a_n, g^q)$.*

Proof. If $\sum_i c_i/(x - a_i) = 0$ in $\mathbf{F}_{q^m}[x]/g^q$ then certainly $\sum_i c_i/(x - a_i) = 0$ in $\mathbf{F}_{q^m}[x]/g^{q-1}$.

Conversely, consider any $(c_1, c_2, \ldots, c_n) \in \mathbf{F}_q^n$ such that $\sum_i c_i/(x - a_i) = 0$ in $\mathbf{F}_{q^m}[x]/g^{q-1}$. Find an extension k of $\mathbf{F}_{q^m}$ so that g splits into linear factors in $k[x]$. Then $\sum_i c_i/(x-a_i) = 0$ in $k[x]/g^{q-1}$, so $\sum_i c_i/(x-a_i) = 0$ in $k[x]/(x-r)^{q-1}$ for each factor $x - r$ of g. The elementary series expansion

$$\frac{1}{x - a_i} = -\frac{1}{a_i - r} - \frac{x - r}{(a_i - r)^2} - \frac{(x - r)^2}{(a_i - r)^3} - \cdots$$

then implies

$$\sum_i \frac{c_i}{a_i - r} + (x - r) \sum_i \frac{c_i}{(a_i - r)^2} + (x - r)^2 \sum_i \frac{c_i}{(a_i - r)^3} + \cdots = 0$$

in $k[x]/(x - r)^{q-1}$; i.e., $\sum_i c_i/(a_i - r) = 0$, $\sum_i c_i/(a_i - r)^2 = 0$, $\ldots$, $\sum_i c_i/(a_i - r)^{q-1} = 0$. Now take the qth power of the equation $\sum_i c_i/(a_i - r) = 0$, and use the fact that $c_i \in \mathbf{F}_q$, to obtain $\sum_i c_i/(a_i - r)^q = 0$. Work backwards to see that $\sum_i c_i/(x - a_i) = 0$ in $k[x]/(x - r)^q$.

By hypothesis g is the product of its distinct linear factors $x - r$. Therefore g^q is the product of the coprime polynomials $(x - r)^q$, and $\sum_i c_i/(x - a_i) = 0$ in $k[x]/g^q$; i.e., $\sum_i c_i/(x - a_i) = 0$ in $\mathbf{F}_{q^m}[x]/g^q$. □

The "wild" terminology. To explain the name "wild Goppa codes" we briefly review the standard concept of wild ramification.

A prime p "ramifies" in a number field L if the unique factorization $p\mathcal{O}_L = Q_1^{e_1} Q_2^{e_2} \cdots$ has an exponent e_i larger than 1, where $\mathcal{O}_L$ is the ring of integers of L and $Q_1, Q_2, \ldots$ are distinct maximal ideals of $\mathcal{O}_L$. Each Q_i with $e_i > 1$ is "ramified over p"; this ramification is "wild" if e_i is divisible by p.

If $\mathcal{O}_L/p$ has the form $\mathbf{F}_p[x]/f$, where f is a monic polynomial in $\mathbf{F}_p[x]$, then the maximal ideals $Q_1, Q_2, \ldots$ correspond naturally to the irreducible factors of f, and the exponents $e_1, e_2, \ldots$ correspond naturally to the exponents in the factorization of f. In particular, the ramification corresponding to an irreducible factor of f is wild if and only if the exponent is divisible by p.

Similar comments apply to more general extensions of global fields. Ramification corresponding to an irreducible factor φ of a monic polynomial f in $\mathbf{F}_{p^m}[x]$ is wild if and only if the exponent is divisible by p, i.e., the local component of f is a power of φ^p. We take the small step of referring to φ^p as being "wild", and referring to the corresponding Goppa codes as "wild Goppa codes". Of course, if the Goppa code for φ^p is wild, then the Goppa code for φ^{p-1} must also be wild, since (by Theorem 4.1) it is the same code.

The traditional concept of wild ramification is defined by the characteristic of the base field. We find it more useful to allow a change of base from $\mathbf{F}_p$ to $\mathbf{F}_q$, generalizing the definition of wildness to use the size of $\mathbf{F}_q$ rather than just the characteristic of $\mathbf{F}_q$.

5 Decrypting Wild-McEliece Ciphertexts

The main problem faced by a wild-McEliece receiver is to decode $\lfloor qt/2 \rfloor$ errors in the code $\Gamma = \Gamma_q(a_1, \ldots, a_n, g^{q-1})$: i.e., to find a codeword $c = (c_1, \ldots, c_n) \in \Gamma$, given a received word $y = (y_1, \ldots, y_n) \in \mathbf{F}_q^n$ at Hamming distance $\lfloor qt/2 \rfloor$ from c. This section presents an asymptotically fast algorithm that decodes $\lfloor qt/2 \rfloor$ errors, and then a "list decoding" algorithm that decodes even more errors.

Classical decoding. Recall from Theorem 4.1 that

$$\begin{aligned}\Gamma &= \Gamma_q(a_1, \ldots, a_n, g^q) \\ &\subseteq \Gamma_{q^m}(a_1, \ldots, a_n, g^q) \\ &= \left\{ \left(\frac{f(a_1)}{h'(a_1)}, \ldots, \frac{f(a_n)}{h'(a_n)} \right) : f \in g^q \mathbf{F}_{q^m}[x], \deg f < n \right\}\end{aligned}$$

where $h = (x - a_1) \cdots (x - a_n)$. We thus view the target codeword $c = (c_1, \ldots, c_n) \in \Gamma$ as a sequence $(f(a_1)/h'(a_1), \ldots, f(a_n)/h'(a_n))$ of function values, where f is a multiple of g^q of degree below n. We are given y, the same sequence with $\lfloor qt/2 \rfloor$ errors, or more generally with $\le \lfloor qt/2 \rfloor$ errors. We reconstruct c from y as follows:

- Interpolate $y_1 h'(a_1)/g(a_1)^q, \ldots, y_n h'(a_n)/g(a_n)^q$ into a polynomial φ: i.e., construct the unique $\varphi \in \mathbf{F}_{q^m}[x]$ such that $\varphi(a_i) = y_i h'(a_i)/g(a_i)^q$ and $\deg \varphi < n$.
- Compute the continued fraction of φ/h to degree $\lfloor qt/2 \rfloor$: i.e., apply the Euclidean algorithm to h and φ, stopping with the first remainder $v_0 h - v_1 \varphi$ of degree $< n - \lfloor qt/2 \rfloor$.
- Compute $f = (\varphi - v_0 h/v_1) g^q$.
- Compute $c = (f(a_1)/h'(a_1), \ldots, f(a_n)/h'(a_n))$.

This algorithm uses $n^{1+o(1)}$ operations in $\mathbf{F}_{q^m}$ if multiplication, evaluation, interpolation, and continued-fraction computation are carried out by standard FFT-based subroutines; see [5] for a survey of those subroutines.

To see that this algorithm works, observe that φ has many values in common with the target polynomial f/g^q: specifically, $\varphi(a_i){=}f(a_i)/g(a_i)^q$ for all but $\lfloor qt/2 \rfloor$ values of i. In other words, the error-locator polynomial

$$\epsilon = \prod_{i:\frac{f(a_i)}{g(a_i)^q} \neq \varphi(a_i)} (x - a_i)$$

has degree at most $\lfloor qt/2 \rfloor$. The difference $\varphi - f/g^q$ is a multiple of h/ϵ, say $\delta h/\epsilon$. Now the difference $\delta/\epsilon - \varphi/h = -(f/g^q)/h$ is smaller than $1/x^{qt}$ and therefore smaller than $1/\epsilon^2$, so δ/ϵ is a "best approximation" to φ/h, so δ/ϵ must appear as a convergent to the continued fraction of φ/h, specifically the convergent at degree $\lfloor qt/2 \rfloor$. Consequently $\delta/\epsilon = v_0/v_1$; i.e., $f/g^q = \varphi - v_0 h/v_1$.

More generally, one can use any Reed–Solomon decoder to reconstruct f/g^q from the values $f(a_1)/g(a_1)^q, \ldots, f(a_n)/g(a_n)^q$ with $\lfloor qt/2 \rfloor$ errors. This is an illustration of the following sequence of standard transformations:

$$\text{Reed–Solomon decoder} \Rightarrow \text{generalized Reed–Solomon decoder}$$
$$\Rightarrow \text{alternant decoder} \Rightarrow \text{Goppa decoder.}$$

The resulting decoder corrects $\lfloor (\deg g)/2 \rfloor$ errors for general Goppa codes $\Gamma_q(a_1, \ldots, a_n, g)$; in particular, $\lfloor q(\deg g)/2 \rfloor$ errors for $\Gamma_q(a_1, \ldots, a_n, g^q)$; and so $\lfloor q(\deg g)/2 \rfloor$ errors for $\Gamma_q(a_1, \ldots, a_n, g^{q-1})$, by Theorem 4.1.

We do not claim that the particular algorithm stated above is the fastest possible decoder, and in particular we do not claim that it is quite as fast as Patterson's algorithm [33] for $q = 2$. However, it has essentially the same scalability in n as Patterson's algorithm, works for general q, and is obviously fast enough to be usable.

An example implementation of a wild-Goppa-code decoder in the Sage computer-algebra system [39] can be found at `http://pqcrypto.org/users/christiane/wild.html`.

List decoding. By switching from a classical Reed–Solomon decoding algorithm to the Guruswami–Sudan list-decoding algorithm [19] we can efficiently correct $n - \sqrt{n(n-qt)} > \lfloor qt/2 \rfloor$ errors in the function values $f(a_1)/g(a_1)^q, \ldots, f(a_n)/g(a_n)^q$. This algorithm is not as fast as a classical decoder but still takes polynomial time. Consequently we can handle $n - \sqrt{n(n-qt)}$ errors in the wild Goppa code $\Gamma_q(a_1, \ldots, a_n, g^{q-1})$.

This algorithm can, at least in theory, produce several possible codewords c. This does not pose a problem for the CCA2-secure variants of the McEliece cryptosystem introduced by Kobara and Imai in [25]: those variants automatically reject all codewords that do not include proper labels cryptographically protected by an "all-or-nothing transform".

As above, we do not claim that this algorithm is the fastest possible decoder. In particular, for $q = 2$ the same error-correcting capacity was obtained by Bernstein in [4] using a more complicated algorithm, analogous to Patterson's algorithm; we do not claim that the $\Gamma(a_1, \ldots, a_n, g^2)$ approach is as fast as that algorithm.

With more decoding effort we can handle a few additional errors by the standard idea of combinatorially guessing those errors. Each additional error produces a noticeable reduction of key size, as shown later in this paper. In many applications, the McEliece decoding time is unnoticeable while the McEliece key size is a problem, so allowing extra errors at the expense of decoding time is a good tradeoff.

6 Attacks

This section discusses several attacks against the wild McEliece cryptosystem. All of the attacks scale poorly to large key sizes; Section 7 presents parameters that are safe against all of these attacks. We do not claim novelty for any of the attack ideas.

We emphasize that the wild McEliece cryptosystem includes, as a special case, the original McEliece cryptosystem. A complete break of the wild McEliece cryptosystem would therefore imply a complete break of the original McEliece cryptosystem, a system that has survived scrutiny for 32 years. It is of course possible that there is a magical dividing line between $q = 2$ and $q = 3$, an attack that breaks every new case of our proposal while leaving the original cryptosystem untouched, but we have not found any such line.

We focus on inversion attacks, i.e., attacks against the one-wayness of wild McEliece encryption. There are several well-known chosen-ciphertext attacks that break semantic security without breaking one-wayness, but all of those attacks are stopped by standard conversions; see [25].

Information-set decoding. The top threat against the original McEliece cryptosystem, the attack algorithm that has always dictated key-size recommendations, is information-set decoding, which as mentioned in the introduction is a generic decoding method that does not rely on any particular code structure. The same attack also appears to be the top threat against the wild McEliece cryptosystem for $\mathbf{F}_3$, $\mathbf{F}_4$, etc.

The exact complexity of information-set decoding is not easy to state concisely. We rely on, and refer the reader to, the recent analysis of state-of-the-art $\mathbf{F}_q$ information-set decoding by Peters in [34], combining various improvements from [40], [11], [7], and [16]. To find the parameters in Section 7 we searched various (n, k, t) and applied the complexity formulas from [34] to evaluate the security level of each (n, k, t).

Generalized birthday attacks. Wagner's "generalized birthday attacks" [43] can also be used as a generic decoding method. The Courtois–Finiasz–Sendrier signature system [13] was attacked by Bleichenbacher using this method. However, information-set decoding is always more efficient than generalized birthday attacks as an attack against code-based encryption. See [16] for further discussion; the analysis is essentially independent of q.

Polynomial-searching attacks. There are approximately q^{mt}/t monic irreducible polynomials g of degree t in $\mathbf{F}_{q^m}[x]$, and therefore approximately q^{mt}/t

choices of g^{q-1}. One can marginally expand the space of polynomials by considering more general squarefree polynomials g, but we focus on irreducible polynomials to avoid any unnecessary security questions.

An attacker can try to guess the Goppa polynomial g^{q-1} and then apply Sendrier's "support-splitting algorithm" [37] to compute the support $(a_1, \ldots, a_n)$. We combine two defenses against this attack:

- We keep q^{mt}/t extremely large, so that guessing g^{q-1} has negligible chance of success. Parameters with q^{mt}/t smaller than 2^{128} are marked with the international biohazard symbol ☣ in Section 7.
- We keep n noticeably lower than q^m, so that there are many possible subsets $\{a_1, \ldots, a_n\}$ of $\mathbf{F}_{q^m}$. The support-splitting algorithm takes $\{a_1, \ldots, a_n\}$ as an input along with g.

The second defense is unusual: it is traditional, although not universal, to take $n = 2^m$ and $q = 2$, so that the only possible set $\{a_1, \ldots, a_n\}$ is $\mathbf{F}_{2^m}$. The strength of the second defense is unclear: we might be the first to ask whether the support-splitting idea can be generalized to handle many sets $\{a_1, \ldots, a_n\}$ simultaneously, and we would not be surprised if the answer turns out to be yes. However, the first defense is well known for $q = 2$ and appears to be strong.

Algebraic attacks. In a recent paper [14], Faugère, Otmani, Perret, and Tillich broke many (but not all) of the "quasi-cyclic" and "quasi-dyadic" variants of the McEliece cryptosystem that had been proposed in the papers [2] and [30] in 2009. Gauthier Umana and Leander in [17] independently broke some of the same systems.

These variants have highly regular support structures allowing very short public keys. The attacks set up systems of low-degree algebraic equations for the code support, taking advantage of the fact that there are not many variables in the support.

The paper [14] indicates that the same attack strategy is of no use against the original McEliece cryptosystem because there are "much more unknowns" than in the broken proposals: for example, 1024 variables in $\mathbf{F}_{1024}$, totalling 10240 bits. Our recommended parameters also have very large supports, with no particular structure, so algebraic attacks do not appear to pose any threat.

7 Parameters

The public key in Kobara and Imai's CCA2-secure variant [25] of the McEliece cryptosystem can be stored in systematic form as $(n-k)k$ entries in $\mathbf{F}_q$. The same is true for the Niederreiter variant; see, e.g., [32, Algorithm 2.3]. The simplest representation of an element of $\mathbf{F}_q$ takes $\lceil \log_2 q \rceil$ bits (e.g., 3 bits for $q = 5$), but a sequence of elements can be compressed: one stores a batch of b elements of $\mathbf{F}_q$ in $\lceil \log_2 q^b \rceil$ bits, at the expense of some easy computation to recover the individual elements. As b grows the storage per field element drops to approximately $\log_2 q$ bits, so $(n-k)k$ elements can be stored using about $\lceil (n-k)k \log_2 q \rceil$ bits.

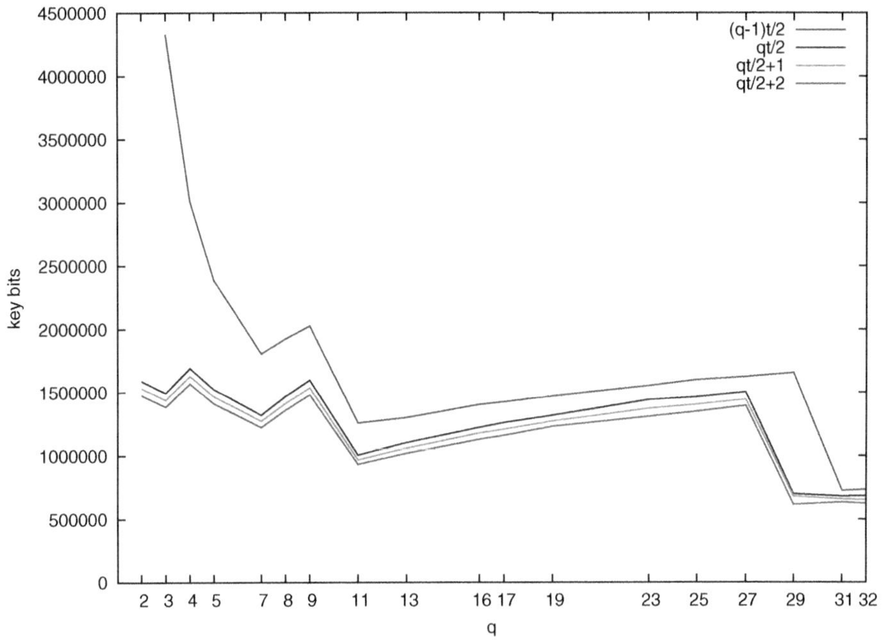

Fig. 7.1. Decrease in key sizes when correcting more errors (128-bit security). See Table 7.1.

Table 7.1 gives parameters (n, k, t) for the McEliece cryptosystem using a code $\Gamma = \Gamma_q(a_1, \ldots, a_n, g^{q-1})$ that provides 128-bit security against the attack in [34]. We chose the code length n, the degree t of g and the dimension $k = n - \lceil \log_q n \rceil t(q-1)$ of Γ to minimize the key size $\lceil (n-k)k \log_2 q \rceil$ for 128-bit security when w errors are added. We compare four cases:

- $w = \lfloor (q-1)t/2 \rfloor$ added errors using classical decoding techniques,
- $w = \lfloor qt/2 \rfloor$ added errors using Theorem 4.1,
- $w = \lfloor qt/2 \rfloor + 1$ added errors, and
- $w = \lfloor qt/2 \rfloor + 2$ added errors,

where the last two cases use Theorem 4.1 together with list decoding as in Section 5. See Figure 7.1 for a graph of the resulting key sizes.

In [7] a Goppa code $\Gamma_2(a_1, \ldots, a_n, g)$ with length 2960, dimension 2288, and g of degree $t = 56$ is proposed for 128-bit security when 57 errors are added by the sender. A key in this setting has 1537536 bits. This is consistent with our table entry for $q = 2$ with $w = \lfloor qt/2 \rfloor + 1$ added errors.

Small q's larger than 2 provide astonishingly good results. For larger q's one has to be careful: parameters optimized against information-set decoding have q^{mt}/t dropping as q grows, reducing the number of suitable polynomials g in

$\mathbf{F}_{q^m}[x]$ significantly. For example, there are only about 2^{28} monic irreducible polynomials g of degree 3 over $\mathbf{F}_{31^2}[x]$, while there are about 2^{227} monic irreducible polynomials g of degree 20 in $\mathbf{F}_{5^5}[x]$. The smallest q for which the g possibilities can be enumerated in less time than information-set decoding is $q = 11$: the parameters $(n, k, t) = (1199, 899, 10)$ satisfy $q^{\lceil \log_q n \rceil t}/t \approx 2^{100}$, so there are about 2^{100} monic irreducible polynomials g in $\mathbf{F}_{11^3}[x]$ of degree $t = 10$. This is one of the cases marked by ☣ in Table 7.1. The security of these cases depends on the strength of the second defense discussed in Section 6.

The ☣ symbol is omitted from the $\lfloor (q-1)t/2 \rfloor$ column because that relatively low error-correcting capability, and relatively high key size, can be achieved by non-wild codes with many more choices of g.

Table 7.1. Decrease in key sizes when correcting more errors (128-bit security). Each entry in the first column states q. Each entry in the subsequent columns states key size, (n, k, t) and the number of errors.

q	$\lfloor (q-1)t/2 \rfloor$	$\lfloor qt/2 \rfloor$	$\lfloor qt/2 \rfloor + 1$	$\lfloor qt/2 \rfloor + 2$
2	—	1590300 bits: (3009, 2325, 57) 57 errors	1533840 bits: (2984, 2324, 55) 56 errors	1477008 bits: (2991, 2367, 52) 54 errors
3	4331386 bits: (3946, 3050, 56) 56 errors	1493796 bits: (2146, 1530, 44) 66 errors	1439876 bits: (2133, 1545, 42) 64 errors	1385511 bits: (2121, 1561, 40) 62 errors
4	3012336 bits: (2886, 2202, 38) errors 57	1691424 bits: (2182, 1678, 28) errors 56	1630044 bits: (2163, 1677, 27) 55 errors	1568700 bits: (2193, 1743, 25) 52 errors
5	2386014 bits: (2395, 1835, 28) 56 errors	1523278 bits: (1931, 1491, 22) 55 errors	1468109 bits: (1877, 1437, 22) 56 errors	1410804 bits: (1919, 1519, 20) 52 errors
7	1806298 bits: (1867, 1411, 19) 57 errors	1319502 bits: (1608, 1224, 16) 56 errors	1273147 bits: (1565, 1181, 16) 57 errors	1223423 bits: (1633, 1297, 14) 51 errors
8	1924608 bits: (1880, 1432, 16) 56 errors	1467648 bits: (1640, 1248, 14) 56 errors	1414140 bits: (1659, 1295, 13) 53 errors	1359540 bits: (1609, 1245, 13) 54 errors
9	2027941 bits: (1876, 1428, 14) 56 errors	1597034 bits: (1696, 1312, 12) 54 errors	1537389 bits: (1647, 1263, 12) 55 errors	1481395 bits: (1601, 1217, 12) 56 errors
11	1258265 bits: (1286, 866, 14) 70 errors	1004619 bits: (1268, 968, 10)☣ 55 errors	968295 bits: (1233, 933, 10)☣ 56 errors	933009 bits: (1199, 899, 10)☣ 57 errors
13	1300853 bits: (1409, 1085, 9) 54 errors	1104093 bits: (1324, 1036, 8)☣ 52 errors	1060399 bits: (1283, 995, 8)☣ 53 errors	1018835 bits: (1244, 956, 8)☣ 54 errors

Table 7.1. *(continued)*

q	$\lfloor (q-1)t/2 \rfloor$	$\lfloor qt/2 \rfloor$	$\lfloor qt/2 \rfloor + 1$	$\lfloor qt/2 \rfloor + 2$
16	1404000 bits: (1335, 975, 8) 60 errors	1223460 bits: (1286, 971, 7)☣ 56 errors	1179360 bits: (1251, 936, 7)☣ 57 errors	1129680 bits: (1316, 1046, 6)☣ 50 errors
17	1424203 bits: (1373, 1037, 7) 56 errors	1260770 bits: (1359, 1071, 6)☣ 51 errors	1208974 bits: (1315, 1027, 6)☣ 52 errors	1160709 bits: (1274, 986, 6)☣ 53 errors
19	1472672 bits: (1394, 1070, 6) 54 errors	1318523 bits: (1282, 958, 6)☣ 57 errors	1274481 bits: (1250, 926, 6)☣ 58 errors	1231815 bits: (1219, 895, 6)☣ 59 errors
23	1553980 bits: (1371, 1041, 5) 55 errors	1442619 bits: (1472, 1208, 4)☣ 46 errors	1373354 bits: (1414, 1150, 4)☣ 47 errors	1310060 bits: (1361, 1097, 4)☣ 48 errors
25	1599902 bits: (1317, 957, 5) 60 errors	1465824 bits: (1384, 1096, 4)☣ 50 errors	1405640 bits: (1339, 1051, 4)☣ 51 errors	1349468 bits: (1297, 1009, 4)☣ 52 errors
27	1624460 bits: (1407, 1095, 4) 52 errors	1502811 bits: (1325, 1013, 4)☣ 54 errors	1446437 bits: (1287, 975, 4)☣ 55 errors	1395997 bits: (1253, 941, 4)☣ 56 errors
29	1656766 bits: (1351, 1015, 4) 56 errors	699161 bits: (794, 514, 5)☣ 72 errors	681478 bits: (781, 501, 5)☣ 73 errors	617003 bits: (791, 567, 4)☣ 60 errors
31	726484 bits: (851, 611, 4) 60 errors	681302 bits: (813, 573, 4)☣ 62 errors	659899 bits: (795, 555, 4)☣ 63 errors	634930 bits: (892, 712, 3)☣ 48 errors
32	735320 bits: (841, 593, 4) 62 errors	685410 bits: (923, 737, 3)☣ 48 errors	654720 bits: (890, 704, 3)☣ 49 errors	624960 bits: (858, 672, 3)☣ 50 errors

References

[1] —- (No Editor), Eleventh International Workshop on Algebraic and Combinatorial Coding Theory, Pamporovo, Bulgaria, June 16–22 (2008), `http://www.moi.math.bas.bg/acct2008/acct2008.html`, See [15]

[2] Berger, T.P., Cayrel, P.-L., Gaborit, P., Otmani, A.: Reducing Key Length of the McEliece Cryptosystem. In: AFRICACRYPT 2009 [35], pp. 77–97 (2009), Citations in This Document: §6

[3] Bernstein, D.J.: Grover vs. McEliece. In: PQCrypto 2010 [36], pp. 73–80 (2010), `http://cr.yp.to/papers.html#grovercode`, Citations in This Document: §1

[4] Bernstein, D.J.: List Decoding for Binary Goppa Codes (2008), `http://cr.yp.to/papers.html#goppalist`, Citations in This Document: §5

[5] Bernstein, D.J.: Fast Multiplication and Its Applications. In: Algorithmic Number Theory [10], pp. 325–384 (2008), http://cr.yp.to/papers.html#multapps, Citations in This Document: §5

[6] Bernstein, D.J., Buchmann, J., Dahmen, E. (eds.): Post-Quantum Cryptography. Springer, Heidelberg (2009) ISBN 978-3-540-88701-0, See [32]

[7] Bernstein, D.J., Lange, T., Peters, C.: Attacking and Defending the McEliece Cryptosystem. In: PQCrypto 2008 [9], pp. 31–46 (2008), http://eprint.iacr.org/2008/318, Citations in This Document: §1, §6, §7

[8] Boyd, C. (ed.): Advances in Cryptology — ASIACRYPT 2001, Proceedings of the 7th International Conference on the Theory and Application of Cryptology and Information Security Held on the Gold Coast, December 9-13, 2001. LNCS, vol. 2248. Springer, Heidelberg (2001) ISBN 3-540-42987-5, See [13]

[9] Buchmann, J., Ding, J. (eds.): Proceedings of Post-Quantum Cryptography, Second International Workshop, PQCrypto 2008, Cincinnati, OH, USA, October 17-19, 2008. LNCS, vol. 5299. Springer, Heidelberg (2008), See [7]

[10] Buhler, J., Stevenhagen, P. (eds.): Algorithmic Number Theory: Lattices, Number Fields, Curves and Cryptography. Cambridge University Press, Cambridge (2008) ISBN 978-0521808545, See [5]

[11] Canteaut, A., Chabaud, F.: A New Algorithm for Finding Minimum-Weight Words in a Linear Code: Application to McEliece's Cryptosystem and to Narrow-Sense BCH Codes of Length 511. IEEE Transactions on Information Theory 44, 367–378 (1998), http://hal.inria.fr/inria-00074006/en/, MR 98m:94043, Citations in This Document: §6

[12] Cohen, G.D., Wolfmann, J. (eds.): Coding Theory and Applications. LNCS, vol. 388. Springer, Heidelberg (1989), See [40]

[13] Courtois, N., Finiasz, M., Sendrier, N.: How to Achieve a McEliece-Based Digital Signature Scheme. In: ASIACRYPT 2001 [8], pp. 157–174 (2001), http://hal.inria.fr/docs/00/07/25/11/PDF/RR-4118.pdf, MR 2003h:94028, Citations in This Document: §6

[14] Faugère, J.-C., Otmani, A., Perret, L., Tillich, J.-P.: Algebraic Cryptanalysis of McEliece Variants with Compact Keys. In: EUROCRYPT 2010 [18], pp. 279–298 (2010), Citations in This Document: §6, §6

[15] Faure, C., Minder, L.: Cryptanalysis of the McEliece Cryptosystem over Hyperelliptic Codes. In: ACCT 2008 [1], pp. 99–107 (2008), http://www.moi.math.bas.bg/acct2008/b17.pdf , Citations in This Document: §4

[16] Finiasz, M., Sendrier, N.: Security Bounds for the Design of Code-Based Cryptosystems. In: ASIACRYPT 2009 [27], pp. 88–105 (2009), http://eprint.iacr.org/2009/414 , Citations in This Document: §6, §6

[17] Gauthier Umana, V., Leander, G.: Practical Key Recovery Attacks on Two McEliece Variants (2009), http://eprint.iacr.org/2009/509, Citations in This Document: §6

[18] Gilbert, H. (ed.): Proceedings of Advances in Cryptology — EUROCRYPT 2010, 29th Annual International Conference on the Theory and Applications of Cryptographic Techniques, French Riviera, May 30-June 3, 2010. LNCS, vol. 6110. Springer, Heidelberg (2010), See [14]

[19] Guruswami, V., Sudan, M.: Improved Decoding of Reed-Solomon and Algebraic-Geometry Codes. IEEE Transactions on Information Theory 45, 1757–1767 (1999), http://theory.lcs.mit.edu/~madhu/bib.html, ISSN 0018-9448, MR 2000j:94033, Citations in This Document: §5

[20] Isaacs, I.M., Lichtman, A.I., Passman, D.S., Sehgal, S.K., Sloane, N.J.A., Zassenhaus, H.J. (eds.): Representation Theory, Group Rings, and Coding Theory: Papers in Honor of S. D. Berman. Contemporary Mathematics, vol. 93. American Mathematical Society, Providence (1989), See [23]

[21] Jacobson Jr., M.J., Rijmen, V., Safavi-Naini, R. (eds.): Selected Areas in Cryptography, 16th Annual International Workshop, SAC 2009, Calgary, Alberta, Canada, August 13-14, 2009. LNCS, vol. 5867. Springer, Heidelberg (2009), See [30]

[22] Janwa, H., Moreno, O.: McEliece Public Key Cryptosystems Using Algebraic-Geometric Codes. Designs, Codes and Cryptography 3, 293–307 (1996), Citations in This Document: §1, §4

[23] Katsman, G.L., Tsfasman, M.A.: A Remark on Algebraic Geometric Codes. In: Representation Theory, Group Rings, and Coding Theory [20], pp. 197–199, Citations in This Document: §4

[24] Kim, K. (ed.): Public Key Cryptography: Proceedings of the 4th International Workshop on Practice and Theory in Public Key Cryptosystems (PKC 2001) Held on Cheju Island, February 13-15, 2001. LNCS, vol. 1992. Springer, Heidelberg (2001), See [25]

[25] Kobara, K., Imai, H.: Semantically Secure McEliece Public-Key Cryptosystems — Conversions for McEliece PKC. In: PKC 2001 [24], pp. 19–35 (2001), MR 2003c:94027, Citations in This Document: §5, §6, §7

[26] Li, Y.X., Deng, R.H., Wang, X.M.: On the Equivalence of McEliece's and Niederreiter's Public-Key Cryptosystems. IEEE Transactions on Information Theory 40, 271–273 (1994), Citations in This Document: §2

[27] Matsui, M. (ed.): Proceedings of Advances in Cryptology — ASIACRYPT 2009, 15th International Conference on the Theory and Application of Cryptology and Information Security, Tokyo, Japan, December 6-10, 2009. LNCS, vol. 5912. Springer, Heidelberg (2009), See [16]

[28] McEliece, R.J.: A Public-Key Cryptosystem Based on Algebraic Coding Theory, JPL DSN Progress Report, pp. 114–116 (1978), `http://ipnpr.jpl.nasa.gov/progress_report2/42-44/44N.PDF`, Citations in This Document: §1, §2

[29] Minder, L.: Cryptography Based on Error-Correcting Codes, Ph.D. Thesis, EPFL, PhD thesis 3846 (2007), Citations in This Document: §4

[30] Misoczki, R., Barreto, P.S.L.M.: Compact McEliece Keys from Goppa Codes. In: SAC 2009 [21], pp. 376–392 (2009), Citations in This Document: §1, §6

[31] Niederreiter, H.: Knapsack-Type Cryptosystems and Algebraic Coding Theory. Problems of Control and Information Theory 15, 159–166 (1986), Citations in This Document: §1, §2

[32] Overbeck, R., Sendrier, N.: Code-Based Cryptography. In: Post-Quantum Cryptography [6], pp. 95–145 (2009), Citations in This Document: §1, §7

[33] Patterson, N.J.: The Algebraic Decoding of Goppa Codes. IEEE Transactions on Information Theory 21, 203–207 (1975), Citations in This Document: §1, §5

[34] Peters, C.: Information-Set Decoding for Linear Codes over $\mathbf{F}_q$. In: PQCrypto 2010 [36], pp. 81–94 (2010), `http://eprint.iacr.org/2009/589`, Citations in This Document: §1, §4, §6, §6, §7

[35] Preneel, B. (ed.): Progress in Cryptology — AFRICACRYPT 2009, Second International Conference on Cryptology in Africa, Gammarth, Tunisia, June 21-25, 2009. LNCS, vol. 5580. Springer, Heidelberg (2009), See [2]

[36] Sendrier, N. (ed.): Post-Quantum Cryptography, Third International Workshop, PQCrypto, Darmstadt, Germany, May 25-28, 2010. LNCS, vol. 6061. Springer, Heidelberg (2010), See [3], [34]
[37] Sendrier, N.: Finding the Permutation between Equivalent Linear Codes: The Support Splitting Algorithm. IEEE Transactions on Information Theory 46, 1193–1203 (2000), http://hal.inria.fr/docs/00/07/30/37/PDF/ RR-3637.pdf , MR 2001e:94017, Citations in This Document: §6
[38] Sidelnikov, V.M., Shestakov, S.O.: On an Encoding System Constructed on the Basis of Generalized Reed-Solomon Codes. Discrete Mathematics and Applications 2, 439–444 (1992), MR 94f:94009, Citations in This Document: §1, §2
[39] Stein, W. (ed.): Sage Mathematics Software (Version 4.4.3). The Sage Group (2010), http://www.sagemath.org, Citations in This Document: §5
[40] Stern, J.: A Method for Finding Codewords of Small Weight. In: [12], pp. 106–113 (1989), Citations in This Document: §6
[41] Sugiyama, Y., Kasahara, M., Hirasawa, S., Namekawa, T.: Further Results on Goppa Codes and Their Applications to Constructing Effcient Binary Codes. IEEE Transactions on Information Theory 22, 518–526 (1976), Citations in This Document: §1, §4, §4, §4
[42] Wagner, D.: A Generalized Birthday Problem (Extended Abstract). In: [45], pp. 288–303 (2002); See Also Newer Version [43], http://www.cs.berkeley.edu/ daw/papers/genbday.html
[43] Wagner, D.: A Generalized Birthday Problem (Extended Abstract) (Long Version) (2002); See Also Older Version [42], http://www.cs.berkeley.edu/~daw/ papers/genbday.html, Citations in This Document: §6
[44] Wirtz, M.: On the Parameters of Goppa Codes. IEEE Transactions on Information Theory 34, 1341–1343 (1988), Citations in This Document: §4
[45] Yung, M. (ed.): Proceedings of Advances in Cryptology — CRYPTO 2002: 22nd Annual International Cryptology Conference, Santa Barbara, California, USA, August 2002. LNCS, vol. 2442. Springer, Heidelberg (2002) ISBN 3-540-44050-X, See [42]

Parallel-CFS
Strengthening the CFS McEliece-Based Signature Scheme

Matthieu Finiasz

ENSTA

Abstract. This article presents a modification of the CFS code based signature scheme. By producing two (or more generally i) signatures in parallel, we show that it is possible to protect this scheme from "one out of many" decoding attacks. With this modification, and at the cost of slightly larger signatures, it is possible to use smaller parameters for the CFS signature, thus making this new Parallel-CFS construction more practical than standard CFS signatures.

Keywords: CFS digital signature scheme, code based cryptography, Syndrome Decoding problem.

Introduction

Published in 2001, the Courtois-Finiasz-Sendrier (CFS) code based signature scheme [4] was the first practical digital signature scheme with a security reduction to the Syndrome Decoding problem. Though practical, this scheme requires much more resources than traditional number theory signatures: both the public key size and the signature time are relatively large. However, it offers the shortest known digital signatures, with sizes down to 81 bits for the original parameters.

Some time after the publication of this construction, D. Bleichenbacher imagined a new attack based on the Generalized Birthday Algorithm [13] which made the original CFS parameters insecure. This unpublished attack is described in [7]. For a given security level, resisting Bleichenbacher's attack only requires a small parameter increase, but this small increase can have a heavy impact on the signature time or the public key size.

This article introduces the concept of parallel signature, that is, producing two CFS signatures (or more) in parallel for a same document. The aim of this construction is simple: make the application of Bleichenbacher's attack impossible, or at least, as expensive as standard decoding attacks. A similar idea was proposed by Naccache, Pointcheval and Stern in [10] under the name Twin-signature, but with a completely different purpose. Their construction allows to sign short messages without having to hash them, and thus, can be proven secure without the need for a random oracle. The main focus of the present article is practical security and we will thus use hash functions and consider them as random oracles.

A. Biryukov, G. Gong, and D.R. Stinson (Eds.): SAC 2010, LNCS 6544, pp. 159–170, 2011.

We start this article by recalling the original CFS signature construction and the existing attacks against it. In Section 2 we introduce Parallel-CFS and detail the gains it offers in terms of security. Finally, in Section 3, we explain how to select secure parameters for Parallel-CFS.

1 The Original CFS Signature Scheme

The hash-and-sign paradigm makes it possible to convert any public key encryption scheme into a digital signature scheme. Producing a signature consists in hashing the document to sign into a ciphertext and then decrypting this "random" ciphertext using a secret key. Verification of the signature simply consists in comparing the hash of the document with the encryption of the signature (as encryption only requires the knowledge of the public key associated to the signer's private key, anyone can verify the signature).

In order for this construction to apply (and be secure), it is necessary to have access to a public cryptographic hash function which outputs ciphertexts uniformly distributed among all the possible ciphertexts. In the case of code based cryptosystems like the McEliece [9] or Niederreiter [11] encryption schemes, designing such a hash function is however impossible: the set of possible ciphertexts is a subset of known size of binary vectors of a given length r, but no simple description of this subset exists. One can thus use a hash function with uniform output among the binary vectors of length r, but then, only a small part of the hashes can be decrypted. The CFS signature scheme proposes two workarounds for this problem.

1.1 The Niederreiter Encryption Scheme

The CFS signature is built upon the Niederreiter encryption scheme which is described by the three following algorithms.

Key Generation. Choose parameters m and t and let $n = 2^m$. Let $\Gamma(g, S)$ be a binary Goppa code defined by its polynomial g of degree t in $\mathbf{F}_{2^m}[x]$ and its support S, a permutation of the n elements of $\mathbf{F}_{2^m}$. This code can correct up to t errors. Let H be a systematic $mt \times n$ binary parity check matrix of $\Gamma(g, S)$. H is the public encryption key, g and S form the private decryption key.

Encryption. To encrypt a plaintext p, first convert it into an error pattern e_p of length n and Hamming weight at most t (using an invertible mapping φ_t). Compute $s = H \times e_p^T$, the syndrome associated to the error pattern e_p with respect to the public parity check matrix H. The syndrome s is the ciphertext.

Decryption. To decrypt the ciphertext s, one simply applies the decoding algorithm associated to g and S to the received syndrome s and obtains e_p. The plaintext p is recovered by applying φ_t^{-1}.

Remark: The classical description of the Niederreiter cryptosystem uses two scrambling matrices to "hide" the structure of the parity check matrix H. In practice, these matrices are not necessary (see [2] for more details): the $n \times n$ permutation matrix simply corresponds to the order of the elements of the support S, and the $mt \times mt$ invertible matrix is not necessary when H is given in systematic form.

1.2 The CFS Signature Scheme

The CFS signature scheme uses the hash-and-sign paradigm. The hash function used should have an output size of $r = mt$ bits. The document hash is then viewed as a ciphertext which has to be decrypted. However, only ciphertexts corresponding to syndromes of error patterns of weight t or less can be decrypted as the decoding algorithm only corrects up to t errors. This means than only $\binom{2^m}{t} \simeq \frac{2^{mt}}{t!}$ out of the 2^{mt} possible syndromes can be decoded. Thus, only one document out of $t!$ can be signed, which makes its direct application impractical. There are two methods to get round this problem, however, both require to perform $t!$ decryption attempts in average. For this reason, only very small values of t are acceptable.

Appending a Counter to the Message. The first method which was proposed consists in appending a counter to the document to sign. We denote by D the document to sign and h the hash function. Instead of computing $s = h(D)$, one computes a sequence of hashes $s_i = h(D \,||\, i)$ where $||$ represents the concatenation. Starting with s_0 and incrementing i each time, the signer tries to decrypt the syndrome s_i, until a decodable syndrome is found. Let i_0 be the first index for which s_{i_0} can be decrypted. The signature is then $(p_{i_0} \,||\, i_0)$ where p_{i_0} is the plaintext corresponding to s_{i_0}, that is $H \times \varphi_t(p_{i_0})^T = s_{i_0}$. In order to verify this signature, one has to verify the equality $H \times \varphi_t(p_{i_0})^T \stackrel{?}{=} h(D \,||\, i_0)$.

Note that by bounding the space in which the counters are selected, L. Dallot was able to formally prove the security of this construction in the random oracle model [5].

Performing Complete Decoding. The idea of this second method is to be able to decode/decrypt any syndrome given by the hash function. For this, one needs to modify the decoding algorithm in order to be able to decode more than t errors. A first step towards complete decoding could be the use of Bernstein's list decoding algorithm [1], however, for code rates close to 1 (which is the case here for very small values of t), this algorithm becomes less efficient than simple exhaustive search. The idea is thus to use exhaustive search for the additional errors we want to decode. Let δ be the smallest integer such that $\binom{2^m}{t+\delta} > 2^{mt}$, then, any syndrome can (with a good probability) be decoded into an error pattern of weight $t + \delta$ or less.

With this method, the signer will go through all error patterns $\varphi_\delta(i)$ of weight δ and try to decode the resulting syndrome $s_i = h(D) + H \times \varphi_\delta(i)^T$. Once a decodable syndrome is found for a given index i_0, as in the previous method, we have found a p'_{i_0} such that $H \times \varphi_t(p'_{i_0})^T = s_{i_0} = h(D) + H \times \varphi_\delta(i_0)^T$. The signature is then $p_{i_0} = \varphi^{-1}_{t+\delta}(\varphi_t(p'_{i_0}) + \varphi_\delta(i_0))$, that is, the message corresponding to the error pattern of weight $t + \delta$.

In order to verify the signature, one simply verifies the equality:

$$H \times \varphi_{t+\delta}(p_{i_0})^T \stackrel{?}{=} h(D).$$

1.3 Existing Attacks - One Out of Many Syndrome Decoding

Two kind of attacks exist against a signature scheme: key recovery attacks, which aim at recovering the private key from the public key, and signature forgeries, which try to produce a valid signature for a message without the knowledge of the private key. Key recovery attacks against McEliece type cryptosystems are traditionally less efficient than decoding attacks, however, recent developments in Goppa code distinguishing [6] could bring new attacks into consideration. For the moment no such attack has been found and we therefore focus on decoding attacks which, in the context of signatures, are signature forgeries.

When forging a CFS signature, one has to find a valid signature/document pair, and therefore has to solve an instance of the Syndrome Decoding problem: find a low weight error pattern corresponding to a given syndrome. However, as opposed to the standard Syndrome Decoding problem, one only has to solve one instance out of many.

Problem 1 (One out of Many Syndrome Decoding (OMSD)). Given parameters n, r, t, and N, a binary $r \times n$ matrix H and a set of N binary vectors S_i of r bits, find a binary error pattern e of Hamming weight t or less such that:

$$\exists i \in [1, N] \ s.t. \ H \times e^T = S_i.$$

In order to solve this problem, one can use the same methods as for the standard single Syndrome Decoding (SD) problem and see how they can be improved when several instances (for the same matrix) are available. As described in [7], when designing a code based cryptosystem the two main attacks to consider are Information Set Decoding (ISD) and the Generalized Birthday Algorithm (GBA) [13].

Information Set Decoding. ISD algorithms are particularly efficient for solving instances of the SD problem which have a single (or a few) solutions. The application of ISD to instances of OMSD has been studied by Johansson and Jönsson in [8]. They modify the Canteaut-Chabaud algorithm [3] so as to take into account the number of target syndromes and study the efficiency of their new algorithm against various code based cryptosystems including the CFS signature scheme. However, the authors do not give any asymptotic analysis of the gain when targeting N syndromes instead of 1. Applying their technique to the "idealized" algorithm described in [7] cannot gain more than an order $\sqrt{N}$, which is exactly what the Generalized Birthday Algorithm described in the following section offers. Both algorithms should thus have a similar asymptotic behavior, but the complexity of the next algorithm is well known and easier to study. The reader should thus keep in mind that the attack complexities given in Section 3.2 might be slightly improved using an idealized version of Johansson and Jönsson's algorithm, but the gain cannot be more than a small constant factor.

In the rest of this article, we will denote by ISD the Information Set Decoding attack targeting a single syndrome. This attack is an exact replacement for the secret decoding algorithm, so any signature the legitimate signer can produce can be forged using this algorithm. Its complexity which is close to $2^{\frac{mt}{2}}$ will thus serve as a reference security level.

Generalized Birthday Algorithm. As opposed to ISD, the GBA algorithm can only work when there are many solutions. When attacking a single instance of SD with the CFS parameters, there is less than a solution in average so GBA cannot be applied directly. However, when attacking OMSD, if enough instances are considered simultaneously, the number of solutions can become very large. This idea came from Daniel Bleichenbacher who proposed to build a list of target syndromes and use this list as one of the starting lists of GBA. Compared to ISD, this allows to significantly decrease the cost of a signature forgery. The complexity of this attack against CFS with a counter is given by the formulas:

$$C_{\text{GBA}} = L\log(L), \text{ with } L = \min\left(\frac{2^r}{\binom{n}{t-\lfloor t/3\rfloor}}, \sqrt{\frac{2^r}{\binom{n}{\lfloor t/3\rfloor}}}\right).$$

The size L of the largest list used in the algorithm is roughly $2^{\frac{mt}{3}}$ (which is what one would expect using GBA with 4 lists). In practice, it is a little larger than this because $\binom{n}{t} < 2^{mt}$ in the counter version of CFS, so lists formed by XORs of columns of H are too small and this has to be compensated by using a larger list of target syndromes.

In the case of CFS using complete decoding, the target is a word of weight $t+\delta$ and, as $\binom{n}{t+\delta} > 2^{mt}$, lists formed of XORs of columns of H are large enough and the size L of the largest list is very close to $2^{\frac{mt}{3}}$.

2 Parallel-CFS: Cost and Gain

The possibilities offered by OMSD against the original CFS signature are not devastating: asymptotically, the security can be decreased from $2^{\frac{mt}{2}}$ to $2^{\frac{mt}{3}}$. However, this is enough to require a slight increase in the parameters m or t, which translates into a significant increase in public key size (which is exponential in m) or signature cost (which is exponential in t). For this reason, keeping the parameters as small as possible is critical. The aim of Parallel-CFS is to make the application of OMSD improvements impossible.

2.1 Description of Parallel-CFS

The idea in Parallel-CFS is very simple: instead of producing one hash (using a function h) from a document D and signing it, one can produce two hashes (using two functions h_1 and h_2) and sign both $h_1(D)$ and $h_2(D)$ in parallel. This way, if one wants to use OMSD, he will have to produce two forgeries, one for h_1 and one for h_2, but these forgeries also have to be for the same document D. More generally, one can also use i different hash functions and produce i signatures in parallel. We will denote the construction using i hash functions as order i Parallel-CFS.

Using CFS with a Counter is Impossible. The first thing to note when using Parallel-CFS is that the version of CFS using a counter is not suitable. If we simply compute two CFS signatures for D using both h_1 and h_2, we will obtain two signatures $(p_{i_1} \,||\, i_1)$ and $(p_{i_2} \,||\, i_2)$. The problem here is that these two signatures are not linked through the hash function: they are signatures for $h_1(D \,||\, i_1)$ and $h_2(D \,||\, i_2)$, and using enough different counter values one simply has to solve two independent instances of OMSD. In order to link the signatures together, they have to be signatures for the exact same message: a single counter has to be used for both signatures. One has to find an index i_0 such that both $h_1(D \,||\, i_0)$ and $h_2(D \,||\, i_0)$ can be decoded. The problem now is that instead of having $t!$ attempts to perform, one needs $t! \times t!$ decodings in average! Of course this is not acceptable, and we therefore propose to use the other version of CFS.

Using CFS with Complete Decoding. When using this second version of CFS, we no longer have any counter problems. Parallel-CFS can thus be described by the following algorithms.

Key Generation. This step is similar to the Niederreiter cryptosystem. Choose parameters m, t and let $n = 2^m$. Select δ such that $\binom{n}{t+\delta} > 2^{mt}$. Choose a Goppa polynomial g of degree t in $\mathbf{F}_{2^m}[x]$ and a support S (a permutation of the n elements of $\mathbf{F}_{2^m}$). Let H be a $mt \times n$ systematic parity check matrix of the Goppa code $\Gamma(g, S)$. H is the public verification key, g and S form the private signature key. The parameters m, t, and δ as well as two cryptographic hash function h_1 and h_2 are also made public.

Signature. When signing a document D, compute $h_1(D)$ and $h_2(D)$. Then, as in the original CFS, using the Goppa code decoding algorithm, compute two error patterns e_1 and e_2 of weight at most $t + \delta$ such that $H \times e_1^T = h_1(D)$ and $H \times e_2^T = h_2(D)$. The signature is $\left(\varphi_{t+\delta}^{-1}(e_1) \,||\, \varphi_{t+\delta}^{-1}(e_2)\right)$.

Verification. When verifying a signature $(p_1 \,||\, p_2)$ for a document D. One verifies if $H \times \varphi_{t+\delta}(p_1)^T \stackrel{?}{=} h_1(D)$ and $H \times \varphi_{t+\delta}(p_2)^T \stackrel{?}{=} h_2(D)$. If both equalities are verified, the signature is valid.

2.2 Cost of Parallel-CFS

The computational cost of Parallel-CFS is easy to evaluate: instead of producing one CFS signature, the signer has to produce two (or more generally i) signatures.

Compared to the original CFS, the signature time is doubled (or multiplied by i) and the signature size is also doubled (or multiplied by i), the key sizes remain the same, and the verification time is doubled (or multiplied by i).

Signature Failure Probability. One of the main issues with the complete decoding version of CFS (as opposed to the version using a counter) is that some documents might not be signable: some syndromes might not correspond to error patterns of weight $t + \delta$. Complete decoding is only possible if $t + \delta$ is equal (or larger) to the *covering radius* of the Goppa code we use. Unfortunately, computing the covering radius of a Goppa code is difficult. When selecting δ we thus consider that the words in the balls or radius $t+\delta$ centered on the codewords are randomly distributed in the space. This way, we can compute an estimate of the probability $\mathrm{P}_{\mathrm{noCFS}}$ of not being able to perform one CFS signature, and the probability $\mathrm{P}_{\mathrm{fail}}$ of not being able to sign with order i Parallel-CFS.

$$\mathrm{P}_{\mathrm{noCFS}} \simeq \left(1 - \frac{1}{2^{mt}}\right)^{\binom{n}{t+\delta}}$$

$$\mathrm{P}_{\mathrm{fail}} = 1 - \left(1 - \mathrm{P}_{\mathrm{noCFS}}\right)^{i}.$$

Even if this probability is negligible for the proposed parameters (see Section 3.2, Table 1), the protocol has to be ready to handle this kind of problem, typically by modifying (or expanding) the document to sign.

2.3 Gain of Parallel-CFS

The only gain compared to the original CFS is on the security side. Security against ISD attacks is the same as before and is easy to evaluate: you need to forge two CFS signatures, so the cost is twice the cost of attacking CFS. Security against GBA and attacks like that of Bleichenbacher is a little more complicated to evaluate. There are two strategies to exploit OMSD in Parallel-CFS: either consider it as one big signature scheme, or try to chain two attacks on the first and second signatures (or, in general, chain i attacks).

Parallel-CFS as One Big Signature. This first strategy considers Parallel-CFS as a single OMSD problem and tries to solve a problem of the form:

$$\left(\begin{array}{c|c} H & 0 \\ \hline 0 & H \end{array}\right) \times \left(\begin{array}{c|c} e_1 & e_2 \end{array}\right)^T = \left(\begin{array}{c} h_1(D) \\ \hline h_2(D) \end{array}\right)$$

In this case, Bleichenbacher's attack applies directly, but on a problem where all parameters are doubled. The size L of the lists used in the attack is roughly $2^{\frac{2mt}{3}}$ which, as intended, is larger than the complexity of $2^{\frac{mt}{2}}$ offered by ISD attacks. This strategy is thus less efficient than applying 2 ISD attacks independently.

Chaining Attacks against Parallel-CFS. This second strategy considers the two signatures sequentially. Bleichenbacher's attack was originally described to produce a single solution, however, GBA can also be used to produce several solutions quite efficiently. The idea is thus to use this attack to produce a large number of valid signatures for the first hash function h_1, and use all these solutions as possible targets of the second hash function. It is then possible to benefit from OMSD also for the second signature. However, the attack against the first signature will cost more than for a single solution.

In order to simplify computations, we will make the following assumptions (similar to those used in [7]):

- it is possible to XOR non-integer numbers of vectors, thus XORs of $\frac{t+\delta}{3}$ columns of H are always possible,
- the number $\binom{n}{t+\delta}$ of syndromes we can build is larger than 2^{mt}, but is not much larger. We consider that we can build 3 lists L_0, L_1, and L_2, respectively of XORs of w_0, w_1, and w_2 columns of H, with $w_0 + w_1 + w_2 = t + \delta$ such that $|L_0| \times |L_1| \times |L_2| = 2^{mt}$. In practice these lists can even be a little larger than 2^{mt}, but we ignore this small factor as the improvement it can yield is negligible.

With these assumptions, the cost of Bleichenbacher's attack against a single CFS signature is exactly $L \log L$ with $L = 2^{\frac{mt}{3}}$.

Now, suppose one has forged 2^c signatures for 2^c different hashes $h_1(D_i)$. Then there are 2^c target hashes $h_2(D_i)$ for the second function. One then builds three lists L_0, L_1, and L_2 of XORs of columns of H such that $|L_0| = |L_1| = 2^{\frac{mt+c}{4}}$ and $|L_2| = 2^{\frac{mt-c}{2}}$. In accord with our assumption, this choice satisfies $|L_0| \times |L_1| \times |L_2| = 2^{mt}$ and is thus possible. Then, if we merge lists L_0 and L_1 together and list L_2 with our 2^c hashes, by zeroing c bits in the first step of a GBA it is possible to find a valid signature with a cost of $2^{\frac{mt-c}{2}}$.

In order to determine the optimal value of c, we need to know the cost of the forgery of 2^c signatures for the first hash function. Thanks to our assumptions this is quite easy: we can find one solution with GBA and a complexity of $2^{\frac{mt}{3}}$ by using $2^{\frac{mt}{3}}$ target syndromes $h_1(D_i)$. If we want more solutions we have to take more syndromes: the number giving the smallest complexity is $2^{\frac{mt+2c}{3}}$ syndromes. Then one can choose $|L_0| = |L_1| = 2^{\frac{mt+c/2}{3}}$ and $|L_2| = 2^{\frac{mt-c}{3}}$ and, by zeroing $\frac{mt-c}{3}$ bits in the first merge, obtain exactly 2^c solutions in average. The complexity of this step is $2^{\frac{mt+2c}{3}}$.

The optimal choice of c is when both steps of the forgery have the same cost, that is: $\frac{mt-c}{2} = \frac{mt+2c}{3}$ and $c = \frac{1}{7}mt$. Chaining two OMSD attacks to forge a Parallel-CFS signature thus costs $2L \log L$ with $L = 2^{\frac{3}{7}mt}$.

Security of Order i Parallel-CFS. Using two CFS signatures in parallel increases the cost of GBA-based attacks from $2^{\frac{1}{3}mt}$ to $2^{\frac{3}{7}mt}$. If one uses i signatures in parallel an attacker has to chain i GBA algorithms and the security of the construction should be even closer to $2^{\frac{1}{2}mt}$. In order to evaluate this more precisely we need to determine the exact cost of a signature forgery starting from 2^{c_j} syndromes and producing $2^{c_{j+1}}$ signatures.

Similarly to the second step of the attack against order 2 Parallel-CFS, one chooses starting lists such that $|L_0| = |L_1| = 2^{\frac{mt+c_j}{4}}$ and $|L_2| = 2^{\frac{mt-c_j}{2}}$, but instead of zeroing c_j bits during the first merge operations, one can only zero $c_j - c_{j+1}$ bits. The complexity of the attack is thus $2^{\frac{mt-(c_j-2c_{j+1})}{2}}$.

When forging an order i Parallel-CFS signature one has to select indices $(c_1, ..., c_i)$ such that each step has the same complexity 2^K, that is:

- for the first signature forgeries $K = \frac{mt+2c_1}{3}$,
- for each of the following steps $\forall j \in [1, i-1]$, $K = \frac{mt-(c_j-2c_{j+1})}{2}$,
- at the end one wants one valid signature, so $c_i = 0$.

Simple computations lead to the solution $c_j - 2c_{j+1} = \frac{mt}{2^{i+1}-1}$ and the global complexity of an attack chaining i OMSD attacks is of order $iL \log L$ with $L = 2^{\frac{2^i-1}{2^{i+1}-1}mt}$.

As one can see, order i Parallel-CFS cannot achieve an asymptotic security of $2^{\frac{mt}{2}}$, but comes very close to it. In practice, order 2 or 3 Parallel-CFS will be the best choice for most parameters. The security gain using 4 parallel signatures can never compensate the cost in signature time and size of a fourth signature.

3 Parameter Selection

3.1 Signature Size

It is always possible to reduce the size of a signature at the cost of an increase in the verification time. As signature verification is exceptionally fast for CFS (one only has to XOR $t + \delta$ columns of H) it is not necessarily a problem to increase its cost. The signature shortening techniques presented in [4] can still be applied for Parallel-CFS. Compared to the original proposition, the replacement of the counter by δ additional positions does not change much and the two following reduction methods can still be applied:

- omit the w first positions of the $t + \delta$ positions of a signature: the verifier has to exhaustively search for $w - 1$ of these positions,
- split the length n in $\frac{n}{s}$ intervals of size s (typically s will be close to m) and only include the interval containing the error in the signature (not the exact position): the verifier has to perform a Gaussian elimination on H (the cost of which is not negligible if less than 3 positions were omitted).

If one wants very fast signature verification ($t + \delta$ column operations on H), omitting a single column is the right choice and the size of the signature of order i Parallel-CFS is $i \times \log_2 \binom{n}{t+\delta-1}$. For the original $t = 9$ and $m = 16$ parameters this is $139 \times i$ bits. If one aims for short signatures with a longer verification ($3\binom{n}{w}/\binom{t+\delta}{2}$ column operations on H), omitting 3 columns and using intervals of size m, the size of the signature of order i Parallel-CFS is $i \times \log_2 \binom{n/m}{t+\delta-3}$. For the original parameters this is $81 \times i$ bits.

3.2 Parameter Examples

Table 1 presents a few sets of parameters that can be used for Parallel-CFS. These parameters are not all intended to be optimal choices but simply serve as examples to illustrate the flexibility of this new construction. If one aims for a security of 2^{80}, four sets of parameters (m, t, δ) stand out:

- Parameters $(20, 8, 2)$: if one wants fast signature, signature time will be 10 times smaller than for other parameters with a same security level. In order to have a sufficient security level 3 signatures have to be produced in parallel leading to a signature size of 294 bits, which is acceptable. The downside of this set of parameters is the public key size: 20 Mbytes is a lot.

Table 1. Some parameter examples for Parallel-CFS. Using $i = 1$ corresponds to the orginal CFS signature scheme and can serve for comparison

parameters				ISD	orig. CFS	security against	sign. failure	public	sign.	sign.
m	t	δ	i[a]	security[b]	security[c]	(chained) GBA	probability	key size	cost[d]	size[e]
20	8	2	1	$2^{81.0}$	$2^{66.4}$	$2^{59.1}$	~ 0	20.0 MB	$2^{15.3}$	98
–	–	–	2	–	–	$2^{75.7}$	~ 0	–	$2^{16.3}$	196
–	–	–	3	–	–	$2^{82.5}$	~ 0	–	$2^{16.9}$	294
16	9	2	1	$2^{76.5}$	$2^{63.3}$	$2^{53.6}$	2^{-155}	1.1 MB	$2^{18.5}$	81
–	–	–	2	–	–	$2^{68.7}$	2^{-154}	–	$2^{19.5}$	162
–	–	–	3	–	–	$2^{74.9}$	2^{-153}	–	$2^{20.0}$	243
18	9	2	1	$2^{84.5}$	$2^{69.5}$	$2^{59.8}$	2^{-1700}	5.0 MB	$2^{18.5}$	96
–	–	–	2	–	–	$2^{76.5}$	2^{-1700}	–	$2^{19.5}$	192
–	–	–	3	–	–	$2^{83.4}$	2^{-1700}	–	$2^{20.0}$	288
19	9	2	1	$2^{88.5}$	$2^{72.5}$	$2^{62.8}$	~ 0	10.7 MB	$2^{18.5}$	103
–	–	–	2	–	–	$2^{80.5}$	~ 0	–	$2^{19.5}$	206
–	–	–	3	–	–	$2^{87.7}$	~ 0	–	$2^{20.0}$	309
15	10	3	1	$2^{76.2}$	$2^{63.1}$	$2^{55.6}$	~ 0	0.6 MB	$2^{21.8}$	90
–	–	–	2	–	–	$2^{71.3}$	~ 0	–	$2^{22.8}$	180
–	–	–	3	–	–	$2^{77.7}$	~ 0	–	$2^{23.4}$	270
16	10	2	1	$2^{86.2}$	$2^{66.2}$	$2^{59.1}$	2^{-13}	1.2 MB	$2^{21.8}$	90
–	–	–	2	–	–	$2^{75.7}$	2^{-12}	–	$2^{22.8}$	180
–	–	–	3	–	–	$2^{82.5}$	$2^{-11.3}$	–	$2^{23.4}$	270
17	10	2	1	$2^{90.7}$	$2^{69.3}$	$2^{62.5}$	2^{-52}	2.7 MB	$2^{21.8}$	98
–	–	–	2	–	–	$2^{80.0}$	2^{-51}	–	$2^{22.8}$	196
–	–	–	3	–	–	$2^{87.2}$	2^{-50}	–	$2^{23.4}$	294

[a] Number of parallel signatures to perform.
[b] Cost of an ISD attack on the associated SD instance. This is an upper bound on the security we can obtain from parallel signatures.
[c] Security against GBA of the original CFS signature (using a counter with no parallel signatures) with the same parameters.
[d] Average number of decoding attempts required to sign a document.
[e] Size in bits of a signature with all size reductions applied (omitting 3 columns and using intervals).

- Parameters $(18, 9, 2)$: these are what we would call parameters for "every-day's use." A key of 5 Mbytes is not negligible, but can be accepted for certain applications and signature time is still reasonable. Order 3 Parallel-CFS still has to be used, leading to signatures of 288 bits.
- Parameters $(19, 9, 2)$: these parameters offer short 206 bits signatures as 2 parallel signatures are enough for 80 bits of security. While the signature time is still reasonable, the key size can already be problematic.
- Parameters $(16, 10, 2)/(17, 10, 2)$: choosing $t = 10$ allows for much smaller keys but significantly increases the cost of the signature. These parameters are similar to the two previous sets, but with a smaller key and larger signature time.

3.3 Hiding the Structure in Parallel-CFS?

A natural idea to improve Parallel-CFS would be to combine the two independent signature problems into one large signature: this way, an attacker would have to solve an instance of OMSD with doubled parameters. Unfortunately, the structure in the combined matrix is too strong and cannot be efficiently hidden (while preserving the legitimate signature algorithm).

The best that can be done in terms of structure hiding is to select a $2n \times 2n$ permutation matrix P, a $2mt \times 2mt$ invertible matrix S, and a random $mt \times n$ binary matrix Y and build the matrix:

$$H' = S \times \left(\begin{array}{c|c} H_1 & 0 \\ \hline Y & H_2 \end{array} \right) \times P.$$

Where H_1 and H_2 are two distinct Goppa code parity check matrices. Signing in that case requires to sign the first hash $h_1(D)$, and then sign the second hash XORed to the product of the first signature by Y.

As we said before, this is unfortunately not sufficient to hide the structure in matrix H'. Raphael Overbeck already studied this structure under the name "permuted reducible codes" and showed in [12] that separating H_1 and H_2 was an easy problem. We leave it as an exercise to the reader to find out how this can be done.

4 Conclusion

With Parallel-CFS we propose to add some flexibility in the parameter choices of the CFS signature scheme. In order to resist OMSD attacks like that of Bleichenbacher, it is possible to increase the number of signatures to produce instead of increasing the signature parameters. In addition to the two previous tradeoffs where security could be gained at the cost of a larger public key or of a much longer signature time, we now have a third tradeoff where increasing security mostly increases the signature size. Thanks to this, parameter sets which had become insecure can be used again, making Parallel-CFS much more practical than standard CFS.

References

1. Bernstein, D.J.: List decoding for binary goppa codes. Preprint (2008), http://cr.yp.to/codes/goppalist-20081107.pdf
2. Biswas, B., Sendrier, N.: McEliece cryptosystem implementation: Theory and practice. In: Buchmann, J., Ding, J. (eds.) PQCrypto 2008. LNCS, vol. 5299, pp. 47–62. Springer, Heidelberg (2008)
3. Canteaut, A., Chabaud, F.: A new algorithm for finding minimum-weight words in a linear code: Application to McEliece's cryptosystem and to narrow-sense BCH codes of length 511. IEEE Transactions on Information Theory 44(1), 367–378 (1998)
4. Courtois, N., Finiasz, M., Sendrier, N.: How to achieve a mcEliece-based digital signature scheme. In: Boyd, C. (ed.) ASIACRYPT 2001. LNCS, vol. 2248, pp. 157–174. Springer, Heidelberg (2001)
5. Dallot, L.: Towards a concrete security proof of courtois, finiasz and sendrier signature scheme. In: Lucks, S., Sadeghi, A.-R., Wolf, C. (eds.) WEWoRC 2007. LNCS, vol. 4945, pp. 65–77. Springer, Heidelberg (2008)
6. Faugère, J.-C., Otmani, A., Perret, L., Tillich, J.-P.: Algebraic cryptanalysis of mcEliece variants with compact keys. In: Gilbert, H. (ed.) EUROCRYPT 2010. LNCS, vol. 6110, pp. 279–298. Springer, Heidelberg (2010)
7. Finiasz, M., Sendrier, N.: Security bounds for the design of code-based cryptosystems. In: Matsui, M. (ed.) ASIACRYPT 2009. LNCS, vol. 5912, pp. 88–105. Springer, Heidelberg (2009)
8. Johansson, T., Jönsson, F.: On the complexity of some cryptographic problems based on the general decoding problem. IEEE Transactions on Information Theory 48(10), 2669–2678 (2002)
9. McEliece, R.J.: A public-key cryptosystem based on algebraic coding theory. DSN Progress Report, Jet Prop. Lab., California Inst. Technol., Pasadena, CA, pp. 114–116 (January 1978)
10. Naccache, D., Pointcheval, D., Stern, J.: Twin signatures: an alternative to the hash-and-sign paradigm. In: ACM Conference on Computer and Communications Security, ACMCCS 2001, pp. 20–27. ACM, New York (2001)
11. Niederreiter, H.: Knapsack-type crytosystems and algebraic coding theory. Prob. Contr. Inform. Theory 15(2), 157–166 (1986)
12. Overbeck, R.: Recognizing the structure of permuted reducible codes. In: Augot, D., Sendrier, N. (eds.) International Workshop on Coding and Cryptography, WCC 2007, pp. 269–276 (2007)
13. Wagner, D.: A generalized birthday problem. In: Yung, M. (ed.) CRYPTO 2002. LNCS, vol. 2442, pp. 288–304. Springer, Heidelberg (2002)

A Zero-Knowledge Identification Scheme Based on the q-ary Syndrome Decoding Problem

Pierre-Louis Cayrel[1], Pascal Véron[2], and Sidi Mohamed El Yousfi Alaoui[1]

[1] CASED – Center for Advanced Security Research Darmstadt,
Mornewegstrasse 32, 64293 Darmstadt, Germany
{pierre-louis.cayrel,elyousfi}@cased.de
[2] IMATH
Université du Sud Toulon-Var.
B.P. 20132, F-83957 La Garde Cedex, France
veron@univ-tln.fr

Abstract. At CRYPTO'93, Stern proposed a 3-pass code-based identification scheme with a cheating probability of 2/3. In this paper, we propose a 5-pass code-based protocol with a lower communication complexity, allowing an impersonator to succeed with only a probability of 1/2. Furthermore, we propose to use double-circulant construction in order to dramatically reduce the size of the public key.

The proposed scheme is zero-knowledge and relies on an NP-complete coding theory problem (namely the q-ary Syndrome Decoding problem). The parameters we suggest for the instantiation of this scheme take into account a recent study of (a generalization of) Stern's information set decoding algorithm, applicable to linear codes over arbitrary fields $\mathbb{F}_q$; the public data of our construction is then 4 Kbytes, whereas that of Stern's scheme is 15 Kbytes for the same level of security. This provides a very practical identification scheme which is especially attractive for light-weight cryptography.

Keywords: post-quantum cryptography, code-based cryptography, Stern's scheme, identification, zero-knowledge.

1 Introduction

Shor's quantum algorithm for integer factorization, which was published in 1994, poses a serious threat to most cryptographic systems in use today. In particular, all constructions whose security relies on number theory (such as variants of the discrete logarithm problem or integer factorization) are vulnerable to this algorithm. If quantum computers will at one point exist, such schemes can be broken in polynomial time, whereas no quantum attacks are known for lattice-based, code-based, and multivariate cryptographic systems. On the other hand, even should such number-theoretic assumptions remain hard, it is not wise to rely on a single type of hard problems. Furthermore, as the capacity of current adversaries increases, so does the key size for classical constructions; it is possible

A. Biryukov, G. Gong, and D.R. Stinson (Eds.): SAC 2010, LNCS 6544, pp. 171–186, 2011.

that alternative post-quantum constructions may provide a better alternative in that sense.

In this paper, we consider a particular type of alternative cryptography, based on error-correcting code theory. Code-based cryptography was initiated a long time ago with the celebrated McEliece encryption algorithm.

We consider the question of public key identification (ID) protocols in this context. Such schemes allow a party holding a secret key to prove its identity to any other entity holding the corresponding public key. The minimum security of such protocols should be that a passive observer who sees the interaction should not then be able to perform his own interaction and successfully impersonate the prover.

Stern's code-based identification scheme, proposed at CRYPTO'93, is still the reference in this area [26]. Stern's scheme is a multiple round zero-knowledge protocol, where each round is a three-pass interaction between the prover and the verifier. This construction has two major drawbacks:

1. Since the probability of a successful impersonation is $2/3$ for Stern's construction instead of $1/2$ as in the case of Fiat-Shamir's protocol based on integer factorization [11], Stern's scheme uses more rounds to achieve the same security, typically 28 rounds for an impersonation resistance of 2^{-16}.
2. There is a common data shared by all users (from which the public identification is derived) which is very large, typically 66 Kbits. In Fiat Shamir's scheme, this common data is 1024 bits long.

The second issue was addressed by Gaborit and Girault in [12] and by Véron in [29]. In this paper, we focus on the first drawback. Using q-ary codes instead of binary ones, we define a 5-pass identification scheme for which the success probability of a cheater is $1/2$. We then propose to use quasi-cyclic construction to address the second drawback.

Organization of the Paper

In Section 2, we give basic facts about code-based cryptography and describe the original scheme due to Stern; in Section 3 we show a new identification scheme which allows us to reduce the number of identification rounds. In Section 4, we describe the properties of our proposal and study its security. Section 5 presents some concluding remarks to our contribution.

2 Code-Based Cryptography

In this section we recall basic facts about code-based cryptography. We refer to [4], for a general introduction to these issues.

2.1 Definitions

Linear codes are k-dimensional subspaces of an n-dimensional vector space over a finite field $\mathbb{F}_q$, where k and n are positive integers with $k < n$, and q a prime power. The error-correcting capability of such a code is the maximum number t of errors that the code is able to decode. In short, linear codes with these parameters are denoted (n, k, t)-codes.

Definition 1 (Hamming weight). *The (Hamming) weight of a vector x is the number of non-zero entries. We use $\mathsf{wt}(x)$ to represent the Hamming weight of x.*

Definition 2 (Generator and Parity Check Matrix). *Let $\mathscr{C}$ be a linear code over $\mathbb{F}_q$. A generator matrix G of $\mathscr{C}$ is a matrix whose rows form a basis of $\mathscr{C}$:*

$$\mathscr{C} = \{xG : x \in \mathbb{F}_q^k\}$$

A parity check matrix H of $\mathscr{C}$ is is an $(n-k) \times n$ matrix whose rows form a basis of the orthogonal complement of the vector subspace $\mathscr{C}$, i.e. it holds that,

$$\mathscr{C} = \{x \in \mathbb{F}_q^n : Hx^T = 0\}$$

Let n and r be two integers such that $n \geq r$, $\mathsf{Binary}(n, r)$ (resp. $\mathsf{q-ary}(n, r)$) be the set of binary (resp. q-ary) matrices with n columns and r rows of rank r. Moreover, denote by $x \overset{\$}{\leftarrow} A$, the random choosing of x amongst the elements of a set A.

We describe here the main hard problems on which the security of code-based cryptosystems mostly relies.

Definition 3 (Binary Syndrome Decoding (SD) problem)
Input : $H \overset{\$}{\leftarrow} \mathsf{Binary}(n, r)$, $y \overset{\$}{\leftarrow} \mathbb{F}_2^r$, *and an integer* $\omega > 0$.
Output : *A word* $s \in \mathbb{F}_2^n$ *such that* $\mathsf{wt}(s) \leq \omega$, $Hs^T = y$.

This problem was proven to be NP-complete in 1978 [3]. An equivalent dual version of the SD problem can be presented as follows:

Definition 4 (General Binary Decoding (G-SD) problem)
Input : $G \overset{\$}{\leftarrow} \mathsf{Binary}(n, n-r)$, $y \overset{\$}{\leftarrow} \mathbb{F}_2^n$, *and an integer* $\omega > 0$.
Output : *A word* $x \in \mathbb{F}_2^{n-r}$, $e \in \mathbb{F}_2^n$ *such that* $\mathsf{wt}(e) \leq \omega$ *and* $xG + e = y$.

Finally, this problem can be considered over an arbitrary finite field.

Definition 5 (q-ary Syndrome Decoding (qSD) problem)
Input : $H \overset{\$}{\leftarrow} \mathsf{q-ary}(n, r)$, $y \overset{\$}{\leftarrow} \mathbb{F}_q^r$, *and an integer* $\omega > 0$.
Output : *A word* $s \in \mathbb{F}_q^n$ *such that* $\mathsf{wt}(s) \leq \omega$ *and* $Hs^T = y$.

In 1994, A. Barg proved that this last problem remains NP-complete [1, in russian].

The problems which cryptographic applications rely upon can have different numbers of solutions. For example, public key encryption schemes usually have exactly one solution, while digital signatures often have more than one possible solution. For code-based cryptosystems, the uniqueness of solutions can be expressed by the Gilbert-Varshamov (GV) bound:

Definition 6 (q-ary Gilbert-Varshamov bound)
Let $H_q(x)$ be the q-ary entropy function, given by:

$$H_q(x) = x \log_q(q-1) - x \log_q(x) - (1-x)\log_q(1-x)$$

Suppose $0 \leq \xi \leq (q-1)/q$. Then there exists an infinite sequence of (n, k, d) q-ary linear codes with $d/n = \xi$ and rate $R = k/n$ satisfying the inequality:

$$R \geq 1 - H_q(\xi) \qquad \forall n.$$

2.2 SD and G-SD Identification Schemes

Stern's scheme is the first practical zero-knowledge identification scheme based on the Syndrome Decoding problem [26]. The scheme uses a binary $(n-k) \times n$ matrix H common to all users. If H is chosen randomly, it will provide a parity check matrix for a code with asymptotically good minimum distance given by the (binary) Gilbert-Varshamov (GV) bound. The private key for a user will thus be a word s of small weight $\mathsf{wt}(s) = \omega$ (e.g. $\omega \approx$ GV bound), which corresponds to the syndrome $Hs^T = y$, the public key. By Stern's 3-pass zero-knowledge protocol, the secret key holder can prove his knowledge of s by using two blending factors: a permutation and a random vector. However, a dishonest prover not knowing s can cheat the verifier in the protocol with probability $2/3$. Thus, the protocol has to be run several times to detect cheating provers. The security of the scheme relies on the hardness of the general decoding problem, that is on the difficulty of determining the preimage s of $y = Hs^T$.

As mentioned in [3], the SD problem stated in terms of generator matrices is also NP-complete since one can go from the parity-check matrix to the generator matrix (or vice-versa) in polynomial time. In [29], the author uses a generator matrix of a random linear binary code as the public key and defines this way a dual version of Stern's scheme in order to obtain, among other things, an improvement of the transmission rate : the G-SD identification scheme.

Fig. 1 sums up the performances of the two 3-pass SD identification schemes for a probability of cheating bounded by 10^{-6}. The prover's complexity is the number of bit operations involved for the prover in the protocol run, while the communication complexity is measured in the number of exchanged bits. We considered that hash values are 160 bits long and seeds used to generate permutations 128 bits long.

2.3 Attacks

For SD identification schemes, since the matrix used is a random one, the cryptanalyst is faced with the problem of decoding a random binary linear code. There are two main families of algorithms to solve this problem: Information Set Decoding (ISD) and (Generalized) Birthday Algorithm (GBA). The Information Set Decoding algorithm has the lowest complexity of the two; the strategy to recover the k information symbols is as follows: the first step is to pick k of the

	SD	G-SD
Rounds	35	35
Public data (bits)	65792	66048
Prover's complexity	$2^{22.14}$	$2^{22.13}$
Communication complexity	43750	37777

Fig. 1. Performances of SD schemes,security level 2^{70}, probability of cheating 10^{-6}

n coordinates randomly in the hope that all of them are error-free. Then try to recover the message by solving a $k \times k$ linear system (binary or over $\mathbb{F}_q$).

In [19], the author describes and analyzes the complexity of a generalization of Stern's information set decoding algorithm from [25] which permit the decoding of linear codes over arbitrary finite fields $\mathbb{F}_q$. We will choose our parameters with regards to the complexity of this attack.

3 An Identification Scheme Based on qSD

To our knowledge, amongst all the identification schemes whose security does not depend upon some number theoretic assumptions, only three of them involve 5-pass, have a probability of cheating bounded by 1/2, and deal with values over a finite field $\mathbb{F}_q$ $(q > 2)$: PKP, Chen's scheme and CLE ([24],[8], [27]). Stern's 5-pass variant of SD is on a binary field, PPP [22] 5-pass variant has a probability of cheating bounded by 2/3 and $\mathcal{MQ}^*$-IP is a 2-pass protocol [30].

PKP, Chen's scheme and CLE have one thing in common : once the commitments sent, the verifier sends a random challenge which is an element $\alpha \in \mathbb{F}_q$. Then the prover sends back his secret vector scrambled by : a random vector, a random permutation and the value α. We proposed in this paper to show how to adapt this common step in the context of the qSD problem. Notice that while it is known since Barg's paper in 1994, that the qSD problem is NP-complete, it's only from the recent works developed in [18,19] that it was possible to set up realistic parameters for the security of an identification scheme based on the qSD problem. To end this remark, we just mention that Chen's scheme based on rank metric codes is not secured [7].

In what follows, we write elements of $\mathbb{F}_q^n$ as n blocks of size $\lceil \log_2(q) \rceil = N$. We represent each element of $\mathbb{F}_q$ as N bits. We first introduce a special transformation that we will use in our protocol.

Definition 7. *Let Σ be a permutation of $\{1, \dots, n\}$ and $\gamma = (\gamma_1, \dots, \gamma_n) \in \mathbb{F}_q^n$ such that $\forall i, \gamma_i \neq 0$. We define the transformation $\Pi_{\gamma,\Sigma}$ as :*

$$\begin{aligned} \Pi_{\gamma,\Sigma} : \mathbb{F}_q^n &\longrightarrow \mathbb{F}_q^n \\ v &\mapsto (\gamma_{\Sigma(1)} v_{\Sigma(1)}, \dots, \gamma_{\Sigma(n)} v_{\Sigma(n)}) \end{aligned}$$

Notice that $\forall \alpha \in \mathbb{F}_q, \forall v \in \mathbb{F}_q^n$, $\Pi_{\gamma,\Sigma}(\alpha v) = \alpha \Pi_{\gamma,\Sigma}(v)$, and $\mathsf{wt}(\Pi_{\gamma,\Sigma}(v)) = \mathsf{wt}(v)$.

Our identification scheme consists of two parts: a key generation algorithm (Fig. 2) and an identification protocol (Fig. 3); in the following we will describe these parts.

3.1 Key Generation

For $r = n - k$, the scheme uses a random $(r \times n)$ q-ary matrix H common to all users which can be considered to be the parity check matrix of a random linear (n, k) q-ary code. We can assume that H is described as $(I_r|M)$ where M is a random $r \times r$ matrix; as Gaussian elimination does not change the code generated by H, there is no loss of generality. Let κ be the security parameter. Fig. 2 describes the key generation process ($\mathrm{WF}_{\mathrm{ISD}}$ denotes the workfactor of the Information Set Decoding algorithm).

KeyGen:
Choose n, k, ω, and q such that $\mathrm{WF}_{\mathrm{ISD}}(n, r, \omega, q) \geq 2^{\kappa}$
$H \xleftarrow{\$} \mathbb{F}_q^{r \times n}$
$s \xleftarrow{\$} \mathbb{F}_q^n$, s.t. $\mathsf{wt}(s) = \omega$.
$y \leftarrow Hs^T$
Output $(\mathrm{sk}, \mathrm{pk}) = (s, (y, H, \omega))$

Fig. 2. Key generation algorithm: parameters n, k, w, q are public

3.2 Identification Protocol

The secret key holder can prove his knowledge of s by using two blending factors: the transformation by means of a permutation and a random vector. In the next section we will show how a dishonest prover not knowing s can cheat the verifier in the protocol with probability of $q/2(q-1)$. Thus, the protocol has to be run several times to detect cheating provers. The security of the scheme relies on the hardness of the general decoding problem, that is on the difficulty of determining the preimage s of $y = Hs^T$. In Fig. 3, h denotes a hash function and S_n the symmetric group of degree n.

4 Properties and Security of the Scheme

4.1 Zero-Knowledge-Proof

Let $I = (H, y, \omega)$ be the public data shared by the prover and the verifier in our construction, and let $P(I, s)$ be the predicate:

$P(I, s) =$ "s is a vector which satisfies $Hs^T = y, \mathsf{wt}(s) = \omega$". We show in this section that the protocol presented in Fig. 3 corresponds to a zero-knowledge interactive proof. To this end, we provide in the following proofs for the completeness, soundness, and zero-knowledge properties of our identification scheme.

Prover $\mathcal{P}$		**Verifier $\mathcal{V}$**
$(\mathrm{sk}, \mathrm{pk}) = (s, (y, H, \omega)) \longleftarrow$ KEYGEN		$\mathrm{pk} = y, H, \omega$
$u \xleftarrow{\$} \mathbb{F}_q^n, \Sigma \xleftarrow{\$} S_n$		
$\gamma \xleftarrow{\$} \mathbb{F}_q^{n*}$		
$c_1 \leftarrow h\left(\Sigma, \gamma, Hu^T\right)$		
$c_2 \leftarrow h\left(\Pi_{\gamma,\Sigma}(u), \Pi_{\gamma,\Sigma}(s)\right)$	$\xrightarrow{c_1, c_2}$	
	$\xleftarrow{\alpha}$	$\alpha \xleftarrow{\$} \mathbb{F}_q^*$
$\beta \longleftarrow \Pi_{\gamma,\Sigma}(u + \alpha s)$	$\xrightarrow{\beta}$	
	$\xleftarrow{\text{Challenge } b}$	$b \xleftarrow{\$} \{0, 1\}$
If $b = 0$:	$\xrightarrow{\Sigma, \gamma}$	**Check** $c_1 \stackrel{?}{=} h(\Sigma, \gamma, H\Pi_{\gamma,\Sigma}^{-1}(\beta)^T - \alpha y)$
Else:	$\xrightarrow{\Pi_{\gamma,\Sigma}(s)}$	**Check** $c_2 \stackrel{?}{=} h(\beta - \alpha\Pi_{\gamma,\Sigma}(s), \Pi_{\gamma,\Sigma}(s))$, $\mathsf{wt}(\Pi_{\gamma,\Sigma}(s)) \stackrel{?}{=} \omega$

Fig. 3. Identification protocol

Completeness. Clearly, each honest prover which has the knowledge of a valid secret s, the blending mask u, and the permutation $\Pi_{\gamma,\Sigma}$ for the public data can answer correctly any of the honest verifier's queries in any given round, thus the completeness property of the scheme is satisfied.

Zero-Knowledge. The zero-knowledge property for our identification protocol (Fig. 3) is proved in the random oracle model assuming that the hash function h has statistical independence properties.

Theorem 1. *The construction in Fig. 3 is a zero-knowledge interactive proof for $P(I, s)$ in the random oracle model.*

Proof. The proof uses the classical idea of resettable simulation [13]. Let M be a polynomial-time probabilistic Turing machine (simulator) using a dishonest verifier. Because of the two interaction with the prover, we have to assume that the dishonest verifier could contrive two strategies : $St_1(c_1, c_2)$ taking as input the prover's commitments and generating a value $\alpha \in \mathbb{F}_q^*$, $St_2(c_1, c_2, \beta)$ taking as input the prover's commitments, the answer β and generating as output a challenge in the set $\{0, 1\}$. M will generate a communication tape representing the interaction between prover and verifier. The goal is to produce a communication tape whose distribution is indistinguishable from a real tape by an honest interaction. The simulator M is constructed as follows :

Step 1. M randomly picks a query b from $\{0, 1\}$.

- If $b = 0$, M randomly chooses: u, γ, and Σ, and solves the equation: $Hs'^T = y$ for some s' not necessarily satisfying the condition $\mathsf{wt}(s') = \omega$. The commitments are taken as $c_1 = h(\Sigma, \gamma, Hu^T)$, and c_2 as a random string. By simulating the verifier, M applies $St_1(c_1, c_2)$ to get $\alpha \in \mathbb{F}_q^*$, and then computes

$\beta = \Pi_{\gamma,\Sigma}(u + \alpha s')$, and has the information needed to derive the simulated communication data between prover and verifier. Therefore the candidates to be written in the communication tape consist of elements $A = c_1 || c_2$, β and $ans = \gamma || \Sigma$. Taking into account the uniform distribution of the random variables used in the computation of A, ans and β, it follows that the distribution of these elements is indistinguishable from those resulting from a fair interaction.

– If $b = 1$ the machine also chooses u, γ, and Σ at random. This time it picks s as random from the set $\mathbb{F}_q^n$ with weight ω. The commitment c_1 will be given uniformly at random value and $c_2 = h(\Pi_{\gamma,\Sigma}(u), \Pi_{\gamma,\Sigma}(s))$. Again, from $St_1(c_1, c_2)$, the machine computes $\beta = \Pi_{\gamma,\Sigma}(u+\alpha s)$, and has the information needed to derive the simulated communication data. The communication set features elements $A = c_1 || c_2$, β and $ans = \Pi_{\gamma,\Sigma}(s)$. The uniformly random character of the choices made will render these elements indistinguishable from those resulting from a fair interaction.

Step 2. M applies the verifier's strategy $St_2(c_1, c_2, \beta)$ obtaining b' as result.
Step 3. When $b = b'$, the machine M writes on its communication tape the values of A, α, β, b and ans. If the values differ, however, nothing is written and the machine returns to step 1.

Therefore, in 2δ rounds on average, M produces a communication tape indistinguishable from another that corresponds to a fair identification process execution that takes δ rounds. This concludes the proof. □

Soundness: We now show that at each round, a dishonest prover is able to cheat a verifier to accept his identity with a probability limited by $q/(2(q-1))$.

Let us suppose that a dishonest prover has devised the following strategies to cope with the challenges that the verifier is expected to send. The first strategy (st_0) corresponds to the actions the prover takes when hoping to receive 0 as challenge. He chooses u, γ, and Σ at random and solves the equation $Hs'^T = y$ without satisfying the condition $\mathsf{wt}(s') = \omega$. Then he computes c_1 according to these values and randomly generates c_2. Thus, he will be able to answer the challenge $b = 0$, regardless of the value of α chosen by the verifier. The second strategy (st_1) is successful in case a value 1 is received as challenge. He chooses u, γ and Σ at random and picks an s' with Hamming weight w. With this choice, the commitment c_2 can be correctly reconstructed, and the Hamming weight of the fake private key validated. The commitment c_1 is randomly generated.

Now, these two strategies can be improved. Indeed a dishonest prover can try to make a guess on the value α sent by the verifier. Let α_c be the guessed value, so that β would be $\Pi_{\gamma,\Sigma}(u + \alpha_c s')$.

In st_0, instead of randomly generating c_2, he computes $c_2 = h(\beta - \alpha_c \tilde{s}, \tilde{s})$ where $\tilde{s}$ is a random word of Hamming weight w which will be sent as answer (if $b = 1$) instead of $\Pi_{\gamma,\Sigma}(s')$. With such a strategy, the cheater can answer to $b = 0$ regardless the value of α chosen by the verifier and to $b = 1$ if $\alpha = \alpha_c$.

In st_1, instead of randomly generating c_1, he computes $c_1 = h(\Sigma, \gamma, Hu^T + \alpha_c(Hs'^T - y))$. With such a strategy, the cheater can answer to $b = 1$ regardless the value of α chosen by the verifier and to $b = 0$ if $\alpha = \alpha_c$.

Therefore, when we consider the probability space represented by the random variables b and α, the success probability of a strategy st for one round is given by:

$$P[\text{successful impersonation}] = \sum_{i=0}^{1} P(st = st_i)P(b = i) + P(st = st_i)P(b = 1 - i)P(\alpha = \alpha_c) = \frac{q}{2(q-1)}.$$

Though it was calculated for the particular strategies above, this value also corresponds to the upper limit for generic cheating strategies as shown below. The security assumptions that we make are as follows: we require that the commitment scheme be computationally binding and that the qSD problem be hard. We now show that if a cheating prover manages to answer more than $(\frac{q}{2(q-1)})^\delta$ of the queries made by a verifier after δ rounds, either of the security assumptions above was broken, as stated in the theorem below.

Let us denote by $\overline{B}$ an honest verifier and by $\tilde{A}$ a cheating prover.

Theorem 2. *If $\overline{B}$ accepts $\tilde{A}$ proof with probability $\geqslant (\frac{q}{2(q-1)})^\delta + \varepsilon$, then there exists a polynomial time probabilistic machine M which, with overwhelming probability, either computes a valid secret s or finds a collision for the hash function.*

Proof. Let T be the execution tree of $(\tilde{A}, \overline{B})$ corresponding to all possible questions of the verifier when the adversary has a random tape RA. $\overline{B}$ may ask $2(q-1)$ possible questions at each stage. Each question is a couple (α, b) where $\alpha \in \mathbb{F}_q^*$ and $b \in \{0, 1\}$. First we are going to show that, unless a hash-collision has been found, a secret key s can be computed from a vertex with $q+1$ sons. Then we will show that a polynomial time M can find such a vertex in T with overwhelming probability.

Let V be a vertex with $q+1$ sons. This corresponds to a situation where 2 commitments c_1, c_2 have been made and where the cheater has been able to answer to $q+1$ queries. That is to say that there exists $\alpha \neq \alpha'$ such that the cheater answered correctly to the queries $(\alpha, 0)$, $(\alpha, 1)$, $(\alpha', 0)$ and $(\alpha', 1)$. Now let :

- (β, Σ, γ) the answer sent for the query $(\alpha, 0)$,
- (β, z) the answer sent for the query $(\alpha, 1)$,
- $(\beta', \Sigma', \gamma')$ the answer sent for the query $(\alpha', 0)$,
- (β', z') the answer sent for the query $(\alpha', 1)$,

the value z (resp. z') represents the expected value $\Pi_{\gamma,\Sigma}(s)$, (resp. $\Pi_{\gamma',\Sigma'}(s)$), hence $\mathrm{wt}(z) = \omega$. Notice also that the same value β (resp. β') is used for $(\alpha, 0)$ and $(\alpha, 1)$ (resp. $(\alpha', 0)$ and $(\alpha', 1)$) since it is sent before the bit challenge b. Then, because commitment c_1 (resp. c_2) is consistent with both queries $(\alpha, 0)$ and $(\alpha', 0)$ (resp. $(\alpha, 1)$ and $(\alpha', 1)$), we have:

$$h(\Sigma, \gamma, H\Pi_{\gamma,\Sigma}^{-1}(\beta)^T - \alpha y) = c_1 = h(\Sigma', \gamma', H\Pi_{\gamma',\Sigma'}^{-1}(\beta')^T - \alpha' y),$$

and

$$h(\beta - \alpha z, z) = c_2 = h(\beta' - \alpha' z', z') .$$

The equations are satisfied by finding collisions on the hash function or having the following equalities:

$$\begin{aligned} \Sigma &= \Sigma' \\ \gamma &= \gamma' \\ z &= z' \\ H\Pi^{-1}_{\gamma,\Sigma}(\beta)^T - \alpha y &= H\Pi^{-1}_{\gamma',\Sigma'}(\beta')^T - \alpha' y \\ \beta - \alpha z &= \beta' - \alpha' z' . \end{aligned}$$

Hence:

$$\begin{aligned} H\Pi^{-1}_{\gamma,\Sigma}(\beta - \beta')^T(\alpha - \alpha')^{-1} &= y \\ (\beta - \beta')^T(\alpha - \alpha')^{-1} &= z . \end{aligned}$$

Then:

$$H\Pi^{-1}_{\gamma,\Sigma}(z) = y .$$

Therefore, the value $s = \Pi^{-1}_{\gamma,\Sigma}(z)$ with $\mathsf{wt}(\Pi^{-1}_{\gamma,\Sigma}(z)) = \mathsf{wt}(z) = \omega$, obtained from the equalities above, constitutes a secret key that can be used to impersonate the real prover.

Now, the assumption implies that the probability for T to have a vertex with $q+1$ sons is at least ε. Indeed, let us consider RA the random tape where $\tilde{A}$ randomly picks its values, and let Q bet the set $\mathbb{F}_q^* \times \{0,1\}$. These two sets are considered as probability spaces both of them with the uniform distribution.

A triple $(c, \alpha, b) \in (RA \times Q)^\delta$ represents the commitments, answers and queries exchanged between $\tilde{A}$ and $\bar{B}$ during an identification process (c represents commitments and answers). We will say that (c, α, b) is "valid", if the execution of $(\tilde{A}, \bar{B})$ leads to the success state.

Let V be the subset of $(RA \times Q)^\delta$ composed of all the valid triples. The hypothesis of the lemma means that:

$$\frac{\mathrm{card}(V)}{\mathrm{card}((RA \times Q)^\delta)} \geq \left(\frac{q}{2(q-1)}\right)^\delta + \varepsilon.$$

Let Ω_δ be a subset of RA^δ such that:

- If $c \in \Omega_\delta$, then $q^\delta + 1 \leq \mathrm{card}\{(\alpha, b),\ (c, \alpha, b) \text{ be valid }\} \leq (2(q-1))^\delta$,
- If $c \in RA^\delta \setminus \Omega_\delta$, then $0 \leq \mathrm{card}\{(\alpha, b),\ (c, \alpha, b) \text{ be valid }\} \leq q^\delta$.

Then, $V = \{\text{valid } (c, \alpha, b), c \in \Omega_\delta\} \cup \{\text{valid } (c, \alpha, b), c \in RA^\delta \setminus \Omega_\delta\}$, therefore:

$$\mathrm{card}(V) \leqslant \mathrm{card}(\Omega_\delta)(2(q-1))^\delta + (\mathrm{card}(RA^\delta) - \mathrm{card}(\Omega_\delta))q^\delta.$$

Thus

$$\frac{\operatorname{card}(V)}{\operatorname{card}((RA \times Q)^{\delta})} \leqslant \frac{\operatorname{card}(\Omega_{\delta})}{\operatorname{card}(RA^{\delta})} + q^{\delta}\left((2(q-1))^{-\delta} - \frac{\operatorname{card}(\Omega_{\delta})}{\operatorname{card}((RA \times Q)^{\delta})}\right)$$

$$\leq \frac{\operatorname{card}(\Omega_{\delta})}{\operatorname{card}(RA^{\delta})} + \left(\frac{q}{2(q-1)}\right)^{\delta}.$$

It follows that:

$$\frac{\operatorname{card}(\Omega_{\delta})}{\operatorname{card}(RA^{\delta})} \geq \varepsilon.$$

This shows that the probability that an intruder might answer to (at least) $q^{\delta}+1$ of the verifier's queries, by choosing random values, is greater than ε. Now, if more than $q^{\delta}+1$ queries are bypassed by an intruder then $T(RA)$ has at least $q^{\delta}+1$ leaves, i.e. $T(RA)$ has at least a vertex with $q+1$ sons.

So, by resetting $\tilde{A}$ $\frac{1}{\varepsilon}$ times, and by repeating again, it is possible to find an execution tree with a vertex with $q+1$ sons with probability arbitrary close to one. This theorem implies that either the hash function h is not collision free, or the qSD problem is not intractable. Therefore, the soundness property was demonstrated, given that one must have the probability negligibly close to 1/2.

4.2 Security and Parameters

As for binary SD identification schemes, the security of our scheme relies on three properties of random linear q-ary codes:

1. Random linear codes satisfy the q-ary Gilbert-Varshamov lower bound [15];
2. For large n almost all linear codes lie over the Gilbert-Varshamov bound [20];
3. Solving the q-ary syndrome decoding problem for random codes is NP-complete [1].

We now have to choose parameters for an instantiation of the construction in Fig. 3. We take into account the bounds corresponding to the Information Set Decoding algorithm over $\mathbb{F}_q$ in [18] and propose parameters for a security level of at least 2^{80}. The number of rounds must then be chosen in order to minimize the success probability of a cheater.

Since we deal with random codes, we have to select parameters with respect to the Gilbert-Varshamov bound (see Definition 6), which is optimal for $k = r = n/2$. We assume this to be true in the remainder of the paper.

Let N be the number of bits needed to encode an element of $\mathbb{F}_q$, ℓ_h the output size of the hash function h, ℓ_{Σ} *(resp.* ℓ_{γ}*)* the size of the seed used to generate the permutation Σ *(resp. the permutation* γ*)*, and δ the number of rounds. We have the following properties for our scheme:

Size of the matrix in bits:

$$k \times k \times N (\text{we use the systematic form of } H)$$

Size of the public identification:

$$kN$$

Size of the secret key:

$$nN$$

Total number of bits exchanged:

$$\delta(2\ell_h + N + nN + 1 + (\ell_\Sigma + \ell_\gamma + nN)/2)$$

Prover's computation complexity over $\mathbb{F}_q$:

$$\delta((k^2 + \mathsf{wt}(s)) \text{ multiplications} + (k^2 + \mathsf{wt}(s)) \text{ additions})$$

To obtain a precise complexity on the workfactor of ISD algorithms over $\mathbb{F}_q$ we've used the code developed by C. Peters, which estimates the number of iterations needed for an attack using a Markov chain implementation [19]. ISD algorithms depend on a set of parameters and this code allows to test which ones can minimize the complexity of the attack.

For our scheme, we suggest the following parameters:

$$q = 256, n = 128, k = 64, \mathsf{wt}(s) = 49.$$

The complexity of an attack using ISD algorithms is then at least 2^{87}. For the same security level in SD schemes, we need to take $n = 700, k = 350, \mathsf{wt}(s) = 75$.

In [26], Stern has proposed two 5-pass variants of his scheme. The first one to lower the computing load. However, this variant slightly increases the probability of cheating rather than lowering it, and thus increases the communication complexity. The other one minimizes the number of rounds and lower the probability of cheating to $(1/2)^\delta$. The following table shows the advantage regarding the communication cost and the size of the matrix of our scheme in comparison with Stern's initial proposal and his second variant, for the same security level of 2^{87} and an impersonation resistance of 2^{-16}. We considered that all seeds used are 128 bits long and that hash values are 160 bits long.

	SD	G-SD	Stern 5-pass	Our scheme
Rounds	28	28	16	16
Matrix size (bits)	122500	122500	122500	32768
Public Id (bits)	350	700	2450	512
Secret key (bits)	700	1050	4900	1024
Communication (bits)	42019	35486	62272	31888
Prover's Computation	$2^{22.7}$op. over $\mathbb{F}_2$	$2^{22.7}$op. over $\mathbb{F}_2$	$2^{21.92}$op. over $\mathbb{F}_2$	2^{16}mult + 2^{16}add op. over $\mathbb{F}_{256}$

Fig. 4. SD schemes vs. q-ary SD scheme, security level 2^{87}, probability of cheating 2^{-16}

To obtain a security level of 2^{128} the indicated parameters are,

$$q = 256, n = 208, k = 104, \mathsf{wt}(s) = 78,$$

which gives a scheme with the following properties:

Number of Rounds : 16
Matrix size (bits) : 86528
Public Id (bits) : 832
Secret key (bits) : 1664
Communication (bits) : 47248
Prover's Computation : $2^{17.4}$mult. and $2^{17.4}$add. over $\mathbb{F}_{256}$

4.3 Comparison with Other Schemes

We compare our scheme to some other zero-knowledge schemes whose security does not depend upon number theoretic assumptions, and where the whole probability of cheating is bounded by $(1/2)^\delta$ (except for PPP). We use some results given in [21], [22], [23] and [14] and try to adapt parameters such that the security level be as near as possible than 2^{87} for a fair comparison. Notice that for CLE, the result given in our table does not fit with what is given in [22] and [23]. Indeed, as mentioned in [27], the zero-knowledge property of the scheme can only be stated if two quantities ($S\sigma$ and $T\tau$) are public in addition to the public identification. For PPP, we considered the 3 pass version instead of the five one because, as stated by the authors in [22], it is more efficient from a computational point of view and furthermore easier to implement. As for our scheme, only a part of the matrix can be stored in PKP. All these schemes uses a random matrix shared by all users. In Fig. 5, we considered that all seeds used are 128 bits long and that hash values are 160 bits long. We have not considered for the prover's complexity the cost of the computation of hash values but the number of hash values to compute is mentioned in Fig. 5.

Notice that for a level of security near from 2^{80} we could have used smaller parameters. This would improve the general performances of our scheme, but we think that the suggested parameters fit well for practical implementation.

	PKP	CLE	PPP	Our scheme
Rounds	16	16	39	16
Matrix size	24×24	24×24	161×177	64×64
over the field	$\mathbb{F}_{251}$	$\mathbb{F}_{257}$	$\mathbb{F}_2$	$\mathbb{F}_{256}$
Public Id (bits)	384	288	245	512
Secret key (bits)	128	192	177	1024
Communication (bits)	13456	16528	51441	31888
Prover's Computation	$2^{13.28}$add., $2^{13.28}$ mul.	$2^{13.28}$add., $2^{13.34}$ mul.	$2^{21.1}$ add., $2^{21.1}$ mul.	2^{16} add. +, 2^{16} mul.
over the field	$\mathbb{F}_{251}$	$\mathbb{F}_{257}$	$\mathbb{F}_{127}$	$\mathbb{F}_{256}$
Number of hash values	2	2	8	2
Security level	2^{85}	$\simeq 2^{84}$	$> 2^{74}$	2^{87}

Fig. 5. qSD scheme vs. other schemes, probability of cheating 2^{-16}

To see how the performances are modified with a lower probability of cheating, interested readers can consult [9].

4.4 Reducing Public Key Size

Double-circulant construction. The authors of [12] propose a variation of the Stern identification scheme by using double-circulant codes. The circulant structure of the matrix used as a public key requires very little storage and greatly simplifies the computation, as the binary matrix needs never to be wholly generated. Still in this context, the authors show that all random double-circulant $[2k, k]$ codes such that k be prime and 2 be a primitive root of $\mathbb{Z}/k\mathbb{Z}$ lie on the Gilbert-Varshamov bound. They propose a scheme with a public key of size 347 bits and a private key of size 694 bits.

We can use this construction in our context by replacing the random q-ary matrix H by a random q-ary double-circulant matrix. In this case, the parameters using this construction are $q = 256, n = 134, k = 67, \mathsf{wt}(s) = 49$; this gives a size for the public data of 1072 bits (536 for the matrix and 536 for the public identification) and a private key of size 1072 bits for almost the same complexity for an ISD attack.

We can also imagine a construction based on double-dyadic codes or embedding the syndrome in the matrix as proposed in [17] and [12].

Against these aforementioned constructions, there are recently several *new* structural attacks appeared in [28] and [10]; these attacks extract the private key of some parameters of the variants presented in [2] and [17]. Since in our context we deal with random codes, we are not addressed by this kind of attacks.

Furthermore in [6] the authors describe a secure implementation of the Stern scheme using quasi-circulant codes. Our proposal inherits the advantages of the original Stern scheme against leakage of information, such as SPA and DPA attacks.

5 Conclusion

We have defined an identification scheme which among all the schemes based on the SD problem has the best parameters for the size of the public data as well as for the communication complexity. Moreover, we propose a variant with a reduced public key size.

The improvement proposed here to the Stern scheme can be applied to all the Stern-based identification and signature schemes (such as identity-based identification and signature scheme [5] or threshold ring signature scheme [16] for example).

We believe that this type of scheme is a realistic alternative to the usual number theory identification schemes in the case of constrained environments such as, for smart cards and for applications like Pay-TV or vending machines.

References

1. Barg, S.: Some new NP-complete coding problems. Probl. Peredachi Inf. 30, 23–28 (1994)
2. Berger, T.P., Cayrel, P.-L., Gaborit, P., Otmani, A.: Reducing key length of the mcEliece cryptosystem. In: Preneel, B. (ed.) AFRICACRYPT 2009. LNCS, vol. 5580, pp. 77–97. Springer, Heidelberg (2009)
3. Berlekamp, E., McEliece, R., van Tilborg, H.: On the inherent intractability of certain coding problems. IEEE Transactions on Information Theory 24(3), 384–386 (1978)
4. Bernstein, D.J., Buchmann, J., Dahmen, E.: Post-Quantum Cryptography. Springer, Heidelberg (2008)
5. Cayrel, P.-L., Gaborit, P., Girault, M.: Identity-based identification and signature schemes using correcting codes. In: Augot, D., Sendrier, N., Tillich, J.-P. (eds.) International Workshop on Coding and Cryptography, WCC 2007, pp. 69–78 (2007)
6. Cayrel, P.-L., Gaborit, P., Prouff, E.: Secure implementation of the stern authentication and signature schemes for low-resource devices. In: Grimaud, G., Standaert, F.-X. (eds.) CARDIS 2008. LNCS, vol. 5189, pp. 191–205. Springer, Heidelberg (2008)
7. Chabaud, F., Stern, J.: The cryptographic security of the syndrome decoding problem for rank distance codes. In: Kim, K.-c., Matsumoto, T. (eds.) ASIACRYPT 1996. LNCS, vol. 1163, pp. 368–381. Springer, Heidelberg (1996)
8. Chen, K.: Improved girault identification scheme. Electronics Letters 30(19), 1590–1591 (1994)
9. Interactive comparison of some zero knowledge identification schemes, `http://tinyurl.com/32gxn8w`
10. Faugère, J.-C., Otmani, A., Perret, L., Tillich, J.-P.: Algebraic cryptanalysis of mcEliece variants with compact keys. In: Gilbert, H. (ed.) EUROCRYPT 2010. LNCS, vol. 6110, pp. 279–298. Springer, Heidelberg (2010)
11. Fiat, A., Shamir, A.: How to prove yourself: Practical solutions to identification and signature problems. In: Odlyzko, A.M. (ed.) CRYPTO 1986. LNCS, vol. 263, pp. 186–194. Springer, Heidelberg (1987)
12. Gaborit, P., Girault, M.: Lightweight code-based authentication and signature. In: IEEE International Symposium on Information Theory – ISIT 2007, Nice, France, pp. 191–195. IEEE, Los Alamitos (2007)
13. Goldreich, O.: Zero-knowledge twenty years after its invention (2002), `http://eprint.iacr.org/`
14. Jaulmes, É., Joux, A.: Cryptanalysis of pkp: a new approach. In: Kim, K.-c. (ed.) PKC 2001. LNCS, vol. 1992, pp. 165–172. Springer, Heidelberg (2001)
15. MacWilliams, F.J., Sloane, N.J.A.: The theory of error correcting codes. North-Holland, Amsterdam (1977)
16. Aguilar Melchor, C., Cayrel, P.-L., Gaborit, P.: A new efficient threshold ring signature scheme based on coding theory. In: Buchmann, J., Ding, J. (eds.) PQCrypto 2008. LNCS, vol. 5299, pp. 1–16. Springer, Heidelberg (2008)
17. Misoczki, R., Barreto, P.S.L.M.: Compact mcEliece keys from goppa codes. In: Jacobson Jr., M.J., Rijmen, V., Safavi-Naini, R. (eds.) SAC 2009. LNCS, vol. 5867, pp. 376–392. Springer, Heidelberg (2009)
18. Niebuhr, R., Cayrel, P.-L., Bulygin, S., Buchmann, J.: On lower bounds for information set decoding over Fq. In: SCC 2010 (2010) (preprint)

19. Peters, C.: Information-set decoding for linear codes over Fq (2009), http://eprint.iacr.org/
20. Pierce, J.N.: Limit distributions of the minimum distance of random linear codes. IEEE Trans. Inf. theory 13, 595–599 (1967)
21. Pointcheval, D.: A new identification scheme based on the perceptrons problem. In: De Santis, A. (ed.) EUROCRYPT 1994. LNCS, vol. 950, pp. 319–328. Springer, Heidelberg (1995)
22. Pointcheval, D., Poupard, G.: A new NP-complete problem and public-key identification. Des. Codes Cryptography 28(1), 5–31 (2003)
23. Poupard, G.: A realistic security analysis of identification schemes based on combinatorial problems. European Transactions on Telecommunications 8(5), 471–480 (1997)
24. Shamir, A.: An efficient identification scheme based on permuted kernels. In: Brassard, G. (ed.) CRYPTO 1989. LNCS, vol. 435, pp. 606–609. Springer, Heidelberg (1990)
25. Stern, J.: A method for finding codewords of small weight. In: Wolfmann, J., Cohen, G. (eds.) Coding Theory 1988. LNCS, vol. 388, pp. 106–113. Springer, Heidelberg (1989)
26. Stern, J.: A new identification scheme based on syndrome decoding. In: Stinson, D.R. (ed.) CRYPTO 1993. LNCS, vol. 773, pp. 13–21. Springer, Heidelberg (1994)
27. Stern, J.: Designing identification schemes with keys of short size. In: Desmedt, Y.G. (ed.) CRYPTO 1994. LNCS, vol. 839, pp. 164–173. Springer, Heidelberg (1994)
28. Gauthier Umana, V., Leander, G.: Practical key recovery attacks on two McEliece variants (2009), http://eprint.iacr.org/2009/509.pdf
29. Véron, P.: Improved identification schemes based on error-correcting codes. Appl. Algebra Eng. Commun. Comput. 8(1), 57–69 (1996)
30. Wolf, C., Preneel, B.: $\mathcal{MQ}^*$-ip: An identity-based identification scheme without number-theoric assumptions (2010), http://eprint.iacr.org/

Optimal Covering Codes for Finding Near-Collisions

Mario Lamberger[1] and Vincent Rijmen[1,2]

[1] Institute for Applied Information Processing and Communications
Graz University of Technology, Inffeldgasse 16a, A–8010 Graz, Austria
[2] Dept. of Electrical Engineering ESAT/COSIC, K.U. Leuven and Interdisciplinary
Institute for BroadBand Technology (IBBT), Kasteelpark Arenberg 10,
B–3001 Heverlee, Belgium
mario.lamberger@iaik.tugraz.at

Abstract. Recently, a new generic method to find near-collisions for cryptographic hash functions in a memoryless way has been proposed. This method is based on classical cycle-finding techniques and covering codes. This paper contributes to the coding theory aspect of this method by giving the optimal solution to a problem which arises when constructing a suitable code as the direct sum of Hamming and trivial codes.

Keywords: Hash functions, memoryless near-collisions, covering codes, direct sum construction, digital expansions.

1 Introduction

The field of hash function research has developed significantly in the light of the attacks on some of the most frequently used hash functions like MD4, MD5 and SHA-1 (cf. [5,6,7,22,23]). As a consequence, academia and industry started to evaluate alternative hash functions, *e.g.* in the SHA-3 initiative organized by NIST [16]. During this ongoing evaluation, not only the three classical security requirements *collision resistance*, *preimage resistance* and *second preimage resistance* are considered. Researchers look at (semi-)free-start collisions, near-collisions, etc. Whenever a 'behavior different from that expected of a random oracle' could be demonstrated, the hash function is considered suspect, and so are weaknesses that are demonstrated only for the compression function and not for the full hash function.

Coding theory has entered the stage of hash function cryptanalysis quite early where an integral part in the attack strategies is based on the search for low-weight code words in a linear code (*cf.* [1,3,18] among others). In this paper, we want to elaborate on a newly proposed application of coding theory to hash function cryptanalysis. In [13], it is demonstrated how to use covering codes to find near-collisions for hash functions in a memoryless way. We also want to refer to the recent paper [10] which look at similar concepts from the viewpoint of locality sensitive hashing.

A. Biryukov, G. Gong, and D.R. Stinson (Eds.): SAC 2010, LNCS 6544, pp. 187–197, 2011.

The rest of the paper is organized as follows: In Section 2 we review some basic definitions and well known generic algorithms. Section 3 gives the main idea on how to use covering codes to find near-collisions for hash functions. Section 4 shows how to construct suitable codes for the method of Section 3. Section 5 finally presents the optimal solution to a problem that arises in Section 4 which asks how to construct a code of given length and covering radius that can be used to find near-collisions. Finally, we conclude in Section 6.

2 Collisions and Near-Collisions of Hash Functions

In all of the following, we will work with binary values, where we identify $\{0,1\}^n$ with $\mathbb{Z}_2^n$. Let "+" denote the n-bit exclusive-or operation. The Hamming weight of a vector $v \in \mathbb{Z}_2^n$ is denoted by $\mathrm{w}(v) = \#\{i \mid v_i = 1\}$ and the Hamming distance of two vectors by $\mathrm{d}(u,v) = \mathrm{w}(u+v)$. The Handbook of Applied Cryptography defines *near-collision resistance* as follows:

Definition 1 (Near-Collision Resistance [15, page 331]). *It should be hard to find any two inputs m, m^* with $m \neq m^*$ such that $H(m)$ and $H(m^*)$ differ in only a small number of bits:*

$$\mathrm{d}(H(m), H(m^*)) \leq \epsilon. \tag{1}$$

For ease of later use we also give the following definition:

Definition 2. *A message pair m, m^* with $m \neq m^*$ is called an ϵ-near-collision for H if* (1) *holds.*

The definitions suggest that a hash function for which an efficient algorithm is known that allows an attacker to construct near-collisions, can no longer be considered to be ideal. Above that, for several designs, near-collisions for the compression function can be converted to collisions for the hash function (*e.g.* [14,23]).

Collisions are of course a special case of near-collisions where the parameter $\epsilon = 0$. The generic method for finding collisions for a given hash function is based on the *birthday paradox* and attributed to Yuval [24]. This birthday attack requires approximately $2^{n/2}$ hash function computations and a table of the same size. In practice, memory is expensive relative to computation, and memoryless algorithms are given the preference over algorithms with large memory requirements. There are well established cycle-finding techniques (due to Floyd, Brent, Nivasch, *cf.* [2,12,17]) that remove the memory requirements from an attack based on the birthday paradox (see also [20]). These methods work by repeated iteration of the underlying hash function where in all of these applications the function is considered to behave like a random function.

Let S_ϵ be the set $\{x \in \mathbb{Z}_2^n \mid \mathrm{w}(x) \leq \epsilon\}$. An approach analogous to the classical birthday attack to find ϵ-near-collisions is to start with an empty table and randomly select messages m^j, compute $H(m^j)$ and check whether or not the entry $(H(m^j) + \delta, m^*)$ is present in the table, $\forall \delta \in S_\epsilon$ and an arbitrary m^* If no match is found, then we add $(H(m^j), m^j)$ to the table and select a new message. Proceeding in this manner, the expected number of messages that we need to hash and store before we find an ϵ-near-collision is about:

$$\frac{2^{n/2}}{\sqrt{\sum_{i=0}^{\epsilon}\binom{n}{i}}}. \tag{2}$$

We see that, depending on ϵ, finding ϵ-near-collisions is clearly easier than finding collisions.

3 Memoryless Near-Collisions Based on Coding Theory

In [13], the question is raised whether or not the above mentioned cycle-finding techniques are also applicable to the problem of finding near-collisions. We now give a short account of the ideas of [13].

Since Definition 2 includes collisions as well, the task of finding near-collisions is easier than finding collisions. The goal is now to find a generic method to construct near-collisions more efficiently than the generic methods to find collisions.

The first straight forward approach is to apply the cycle-finding algorithms to the problem of finding near-collisions is a projection based approach. The basic idea is to fix ϵ bit positions in $\mathbb{Z}_2^n$ and define the map π to set the bits of an $x \in \mathbb{Z}_2^n$ to zero at these ϵ positions. Then, we can apply a cycle-finding algorithm to the map $\pi \circ H$ which can find an ϵ-near-collision in a memoryless way with a complexity of about $2^{(n-\epsilon)/2}$. This can be even improved by setting $2\epsilon + 1$ bits to zero, since the probability is still $\frac{1}{2}$ that a collision for $\pi \circ H$ is an ϵ-near-collision, thus improving the complexity to about

$$2^{(n-1)/2-\epsilon}. \tag{3}$$

A drawback to this solution is of course that we can only find ϵ-near-collisions of a limited shape (depending on the fixed bit positions), so only a fraction of all possible ϵ-near-collisions can be detected, namely

$$\frac{2^{\epsilon}}{\sum_{i=0}^{\epsilon}\binom{n}{i}}. \tag{4}$$

To circumvent this drawback, there is the following nice solution. The idea is to replace the projection π by a more complicated function g. The choice for g is to be the decoding operation of a certain *covering code* $\mathcal{C}$. These codes are concerned with the so called *covering radius*

$$R(\mathcal{C}) = \max_{x\in\mathbb{Z}_2^n} \min_{c\in\mathcal{C}} \mathrm{d}(x, c)\,, \tag{5}$$

that is, R is the smallest radius such that the union of Hamming spheres $B_R(c)$ around the codewords of $\mathcal{C}$ cover the whole space $\mathbb{Z}_2^n$. If the minimum distance between codewords is the parameter of importance, then we speak of error-correcting codes. Covering codes are a well researched topic in coding theory, see for example the monograph [4] for a thorough introduction.

The decoding function g of a covering code with covering radius R groups possible outputs of the hash function H into classes where for every two elements x, y in such a class we have $\mathrm{d}(x, y) \leq 2R$. Now instead of iterating the function on the output space of the hash function, one does so on the function over classes represented by their canonical members. If two different inputs are mapped into the same class, it corresponds to an ϵ-near-collision with $\epsilon = 2R$. In other words, we apply the cycle-finding algorithms mentioned in Section 2 to the function $g \circ H$ under the assumption that H acts as a random function. The main idea can thus be summarized as follows:

Theorem 1 ([13]). *Let H be a hash function of output size n. Let $\mathcal{C}$ be a covering code of the same length n, size K and covering radius $R(\mathcal{C})$ and assume there exists an efficiently computable map g satisfying*

$$\begin{aligned} g : \mathbb{Z}_2^n &\to \mathcal{C} \\ x &\mapsto c \quad \textit{with} \\ \mathrm{d}(x, c) &\leq R(\mathcal{C}). \end{aligned} \tag{6}$$

Then, we can find $2R(\mathcal{C})$-near-collisions for H with a complexity of about $\sqrt{K}$ and with virtually no memory requirements.

In order to be efficient, the task is thus to find a code $\mathcal{C}$ with K as small as possible. However, also the computability of the function g defined in (6) plays a crucial role. An evaluation of g should be efficient when compared to a hash function call. The actual task is thus to find a code $\mathcal{C}$ with given length n and covering radius R, such that the size of $\mathcal{C}$ is as small as possible and decoding can be done efficiently.

A general bound for the size of a covering code is the so called *Sphere Covering Bound*, which states that if a code $\mathcal{C}$ of length n and covering radius $R = R(\mathcal{C})$ exists, the size $K(n, R)$ must be

$$K(n, R) \geq \frac{2^n}{\sum_{i=0}^{R} \binom{n}{i}} . \tag{7}$$

An extensive amount of work in the theory of covering codes is devoted to derive better bounds and to construct codes achieving these bounds (*cf.* [4,19,21]).

4 Direct Sum Constructions of Covering Codes

In the rest of this paper, we will restrict ourselves to linear covering codes in $\mathbb{Z}_2^n$. We will use the notation $\mathcal{C} = [n, k]R$ for a code of length n, dimension k (that is, the size $K = 2^k$) and covering radius R. It is well known that *perfect codes* are good covering codes, non-trivial examples in the binary case are the Hamming codes $\mathcal{H}_i$ for $i \geq 1$ which are $[2^i - 1, 2^i - 1 - i]1$ codes and the $[23, 12]3$ Golay code. For other lengths n, no non-trivial perfect codes exist.

Fortunately, the bitlength of a hash value is very often of the form $n = 2^i$. For these lengths, explicit and almost explicit results in the case when the covering radius is $R = 1$ and $R = 2$ are known:

Proposition 1. *Let $n = 2^i$ for $i \geq 1$ and let $k(n, R)$ be the minimum dimension k such that an $[n, k]R$ code exists. Then,*

$$k(2^i, 1) = 2^i - i \tag{8}$$

$$k(2^i, 2) \in \{2^i - 2i, 2^i - 2i + 1, 2^i - 2i + 2\}. \tag{9}$$

For a proof of (8) we refer to [21], (9) is shown in [11]. One basic construction principle when deriving such bounds is the so called *direct sum* of linear codes (*cf.* [11]):

Lemma 1. *For linear codes $\mathcal{C}_1 = [n_1, k_1]R_1$ and $\mathcal{C}_2 = [n_2, k_2]R_2$, the direct sum of $\mathcal{C}_1$ and $\mathcal{C}_2$ is defined as*

$$\mathcal{C}_1 \oplus \mathcal{C}_2 = \{(c_1, c_2) \mid c_1 \in \mathcal{C}_1, c_2 \in \mathcal{C}_2\}.$$

Then, $\mathcal{C}_1 \oplus \mathcal{C}_2$ is a linear code with parameters $[n_1 + n_2, k_1 + k_2]R_1 + R_2$.

For (linear) codes of length $n \leq 33$ and for relatively small covering radii R we can find extensive tables of the values of $k(n, R)$ (see *e.g.* [4] or [9]). However, since the length of the code is determined by the output size of the hash function, we will deal with lengths n that are significantly larger than 33.

In [13], a direct sum construction was proposed that would be applicable for all lengths n and covering radii R and only combines Hamming codes and the trivial codes $\mathbb{Z}_2^q$. This construction looks as follows. Let the numbers $N_i = 2^i - 1$ denote the lengths of the Hamming codes $\mathcal{H}_i$ for $i = 1, 2, \ldots$. Let $\mathcal{D} = \{0, 1, \ldots, R\}$ be the set of digits. We denote by

$$\mathcal{X} := \left\{x = \sum\nolimits_{i \geq 1} d_i N_i \mid d_i \in \mathcal{D}, d_i \neq 0 \text{ for finitely many } i\right\} \tag{10}$$

the set of possible expansions in the base $(N_i)_{i \geq 1}$ and with digits in $\mathcal{D}$. Furthermore, we also introduce

$$\mathcal{X}_n := \{x \in \mathcal{X} \mid x \leq n\}. \tag{11}$$

For ease of notation, we will denote by $d \cdot \mathcal{H}_i$ the direct sum of d copies of $\mathcal{H}_i$. Then, the following optimization problem can be formulated:

Problem 1. *Let n and $R < \lfloor \frac{n}{4} \rfloor$ be given. Find an expansion*

$$x = \sum\nolimits_{i \geq 1} d_i N_i \in \mathcal{X}_n \tag{12}$$

that additionally satisfies the following properties:

$$\sigma(x) := \sum\nolimits_{i \geq 1} d_i = R, \tag{13}$$

$$e(x) := \sum\nolimits_{i \geq 1} d_i \cdot i \rightarrow \textit{max}. \tag{14}$$

Then, the code

$$\mathcal{C} = \bigoplus_{i \geq 1} d_i \cdot \mathcal{H}_i \oplus \mathbb{Z}_2^{n-x} \tag{15}$$

has length n, covering radius R and the dimension of the code is

$$k = n - \sum_{i \geq 1} d_i \cdot i\,.$$

From Lemma 1 it follows that the code (15) has length $x + (n - x) = n$, and that the covering radius is exactly R. For the dimension of the code we get

$$\begin{aligned} k &= \sum\nolimits_{i \geq 1} d_i(N_i - i) + n - \sum\nolimits_{i \geq 1} d_i N_i \\ &= n - \sum\nolimits_{i \geq 1} d_i \cdot i. \end{aligned}$$

Clearly, the dimension is minimal if $\sum_{i \geq 1} d_i \cdot i$ is maximal.

5 The Optimal Solution for Problem 1

We now give a complete solution of the optimization question formulated in Problem 1. We start by stating the main theorem.

Theorem 2. *Let n, R be given as in Problem 1. Define*

$$\ell := \left\lfloor \log_2 \left(\frac{n}{R} + 1 \right) \right\rfloor \quad \textit{and} \quad r := \left\lfloor \frac{n - R(2^\ell - 1)}{2^\ell} \right\rfloor . \tag{16}$$

Then, the expansion

$$x = (R - r)(2^\ell - 1) + r(2^{\ell+1} - 1) \tag{17}$$

satisfies all conditions (12), (13) *and* (14). *The resulting code*

$$\mathcal{C} = (R - r) \cdot \mathcal{H}_\ell \oplus r \cdot \mathcal{H}_{\ell+1} \oplus \mathbb{Z}_2^{n-x} \tag{18}$$

has dimension $k = n - R \cdot \ell - r$ and is an optimal solution subject to this construction.

The proof of Theorem 2 is split into two auxiliary results for the expansions $x \in \mathcal{X}_n$ which satisfy (13) and (14) which will be shown in Proposition 2 and Proposition 3. Remember that for a given expansion $x \in \mathcal{X}_n$ we denote by $e(x) = \sum_{i \geq 1} d_i \cdot i$ the value of the expansion, which has to be maximized.

Proposition 2. *Assume $x^* \in \mathcal{X}_n$ is an optimal expansion satisfying* (13) *and* (14). *Then we have*

$$R\,\ell \leq e(x^*) < R(\ell + 1). \tag{19}$$

Proof. The left hand side of the inequality is easy to see, since from (16) we know that ℓ is chosen in such a way that

$$R(2^\ell - 1) \leq n < R(2^{\ell+1} - 1).$$

So $x = R(2^\ell - 1) \in \mathcal{X}_n$ is a valid expansion and $e(x) = R\,\ell$.

For the right hand side, we assume there is an expansion $x^* \in \mathcal{X}_n$ with $e(x^*) \geq R(\ell + 1)$, that is, we have

$$\sum_{i \geq 1} d_i(2^i - 1) \leq n, \tag{20}$$

$$\sum_{i \geq 1} d_i = R, \tag{21}$$

$$\sum_{i \geq 1} d_i \cdot i \geq R(\ell + 1). \tag{22}$$

Since $d_i \geq 0$ and because of (21) we can interpret the sequence

$$\left(\frac{d_1}{R}, \frac{d_2}{R}, \dots\right)$$

as a discrete probability distribution for a random variable X. In other words, we consider X with $\mathbb{P}\,(X = i) = \frac{d_i}{R}$ for $i \geq 1$. In this light, we can read (22) as an inequality for the expected value $\mathbb{E}(X) \geq \ell + 1$. Now Jensen's inequality (cf. [8]) states, that for a convex function ϕ we have

$$\mathbb{E}(\phi(X)) \geq \phi\left(\mathbb{E}(X)\right). \tag{23}$$

Applying this to the random variable X from above and the convex function $\phi(x) = 2^x - 1$ we can derive

$$\textstyle\sum_{i \geq 1} \frac{d_i}{R}(2^i - 1) = \mathbb{E}(\phi(X)) \geq \phi(\mathbb{E}(X)) \geq \phi(\ell + 1) = 2^{\ell+1} - 1.$$

After multiplying this inequality by R, we end up with

$$x^* \geq R(2^{\ell+1} - 1) > n,$$

by the definition of ℓ. This contradiction proves the proposition. ∎

The last proposition specifies the interval in which $e(x^*)$ must lie for an optimal solution x^*. The next proposition will give the explicit solution.

Proposition 3. *For given n and R, the expansion*

$$x^* = (R - r)(2^\ell - 1) + r(2^{\ell+1} - 1)$$

with ℓ and r as in (16) is optimal, that is, it reaches the maximal value $e(x^*) = R\,\ell + r$. Depending on n and R, this optimum can also be attained by other expansions than x^*.

Proof. We want to address first, that in general there is not a unique optimal expansion. This is easy to see since for certain values of n and R it might occur, that

$$x^{**} = (2^{\ell-1} - 1) + (R - r - 2)(2^{\ell} - 1) + (r + 1)(2^{\ell+1} - 1) \leq n$$

holds. This expansion also has

$$e(x^{**}) = \ell - 1 + (R - r - 2)\ell + (r + 1)(\ell + 1) = R\ell + r.$$

For example in the case $n = 160$ and $R = 2$ we would have $x^* = 2(2^6 - 1) = 126$ and $x^{**} = (2^5 - 1) + (2^7 - 1) = 158$ which both are ≤ 160 and have $e(x^*) = e(x^{**}) = 12$.

By definition in (16), we see that $r \in \{0, \dots, R-1\}$. Actually, r is chosen in such a way that

$$(R-r)(2^{\ell}-1)+r(2^{\ell+1}-1) \leq n < (R-r-1)(2^{\ell}-1)+(r+1)(2^{\ell+1}-1). \quad (24)$$

Thus, Proposition 2 states that $R\ell + r$ would be a possible optimal value for $e(x^*)$. Let us now assume that there exists an expansion $x' \in \mathcal{X}_n$ such that $e(x') > R\ell + r$. Let $e(x') = R\ell + r + \delta$ with $0 < \delta < R - r$. Then, another expansion x'' having $e(x'') = e(x')$ is

$$x'' = (R - r - \delta)(2^{\ell} - 1) + (r + \delta)(2^{\ell+1} - 1). \quad (25)$$

Now we will show that any x' with $e(x') = e(x'') = R\ell + r + \delta$ satisfies $x' \geq x''$.

Let us consider the digits of the expansion (25) as units, that is, we have a total of R digits (because of (21)) and these digits are distributed at positions ℓ and $\ell + 1$. Any other x' satisfying $e(x') = e(x'')$ can be seen to result from x'' by moving the digits of the expansion of x'' to other positions.

To be even more specific we can describe a "unit move" by S_j^i which denotes the process of moving one digit of x'' at position i to $i+1$ and simultanously moving one digit from position j to $j-1$ (see also Fig. 1). Any such step has the property of maintaining the value $e(x'')$. Starting from x'', i and j can only be ℓ or $\ell+1$. In this case only the moves S_ℓ^ℓ, $S_\ell^{\ell+1}$ and $S_{\ell+1}^{\ell+1}$ make sense, since $S_{\ell+1}^{\ell}$ would be redundant by leaving x'' unchanged. In general, we only have to consider moves S_j^i with $i \geq j$ since any move with $i < j$ results in a previous configuration of digits. (This can be shown by induction over the number of non-zero digits of a given expansion in $\mathcal{X}$.) When applying a unit move S_j^i with $i \geq j$ to x'', the digit going from i to $i+1$ increases the value of the resulting expansion x' by $2^{i+1} - 1 - 2^i + 1 = 2^i$ whereas the digit going from j to $j-1$ decreases the value of x' by 2^j. Therfore, the overall change of one unit move is $2^i - 2^j$ which is always non-negative, since we assumed $i \geq j$. Since any x' with $e(x') = e(x'')$ results from x'' by a series of unit moves S_j^i with $i \geq j$, we can therefore deduce that we have $x' \geq x''$. But $x' \geq x''$ also implies $x' > n$ because

$$x'' \geq (R - r - 1)(2^{\ell} - 1) + (r + 1)(2^{\ell+1} - 1) > n$$

by (24) and since $\delta > 0$. This proves the proposition. ∎

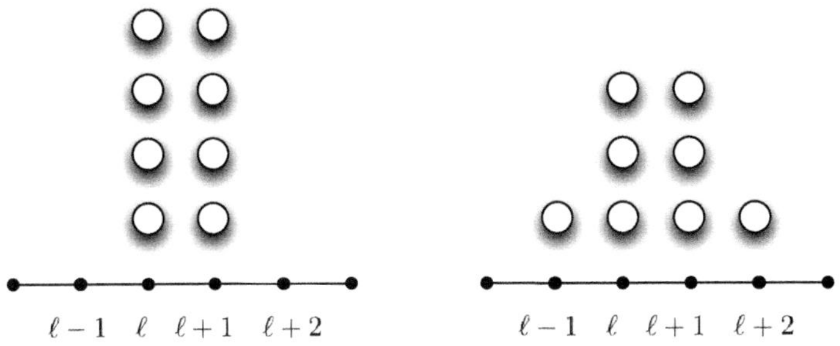

Fig. 1. Example of the unit move $S_\ell^{\ell+1}$ with $R = 8$

Table 1. For given $\epsilon \in \{2,4,6,8\}$, the table compares the base-2 logarithms of the complexity of the standard table-based approach (2), the projection based approach (3) and our construction (15) for $n = 128, 160$ and 512

	$n = 128$			$n = 160$			$n = 512$		
ϵ	(2)	(3)	(15)	(2)	(3)	(15)	(2)	(3)	(15)
2	57.5	61.5	60.5	73.2	77.5	76.5	247.5	253.5	251.5
4	52.3	59.5	58.0	67.7	75.5	74.0	240.3	251.5	248.0
6	47.8	57.5	56.0	62.8	73.5	71.5	233.8	249.5	245.0
8	43.8	55.5	54.0	58.5	71.5	69.5	227.7	247.5	242.0

We conclude this section by giving a table which compares the dimension of the codes (18) with the projection based approach and the complexity of a table-based near-collision search for several values of ϵ and n.

Remark 1. It is of course natural to compare the codes resulting from Theorem 2 with other well known codes. Binary BCH codes with parameters e, m (see [4, Sect. 10.1]) are algebraic codes of length $n = 2^m - 1$, dimension $k \geq n - m \cdot e$ and minimum distance $d \geq 2e + 1$. For $e \in \{2, 3\}$ the exact covering radius of $BCH(e, m)$ is known, namely $R(BCH(2, m)) = 3$ and $R(BCH(3, m)) = 5$. If we now consider for example $\mathcal{B}_1 = BCH(2, 7) \oplus \mathbb{Z}_2$ and $\mathcal{B}_2 = BCH(2, 9) \oplus \mathbb{Z}_2$, we see that $\mathcal{B}_1$ is a $[128, 114]$ $R = 3$ code and $\mathcal{B}_2$ has parameters $[512, 494]$ $R = 5$, so their dimension is higher than that of (15).

One possible way to achieve an improvement is to move from the direct sum construction of Section 4 to blockwise or amalgamated direct sum constructions (cf. [4]).

6 Conclusion

In this paper, we have solved a problem concerning the direct sum of Hamming codes and trivial codes $\mathbb{Z}_2^q$. This problem arose in the context of a newly proposed method that allows us to find near-collisions for a cryptographic hash function

H in a memoryless way by applying the standard cycle-finding algorithms to the composition of the decoding operation of a covering code and the hash function H. This method is then able to find ϵ-near-collisions for H with $\epsilon = 2R$ where R is the covering radius of the underlying code. The efficiency of the method is determined by the size of this code. The question of finding the right combination of Hamming and trivial $\mathbb{Z}_2^q$ codes has been translated into an optimization problem for digital expansions and this has been solved by Theorem 2.

Acknowledgements

The authors wish to thank the anonymous referees, Florian Mendel and René Struik for valuable comments and discussions. The work in this paper has been supported in part by the European Commission under contract ICT-2007-216646 (ECRYPT II), in part by the Austrian Science Fund (FWF), project P21936 and in part by the IAP Programme P6/26 BCRYPT of the Belgian State (Belgian Science Policy).

References

1. Biham, E., Chen, R.: Near-Collisions of SHA-0. In: Franklin, M. (ed.) CRYPTO 2004. LNCS, vol. 3152, pp. 290–305. Springer, Heidelberg (2004)
2. Brent, R.P.: An improved Monte Carlo factorization algorithm. BIT 20(2), 176–184 (1980)
3. Chabaud, F., Joux, A.: Differential Collisions in SHA-0. In: Krawczyk, H. (ed.) CRYPTO 1998. LNCS, vol. 1462, pp. 56–71. Springer, Heidelberg (1998)
4. Cohen, G., Honkala, I., Litsyn, S., Lobstein, A.: Covering codes. North-Holland Mathematical Library, vol. 54. North-Holland Publishing Co., Amsterdam (1997)
5. De Cannière, C., Mendel, F., Rechberger, C.: Collisions for 70-Step SHA-1: On the Full Cost of Collision Search. In: Adams, C., Miri, A., Wiener, M. (eds.) SAC 2007. LNCS, vol. 4876, pp. 56–73. Springer, Heidelberg (2007)
6. De Cannière, C., Rechberger, C.: Finding SHA-1 Characteristics: General Results and Applications. In: Lai, X., Chen, K. (eds.) ASIACRYPT 2006. LNCS, vol. 4284, pp. 1–20. Springer, Heidelberg (2006)
7. Dobbertin, H.: Cryptanalysis of MD4. J. Cryptology 11(4), 253–271 (1998)
8. Feller, W.: An introduction to probability theory and its applications, 3rd edn., vol. I. John Wiley & Sons Inc., New York (1968)
9. Kéri, G.: Tables for bounds on covering codes, `http://www.sztaki.hu/~keri/codes/` (accessed May 17, 2010)
10. Gordon, D., Miller, V., Ostapenko, P.: Optimal hash functions for approximate matches on the n-cube. IEEE Trans. Inform. Theory 56(3), 984–991 (2010)
11. Graham, R.L., Sloane, N.J.A.: On the covering radius of codes. IEEE Trans. Inform. Theory 31(3), 385–401 (1985)
12. Knuth, D.E.: The art of computer programming. Seminumerical algorithms, Addison-Wesley Series in Computer Science and Information Processing, vol. 2. Addison-Wesley Publishing Co., Reading (1997)

13. Lamberger, M., Mendel, F., Rijmen, V., Simoens, K.: Memoryless Near-Collisions via Coding Theory (December 2009), http://asiacrypt2009.cipher.risk.tsukuba.ac.jp/rump/slides/13_NC-talk.pdf, (short talk) presented at the ASIACRYPT 2009 rump session
14. Mendel, F., Schläffer, M.: On Free-Start Collisions and Collisions for TIB3. In: Samarati, P., Yung, M., Martinelli, F., Ardagna, C.A. (eds.) ISC 2009. LNCS, vol. 5735, pp. 95–106. Springer, Heidelberg (2009)
15. Menezes, A., van Oorschot, P.C., Vanstone, S.A.: Handbook of Applied Cryptography. CRC Press, Boca Raton (1996)
16. National Institute of Standards and Technology (NIST). Cryptographic Hash Project (2007), http://www.nist.gov/hash-competition
17. Nivasch, G.: Cycle detection using a stack. Inf. Process. Lett. 90(3), 135–140 (2004)
18. Pramstaller, N., Rechberger, C., Rijmen, V.: Exploiting Coding Theory for Collision Attacks on SHA-1. In: Smart, N.P. (ed.) Cryptography and Coding 2005. LNCS, vol. 3796, pp. 78–95. Springer, Heidelberg (2005)
19. Struik, R.: An improvement of the Van Wee bound for binary linear covering codes. IEEE Transactions on Information Theory 40(4), 1280–1284 (1994)
20. van Oorschot, P.C., Wiener, M.J.: Parallel Collision Search with Cryptanalytic Applications. J. Cryptology 12(1), 1–28 (1999)
21. van Wee, G.J.M.: Improved sphere bounds on the covering radius of codes. IEEE Transactions on Information Theory 34(2), 237–245 (1988)
22. Wang, X., Yin, Y.L., Yu, H.: Finding Collisions in the Full SHA-1. In: Shoup, V. (ed.) CRYPTO 2005. LNCS, vol. 3621, pp. 17–36. Springer, Heidelberg (2005)
23. Wang, X., Yu, H.: How to Break MD5 and Other Hash Functions. In: Cramer, R. (ed.) EUROCRYPT 2005. LNCS, vol. 3494, pp. 19–35. Springer, Heidelberg (2005)
24. Yuval, G.: How to swindle Rabin? Cryptologia 3(3), 187–191 (1979)

Tweaking AES

Ivica Nikolić

University of Luxembourg

Abstract. In this paper we present a tweak for the key schedule of AES in a form of a few additional basic operations such as rotations and S-boxes. This leads to a new cipher, which we call xAES, and which is resistant against the latest related-key differential attacks found in AES. xAES has a speed benchmark close to the one of AES even in the applications which use a frequent change of the master key.

Keywords: AES, tweak, key schedule.

1 Introduction

The Advanced Encryption Standard (AES) [6] is a block cipher adopted by NIST [15]. Eight years after the adoption, AES is widely used for commercial and governmental purposes while being implemented in both software and hardware. It is an elegant design and a very efficient cipher.

Recently, a few cryptanalytical results were obtained regarding the security resistance of AES [4,3]. It was shown that AES-192 and AES-256, i.e. the versions of AES with 192 and 256 key bits, do not have the ideal security level in the framework where related-key attacks are permitted. Despite the fact that so far these attacks are only theoretical and require a computational power beyond our reach, finding an efficient fix for AES that will produce a cipher that is ideal by the cryptographic standards, seems a good open problem.

In this paper we propose such fix. Since the recent attacks are mostly based on the property of the key schedule of AES, we tweak only this part of the cipher, while keeping intact the round function. We introduce only a few additional operations in the key schedule which result in a cipher that is: 1)resistant against related-key differential attacks, 2)has a speed close to the speed of AES.

The rest of the paper is structured as follows. In section 2 we give a brief facts on efficiency and security of AES. In section 3, we present our tweak for the key schedule. First, we focus on choosing a tweak that will produce a secure and efficient key schedule, then we prove the resistance of the new cipher against related-key differential attacks and finally we give theoretical and empirical estimates of its efficiency. In section 4 we conclude.

2 Efficiency and Security of AES

The block cipher AES has 128-bit state and supports three key sizes: 128, 192, and 256 bits. It is a byte oriented cipher and depending on the key size it has

A. Biryukov, G. Gong, and D.R. Stinson (Eds.): SAC 2010, LNCS 6544, pp. 198–210, 2011.

10 rounds for 128-bit keys, 12 rounds for 192-bit keys, and 14 rounds for 256-bit keys. In each round of AES the state, which can be seen as 4x4 matrix of bytes, undergoes four basic transformations:

1. SubBytes - bytewise application of S-boxes,
2. ShiftRows - cyclic shift of each row of the state matrix on some amount,
3. MixColumns - columnwise matrix multiplication,
4. AddRoundKey – xor of the subkey to the state.

The choice of these transformations permits to implement a round of AES as a combination of simple table lookups and xors (See [6]) leading to significant performance benefits. Moreover, Intel has announced that a new AES instruction set[11], called AES-NI, will be introduced in the new processors. Among other, the new instructions will significantly increase the efficiency of the round function of AES. Yet, no special instructions will be available to perform the key schedule routine.

Security analysis of AES has been the target of many cryptographic papers. The initial analysis was done by the submitters of Rijndael [6]. Using the property of the MixColumns transform, which is based on maximum distance separable code, the designers proved that *in the fixed-key model, differential characteristics exist only for a reduced number of rounds.* Hence the further analysis of AES was mainly focused either on other (non-differential) fixed-key attacks, or on related-key differential attacks.

In the fixed-key model, square attacks on 6 rounds of AES [6], boomerang attack on 6 rounds [2], collisions attacks on 7-8 rounds of AES [10,7], impossible differentials on 7-8 rounds of AES [13] and partial sum attacks [8] on 7,8,9 rounds of AES-128,-192,-256 respectively, were obtained.

In the related-key model, until recently, the best attacks were the boomerang and rectangle attacks found up to 10 rounds of AES-192 and 10 rounds of AES-256 [1,12,9]. The first attack on full-round AES-256 was given in [4]. In the paper, the authors present a related-key differential characteristic on all 14 rounds of AES-256, which leads to a key-recovery attack. Since some of the differences of the characteristic are in the subkey bytes which afterwards go through S-boxes, the attack works only for a class of keys. The second attack, in a form of related-key boomerang attack, on full-round AES [3] focuses on both AES-192 and AES-256. The attack leads to a key-recovery and works for all keys.

3 xAES – A New and Improved AES

In this section we present our proposal xAES. Although the security of the new version is our main concern, we would like to obtain an efficient primitive as well.

AES is widely implemented in both software and hardware. The round function is elegant with good security properties and it allows a fast implementation through a low number of table lookups and xors. The implementation is made even faster in software on the upcoming new Intel processors. Therefore, to gain the necessary level of security for our proposal, we will focus on *improving the current key schedule of AES while keeping unchanged the round function.*

Let us define our main objectives. First, it is creating a new key schedule for AES such that no related-key differential characteristics exist on the full-round version of 128, 192, and 256 key sizes. We take a conservative approach and require that no such characteristics exist in any weak key class. Second, the new key schedule should be efficient – the speed of the new proposal should be comparable with the speed of AES. Note that when talking about the speed of a cipher, regarding the key agility we can go into two directions. One is to measure the efficiency of a cipher in *the encryption mode*, where the master key is fixed and the subkeys are computed once and used in all of the iterations. In this case, the efficiency of the key schedule is irrelevant[1] and the designer can spend a lot of computational power to produce the subkeys from the master key since the key setup is done only once. The second is when the cipher is used as an underlying primitive for other cryptographic constructions, e.g. hash functions. Then the master key is changed on every iteration, and sequentially, the subkeys have to be recomputed. In this case, the efficiency of the key schedule comes to a forefront and it has a significant impact on the efficiency of the whole cipher (the whole cryptographic construction). To measure the efficiency of a cipher, we take into account the second, more conservative direction, i.e. we measure the speed with the assumption that the master key is frequently changed – *a hash mode.*

Further, we present some ideas on possible approaches to build a secure and fast key schedule for AES. Then we present our proposal xAES, and give a security and efficiency analysis of the new cipher.

3.1 Methods to Improve the Key Schedule of AES

There are a few approaches to raise the security level of AES against related-key differential attacks. Further we present each approach and give an evaluation of its efficiency.

1. Increase the number of rounds. One can simply add a few more rounds at the top of the regular number of rounds of AES and obtain a cipher that is secure against related-key differential attacks. Note that the current key schedule of AES can easily produce a few more subkeys without the necessity of any substantial change. This approach has many positive sides, one of which is that the new cipher does not have to be reevaluated against the rest of the related-key non-differential attacks because the key schedule has not been changed. Yet, our second objective, efficiency, seems to suffer. Obviously each added round reduces the speed (in both the encryption and hash modes) by a factor of $\frac{1}{10}, \frac{1}{12}, \frac{1}{14}$ for AES-128, AES-192, and AES-256 respectively.
2. Create a key-schedule provably secure against differential attacks. One can design a key schedule full of S-box transformations and then prove the any related-key differential characteristic on the full number of rounds of the

[1] It is important only for encryption of short messages.

cipher, alone in the key schedule has a low probability because it has a high number of active S-boxes in the characteristic of the key schedule. This way, the related-key differential attacks on full rounds become impossible. A similar approach was used in [14] although the resistance of the key schedule was not formally proven. Again, with this approach, the designer meets our security objective, but might suffer a strong efficiency drawback in the hash mode due to the high number of S-boxes in the key schedule which may reduce the speed significantly.

3. Slightly change the current key schedule of AES, but keep unchanged the number of rounds. One can alter the key schedule by introducing additional (but small) number of S-boxes and/or other simple operations. These can be any operations that are sufficiently fast in software and hardware, e.g. ANDs, ORs, rotations, XORs, etc. This way the efficiency will not change significantly. Yet, in this approach, the proof of security against differential attacks is not trivial.

Further, we will use the third approach, i.e. we will introduce a small change in the current AES key schedule. This way we can easily meet our second objective – efficiency. To fulfill the security objective, we will analyze the resistance of the new cipher against related-key differential attacks using the tool for search of differential characteristics proposed in [5].

3.2 Specification of xAES

Now we can give a complete specification of our proposal xAES. Similarly to AES, xAES supports three key sizes: 128,192,256, denoted as xAES-128, xAES-192, and xAES-256 respectively. Although in [5] it was proven that no differential characteristic exist on the full round AES-128, we introduce xAES-128 to have a complete family of ciphers supporting the standard key sizes of 128,192, and 256 bits. The number of internal rounds in xAES for different key sizes is the same as the number of rounds in AES, i.e. 10 rounds for xAES-128, 12 rounds for xAES-192, and 14 rounds for xAES-256. Each internal round is defined same as in AES – through the four transformations SubBytes, ShiftRows, MixColumns and AddRoundKey. The only difference between AES and xAES is in the key schedule. Yet, the difference is small. In short, for obtaining each next column of the new subkey, xAES *always* uses rotation by one byte up of the previous subkey column, while AES uses a rotation only when obtaining the subkey column with an index multiple of N_k ($N_k = 4, 6, 8$ for AES-128,-192,-256). Let us give a formal definition of the new key schedules. We assume that the master key K is given as an array $K[4][N_k]$ and the key schedule produces a subkey array $W[4][4(N_r + 1)]$. The s-th subkey is given by the columns $4 \cdot s$ to $4 \cdot (s + 1) - 1$ of W. The round constant $RC[i][j]$ is the same as in AES.

The key schedule of xAES-128 is defined as follows. Let $K[4][4]$ be the master key. Then the subkey array $W[4][44]$ is defined as:

$$W[i][j] = \begin{cases} K[i][j], & \text{if } j < 4 \\ S(W[i-1 \bmod 4][j-1]) \oplus W[i][j-4] \oplus RC[i][j/4], & \text{if } j \bmod 4 == 0 \\ W[i-1 \bmod 4][j-1] \oplus W[i][j-4], & \text{otherwise} \end{cases}$$

The key schedule of xAES-192 is defined as follows. Let $K[4][6]$ be the master key. Then the subkey array $W[4][52]$ is defined as:

$$W[i][j] = \begin{cases} K[i][j], & \text{if } j < 6 \\ S(W[i-1 \bmod 4][j-1]) \oplus W[i][j-6] \oplus RC[i][j/4], & \text{if } j \bmod 6 == 0 \\ S(W[i-1 \bmod 4][j-1]) \oplus W[i][j-6], & \text{if } j \bmod 6 == 3 \\ W[i-1 \bmod 4][j-1] \oplus W[i][j-6], & \text{otherwise} \end{cases}$$

The key schedule of xAES-256 is defined as follows. Let $K[4][8]$ be the master key. Then the subkey array $W[4][60]$ is defined as:

$$W[i][j] = \begin{cases} K[i][j], & \text{if } j < 8 \\ S(W[i-1 \bmod 4][j-1]) \oplus W[i][j-8] \oplus RC[i][j/4], & \text{if } j \bmod 8 == 0 \\ S(W[i-1 \bmod 4][j-1]) \oplus W[i][j-8], & \text{if } j \bmod 8 == 4 \\ W[i-1 \bmod 4][j-1] \oplus W[i][j-8], & \text{otherwise} \end{cases}$$

To clearly understand the idea of the additional operations, in Fig. 1 we give a pictorial representation of how the $s+1$-th subkey is obtained from the s-th subkey, for all three key schedules of xAES as well as for the key schedule of AES-256 so the reader can compare the changes.

Besides the additional rotations, the difference between AES and xAES is in the 192-bit key version. We introduce additional layer of S-boxes to meet our security level.

3.3 Security Analysis of xAES

For a security analysis of xAES first we will focus on proving the resistance of xAES against related-key differential attacks. Then we will provide an evaluation of the security against other attacks.

Related-key Differential Attacks in xAES. Let us give a formal definition of an r-round related-key differential characteristic for a cipher. Let $E_K(P)$ be an R-round block cipher, where P is the plaintext and K is the master key. The key schedule function $KS(K)$ of the cipher $E_K(P)$ given key K, produces a set of (round) subkeys $K_0, \dots, K_R$, i.e. $KS(K) = (K_0, \dots, K_R)$. Let S_i be the value of state of $E_K(P)$ at the beginning of round i and $S_0 = P$ and let $E^1_{K_i}(S_i)$ be one round of the cipher. Let $p_K^{\Delta^K, \Delta_i^K}$ be probability that a given difference Δ^K in the master key K produces a set of differences $\Delta_i^K, i = 0, \dots, R$ in the subkeys K_i, i.e.

$$p_K^{\Delta^K, \Delta_i^K} = \mathbf{P}(KS(K) \oplus KS(K \oplus \Delta^K) = (\Delta_0^K, \dots, \Delta_R^K)) \quad (1)$$

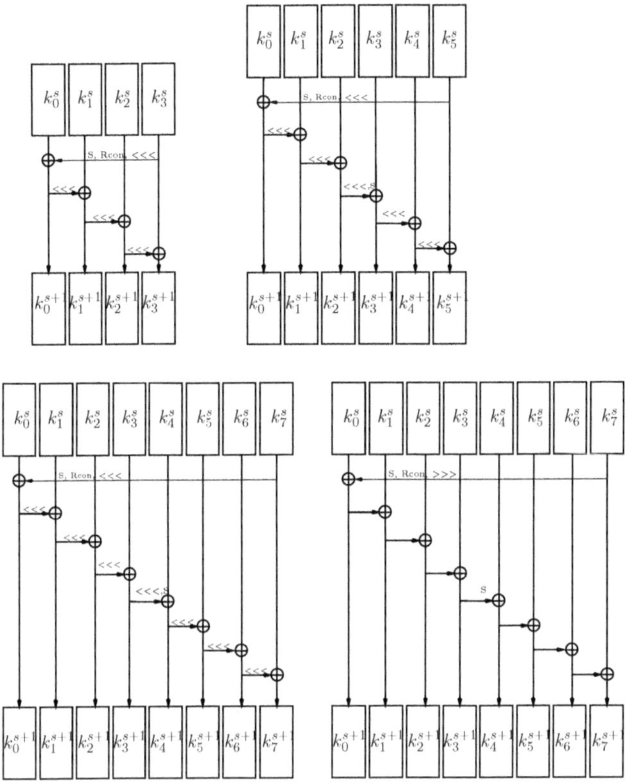

Fig. 1. One subkey round for xAES-128 (top left), xAES-192 (top right), xAES-256 (bottom-left), and AES-256 (bottom-right). Each k_i^j is a subkey column – 4 bytes. $\lll$ ($\ggg$) stand for a word rotation on 8 bits to the left(right), S for S-box, and Rcon for xor of the round constant.

Let $p_i^{\Delta_i^K,\Delta_i^S,\Delta_{i+1}^S}$ be the probability that a difference Δ_i^S in the state S_i and Δ_i^K in the subkey K_i produces difference Δ_{i+1}^S in the state S_{i+1}, i.e.

$$p_i^{\Delta_i^K,\Delta_i^S,\Delta_{i+1}^S} = \mathbf{P}(E^1_{K_i\oplus\Delta_i^K}(S_i\oplus\Delta_i^S)\oplus E^1_{K_i}(S_i)=\Delta_{i+1}^S), i=0,\ldots,R-1 \quad (2)$$

For a cipher $E_K(P)$ an r-round related-key differential characteristic is defined as a set $(\Delta_i^S,\Delta_i^K,p_i^{\Delta_i^K,\Delta_i^S,\Delta_{i+1}^S},p_K^{\Delta^K,\Delta_i^K}), i=0,\ldots,r$ where (1),(2) are satisfied. The probability of this characteristic is given as:

$$p = p_K^{\Delta^K,\Delta_i^K}\cdot\prod_{0\leq i<r} p_i^{\Delta_i^K,\Delta_i^S,\Delta_{i+1}^S} \quad (3)$$

To prove the resistance of xAES against related-key differential attacks, we will use the technique provided in [5]. In the paper, the authors specify a tool for

Algorithm 1. Search for RK differential characteristic

```
FirstRound()
{
for all ΔP do
  for all ΔS_1 do
    ΔK_0 = ΔP ⊕ ΔS_1
    Call NextRound(ΔS_1, ΔK_0, W(ΔS_1) + W(ΔK_0), 2)
  end for
end for
}

NextRound(ΔS_old,ΔK_old, w, r)
{
S̃ ← StateRound(ΔS_old)
for all S_new|W(S_new) + w + W_{n−r} ≤ W̃_n do
  ΔK_new ← ΔS̃ ⊕ ΔS_new
  if ΔK_new == SubkeyRound(ΔK_old) then
    if r == n then
      W̃_n ← w + W(ΔS_new) + W(ΔK_new)
    else
      Call NextRound(ΔS_new, ΔK_new, w + W(ΔS_new) + W(ΔK_new), r + 1)
    end if
  end if
end for
}
```

search of the best related-key differential characteristics in byte-oriented block ciphers. Depending on the key schedule of the analyzed cipher, the authors give three versions of the tool. Since, the key schedule of xAES is almost the same as the one in AES, we will use the same version as did the authors when analyzing AES. That is the version 2 of the tool. On Alg. 1 we give a short description of the tool in pseudo code. Given the weights W_i (which are actually the number of active S-boxes) of the best differential characteristics (the best is considered the characteristic that holds with highest probability) for the first $n-1$ rounds, and some weight $\tilde{W}_n$ of the n-round characteristic, the tool produces the best characteristic for n rounds. It starts with the procedure FirstRound, which fixes a certain difference ΔS_1 in the state at the begining of round 1, and a difference ΔK_0 in the whitening key. For each pair $(\Delta S_1, \Delta K_0)$ NextRound is called. This procedure, under certain weight conditions, extends the characteristic for an additional round as follows. First, from ΔS_{old} produces the difference $\Delta\tilde{S}$ in the state at the end of the round (just before the subkey addition). Then it takes all possible differences ΔS_{new} at the begining of the next round, and produces the difference ΔK_{new} in the subkey as an xor of $\Delta\tilde{S}$ and ΔS_{new} (recall the subkey addition defined in AES). Finally, it checks if ΔK_{new} can be obtained from ΔK_{old}, that is it checks if the difference in the following subkey can be produced from the difference in the previous subkey. The conditions on the weights ($W(S_{new}) + w + W_{n-r} \leq \tilde{W_n}$) are introduced to stop extending unnecessarily some characteristics – the number of active Sboxes in the first r rounds ($W(S_{new}) + w$) plus the minimal number of active Sboxes in the rest $n - r$ rounds (W_{n-r}) should not exceed the number of active Sboxes of the best known characteristic $(\tilde{W_n})^2$.

Since the only difference between AES and xAES is in the key schedule, to implement the tool for xAES, we have to find method that checks $\Delta K_{new} == SubkeyRound(\Delta K_{old})$, i.e. if the difference in the next subkey can be obtained from the difference of the previous subkey. Taking into consideration that the subkeys columns are produced one by one (see Fig. 1), this problem is reduced to the problem of checking if the differences in three subkey columns $k_j^i, k_{j+1}^i, k_{j+1}^{i-1}$ (where k_j^i, k_{j+1}^i are the j and $j+1$-th columns of the i-th subkey, and k_{j+1}^{i-1} is the $j+1$-th column of the $i-1$-th subkey) are related as:

$$(\Delta k_j^i) \lll 8 \oplus \Delta k_{j+1}^i = \Delta k_{j+1}^{i-1}. \qquad (4)$$

The authors of the tool proposed a so-called compact representation of a difference in the subkey column. This difference is described with an 8-bit vector $\tilde{c} = (\tilde{a}, \tilde{b}) = (a_1, \ldots, a_4, b_1, \ldots, b_4), a_i, b_i \in \{0, 1\}$. The compact $\tilde{c}$ describes (is a set of) all subkey column differences $\Delta\tilde{d} = (\Delta d_1, \Delta d_1, \Delta d_2, \Delta d_3), \Delta d_i \in Z_{2^8}$, such that:

$$\Delta\tilde{d}^T = MC \cdot (x_1, x_2, x_3, x_4)^T \oplus (y_1, y_2, y_3, y_4)^T = MC \cdot \tilde{x}^T \oplus \tilde{y}^T, \qquad (5)$$

where MC is the matrix of the MixColumns transform, $x_i, y_i \in Z_{2^8}$ and $x_i > 0$ **iff** $a_i > 0$, $y_i > 0$ **iff** $b_i > 0$. Note that for example the vector $(\tilde{0}, \tilde{b})$ is a simple truncated representation of a difference. In our implementation we will use the same compact representation for the differences in the subkey columns. To check (4) we have to deal with the rotation of the key Δk_j^i since in the key schedule of AES there is no such rotation. Let us see how this rotation influences the compact representation. If the difference Δk_j^i in the subkey is $\Delta\tilde{d}$ (see (5)), then the rotation of this difference is:

$$\Delta\tilde{d}^T \lll 8 = (MC \cdot \tilde{x}^T \oplus \tilde{y}^T) \lll 8 = (MC \cdot \tilde{x}^T) \lll 8 \oplus \tilde{y}^T \lll 8 \qquad (6)$$

The matrix MC has the property $(MC \cdot X) \lll 8 = MC \cdot (X \lll 8)$. Hence (6) can be rewritten as:

$$\Delta\tilde{d}^T \lll 8 = MC \cdot (\tilde{x}^T \lll 8) \oplus \tilde{y}^T \lll 8 \qquad (7)$$

Therefore, if the initial difference Δk_j^i had a compact representation $\tilde{c_1} = (a_1, a_2, a_3, a_4, b_1, b_2, b_3, b_4)$ then the rotation of this difference $\Delta k_j^i \lll 8$ has

[2] If it exceeds than this r round characteristic cannot be extend to n rounds because the next $n - r$ rounds will have at least W_{n-r} active S-boxes, so the total weight will be more than $\tilde{W_n}$.

a compact representation $\tilde{c_1} = (a_2, a_3, a_4, a_1, b_2, b_3, b_4, b_1)$. Hence, all the differences in (4) have a compact representation and this condition can easily be checked[3].

We have implemented the tool in practice and we searched for the best *round-reduced* related-key differential characteristics. To prove the resistance of r-round xAES against related-key differential attacks, these characteristics have to have certain properties:

1. No two characteristics exist with probability $2^{-p_1}, 2^{-p_2}$ on r_1 and r_2 rounds such that $r_1 + r_2 \geq r - 2$ and $2p_1 + 2p_2 \leq k$, where k is the key size. This restriction was introduced to stop the boomerang attacks on the full r rounds. We assume that two rounds can be obtained for free by various techniques, but the rest $r_1 + r_2$ rounds are part of the boomerang.
2. No characteristics exist on $r/2$ rounds with probability higher than $2^{-k/2}$. Obviously, this was introduced to stop the related-key differential attacks on the full r-round cipher which always can be seen as a concatenation of two $r/2$-round ciphers.

Each characteristic found by the tool is presented in a compact form. To find the probability of a characteristic one has to count the number of active bytes, i.e. the position of the bytes with 1 that go through the S-boxes. For example, a characteristics with s active bytes has a probability at most $2^{-6 \cdot s}$ because the maximal differential propagation of an S-box in AES is 2^{-6}. In table Tbl. 1 we give the probabilities (in terms of active bytes) of the best related-key differential characteristics for xAES-128, xAES-192, and xAES-256[4]. Using these results we can prove the differential resistance of xAES.

In case of xAES-128, to have a valid differential characteristic[5], the number of active bytes in the differential attack should not exceed $\lfloor \frac{128}{6} \rfloor = 21$ (because the key size is 128 bits and the maximal differential propagation of the S-box

Table 1. The number of active S-boxes in the best round-reduced related-key differential characteristics in xAES-128, xAES-192, and xAES-256

$rounds$	$xAES-128$	$xAES-192$	$xAES-256$
2	1	0	0
3	5	1	1
4	10	4	3
5	> 11	9	7
6	> 11	> 16	13
7	> 11	> 16	18
8	> 11	> 16	> 21

[3] Note that now checking (4) is reduced to checking for the case where all three subkey columns have a compact representation, which was solved for AES.

[4] For example, the best differential characteristic for xAES-192 on 5 rounds has 9 active S-boxes – in Tbl. 1 the intersection of row 5 and column xAES-192 is 9.

[5] A valid characteristic has a probability higher than 2^{-128}.

is 2^{-6}). In a boomerang attack (recall that since xAES-128 has 10 rounds, we try to build a boomerang on $10 - 2 = 8$ rounds), at least one of characteristics (upper or lower) has to be on 4 rounds, for which the attacker has to pay at least $2 \cdot 10 = 20$ active S-boxes. Hence, he has only $21 - 20 = 1$ active S-box left which is insufficient for a boomerang on 8 rounds and therefore xAES-128 is resistant against boomerang-type attacks. Now let us try to build a differential characteristic on all 10 rounds. Note that the characteristic on 5 rounds has more than 11 active S-boxes, hence the characteristic on 10 rounds would have more than $2 \cdot 11 = 22$, and therefore no related-key differential characteristic exist on all 10 rounds of xAES-128.

In xAES-192, the number of active S-boxes in a valid differential characteristic is bounded by $\lfloor \frac{192}{6} \rfloor = 32$. For a boomerang attack, in case one of the characteristics has 6 or more rounds, the number of active S-boxes becomes greater than 32, hence the attack does not work. When both characteristics have 5 rounds, then this number is $2 \cdot 9 + 2 \cdot 9 = 36$ which is again higher than 32, and therefore the boomerang with 10 rounds has lower probability than 2^{-192}. Similarly, any differential characteristic on 12 rounds (which can be seen as $6 + 6$ rounds), has more than $16 + 16 = 32$ active S-boxes, hence its probability is less than 2^{-192}.

In xAES-256, the number of active S-boxes is bounded by $\lfloor \frac{256}{6} \rfloor = 42$. Regarding the boomerang attack, when one of the characteristics is on at least 8 rounds, the attacker only for this characteristic has to pay more then $2 \cdot 21 = 42$ active S-boxes. When the characteristics are on 7 and 5 rounds, then the attacker pays $2 \cdot 18 + 2 \cdot 7 = 50$, while when both are on 6 rounds, he pays $2 \cdot 13 + 2 \cdot 13 = 52$ active S-boxes. In each of these cases, the total probability of the boomerang is less than 2^{-256}. The best characteristic on 7 rounds has only 18 active S-boxes. Hence, we cannot trivially prove that it does not exist a characteristic on 14 rounds (because $18 + 18 = 36$ which is less than 42). That is why we have to take a different approach. Any characteristic on 14 rounds, is composed of two 7-round characteristics, one of which has to have no more than 21 S-boxes (otherwise the total sum will be more than 42). First, we build all characteristics on 7 rounds that have no more than 21 active S-box. Then, we try to extend upward and downward each such characteristic for 7 additional rounds. Our search did not find any good candidate, i.e. no characteristic on 7 rounds with at most 21 active S-box can be extended to a characteristic on 14 rounds (with no more that 42 active S-boxes) and therefore no related-key differential characteristic exists on 14 rounds in xAES-256. This concludes our proof for the related-key differential resistance of full-round xAES.

The search for the best related-key differential characteristics for different version of xAES, i.e. running the tool in practice and obtaining the results of Tbl. 1, required different amount of computational effort. While finding the probabilities and the actual values for the round-reduced characteristics in xAES-128 and xAES-192 was performed in a few hours, in xAES-256 the search required a few days on a single core. The search for all good characteristics on 7 rounds of xAES-256 with no more than 21 active S-boxes produced around 2^{15} candidates and required two weeks on 8 cores. Extending these 7-round characteristics to

14 rounds, as mentioned before, did not give any good candidate, and required a few days on a single core.

Resistance of xAES Against Other Attacks. The round function of xAES is the same as the one of AES. Therefore all fixed-key attacks on xAES, which are based on vulnerabilities of the round function and do not exploit any properties of the key schedule, have the same security margin as in AES, that is the number of attacked rounds cannot be increased in xAES. This includes all of the fixed-key attacks mentioned in section 2.

3.4 Efficiency of xAES

Let us compare the speed of xAES with the speed of AES in software. We assume that both use optimal implementation with table lookups and xors. First let us give a theoretical comparison of the efficiency. Recall that since the round functions of AES and xAES are identical, in an environment where the master key is fixed and the encrypted message is longer (encryption mode), their speed is the same. Now let assume that the master key is frequently changed (hash mode). One round of AES (and therefore of xAES) has 16 table lookups and 16 xors.

One out of 10 subkey rounds of AES-128 has 4 table lookups and 8 xors. In xAES one such round has 4 table lookups, 8 xors and 3 rotations. If we assume that rotations have the same cost as xors, then for encrypting 16 bytes, AES uses $10 \cdot 16 + 10 \cdot 4 = 200$ lookups and $10 \cdot 16 + 10 \cdot 8 = 240$ operations. In xAES these numbers are $10 \cdot 16 + 10 \cdot 4 = 200$ lookups and $10 \cdot 16 + 10 \cdot 4 + 10 \cdot 3 = 270$ operations.

In AES-192, one subkey round (out of 8) has 4 table lookups and 10 xors while in xAES-192 one subkey round has 8 table lookups, 10 xors and 5 rotations. Hence, for 16 bytes, AES-192 spends $12 \cdot 16 + 8 \cdot 4 = 224$ lookups and $12 \cdot 16 + 8 \cdot 10 = 272$ operations, while xAES-192 spends $12 \cdot 16 + 8 \cdot 8 = 256$ lookups and 312 operations.

Finally, AES-256 has 7 subkey rounds and in each it has 8 table lookups and 16 xors. xAES-256 has the same number of subkey rounds and in each uses 8 table lookups , 16 xors and 7 rotations. For 16 bytes, AES-256 uses $14 \cdot 16 + 7 \cdot 8 = 280$ lookups and $14 \cdot 16 + 7 \cdot 16 = 336$ operations, while xAES-256 uses $14 \cdot 16 + 7 \cdot 8 = 280$ lookups and $14 \cdot 16 + 7 \cdot 16 + 7 \cdot 7 = 385$ operations.

These numbers indicate that one can expect that xAES-128 is around 6%, xAES-192 is around 12.5%, and xAES-256 is 7% slower than AES-128, AES-192, and AES-256 respectively. The actual implementation results obtained based on optimal implementation on C, together with the theoretical estimates, are given in Tbl. 2. In the table, the "Hash mode" entries indicate the speed of xAES compared to the speed of AES where the master key is changed on every iteration (16 bytes of plaintext), while the "Encryption mode" entries compare the speed when the master key is fixed[6]. The difference between the theoretical estimate and the actual implementation comes from the fact that the modern

[6] For short messages in the encryption mode, refer to the speed of "Hash mode".

Table 2. Comparison of the speed of xAES with the speed of AES. The abbreviations "tb" and "op" stand for table lookups and operations, respectively.

xAES/AES			
	128	192	256
		Hash mode	
Theoretical	$\frac{200tl+240op}{200tl+270op} \approx$ $\approx 94\%$	$\frac{224tl+272op}{256tl+312op} \approx$ $\approx 87\%$	$\frac{280tl+336op}{280tl+385op} \approx$ $\approx 93\%$
Implementation	96%	83%	97%
		Encryption mode	
Theoretical, Implementation	100%	100%	100%

processors in one clock cycle can perform several xor operations but only one table lookup.

4 Conclusion

We have presented a tweak in the key schedule of AES that leads to a cipher that is resistant against the latest related-key differential attacks found in AES and it has the same security level against the other published attacks on AES. The resistance of xAES against the related-key attacks comes from the additional rotations of the columns in the key schedule which stop potential local collisions found in AES.

The low number of operations introduced by the tweak, keeps the speed of the new cipher on a level that is close to the speed of AES. More precisely, xAES is efficient as AES in the encryption mode, and slightly less efficient than AES in the hash mode.

Acknowledgements. The author would like to thank the anonymous reviewers of SAC 2010 for their valuable comments and Aleksandar and Antonio Nikolić for providing additional computational power. Ivica Nikolić is supported by the Fonds National de la Recherche Luxembourg grant TR-PHD-BFR07-031.

References

1. Biham, E., Dunkelman, O., Keller, N.: Related-key boomerang and rectangle attacks. In: Cramer, R. (ed.) EUROCRYPT 2005. LNCS, vol. 3494, pp. 507–525. Springer, Heidelberg (2005)
2. Biryukov, A.: The Boomerang Attack on 5 and 6-Round Reduced AES. In: Dobbertin, H., Rijmen, V., Sowa, A. (eds.) AES 2005. LNCS, vol. 3373, pp. 11–15. Springer, Heidelberg (2005)

3. Biryukov, A., Khovratovich, D.: Related-key cryptanalysis of the full AES-192 and AES-256. In: Matsui, M. (ed.) ASIACRYPT 2009. LNCS, vol. 5912, pp. 1–18. Springer, Heidelberg (2009)
4. Biryukov, A., Khovratovich, D., Nikolić, I.: Distinguisher and related-key attack on the full AES-256. In: Halevi, S. (ed.) CRYPTO 2009. LNCS, vol. 5677, pp. 231–249. Springer, Heidelberg (2009)
5. Biryukov, A., Nikolić, I.: Automatic search for related-key differential characteristics in byte-oriented block ciphers: Application to AES, Camellia, Khazad and others. In: Gilbert, H. (ed.) EUROCRYPT 2010. LNCS, vol. 6110, pp. 322–344. Springer, Heidelberg (2010)
6. Daemen, J., Rijmen, V.: The Design of Rijndael: AES - The Advanced Encryption Standard. Springer, Heidelberg (2002)
7. Demirci, H., Selçuk, A.A.: A meet-in-the-middle attack on 8-round AES. In: Nyberg, K. (ed.) FSE 2008. LNCS, vol. 5086, pp. 116–126. Springer, Heidelberg (2008)
8. Ferguson, N., Kelsey, J., Lucks, S., Schneier, B., Stay, M., Wagner, D., Whiting, D.: Improved cryptanalysis of rijndael. In: Schneier, B. (ed.) FSE 2000. LNCS, vol. 1978, pp. 213–230. Springer, Heidelberg (2001)
9. Fleischmann, E., Gorski, M., Lucks, S.: Attacking 9 and 10 rounds of AES-256. In: Boyd, C., González Nieto, J. (eds.) ACISP 2009. LNCS, vol. 5594, pp. 60–72. Springer, Heidelberg (2009)
10. Gilbert, H., Minier, M.: A collision attack on 7 rounds of Rijndael. In: AES Candidate Conference, pp. 230–241 (2000)
11. Gueron, S.: Intel's new AES instructions for enhanced performance and security. In: Dunkelman, O. (ed.) FSE 2009. LNCS, vol. 5665, pp. 51–66. Springer, Heidelberg (2009)
12. Kim, J., Hong, S., Preneel, B.: Related-key rectangle attacks on reduced AES-192 and AES-256. In: Biryukov, A. (ed.) FSE 2007. LNCS, vol. 4593, pp. 225–241. Springer, Heidelberg (2007)
13. Lu, J., Dunkelman, O., Keller, N., Kim, J.: New impossible differential attacks on AES. In: Chowdhury, D.R., Rijmen, V., Das, A. (eds.) INDOCRYPT 2008. LNCS, vol. 5365, pp. 279–293. Springer, Heidelberg (2008)
14. May, L., Henricksen, M., Millan, W., Carter, G., Dawson, E.: Strengthening the key schedule of the AES. In: Batten, L.M., Seberry, J. (eds.) ACISP 2002. LNCS, vol. 2384, pp. 226–240. Springer, Heidelberg (2002)
15. National Institute of Standards and Technology. Advanced encryption standard (AES). FIPS 197 (November 2001)

On the Diffusion of Generalized Feistel Structures Regarding Differential and Linear Cryptanalysis

Kyoji Shibutani*

Sony Corporation
1-7-1 Konan, Minato-ku, Tokyo 108-0075, Japan
Kyoji.Shibutani@jp.sony.com

Abstract. This paper studies the security of blockciphers with generalized Feistel structures (GFS) consisting of SP-type F-functions. While GFS leads to compact implementations, the security is not well understood, in particular for larger values of the partitioning number which indicates the number of subblocks. For both differential and linear cryptanalysis, we first prove tighter lower bounds on the minimum number of active S-boxes for four and six rounds of the GFS utilizing word-based rotation as a round permutation. These bounds are almost twice as large as the previous results in literature. Then we present a new approach to derive the first tight lower bounds for the minimum number of active S-boxes in several types of GFS with large parameters. The proposed algorithm exploits word-based truncated differential search and three-round relations of Feistel connections. By applying our results, the number of rounds required to be secure against differential and linear attacks can be reduced significantly. Thus the results enable us to design a more efficient symmetric key primitive. Moreover, we show that the improved GFS proposed by Suzaki and Minematsu at FSE 2010 have more active S-boxes than the standard GFS.

Keywords: blockcipher, generalized Feistel structure, diffusion, lightweight cryptography.

1 Introduction

It is well known that Type-II generalized Feistel structures (GFS) [18] have several desirable implementation properties, notably compactness. For instance, the GFS has smaller F-functions compared to the Feistel structure for the same block size. Also GFS do not need inverse F-functions for decryption, in contrast to Substitution Permutation Networks (SPNs). Recently, lightweight cryptography has become a hot topic. Thus the GFS is an attractive structure for a lightweight symmetric key primitive such as a blockcipher or a hash function.

* This work was done while the author stayed at ESAT/COSIC, Katholieke Universiteit Leuven, Belgium.

A. Biryukov, G. Gong, and D.R. Stinson (Eds.): SAC 2010, LNCS 6544, pp. 211–228, 2011.

This might be one of the reasons why recent blockciphers such as CLEFIA [16] and HIGHT [6] utilize the GFS.

The GFS divides a plaintext into d subblocks, where $d > 2$, instead of $d = 2$ as used in Feistel structures. The size of the F-functions used in the GFS depends on the partitioning number d and the block size. If the partitioning number d of the GFS is larger, then smaller F-functions will be used. However, a large value of d generally requires a large number of rounds due to its slow diffusion. Hence there is a trade-off between the partitioning number and the required number of rounds. However, this relation has not been clear so far.

Recently, Suzaki and Minematsu introduced a GFS with the optimal round permutation with respect to full diffusion property, which is a property that all outputs are affected by all inputs [17]. Their paper showed that the improved GFS can be more secure against impossible differential and saturation attacks than the standard GFS. However, they expect that the minimum number of active S-boxes remains about the same. Thus their structures still require at least same number of rounds as the standard GFS to be secure against differential and linear attacks [3,10].

It is well understood how to practically evaluate the security against differential and linear attacks by determining the maximum differential and linear characteristic probabilities [4,7]. For instance, counting the number of active S-boxes is a well used technique to evaluate the immunity against those attacks [16]. This approach was used to design many blockciphers and hash functions, including AES [5] and Whirlpool [1]. In SPN structures, it is relatively easy to evaluate the minimum number of active S-boxes by evaluating the permutation layers as discussed in [4]. However, in Feistel structures, this is more complicated due to differential cancellations caused by the XOR operation after the F-function. Kanda showed that the minimum number of active S-boxes of certain consecutive rounds of Feistel structures with SP-type F-function can be represented as the branch number of the matrices used in the structure [7]. Shirai and Araki extended his result to three types of generalized Feistel structures [14], which are known as Type-I, Type-II and Nyberg's constructions [13,18]. They showed that any six consecutive rounds of Type-II GFS with any partitioning number have at least the same number of active S-boxes as the Feistel structure. They also introduced an efficient weight-based active S-box search algorithm. However, their algorithm only works for small parameter sets of the GFS and the bound shown in the paper is not tight. Therefore, to design a secure symmetric key primitive, a large number of rounds is still required.

In this paper, we show the first tight bounds on the minimum number of differential and linear active S-boxes of GFS with large parameter sets. We first prove tight lower bounds for four and six rounds of the standard GFS manually. The obtained bound of six rounds of the standard GFS is almost twice as large as the previous bound. This enables the required number of rounds to be almost halved. Then we show a novel approach to efficiently derive tight lower bounds on the minimum number of active S-boxes of several types of GFS with large parameters including recently proposed GFS utilizing optimal round permutations [17].

Table 1. Summary of our results, where $\mathcal{B}$ is the differential or the linear branch number of the matrices used in GFS

rounds	Feistel [7,15]	$\mathrm{GFS}_d^{\mathrm{std}}$ [14]	$\mathrm{GFS}_4^{\mathrm{std}}$ **(this paper)**	$\mathrm{GFS}_8^{\mathrm{std}}$ **(this paper)**	$\mathrm{GFS}_6^{\mathrm{imp}}$ **(this paper)**	$\mathrm{GFS}_8^{\mathrm{imp}}$ **(this paper)**
4	$\mathcal{B}$	-	$\mathcal{B}+1$	$\mathcal{B}+1$	$\mathcal{B}+1$	$\mathcal{B}+1$
5	$\mathcal{B}+1$	-	$\mathcal{B}+3$	$\mathcal{B}+3$	$\mathcal{B}+3$	$\mathcal{B}+3$
6	$\mathcal{B}+2$	$\mathcal{B}+2$	$2\mathcal{B}+2$	$2\mathcal{B}+2$	$2\mathcal{B}+2$	$2\mathcal{B}+2$
7	-	-	$2\mathcal{B}+2$	$2\mathcal{B}+4$	$2\mathcal{B}+4$	$2\mathcal{B}+4$
8	$2\mathcal{B}+1$	-	$2\mathcal{B}+3$	$3\mathcal{B}+3$	$4\mathcal{B}+2$	$4\mathcal{B}+3$
9	$2\mathcal{B}+2$	-	$2\mathcal{B}+4$	$3\mathcal{B}+6$	$4\mathcal{B}+4$	$4\mathcal{B}+6$
10	-	-	$3\mathcal{B}+3$	$4\mathcal{B}+5$	$4\mathcal{B}+6$	$5\mathcal{B}+4$
11	-	-	$3\mathcal{B}+5$	$4\mathcal{B}+8$	$4\mathcal{B}+8$	$5\mathcal{B}+7$
12	$3\mathcal{B}+1$	$2\mathcal{B}+4$	$4\mathcal{B}+4$	$6\mathcal{B}+6$	$6\mathcal{B}+2$	$7\mathcal{B}+4$
⋮	⋮	⋮	⋮	⋮	⋮	⋮
18	$4\mathcal{B}+4$	$3\mathcal{B}+6$	$6\mathcal{B}+6$	$8\mathcal{B}+8$	$8\mathcal{B}+10$	$10\mathcal{B}+6$

The proposed algorithm exploits word-based truncated differential search and three-round relations of Feistel connections. By using our results, the required number of rounds to be secure against differential and linear attacks can be reduced significantly. Therefore, our results are useful not only for a deeper understanding the security of GFS, but also for designing an efficient symmetric primitive. Our results are summarized in Table 1. More detailed results are listed in Appendix A.

This paper is organized as follows. In Sect. 2, definitions and some properties are introduced. In Sect. 3, related work on GFS is explained. Section 4 and 5 describe the lower bounds on the number of differential and linear active S-boxes in GFS, respectively. In Sect. 6, we discuss the result obtained in this paper. Finally, we conclude in Sect. 7.

2 Preliminaries

2.1 Target Structures

In this paper, we focus on GFS with SP-type F-functions [7] and an *even-odd* shuffle [17] as shown in Fig. 1. Let d be an even integer. A dmn-bit plaintext P is divided into d subblocks as $P = (x_0^{(1)}, x_1^{(1)}, ..., x_{d-1}^{(1)})$, where $x_j^{(i)} \in \{0,1\}^{mn}$. Then the i-th round output is calculated as follows:

$$(x_0^{(i+1)}, x_1^{(i+1)}, ..., x_{d-1}^{(i+1)}) \leftarrow \pi(x_0^{(i)}, F_0^{(i)}(x_1^{(i)}) \oplus x_0^{(i)}, ..., F_{d/2-1}^{(i)}(x_{d-2}^{(i)}) \oplus x_{d-1}^{(i)}),$$

where $F_j^{(i)} : \{0,1\}^{mn} \rightarrow \{0,1\}^{mn}$ is a j-th round function in the i-th round, and $\pi : (\{0,1\}^{mn})^d \rightarrow (\{0,1\}^{mn})^d$ is a deterministic permutation. We assume that each round function is the SP-type F-function which consists of an mn-bit round

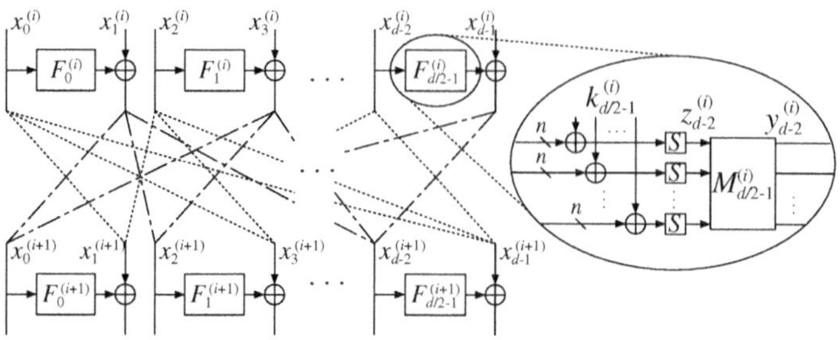

Fig. 1. GFS_d with SP-type F-function and *even-odd* shuffle, where dotted lines show possible connections, each set of outputs and inputs is connected by exactly one line. The sub-diagram on the right is a zoom in on an F-function.

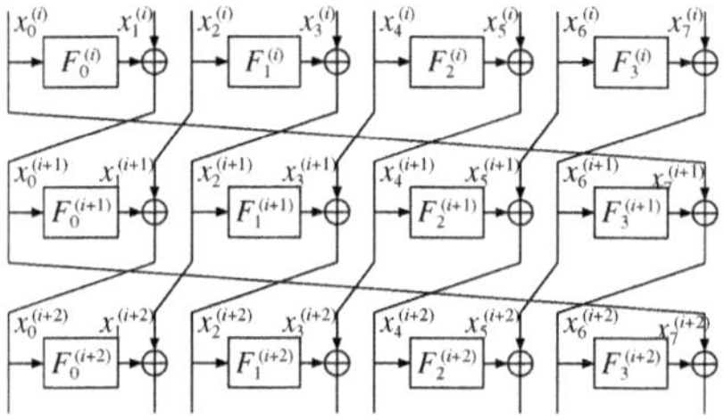

Fig. 2. $\mathrm{GFS}_8^{\mathrm{std}}$

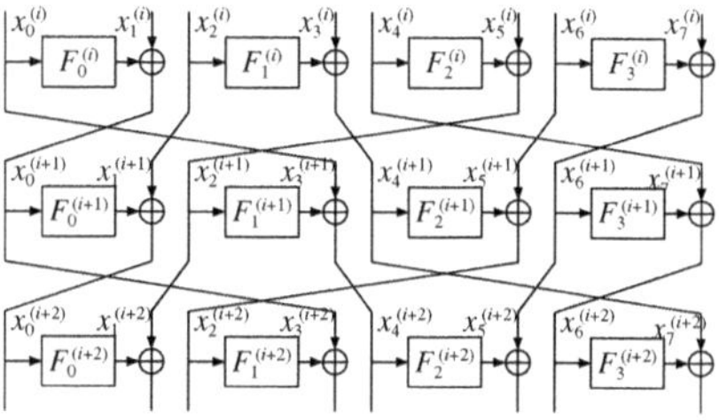

Fig. 3. $\mathrm{GFS}_8^{\mathrm{imp}}$ [17]

key addition, m n-bit bijective S-boxes and an mn-bit linear Boolean function [7]. $S(\cdot)$ denotes an n-bit bijective S-box and $M_j^{(i)}$ denotes a non-singular $m \times m$ matrix over a chosen field $\mathrm{GF}(2^n)$. $z_{2j}^{(i)}$ and $y_{2j}^{(i)}$ denote an output of the S-boxes and the linear function $M_j^{(i)}$ in $F_j^{(i)}$, respectively. We also restrict π to be a word-based permutation. For instance, π of GFS with the partitioning number eight and the word-based rotation shown in Fig. 2 is represented as $\pi(x_0, x_1, ..., x_7) = (x_1, x_2, ..., x_7, x_0)$. We treat several types of π in this paper. Hereafter mn denotes the bit length of subblock, GFS_d denotes the GFS with the partitioning number d, $\mathrm{GFS}_d^{\mathrm{std}}$ denotes the GFS_d with the word-based rotation, i.e., standard Type-II GFS, and $\mathrm{GFS}_d^{\mathrm{imp}}$ denotes the GFS_d with the optimal round permutation proposed by Suzaki and Minematsu [17][1].

2.2 Definitions

In this section, we give some definitions used in the following sections. We first give the definitions of bundle weight and branch number [5].

[1] We treat GFS_d with the round permutations No.1 given in Appendix A of [17] as $\mathrm{GFS}_d^{\mathrm{imp}}$.

Definition 1 (Bundle Weight). *Let $x \in \{0,1\}^{pn}$ be represented as $x=(x_0, x_1, \ldots, x_{p-1})$, where $x_i \in \{0,1\}^n$, then the bundle weight $w_n(x)$ is defined as*

$$w_n(x) = \sharp\{i | 0 \leq i \leq p-1, x_i \neq 0\}. \tag{1}$$

Definition 2 (Branch Number). *Let $P : \{0,1\}^{pn} \rightarrow \{0,1\}^{qn}$. The branch number of P is defined as*

$$\mathcal{B}_n(P) = \min_{a \neq 0}\{w_n(a) + w_n(P(a))\}. \tag{2}$$

We give the definitions of $\mathcal{B}^D$ and $\mathcal{B}^L$ in r-round GFS to show the minimum number of differential and linear active S-boxes, respectively.

Definition 3 (Differential Branch Number)

$$\mathcal{B}^D = \min_{1 \leq i \leq r, 0 \leq j \leq d/2-1} \mathcal{B}_n(M_j^{(i)}). \tag{3}$$

Definition 4 (Linear Branch Number)

$$\mathcal{B}^L = \min_{1 \leq i \leq r, 0 \leq j \leq d/2-1} \mathcal{B}_n({}^t M_j^{(i)}), \tag{4}$$

where ${}^t M$ is the transpose matrix of M.

Since each active S-box reduces the differential and linear characteristic probabilities, the maximum differential and linear characteristic probabilities are bounded by the minimum number of differential and linear active S-boxes, respectively. On the other hand, the minimum number of active S-boxes is relevant to the branch number of the linear function. Thus the motivation of this paper is to clarify the minimum number of differential and linear active S-boxes for GFS by using $\mathcal{B}^D$ and $\mathcal{B}^L$, respectively.

It is well known that the upper bounds on the security against linear attacks are derived from the upper bounds on the security against differential attacks because of its duality [2,11,7]. Thus, in this paper, we mainly discuss the security against differential attacks. We discuss the security against linear attacks in Sect. 5.

2.3 Properties of Generalized Feistel Structures

In this section, we present several properties of GFS. Hereafter we refer to an F-function which has non-zero input difference or non-zero output mask value as a differential or a linear active F-function, respectively. From the bijectivity of F-functions, the following property holds:

Property 1. Any two consecutive rounds of GFS have at least one differential active F-function if a non-zero input difference is given.

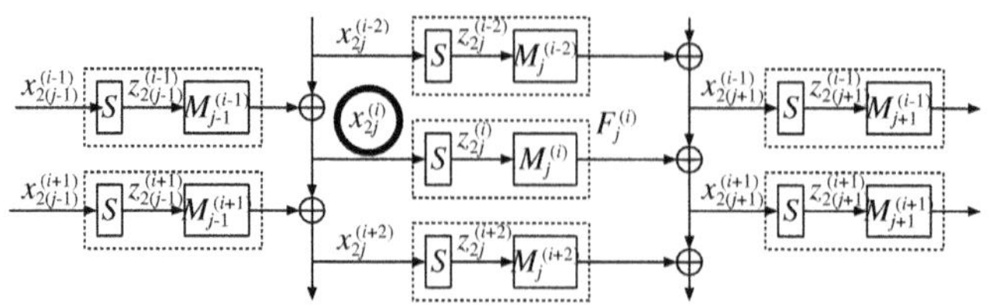

Fig. 4. Five Rounds of $\mathrm{GFS}_d^{\mathrm{std}}$ (Untwisted Form)

We consider the five-round structure of $\mathrm{GFS}_d^{\mathrm{std}}$ shown in Fig. 4, and focus on the value $x_{2j}^{(i)}$ in the center of the structure, where $x_{2j}^{(i)}$ and $z_{2j}^{(i)}$ denote an input of $F_j^{(i)}$ and an output of S-boxes in $F_j^{(i)}$, respectively. Let $D_j^{(i)}$ denote the number of differential active S-boxes in $F_j^{(i)}$. Since all S-boxes are bijective, we have the following relations.

Property 2

$$D_j^{(i)} = w_n(\Delta x_{2j}^{(i)}) = w_n(\Delta z_{2j}^{(i)}). \tag{5}$$

Then the following property is derived [14].

Property 3 (Three-round relation of Feistel connection). If $D_j^{(i)} \neq 0$, then $D_j^{(i)} + D_{j+1}^{(i-1)} + D_{j+1}^{(i+1)} \geq \mathcal{B}^D$.

Proof

$$M_j^{(i)}(\Delta z_{2j}^{(i)}) = \Delta x_{2(j+1)}^{(i-1)} \oplus \Delta x_{2(j+1)}^{(i+1)}. \tag{6}$$

From the definition of $\mathcal{B}^D$, $w_n(\Delta z_{2j}^{(i)}) + w_n(M_j^{(i)}(\Delta z_{2j}^{(i)})) \geq \mathcal{B}^D$ if $\Delta z_{2j}^{(i)} \neq 0$. Also, $w_n(a) + w_n(b) \geq w_n(a \oplus b)$ holds, then we have

$$w_n(\Delta z_{2j}^{(i)}) \neq 0 \Rightarrow w_n(\Delta z_{2j}^{(i)}) + w_n(\Delta x_{2(j+1)}^{(i-1)}) + w_n(\Delta x_{2(j+1)}^{(i+1)}) \geq \mathcal{B}^D. \tag{7}$$

□

In this paper, we refer to this relation of three values $\Delta x_{2j}^{(i)}$, $\Delta x_{2(j+1)}^{(i-1)}$ and $\Delta x_{2(j+1)}^{(i+1)}$ as the three-round relation of the Feistel connection. The following properties are also obtained.

Property 4. If $D_j^{(i)} \neq 0$, then $D_{j-1}^{(i-1)} + D_j^{(i-2)} \geq 1$, $D_{j-1}^{(i+1)} + D_j^{(i+2)} \geq 1$, and $D_{j+1}^{(i-1)} + D_{j+1}^{(i+1)} \geq 1$.

Proof

$$M_{j-1}^{(i-1)}(\Delta z_{2(j-1)}^{(i-1)}) \oplus \Delta x_{2j}^{(i-2)} = \Delta x_{2j}^{(i)} \neq 0, \tag{8}$$

$$M_{j-1}^{(i-1)}(\Delta z_{2(j-1)}^{(i-1)}) \neq \Delta x_{2j}^{(i-2)}. \tag{9}$$

Then $M_{j-1}^{(i-1)}(\Delta z_{2(j-1)}^{(i-1)})$ and $\Delta x_{2j}^{(i-2)}$ cannot be 0 simultaneously. Thus, $D_{j-1}^{(i-1)} + D_j^{(i-2)} \geq 1$. The other properties can be proved in a similar way. □

We give some definitions of round permutations to use three-round relation of the Feistel connections in GFS. Let π_E, π_O be index mappings. π_E is the index mapping of π from even numbered blocks to odd-number blocks and all indexes are divided by two. For example, π_E of $\mathrm{GFS}_8^{\mathrm{std}}$ shown in Fig. 2 is represented as $\pi_E[0] = 3$, $\pi_E[1] = 0$, $\pi_E[2] = 1$ and $\pi_E[3] = 2$. Similarly, π_O is the index mapping of π from odd numbered blocks to even-number blocks and all indexes are divided by two. For example, π_O of $\mathrm{GFS}_8^{\mathrm{std}}$ is the identity mapping, and π_O of $\mathrm{GFS}_8^{\mathrm{imp}}$ is represented as $\pi_O[0] = 0$, $\pi_O[1] = 2$, $\pi_O[2] = 1$ and $\pi_O[3] = 3$. By using these mappings π_E and π_O, the three-round relations of the Feistel connections in GFS can easily be represented. For instance, the three F-functions input differences $\Delta x_{2\pi_E^{-1}[j/2]}^{(i)}$, $\Delta x_j^{(i+1)}$ and $\Delta x_{2\pi_O[j/2]}^{(i+2)}$ in Figs. 2 and 3 satisfy the three-round relation shown in Property 3 independently, where $j = \{0, 2, 4, 6\}$ and π_E^{-1} is an inverse mapping of π_E.

Let $\boldsymbol{\Delta x}^{(i)} = (\Delta x_0^{(i)}, \Delta x_2^{(i)}, ..., \Delta x_{d-2}^{(i)})$. Then the following property is derived.

Property 5. Any three consecutive rounds of $(i-1)$ to $(i+1)$-round of GFS_d have at least $w_{mn}(\boldsymbol{\Delta x}^{(i)}) \cdot \mathcal{B}^D$ differential active S-boxes, specifically,

$$\sum_{s=0}^{d/2-1} \sum_{t=i-1}^{i+1} D_s^{(t)} \geq w_{mn}(\boldsymbol{\Delta x}^{(i)}) \cdot \mathcal{B}^D. \tag{10}$$

Proof. From the definition of the *even-odd* shuffle, each i-th round output after the XOR operation is mapped to the corresponding F-function of $(i-1)$-th round and $(i+1)$-th round respectively. In other words, there exist d independent three-round relations shown in Property 3. Thus the number of active S-boxes in three consecutive rounds is bounded by the bundle weight of the differentials in the center. □

The mappings π_E, π_O, and the Property 5 are useful to evaluate the minimum number of active S-boxes of GFS.

3 Related Work

In this section, we discuss previous results related to GFS. The formal definition of GFS was given by Zheng et al. [18]. Several cryptographic properties of these structures were analyzed in [8,12]. Provable security of $\mathrm{GFS}_4^{\mathrm{std}}$ against differential and linear attacks was discussed by Lee et al. [9]. In their results, more than five rounds of $\mathrm{GFS}_4^{\mathrm{std}}$ have the maximum differential probability $p^4 + 2p^5$ and the maximum linear probability $q^4 + 2q^5$, where p and q are the maximum average differential probability and the maximum average linear probability of the F-functions used in the structure, respectively.

The practical security of $\mathrm{GFS}_d^{\mathrm{std}}$ against differential and linear attacks was discussed by Shirai and Araki [14]. They showed the lower bounds on the number of active S-boxes in three types of generalized Feistel structures, Type-I, Type-II and Nyberg's constructions [13,18]. In their results, any six consecutive rounds of $\mathrm{GFS}_d^{\mathrm{std}}$ have at least $\mathcal{B}^D + 2$ active S-boxes[2]. Moreover, they introduced efficient weight-based active S-box search algorithms that can derive the minimum number of active S-boxes of GFS. Though their algorithm is efficient, still a large computation is required to evaluate large parameter sets of GFS, namely, it requires to search at most $(m+1)^{d(r+1)/2}$ values to evaluate r-round $\mathrm{GFS}_d^{\mathrm{std}}$. Thus the algorithm does not work for $\mathrm{GFS}_d^{\mathrm{std}}$ with large parameters. We use this algorithm to verify the tightness of our results in Sect. 4.4.

Suzaki and Minematsu discussed round permutations of GFS [17]. They mainly focused on full diffusion property, which is a property that all outputs are affected by all inputs. They showed that the diffusion property of the GFS_d $(d > 4)$ could be better than $\mathrm{GFS}_d^{\mathrm{std}}$ by replacing its round permutation from the word-based rotation used in $\mathrm{GFS}_d^{\mathrm{std}}$. In their paper, although the improved GFS has better properties with respect to full diffusion, they have about the same number of active S-boxes[3] as $\mathrm{GFS}_d^{\mathrm{std}}$.

4 Differential Active S-Boxes in GFS

In this section, we present the minimum number of differential active S-boxes in several types of GFS. First, we show better lower bounds for four and six rounds of $\mathrm{GFS}_d^{\mathrm{std}}$. Then, we introduce an exhaustive search algorithm that determines the minimum number of differential active S-boxes for all types of GFS efficiently. By using this algorithm, we present several lower bounds on GFS. Finally, we compare the results obtained from the new algorithm with the results obtained from weight-based exhaustive active S-box search to verify the tightness of the new bounds.

4.1 The Lower Bounds for Four and Six Rounds of $\mathrm{GFS}_d^{\mathrm{std}}$

Theorem 1. *Let $d \geq 4$. Any four consecutive rounds of $\mathrm{GFS}_d^{\mathrm{std}}$ have at least $\mathcal{B}^D + 1$ differential active S-boxes.*

Proof. We consider four consecutive rounds that start from the i-th round as described in Fig. 5. From Property 1, there is at least one active F-function in any two consecutive rounds, i.e., there is at least one active F-function in the $(i+1)$-th round or the $(i+2)$-th round. As shown on the left side of Fig. 5, suppose that

[2] Their results were given by $\mathcal{B}^D$, and $\mathcal{B}_2^D$ which is a branch number of two consecutive matrices. If matrices used in each F-function are different, $\mathcal{B}_2^D$ can be more than two. However, in our model, $\mathcal{B}_2^D = 2$.

[3] Note that, they evaluated the number of active S-boxes by counting the number of active F-functions as active S-boxes.

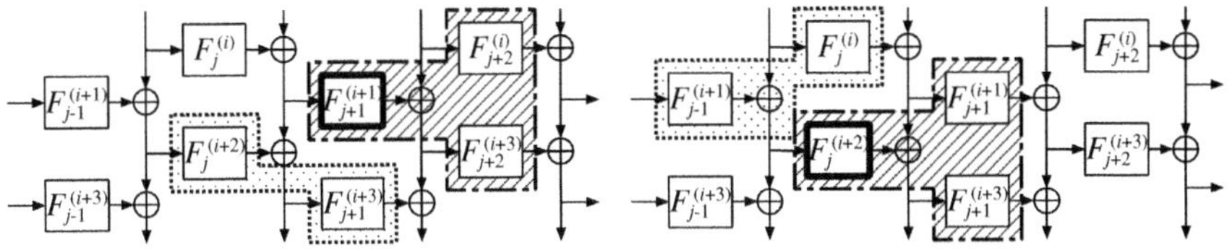

Fig. 5. Four Rounds of $\mathrm{GFS}_d^{\mathrm{std}}$ (Untwisted Form)

the j-th F-function in the $(i+1)$-th round is active, namely, $D_j^{(i+1)} \neq 0$. In that case, $D_{j+1}^{(i+1)} + D_{j+2}^{(i)} + D_{j+2}^{(i+3)} \geq \mathcal{B}^D$ from Property 3, and $D_j^{(i+2)} + D_{j+1}^{(i+3)} \geq 1$ from Property 4. Thus these four rounds have at least $\mathcal{B}^D + 1$ differential active S-boxes. Similarly, in the case of an active F-function in the $(i+2)$-th round, we have the same bound as shown in the right side of Fig. 5. Therefore, we obtain $\Sigma_{s=0}^{d/2-1} \Sigma_{t=i}^{i+3} D_s^{(t)} \geq \mathcal{B}^D + 1$. □

Theorem 2. *Let $d \geq 4$. Any six consecutive rounds of GFS_d^{std} have at least $2\mathcal{B}^D + 2$ differential active S-boxes.*

See Appendix B for a proof. The bound given by this theorem is almost twice as large as the previous result. Thus, the required number of rounds of $\mathrm{GFS}_d^{\mathrm{std}}$ to be secure against differential attacks can be almost halved by using this bound.

While it might be possible to prove the minimum number of active S-boxes of a large number of rounds of $\mathrm{GFS}_d^{\mathrm{std}}$ in a similar way, such proofs would be quite complex when the number of rounds is large. In other words, the number of cases to be considered would be increased drastically. Also, using the approaches so far, the relation between the partitioning number d and the minimum number of active S-boxes is still unclear. If all possible cases are checked efficiently, the minimum number of active S-boxes of the structures can be derived easily. Therefore, we propose another approach to efficiently derive the minimum number of active S-boxes of GFS with large parameter sets in the following section.

4.2 The Search for the Minimum Number of Differential Active S-Boxes

In this section, we introduce the search algorithm of the minimum number of differential active S-boxes for GFS. This algorithm consists of the following two steps: (a) searching active F-function paths of GFS exhaustively by word-based truncated differential search, (b) determining the minimum number of differential active S-boxes from a given path.

Let $X^{(i)} \in \{0,1\}^{d/2}$ be the input differences of the mn-bit truncated differentials of the i-th F-function, i.e., $X^{(i)} = (w_{mn}(\Delta x_0^{(i)}), w_{mn}(\Delta x_2^{(i)}), \ldots, w_{mn}(\Delta x_{d-2}^{(i)}))$, where $X^{(0)}$ is the first input differences to XOR operation side, namely, $X^{(0)} = (w_{mn}(\Delta x_1^{(1)}), w_{mn}(\Delta x_3^{(1)}), \ldots, w_{mn}(\Delta x_{d-1}^{(1)}))$. Let $\mathrm{BD}(R)$ be the minimum number of differential active S-boxes in R-round GFS, then $\mathrm{BD}(R)$ is calculated as follows:

Step 1. Initialize BD(R) to a sufficiently large value, such as the total number of S-boxes.

Step 2. Choose a possible active F-function path by searching mn-bit truncated differential paths of GFS. First, $X^{(0)}$ and $X^{(1)}$ are chosen exhaustively. Then, i-th round truncated differential path $X^{(i)}$ ($i \geq 3$) can be determined by $X^{(i-2)}$ and $X^{(i-1)}$ as follows:

$$X_j^{(i)} = \begin{cases} X^{(i-1)}_{\pi_O^{-1}[j]} \oplus X^{(i-2)}_{\pi_E^{-1}[\pi_O^{-1}[j]]} &, \text{ if } X^{(i-1)}_{\pi_O^{-1}[j]} \wedge X^{(i-2)}_{\pi_E^{-1}[\pi_O^{-1}[j]]} = 0, \\ 0, 1 &, \text{ otherwise,} \end{cases}$$

where $X_j^{(i)}$ is a j-th bit of $X^{(i)}$ and $X_0^{(i)}$ is the most significant bit of $X^{(i)}$. In the case of $i = 2$, $X^{(i-2)}_{\pi_E^{-1}[\pi_O^{-1}[j]]}$ is replaced by $X^{(i-2)}_{\pi_O^{-1}[j]}$. Thus R-round path of $X^{(i)}(0 \leq i \leq R)$ is calculated by using the previous algorithm repeatedly.

Step 3. Determine the minimum number of active S-boxes from a given truncated differential path. This step is described in Fig. 6. If the bound obtained from the algorithm Fig. 6 is less than BD(R), then BD(R) is updated. The detailed explanation of this step is presented in the following section.

Step 4. If all possible truncated differential paths have been checked, terminate the program. Otherwise, go to Step 2.

We give an improvement of Step 2. From Property 5, it is easy to derive a rough bound on the number of $\mathcal{B}^D$ in the structure by checking some Hamming weights of $X^{(i)}$. Then if the obtained rough bound is more than the current bound BD(R), we can simply skip this path. For example, in the case of $R = 6$, we check max(Hw($X^{(2)}$)+ Hw($X^{(5)}$), Hw($X^{(3)}$), Hw($X^{(4)}$)), where Hw(X) denotes a Hamming weight of X. This improvement results in a speed-up in practice.

4.3 Detailed Explanation of the Algorithm

We explain the algorithm presented in the previous section in detail. The most important part of this algorithm is Step 3. In this step, we focus on three-round relations in GFS. As discussed in Sect. 2.3, we find three-round relations in any three consecutive rounds by using π_E^{-1} and π_O. Then we count the number of $\mathcal{B}^D$ in GFS greedily from top to bottom. Finally, we count the remaining constants in the structure. We exploit fact that there exist $d/2$ independent three-round relations in any three consecutive rounds of GFS$_d$ and these relations can be obtained by using the mappings π_E^{-1} and π_O. Once $d/2$ independent three-round relations are obtained, the number of $\mathcal{B}^D$ in three consecutive rounds is easily derived from Property 3 and 5. However, in this algorithm, there should be some overlapping values. To avoid this problem, we use a flag for each bit of truncated differentials. Once a value is used for counting the number of $\mathcal{B}^D$ in the certain three consecutive rounds, then the flag is set. Then this value cannot be used twice, and the algorithm works correctly.

Note that the comparison phase in Step 3 depends on the value of $\mathcal{B}^D$. Suppose that the current BD(R) $= 2\mathcal{B}^D$, and a new value of $\mathcal{B}^D + 3$ is obtained. In that

Algorithm $CountBD(r, X^{(1)}, ..., X^{(r)})$ **:**
Clear flags of $X_j^{(i)}, (1 \le i \le r, 0 \le j \le d/2 - 1)$
$S = 0$
for $i \leftarrow 2$ to $(r-1)$ do
  for $j \leftarrow 0$ to $(d/2 - 1)$ do
    if $(X_j^{(i)} = 1) \wedge$ (flags of $X^{(i-1)}_{\pi_E^{-1}[j]}$ and $X_j^{(i)}$ are not set) then
      $S \leftarrow S + 1$
      Set flags of $X_j^{(i)}$, $X^{(i-1)}_{\pi_E^{-1}[j]}$ (if $X^{(i-1)}_{\pi_E^{-1}[j]} = 1$), and $X^{(i+1)}_{\pi_O[j]}$ (if $X^{(i+1)}_{\pi_O[j]} = 1$)
$T = 0$
for $i \leftarrow 1$ to r do
  for $j \leftarrow 0$ to $(d/2 - 1)$ do
    if $X_j^{(i)} = 1 \wedge$ (flag of $X_j^{(i)}$ is not set) then
      $T \leftarrow T + 1$
return $S \cdot \mathcal{B}^D + T$

Fig. 6. Algorithm $CountBD(r, X^{(0)}, ..., X^{(r)})$

case, the BD(R) is updated when $\mathcal{B}^D > 2$, because $2\mathcal{B}^D \le \mathcal{B}^D + 3$. However, when $\mathcal{B}^D = 2$, it should not be updated. This paper contains results for $\mathcal{B}^D > 2$.

We now show that this algorithm does not always give the best bound in the structure from a given path. The path in the left of Fig. 7 is the case, where an F-function indicated by bold line is determined to be active and an F-function indicated by dotted line is determined to be non-active. In this case, the algorithm (Fig. 6) outputs $\mathcal{B}^D + 4$ instead of $2\mathcal{B}^D + 2$ as the path in the center of Fig. 7, where there is at least $\mathcal{B}^D$ active S-boxes in the area encircled by chain line. However, because the purpose of this algorithm is to find a lower bound on the number of differential active S-boxes, the best bound in this step is not necessary. We can avoid this problem by adding search patterns to the algorithm. For example, if we compute the bound both way, i.e., from top to bottom and from bottom to top, the algorithm outputs the best bound from the path at the right of Fig. 7. However, from our calculations, it seems that this change does not provide an improvement in practice. In other words, the obtained lower bound is the same even if we add some search patterns to the algorithm, e.g., the path in Fig. 7 is not the minimum path for $\text{GFS}_4^{\text{std}}$.

4.4 Comparison of Results

We verified the tightness of the obtained lower bounds by comparing with the results obtained by the weight-based exhaustive active S-box search [14] for as many parameters as possible. Consequently, the actual number of active S-boxes from the obtained bounds completely corresponded to the results from the exhaustive search with the following parameters: $\text{GFS}_4^{\text{std}}$ with $m = 2, 3, ..., 8,$[4]

[4] The case of $\text{GFS}_4^{\text{std}}$ with $m = 4$ is in Table 4 of [14].

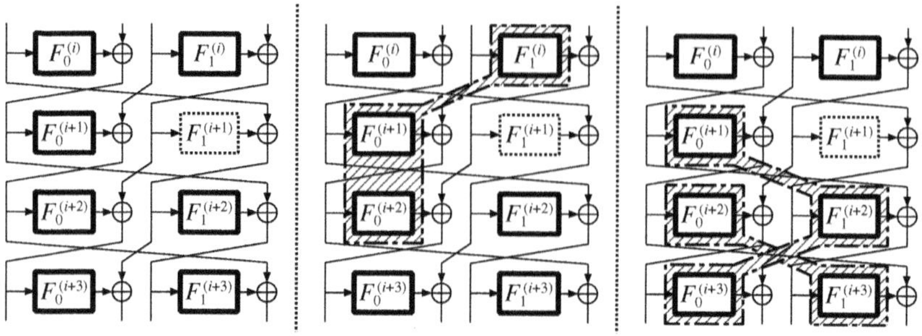

Fig. 7. An Example Path of $\mathrm{GFS}_4^{\mathrm{std}}$

$\mathrm{GFS}_6^{\mathrm{std}}$ with $m = 2, 3, 4$, $\mathrm{GFS}_8^{\mathrm{std}}$ with $m = 2$, $\mathrm{GFS}_6^{\mathrm{imp}}$ with $m = 2, 3, 4$, and $\mathrm{GFS}_8^{\mathrm{imp}}$ with $m = 2$ and $r = 1$ up to 20, where $\mathcal{B}^D = m + 1$. While we have not confirmed the tightness of the other bounds due to computational restrictions of the weight-based exhaustive search, it seems that the obtained bounds are tight as well.

5 Linear Active S-Boxes in GFS

It was shown by Kanda [7] that the lower bounds on the minimum number of linear active S-boxes of Feistel structure with SP-type F-functions can be obtained by simply replacing differential branch number $\mathcal{B}^D$ by linear branch number $\mathcal{B}^L$. In his work, Feistel structures with SP-type F-functions can be represented as Feistel structures with PS-type F-functions by using an equivalent transformation. Then the minimum number of active S-boxes is derived by evaluating the transformed cipher using the concatenation rules [2,11].

GFS with SP-type F-functions can be represented as GFS with PS-type F-functions in a similar way. Note that, in contrast to Feistel structures, depending on the original round permutation used in GFS, the transformed round permutation can be different. However, we can use the same algorithm to determine the lower bounds on the minimum number of linear active S-boxes by replacing the original round permutation by the transformed round permutation. This is not the case for the structures in the tables shown in this paper: the transformed round permutation is the same as the original round permutation. Thus, the minimum number of linear active S-boxes is obtained by simply replacing differential branch numbers $\mathcal{B}^D$ by linear branch numbers $\mathcal{B}^L$.

6 Discussion

In this section, we discuss the obtained results. We first give an example of the parameter $m = 4$ and $n = 8$ of $\mathrm{GFS}_8^{\mathrm{std}}$, i.e., 256-bit blockcipher, to show applicability of our results. We assume that this example cipher consists of the MDS matrices and the inversion S-boxes over GF(2^8) , specifically, $\mathcal{B}^D = \mathcal{B}^L = 5$ and the maximum differential and linear probability of the S-box is 2^{-6}. In this case, at least 22 active S-boxes are required to be secure against differential and linear attacks, as $(2^{-6})^{22} = 2^{-132} < 2^{-128}$ when the key size is 128-bit. Though the previous result shows that 24 rounds are required to have more than 22 active S-boxes, our results show that only 10 rounds are required to be secure against differential and linear attacks. Thus, our results are useful to design an efficient symmetric primitive, since the required number of rounds with respect to differential and linear cryptanalysis is reduced. While many types of attacks must be considered when constructing a secure symmetric primitive, actually, differential, linear, impossible differential and saturation attacks tend to be the bottleneck in GFS. Therefore, it can be said that at least two of them can be improved by using the new bounds. If the parameters (the dimension of the matrices m and the partitioning number d) are larger, the effects of our results become even more noticeable.

Moreover, according to our results, most of the bounds on a sufficiently large number of rounds can be derived from bounds on a smaller number of rounds. For example, most of rounds of the minimum number of active S-boxes for more than seven rounds of $\mathrm{GFS}_4^{\mathrm{std}}$ can be derived from the bounds on one to the bounds on six consecutive rounds, e.g. the minimum number of active S-boxes in ten rounds of $\mathrm{GFS}_4^{\mathrm{std}}$ can be represented as active S-boxes in four rounds and six rounds of $\mathrm{GFS}_4^{\mathrm{std}}$. Thus it seems that determining tight bounds for a small of rounds is important. Therefore, our algorithm works well even if the number of rounds is large, whereas it needs a lot of computation to derive bounds of GFS with large number of rounds, e.g., more than 30 rounds.

Furthermore, the results show that the number of active S-boxes increases about 1.5 times when the partitioning number is doubled, assuming the number of S-boxes used in each F-function remains the same and the number of rounds is sufficiently large.

7 Conclusion

In this paper, we have shown the first tight bounds on the minimum number of active S-boxes of GFS with large parameter sets. We first proved tight lower bounds for four and six rounds of the standard GFS manually. Then, we introduced a novel approach to evaluate the minimum number of active S-boxes of GFS by using the branch number of the matrices used in the structure. The proposed algorithm uses three-round relations of the Feistel connection and well known truncated differential search. By using our algorithm, all types of the GFS can be evaluated precisely, including recently proposed GFS that utilize optimal round permutations instead of the word-based rotation used in the standard GFS. Moreover, we confirmed the tightness of the obtained bounds by comparing with the results obtained by the weight-based exhaustive active S-box search algorithm.

By applying our results, the required number of rounds to be secure against differential and linear attacks can be reduced significantly. Moreover, all bounds obtained in this paper depend only on the branch number of the matrices used in GFS. The results can therefore be widely used to design an efficient symmetric primitive. In other words, our results are useful not only for more thoroughly understanding the security of the GFS, but also for designing an efficient symmetric key primitive, because the GFS can be implemented compactly and evaluating its security against differential attacks is essential to both blockcipher and hash function design.

Acknowledgments. The author would like to thank Bart Preneel, Nicky Mouha and the anonymous reviewers for their helpful comments.

References

1. Barreto, P.S.L.M., Rijmen, V.: The Whirlpool hashing function. Primitive submitted to NESSIE (September 2000), `http://www.larc.usp.br/~pbarreto/WhirlpoolPage.html` (revised May 2003)
2. Biham, E.: On Matsui's linear cryptanalysis. In: De Santis, A. (ed.) EUROCRYPT 1994. LNCS, vol. 950, pp. 341–355. Springer, Heidelberg (1995)
3. Biham, E., Shamir, A.: Differential Cryptanalysis of the Data Encryption Standard. Springer, Heidelberg (1993)
4. Daemen, J., Rijmen, V.: The wide trail design strategy. In: Honary, B. (ed.) Cryptography and Coding 2001. LNCS, vol. 2260, pp. 222–238. Springer, Heidelberg (2001)
5. Daemen, J., Rijmen, V.: The Design of Rijndael: AES - The Advanced Encryption Standard (Information Security and Cryptography). Springer, Heidelberg (2002)
6. Hong, D., Sung, J., Hong, S., Lim, J., Lee, S., Koo, B., Lee, C., Chang, D., Lee, J., Jeong, K., Kim, H., Kim, J., Chee, S.: HIGHT: A new block cipher suitable for low-resource device. In: Goubin, L., Matsui, M. (eds.) CHES 2006. LNCS, vol. 4249, pp. 46–59. Springer, Heidelberg (2006)
7. Kanda, M.: Practical security evaluation against differential and linear cryptanalyses for Feistel ciphers with SPN round function. In: Stinson, D.R., Tavares, S. (eds.) SAC 2000. LNCS, vol. 2012, pp. 324–338. Springer, Heidelberg (2001)
8. Kim, J., Hong, S., Sung, J., Lee, S., Lim, J., Sung, S.: Impossible differential cryptanalysis for block cipher structures. In: Johansson, T., Maitra, S. (eds.) INDOCRYPT 2003. LNCS, vol. 2904, pp. 82–96. Springer, Heidelberg (2003)
9. Lee, C., Kim, J., Sung, J., Hong, S., Lee, S.: Provable security for an RC6-like structure and a MISTY-FO-like structure against differential cryptanalysis. In: Gavrilova, M., et al. (eds.) ICCSA 2006. LNCS, vol. 3982, pp. 446–455. Springer, Heidelberg (2006)
10. Matsui, M.: Linear cryptanalysis of Data Encryption Standard. In: Helleseth, T. (ed.) EUROCRYPT 1993. LNCS, vol. 765, pp. 386–397. Springer, Heidelberg (1994)
11. Matsui, M.: On correlation between the order of S-boxes and the strength of DES. In: De Santis, A. (ed.) EUROCRYPT 1994. LNCS, vol. 950, pp. 366–375. Springer, Heidelberg (1995)

12. Moriai, S., Vaudenay, S.: On the pseudorandomness of top-level schemes of block ciphers. In: Okamoto, T. (ed.) ASIACRYPT 2000. LNCS, vol. 1976, pp. 289–302. Springer, Heidelberg (2000)
13. Nyberg, K.: Generalized Feistel network. In: Kim, K., Matsumoto, T. (eds.) ASIACRYPT 1996. LNCS, vol. 1163, pp. 91–104. Springer, Heidelberg (1996)
14. Shirai, T., Araki, K.: On generalized Feistel structures using the diffusion switching mechanism. IEICE Trans. Fundamentals E91-A(8), 2120–2129 (2008)
15. Shirai, T., Shibutani, K.: On Feistel structures using a diffusion switching mechanism. In: Robshaw, M.J.B. (ed.) FSE 2006. LNCS, vol. 4047, pp. 41–56. Springer, Heidelberg (2006)
16. Shirai, T., Shibutani, K., Akishita, T., Moriai, S., Iwata, T.: The 128-bit blockcipher CLEFIA. In: Biryukov, A. (ed.) FSE 2007. LNCS, vol. 4593, pp. 181–195. Springer, Heidelberg (2007)
17. Suzaki, T., Minematsu, K.: Improving the generalized Feistel. In: Hong, S., Iwata, T. (eds.) FSE 2010. LNCS, vol. 6147, pp. 19–39. Springer, Heidelberg (2010)
18. Zheng, Y., Matsumoto, T., Imai, H.: On the construction of block ciphers provably secure and not relying on any unproved hypotheses. In: Brassard, G. (ed.) CRYPTO 1989. LNCS, vol. 435, pp. 461–480. Springer, Heidelberg (1990)

A Lower Bounds on the Number of Active S-Boxes

Several lower bounds obtained in this paper are shown in Table 2 and 3. In these tables, $\mathcal{B}$ denotes either the differential or the linear branch number of the matrices used in the GFS.

B A Proof of Theorem 2

Proof. We consider six consecutive rounds that start from the i-th round. From Property 1, there is at least one active F-function in any two consecutive rounds, i.e., there is at least one active F-function in the $(i+2)$-th round or the $(i+3)$-th round. Suppose that the j-th F-function in the $(i+2)$-th round is active, i.e., $D_j^{(i+2)} \neq 0$ as shown in Fig. 8. Then we consider the following cases.

Case 1. If $D_{j+1}^{(i+3)} = 0$, then $D_{j+1}^{(i+1)} \neq 0$ from Property 4 , also $D_j^{(i)} + D_{j-1}^{(i+1)} \geq 1$ and $D_{j-1}^{(i+3)} + D_j^{(i+4)} \geq 1$. Then $D_{j+1}^{(i+1)} + D_{j+2}^{(i)} + D_{j+2}^{(i+2)} \geq \mathcal{B}^D$ from the fact $D_{j+1}^{(i+1)} \neq 0$ and Property 3. We then consider the following two cases.

Case 1-1. If $D_j^{(i+4)} \neq 0$, then $D_j^{(i+4)} + D_{j+1}^{(i+5)} \geq \mathcal{B}^D$ from Property 3. Thus we have $\Sigma_{s=0}^{d/2-1} \Sigma_{t=i}^{i+5} D_s^{(t)} \geq 2\mathcal{B}^D + 2$.

Case 1-2. If $D_{j-1}^{(i+3)} \neq 0$, then $D_{j-1}^{(i+3)} + D_j^{(i+2)} + D_j^{(i+4)} \geq \mathcal{B}^D$ from Property 3 and $D_{j-2}^{(i+4)} + D_{j-1}^{(i+5)} \geq 1$ from Property 4. Thus we obtain $\Sigma_{s=0}^{d/2-1} \Sigma_{t=i}^{i+5} D_s^{(t)} \geq 2\mathcal{B}^D + 2$.

Case 2. $D_{j+1}^{(i+3)} \neq 0$, then $D_{j+2}^{(i+2)} + D_{j+2}^{(i+4)} \geq 1$. Then we consider the following cases.

Table 2. The Minimum Number of Active S-boxes in $\text{GFS}_d^{\text{std}}$, assuming $\mathcal{B} > 2$

rounds	Feistel	$\text{GFS}_4^{\text{std}}$	$\text{GFS}_6^{\text{std}}$	$\text{GFS}_8^{\text{std}}$	$\text{GFS}_{10}^{\text{std}}$	$\text{GFS}_{12}^{\text{std}}$	$\text{GFS}_{14}^{\text{std}}$	$\text{GFS}_{16}^{\text{std}}$
1	0	0	0	0	0	0	0	0
2	1	1	1	1	1	1	1	1
3	2	2	2	2	2	2	2	2
4	$\mathcal{B}$	$\mathcal{B}+1$	$\mathcal{B}+1$	$\mathcal{B}+1$	$\mathcal{B}+1$	$\mathcal{B}+1$	$\mathcal{B}+1$	$\mathcal{B}+1$
5	$\mathcal{B}+1$	$\mathcal{B}+3$	$\mathcal{B}+3$	$\mathcal{B}+3$	$\mathcal{B}+3$	$\mathcal{B}+3$	$\mathcal{B}+3$	$\mathcal{B}+3$
6	$\mathcal{B}+2$	$2\mathcal{B}+2$	$2\mathcal{B}+2$	$2\mathcal{B}+2$	$2\mathcal{B}+2$	$2\mathcal{B}+2$	$2\mathcal{B}+2$	$2\mathcal{B}+2$
7	$\mathcal{B}+3$	$2\mathcal{B}+2$	$2\mathcal{B}+4$	$2\mathcal{B}+4$	$2\mathcal{B}+4$	$2\mathcal{B}+4$	$2\mathcal{B}+4$	$2\mathcal{B}+4$
8	$2\mathcal{B}+1$	$2\mathcal{B}+3$	$3\mathcal{B}+3$	$3\mathcal{B}+3$	$3\mathcal{B}+3$	$3\mathcal{B}+3$	$3\mathcal{B}+3$	$3\mathcal{B}+3$
9	$2\mathcal{B}+2$	$2\mathcal{B}+4$	$3\mathcal{B}+6$	$3\mathcal{B}+6$	$3\mathcal{B}+6$	$3\mathcal{B}+6$	$3\mathcal{B}+6$	$3\mathcal{B}+6$
10	$2\mathcal{B}+3$	$3\mathcal{B}+3$	$4\mathcal{B}+5$	$4\mathcal{B}+5$	$4\mathcal{B}+5$	$4\mathcal{B}+5$	$4\mathcal{B}+5$	$4\mathcal{B}+5$
11	$2\mathcal{B}+4$	$3\mathcal{B}+5$	$4\mathcal{B}+7$	$4\mathcal{B}+8$	$4\mathcal{B}+8$	$4\mathcal{B}+8$	$4\mathcal{B}+8$	$4\mathcal{B}+8$
12	$3\mathcal{B}+2$	$4\mathcal{B}+4$	$5\mathcal{B}+5$	$6\mathcal{B}+6$	$6\mathcal{B}+6$	$6\mathcal{B}+6$	$6\mathcal{B}+6$	$6\mathcal{B}+6$
13	$3\mathcal{B}+3$	$4\mathcal{B}+4$	$5\mathcal{B}+6$	$6\mathcal{B}+6$	$6\mathcal{B}+9$	$6\mathcal{B}+9$	$6\mathcal{B}+9$	$6\mathcal{B}+9$
14	$3\mathcal{B}+4$	$4\mathcal{B}+5$	$6\mathcal{B}+5$	$6\mathcal{B}+7$	$7\mathcal{B}+8$	$7\mathcal{B}+8$	$7\mathcal{B}+8$	$7\mathcal{B}+8$
15	$3\mathcal{B}+5$	$4\mathcal{B}+6$	$6\mathcal{B}+7$	$6\mathcal{B}+8$	$7\mathcal{B}+12$	$7\mathcal{B}+12$	$7\mathcal{B}+12$	$7\mathcal{B}+12$
16	$4\mathcal{B}+3$	$5\mathcal{B}+5$	$7\mathcal{B}+6$	$7\mathcal{B}+7$	$9\mathcal{B}+9$	$9\mathcal{B}+9$	$9\mathcal{B}+9$	$9\mathcal{B}+9$
17	$4\mathcal{B}+4$	$5\mathcal{B}+7$	$7\mathcal{B}+8$	$7\mathcal{B}+9$	$9\mathcal{B}+13$	$9\mathcal{B}+13$	$9\mathcal{B}+13$	$9\mathcal{B}+13$
18	$4\mathcal{B}+5$	$6\mathcal{B}+6$	$8\mathcal{B}+7$	$8\mathcal{B}+8$	$10\mathcal{B}+8$	$10\mathcal{B}+12$	$10\mathcal{B}+12$	$10\mathcal{B}+12$

Table 3. The Minimum Number of Active S-boxes in $\text{GFS}_d^{\text{imp}}$, assuming $\mathcal{B} > 2$

rounds	$\text{GFS}_6^{\text{imp}}$	$\text{GFS}_8^{\text{imp}}$	$\text{GFS}_{10}^{\text{imp}}$	$\text{GFS}_{12}^{\text{imp}}$	$\text{GFS}_{14}^{\text{imp}}$	$\text{GFS}_{16}^{\text{imp}}$
1	0	0	0	0	0	0
2	1	1	1	1	1	1
3	2	2	2	2	2	2
4	$\mathcal{B}+1$	$\mathcal{B}+1$	$\mathcal{B}+1$	$\mathcal{B}+1$	$\mathcal{B}+1$	$\mathcal{B}+1$
5	$\mathcal{B}+3$	$\mathcal{B}+3$	$\mathcal{B}+3$	$\mathcal{B}+3$	$\mathcal{B}+3$	$\mathcal{B}+3$
6	$2\mathcal{B}+2$	$2\mathcal{B}+2$	$2\mathcal{B}+2$	$2\mathcal{B}+2$	$2\mathcal{B}+2$	$2\mathcal{B}+2$
7	$2\mathcal{B}+4$	$2\mathcal{B}+4$	$2\mathcal{B}+4$	$2\mathcal{B}+4$	$2\mathcal{B}+4$	$2\mathcal{B}+4$
8	$4\mathcal{B}+2$	$4\mathcal{B}+3$	$4\mathcal{B}+3$	$3\mathcal{B}+3$	$4\mathcal{B}+3$	$4\mathcal{B}+3$
9	$4\mathcal{B}+4$	$4\mathcal{B}+6$	$5\mathcal{B}+4$	$3\mathcal{B}+6$	$5\mathcal{B}+4$	$5\mathcal{B}+6$
10	$4\mathcal{B}+6$	$5\mathcal{B}+4$	$6\mathcal{B}+4$	$5\mathcal{B}+4$	$7\mathcal{B}+2$	$7\mathcal{B}+5$
11	$4\mathcal{B}+8$	$5\mathcal{B}+7$	$6\mathcal{B}+6$	$5\mathcal{B}+7$	$7\mathcal{B}+5$	$8\mathcal{B}+8$
12	$6\mathcal{B}+2$	$7\mathcal{B}+4$	$7\mathcal{B}+10$	$7\mathcal{B}+4$	$9\mathcal{B}+4$	$10\mathcal{B}+4$
13	$6\mathcal{B}+3$	$7\mathcal{B}+5$	$8\mathcal{B}+4$	$8\mathcal{B}+5$	$10\mathcal{B}+4$	$11\mathcal{B}+5$
14	$6\mathcal{B}+8$	$8\mathcal{B}+4$	$9\mathcal{B}+3$	$9\mathcal{B}+8$	$11\mathcal{B}+5$	$12\mathcal{B}+3$
15	$6\mathcal{B}+10$	$8\mathcal{B}+6$	$9\mathcal{B}+5$	$9\mathcal{B}+12$	$11\mathcal{B}+8$	$12\mathcal{B}+10$
16	$8\mathcal{B}+6$	$9\mathcal{B}+5$	$10\mathcal{B}+4$	$10\mathcal{B}+10$	$13\mathcal{B}+6$	$15\mathcal{B}+1$
17	$8\mathcal{B}+8$	$9\mathcal{B}+7$	$10\mathcal{B}+6$	$10\mathcal{B}+14$	$14\mathcal{B}+6$	$15\mathcal{B}+3$
18	$8\mathcal{B}+10$	$10\mathcal{B}+6$	$12\mathcal{B}+5$	$12\mathcal{B}+8$	$16\mathcal{B}+3$	$17\mathcal{B}+2$

Case 2-1. If $D_{j+2}^{(i+2)} \neq 0$, then $D_{j+3}^{(i+1)} + D_{j+3}^{(i+3)} \geq 1$. We consider the following two cases.

Case 2-1-1. If $D_{j+3}^{(i+1)} \neq 0$, then $D_{j+3}^{(i+1)} + D_{j+4}^{(i)} + D_{j+4}^{(i+2)} \geq \mathcal{B}^D$. Also, $D_{j+1}^{(i+3)} + D_{j+2}^{(i+2)} + D_{j+2}^{(i+4)} \geq \mathcal{B}^D$, $D_{j+1}^{(i+1)} + D_{j+2}^{(i)} \geq 1$, and $D_{j}^{(i+4)} + D_{j+1}^{(i+5)} \geq 1$. Therefore, we have $\Sigma_{s=0}^{d/2-1} \Sigma_{t=i}^{i+5} D_s^{(t)} \geq 2\mathcal{B}^D + 2$.

Case 2-1-2. If $D_{j+3}^{(i+3)} \neq 0$, then $D_{j+2}^{(i+4)} + D_{j+3}^{(i+5)} \geq 1$. Also, $D_{j}^{(i+2)} + D_{j+1}^{(i+1)} + D_{j+1}^{(i+3)} \geq \mathcal{B}^D$, $D_{j+2}^{(i+2)} + D_{j+3}^{(i+1)} + D_{j+3}^{(i+3)} \geq \mathcal{B}^D$, and $D_{j}^{(i+4)} + D_{j+1}^{(i+5)} \geq 1$. Thus, we obtain $\Sigma_{s=0}^{d/2-1} \Sigma_{t=i}^{i+5} D_s^{(t)} \geq 2\mathcal{B}^D + 2$.

Case 2-2. If $D_{j+2}^{(i+4)} \neq 0$, then $D_{j+2}^{(i+4)} + D_{j+3}^{(i+3)} + D_{j+3}^{(i+5)} \geq \mathcal{B}^D$. Also, $D_{j}^{(i+2)} + D_{j+1}^{(i+1)} + D_{j+1}^{(i+3)} \geq \mathcal{B}^D$, $D_{j-1}^{(i+1)} + D_{j}^{(i)} \geq 1$, and $D_{j}^{(i+4)} + D_{j+1}^{(i+5)} \geq 1$. Therefore, we have $\Sigma_{s=0}^{d/2-1} \Sigma_{t=i}^{i+5} D_s^{(t)} \geq 2\mathcal{B}^D + 2$.

Considering all cases, we conclude that any six consecutive rounds in $\mathrm{GFS}_d^{\mathrm{std}}$ have at least $2\mathcal{B}^D + 2$ differential active S-boxes when there is at least one active F-function in the $(i+2)$-th round. Similarly, in the case that there exists at least one active F-function in the $(i+3)$-th round, we have the same bound. Finally, we conclude that any six consecutive rounds in $\mathrm{GFS}_d^{\mathrm{std}}$ have at least $2\mathcal{B}^D + 2$ differential active S-boxes. □

All cases used for this proof of the minimum number of active S-boxes in six rounds of $\mathrm{GFS}_4^{\mathrm{std}}$ are shown in Figs. 9-13. In these figures, the F-function indicated by the bold line is determined to be active and the F-function indicated by the dotted line is determined to be non-active. Also, there is at least one active S-box in the area encircled by dotted line, and there are at least $\mathcal{B}^D$ active S-boxes in the area encircled by chain line.

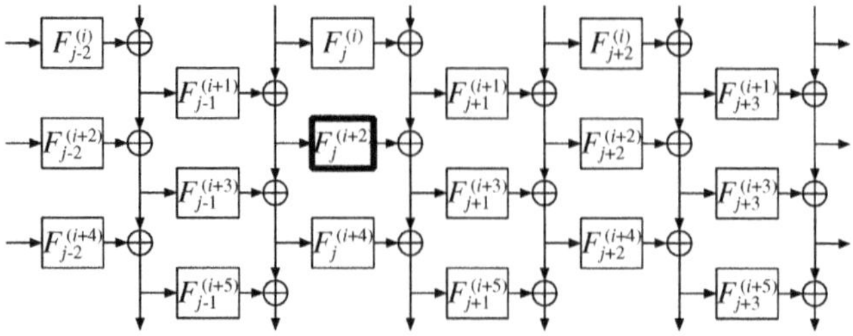

Fig. 8. Six Rounds of $\mathrm{GFS}_d^{\mathrm{std}}$ (Untwisted Form)

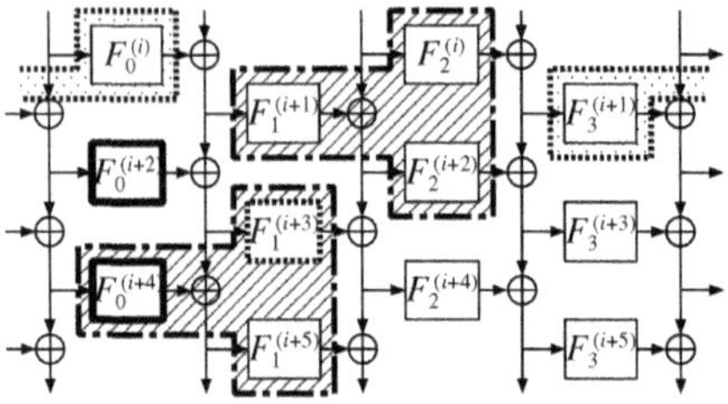

Fig. 9. Case 1-1

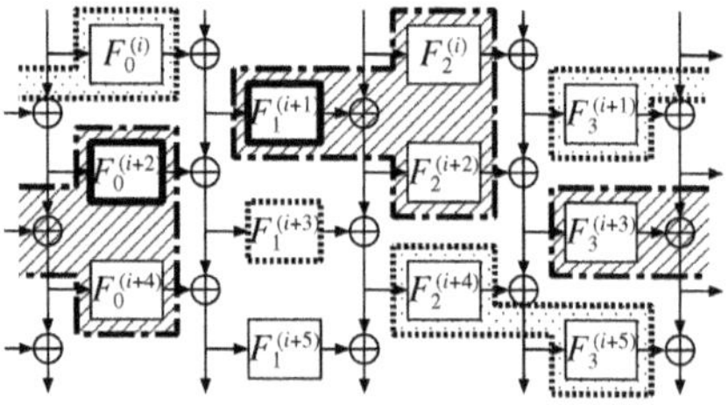

Fig. 10. Case 1-2

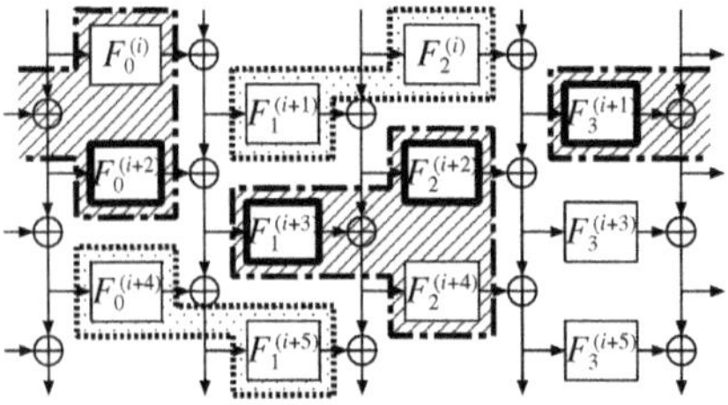

Fig. 11. Case 2-1-1

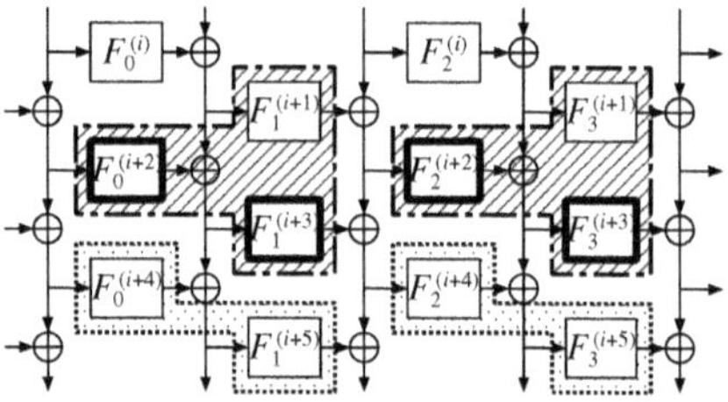

Fig. 12. Case 2-1-2

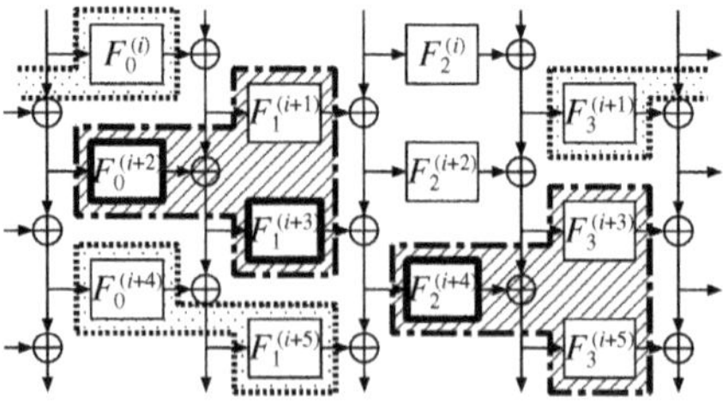

Fig. 13. Case 2-2

A 3-Subset Meet-in-the-Middle Attack: Cryptanalysis of the Lightweight Block Cipher KTANTAN

Andrey Bogdanov and Christian Rechberger

Katholieke Universiteit Leuven, ESAT/COSIC and IBBT, Belgium
{andrey.bogdanov,christian.rechberber}@esat.kuleuven.be

Abstract. In this paper we describe a variant of existing meet-in-the-middle attacks on block ciphers. As an application, we propose meet-in-the-middle attacks that are applicable to the KTANTAN family of block ciphers accepting a key of 80 bits. The attacks are due to some weaknesses in its bitwise key schedule[1]. We report an attack of time complexity $2^{75.170}$ encryptions on the full KTANTAN32 cipher with only 3 plaintext/ciphertext pairs and well as $2^{75.044}$ encryptions on the full KTANTAN48 and $2^{75.584}$ encryptions on the full KTANTAN64 with 2 plaintext/ciphertext pairs. All these attacks work in the classical attack model without any related keys.

In the differential related-key model, we demonstrate 218- and 174-round differentials holding with probability 1. This shows that a strong related-key property can translate to a successful attack in the non-related-key setting. Having extremely low data requirements, these attacks are valid even in RFID-like environments where only a very limited amount of text material may be available to an attacker.

Keywords: cryptanalysis, meet-in-the-middle attacks, block cipher, key schedule, lightweight cipher, key-recovery, RFID.

1 Introduction

A number of new cipher designs have been proposed recently, targeting use cases with severe implementation constraints imposed. Block cipher design methods have advanced to a stage where strong arguments for the resistance of the design against large classes of attacks such as differential and linear cryptanalysis are possible. However, if aggressive design decisions have been made forced by a restrictive application scenario, some other, more dedicated analysis techniques may turn out useful for attacking the cipher.

Cryptographic techniques move into applications like sensor nodes, RFID tags, or the "the Internet of things" at large. The ever increasing demand for security

[1] The SAC 2010 pre-proceedings version of this paper [6] was based on a key-schedule from a previous version of the reference code which contained errors. This paper is based on the corrected reference code available under [1].

A. Biryukov, G. Gong, and D.R. Stinson (Eds.): SAC 2010, LNCS 6544, pp. 229–240, 2011.

and privacy in these very constrained environments requires new cryptographic primitives, like tiny yet efficient ciphers. A number of designs and implementation techniques have been proposed recently to address this need. Stream ciphers like Trivium [10,8], Grain [17,18], or Mickey [3], or block ciphers like DESL [22], PRESENT [4], HIGHT [19], mCrypton [23], KATAN and KTANTAN [9], or the hash functions based on PRESENT [5] are among the important ones.

Motivation. The economical and physical constraints force designers to make design decisions which are often considered to be "on the edge". In this context it is often argued that block ciphers are better understood than stream ciphers and are hence more trustworthy. Some recent designs like PRESENT and KATAN/KTANTAN have come with strong arguments that large classes of attacks shown powerful in the past are not applicable. The technique used is to provide bounds on various non-random properties, like differential or linear characteristics. Indeed, whereas in the eStream project a number of lightweight stream ciphers were broken, sometimes even with practical attack complexities, none of the recently proposed block ciphers have been broken so far.

KTANTAN [9] accepts a key of 80 bits. It was designed to resist differential and linear attacks, and exhibits strong bounds in the non-related-key model, an upper bound 2^{-b} on the probability of every differential/linear characteristic over 128 rounds being an essential design criterion ($b \in \{32, 48, 64\}$ is the block size of the cipher). Even if related keys are considered, a much less realistic setting, designers report no differential characteristic with a higher probability than 2^{-b} for 150 out of the 254 rounds. In [2], Albrecht et al. study algebraic approaches to amplify differential attacks on this family of ciphers.

Contributions and Outline. Section 2 considers a framework for MITM attacks. In Section 4, based on this framework, we propose a key-recovery attack on the KTANTAN block cipher family (briefly described in Section 3), requiring only very few known plaintext/ciphertext pairs. Hence this kind of attacks is even valid in very restrictive RFID-like environments and protocols where only a very limited number of transactions are foreseen in the lifetime of a tag. The parameters and complexities of our attacks are provided in Table 1. Some properties we use translate to probability-1 related-key differentials over many rounds which are outlined in Table 4. Note that the data complexity of our attacks is

Table 1. Results on MITM cryptanalysis for KTANTAN

attack/bound	cipher $b \in \{32, 48, 64\}$	#rounds (of 254)	time [encryptions]	data compl. [PT/CT pars]
[9], RK diff. bound	KTANTANb	150	$\mathcal{O}(2^b)$	$\mathcal{O}(2^b)$
[9], DC and LC bound	KTANTANb	128	$\mathcal{O}(2^b)$	$\mathcal{O}(2^b)$
this paper, MITM attack	KTANTAN32	254	$2^{75.170}$	3
this paper, MITM attack	KTANTAN48	254	$2^{75.044}$	2
this paper, MITM attack	KTANTAN64	254	$2^{75.584}$	2

the lowest possible and exactly corresponds to that of a brute-force attack. We conclude with a discussion on links to other works, high-level design choices for low-resource ciphers, and future work in Section 5.

2 Framework for MITM Attacks

2.1 Basic MITM Attack

The basic meet-in-the-middle (MITM) approach will be a starting point for our attack. MITM techniques are arguably much less common than differential or linear attacks on ciphers. There are some applications of MITM principles to block ciphers like DES or AES, see e.g. [7,11,12,14,15,20] for dedicated attacks, and e.g. [24,25] for meet-in-the-middle attacks on a higher level.

The basic MITM technique is due to Diffie and Hellman [13]. Let $\varphi_{i,j}$ denote the partial transform of an R-round block cipher beginning in round i and ending directly after round j under some fixed key, $1 \leq i \leq j \leq R$, see Figure 1. Then if $\varphi_{1,\alpha}$ and $\varphi_{\alpha+1,R}$ use subkeys with distinct key bits, the key can be as a rule recovered much more efficiently than by brute force over two subkeys. The central idea here, as also applied to reduced DES in [15], is that the subkeys in both parts of the cipher can be guessed independently. Each guess of the first subkey allows the adversary to compute $\varphi_{1,\alpha}(p)$ and of the second subkey to obtain $\varphi^{-1}_{\alpha+1,R}(c)$. The right key will be among those fulfilling the equation $\varphi_{1,\alpha}(p) = \varphi^{-1}_{\alpha+1,R}(c)$.

2.2 The 3-Subset MITM Approach

Here we consider a variant of the basic MITM attack. The idea is to remove restrictions on the choice of key bits, thereby potentially allowing attacks where an attack is not possible with the basic MITM approach. Instead of considering two subsets of key bits, we consider three subsets. The attack consists of two parts. In the *MITM stage*, we filter out some wrong key candidates and reduce the key space. In the *key testing stage*, we look for the right key in the reduced key space.

Let $K = k_{\ell-1}k_{\ell-2}\ldots k_1k_0$ be the ℓ-bit key. Then if $K_1 = \{k_i : k_i \text{ used by } \varphi_{1,\alpha}\}$ and $K_2 = \{k_i : k_i \text{ used by } \varphi_{R-\beta+1,R}\}$, then $A_0 = K_1 \cap K_2$ is the set of key

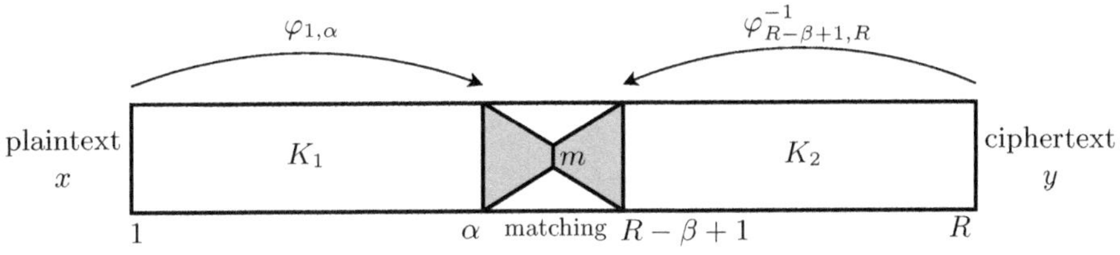

Fig. 1. MITM

bits used both by the first α and last β rounds, see Figure 1. Moreover, $A_1 = K_1 \backslash K_1 \cap K_2$ and $A_2 = K_2 \backslash K_1 \cap K_2$ are the sets of key bits used by K_1 only and by K_2 only, respectively. We further assume that $K_1 \cup K_2 = K$.

For the attack we need n plaintext/ciphertext pairs $\{(x_i, y_i)\}$, $i = 1, \ldots, n$. Let x_i be plaintext and y_i ciphertext.

MITM Stage. The meet-in-the-middle part of the attack on R rounds of the cipher can be performed as follows:

- For each guess of key bits in A_0:
  - For each guess of key bits in A_1:
    - Compute $v = \varphi_{1,\alpha}(x)$
  - For each guess of key bits in A_2:
    - Compute $u = \varphi^{-1}_{R-\beta+1,R}(y)$
  - Perform matching in the middle between the values of v and the values of u on m bits, $1 \leq m \leq b$ (see Subsection 4.3) and add surviving key candidates to the list $\mathcal{K}$ of surviving keys. We expect to have false positives with probability 2^{-m} which is called the *false positive rate* of a MITM attack.

Key Testing Stage. In this stage, we test the surviving key candidates from $\mathcal{K}$ using some plaintext-ciphertext pairs in a brute-force manner. Generally speaking, it is not necessary to use additional plaintext-ciphertext pairs. The number of the texts needed is defined by the unicity distance of the cipher which essentially depends on the block size and key length. If we can significantly reduce the key space in the MITM stage (by ruling out a large part of the keys), the complexity of the key testing stage will be negligible with respect to the MITM stage. Generally speaking, however, this is not necessarily the case.

Attack Complexity. The computational complexity of the attack will be dominated by

$$C_{\text{comp}} = \underbrace{2^{|A_0|}(2^{|A_1|} + 2^{|A_2|})}_{\text{MITM stage}} + \underbrace{(2^{\ell-m} + 2^{\ell-m-b} + 2^{\ell-m-2b} + \ldots)}_{\text{key testing stage}}. \qquad (1)$$

If A_1 and A_2 are both non-empty and $|A_1| + |A_2| > 2$, then the attack becomes more efficient than exhaustive search provided that the false positive rate is low enough.

The MITM stage requires exactly one plaintext/ciphertext pair. However, of the b bits only m are used for matching. That is, the information contained in the other $b - m$ state bits is not used in this stage and can be used in the key testing stage. For the key testing stage, more pairs might be required, depending on the relation between the key length and the block size. This results in data complexity

$$C_{\text{data}} = \left\lceil \frac{\ell}{b} \right\rceil$$

depending on the block size b and the key length ℓ. The memory complexity is defined by matching in the MITM stage. For small sets A_1 and A_2, it is negligible.

3 A Short Description of KTANTAN

KTANTAN is a block cipher which accepts an 80-bit user-supplied key. Versions with block size $b \in \{32, 48, 64\}$ bit have been specified. Each version has 254 rounds. While the definition of a round transform differs from version to version, the key schedule remains the same. Throughout the paper, we refer to the KTANTAN version with b-bit blocks as KTANTANb.

3.1 Round Transform

KATAN and KTANTAN share the specification of a round transform, as the operations on the state are exactly the same up to the key schedule. The state of the cipher is represented as two disjunct parts L_1 and L_2. The transform of round r is based on two Boolean functions $f_{1,r}$ and $f_{2,r}$, having L_1 and L_2 as their domain, correspondingly:

$$f_{1,r}(L_1) = L_1[x_1] \oplus L_1[x_2] \oplus (L_1[x_3] \cdot L_1[x_4]) \oplus (L_1[x_5] \cdot IR_r) \oplus \kappa_{1,r}$$
$$f_{2,r}(L_2) = L_2[y_1] \oplus L_2[y_2] \oplus (L_2[y_3] \cdot L_2[y_4]) \oplus (L_2[y_5] \cdot L_2[y_6]) \oplus \kappa_{2,r},$$

where x_i, y_i are the numbers of active bit positions, IR_r is the round constant bit in round r, and $\kappa_{1,r}$, $\kappa_{2,r}$ are the bits of the extended key defined by the key schedule for round r. The lengths of L_1 and L_2 as well as the bit positions x_i, y_i are specific for each KTANTAN version.

Once $f_{1,r}$ and $f_{2,r}$ are computed, the registers L_1 and L_2 are shifted, the MSB of each register falls off and the LSB is set to the output of $f_{2,r}$ and the output of $f_{1,r}$, respectively. KTANTAN32 applies transformations $f_{1,r}$ and $f_{2,r}$ once in a round. One round of KTANTAN48 and KTANTAN64 updates the registers using $f_{1,r}$ and $f_{2,r}$ two and three times, respectively.

Table 2. Version-specific parameters of KTANTAN

b	$\|L_1\|$	$\|L_2\|$	x_1	x_2	x_3	x_4	x_5	y_1	y_2	y_3	y_4	y_5	y_6
32	13	19	12	7	8	5	3	18	7	12	10	8	3
48	19	29	18	12	15	7	6	28	19	21	13	15	6
64	25	39	24	15	20	11	9	38	25	33	21	14	9

Table 3. Round constant bits IR_r: IR_1 first, IR_{254} last

```
1111111000 1101010101 1110110011 0010100100 0100011000 1111000010
0001010000 0111110011 1111010100 0101010011 0000110011 1011111011
1010010101 1010011100 1101100010 1110110111 1001011011 0101110010
0100110100 0111000100 1111010000 1110101100 0001011001 0000001101
1100000001 0010
```

3.2 Key Schedule

The functions $f_{1,r}$ and $f_{2,r}$ require input from the key schedule, which is a function mapping the 80-bit user-supplied key $K = k_{79}k_{78} \dots k_1 k_0$ to $\kappa_{1,r}$ and $\kappa_{2,r}$ for each round r. It is exactly this part where KTANTAN differs from KATAN. This difference, together with some properties of the data transform, makes KTANTAN vulnerable to our attack.

An 8-bit round counting LFSR is used to control the key schedule. It is defined by the feedback polynomial

$$\zeta^8 + \zeta^7 + \zeta^5 + \zeta^3 + 1$$

and its initial state is all ones. The value of IR_r is specified as the most significant bit of this LFSR in round r. Let $l_{7,r}l_{6,r}...l_{1,r}l_{0,r}$ denote the 8-bit state of the LFSR in round r.

The key schedule of KTANTAN chooses two bits of K in each round. This is done by applying two layers of MUX logic. First, K is divided into 5 chunks W_i of 16 bits each: $K = W_4||W_3||W_2||W_1||W_0$. One bit out of each chunk is selected:

$$\omega_{i,r} = \text{MUX16to1}(W_i, l_{7,r}l_{6,r}l_{5,r}l_{4,r}), i = 0, \dots, 4,$$

where the LFSR bits define the position in W_i to choose. Second, two out of these five bits are chosen controlled by the other half of the LFSR state:

$$\begin{aligned}\kappa_{1,r} &= \overline{l_{3,r}} \cdot \overline{l_{2,r}} \cdot \omega_{0,r} \oplus (l_{3,r} \vee l_{2,r}) \cdot \text{MUX4to1}(\omega_{4,r}\omega_{3,r}\omega_{2,r}\omega_{1,r}, l_{1,r}l_{0,r})\\ \kappa_{2,r} &= \overline{l_{3,r}} \cdot l_{2,r} \cdot \omega_{4,r} \oplus (l_{3,r} \vee \overline{l_{2,r}}) \cdot \text{MUX4to1}(\omega_{3,r}\omega_{2,r}\omega_{1,r}\omega_{0,r}, \overline{l_{1,r}l_{0,r}}).\end{aligned}$$

4 Low Data-Complexity Attacks on KTANTAN

In here, we apply the MITM framework described in Section 2 to all 3 variants of the full KTANTAN with 254 rounds. The resulting attack requires an extremely small number of known plaintext/ciphertext pairs (basically, the minimum due to the unicity distance) and negligible memory. The MITM techniques make use of the fact that several key bits remain unused by the KTANTAN key schedule in large connected parts of the cipher. More precisely, it is the rounds at the beginning and end of KTANTAN which we are most interested in to make the attack work.

4.1 Related-Key Differentials of Probability 1

We start with a note on probability-1 related-key differentials of KTANTAN over many rounds.

The key observation here is that if certain key bits are not used over many rounds, they can be flipped without affecting the data transformation. In other words, the R-round related-key differential $(0, \Delta) \mapsto 0$ holds with probability 1, where 0 is the zero input and output difference in the data transformation and Δ is the key difference with ones at key bit position not used in the R rounds

Table 4. Related key differentials for KTANTANb, $b \in \{32, 48, 64\}$

covered rounds	#rounds	differential	probability
$\varphi_{1,218}$	218	$(0, 00000000800000000000) \mapsto 0$	1
$\varphi^{-1}_{81,254}$	174	$(0, 00000000000000010000) \mapsto 0$	1

(first key bit positions are on the left-hand side). Some of the longest related-key differentials of this type we found for KTANTANb are given in Table 4. These differentials are due to the fact that the first 218 and last 174 rounds of KTANTAN do not use key bits k_{32} and k_{63}, respectively.

We notice that it seems possible that these properties can be turned into low-complexity differential related-key attacks on KTANTAN. However, we are mostly concerned with attacks that do not require related keys, and hence continue by exploiting this property in another way.

4.2 Application of the MITM Framework to KTANTAN

Depending on the KTANTAN version, different properties of the key schedule are exploited in our attack. This is due to the fact that all three versions of KTANTAN have different numbers of register clocks in one round. The versions with a larger block size have heavier rounds with more diffusion which complicates the partial matching phase. Effectively, this might reduce the number of rounds in the middle for which matching is possible.

In Table 5 we give a summary of the properties and parameters of our attacks. We aim for the full, and if this is not possible for the highest number of rounds. Considering variants with a more reduced number of rounds would lead to more neutrals key bits, and generally lower attack complexities.

To illustrate the meaning of this table, let us consider the first entry. We attack the full 254-round KTANTAN32. The two basic properties of the KTANTAN key schedule which make our attack on KTANTAN32 possible can be formulated as:

Fact 1. $\varphi_{1,\alpha}$ *does not use key bits* $\{k_{32}, k_{39}, k_{44}, k_{61}, k_{66}, k_{75}\}$ *for* $1 \leq \alpha \leq 111$.

Fact 2. $\varphi_{254-\beta+1,254}$ *does not use key bits* $\{k_3, k_{20}, k_{41}, k_{47}, k_{63}, k_{74}\}$ *for* $1 \leq \beta \leq 131$.

Table 5. Details of the proposed attacks

b	R	α	A_1	$R-\beta$	A_2	matching bits m	complexity C_{comp} MITM	key test	total
32	254	111	32,39,44,61,66,75	131	3,20,41,47,63,74	8	75.000	72	75.170
48	254	111	32,39,44,61,66,75	131	3,20,41,47,63,74	10	75.000	70	75.044
64	254	123	32,44,61,66,75	131	3,20,41,47,63,74	47	75.584	33	75.584

This means that if we fix $\alpha = 111$ and $\beta = 131$, then $\varphi_{1,111}$ and $\varphi_{123,254}$ will have 6 *neutral* key bits in each direction. Moreover, one can efficiently match v and u in 8 bits, despite being 21 rounds apart due to the slow diffusion in one round of KTANTAN32, which is demonstrated in Subsection 4.3.

4.3 Partial-Matching Phase

In here, we describe in more detail the matching procedure that is used as a sub-routine in the MITM stage.

Procedure. The starting point are two completely determined internal states u and v several rounds apart (for KTANTAN32, one at round 111 and the other one at round 131). If we considered a cipher where those middle rounds were cut away, then the matching phase would be trivial as we would simply check if the $u = v$. With a probability of about 2^{-b} this check would give a false positive, but overall the number of key candidates is reduced to about 2^{80-b}. Remember that $b \in \{32, 48, 64\}$. Hence the number of key candidates is small enough to not influence the attack complexity during the key testing state.

In order to bridge this gap and to obtain a result on the full cipher, we drop the requirement to match on every state bit but allow for a much smaller number of matched bits m. This will increase the number of false positives, but in a way that does not noticeably influence any property of the attack. In more detail, we find that m bits (for KTANTAN32, $m = 8$) will still match with probability 1 (see below for details). This means that we will have reduced the number of key candidates to 2^{80-m} after the MITM stage. In total, we hence need only between 2 (for block size $b = \{48, 64\}$) or 3 (for $b = 32$) known plaintext/ciphertext pairs.

We note that this procedure can be implemented in an essentially memoryless way, as every match can immediately be tested with another plaintext/ciphertext pair. Also in our estimate of the attack complexity, we do not consider any implementation optimizations that e.g. would also be possible for a brute force search that does not use any shortcut attacks. Examples of such optimizations would e.g. be a reuse of computations from one key guess to the next.

Details on the Partial Matching Phase. In the following we trace those bits that remain unaffected during the middle rounds for the block size of $b = 32$. '1' means affected, '0' means not affected. $k1$ and $k2$ denote disturbances caused by the unknown neutral bits from the opposite chunk at the respective rounds. For other block sizes, we refer to Appendix A.

```
10 bits match as follows

forward part:
forward R=111: k1=1, k2=1  0 0 0 0 0 0 0 0 0 0 0 0 0   0 0 0 0 0 0 0 0 0 0 0 0 0 0 0 0 0 0 0
forward R=112: k1=0, k2=0  1 0 0 0 0 0 0 0 0 0 0 0 0   1 0 0 0 0 0 0 0 0 0 0 0 0 0 0 0 0 0 0
forward R=113: k1=0, k2=0  0 1 0 0 0 0 0 0 0 0 0 0 0   0 1 0 0 0 0 0 0 0 0 0 0 0 0 0 0 0 0 0
forward R=114: k1=0, k2=0  0 0 1 0 0 0 0 0 0 0 0 0 0   0 0 1 0 0 0 0 0 0 0 0 0 0 0 0 0 0 0 0
forward R=115: k1=0, k2=0  0 0 0 1 0 0 0 0 0 0 0 0 0   0 0 0 1 0 0 0 0 0 0 0 0 0 0 0 0 0 0 0
forward R=116: k1=0, k2=0  1 0 0 0 1 0 0 0 0 0 0 0 0   1 0 0 0 1 0 0 0 0 0 0 0 0 0 0 0 0 0 0
forward R=117: k1=0, k2=0  0 1 0 0 0 1 0 0 0 0 0 0 0   0 1 0 0 0 1 0 0 0 0 0 0 0 0 0 0 0 0 0
forward R=118: k1=0, k2=0  0 0 1 0 0 0 1 0 0 0 0 0 0   1 0 1 0 0 0 1 0 0 0 0 0 0 0 0 0 0 0 0
forward R=119: k1=0, k2=0  0 0 0 1 0 0 0 1 0 0 0 0 0   0 1 0 1 0 0 0 1 0 0 0 0 0 0 0 0 0 0 0
forward R=120: k1=0, k2=0  1 0 0 0 1 0 0 0 1 0 0 0 0   1 0 1 0 1 0 0 0 1 0 0 0 0 0 0 0 0 0 0
forward R=121: k1=0, k2=0  1 1 0 0 0 1 0 0 0 1 0 0 0   1 1 0 1 0 1 0 0 0 1 0 0 0 0 0 0 0 0 0
forward R=122: k1=0, k2=0  1 1 1 0 0 0 1 0 0 0 1 0 0   1 1 1 0 1 0 1 0 0 0 1 0 0 0 0 0 0 0 0
forward R=123: k1=1, k2=0  1 1 1 1 0 0 0 1 0 0 0 1 0   0 1 1 1 0 1 0 1 0 0 0 1 0 0 0 0 0 0 0
forward R=124: k1=0, k2=0  1 1 1 1 1 0 0 0 1 0 0 0 1   1 0 1 1 1 0 1 0 1 0 0 0 1 0 0 0 0 0 0
forward R=125: k1=0, k2=0  1 1 1 1 1 1 0 0 0 1 0 0 0   1 1 0 1 1 1 0 1 0 1 0 0 0 1 0 0 0 0 0
forward R=126: k1=0, k2=0  1 1 1 1 1 1 1 0 0 0 1 0 0   1 1 1 0 1 1 1 0 1 0 1 0 0 0 1 0 0 0 0
forward R=127: k1=0, k2=1  1 1 1 1 1 1 1 1 0 0 0 1 0   1 1 1 1 0 1 1 1 0 1 0 1 0 0 0 1 0 0 0

backward part:
backward R=131: k1=0, k2=1  0 0 0 0 0 0 0 0 0 0 0 0 0   0 0 0 0 0 0 0 0 0 0 0 0 0 0 0 0 0 0 0
backward R=130: k1=1, k2=1  0 0 0 0 0 0 0 0 0 0 0 0 0   0 0 0 1 0 0 0 1 1 0 1 0 1 0 0 0 0 0 1
backward R=129: k1=0, k2=0  0 0 0 1 0 1 0 1 1 0 0 0 1   0 0 1 1 0 0 1 1 1 1 1 1 1 0 0 0 0 1 1
backward R=128: k1=0, k2=0  0 0 1 0 1 0 1 1 0 0 0 1 0   0 1 1 0 0 1 1 1 1 1 1 1 0 0 0 0 1 1 0
backward R=127: k1=0, k2=0  0 1 0 1 0 1 1 0 0 0 1 0 0   1 1 0 0 1 1 1 1 1 1 1 0 0 0 0 1 1 0 0

The highest number of matching bits is obtained at round 127:
 forward R=127: k1=0, k2=1  1 1 1 1 1 1 1 1 0 0 0 1 0   1 1 1 1 0 1 1 1 0 1 0 1 0 0 0 1 0 0 0
backward R=127: k1=0, k2=0  0 1 0 1 0 1 1 0 0 0 1 0 0   1 1 0 0 1 1 1 1 1 1 1 0 0 0 0 1 1 0 0
```

As can be seen, at three positions in the state both in the forward and in the backward part no changes happen, which is the property needed for the matching part.

5 Discussion and Future Work

The recently proposed lightweight block cipher KTANTAN is susceptible to a class of meet-in-the-middle attacks that seems to put less constraints on the selection of key bits than some earlier meet-in-the-middle attacks on block ciphers. We proposed key-recovery attacks with an extremely low number of known plaintexts. The approach we describe is inspired by recent advances in MITM preimage attacks on hash functions like those that succeeded in breaking MD5 or Tiger [16,27], even though it remains an open problem to transfer most of the techniques there from the key-less hash setting to the cipher setting. The MITM approach may be seen as a way to turn very strong related-key properties into attacks in the single-key setting, complementing e.g. the work on the self-synchronized stream-cipher Moustique [21]. Even though the time complexity of our attack remains high, optimizations may result in reduced time complexities, by e.g. allowing the attacker to choose the plaintext instead (possible in many protocols), or asking for more plaintext/ciphertext pairs. Also, implementation techniques that speed-up brute force search, such as determining a good sequence of keys to guess and save computations that way, are likely to carry over to the meet-in-the-middle attack.

Among the ciphers most vulnerable to the meet-in-the-middle attacks, are those with little key-dependency in the sense that large parts of the cipher depend on a subset of key bits only. This is opposed to substitution-permutation networks which usually use subkeys of the block length in each round. For such ciphers, it is often difficult to mount a meet-in-the-middle attack even on a small number of rounds because of the strong key dependency. However, this approach as a rule results in a much higher number of XOR-operations needed for the key addition which in turn leads to higher area and/or time requirements and, thus, to a lower efficiency. An optimal trade-off between the level of resistance and the amount of key dependency remains, however, an area of research.

Acknowledgements. Andrey Bogdanov was supported in part by a visiting postdoctoral fellow grant from the Fund for Scientific Research - Flanders (FWO) within the FWO research project "Linear codes and cryptography" G.0317.06. This work was also sponsored by the Research Fund K.U.Leuven grant (OT/08/027) "A mathematical theory for the design of symmetric primitives", by the IAP Programme P6/26 BCRYPT of the Belgian State (Belgian Science Policy), and by the European Commission under contract ICT-2007-216646 (ECRYPT II).

The authors are grateful to the designers of KATAN/KTANTAN for clarifying the issues with the KTANTAN key schedule and would like to thank the anonymous reviewers of SAC 2010 whose insightful comments improved the presentation of the paper.

References

1. Bit-sliced reference code of KATAN and KTANTAN (2010), `http://www.cs.technion.ac.il/~orrd/KATAN/katan.c`
2. Albrecht, M., Cid, C., Dullien, T., Faugre, J.C., Perret, L.: Algebraic Precomputations in Differential Cryptanalysis. In: ECRYPT Tools for Cryptanalysis Workshop 2010 (2010)
3. Babbage, S., Dodd, M.: The MICKEY Stream Ciphers. In: Robshaw and Billet [26], pp. 191–209
4. Bogdanov, A., Knudsen, L.R., Leander, G., Paar, C., Poschmann, A., Robshaw, M.J.B., Seurin, Y., Vikkelsoe, C.: PRESENT: An Ultra-Lightweight Block Cipher. In: Paillier, P., Verbauwhede, I. (eds.) CHES 2007. LNCS, vol. 4727, pp. 450–466. Springer, Heidelberg (2007)
5. Bogdanov, A., Leander, G., Paar, C., Poschmann, A., Robshaw, M.J.B., Seurin, Y.: Hash Functions and RFID Tags: Mind the Gap. In: Oswald, E., Rohatgi, P. (eds.) CHES 2008. LNCS, vol. 5154, pp. 283–299. Springer, Heidelberg (2008)
6. Bogdanov, A., Rechberger, C.: Generalized Meet-in-the-Middle Attacks: Cryptanalysis of the Lightweight Block Cipher KTANTAN. In: Biryukov, A., Gong, G., Stinson, D.R. (eds.) SAC 2010. LNCS, vol. 6544. Springer, Heidelberg (2010)
7. Chaum, D., Evertse, J.H.: Cryptanalysis of DES with a Reduced Number of Rounds. In: Williams, H.C. (ed.) CRYPTO 1985. LNCS, vol. 218, pp. 192–211. Springer, Heidelberg (1986)
8. De Cannière, C.: Trivium: A Stream Cipher Construction Inspired by Block Cipher Design Principles. In: Katsikas, S.K., López, J., Backes, M., Gritzalis, S., Preneel, B. (eds.) ISC 2006. LNCS, vol. 4176, pp. 171–186. Springer, Heidelberg (2006)
9. De Cannière, C., Dunkelman, O., Knezevic, M.: KATAN and KTANTAN - A Family of Small and Efficient Hardware-Oriented Block Ciphers. In: Clavier, C., Gaj, K. (eds.) CHES 2009. LNCS, vol. 5747, pp. 272–288. Springer, Heidelberg (2009)

10. De Cannière, C., Preneel, B.: Trivium. In: Robshaw and Billet [26], pp. 244–266
11. Demirci, H., Selçuk, A.A.: A Meet-in-the-Middle Attack on 8-Round AES. In: Nyberg, K. (ed.) FSE 2008. LNCS, vol. 5086, pp. 116–126. Springer, Heidelberg (2008)
12. Demirci, H., Taskin, I., Çoban, M., Baysal, A.: Improved Meet-in-the-Middle Attacks on AES. In: Roy, B., Sendrier, N. (eds.) INDOCRYPT 2009. LNCS, vol. 5922, pp. 144–156. Springer, Heidelberg (2009)
13. Diffie, W., Hellman, M.: Exhaustive Cryptanalysis of the NBS Data Encryption standard. Computer 10(6), 74–84 (1977)
14. Dunkelman, O., Keller, N., Shamir, A.: Improved Single-Key Attacks on 8-round AES. Cryptology ePrint Archive, Report 2010/322 (2010), `http://eprint.iacr.org/`
15. Dunkelman, O., Sekar, G., Preneel, B.: Improved Meet-in-the-Middle Attacks on Reduced-Round DES. In: Srinathan, K., Rangan, C.P., Yung, M. (eds.) INDOCRYPT 2007. LNCS, vol. 4859, pp. 86–100. Springer, Heidelberg (2007)
16. Guo, J., Ling, S., Rechberger, C., Wang, H.: Advanced Meet-in-the-Middle Preimage Attacks: First Results on Full Tiger, and Improved Results on MD4 and SHA-2. Cryptology ePrint Archive, Report 2010/016 (2010), `http://eprint.iacr.org/`
17. Hell, M., Johansson, T., Maximov, A., Meier, W.: The Grain Family of Stream Ciphers. In: Robshaw and Billet [26], pp. 179–190
18. Hell, M., Johansson, T., Meier, W.: Grain: a stream cipher for constrained environments. IJWMC 2(1), 86–93 (2007)
19. Hong, D., Sung, J., Hong, S., Lim, J., Lee, S., Koo, B., Lee, C., Chang, D., Lee, J., Jeong, K., Kim, H., Kim, J., Chee, S.: HIGHT: A New Block Cipher Suitable for Low-Resource Device. In: Goubin, L., Matsui, M. (eds.) CHES 2006. LNCS, vol. 4249, pp. 46–59. Springer, Heidelberg (2006)
20. Indesteege, S., Keller, N., Dunkelman, O., Biham, E., Preneel, B.: A Practical Attack on KeeLoq. In: Smart, N.P. (ed.) EUROCRYPT 2008. LNCS, vol. 4965, pp. 1–18. Springer, Heidelberg (2008)
21. Käsper, E., Rijmen, V., Bjørstad, T.E., Rechberger, C., Robshaw, M.J.B., Sekar, G.: Correlated Keystreams in Moustique. In: Vaudenay, S. (ed.) AFRICACRYPT 2008. LNCS, vol. 5023, pp. 246–257. Springer, Heidelberg (2008)
22. Leander, G., Paar, C., Poschmann, A., Schramm, K.: New Lightweight DES Variants. In: Biryukov, A. (ed.) FSE 2007. LNCS, vol. 4593, pp. 196–210. Springer, Heidelberg (2007)
23. Lim, C.H., Korkishko, T.: mCrypton – A Lightweight Block Cipher for Security of Low-Cost RFID Tags and Sensors. In: Song, J., Kwon, T., Yung, M. (eds.) WISA 2005. LNCS, vol. 3786, pp. 243–258. Springer, Heidelberg (2006)
24. Merkle, R.C., Hellman, M.E.: On the Security of Multiple Encryption. Commun. ACM 24(7), 465–467 (1981)
25. van Oorschot, P.C., Wiener, M.J.: A Known-Plaintext Attack on Two-Key Triple Encryption. In: Damgård, I.B. (ed.) EUROCRYPT 1990. LNCS, vol. 473, pp. 318–325. Springer, Heidelberg (1991)
26. Robshaw, M.J.B., Billet, O. (eds.): New Stream Cipher Designs. LNCS, vol. 4986. Springer, Heidelberg (2008)
27. Sasaki, Y., Aoki, K.: Finding Preimages in Full MD5 Faster Than Exhaustive Search. In: Joux, A. (ed.) EUROCRYPT 2009. LNCS, vol. 5479, pp. 134–152. Springer, Heidelberg (2009)

A More Details on Partial Matching

A.1 Block Size 48 Bits

The details for the partial matching phase for the attack on KTANTAN with $b = 48$ are as follows:

```
10 bits match as follows

forward part:
forward R=111: k1=1, k2=1  0000000000000000000   00000000000000000000000000000
forward R=112: k1=0, k2=0  1100000000000000000   11000000000000000000000000000
forward R=113: k1=0, k2=0  0011000000000000000   00110000000000000000000000000
forward R=114: k1=0, k2=0  0000110000000000000   00001100000000000000000000000
forward R=115: k1=0, k2=0  1000001100000000000   10000011000000000000000000000
forward R=116: k1=0, k2=0  0110000011000000000   11100000110000000000000000000
forward R=117: k1=0, k2=0  0001100000110000000   00111000001100000000000000000
forward R=118: k1=0, k2=0  0000011000001100000   10001110000011000000000000000
forward R=119: k1=0, k2=0  1100000110000011000   11100011100000110000000000000
forward R=120: k1=0, k2=0  1111000001100000110   11111000111000001100000000000
forward R=121: k1=0, k2=0  0011110000011000001   10111110001110000011000000000
forward R=122: k1=0, k2=0  1100111100000110000   11101111100011100000110000000
forward R=123: k1=1, k2=0  1111001111000001100   11111011111000111000001100000

backward part:
backward R=131: k1=0, k2=1  0000000000000000000  00000000000000000000000000000
backward R=130: k1=1, k2=1  0000000000000000000  00000110000011110011110000011
backward R=129: k1=0, k2=0  0000011100011011011  00011110001111111111110001111
backward R=128: k1=0, k2=0  0001110001101101100  01111000111111111111000111100
backward R=127: k1=0, k2=0  0111000110110110000  11100011111111111100011110000
backward R=126: k1=0, k2=0  1100011111011011011  10001111111111110001111000000
backward R=125: k1=0, k2=0  0001111101111111111  00111111111111110111110000011
backward R=124: k1=0, k2=0  0111110111111111100  11111111111111011111000001100
backward R=123: k1=0, k2=0  1111101111111111011  11111111111101111100000110000

The highest number of matching bits is obtained at round 123:
 forward R=123: k1=1, k2=0  1111001111000001100  11111011111000111000001100000
backward R=123: k1=0, k2=0  1111101111111111011  11111111111101111100000110000
```

A.2 Block Size 64 Bits

The details for the partial matching phase for the attack on KTANTAN with $b = 64$ are as follows:

```
47 bits match as follows

forward part:
forward R=123: k1=1, k2=0  0000000000000000000000000  000000000000000000000000000000000000000
forward R=124: k1=0, k2=0  0000000000000000000000000  111000000000000000000000000000000000000
forward R=125: k1=0, k2=0  0000000000000000000000000  000111000000000000000000000000000000000
forward R=126: k1=0, k2=0  0000000000000000000000000  000000111000000000000000000000000000000
forward R=127: k1=0, k2=1  1100000000000000000000000  000000000111000000000000000000000000000
forward R=128: k1=0, k2=0  1111100000000000000000000  000000000000111000000000000000000000000
forward R=129: k1=0, k2=0  1111111100000000000000000  000000000000000111000000000000000000000
forward R=130: k1=0, k2=0  0001111111100000000000000  100000000000000000111000000000000000000
forward R=131: k1=0, k2=0  1100001111111100000000000  111100000000000000000111000000000000000

backward part:
backward R=131: k1=0, k2=1  0000000000000000000000000  000000000000000000000000000000000000000

The highest number of matching bits is obtained at round 131:
 forward R=131: k1=0, k2=0  1100001111111100000000000  111100000000000000000111000000000000000
backward R=131: k1=0, k2=1  0000000000000000000000000  000000000000000000000000000000000000000
```

Improving DPA by Peak Distribution Analysis

Jing Pan[1], Jasper G.J. van Woudenberg[1], Jerry I. den Hartog[2], and Marc F. Witteman[1]

[1] Riscure BV, 2628 XJ Delft, The Netherlands
{pan,vanwoudenberg,witteman}@riscure.com
[2] Eindhoven University of Technology, 5600 MB Eindhoven, The Netherlands
j.d.hartog@tue.nl

Abstract. Differential Power Analysis (DPA) attacks extract secret key information from cryptographic devices by comparing power consumption with predicted values based on key candidates and looking for peaks which indicate a correct prediction. A general obstacle in the use of DPA is the occurrence of so called ghost peaks, which may appear when evaluating incorrect key candidates. Some ghost peaks can be expected from the structure and may actually leak information. We introduce a DPA enhancement technique—Euclidean Differential Power Analysis (EDPA), which makes use of the information leaked by the ghost peaks to diminish the ghost peaks themselves and bring forward the correct key candidate. The EDPA can be combined with any standard DPA attack irrespective of the distinguisher used. We illustrate that EDPA improves on DPA with both simulations and experiments on smart cards.

Keywords: Differential power analysis, Euclidean similarity, ghost peaks.

1 Introduction

Side-channel attacks (SCA) reveal the secret key of a cryptosystem based on information gained from physical implementation of the cryptosystem on a smart card or other device. Information provided by sources such as timing [8], power consumption [9] and electromagnetic emulation [15] can be exploited by SCA attacks to break cryptosystems. Differential power analysis (DPA) [9] is a form of SCA that can extract secrets from power consumption measurements which may contain a lot of noise. Using DPA, an adversary can obtain intermediate values within cryptographic computations by statistically analyzing the power consumption measurements collected from multiple cryptographic operations performed by a vulnerable device.

A successful DPA attack would typically result in a vector of statistical test results amongst which the highest value occurs for the correct key candidate and the correct time (the moment in time during which the examined intermediate value is manipulated on the device). This highest value is usually referred to as *the correct peak* and the location in the vector where this peak occurs as *the correct time*. An unsuccessful attack normally implies a '*ghost peak*' problem,

A. Biryukov, G. Gong, and D.R. Stinson (Eds.): SAC 2010, LNCS 6544, pp. 241–261, 2011.

where the highest peak does not accord to the correct key candidate and thus erroneous conclusions can be drawn from the attack results.

Both academic research and practical experimentation have been conducted to make a clearer distinction between the correct peak and the ghost peaks resulted from a DPA attack. Proposed solutions include, for example, improvement on measurement techniques such that strong noises are filtered out from the power traces [13], improvement on the trace alignment such that power signals that correspond to the same intermediate result are located at the same position for all the traces [18], and improvement on DPA algorithms so that suitable power models or statistic tools are applied in specific attacks [2,5]. Such solutions attempt to reduce noise but at best can achieve the theoretical distinctions between the correct peak and the ghost peaks obtained in an attack using noise-free measurements. No solutions have, to the best of our knowledge, involved strengthening the correct peak by analyzing the distribution of the DPA results of all key hypotheses.

Here we propose a novel approach which treats the ghost peaks as a source of information as well and allows an attack to reduce ghost peaks based on information provided by the ghost peaks themselves. The proposed approach is built upon a standard DPA attack with additional adjustment made as suggested by the characteristics of the ghost peaks. Typically, the distribution of the DPA results at the correct time shows a predictable pattern with the real key giving the highest peak and some of the incorrect keys giving ghost peaks. Our attack exploits this information by comparing the distribution of the peaks in a real attack to the distribution of the peaks predicted by a hypothetical noise free attack. We use *Euclidean similarity* [6] to match the hypothesis with the actually observed pattern of peaks and hence refer to this method as the Euclidean Differential Power Analysis (EDPA).

The distribution of the DPA results at the correct time will always reflect the correct key. The DPA attack, however, only looks which peak is the highest and ignores the distribution of other peaks. Hence, there is always additional information about the key that an EDPA attack regards and a DPA attack ignores. We apply EDPA to Correlation Power Analysis (CPA) [2], calling the resulting method ECPA, and show that ECPA improves on CPA, almost always providing a clearer distinction between the correct peak and ghost peaks. We show this using both simulation and physical experiments on smart cards.

Commonly used measures to evaluate the effectiveness of SCA attacks, so called SCA security metrics, are success rate and guessing entropy [17]. As an additional result we propose a new measure 'oth-order guessing entropy' and argue that it is more practical than the original guessing entropy.

The remainder of this paper is organized as follows. Section 2 recaps success rate and guessing entropy, analyzes their relation and introduces oth-order guessing entropy. Section 3 explains an EDPA attack in more detail. Section 4 demonstrates ECPA in simulation and compares it to CPA. In Section 5, the two attacks are applied and compared using experiments on smart cards. Finally, Section 6 provides conclusions.

2 SCA Security Metrics

Soon after the introduction of SCA attacks [8] many different attacks and optimizations of attacks were proposed e.g. [12,1,2]. To be able to compare different attacks several SCA security metrics have been proposed such as success rate [17], guessing entropy [17], signal-to-noise ratios [12] and number of traces needed [3]. How meaningful a metric is and how easy it is to evaluate depends a lot on the type of adversary and the conditions under which the attack is performed. Thus often several metrics are combined when evaluating a SCA attack, see e.g. [10,16].

Here we have chosen to use o-th order success rate (SR in short) and guessing entropy (GE in short) as our security metrics. SR makes sense if the adversary only looks at the top results. GE is compatible if the adversary only uses the DPA as a method to sort key candidates for a brute-force attack. Additionally, we introduce a new security metric, called oth-order guessing entropy, which is similar to guessing entropy but better reflects the fact that the computational ability of an attacker will have some limit. Below we first quickly recall success rate and guessing entropy and then discuss the need for and define o-th order guessing entropy.

2.1 Success Rate and Guessing Entropy

An SCA attack executes a set of queries, obtains side channel information during the execution[1] and based on this information sorts key candidates according to their likelihood of being correct. Let random variable $\mathbf{g}_q$ denote the vector resulting from sorting all possible key candidates based on an attack using q queries. (Note that in practice $\mathbf{g}_q$ is built by combining the results from many sub-SCA, where each sub-attack targets a different sub-key. See also Section 2.2.) The success rate of order o, $sr^o_{\mathbf{g}_q}$, is the probability that the correct key s is ranked amongst the first o candidates in attack $\mathbf{g}_q$. The guessing entropy, $ge_{\mathbf{g}_q}$, gives the expected index of the correct key in $\mathbf{g}_q$. Intuitively, SR measures the probability of success with a fixed limit on the amount of computation, while GE measures the average cost of a brute-force key search with no limit on the computational ability.

Note that the GE of an attack can be calculated based on the SR of the attack for the various orders of SR. For $S = |\mathbf{g}_q|$ and $i = 1, 2, ..., S$ let $\mathcal{P}(\mathbf{g}_q[i] = s)$ denote the probability that the correct key s is ranked at position i in $\mathbf{g}_q$, then

$$\begin{aligned} sr^0_{\mathbf{g}_q} &= 0\,, \\ sr^i_{\mathbf{g}_q} &= sr^{i-1}_{\mathbf{g}_q} + \mathcal{P}(\mathbf{g}_q[i] = s)\,, \\ ge_{\mathbf{g}_q} &= \sum_{i=1}^{S} i \cdot \mathcal{P}(\mathbf{g}_q[i] = s) \;=\; \sum_{i=1}^{S} i \cdot (sr^i_{\mathbf{g}_q} - sr^{i-1}_{\mathbf{g}_q})\,. \end{aligned}$$

[1] This may involve optimizations to reduce noise such as running the algorithm multiple times with the same input and averaging the measurements.

2.2 Sorting Key Candidates

An SCA attack divides a secret key into several *sub-keys* each of which contains a small number of bits. A series of *sub-SCA attacks* are applied to rate the likelihood of each possible sub-key. The full keys are then sorted and tested in an order derived from the likelihood of the sub-keys. It is reasonable to assume that, to improve the attack, an adversary will not just use the ranking in the sub-attacks for sorting full keys but will also perform some global optimization combining and comparing ratings across different sub-attacks.

For independent sub-attacks combined with naive sorting, the product of GEs can be used as an approximation of the full GE. When using global optimizations there is no guarantee this is still a good estimation. Only when there is a consistent and similar improvement in GE across the sub-attacks is it reasonable to assume this translates into a proportional advantage in the overall GE. (See also Section 4.3.)

Without loss of generality, we focus on two sorting algorithms that can be used to sort the key candidates in $\mathbf{g}_q$. The first is an *optimal* solution, which performs a full global-optimization by sorting the key candidates in descending order of their combined sub-SCA results. The cost of sorting ($O(N \log(N))$ where N is the size of the key space) is acceptable compared to the effort needed for a brute-force attack, so an attacker will likely want to do this to optimize attack. However, note that N is exponential in the key size ($N = 2^{|k|}$) which means that actually doing the sorting will quickly become unfeasible. This means that estimating the guessing entropy with experiments is not realistically possible.

We address this problem in two ways. The first is to introduce a second, *sub-optimal*, sorting algorithm. It sorts the key candidates by a heuristic search in which optimal next key candidates are only selected at fixed points in the sorting rather than at every step. With this algorithm we are able to calculate the index of the correct key (in time polynomial in the key size) without actually having to do the sorting. However, the index of a key may increase a lot compared to its optimal ranking which may, especially for very noisy sub-SCA results, cause a much higher index of the correct key. (We refer the interested readers to Appendix A for a more detailed description of the sorting algorithms.)

The second way we address the problem with computing guessing entropy is to propose an enhanced alternative security measure called o-th order guessing entropy.

2.3 The oth-Order Guessing Entropy Security Metric

The GE of an attack measures the average brute-force cost after an SCA attack without a limit on the amount of computation. In the other words, it assumes that the adversary can always test as many key candidates as it is necessary to find the correct key. This is usually not a practical assumption. Considering the usually large key space (56-bit DES key or 128-bit AES key) an adversary will likely have to limit the number of candidates tested before considering the attack a failure. To capture this in a security measure, we introduce o-th order GE.

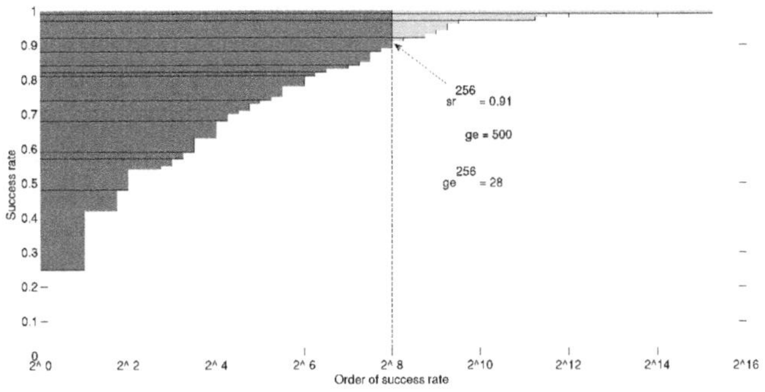

Fig. 1. An example of $sr^o_{\mathbf{g}_q}$, $ge_{\mathbf{g}_q}$ and $ge^o_{\mathbf{g}_q}$

The oth-order guessing entropy of an attack $\mathbf{g}_q$, written as $ge^o_{\mathbf{g}_q}$, measures the average number of key candidates to test after an SCA attack with q queries, given that in maximum o candidates can be tested. Intuitively, it merges the concept of the 'average cost' from the guessing entropy and the 'maximum cost limit' from the success rate. It allows an easily interpretable measurement when characterizing the average cost of a post-SCA brute-force attack in practical scenarios where the adversary does not test all possible key candidates.

Like $ge_{\mathbf{g}_q}$, the $ge^o_{\mathbf{g}_q}$ of an attack can be calculated from the success rates $sr^o_{\mathbf{g}_q}$ of the attack for the various order o:

$$\begin{aligned} ge^o_{\mathbf{g}_q} &= \sum_{i=1}^{o} i \cdot \mathcal{P}(\mathbf{g}_q[i] = s) + o \cdot \sum_{i=o+1}^{S} \mathcal{P}(\mathbf{g}_q[i] = s) \\ &= \sum_{i=1}^{o} i \cdot (sr^i_{\mathbf{g}_q} - sr^{i-1}_{\mathbf{g}_q}) + o \cdot (1 - sr^o_{\mathbf{g}_q})\,. \end{aligned}$$

Figure 1 illustrates the relation between $sr^o_{\mathbf{g}_q}$, $ge_{\mathbf{g}_q}$ and $ge^o_{\mathbf{g}_q}$ using results from a simulated CPA attack that targets eight DES S-boxes (see Section 4.2). The curve formed by the bottom of the colored area depicts the sr^o for various o. The (dark and light) gray region visualizes the calculation of the ge based on Eq. (1) with each of the horizontal bars marking an area equal to $i \cdot (sr^i - sr^{i-1})$ for some order i. As the summation of those small bars, the ge is then equal to the entire gray area. The oth-order guessing entropy, ge^o, limits the maximum computation to o and thus is equal to the dark gray area between the axis $x = 0$ and the line $x = o$. Compared to ge, the light gray area to the right of the line $x = o$ is omitted from ge^o. (Note that this area is much larger than it appears due to the logarithmic scale.)

3 The EDPA Attack

The result of a DPA attack $\mathcal{S}$ is calculated based on some distinguisher $\mathcal{D}$ that compares the real power measurement $\mathcal{T}$ to the hypothetical power consumption values $\mathcal{H}$: $\mathcal{S} = \mathcal{D}(\mathcal{T}, \mathcal{H})$. The distinguisher $\mathcal{D}$ can be various statistical tests, such as difference-of-means [9], Pearson's correlation coefficient [2], mutual information [7], variance test [16], etc. An EDPA attack can be built on top of any DPA attack independently from the distinguisher used. In this section, we demonstrate the construction of an EDPA attack with emphasis on ECPA, where Pearson's correlation coefficient is used as the distinguisher $\mathcal{D}$. Note that all attacks mentioned in this section are actually sub-attacks using the terminology of Section 2.

3.1 Description of the Attack

We use the block representations of [11, Ch. 6] to describe our attack. (See appendix B for a graphical representation.) The hypothetical power consumption values are contained in a $q \times n$ matrix $\mathbf{H}$, with q being the number of queries used and n being the number of key candidates in this attack. A column of $\mathbf{H}$, written as $\boldsymbol{h}_i$, corresponds to a key hypothesis k_i. The result of a DPA attack can be represented as an $n \times m$ matrix $\mathbf{S}$, calculated based on n key hypotheses and m time samples. In $\mathbf{S}$, $s_{i,j}$ corresponds to the DPA result for key hypothesis k_i and time sample t_j. Let (ck, ct) be the index of the correct peak in $\mathbf{S}$, i.e. k_{ck} is the correct key and t_{ct} is the correct time.

After obtaining the results of DPA, an EDPA attack continues with the following three steps.

Step 1: Generate hypothetical attack results. The hypothetical power consumption values of a DPA attack model the power consumption of the device caused by the processing of the targeted intermediate value. We use this model to simulate the attack with each of the n key candidate as the correct key. As each attack gives a result for every key candidate this yields an n-by-n matrix $\mathbf{C}$ of DPA results, where $c_{i,j} = \mathcal{D}(\boldsymbol{h}_j, \boldsymbol{h}_i)$. The ck-th column $\mathbf{c}_{ck}$ in $\mathbf{C}$ thus models the expected DPA results at the correct time ct. For ECPA this means that, for candidate k_i given correct key k_j, we calculate the correlation between columns $\boldsymbol{h}_j$ and $\boldsymbol{h}_i$ of $\mathbf{H}$, $c_{i,j} = \rho(\boldsymbol{h}_j, \boldsymbol{h}_i)$ $(i, j = 1..n)$. In this case we refer to $\mathbf{C}$ as inter-data correlation.

Step 2: Compare the actual and the hypothetical attacks. Next we match the DPA results predicted for each key candidate (i.e. each column of $\mathbf{C}$) with the actually observed DPA results at each point in time (i.e. each column of $\mathbf{S}$) using Euclidean similarity [6]. In ECPA a similarity $e_{i,j}$ is assigned to column i of the inter-data correlation $\mathbf{C}$ and column j of DPA results $\mathbf{S}$, as defined in Eq. (1) ($i = 1..n$ and $j = 1..m$) resulting in an $n \times m$ matrix $\mathbf{E}$. Like in $\mathbf{S}$, $e_{i,j}$ corresponds to key hypothesis k_i and time sample t_j.

$$e_{i,j} = 1 - \frac{d_{i,j}}{\max\{d_{x,j} \mid x = 1..n\}}, \quad \text{where} \quad d_{i,j} = \sqrt{\sum_{p=1}^{n} (c_{p,i} - s_{p,j})^2}\,. \qquad (1)$$

Here $d_{i,j}$ is the *Euclidean distance* between vectors $\boldsymbol{c}_i$ and $\boldsymbol{s}_j$.

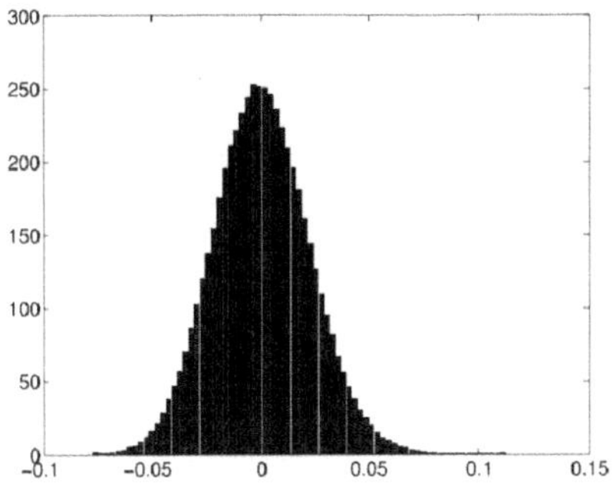

Fig. 2. Histogram of the distribution of **S**

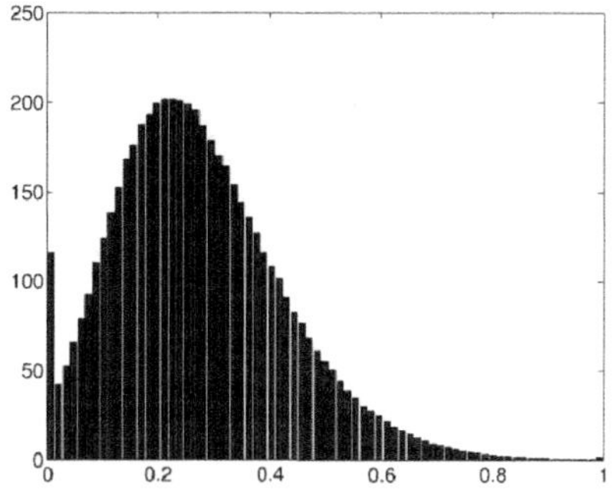

Fig. 3. Histogram of the distribution of $\hat{\mathbf{E}}$

Step 3: Combine the DPA and Euclidean similarity results. Finally, the DPA **S** is scaled using the Euclidean similarity **E** by Eq. (2) resulting the final result **R** of the attack.

$$r_{i,j} = \frac{1}{2} s_{i,j} + \frac{1}{2} s_{i,j} \cdot \hat{e}_{i,j} \,, \quad \text{where} \quad \hat{e}_{i,j} = \frac{e_{i,j}}{\max\{e_{x,y} \mid x = 1..n,\; y = 1..m\}} \,. \tag{2}$$

The highest value in **R** now reveals the location (ck, ct) and hence k_{ck} and t_{ct}. Let $\hat{\mathbf{E}}$ be the matrix of the normalized Euclidean similarity $\hat{e}_{i,j}$. The mixing function Eq. (2) scales down the DPA values by factors of 0 to 1/2, linearly to the corresponding normalized Euclidean similarity: $s_{i,j}$ remains unaltered if $\hat{e}_{i,j} = 1$ and $s_{i,j}$ is halved if $\hat{e}_{i,j} = 0$.

Remark 1. In contrast to DPA attacks where only the highest correlation value is used to indicate the correct key hypothesis, EDPA attacks determine the correct key based on the correlation values of all key candidates. As presence of DPA peaks where they are expected more strongly indicates the correct key than absence of DPA peaks where none is expected, Euclidean similarity is used to ensure that higher DPA values contribute more than lower ones. The Euclidean similarity values are then used to tune the DPA values such that only the peaks that are significant in both are retained.

Remark 2. In choosing the mixing function in Eq. (2) we note that the Euclidean similarity measure is more sensitive to noise, as illustrated in Figures 2 and 3. These figures plot distributions of the DPA results **S** and the normalized Euclidean similarity $\hat{\mathbf{E}}$. (For 100 repetitions of a simulated attack on DES with high noise levels, see Section 4 for a detailed description of such simulated attacks.) These graphs show the typical distribution of values for **S** and $\hat{\mathbf{E}}$ for correlated and/or uncorrelated time. They show that random $\hat{\mathbf{E}}$ values have a much higher chance of being close to the expected peak $\hat{e}_{ck,ct} = 1$ and thus overtaking the correct value due to noise.

We view $s_{i,j}$ and $\hat{e}_{i,j}$ as independent indicators for the 'likelyhood' of a key candidate, making their product a good choice for a combined indicator where only peaks which occur in both stand out. However, as $\mathbf{S}$ is less sensitive to noise we weight this indicator stronger than the indicator $\hat{\mathbf{E}}$ which we do by adding it again to the combined result resulting in the mixing function in Eq. (2). Note that the factors $(\frac{1}{2}, \frac{1}{2})$ in this function are determined based on empirical study and may not be the optimal solution.

Remark 3. The EDPA attack as given in this section assumes that the correct peak has a positive sign. The attack can be easily adjusted to cope with unknown or negative signs (for the correct peak). E.g. when this sign is unknown, one can modify the mixing function in *Step 3* so that $\{e_{i,j} \mid i = 1..n, j = 1..m\}$ that are of the same distance to their mean factorize their corresponding $s_{i,j}$ by the same amount.

4 Evaluating ECPA Using Simulation

In this section, we show results of simulated attacks on DES and AES using ECPA and CPA and compare the attacks using the security metrics described in Section 2.

4.1 Simulation Setup

We model the power consumption of a device as the summation of the Hamming-weight of the processed intermediate value v, some constant value and noise (see e.g. [2]). The constant value is determined by the operation applied to v. The noise is a normally distributed variable with expectation 0 and some standard deviation σ.

For DES, we let[2] $\sigma = 10$ and simulate the power consumption for the first three rounds of an encryption. To be precise 28 power consumption values are generated per encryption round: 1 for the left half of the round input, 1 for the right half of the round input, 8 for the output of the expansion, 8 for the input of the S-box substitution, 8 for the output of the substitution, 1 for the output of the permutation, and 1 for the XOR of the permutation output and the left half of the round input.

For AES, we let[2] $\sigma = 12$ and simulate the power consumption for the first round of an encryption. To be precise 108 power consumption values are generated: 16 each for the outputs of the initial KeyAddition, and the SubBytes, 12 for the output of the ShiftRows, 32 for the intermediate values of the MixColumns and 16 each for the outputs of the MixColumns, and the KeyAddition at the end of the first round.

[2] We choose $\sigma = 10$ (resp. $\sigma = 12$) for DES (resp. AES) to demonstrate the increase of success rate from 0 to 1 within query span $0 \leq q \leq 3000$, providing a good trade-off between the practicality of the simulation and the cost of the computation.

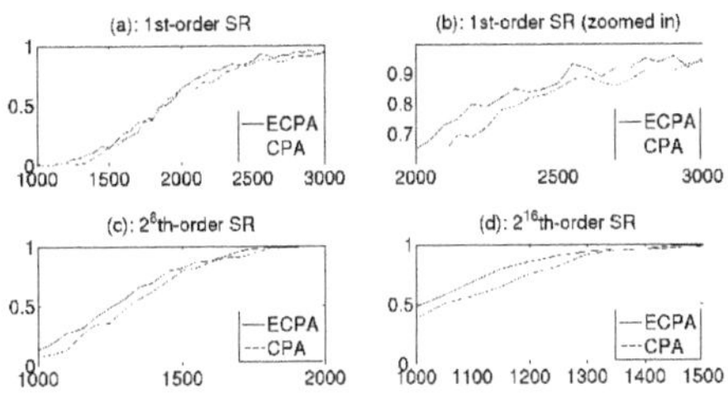

Fig. 4. DES with optimal sorting: SR for different number of queries

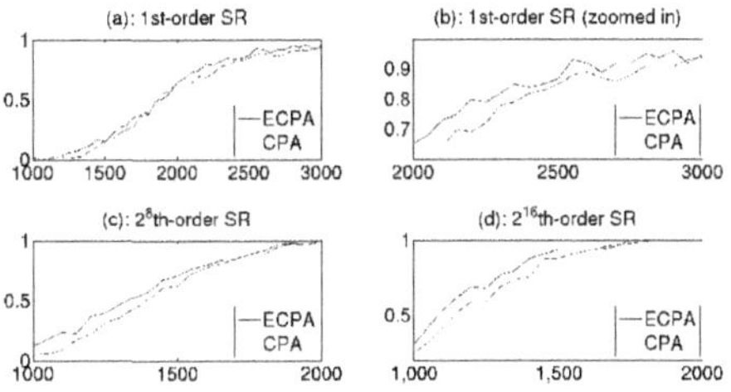

Fig. 5. DES with sub-optimal sorting: SR for different number of queries

To estimate SR and GE, we generate for each algorithm 100 sets of power traces, each containing 3000 simulated traces based on 3000 random plaintexts and one fixed randomly chosen key. Using statistical tests based on one random key is sufficient as, given the same amount of measurements, it is equally difficult to attack one key as an another key for DES and AES.

4.2 Comparing ECPA and CPA on DES

For attacks on DES, we target the eight 4-bit output of the S-boxes in the first round aiming to find the 48-bit round key used in this round. Hence, we perform eight sub-attacks each targeting a 6-bit sub-key used in an S-box. In this experiment, we refer to the SR (resp. the GE) of an attack as the probability (resp. the average cost) of recovering this 48-bit round key. In practice, the remaining 8 bits of the secret key can be found either by another SCA on the second encryption round or by a brute-force attack. Which method is used is immaterial for our comparison of ECPA and CPA.

We use both the optimal and the sub-optimal sorting algorithm for the evaluation of the success rate $sr^o_{\mathbf{g}_q}$ and the guessing entropies $ge_{\mathbf{g}_q}$ and $ge^o_{\mathbf{g}_q}$. Because the computational cost of sorting all the 2^{48} key candidates by the optimal sorting algorithm is too high to be practical, we limit the number of candidates to sort by this algorithm to 2^{16}. Recall that checking a single candidate already requires a significant amount of work from an attacker (e.g. 2^8 encryptions to find the remaining 8 bits).

Figures 4 and 5 show the SR of the ECPA attack and the CPA attack for various q and o using the two sorting algorithms. A 2^8th-order SR (resp. GE) corresponds to the success rate (resp. average cost) of a SCA attack provided that the adversary tests, on average, 2 candidates per S-box after the attack. A 2^{16}th-order SR (resp. GE) corresponds to the success rate (resp. average cost) of an attack provided that on average 4 candidates are tested per S-box.

For both sorting algorithms, ECPA results in a higher success rate than CPA in most of the cases. Comparing the graphs between the figures, we observe that for both sorting algorithms the 1st-order SRs are equal for every attack and every q. This is because both algorithms sort the same candidate the first. The higher-order SRs (see graphs (c) and (d) in Figures 4 and 5) differ per sorting algorithm. It is obvious that the optimal sorting algorithm almost always results in a higher success rate than the sub-optimal sorting algorithm. This gives us an empirical proof that the optimal sorting algorithm is indeed better than the sub-optimal sorting algorithm with respect to the success rate of an attack.

The guessing entropy with the ECPA and CPA attack are shown in Figures 6 and 7 for the two sorting algorithms used. Figure 6 show the GE of order 2^{16} while Figure 7 show the GE of order 2^{48}, i.e. the full GE. The interesting range is roughly $2^{32} \geq GE \geq 2^8$, as above this range a brute-force attack is too expensive and below this range the cost is too small for differences to matter. Both Figure 6 and Figure 7 show that ECPA improves on CPA, especially in this range.

4.3 Comparing ECPA and CPA on AES

For the attack on AES, we target the 8-bit output of the first S-box in the first round. Since the same S-box is used for every byte of the state and the power consumption caused by each of the 16 S-box substitution is simulated based on the same function, we consider that it is as difficult to attack one S-box as attacking another in the same round. We, therefore, only look at the SR (resp. GE) of a sub-attack recovering one byte of the secret key of AES. An advantage in the sub-attack will translate to a proportional advantage in a full attack.

Figure 8 shows the 1st, the 2nd and the 4th-order SRs and the GE of the attacks. The 1st-order SR of the ECPA attack is approximately equal to the 1st-order SR of the CPA attack. For the higher-order SRs, the advantage of ECPA over CPA also does not seem that large. However, when all are added in the GE, a clear benefit of ECPA can be seen. Note that this is only the advantage for the sub-attack and for a full attack, which repeats this attack 16 times, the advantage can grow quickly.

The advantage of ECPA over CPA is greater for DES S-boxes than for the AES S-box. Recall that the advantage of ECPA relies on the information leaked by the ghost peaks. The greater the ghost peaks caused structure in the analyzed instruction, the more information an ECPA attack gains in addition to a CPA attack. Because of their mathematical structure, with the same level of noise, a CPA attack on DES S-boxes leads to higher and more 'telling' ghost peaks,

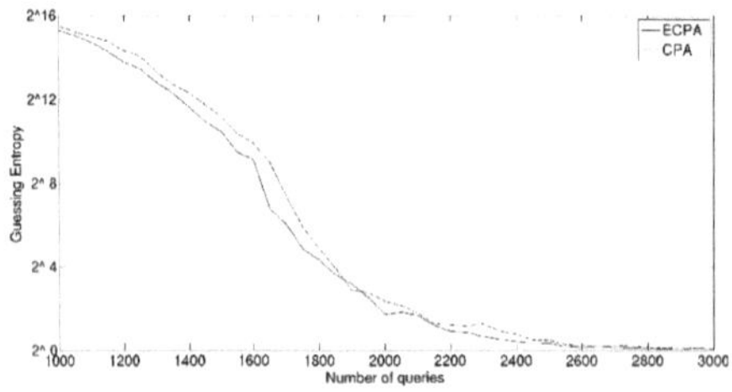

Fig. 6. DES with optimal sorting: 2^{16}th-order GE for different number of queries

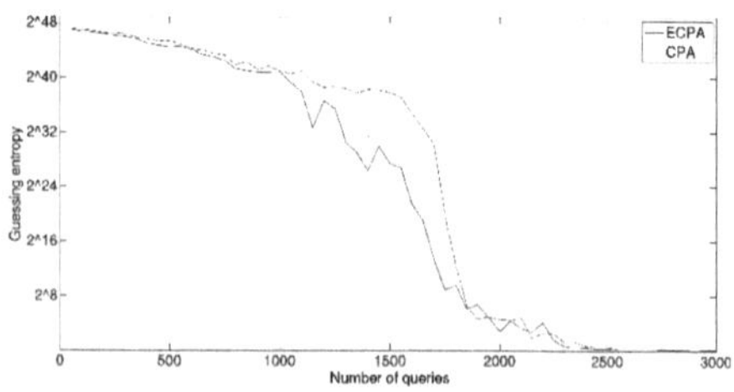

Fig. 7. DES with sub-optimal sorting: GE for different number of queries

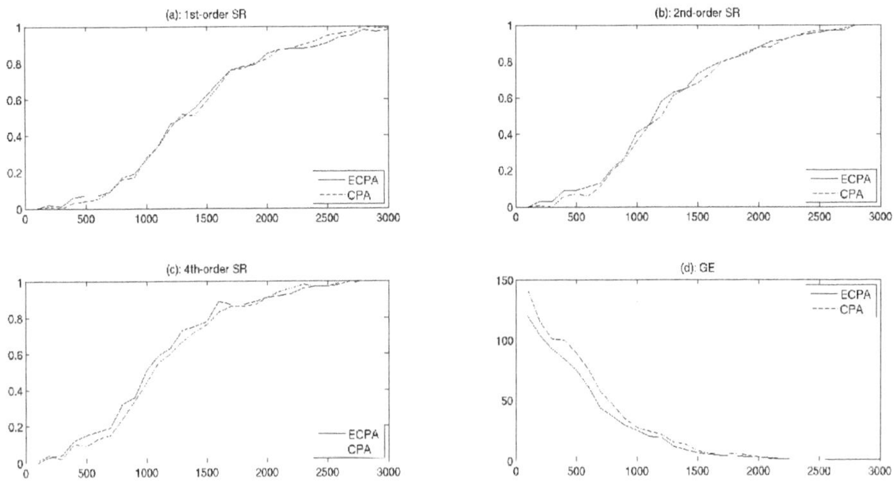

Fig. 8. AES: SR and GE for different number of queries

whereas the AES S-box would result in lower and more uniformly distributed peaks (see e.g. [14]). Hence, the ECPA attack is more effective on DES S-boxes.

5 Evaluating ECPA Using Physical Experiments

To validate our theoretical motivation, we performed CPA and ECPA attacks on two smart cards running a hardware DES and a software AES implementation respectively. The experiment shows that for both devices, with the tested number of traces, ECPA successfully finds the correct key while CPA does not[3].

5.1 Attacking a Hardware DES Implementation

The attacked smart card has an 8-bit processor, with a DES accelerator containing two 32-bit registers. The hardware-implemented DES is countermeasure free. The DES accelerator is clocked at 30.76 MHz. For the power measurement, the oscilloscope collects samples at a frequency of 250 MHz which are then compressed to one sample per internal clock period of the smart card, i.e. 30.76 MHz.

In the smart card that we attack, one round of DES encryption is completed within one clock cycle of the DES accelerator. Therefore, it is very difficult to exploit the leakage caused by the S-boxes substitution. Instead, we target the XOR of the 32-bit permutation output and the 32-bit left half of the round input that takes place at the end of the first round. Assuming that the result of this

[3] Though the comparison performed in this section considers both positive and negative peaks, advantage of ECPA over CPA can also be concluded even when only the positive peaks are regarded, which is the case when the power model of the attacked device is known beforehand.

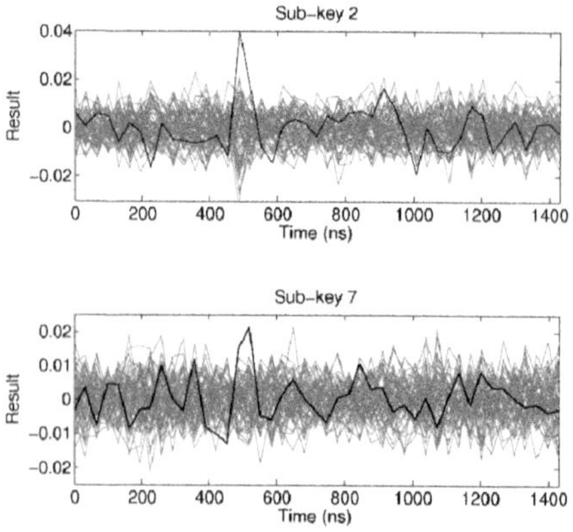

Fig. 9. CPA result of DES S-boxes 2 and 7

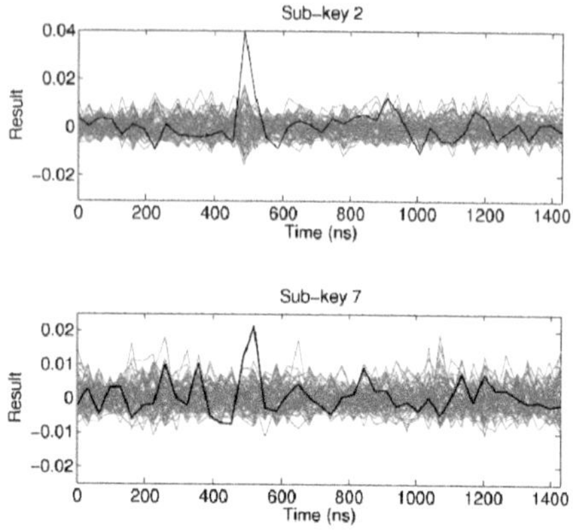

Fig. 10. ECPA result of DES S-boxes 2 and 7

XOR is written in the same register that previously contained the right half of the round input, we use the Hamming distance of these two 32-bit values as our power model. We use eight sub-attacks each targeting 6 key bits (used in the same S-box thus allowing prediction of 4 bits of the 32-bit intermediate value).

The attacks were performed using the same set of 23,000 power traces. We take sub-keys 2 and 7 as examples and show their attack results in Figures 9 and 10, where the results of the correct key candidate is plotted in black and the others are plotted in gray. The attack results for all sub-keys can be found in Appendix C. Though CPA and ECPA both reveal the correct sub-key 2, ECPA significantly lowers the incorrect peaks compared to CPA and therefore raises the confidence level of the correct key.

Sub-key 7 is ranked second by CPA but correctly found by ECPA, showing an improvement of ECPA on CPA. Decreasing the number power traces used, we find that for this sub-key the correct key is always sorted earlier by ECPA than by CPA (see Table 1). Experiments described in Table 1 show that on average ECPA approximately halfs the rank of the correct key compared to CPA. Concerning a global sorting that regards all the eight sub-keys, the difference of the ranking for sub-key 7 can add up to a much more significant difference of the overall ranking for the secret DES key.

Table 1. The rank of the correct sub-key 7 using decreasing numbers of power traces

Number of Traces	22K	21K	20K	19K	18K	17K	16K	15K	10K
CPA	9	5	5	8	22	15	13	13	30
ECPA	3	2	3	5	18	14	6	3	17

Table 2. The results of CPA (top) and ECPA (bottom) of an AES software-implementation. The attack results are written outside the brackets, and the sub-key candidates are written inside the brackets in hexadecimal numbers. The correct peaks and candidates are written in bold.

Rank	Byte 1	Byte 2	Byte 3	Byte 4	Byte 5	Byte 6	Byte 7	Byte 8
1	**.5845(8d)**	**.4699(f5)**	**.5186(91)**	**.5227(54)**	**.4659(6e)**	**.5832(c3)**	**.4826(3e)**	**.5384(5c)**
2	.4353(d8)	.4212(8a)	.4692(45)	-.4468(c1)	.4613(2e)	.4725(68)	-.4398(46)	-.4389(71)
3	.4255(66)	-.4211(ac)	.4123(82)	.4394(5c)	.4339(b3)	-.4587(2c)	-.4279(3d)	-.4351(56)
4	.4247(8b)	.4188(20)	-.4117(7d)	-.4304(23)	-.4313(0b)	.4414(f0)	-.4210(71)	.4149(68)
Rank	Byte 9	Byte 10	Byte 11	Byte 12	Byte 13	Byte 14	Byte 15	Byte 16
1	.4788(f5)	**.4843(69)**	**.5219(7c)**	**.4576(c8)**	**.5445(ac)**	**.5525(1c)**	**.4886(61)**	**.5023(84)**
2	**.4685(d4)**	-.4653(8c)	-.4220(d8)	.4487(4a)	-.4399(91)	-.4194(93)	-.4869(56)	-.4395(fe)
3	-.4289(e4)	.4440(d9)	-.4205(94)	-.4449(4f)	.4160(6b)	.4160(6b)	-.4532(72)	-.4260(91)
4	.4211(cc)	-.4087(41)	.4199(a6)	-.4190(5b)	-.4103(85)	-.4103(85)	.4527(e5)	-.4228(a5)

Rank	Byte 1	Byte 2	Byte 3	Byte 4	Byte 5	Byte 6	Byte 7	Byte 8
1	**.5845(8d)**	**.4612(f5)**	**.5181(91)**	**.5227(54)**	**.4659(6e)**	**.5832(c3)**	**.4887(3e)**	**.5234(5c)**
2	.3995(8b)	.3945(20)	.4417(45)	.4177(63)	.4065(25)	.4118(68)	.4098(84)	.3654(c8)
3	.3912(d8)	.3914(73)	.3834(f8)	.4108(5c)	.4043(2e)	.4002(f0)	-.4005(d8)	.3643(5d)
4	.3792(66)	.3911(3b)	.3770(82)	.3906(5d)	.3980(b3)	.3802(76)	.3935(45)	.3643(85)
Rank	Byte 9	Byte 10	Byte 11	Byte 12	Byte 13	Byte 14	Byte 15	Byte 16
1	**.4613(d4)**	**.4659(69)**	**.5219(7c)**	**.4418(c8)**	**.5445(ac)**	**.5525(1c)**	**.4769(61)**	**.4928(84)**
2	.4224(f5)	.4186(d9)	.3995(a6)	.4296(4a)	.3871(c2)	.3723(6b)	.4271(e5)	-.4147(9d)
3	.3950(df)	.3600(13)	.3855(89)	.3859(5a)	.3827(05)	.3648(2c)	.4062(0a)	.4037(f5)
4	.3867(cc)	.3597(fa)	.3683(1b)	.3764(22)	.3783(75)	.3645(95)	.3988(c0)	.3763(a8)

5.2 Attacking a Software AES Implementation

The attacked smart card for the AES experiment shows quite a lot of side-channel leakage allowing us to suffice with 110 traces. Unlike the card we attacked in Section 5.1, this card does not have an accelerator embedded. The card works on its external clock, which is set at 4 MHz. The oscilloscope was set at frequency 200 MHz and the signals were compressed to one sample per clock period of the card: 4 MHz.

For both ECPA and CPA attacks, we target the 16 bytes of the output of the S-boxes in the first encryption round. We use the Hamming weight of the bytes as our power model.

Table 2 lists the top candidates resulted from both attacks. The attacks use the same set of 110 traces. As in the previous experiment ECPA gives better results than CPA: all the correct sub-keys are ranked the first by ECPA and all the correct peaks stand out more significantly from the ghost peaks. The CPA attack fails to sort the correct candidate of byte 9 the first, resulting that the correct full key of AES will be sorted the 6th and the 9th candidate after the CPA attack according to the optimal and the sub-optimal sorting algorithms respectively.

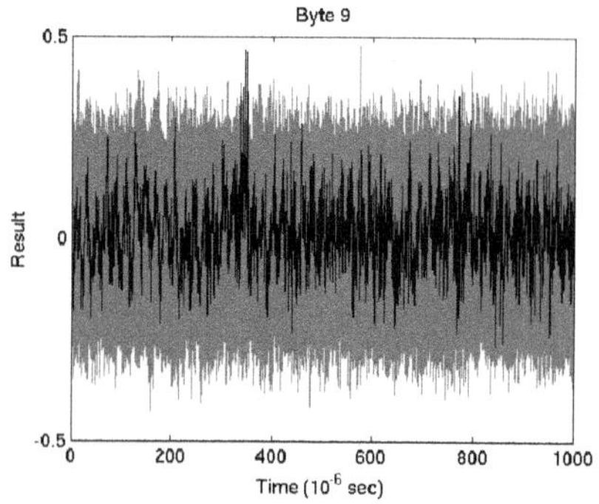

Fig. 11. CPA result of AES for byte 9 of AES

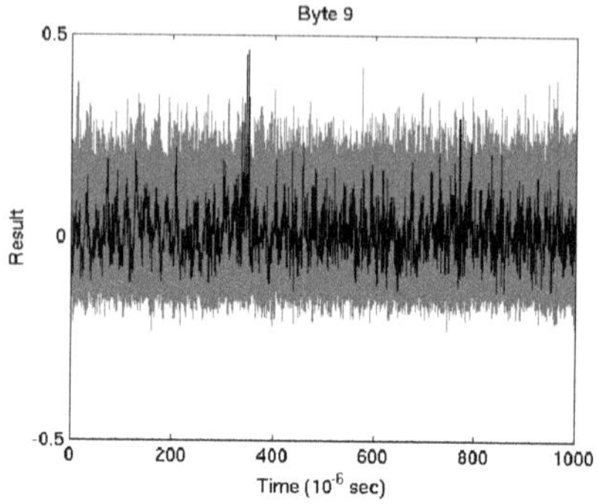

Fig. 12. ECPA result of AES for byte 9

Figures 11 and 12 plot the results of the attacks for byte 9, where the black (resp. gray) curves correspond to the correct (resp. incorrect) key candidates. Observe that the 'bandwidth' of the gray region is narrower in case of ECPA. Additionally, the highest ghost peak in CPA (Figure 11, $t \approx 570\mu s$), which is higher than the correct peak, gets reduced by ECPA (Figure 12, $t \approx 570\mu s$) and is now lower than the correct peak. Plots of the results for the other bytes can be found in Appendix C.

6 Conclusion

We introduce a new SCA attack—EDPA, which is able to extract more information from SCA leakage compared with a standard DPA attack and effectively diminishes ghost peaks using the information leaked by the ghost peaks themselves. We show with simulation and experiment that the extra information indeed improves the effectiveness of the attack. To help evaluate this effectiveness we introduce o-th order guessing entropy. We argue that the o-th order guessing entropy is more realistic and show that it is more practical with a scenario where the o-th order guessing entropy is possible but the original (full) guessing entropy cannot be used. Our results show a consistent advantage of EDPA over DPA but the advantage is not huge, which is to be expected as the attack simply improves the use of the same leaked information. Still, the limited computational overhead of an EDPA attack with respect to a DPA attack, and its efficiency in reducing the noise in the final result suggest that EDPA is at least an effective tool for further eliminating ghost peaks after an ambiguous DPA attack. Finally, since EDPA is based on the same leakage information as a DPA attack, countermeasures that prevent a standard DPA attack can also be used to thwart an ECPA attack.

References

1. Bevan, R., Knudsen, E.: Ways to enhance differential power analysis. In: Lee, P.J., Lim, C.H. (eds.) ICISC 2002. LNCS, vol. 2587, pp. 327–342. Springer, Heidelberg (2003)
2. Brier, É., Clavier, C., Olivier, F.: Correlation power analysis with a leakage model. In: Joye, M., Quisquater, J.-J. (eds.) CHES 2004. LNCS, vol. 3156, pp. 16–29. Springer, Heidelberg (2004)
3. Clavier, C., Coron, J.-S., Dabbous, N.: Differential power analysis in the presence of hardware countermeasures. In: Paar, C., Koç, Ç.K. (eds.) CHES 2000. LNCS, vol. 1965, pp. 252–263. Springer, Heidelberg (2000)
4. Cormen, T., Leiserson, C., Rivest, R.: Introduction to Algorithms. The MIT Press, Cambridge (1990)
5. Coron, J.-S., Naccache, D., Kocher, P.C.: Statistics and secret leakage. ACM Trans. Embedded Comput. Syst. 3(3), 492–508 (2004)
6. Elmore, K.L., Richman, M.B.: Euclidean distance as a similarity metric for principle component analysis. American Meteorological Society 129(3), 540–549 (2001)
7. Gierlichs, B., Batina, L., Tuyls, P., Preneel, B.: Mutual information analysis. In: Oswald, E., Rohatgi, P. (eds.) CHES 2008. LNCS, vol. 5154, pp. 426–442. Springer, Heidelberg (2008)
8. Kocher, P.C.: Timing attacks on implementations of diffie-hellman, rsa, dss, and other systems. In: Koblitz, N. (ed.) CRYPTO 1996. LNCS, vol. 1109, pp. 104–113. Springer, Heidelberg (1996)
9. Kocher, P.C., Jaffe, J., Jun, B.: Differential power analysis. In: Wiener, M. (ed.) CRYPTO 1999. LNCS, vol. 1666, pp. 388–397. Springer, Heidelberg (1999)
10. Mangard, S.: Hardware countermeasures against dpa - a statistical analysis of their effectiveness. In: Okamoto, T. (ed.) CT-RSA 2004. LNCS, vol. 2964, pp. 222–235. Springer, Heidelberg (2004)
11. Mangard, S., Oswald, E., Popp, T.: Power Analysis Attacks: Revealing the Secrets of Smart Cards. In: Advances in Information Security. Springer, Heidelberg (2007)
12. Messerges, T.S., Dabbish, E.A., Sloan, R.H.: Examining smart-card security under the threat of power analysis attacks. IEEE Trans. Computers 51(5), 541–552 (2002)
13. Orfanidis, S.J.: Introduction to signal processing. Prentice-Hall, Inc., Upper Saddle River (1995)
14. Pan, J., den Hartog, J.I., de Vink, E.P.: An operation-based metric on cpa resistance. In: Jajodia, S., Samarati, P., Cimato, S. (eds.) SEC, International Federation for Information Processing, pp. 429–443. Springer, Boston (2008)
15. Quisquater, J.-J., Samyde, D.: Electromagnetic analysis (ema): Measures and counter-measures for smart cards. In: Attali, I., Jensen, T.P. (eds.) E-smart 2001. LNCS, vol. 2140, pp. 200–210. Springer, Heidelberg (2001)
16. Standaert, F.-X., Gierlichs, B., Verbauwhede, I.: Partition vs. comparison side-channel distinguishers: An empirical evaluation of statistical tests for univariate side-channel attacks against two unprotected cmos devices. In: Lee, P.J., Cheon, J.H. (eds.) ICISC 2008. LNCS, vol. 5461, pp. 253–267. Springer, Heidelberg (2009)
17. Standaert, F.-X., Malkin, T., Yung, M.: A unified framework for the analysis of side-channel key recovery attacks. In: Joux, A. (ed.) EUROCRYPT 2009. LNCS, vol. 5479, pp. 443–461. Springer, Heidelberg (2009)
18. van Woudenberg, J.G.J., Witteman, M.F., Bakker, B.: Improving differential power analysis by elastic alignment (2009), http://www.riscure.com/fileadmin/images/Docs/elastic_paper.pdf

A The Sorting Algorithms

In this section we present the two key sorting algorithms. We take a fixed number of sub-key candidates for each sub-attack, and assume all sub-attacks use the same set of traces and that none of the peaks are exactly the same. All of these assumptions can be easily removed at the cost of complicating the notation.

A.1 Pre Processing Sub-SCA Results

Depending on the implementation, the measurement, and other factors, the amount of exploitable information can be different for different sub-attacks. Rather than using the actual SCA result, a normalized SCA result gives better estimation of relative likelihood, which is what we want to sort on. E.g. Consider two sub-attacks where the top two candidates of the attacks have peaks $(0.8, 0.7)$ and $(0.2, 0.1)$, respectively. Clearly we want to try the second candidate from attack 1 (0.7) before that of attack 2 (0.1) as it seems more likely to be the correct key.

Hence, the sorting algorithms presented in this section take as reference the relative SCA value of a key candidate that is with respect to the highest SCA value within the same sub-attack. That is, we sort a key candidate by the ratio between the SCA result of a key candidate and the highest SCA value resulted from the same attack. See Table 3 for an description. We do not give an implementation of this computation since it is relatively trivial.

Table 3. Pre processing sub-SCA results

INPUT: A list of SCA results $r_{i,j}^{(a)}$ $(a = 1..A, i = 1..n, j = 1..m)$, where A is the number of sub-attacks performed, n is the number of sub-key candidates per sub-attack and m is the number of leakage samples per power trace.
OUTPUT: Normalized maximal SCA peaks for each sub-key candidate $rr_i^{(a)} = pk_i^{(a)} / \max\{pk_{i'}^{(a)} \mid i' = 1..n\}$ where $pk_i^{(a)} = \max\{\lvert r_{i,j}^{(a)}\rvert \mid j = 1..m\}$.

A.2 The Sub-optimal Sorting Algorithm

According to the normalized SCA peaks, the sub-optimal algorithm first rates every sub-key candidates with its global ranking concerning all sub-attacks. The vector $\mathbf{g}$ is initialized with the top candidate from every sub-attack: $(k_{\max}^{(1)}, \ldots, k_{\max}^{(A)})$. Next, the rest of sub-key candidates are brought into consideration in the order of their global ratings. Before considering any combination which uses a sub-key with a global rating x, the algorithm will tests all candidates whose sub-keys all have a global ranking lower than x. To add a sub-key $k_i^{(a)}$ into $\mathbf{g}$, we first find all the items in $\mathbf{g}$ that use $k_{\max}^{(a)}$, then we replace $k_{\max}^{(a)}$ with $k_i^{(a)}$ and append the updated items into $\mathbf{g}$ in the order of their original items in $\mathbf{g}$.

Table 4. The sub-optimal sorting algorithm

INPUT: Sub-key candidates $k_i^{(a)}$ and normalized maximal SCA peaks $rr_i^{(a)}$ where $a = 1..A$, $i = 1..n$, A is the number of sub-attacks performed and n is the number of sub-key candidates per sub-attack.
OUTPUT: A sorted list of full key candidates $\mathbf{g}$.

```
For each a = 1..A let k_max^(a) = k_i^(a) with i such that rr_i^(a) = max{rr_p^(a) | p = 1..n};
Let G be a list of all A × n sub-key candidate indexes (a, i) sorted in descending order
of rr_i^a (a = 1..A, i = 1..n);
Initialize g to [(k_max^(1), ..., k_max^(A))];
For p = A + 1 to A × n
  Let (a, i) = G[p];
  For c = 1 to |g|
    If g[c][a] == k_max^(a)
      Append (g[c][1], ..., g[c][a − 1], k_i^(a), g[c][a + 1], ..., g[c][A]) to g;
    End
  End
End
Return g;
```

To estimate the SR and GE of an attack with a known key, we do not need the whole vector $\mathbf{g}$ but only the position of the real key in this vector. This ranking cr of the correct key can be computed by Eq (3).

$$cr = 1 + \sum_{a=1}^{A} \prod_{\substack{b=1,\\ b \leq_G a}}^{A} \#\{i \mid i = 1..n,\ (b,i) <_G (a, ck_a)\}\,. \tag{3}$$

There we write ck_a for the index of correct key candidate in sub-attack a ($a = 1..A$), i.e. the correct key is $(k_{ck_1}^{(1)}, \ldots, k_{ck_A}^{(A)})$, we write $(a,i) <_G (a',i')$ if (a,i) appears before (a',i') on list G and we write $a <_G b$ if $(a, ck_a) <_G (b, ck_b)$ i.e. if the correct index of sub-attack a appears before the correct index of sub-attack b on list G.

A.3 The Optimal Sorting Algorithm

The optimal sorting algorithm (in Table 5) outputs the full key candidates based on their monotonically non-increasing sum (for $a = 1..A$) of normalized sub-SCA results $rr_i^{(a)}$.

The algorithm works by creating a sub-key-specific set of candidates L sorted by decreasing SCA value. Next, a key candidate indexes set H is initialized with the best candidate, which by definition consists of the top sub-key in each $L^{(a)}$.

The set H is now iteratively updated by first removing the candidate h with the highest sum and adding the corresponding key to $\mathbf{g}$. The candidate h is now expanded to all its successors, represented by $E(h)$. This set contains for each sub-key the next best candidate. The set $E(h)$ contains A elements unless all n

Table 5. The optimal sorting algorithm

INPUT: Sub-key candidates $k_i^{(a)}$ and normalized maximal SCA peaks $rr_i^{(a)}$ where $a = 1..A$, $i = 1..n$, A is the number of sub-attacks performed and n is the number of sub-key candidates per sub-attack.
OUTPUT: A sorted list of full key candidates **g**.
For each $a = 1..A$ let $L^{(a)}$ be a list of candidate indexes i sorted in descending order of rr_i^a $(i = 1..n)$;
Let $H = \{(1, \ldots, 1)\}$;
Define $E(i_1, \ldots, i_A) = \{(i_1, \ldots, i_{a-1}, i_a + 1, i_{a+1}, \ldots, i_A) \mid a = 1, \ldots, A,\ i_a + 1 \leq n\}$;
Define $c(i_1, \ldots, i_A) = \sum_{a=1}^{A} rr^{(a)}_{L[i_a]}$;
While $\lvert H \rvert > 0$ do
Let $h = (i_1, \ldots, i_A)$ be such that $c(h) = \max\{c(h') \mid h' \in H\}$;
Let $H := H \cup E(h) \backslash h$;
Append $(k^{(1)}_{L[i_1]}, \ldots, k^{(A)}_{L[i_A]})$ to **g**;
End
Return **g**;

candidates for a sub-key have already been tried. Next, $E(h)$ is added to the set H.

Note that H is a set, and can therefore not contain duplicate items. Because of the construction of the search, the entire space is guaranteed to be visited; the **g** contains all possible keys without duplicates. By sorting vectors $L^{(a)}$ and incrementally walking through the elements, we also guarantee a non-increasing sum.

The complexity of this sorting algorithm is $O(N \log N)$, with $N = n^A$ being the number of possible keys. The loop of the algorithm walks though all N candidates. As $\lvert H \rvert < N$, the set query max, insertion and deletion are $O(\log N)$ if implemented using e.g. a red-black tree [4].

We are not aware of an effective method (i.e. polynomial in the key size n) to determine the ranking of the correct key for this algorithm.

B Block Diagram of ECPA

The block diagram of the ECPA attack is plotted in Figure 15.

C Graphical Presentation of the Practical Experiment Results

In this section we show the plotting of the attack results from the physical experiments described in Section 5, where a DES hardware implementation and an AES software implementation were attacked by both ECPA and CPA.

In the experiment on the DES implementation, the same set of 23,000 power traces were used in both attacks to reveal the sub-keys used in the first encryption

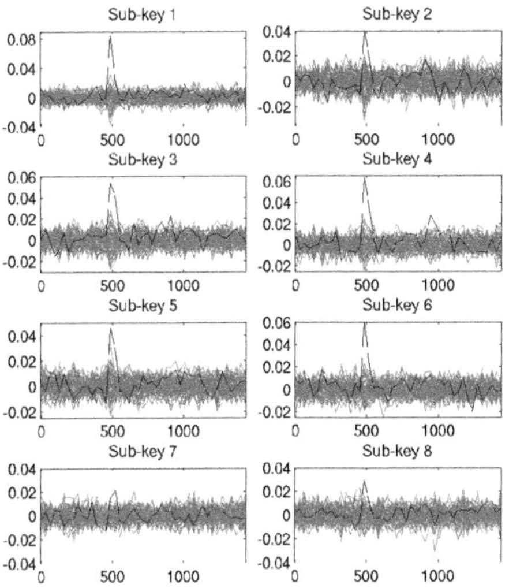

Fig. 13. CPA result of a DES implementation: x-axis is time (ns), y-axis is correlation

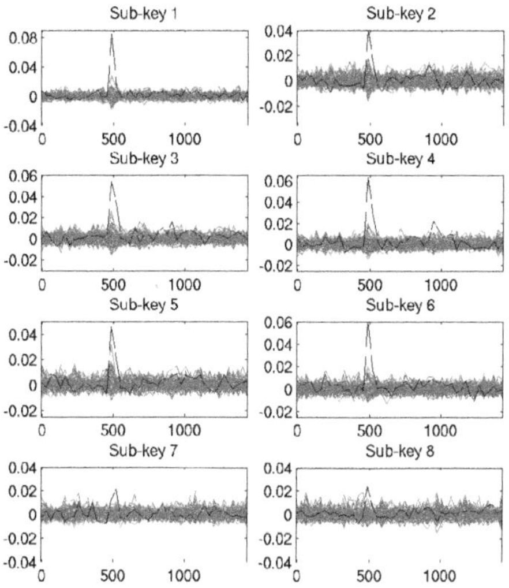

Fig. 14. ECPA result of a DES implementation: x-axis is time (ns), y-axis is correlation

round. Figures 13 and 14 show the results of the attacks. Every graph in these figures shows the results of 64 sub-key candidates that were involved in one of the S-box substitutions. In case of the AES experiment, 110 power traces were used to reveal the first round key of an AES encryption. Figures 16 and 17 show the results of the attacks for all key candidates and a selected range of samples in time, where each graph corresponds to one key byte.

In all the graphs shown in this section, the black curves correspond to the correct key candidates and the gray curves correspond to the incorrect key candidates. One can observe that for every attacked sub-key the gray band formed by the ghost peaks is reduced by ECPA compared to CPA.

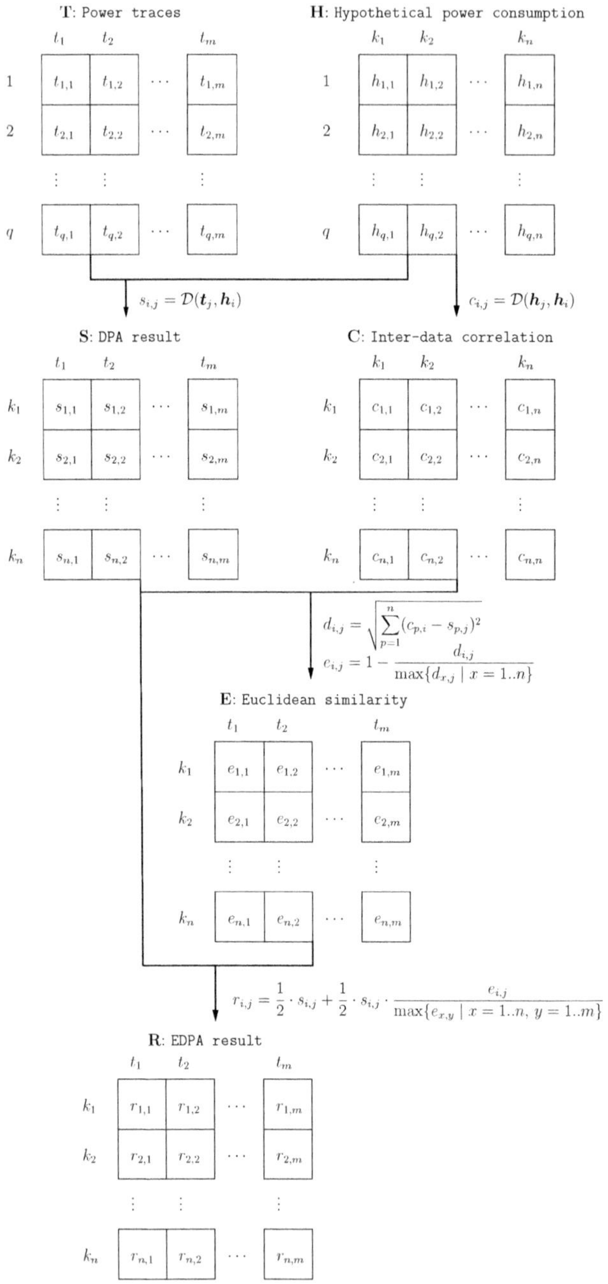

Fig. 15. Block diagram illustrating the last steps of an ECPA attack

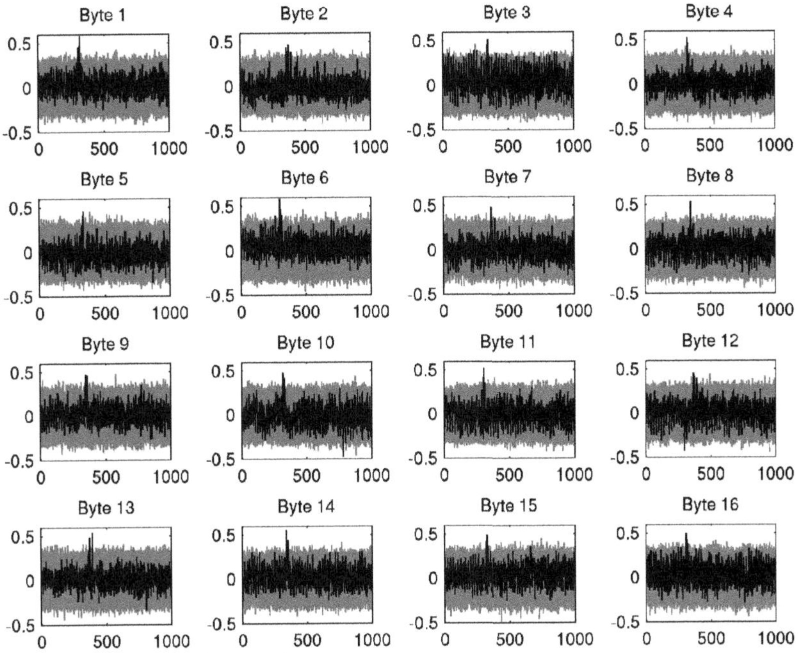

Fig. 16. CPA result on AES: x-axis is time (μs), y-axis is correlation

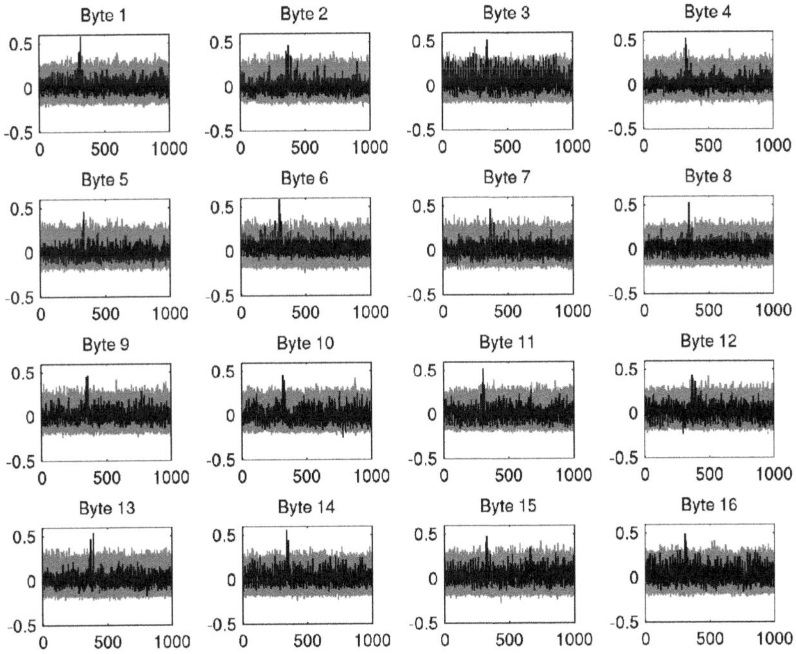

Fig. 17. ECPA result on AES: x-axis is time (μs), y-axis is correlation

Affine Masking against Higher-Order Side Channel Analysis

Guillaume Fumaroli[1], Ange Martinelli[1],
Emmanuel Prouff[2], and Matthieu Rivain[3]

[1] Thales Communications
{guillaume.fumaroli,jean.martinelli}@fr.thalesgroup.com
[2] Oberthur Technologies
e.prouff@oberthur.com
[3] CryptoExperts
matthieu.rivain@cryptoexperts.com

Abstract. In the last decade, an effort has been made by the research community to find efficient ways to thwart side channel analysis (SCA) against physical implementations of cryptographic algorithms. A common countermeasure for implementations of block ciphers is Boolean masking which randomizes the variables to be protected by the bitwise addition of one or several random value(s). However, advanced techniques called *higher-order SCA* attacks exist that overcome such a countermeasure. These attacks are greatly favored by the very nature of Boolean masking. In this paper, we revisit the *affine masking* initially introduced by Von Willich in 2001 as an alternative to Boolean masking. We show how to apply it to AES at the cost of a small timing overhead compared to Boolean masking. We then conduct an in-depth analysis pinpointing the leakage reduction implied by affine masking. Our results clearly show that the proposed scheme provides an excellent performance-security trade-off to protect AES against higher-order SCA.

1 Introduction

Side Channel Analysis is a cryptanalytic technique that consists in analyzing the *side channel leakage* (*e.g.* the power consumption, the electromagnetic emanations) produced during the execution of a cryptographic algorithm embedded on a physical device. SCA exploits the fact that this leakage is statistically dependent on the intermediate variables that are processed. Some of these variables are *sensitive* in the sense that they are related to secret data, and recovering information on them therefore enables efficient key recovery attacks [13,2,10].

A very common countermeasure to protect implementations of block ciphers against SCA is to randomize the sensitive variables by masking techniques [3,12]. The principle is to add one or several random value(s) (called *mask(s)*) to every sensitive variable occurring during the computation. Masks and masked variables propagate throughout the cipher in such a way that every intermediate variable is independent of any sensitive variable. This strategy ensures that the

A. Biryukov, G. Gong, and D.R. Stinson (Eds.): SAC 2010, LNCS 6544, pp. 262–280, 2011.

instantaneous leakage is independent of any sensitive variable, thus rendering SCA difficult to perform. The masking can be characterized by the number of random masks used per sensitive variable. A masking that involves d random masks is called a dth*-order masking*. Such a masking can always be theoretically broken by a $(d+1)^{th}$*-order SCA*, namely an SCA that targets $d+1$ intermediate variables at the same time [16,24,20]. However, the noise effects imply that the difficulty of carrying out a dth-order SCA in practice increases exponentially with d [3]. The dth-order SCA resistance (for a given d) is thus a good security criterion for implementations of block ciphers. Unfortunately, only a few higher-order masking schemes exist and they are costly in timings [24,5,21,22].

Instead of looking for perfect security against d^{th}-order SCA, an alternative approach consists in looking for practical resistance to these attacks. It may for instance be observed that the efficiency of higher-order SCA is related to the way the masks are introduced to randomize sensitive variables. Merely all masking schemes proposed in the literature are based on *Boolean masking* where masks are introduced by exclusive-or (XOR). This masking enables securing implementations against first-order SCA quite efficiently, however it is especially vulnerable to higher-order SCA [16,18] due to the intrinsic physical properties of electronic devices.

A first work towards the direction of practical – instead of perfect – security against d^{th}-order SCA has been published by von Willich [27]. It argues that affine masking offers an improved SCA resistance compared to standard first-order masking schemes. However, implementation issues are not taken into account and the paper does not explain how to apply affine masking to usual block ciphers such as AES or DES. Moreover, von Willich defines the affine masking over the vector space $\text{GF}(2)^n$. When defined in such a way, it implies the generation of an invertible $n \times n$ binary matrix, and n scalar products over GF(2) each time a sensitive variable must be masked. Those steps, and especially the scalar products, are very costly when applied in software. A natural idea to deal with this issue is to define the operations over the field $\text{GF}(2^n)$ in place of the vector space $\text{GF}(2)^n$. The addition operation stays unchanged and the field multiplication is a particular case of the matrix product (the security analysis conducted in this paper shows that both operations offer similar SCA resistance). The idea of masking sensitive data with a multiplicative mask in a field structure was first proposed in [1] to protect an AES implementation. However it was shown in [11] that such a masking is insecure since, by nature, it fails in masking the zero value. A similar zero-value first-order flaw was subsequently exploited in [8] to break the linear masking proposed to protect DES in [12]. These works clearly show that letting the zero value unmasked renders a masking scheme insecure.

Our contribution. In this paper, we propose a practical application of affine masking to AES. Namely, we present an implementation of the block cipher such that every 8-bit intermediate result $z \in \text{GF}(256)$ is manipulated under the form $G(z) = r_1 \cdot z \oplus r_0$, where $(r_1, r_0) \in \text{GF}(2^n)^* \times \text{GF}(2^n)$ is a pair of random values generated before each new execution of the algorithm. Our scheme is very efficient as it maintains the same compatibility as Boolean masking (which is a particular case of our scheme for $r_1 = 1$) with the linear transformations of the algorithm. In the second part of the paper, we conduct an in-depth analysis which shows that the joint use of a multiplicative mask with a Boolean mask greatly improves the resistance of the scheme to higher-order SCA. As we argue, the multiplicative mask enables to complicate the relationship between the unmasked data and the leakage while the Boolean mask prevents the zero-value leakage. Our analysis pinpoints the leakage reduction resulting from affine masking as well as its improved higher-order SCA resistance.

Length constraints do not permit us to give all proofs in details. They can be found in the extended version [7] of this paper.

2 Securing AES with Affine Masking

The AES is an iterated block cipher algorithm. It is composed of several *rounds* that operate on a 4×4 array of bytes denoted by $\mathbf{s} = (s_{i,j})_{0 \leq i,j \leq 3}$ and termed the *state*. At the beginning of AES in encryption mode, the state is initialized with the plaintext.

Let us first briefly introduce the outlines of our method. Initially, both the state $\mathbf{s}$ and the master key $\mathbf{k} = (k_{i,j})_{0 \leq i,j \leq 3}$ are masked by applying a randomly generated affine transformation G to each $s_{i,j}$ and $k_{i,j}$. Then, all the original transformations of the cipher are adapted in order to process on and to return affinely masked variables. Should the additive part of the mask cancel out within the computation, a temporary additive mask is introduced in order to avoid any potential zero-value first-order flaw. Eventually, the ciphertext $(c_{i,j})_{0 \leq i,j \leq 3}$ is simply recovered by applying the inverse mapping G^{-1} to each coordinate of the final value of the masked state (which contains the values $G(c_{i,j})$).

In the following section, we explain how the AES implementation can be adapted to securely operate on a state masked by an affine transformation G.

2.1 Affine Masking Applied to AES

A round of the AES is composed of the four following transformations whose description can be found in [7, Section 2.1]: AddRoundKey, SubBytes, ShiftRows and MixColumns. Each of them operates on the state $\mathbf{s}$ and updates it. To distinguish the updated state from the state at input of the transformation, we denote it by $\mathbf{s}' = (s'_{i,j})_{0 \leq i,j \leq 3}$.

To secure the state manipulations thanks to the affine masking countermeasure every manipulation of $\mathbf{s}$ is replaced by a manipulation of $\mathbf{G}(\mathbf{s}) = (G(s_{i,j}))_{0 \leq i,j \leq 3}$. In the following, we assume that G is defined with respect to a pair (r_1, r_0) of random elements of $\mathrm{GF}(256)^* \times \mathrm{GF}(256)$ as:

$$G : x \in \mathrm{GF}(256) \longmapsto r_1 \cdot x \oplus r_0 \in \mathrm{GF}(256) \ .$$

In the sequel, $G(x)$ shall be called the *G-representation* of x and the variables r_1 and r_0 shall be referred to as the *multiplicative mask* and and the *additive mask* respectively.

Let us now explain how the four main AES primitives can be easily adapted to securely operate on a state masked by an affine transformation G. We shall denote by $\mathbf{G}(\mathbf{s}) = (G(s_{i,j}))_{0\leq i,j\leq 3}$ the masked state at the input of each transformation and by $\mathbf{G}(\mathbf{s}') = (G(s'_{i,j}))_{0\leq i,j\leq 3}$ the masked state at the output.

1. To securely compute the G-representation of the output of AddRoundKey from the G-representations of the input state and the round key, each byte $G(s)$ of the state is XOR-ed with the corresponding round key byte $G(k)$ as follows:
$$G(s') \leftarrow (((G(s) \oplus r) \oplus G(k)) \oplus r_0) \oplus r \ .$$
where r is randomly chosen in GF(256). The method is essentially based on the following observation: each masked output byte $G(s')$ can be computed as $G(s') = G(s \oplus k) = G(s) \oplus G(k) \oplus r_0$. A temporary random mask has to be introduced to ensure that the state bytes are always masked affinely and not only linearly.
2. To process the s-box transformations, we propose to use a new look-up table $\tilde{\mathsf{S}}$ that is recomputed at each new AES execution from both G and S such that for every $x \in \mathrm{GF}(256)$, we have:
$$\tilde{\mathsf{S}}[G(x)] = G(\mathsf{S}[x]) \ . \qquad (1)$$
It can be easily checked that processing $\tilde{\mathsf{S}}$ on the G-representation of a byte $s_{i,j}$ results in the G-representation of $s'_{i,j} = \mathsf{S}[s_{i,j}]$. Securing the SubBytes transformation with the affine masking thus simply consists in applying $\tilde{\mathsf{S}}$ to each byte of the state:
$$G(s'_{i,j}) \leftarrow \tilde{\mathsf{S}}[G(s_{i,j})] \ .$$
3. Since we have $\mathsf{ShiftRows}(\mathbf{G}(\mathbf{s})) = \mathbf{G}(\mathsf{ShiftRows}(\mathbf{s}))$ and since ShiftRows operates on each byte separately, it can be directly applied on $\mathbf{G}(\mathbf{s})$ without introducing any flaw:
$$\mathbf{G}(\mathbf{s}') \leftarrow \mathsf{ShiftRows}(\mathbf{G}(\mathbf{s})) \ .$$
4. Since each output byte of MixColumns can be expressed as a linear function of the bytes of the input state over GF(256), it can be checked that we have:
$$\mathsf{MixColumns}(G(s_{0,c}), G(s_{1,c}), G(s_{2,c}), G(s_{3,c})) \\ = (G(s'_{0,c}), G(s'_{1,c}), G(s'_{2,c}), G(s'_{3,c})).$$
This suggests to perform the following steps to securely process MixColumns on the G-representation of the state columns.
$$\begin{cases} tmp \leftarrow r \oplus G(s_{0,c}) \oplus G(s_{1,c}) \oplus G(s_{2,c}) \oplus G(s_{3,c}) \\ G(s'_{0,c}) \leftarrow \mathsf{xtimes}(G(s_{0,c}) \oplus r' \oplus G(s_{1,c})) \oplus tmp \oplus G(s_{0,c}) \oplus r \oplus \mathsf{xtimes}(r') \\ G(s'_{1,c}) \leftarrow \mathsf{xtimes}(G(s_{1,c}) \oplus r' \oplus G(s_{2,c})) \oplus tmp \oplus G(s_{1,c}) \oplus r \oplus \mathsf{xtimes}(r') \\ G(s'_{2,c}) \leftarrow \mathsf{xtimes}(G(s_{2,c}) \oplus r' \oplus G(s_{3,c})) \oplus tmp \oplus G(s_{2,c}) \oplus r \oplus \mathsf{xtimes}(r') \\ G(s'_{3,c}) \leftarrow r \oplus G(s'_{0,c}) \oplus G(s'_{1,c}) \oplus G(s'_{2,c}) \oplus tmp \end{cases}$$

where xtimes denotes a look-up table for a multiplication by some constant in the field GF(256) (see [6] for more details). To ensure that the state bytes are always masked affinely and not only linearly, two temporary random masks $r, r' \in \mathrm{GF}(256)$ have to be introduced. Moreover, the operations above must be processed from left to right.

Finally, since the round key derivation is a composition of the previous transformations, it can be protected by the exact same methods as previously described.

2.2 Time-Memory Trade-Offs

Affine masking requires 32 computations of G in order to mask both the plaintext and the key, and eventually 16 computations of G^{-1} in order to unmask the ciphertext. Field multiplications and inversions involved in affine masking can be efficiently implemented with the well-known log/alog tables technique as long as conditional statements are avoided to thwart timing attacks (see Appendix A in [7] for an example of such an implementation).

Essentially, the processing of $G(s_{i,j})$, $G^{-1}(s_{i,j})$ and $\tilde{S}(s_{i,j})$ may be conducted on-the-fly or may involve pre-computations. Both strategies have different impacts on time and storage costs.

The best time-memory trade-off consists in using two look-up tables for G and $\tilde{\mathsf{S}}$, and in processing one field multiplication and one addition each time G^{-1} must be performed on a state element. The different steps of the look-up table generations of G and $\tilde{S}$ are summarized in Algorithm 1.

Algorithm 1

INPUT: $r_0 \in \mathrm{GF}(256)$, $r_1 \in \mathrm{GF}(256)^*$, and the LUT S for the AES s-box
OUTPUT: The LUTs for G and $\tilde{\mathsf{S}}$

1. **for** $i = 0$ **to** 255 **do**
2. $\quad G[i] \leftarrow r_1 \cdot i \oplus r_0$
3. **for** $i = 0$ **to** 255 **do**
4. $\quad \tilde{\mathsf{S}}[G[i]] \leftarrow G[\mathsf{S}[i]]$
5. **return** $(G, \tilde{\mathsf{S}})$

As G^{-1} is not stored as a look-up table, each byte $\tilde{s}$ of the final output state has to be unmasked using $s \leftarrow r_1^{-1} \cdot (\tilde{s} \oplus r_0)$.

This way of implementing the affine masking requires the storage of 512 bytes for the look-up tables G and $\tilde{\mathsf{S}}$. It also involves 256 multiplications in the field GF(256) and 256 XORs to generate G, while $\tilde{\mathsf{S}}$ is generated using look-ups only. The initial masking of the plaintext and the key only requires 32 table look-ups. Unmasking implies a total of 16 inversions and 16 multiplications in the field GF(256).

As an alternative to the previous algorithm, two variants can be proposed.

1. **First variant.** $\tilde{\mathsf{S}}$, G and G^{-1} are pre-computed using three look-up tables in order to save on-the-fly computations. Masking both the plaintext and

the key involves 32 table look-ups and unmasking the ciphertext involves 16 table look-ups. This method requires the storage of 3×256 bytes for these look-up tables. It also involves 256 multiplications in the field GF(256) to generate G.

2. **Second variant.** This variant involves a single look-up table for $\tilde{\mathsf{S}}$ and performs every other operation on-the-fly. It requires the storage of 256 bytes for this look-up table. It also involves 2×256 multiplications in the field GF(256) to generate $\tilde{\mathsf{S}}$, and 32 multiplications for the initial masking of the plaintext and the key. Unmasking implies a total of 16 inversions and 16 multiplications in the field GF(256).

2.3 Implementation Results

In this section, we compare several AES implementations protected by affine masking, first-order Boolean masking and second-order Boolean masking. The codes are written in assembly language for an 8051-based 8-bit architecture. More details about these countermeasures can be found in the respective papers [15,21,24]. Table 1 lists the timing and memory performances of each implementation.

Table 1. Comparison of AES implementations

Method	Reference	Cycles	RAM (bytes)	ROM (bytes)
Unprotected Implementation				
No Masking	Na.	2×10^3	32	1150
Provably Secure First-Order SCA Resistant Implementation				
First-Order Boolean Masking	[15]	9×10^3	$256 + 35$	1744
Affine Masking (ref. implem.)	This paper	29×10^3	$512 + 37$	2857
Affine Masking (1st var.)	This paper	28×10^3	$768 + 36$	2985
Affine Masking (2nd var.)	This paper	38×10^3	$256 + 37$	3252
Provably Secure Second-Order SCA Resistant Implementation				
Second-Order Boolean Masking	[24]	594×10^3	$512 + 90$	2336
Second-Order Boolean Masking	[21]	672×10^3	$256 + 86$	2215

Table 1 shows that the implementation of AES protected by affine masking is 3.2 to 4.2 times slower than the one protected by first-order Boolean masking, whereas the memory overhead is either +0% (2nd variant) or +100% (reference implementation) or +200% (3rd variant). When compared to the second-order Boolean masking proposed in [24] and [21], the affine masking of AES is 17.7 times faster with the third variant and 20.5 times faster with the first variant.

As every intermediate variable of the computation is affinely masked, we keep a perfect security with respect to first-order SCA. Moreover, as argued in the next section, we significantly increase the resistance of the implementation against higher-order SCA. In view of the implementation performances depicted in Table 1, this rise in security has been obtained at the cost of a very small overhead when compared to the overhead of provably secure second-order Boolean masking.

3 Resistance to Higher-Order SCA

Affine masking is not inherently perfectly secure against higher-order SCA. It can for instance be checked that several pairs of intermediate variables of the scheme proposed in Sect. 2 depend on sensitive variables. We however argue in this section that affine masking is much more resistant than the widely-used Boolean masking. To highlight this statement, we quantify the information leakage reduction provided by affine masking and we study the efficiency of higher-order DPA [16,20] against it. For comparison purposes, we apply the same analysis to Boolean masking. We eventually give the results of several attack experiments in order to check the reliability of our theoretical analysis with respect to practical attack scenarios.

3.1 Leakage of Affine Masking

In what follows, we shall consider that an intermediate variable U_i is associated with a leakage variable L_i representing the information leaking about U_i through side channel. We will assume that the leakage can be expressed as a deterministic *leakage function* φ of the intermediate variable U_i with an independent additive noise B_i. Namely, we will assume that the leakage variable L_i satisfies:

$$L_i = \varphi(U_i) + B_i \ . \tag{2}$$

In the following, we shall call d^{th}*-order leakage* a tuple of d leakage variables L_i corresponding to d different intermediate variables U_i that jointly dependent on some sensitive variable. As already argued in Sect. 2, when an implementation is correctly protected by affine masking (*i.e.* when every sensitive variable is affinely masked), no first-order leakage of sensitive information occurs. This is a consequence of the action of the random additive mask R_0. However, as detailed hereafter, second-order and third-order information leakages do occur in the presence of affine masking.

Second-order leakage. To recover sensitive information when affine masking is applied, one must at least consider the joint leakage of two different intermediate variables U_1 and U_2 that share common masks. Those variables can thus be assumed to satisfy:

$$\begin{cases} U_1 = G(Z_1) = R_1 \cdot Z_1 \oplus R_0 \\ U_2 = G(Z_2) = R_1 \cdot Z_2 \oplus R_0 \end{cases} , \tag{3}$$

where R_1 and R_0 are random variables defined over $\mathrm{GF}(2^n)^*$ and over $\mathrm{GF}(2^n)$ respectively and where Z_1 and Z_2 are sensitive variables. A particular case is $Z_2 = 0$ which amounts to target the pair $(G(Z_1), R_0)$.

In the following, we shall assume that R_1 and R_0 are uniformly distributed over $\mathrm{GF}(2^n)^*$ and over $\mathrm{GF}(2^n)$ respectively and that they are mutually independent of the pair (Z_1, Z_2), and of each other. After denoting by Z the sensitive variable $Z_1 \oplus Z_2$, we obtain the following lemma.

Lemma 1. *The pairs* (U_1, U_2) *and* $(G(Z), R_0)$ *are identically distributed.*

Lemma 1 shows that the second-order leakage corresponding to a pair of sensitive variables (Z_1, Z_2) both affinely masked is equivalent to the the second-order leakage on a sensitive variable $Z = Z_1 \oplus Z_2$ that is affinely masked and on the corresponding additive mask R_0. For this reason, in the following, we shall only consider a second-order leakage corresponding to a pair $(G(Z), R_0)$, with Z being possibly the sum of two sensitive variables. The analysis hereafter shall further make use of the following lemma.

Lemma 2. *The random pair* $\big((L_1, L_2)|Z = z\big)$ *is identically distributed for every* $z \in \mathrm{GF}(2^n)^*$ *and the random pair* $\big((L_1, L_2)|Z = 0\big)$ *has a distinct distribution.*

Lemma 2 shows that the second-order leakage (L_1, L_2) only reveals information about whether Z equals 0 or not (*i.e.* whether Z_1 equals Z_2 or not). Such a leakage can be thought as a *zero-value second-order leakage* analogously to the *zero-value first-order leakage* of multiplicative masking [1,11]. Intuitively, we have the following diagram where each arrow indicates an additional security level.

No countermeasure
1st-*order leakage*

↙ ↘

Boolean masking — 2nd-*order leakage*
Multiplicative masking — *zero-value* 1st-*order leakage*

↘ ↙

Affine masking
zero-value 2nd-*order leakage*

Third-order leakage. To get more information about Z, a natural idea is to exploit (L_1, L_2) together with the leakage L_3 on the multiplicative mask $U_3 = R_1$. Indeed, while the pair (U_1, U_2) only reveals whether Z equals 0 or not, the triplet (U_1, U_2, U_3) does reveal the full value of Z by:

$$Z = U_3^{-1} \cdot (U_1 \oplus U_2) = R_1^{-1} \cdot (G(Z_1) \oplus G(Z_2)). \tag{4}$$

However, the information about the U_i's that leak through the L_i's does not enable a simple recovery as in (4). In fact, we expect that extracting information on Z through side channels is more difficult when affine masking is applied in place of Boolean masking. Indeed, when the mask is introduced by bitwise addition, then each bit of the mask acts on a single bit of the sensitive variable. In this case, every bit of the masked variable depends on a single bit of the mask. Since bits of processed variables usually contribute to the leakage independently, the information leaking about the mask and the information leaking about the masked variable can be efficiently combined to unmask the variable. This can be illustrated in the Hamming weight leakage model (where $\varphi = \mathrm{HW}$) by the important correlation between $\mathrm{HW}(Z)$ and either $|\mathrm{HW}(Z \oplus R_0) - \mathrm{HW}(R_0)|$ or $(\mathrm{HW}(Z \oplus R_0) - n/2)(\mathrm{HW}(R_0) - n/2)$ [16,20]. When a further mask is introduced by multiplication in $\mathrm{GF}(2^n)^*$, the additive mask still prevents from a zero-value first-order leakage (as for multiplicative masking [11]), and the new multiplicative mask ensures that every bit of the masked variable depends on every bit of both the sensitive variable and the multiplicative mask. In this case, it is legitimate to expect that the information leaked by side channel is much more difficult to exploit to recover information about Z. For instance, there is no evident way to combine $\mathrm{HW}(Z \cdot R_1)$ and $\mathrm{HW}(R_1)$ to construct a variable with high correlation with $\mathrm{HW}(Z)$. In order to validate this intuition, we conduct in the next section an information theoretic evaluation of the leakages resulting from affine masking and different kinds of masking.

3.2 Information Theoretic Evaluation

In order to evaluate the information revealed by affine masking leakages (first-order and second-order) we follow the information theoretic approach suggested in [25]. Namely we compute the mutual information between the sensitive variable Z and either the pair of leakages (L_1, L_2) or the triplet of leakages (L_1, L_2, L_3). For comparison purposes, we proceed similarly for Boolean masking and multiplicative masking. We list hereafter the leakages we consider and the underlying leaking variables:

- 2nd-order leakage of 1st-order Boolean masking: $(Z \oplus R_0, R_0)$
- 3rd-order leakage of 2nd-order Boolean masking: $(Z \oplus R_0 \oplus R_0', R_0, R_0')$
- 1st-order leakage of multiplicative masking: $R_1 \cdot Z$
- 2nd-order leakage of multiplicative masking: $(R_1 \cdot Z, R_1)$
- 2nd-order leakage of affine masking: $(R_1 \cdot Z \oplus R_0, R_0)$
- 3rd-order leakage of affine masking: $(R_1 \cdot Z \oplus R_0, R_0, R_1)$

The variables Z, R_0, R_0' and R_1 are assumed to be uniformly distributed (over $\mathrm{GF}(256)$ for the former and over $\mathrm{GF}(256)^*$ for R_1) and mutually independent. For each kind of leakage, we computed the mutual information between Z and the tuple of leakages in the Hamming weight model with Gaussian noise: the leakage L_i related to a variable U_i is distributed according to (2) with $\varphi = \mathrm{HW}$ and $B_i \sim \mathcal{N}(0, \sigma^2)$ (the different B_i's are also assumed to be mutually independent). In this context, the signal-to-noise *ratio* (SNR) of the leakage is defined as $\mathrm{Var}\left[\varphi(U_i)\right]/\mathrm{Var}\left[B_i\right] = 2/\sigma^2$. Fig. 1 shows the mutual information values obtained for each kind of leakage with respect to an increasing noise standard deviation over $[0.1, 4.47]$ (*i.e.* a decreasing SNR over $[\frac{1}{10}, 200]$). These results demonstrate the information leakage reduction implied by the use of affine masking. As expected, affine masking leaks less information than multiplicative masking and first-order Boolean masking for all SNRs. We further observe that affine masking leaks less information than second-order Boolean masking when σ is lower than 2.36, that is when the SNR is greater than 0.36. This first analysis allows us to conclude that affine masking is less leaky than 2nd-order Boolean masking when the amount of noise in the leakage is small. On the other hand, these results illustrate that a 2nd-order SCA security is asymptotically better than a 1st-order SCA security even if the masking relation is more complicated

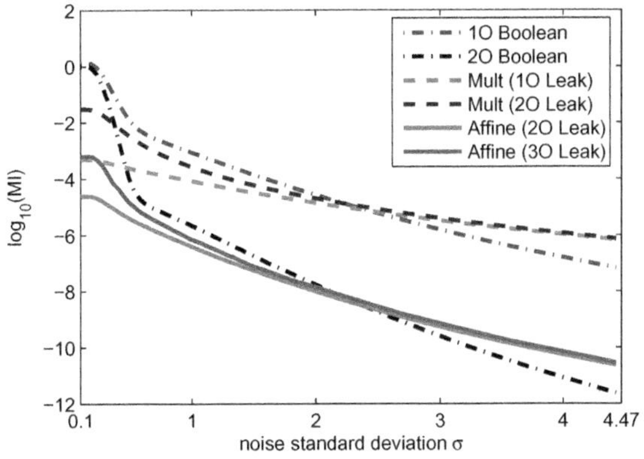

Fig. 1. Mutual information ($\log_{10}$) between the leakage and the sensitive variable over an increasing noise standard deviation

in the latter case. Similarly, we see that for a low noise amount, multiplicative masking is more resistant than 1st-order Boolean masking although it does not thwart 1st-order SCA while Boolean masking does.

Fig. 1 also confirms our intuition regarding the information provided by the leakage on the multiplicative mask. Observing the obtained mutual information for affine masking and for multiplicative masking, we note that the information gained from the leakage on the multiplicative mask is low. This phenomenon amplifies when σ increases and, beyond $\sigma \approx 2$ the distance between the mutual information curves almost vanishes for both kinds of masking. This means that when the noise is sufficiently strong, the leakage on the multiplicative mask does not provide useful information anymore and only the zero-value leakage reveals sensitive information.

In this section, we have quantified the impact of affine masking on the reduction of the information leakage. We will now see to which extent this reduction also applies to the efficiency of side channel attacks on affine masking.

3.3 Higher-Order DPA Evaluation

Let us assume that Z depends on the plaintext and of a subkey $k^\star$, and let us denote by $Z(k)$ the hypothetic value of Z for a guess k on $k^\star$. In a *higher-order DPA* (HO-DPA) [16,20], the attacker tests the guess k by estimating the correlation coefficient $\rho\left[\hat{\varphi}(Z(k)), \mathcal{C}(\mathbf{L})\right]$, where $\mathcal{C}$ is a *combining function* that converts the multivariate leakage $\mathbf{L}$ into a univariate signal and where $\hat{\varphi}$ is a *prediction function* chosen such that $\hat{\varphi}(Z)$ is as much as possible correlated to $\mathcal{C}(\mathbf{L})$. The guess k leading to the greatest correlation in absolute value is selected as key-candidate. In [14], the authors show that the number of traces required to mount a successful DPA attack is roughly quadratic in ρ^{-1} where ρ is the correlation coefficient $\rho\left[\hat{\varphi}(Z), \mathcal{C}(\mathbf{L})\right]$ (that is the expected correlation for the correct key guess). The latter can therefore be used as a metric for the efficiency of a (HO-)DPA attack.

The analysis conducted in [20] states that a good choice for $\mathcal{C}$ is the *normalized product combining*:

$$\mathcal{C} : \mathbf{L} \mapsto \prod_i (L_i - \mathrm{E}[L_i]). \tag{5}$$

Although the effectiveness of the normalized product combining has been only studied in [20] in the context of Boolean masking, this combining function stays a natural choice against any kind of masking since $\rho\left[\hat{\varphi}(Z(k)), \mathcal{C}(\mathbf{L})\right]$ is related to the *multivariate correlation*[1] between $\hat{\varphi}(Z(k))$ and every coordinate of $\mathbf{L}$ [26]. Besides, in the presence of (even little) noise in the side-channel leakage, the HO-DPA with normalized product combining is nowadays the most efficient unprofiled attack against Boolean masking in the literature (see for instance [20,26,22]). For those reasons, it is natural to study how efficient is a HO-DPA with normalized product combining against affine masking compared to Boolean masking.

In [20], it is also shown that the best choice for $\hat{\varphi}$ given $\mathcal{C}$ is:

$$\hat{\varphi} : z \mapsto \mathrm{E}\left[\mathcal{C}(\mathbf{L}) | Z = z\right]. \tag{6}$$

As explained in [20], the attacker may not be able to evaluate $\hat{\varphi}$ without knowing the exact distribution of $\mathbf{L}$ given Z (as in a profiled attack scenario). In a security evaluation context, it however makes sense to assume that the attacker has this ability. As proved in [7, Appendix B], the optimal prediction function $\hat{\varphi}$ computed according to (6) for the zero-value 2nd-order leakage of affine masking is an affine transformation of the dirac function δ_0 defined as[2]:

$$\delta_0(z) = \begin{cases} 1 & \text{if } z = 0 \, , \\ 0 & \text{if } z \neq 0 \, . \end{cases} \tag{7}$$

Therefore, we have $\rho\left[\hat{\varphi}(Z(k)), \mathcal{C}(\mathbf{L})\right] = \pm\rho\left[\delta_0(Z(k)), \mathcal{C}(\mathbf{L})\right]$, that is, the attack performs similarly with $\hat{\varphi}$ and δ_0.

Remark 1. Computing $\rho\left[\delta_0(Z(k)), \mathcal{C}(\mathbf{L})\right]$ amounts to performing a zero-value DPA attack as in [11] but on the combined leakage $\mathcal{C}(\mathbf{L})$. After assuming that $Z(k)$ is uniformly distributed over $\mathrm{GF}(2^n)$, it can indeed be checked that the covariance between $\delta_0(Z(k))$ and $\mathcal{C}(\mathbf{L})$ (which is the discriminating element in the correlation) equals $\frac{2^n-1}{2^n}\mathrm{E}\left[\mathcal{C}(\mathbf{L})|Z(k) \neq 0\right] - \frac{1}{2^n}\mathrm{E}\left[\mathcal{C}(\mathbf{L})|Z(k) = 0\right]$.

When the leakage satisfies (2) with $\varphi = \mathrm{HW}$ and $B_i \sim \mathcal{N}(0, \sigma^2)$ (*i.e.* when the Hamming weight leakage model with Gaussian noise is assumed), it is shown in

[1] What we call multivariate correlation here is the straightforward generalization of the correlation coefficient to more than two variables (see [26]).

[2] This is actually true whatever the leakage function and noise distribution as a direct consequence of Lemma 2.

[7, Appendix B] that the coefficient ρ_{aff} obtained for the zero-value second-order leakage of affine masking satisfies:

$$\rho_{\text{aff}} = \frac{n}{(4\sigma^2 + n)\sqrt{2^n - 1}}, \tag{8}$$

where n is the bit-size of Z.

We also computed the correlation coefficient corresponding to the 3rd-order leakage of affine masking. We did not obtained explicit formulae for this coefficient but we observed for several values of n and σ that it was always lower that ρ_{aff}. This suggests that HO-DPA with normalized product combining works better against the 2nd-order leakage of affine masking than against the 3rd-order one. From our analysis, we therefore concluded that ρ_{aff} not only quantifies the resistance of affine masking against 2nd-order DPA, but also that against HO-DPA in general.

Regarding Boolean masking, it has been shown in [23] that the correlation ρ_{bool} corresponding to HO-DPA with normalized product combining against d^{th}-order Boolean masking satisfies (in the Hamming weight model):

$$\rho_{\text{bool}} = (-1)^d \frac{\sqrt{n}}{(n + 4\sigma^2)^{\frac{d+1}{2}}} . \tag{9}$$

Let us denote by N_{aff} (resp. N_{bool}) the number of leakage measurements for a successful attack on affine masking (resp. Boolean masking). Since, according to [14], N_{aff} and N_{bool} are respectively roughly quadratic in the values of the inverse of the correlation coefficients, the *ratio* $\frac{N_{\text{aff}}}{N_{\text{bool}}}$ satisfies:

$$\frac{N_{\text{aff}}}{N_{\text{bool}}} \approx \left(\frac{\rho_{\text{bool}}}{\rho_{\text{aff}}}\right)^2 = \frac{2^n - 1}{n} \left(\frac{1}{n + 4\sigma^2}\right)^{1-d} . \tag{10}$$

Let ν denote the value $\frac{2^n-1}{n}\left(\frac{1}{n+4\sigma^2}\right)^{1-d}$. In view of (10), affine masking is more resistant to HO-DPA than d^{th}-order Boolean masking if and only if $\nu \geq 1$. Comparing the resistance of Boolean masking and affine masking against HO-DPA thus amounts to study when $\nu \geq 1$ is satisfied. Let us study this inequality with respect to d:

- When $d = 1$, we have $\nu \geq 1$ for all $n \geq 1$ whatever σ. We deduce that affine masking is more resistant to HO-DPA than first-order Boolean masking for all SNRs. Moreover, from (10), we expect that HO-DPA against first-order Boolean masking required around 32 times more leakage measurements than against affine masking whatever σ.
- For $d = 2$, $\nu \geq 1$ if and only if $\sigma^2 \leq (2^n - n^2 - 1)/4n$. This implies that for the case of AES where $n = 8$, affine masking is more resistant to HO-DPA than 2nd-order Boolean masking if $\sigma \leq 2.44$, which corresponds to a SNR greater than 0.335.
- For $d \geq 3$, ν is always smaller than 1 for every $n \geq 1$. Affine masking is hence less resistant to HO-DPA than 3rd-order Boolean masking for all SNRs.

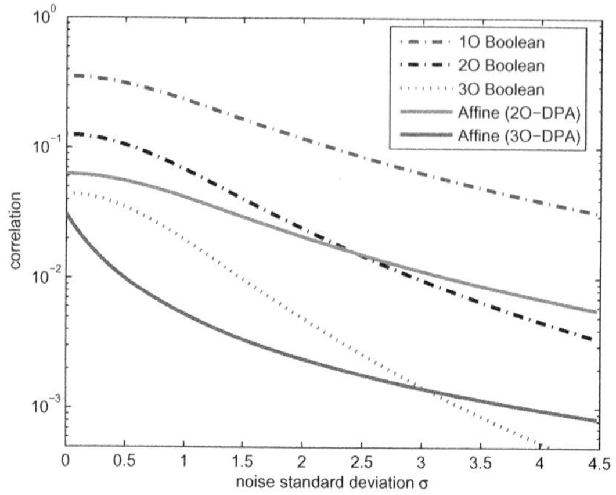

Fig. 2. Correlation values with respect to σ (logarithmic scale)

Eventually Fig. 2 plots the correlation values ρ_{bool} for $d \in \{1, 2, 3\}$, ρ_{aff} (2O-DPA against affine masking) as well as the correlation values obtained for the third-order DPA against affine masking. It illustrates the fact that the correlation corresponding to the 3rd-order leakage of affine masking is always lower than that corresponding to the 2nd-order leakage of affine masking. Moreover and as expected, it shows that the coefficient ρ_{aff} is always lower than ρ_{bool} for $d = 1$, always greater than ρ_{bool} for $d = 3$, and lower than ρ_{bool} $d = 2$ only when $\sigma \leq 2.44$.

3.4 Attack Experiments

In order to confront the theoretical analyses conducted in the previous sections to practice, we performed several attack experiments. In a first place, we applied several side-channel distinguishers to leakage measurements simulated in the Hamming weight model with Gaussian noise. We not only applied (HO)-DPA, but also two other kinds of attacks, namely (higher-order) *Mutual Information Analysis* (MIA) and *Template Attacks* (TA). We chose to test these three side-channel distinguishers against the different kinds of masking firstly because they are the most widely used in the literature, and secondly because they represent a brand spectrum of adversary capabilities. As already mentioned, HO-DPA with normalized product combining is the most efficient unprofiled attack against Boolean masking. On the other hand HO-MIA does not rely on a specific combining function, which is of interest for a fair comparison between Boolean and affine masking. Eventually, assuming that the adversary's templates are perfect, template attacks are the best possible attacks and hence they give the maximal security level reached by each kind of masking. Our methodology enabled us to observe how the different attacks perform against affine masking and to compare its resistance with that of the Boolean/multiplicative masking for different

SNRs. Afterward, we performed some attacks against real power consumption measurements of smart-card implementations in order to check our observations in a real-world context.

Attack simulations. The leakage measurements have been simulated as samples of the random variables L_i defined according to (2) with $\varphi = \mathrm{HW}$ and $B_i \sim \mathcal{N}(0, \sigma^2)$ (the different B_i's are also assumed independent). For all the attacks, the sensitive variable Z was chosen to be an AES s-box output of the form $\mathsf{S}(X \oplus k^\star)$ where X represents a varying plaintext byte and $k^\star$ represents the key byte to recover.

Side-channel distinguishers. We applied higher-order DPA such as described in Sect. 3.3 and we also applied higher-order MIA (HO-MIA) and template attacks. In a higher-order MIA [19,9], the correlation coefficient is replaced by the mutual information: the guess k is tested by estimating $\mathrm{I}(\hat{\varphi}(Z(k)); \mathbf{L})$. Since the mutual information is a multivariate operator, this approach does not involve a combining function. In a template attack [4,17], the attacker owns some *templates* of the leakage that he previously acquired during a profiling phase. More precisely, he has some estimations of the probability distributions $(\ell, z) \mapsto \Pr[\mathbf{L} = \ell | Z = z]$. Based on those estimations, the attacker tests a guess k by estimating the likelihood $\Pr[k^\star = k | \mathbf{L}, X]$.

Target variables. Each attack was applied against the leakages of affine masking, multiplicative masking and Boolean masking. The target variables are those listed in Sect. 3.2 for Z being $\mathsf{S}(X \oplus k^\star)$.

Prediction functions. For each (HO-)DPA, we chose $\hat{\varphi}$ to be the optimal prediction function (6). As explained in Sect. 3.3, this leads us to select the dirac function δ_0 in the attacks against the zero-value 2nd-order leakage of affine masking (resp. the zero-value 1st-order leakage of multiplicative masking) and, according to [23], to select the Hamming weight function in the attacks against Boolean masking of any order.

For the (HO-)MIA attacks, we chose $\hat{\varphi}$ such that it maximizes the mutual information $\mathrm{I}(\hat{\varphi}(Z(k)); \mathbf{L})$ for $k = k^\star$ while ensuring discrimination (*i.e.* the mutual information must be lower for $k \neq k^\star$). As a direct consequence of Lemma 2, we chose $\hat{\varphi} = \delta_0$ to attack the zero-value 2nd-order leakage. Naturally, we did the same choice for the zero-value 1st-order leakage of multiplicative masking. For the third-order MIA on affine masking (and second-order MIA on multiplicative masking), $\hat{\varphi}$ was chosen to be the identity function since it maximizes $\mathrm{I}(\hat{\varphi}(Z); \mathbf{L})$. However, for the attack to succeed with such a choice, the target sensitive variable Z must be such that the function $X \mapsto Z = f_{k^\star}(X)$ (where X is the plaintext part involved in Z) is not injective [10,19]. This constrained us to slightly modify the target variables for these attacks. Against affine masking, we targeted an affinely masked s-box output $G(\mathsf{S}(X \oplus k^\star))$ and an affinely masked plaintext byte $G(X')$ (together with the multiplicative mask R_1), which by Lemma 1 yields a non-injective function $(X, X') \mapsto Z = \mathsf{S}(X \oplus k^\star) \oplus X'$. Against multiplicative masking, we targeted the bitwise addition between two s-box outputs, which yields a non-injective function $(X, X') \mapsto Z = \mathsf{S}(X \oplus k^\star) \oplus \mathsf{S}(X' \oplus k^{\star\prime})$. Eventually, every HO-MIA against Boolean masking was performed with $\hat{\varphi} = \mathrm{HW}$ since the distribution of $(\mathrm{HW}(Z \oplus R_0), \mathrm{HW}(R_0))$ only depends on $\mathrm{HW}(Z)$, and therefore $\mathrm{I}(Z; (\mathrm{HW}(Z \oplus R_0), \mathrm{HW}(R_0))) = \mathrm{I}(\mathrm{HW}(Z); (\mathrm{HW}(Z \oplus R_0), \mathrm{HW}(R_0)))$ (the same argument holds for every masking order).

Pdf estimation method. For the (HO-)MIA attacks, we used the histogram estimation method with rule of [10] for the *bin-widths* selection.

Leakage templates. For the template attacks, the attacker's templates were assumed to be perfect. In our context, this means that the attacker is aware of $\varphi = \mathrm{HW}$ and $B_i \sim \mathcal{N}(0, \sigma^2)$ for every i, and he uses this knowledge to evaluate the real probabilities $\Pr[\mathbf{L}|Z]$.

Attack simulation results. Each attack simulation was performed 100 times for various SNR values ($+\infty$, 1, 1/2, 1/5 and 1/10), that is, for several noise standard deviation values (0, $\sqrt{2}$, 2, $\sqrt{10}$ and $2\sqrt{5}$). Table 2 summarizes the number of leakage measurements required to observe a success rate of 90% in retrieving $k^\star$ for the different attacks.

The results presented in Table 2 show the significant gain of security induced by affine masking compared to multiplicative and first-order Boolean masking. Some more specific observations are reported hereafter.

- **Affine masking *versus* multiplicative masking.** In all scenarios, affine masking is more resistant than multiplicative masking. When the SNR decreases, the resistance of affine masking increases faster than that of multiplicative masking. This is a consequence of the fact that affine masking is perfectly secure against first-order attacks which is not the case of multiplicative masking.
- **Affine masking *versus* Boolean masking.** When compared to first-order Boolean masking, a successful HO-DPA requires between 30 and 40 more leakage measurements against affine masking. For low noises (*i.e.* high SNRs), HO-DPA is also less efficient against affine masking than against second-order masking. The tide is turned when noise increases, which corroborates that higher-order masking combined with noise provides good resistance to SCA [3]. These results validate the theoretical analysis done in Sect. 3.3, where it is expected that affine masking is around 32 times more resistant than first-order Boolean masking and more resistant than second-order Boolean masking only when the SNR is greater than 0.335. On the other hand, the results of template attacks confirm that affine masking is always more resistant than first-order Boolean masking, and that it is also more resistant than second-order Boolean masking for high SNRs. It is interesting to note the strong correlation between the information theoretic evaluation of Sect. 3.2 and the efficiency of template attacks. We see that template attacks are more efficient against second-order Boolean masking

Table 2. Number of leakage measurements for a 90% success rate

Attack \ SNR	$+\infty$	1	1/2	1/5	1/10
Unprofiled Attacks against Boolean Masking					
2O-DPA on 1O Boolean Masking	150	500	1500	6000	20 000
2O-MIA on 1O Boolean Masking	100	5000	15 000	50 000	160 000
3O-DPA on 2O Boolean Masking	1500	9000	35 000	280 000	$> 10^6$
3O-MIA on 2O Boolean Masking	160	160 000	650 000	$> 10^6$	$> 10^6$
Unprofiled Attacks against Multiplicative Masking					
1O-DPA on Multiplicative Masking	900	1500	2500	4000	7500
1O-MIA on Multiplicative Masking	700	2500	3500	5500	15000
2O-DPA on Multiplicative Masking	2500	7500	20 000	60 000	220 000
2O-MIA on Multiplicative Masking	4000	35 000	55 000	100 000	200 000
Unprofiled Attacks against Affine Masking					
2O-DPA on Affine Masking	6500	20 000	45 000	170 000	650 000
2O-MIA on Affine Masking	5500	100 000	600 000	$> 10^6$	$> 10^6$
3O-DPA on Affine Masking	$> 10^6$	$> 10^6$	$> 10^6$	$> 10^6$	$> 10^6$
3O-MIA on Affine Masking	100 000	$> 10^6$	$> 10^6$	$> 10^6$	$> 10^6$
Profiled Attacks					
2O-TA on Boolean Masking	20	500	1200	7000	20 000
3O-TA on 2O Boolean Masking	20	8000	35 000	300 000	$> 10^6$
1O-TA on Multiplicative Masking	500	1300	1900	4000	7000
2O-TA on Multiplicative Masking	60	900	1400	4000	8000
2O-TA on Affine Masking	1300	15 000	45 000	200 000	$> 10^6$
3O-TA on Affine Masking	260	15 000	35 000	200 000	10^6

than against affine masking when the SNR is greater than 1/2 (*i.e.* $\sigma < 2$) which corresponds to the situation where the information leakage of affine masking is lower than that of second-order Boolean masking according to Fig. 1. This observation is in accordance with the argumentation of [25] that the mutual information metric is related to the efficiency of template attacks.

- **3rd-order attacks against affine masking.** It can be observed that targeting the multiplicative mask to mount a third-order attack against affine masking does not improve the efficiency of unprofiled attacks. On the contrary, they become clearly inefficient. This is quite natural for the third-order DPA using the product combining since unlike for an additive mask, such a combination is not suitable to remove a multiplicative mask. Therefore, the contribution of the third leakage to the combined leakage mainly acts as a noise, which renders the attack inefficient. For third-order MIA, the efficiency loss may result from the fact that precise estimations of 3-variate densities require significantly more samples than for bivariate densities which slows down the attack efficiency convergence. For template attacks, targeting the multiplicative mask improves the attack efficiency for high SNRs. However when the noise increases the efficiency of 2O-TA and 3O-TA against affine masking become similar. Once again, this corroborates the information theoretic evaluation of Sect. 3.2 which shows that the information provided by the third-order leakage of affine masking get closer to that provided by the second-order leakage as the noise increases.

– **(HO-)MIA *versus* (HO-)DPA.** (HO-)MIA attacks are always less efficient than the corresponding (HO-)DPA. A possible explanation is that the measurements are simulated in the Hamming weight model which is a situation more favorable to DPA attacks than to MIA attacks. A second possible explanation is that the rule proposed in [10] for the bin-widths selection in the MIA is not suitable when targeting affine masking. This point is let for further research.

Practical attacks. In order to confirm our simulation results, we performed several attacks against software implementations of the AES s-box executed on a 8051 microcontroller. Results of these attacks are reported in [7, Figure 5] and corroborate quite well the attack simulations we performed for an SNR equal to 1/2 (which was approximately the observed SNR on the test device).

4 Conclusion

In this paper, we introduced affine masking as an alternative to the commonly used Boolean masking to protect implementations of block ciphers against side channel analysis. The principle is to mask each sensitive variable both additively and multiplicatively in order to complicate the masking relation and therefore achieve better higher-order resistance in practice. We described an affine masking scheme for AES and we provided some implementation results for our scheme. Moreover, we conducted an in-depth analysis which demonstrates that affine masking significantly improves the resistance to higher-order SCA compared to Boolean masking. This analysis together with our implementation tests clearly show that the proposed scheme provides a good performance-security trade-off compared to existing countermeasures.

References

1. Akkar, M.-L., Giraud, C.: An Implementation of DES and AES, Secure against Some Attacks. In: Koç, Ç.K., Naccache, D., Paar, C. (eds.) CHES 2001. LNCS, vol. 2162, pp. 309–318. Springer, Heidelberg (2001)
2. Brier, E., Clavier, C., Olivier, F.: Correlation Power Analysis with a Leakage Model. In: Joye, M., Quisquater, J.-J. (eds.) CHES 2004. LNCS, vol. 3156, pp. 16–29. Springer, Heidelberg (2004)
3. Chari, S., Jutla, C., Rao, J., Rohatgi, P.: Towards Sound Approaches to Counteract Power-Analysis Attacks. In: Wiener, M. (ed.) CRYPTO 1999. LNCS, vol. 1666, pp. 398–412. Springer, Heidelberg (1999)
4. Chari, S., Rao, J., Rohatgi, P.: Template attacks. In: Kaliski Jr., B.S., Koç, Ç., Paar, C. (eds.) CHES 2002. LNCS, vol. 2523, pp. 13–28. Springer, Heidelberg (2003)

5. Coron, J.-S., Prouff, E., Rivain, M.: Side Channel Cryptanalysis of a Higher Order Masking Scheme. In: Paillier, P., Verbauwhede, I. (eds.) CHES 2007. LNCS, vol. 4727, pp. 28–44. Springer, Heidelberg (2007)
6. Daemen, J., Rijmen, V.: The Design of Rijndael. Springer, Heidelberg (2002)
7. Fumaroli, G., Martinelli, A., Prouff, E., Rivain, M.: Affine masking against higher-order side channel analysis (extended version). Cryptology ePrint Archive, Report 2010/523 (2010), `http://eprint.iacr.org/`
8. Fumaroli, G., Mayer, E., Dubois, R.: First-Order Differential Power Analysis on the Duplication Method. In: Srinathan, K., Rangan, C.P., Yung, M. (eds.) INDOCRYPT 2007. LNCS, vol. 4859, pp. 210–223. Springer, Heidelberg (2007)
9. Gierlichs, B., Batina, L., Preneel, B., Verbauwhede, I.: Revisiting Higher-Order DPA Attacks: Multivariate Mutual Information Analysis. Cryptology ePrint Archive, Report 2009/228 (2009), `http://eprint.iacr.org/`
10. Gierlichs, B., Batina, L., Tuyls, P., Preneel, B.: Mutual Information Analysis. In: Oswald, E., Rohatgi, P. (eds.) CHES 2008. LNCS, vol. 5154, pp. 426–442. Springer, Heidelberg (2008)
11. Golić, J., Tymen, C.: Multiplicative Masking and Power Analysis of AES. In: Kaliski Jr., B.S., Koç, Ç., Paar, C. (eds.) CHES 2002. LNCS, vol. 2523, pp. 198–212. Springer, Heidelberg (2003)
12. Goubin, L., Patarin, J.: DES and Differential Power Analysis. In: Koç, Ç.K., Paar, C. (eds.) CHES 1999. LNCS, vol. 1717, pp. 158–172. Springer, Heidelberg (1999)
13. Kocher, P., Jaffe, J., Jun, B.: Differential Power Analysis. In: Wiener, M. (ed.) CRYPTO 1999. LNCS, vol. 1666, pp. 388–397. Springer, Heidelberg (1999)
14. Mangard, S., Oswald, E., Popp, T.: Power Analysis Attacks – Revealing the Secrets of Smartcards. Springer, Heidelberg (2007)
15. Messerges, T.: Securing the AES Finalists against Power Analysis Attacks. In: Schneier, B. (ed.) FSE 2000. LNCS, vol. 1978, pp. 150–164. Springer, Heidelberg (2001)
16. Messerges, T.: Using Second-order Power Analysis to Attack DPA Resistant Software. In: Paar, C., Koç, Ç. (eds.) CHES 2000. LNCS, vol. 1965, pp. 238–251. Springer, Heidelberg (2000)
17. Oswald, E., Mangard, S.: Template Attacks on Masking—Resistance is Futile. In: Abe, M. (ed.) CT-RSA 2007. LNCS, vol. 4377, pp. 243–256. Springer, Heidelberg (2006)
18. Oswald, E., Mangard, S., Herbst, C., Tillich, S.: Practical Second-order DPA Attacks for Masked Smart Card Implementations of Block Ciphers. In: Pointcheval, D. (ed.) CT-RSA 2006. LNCS, vol. 3860, pp. 192–207. Springer, Heidelberg (2006)
19. Prouff, E., Rivain, M.: Theoretical and Practical Aspects of Mutual Information Based Side Channel Analysis. In: Abdalla, M., Pointcheval, D., Fouque, P.-A., Vergnaud, D. (eds.) ACNS 2009. LNCS, vol. 5536, pp. 499–518. Springer, Heidelberg (2009)
20. Prouff, E., Rivain, M., Bévan, R.: Statistical Analysis of Second Order Differential Power Analysis. IEEE Trans. Comput. 58(6), 799–811 (2009)
21. Rivain, M., Dottax, E., Prouff, E.: Block Ciphers Implementations Provably Secure Against Second Order Side Channel Analysis. In: Nyberg, K. (ed.) FSE 2008. LNCS, vol. 5086, pp. 127–143. Springer, Heidelberg (2008)
22. Rivain, M., Prouff, E.: Provably secure higher-order masking of aes. In: Mangard, S., Standaert, F.-X. (eds.) CHES 2010. LNCS, vol. 6225, pp. 413–427. Springer, Heidelberg (2010)

23. Rivain, M., Prouff, E., Doget, J.: Higher-Order Masking and Shuffling for Software Implementations of Block Ciphers. In: Clavier, C., Gaj, K. (eds.) CHES 2009. LNCS, vol. 5747, pp. 171–188. Springer, Heidelberg (2009)
24. Schramm, K., Paar, C.: Higher Order Masking of the AES. In: Pointcheval, D. (ed.) CT-RSA 2006. LNCS, vol. 3860, pp. 208–225. Springer, Heidelberg (2006)
25. Standaert, F.-X., Malkin, T., Yung, M.: A Unified Framework for the Analysis of Side-Channel Key Recovery Attacks. In: Joux, A. (ed.) EUROCRYPT 2009. LNCS, vol. 5479, pp. 443–461. Springer, Heidelberg (2009)
26. Standaert, F.-X., Veyrat-Charvillon, N., Oswald, E., Gierlichs, B., Medwed, M., Kasper, M., Mangard, S.: The world is not enough: Another look on second-order dpa. Cryptology ePrint Archive, Report 2010/180 (2010), http://eprint.iacr.org/
27. von Willich, M.: A technique with an information-theoretic basis for protecting secret data from differential power attacks. In: Honary, B. (ed.) Cryptography and Coding 2001. LNCS, vol. 2260, pp. 44–62. Springer, Heidelberg (2001)

Search on Encrypted Data in the Symmetric-Key Setting

Alexandra Boldyreva

Georgia Institute of Technology, USA
aboldyre@cc.gatech.edu

Abstract. With cloud storage and computing on the rise, the need for searching on encrypted data is becoming more urgent. In this talk we will survey the existing solutions for the problem of searchable encryption in the symmetric-key setting. We will discuss various tradeoffs between functionality, efficiency and security. We will look at several schemes permitting searches of various types, and will discuss their efficiency and security. Finally we will identity some open problems related to the topic.

A. Biryukov, G. Gong, and D.R. Stinson (Eds.): SAC 2010, LNCS 6544, p. 281, 2011.

Preimages for the Tillich-Zémor Hash Function

Christophe Petit* and Jean-Jacques Quisquater

UCL Crypto Group**
Universit catholique de Louvain
Place du levant 3
1348 Louvain-la-Neuve, Belgium
christophe.petit@uclouvain.be, jjq@uclouvain.be

Abstract. After 15 years of unsuccessful cryptanalysis attempts by the research community, Grassl et al. have recently broken the collision resistance property of the Tillich-Zémor hash function. In this paper, we extend their cryptanalytic work and consider the preimage resistance of the function.

We present two algorithms for computing preimages, each algorithm having its own advantages in terms of speed and preimage lengths. We produce theoretical and experimental evidence that both our algorithms are very efficient and succeed with a very large probability on the function parameters. Furthermore, for an important subset of these parameters, we provide a full proof that our second algorithm always succeeds in deterministic cubic time.

Our attacks definitely break the Tillich-Zémor hash function and show that it is not even one-way. Nevertheless, we point out that other hash functions based on a similar design may still be secure.

1 Introduction

The Tillich-Zémor hash function was one of the oldest unbroken cryptographic hash functions in the literature. It was proposed at CRYPTO'94, following the cryptanalysis of a related scheme of Zémor [15,16,14,12]. It received significant cryptanalytic attention over the years [3,5,1,11,10] but although closely related schemes had been completely broken [2,13,9], it remained essentially intact during 15 years.

In August 2009, Grassl et al. introduced a new and very elegant algorithm finding collisions for the Tillich-Zémor hash function [6]. The authors discovered a particular structure in the hash values of *palindromic* messages (messages such that their bitstring representation can be reversed without changing) and exploited their finding with a nice result of Mesirov and Sweet [8] on the Euclidean algorithm applied to polynomials in characteristic 2.

In this paper, we extend the work of Grassl et al. to the problem of finding preimages for the Tillich-Zémor hash function. We first show that a tiny

* Research Fellow of the Belgian Fund for Scientific Research (F.R.S.-FNRS) at Universit catholique de Louvain (UCL).

** Supported by the Interuniversity Attraction Pole (IAP) projet BCrypt.

A. Biryukov, G. Gong, and D.R. Stinson (Eds.): SAC 2010, LNCS 6544, pp. 282–301, 2011.

modification of their algorithm actually provides a second preimage algorithm. Inspired by previous work on a similar hash function [9], we then reduce the problem of finding preimages to any hash value to the problem of precomputing preimages to a few hash values with certain characteristics. Finally, we provide two algorithms for this precomputing part.

Both our precomputing algorithms are very efficient and successful for random choices of the function parameters. Each algorithm has its own advantages resulting from different approaches. The first algorithm produces shorter preimages than the second one and it is therefore more interesting from a practical point of view. On the other hand, the second algorithm is deterministic and it is faster than the first one. It is also more interesting from a theoretical point of view since we have a proof that it always succeeds in deterministic cubic time for an important subset of the function parameters.

The remainder of this paper is organized as follows. In Section 2 we introduce our notations, the Tillich-Zémor hash function, the essential of Grassl et al.'s algorithm, and we briefly sketch out our algorithms. In Section 3, we modify Grassl et al.'s algorithm into a second preimage algorithm. In Section 4, we reduce the preimage problem to a precomputation part. In Sections 5 and 6 we give our two precomputation algorithms. We conclude the paper in Section 7 with a discussion of our results and the security of Tillich-Zémor-like hash functions. Finally, we illustrate our algorithms with a toy example in Appendix A.

2 Preliminaries

2.1 The Tillich-Zémor Hash Function

Let n be a positive integer and let $p(X)$ be an irreducible polynomial of degree n over the field $\mathbb{F}_2$. Let A_0 and A_1 be the following two matrices

$$A_0 := \begin{pmatrix} X & 1 \\ 1 & 0 \end{pmatrix} \text{ and } A_1 := \begin{pmatrix} X & X+1 \\ 1 & 1 \end{pmatrix}$$

that have determinant 1. We call these matrices the *generators* of the Tillich-Zémor hash function. Let $m = m_1 m_2 ... m_k \in \{0,1\}^*$ be the bitstring representation of a message. The Tillich-Zémor hash value of m is defined as

$$H(m_1 m_2 ... m_k) := A_{m_1} A_{m_2} ... A_{m_k} \bmod p(X).$$

2.2 Notations

Let $K := \mathbb{F}_2[X]/(P(X)) \approx \mathbb{F}_{2^n}$. The images of the Tillich-Zémor hash functions are the matrices of the group $SL(2, K)$, that is the group of matrices with elements in K and determinant 1. Let

$$h(m_1 ... m_k) := A_{m_1} A_{m_2} ... A_{m_k}$$

be the Tillich-Zémor hash function without modular reduction. Its images are elements of $SL(2, \mathbb{F}_2[X])$. In this paper, we sometimes identify the elements of K to their unique representatives of degree smaller than n in $\mathbb{F}_2[X]$. To remove any ambiguity when it may appear, we use the symbol $=$ to mean an equality over $\mathbb{F}_2[X]$ and $\equiv$ to mean an equality over K. For $q(X) \in \mathbb{F}_2[X]$, we write q_i for the coefficient of the term of degree i of $q(X)$. Finally, if $m, m' \in \{0,1\}^*$ are two bitstrings, we write mm' for their concatenation.

2.3 Grassl et al.'s Collision Algorithm

Grassl et al. [6] first observed that two messages collide for the Tillich-Zémor hash function if and only if they collide for the following modified function

$$H'(m_1...m_k) := A'_{m_1} A'_{m_2} ... A'_{m_k} \bmod p(X)$$

where

$$A'_0 := A_0 = \begin{pmatrix} X & 1 \\ 1 & 0 \end{pmatrix} \text{ and } A'_1 := A_0^{-1} A_1 A_0 = \begin{pmatrix} X+1 & 1 \\ 1 & 0 \end{pmatrix}.$$

Grassl et al. then observed the following property of palindromic messages. Let h' be the modified Tillich-Zémor hash function without reduction.

Proposition 1. [6] *Let $m \in \{0,1\}^{2k}$ be a palindrome of even length, say $m = m_k...m_1m_1...m_k$. Let $a_{(0)}, ..., a_{(k)}$ be the following polynomials*

$$a_{(i)} = \begin{cases} 1, & \text{if } i = 0; \\ X + m_1 + 1, & \text{if } i = 1; \\ (X + m_i)a_{(i-1)} + a_{(i-2)}, & \text{if } 1 < i \leq k. \end{cases}$$

Then $h'(m) = \begin{pmatrix} a^2 & b \\ b & d^2 \end{pmatrix}$ for $a = a_{(k)}$, $d = a_{(k-1)}$ and some $b \in \mathbb{F}_2[X]$. Moreover, $h'(0m0) + h'(1m1) = \begin{pmatrix} a^2 & a^2 \\ a^2 & 0 \end{pmatrix}$.

From Proposition 1, we see that the square roots of the upper left entries of $h'(m_1m_1)$, $h'(m_2m_1m_1m_2)$, $h'(m_3m_2m_1m_1m_2m_3)$, etc. satisfy a Euclidean algorithm sequence (in reverse order) where each quotient is either X or $X+1$. Those sequences are often called *maximal length sequences for the Euclidean algorithm* or *maximal length Euclidean sequences*, and they have long been a topic of interest in number theory. Mesirov and Sweet [8] showed that, when $a \in \mathbb{F}_2[X]$ is irreducible, there exist exactly two polynomials d such that a, d are the first terms of a maximal length Euclidean sequence. They also provide an algorithm to compute them, which we will give below.

In their collision algorithm, Grassl et al. apply Mesirov and Sweet's algorithm to the irreducible polynomial $a = p(X)$ in order to recover d. The corresponding bit sequence $m_1...m_n$ can be recovered by applying the Euclidean algorithm to a and d. By Proposition 1, we have

$$h'(0m_n...m_1m_1...m_n0) = h'(1m_n...m_1m_1...m_n1) + \begin{pmatrix} a^2 & a^2 \\ a^2 & 0 \end{pmatrix}$$

hence

$$H'(0m_n...m_1m_1...m_n0) \equiv H'(1m_n...m_1m_1...m_n1).$$

2.4 Maximal Length Sequences in the Euclidean Algorithm in $\mathbb{F}_2[X]$

The Mesirov and Sweet's algorithm, as described by Grassl et al., is the following one. To find a maximal length Euclidean sequence starting from a given polynomial $a(X)$ of degree k,

1. Construct a matrix $A \in \mathbb{F}_2^{(k+1)\times k}$ from the $k+1$ polynomials

$$g_0 = 1,$$
$$g_i = X^{i-1} + X^{2i-1} + X^{2i} \bmod a(X), \qquad \text{for } i = 1, 2, ..., k,$$

placing in the ith row of A the coefficients $g_{i,0}, g_{i,1}, ..., g_{i,k-1}$ of the polynomial $g_i(X) = g_{i,0} + g_{i,1}X + ... + g_{i,k-1}X^{k-1}$.
2. Solve the linear system $Au^t = (1, 0, ..., 0, 1)^t$ where $u = (u_1, ..., u_k)$.
3. Compute $d(X)$ by multiplying $a(X)$ by $\sum_{i=1}^{k} u_i X^{-i}$ and taking only the non-negative powers.

Mesirov and Sweet showed in [8] that polynomials d such that a, d are the first terms of a maximal length sequence for the Euclidean algorithm, are in one-to-one correspondence with the solutions of the equation $Au^t = (1, 0, ..., 0, 1)^t$. Moreover, they proved that when a is irreducible, this equation has exactly two solutions.

Maximal length Euclidean sequences are closely connected to the matrices A'_0 and A'_1. If m_i and $a_{(i)}$ are as in Proposition 1, we have

$$\begin{pmatrix} a_{(1)} & a_{(0)} \end{pmatrix} = \begin{pmatrix} 1 & 0 \end{pmatrix} \begin{pmatrix} X+1+m_1 & 1 \\ 1 & 0 \end{pmatrix} = \begin{pmatrix} 1 & 0 \end{pmatrix} A'_{\overline{m_1}}$$

(where $\overline{m_1} := 1 - m_1$) and for $1 < i \leq k$ we have

$$\begin{pmatrix} a_{(i)} & a_{(i-1)} \end{pmatrix} = \begin{pmatrix} a_{(i-1)} & a_{(i-2)} \end{pmatrix} \begin{pmatrix} X+m_i & 1 \\ 1 & 0 \end{pmatrix} = \begin{pmatrix} a_{(i-1)} & a_{(i-2)} \end{pmatrix} A'_{m_i}.$$

Therefore, the first row of any product of A'_0 and A'_1 is the beginning of a maximal length Euclidean sequence. By induction, we have

$$\begin{pmatrix} a_{(k)} & a_{(k-1)} \end{pmatrix} = \begin{pmatrix} 1 & 0 \end{pmatrix} h'(\overline{m_1} m_2 ... m_k). \tag{1}$$

2.5 Ideas behind Our Algorithms

Before going into the details of our algorithms, we provide some intuition behind them. Let m be the palindromic message used in Grassl et al.'s collision attack. In Section 3, we first observe that the hash values of $m0$ and $0m$ have the form $L := \begin{pmatrix} 1 & 0 \\ \alpha & 1 \end{pmatrix}$ and $U := \begin{pmatrix} 1 & \alpha \\ 0 & 1 \end{pmatrix}$ for some $\alpha \in \mathbb{F}_{2^n}$. Since L and U have order 2, we obtain an algorithm finding preimages to the identity matrix, hence a second preimage algorithm for the Tillich-Zémor hash function.

We then observe that the set of matrices $\mathcal{L} := \{L_\alpha := \begin{pmatrix} 1 & 0 \\ \alpha & 1 \end{pmatrix}, \alpha \in K\}$ forms an Abelian subgroup of $SL(2, K)$ that is isomorphic to the additive group $(K, +)$. Finding n matrices L_{α_i} (together with their preimages) such that the set $\{\alpha_i, i =$

$1, ..., n\}$ is a basis of K over $\mathbb{F}_2$, therefore suffices to generate the whole subgroup $\mathcal{L}$. The same holds for the set $\mathcal{U} := \{U_\alpha := \left(\begin{smallmatrix} 1 & \alpha \\ 0 & 1 \end{smallmatrix}\right), \alpha \in K\}$. Moreover, inspired by previous work on a similar function [9], we prove in Proposition 3 that any matrix of $SL(2, K)$ can be written as a small product of A_0 and matrices of the sets $\mathcal{L}$ and $\mathcal{U}$. At this point, it remains to obtain n matrices L_{α_i} and U_{α_i} generating $\mathcal{L}$ and $\mathcal{U}$. We solve this problem in two different ways and obtain two algorithms, each of them having its own advantages but both of them being very efficient and successful.

As observed above, Grassl et al.'s paper indirectly provides one matrix $L \in \mathcal{L}$ after applying Mesirov and Sweet's algorithm to $a = p$. In our first precomputing algorithm, we obtain n different matrices after applying Mesirov and Sweet's algorithm to $a_i = pp'_i$, where p'_i are randomly-chosen small degree polynomials. This idea is quite simple but proving its correctness requires solving two issues. First, Mesirov and Sweet only guarantee the success of their algorithm when applied to an irreducible polynomial. Second, the α_i values obtained by this way should not be restricted to any vectorial subspace of K. In this paper, we extend Mesirov and Sweet's result in Proposition 5 and then argue on the correctness of our algorithm.

In our second precomputing algorithm, we follow a different approach and obtain n matrices recursively from the first one. In particular, we exhibit a sequence of messages with increasing lengths hashing to matrices of the required form, such that the corresponding values α_i satisfy a very simple recurrence. By studying the elements of this recurrence, we identify a subset $I \subset \{1, ..., 2n\}$ such that the corresponding matrices $\{L_{\alpha_i}, i \in I\}$ generate the whole subgroup when n is prime. This important result is proved through Lemma 6, Lemma 7 and Proposition 9. Matrices $\{U_{\alpha_i}, i \in I\}$ and their preimages are recovered at the same time.

Due to the way it constructs matrices L_{α_i} and U_{α_i}, our second precomputing algorithm produces larger preimages than the first one. On the other hand, it is deterministic, faster than the first one, and it is guaranteed to always succeed when parameter n is prime.

3 Second Preimages for Tillich-Zémor Hash Function

The following proposition constructs collisions with the void message from the palindromic messages used in Grassl et al.'s attack.

Proposition 2. *Let* $\begin{pmatrix} a^2 & b \\ b & d^2 \end{pmatrix} = H'(m)$ *with* $a \equiv 0$ *be the modified Tillich-Zémor hash value of some message* $m \in \{0,1\}^*$. *Then*

$$H(0m0m) = H(1m1m) = H(m0m0) = H(m1m1) = I = H().$$

Proof: We have $1 = \det(h'(m)) = a^2d^2 + b^2 \equiv b^2$ hence $b \equiv 1$. By a straightforward computation, we have $H'(0m) = \left(\begin{smallmatrix} 1 & X+d^2 \\ 0 & 1 \end{smallmatrix}\right)$, $H'(m0) = \left(\begin{smallmatrix} 1 & 0 \\ X+d^2 & 1 \end{smallmatrix}\right)$, $H'(1m) = \left(\begin{smallmatrix} 1 & X+1+d^2 \\ 0 & 1 \end{smallmatrix}\right)$, $H'(m1) = \left(\begin{smallmatrix} 1 & 0 \\ X+1+d^2 & 1 \end{smallmatrix}\right)$, and all these matrices have order 2. Finally, we observe that for any $\tilde{m} \in \{0,1\}^*$ such that $H'(\tilde{m}) = I$, we have

$H(\tilde{m}) = A_0 H'(\tilde{m}) A_0^{-1} = A_0 A_0^{-1} = I.$ □

The message m in Proposition 2 can be obtained by applying Mesirov and Sweet's algorithm to $a = p(X)$ as in Grassl et al.'s attack (see Proposition 1). We therefore obtain a message $\tilde{m}$ colliding with the void message for the Tillich-Zémor hash function. A second preimage algorithm is straightforwardly deduced, since for any $m \in \{0,1\}^*$ we have $H(m\tilde{m}) = H(m)$.

4 Preimage Algorithm from a Few Precomputed Preimages

For the remaining of the paper, we define $L_\alpha := \left(\begin{smallmatrix} 1 & 0 \\ \alpha & 1 \end{smallmatrix}\right)$ and $U_\beta := \left(\begin{smallmatrix} 1 & \beta \\ 0 & 1 \end{smallmatrix}\right)$ for any $\alpha, \beta \in K$. In [9], preimages for the LPS hash function (a function similar to Tillich-Zémor, with different matrix generators) were computed by decomposing any matrix into a product of generators and diagonal matrices, a subset of matrices for which computing preimages appeared to be easier. In the case of Tillich-Zémor, the proof of Proposition 2 suggests the following decomposition.

Proposition 3. *Given a preimage of length at most L for every matrix among a set $\mathcal{S} = \{L_{\alpha_i}, U_{\beta_i}, i = 1, ..., n\}$ where $\{\alpha_i, i = 1, ..., n\}$ and $\{\beta_i, i = 1, ..., n\}$ are two basis of K as a vector space over $\mathbb{F}_2$, there is a deterministic algorithm computing preimages of length at most $3nL + 5$ for the Tillich-Zémor hash function, in time $O(n^3)$.*

Proof: We first observe that it is sufficient to have an algorithm with the same characteristics for the modified Tillich-Zémor hash function. Indeed, for any A, B, C, D with $AD + BC = 1$,

$$H(m) = \left(\begin{smallmatrix} A & B \\ C & D \end{smallmatrix}\right) \Leftrightarrow H'(m) = A_0^{-1} \left(\begin{smallmatrix} A & B \\ C & D \end{smallmatrix}\right) A_0.$$

Now, suppose we are given $M = \left(\begin{smallmatrix} A & B \\ C & D \end{smallmatrix}\right)$ with $\det(M) = 1$ and we want to find a preimage of M for the modified Tillich-Zémor function. If $B \neq 0$, it is easily checked that

$$\begin{pmatrix} A & B \\ C & D \end{pmatrix} = \begin{pmatrix} 1 & 0 \\ \alpha & 1 \end{pmatrix} \begin{pmatrix} X & 1 \\ 1 & 0 \end{pmatrix} \begin{pmatrix} 1 & \beta \\ 0 & 1 \end{pmatrix} \begin{pmatrix} X & 1 \\ 1 & 0 \end{pmatrix}^3 \begin{pmatrix} 1 & 0 \\ \gamma & 1 \end{pmatrix}$$

with

$$\begin{cases} \alpha = (DX + X + B)/(XB) \\ \beta = (B + X^3)/X^2 \\ \gamma = (X + B + X^2B + AX)/(XB) \end{cases}$$

while if $B = 0$, we have

$$\begin{pmatrix} A & 0 \\ C & D \end{pmatrix} = \begin{pmatrix} X & 1 \\ 1 & 0 \end{pmatrix} \begin{pmatrix} C & D \\ A + CX & DX \end{pmatrix}$$

and $D \neq 0$, so we may apply the above decomposition to the last matrix.

Since $\{\alpha_i, i = 1, ..., n\}$ and $\{\beta_i, i = 1, ..., n\}$ are two basis of K, we may write $\alpha = \sum_{i \in I_\alpha} \alpha_i$, $\beta = \sum_{i \in I_\beta} \beta_i$ and $\gamma = \sum_{i \in I_\gamma} \alpha_i$, for some $I_\alpha, I_\beta, I_\gamma \subset \{1, ..., n\}$. Moreover, those decompositions can be recovered in time $O(n^3)$ by solving three corresponding linear systems over $\mathbb{F}_2$. Finally, we observe that for any $I \subset \{1, ..., n\}$, we have

$$\begin{pmatrix} 1 & 0 \\ \sum_{i \in I} \alpha_i & 1 \end{pmatrix} = \prod_{i \in I} \begin{pmatrix} 1 & 0 \\ \alpha_i & 1 \end{pmatrix} \quad \text{and} \quad \begin{pmatrix} 1 & \sum_{i \in I} \beta_i \\ 0 & 1 \end{pmatrix} = \prod_{i \in I} \begin{pmatrix} 1 & \beta_i \\ 0 & 1 \end{pmatrix}.$$

Putting together what we have seen so far, we obtain a decomposition of any matrix into at most 5 matrices A_0' and $3n$ matrices from the set $\mathcal{S}$. A preimage is obtained by concatenating the preimages of the corresponding matrices, and the maximal length of this preimage follows. □

Let $\mu_L, \mu_U : \{0,1\}^* \to \{0,1\}^*$ be two transformations on bitstrings defined as follows:

$$\begin{aligned} \mu_L(m_1 m_2 ... m_k) &= m_k ... m_2 \overline{m_1} \overline{m_1} m_2 ... m_k 0; \\ \mu_U(m_1 m_2 ... m_k) &= 0 m_k ... m_2 \overline{m_1} \overline{m_1} m_2 ... m_k. \end{aligned}$$

Lemma 4. *Let $m \in \{0,1\}^*$ such that $\left(\begin{smallmatrix} 1 & 0 \end{smallmatrix} \right) H'(m) = \left(\begin{smallmatrix} 0 & q \end{smallmatrix} \right)$ for some $q \in K$. Then*

$$H'(\mu_L(m)) = \begin{pmatrix} 1 & 0 \\ X+q^2 & 1 \end{pmatrix} \quad \textit{and} \quad H'(\mu_U(m)) = \begin{pmatrix} 1 & X+q^2 \\ 0 & 1 \end{pmatrix}.$$

Proof: Let $m = m_1 ... m_k$ be the bitwise representation of m. According to Equation 1 and Proposition 1 we have $H'(m_k ... m_2 \bar{m}_1 \bar{m}_1 m_2 ... m_k) = \left(\begin{smallmatrix} 0 & b \\ b & q^2 \end{smallmatrix} \right)$. Moreover $b = 1$ since the determinant of any hash value is 1. Multiplying left and right by A_0 we obtain the result. □

Proposition 3 reduces the preimage problem to the problem of precomputing the preimages of some set of matrices. Lemma 4 further reduces the precomputation to find n messages $m_i, i = 1, ..., n$ such that

$$\left(\begin{smallmatrix} 1 & 0 \end{smallmatrix} \right) H'(m_i) = \left(\begin{smallmatrix} 0 & q_i \end{smallmatrix} \right) \text{ for some } q_i \in K \tag{2}$$

and $\{q_i^2 + X \bmod p, i = 1, ..., n\}$ is a basis of K. In Sections 5 and 6, we give two algorithms for finding these messages.

5 First Precomputing Algorithm

As observed in Section 3, we can obtain one message satisfying Equation 2 by applying Mesirov and Sweet's algorithm to $a = p$. In order to obtain more messages satisfying the equation, a natural idea is to apply the algorithm to a small multiple of p. This leads us to the following algorithm.

1. Take R large enough.
2. Construct a set $T = \{\alpha_i, i = 1, ..., n\}$ containing elements of K that are linearly independent over $\mathbb{F}_2$, as well as preimages to L_{α_i} and U_{α_i}. To this aim, start from an empty set T, then until the set contains n elements:
   (a) Generate a random irreducible polynomial p' of degree R.
   (b) Construct a matrix A by applying the first step of Mesirov and Sweet's algorithm to $a = pp'$.
   (c) If $Au^t = (1, 0, ..., 0, 1)^t$ has solutions, compute $\alpha := d^2 + X$ where d is obtained by completing Mesirov and Sweet's algorithm.
   (d) Check whether α is independent of the elements of T; if it is, add it to the list and compute the corresponding preimages.

The algorithm is conceptually simple but it is not a trivial task to prove its correctness. First, Mesirov and Sweet only guarantee the success of their algorithm for irreducible polynomials while in Step 2(b) we apply it to a more general polynomial. Second, the above algorithm succeeds only if it is possible to generate n independent α_i values in Step 2(d). This last condition seems particularly hard to prove given our current understanding of maximal length Euclidean sequences in $\mathbb{F}_{2^n}$.

In Section 5.1 below, we extend Mesirov and Sweet's result and argue that in Step 2(c) of our algorithm, the system $Au^t = (1, 0, ..., 0, 1)^t$ has solutions with a probability ρ at least 1/2 on average. In Section 5.2, we provide intuitive arguments and experimental evidence showing that if R is $O(\log n)$, the loop of Step 2 must only be repeated $O(n)$ times. Since each loop requires solving at most two linear systems of size n, we expect the whole algorithm to run in probabilistic $O(n^4)$ time.

All the messages constructed by this algorithm have length exactly $R + n$. These messages can be used in Lemma 4 and Proposition 3 to compute preimages of length $O(n^2 + nR) \approx O(n^2)$ for any matrix.

5.1 Mesirov and Sweet's Algorithm for $a = pp'$

In this section, we argue that for a parameter p chosen at random, the probability that $Au^t = (1, 0, ..., 0, 1)^t$ has solutions in Step 2(c) of our algorithm is $\rho \approx 1/2$. Let us consider the arithmetic sequence

$$1 + p + \ell X(X+1)p, \qquad \ell \in \mathbb{F}_2[X], \qquad \deg(\ell) \leq R - 1.$$

For any $\ell \in \mathbb{F}_2[X]$, let $N(\ell)$ be the number of distinct irreducible polynomials of degree R in the factorization of $1+p+\ell X(X+1)p$. Let $N_0 := \sum_{\deg(\ell) \leq R-2} N(\ell)$ and $N_1 := \sum_{\deg(\ell)=R-1} N(\ell)$. Although a priori there may exist some R and p such that $N_0 \approx 0$, for most values R and random polynomials p it seems reasonable to expect $N_0 \approx N_1$. In the following, we show that the probability that $Au^t = (1, 0, ..., 0, 1)^t$ has solutions is at least $\frac{N_0}{N_0+N_1}$, hence for a parameter p chosen at random we expect to have ρ at least equal to 1/2.

By simple linear algebra the system $Au^t = (1, 0, ..., 0, 1)^t$ has solutions if both 1) the first row of A is a linear combination of its last row and some other rows and 2) the last row of A is not a linear combination of its middle rows. In other terms,

1. There exists $v = (v_0, ..., v_{n+R}) \in \mathbb{F}_2^{(n+R+1)\times 1}$ such that $vA = 0$ and $v_0 = v_{n+R} = 1$.
2. For any $w = (w_0, ..., w_{n+R}) \in \mathbb{F}_2^{(n+R+1)\times 1}$ such that $wA = 0$ and $w_0 = 0$, we have $w_{n+R} = 0$.

Following Mesirov and Sweet [8], let us consider the following equations in the (polynomial) variables $r(X)$ and $s(X)$:

$$r(X) + Xr(X)^2 + X^2r(X)^2 = 1 \bmod a(X), \tag{3}$$
$$s(X) + Xs(X)^2 + X^2s(X)^2 = 0 \bmod a(X). \tag{4}$$

Remembering the definition of A, we see that $Au^t = (1, 0, ..., 0, 1)^t$ has solutions if

1. For some $r(X) = r_{n+R-1}X^{n+R-1} + ... + r_1X + r_0$ solution to Equation 3, we have $r_{n+R-1} = 1$.
2. For any $s(X) = s_{n+R-1}X^{n+R-1} + ... + s_1X + s_0$ solution to Equation 4, we have $s_{n+R-1} = 0$.

Since X does not divide $a = pp'$, it must divide $a+1$. The polynomial $(a+1)/X$ has degree $n + R - 1$ and is a solution to Equation 3; it therefore satisfies the first condition. Equation 4 has four solutions s_{00}, s_{01}, s_{10} and s_{11} characterized as follows:

$$\begin{cases} s_{00} = 0 \bmod p, \\ s_{00} = 0 \bmod p'; \end{cases} \qquad \begin{cases} s_{10} = 0 \bmod p, \\ 1 + X(X+1)s_{10} = 0 \bmod p'; \end{cases}$$

$$\begin{cases} 1 + X(X+1)s_{01} = 0 \bmod p, \\ s_{01} = 0 \bmod p'; \end{cases} \qquad \begin{cases} 1 + X(X+1)s_{11} = 0 \bmod p, \\ 1 + X(X+1)s_{11} = 0 \bmod p'. \end{cases}$$

Clearly, $s_{00} = 0 \bmod a$. Since $X+1$ does not divide $a = pp'$, it must divide $a+1$. The polynomial $(a+1)/X(X+1)$ has degree $n + R - 2$ and is a solution to Equation 4. Reducing it modulo p and p', we see that $(a+1)/X(X+1) = s_{11}$. As Equation 4 is homogeneous, its solutions form a vector space, hence $s_{01} = s_{10} + s_{11}$. Since the coefficient $n + R - 1$ of s_{11} is zero, the coefficient $N + R - 1$ of s_{01} and s_{10} are equal. Using Chinese Remainder Theorem, we have

$$s_{10} = \left[(X(X+1)p')^{-1} \bmod p\right] p'$$

hence the coefficient $N + R - 1$ of s_{10} is equal to the coefficient $N - 1$ of $(X(X+1)p')^{-1} \bmod p$. We have proved the following proposition that extends Mesirov and Sweet's result on irreducible polynomials to polynomials with two distinct nonlinear irreducible factors:

Proposition 5. *Let p, p' be nonlinear irreducible polynomials and let $a = pp'$. If*

$$\deg\left(\left[X(X+1)p'\right]^{-1} \bmod p\right) \leq \deg(p) - 2.$$

then the corresponding Mesirov and Sweet system $Au^t = (1, 0, ..., 0, 1)^t$ has solutions.

Let $y := \left[X(X+1)p'\right]^{-1} \bmod p$. By definition, we have

$$yX(X+1)p' = 1 + kp$$

for some unique $k \in \mathbb{F}_2[X]$. As $\deg(y) \leq N-1$, we have $\deg(k) \leq R+1$. We easily see that $X(X+1)$ divides $1+kp$ if and only if $k = 1 + X(X+1)\ell$ for some $\ell \in \mathbb{F}_2[X]$ with $\deg(\ell) \leq R-1$. Therefore for any p' (randomly generated in our algorithm), there exists exactly one polynomial ℓ with $\deg(\ell) \leq R-1$ such that

$$yX(X+1)p' = 1 + p + X(X+1)\ell p.$$

If $\ell \neq 0$, then by Proposition 5, the system $Au^t = (1, 0, ..., 0, 1)^t$ has solutions if $\deg(\ell) = \deg(y) + R - \deg(p) \leq R - 2$. For $\ell = 0$ we have $\deg(y) = \deg(p) - 2 - R$ which satisfies the condition of Proposition 5. Defining N_0 and N_1 as above, N_0 (respectively N_1) is precisely the number of irreducible polynomials p' of degree R such that the corresponding polynomial ℓ satisfies $\deg(\ell) \leq R-2$ (respectively $\deg(\ell) = R-1$). We finally obtain $\rho \geq \frac{N_0}{N_0+N_1}$.

Remark. It is possible to remove the irreducibility condition on p' in Step 2(a) of our algorithm. However, the probability that Mesirov and Sweet system $Au^t = (1, 0, ..., 0, 1)^t$ has solutions in Step 2(c) is maximal when p' is irreducible, as can be seen by further extending Proposition 5.

5.2 Correctness of the Algorithm

Even after finding many different α values in Step 2(c), our algorithm could still fail if all these values belonged to a vector subspace of K. However, the algorithm will always succeed if the following hypothesis holds.

Hypothesis 1. *The polynomials d resulting from applying the Mesirov and Sweet's algorithm to $a = pp'$ (with p and p' irreducible, p fixed and p' random), form a set without any particular structure. In particular, this set can be thought of as a random set of polynomials of degree $n + R - 1$.*

If each d value constructed can be considered as a random polynomial of degree $n + R - 1$, then the corresponding value $\alpha := d^2 + X \bmod p$ can be considered as a random polynomial of degree at most $n - 1$. In that case, every new value α is (very) likely to be independent from the previous one: if there are already i independent elements in T, the new value will be independent from the previous ones with a probability $1 - 2^{i-n}$. After generating a little more than n polynomials d, our algorithm will be likely to succeed in finding n linearly independent

α values. By the analogue of the prime number theorem for irreducible polynomials over a finite field, the number of irreducible polynomials p' of degree R is roughly $2^R/R$. By our analysis in Section 5.1, the Mesirov and Sweet's system has solutions for at least one half of the corresponding polynomials $a = pp'$. Therefore, we must have

$$\frac{2^R}{R} \geq 2n. \tag{5}$$

Assuming Hypothesis 1 is correct, taking a value $O(\log n)$ for R in Step 1 should be sufficient to guarantee the success of our algorithm.

Hypothesis 1 seems very likely to hold. Of course, there is a strong relationship between two polynomials a and d such that all their partial quotients are X or $X+1$. However, this relation does not seem to restrict d to any vector subspace of K, even if a is only chosen among the multiples of p. Today, the "simplest" relation known to hold between two consecutive terms of a maximal length Euclidean sequence is precisely given by the Mesirov and Sweet's algorithm, and it does not seem to impose such a restriction.

A theoretical analysis of our algorithm based on firmer grounds than Hypothesis 1 would be very valuable, but given current understanding of maximal length Euclidean sequences in $\mathbb{F}_{2^n}$, we believe that it is far from reach. To prove the efficiency of our algorithm, we therefore complete our arguments with experimental results. In our experiments, we took p the shortest irreducible polynomial of degree n, that is the polynomial $p = X^n + ... + p_0$ for which $\sum p_i 2^i$ is minimal. For some values of n between 5 and 2039, we tried different values of R until we found one that was large enough. The results are given in Figure 1.

n	R	n	R	n	R
5	5	67	11	257	13
7	7	73	11	277	13
11	8	83	11	307	13
13	9	97	11	331	14
17	9	103	12	353	14
19	9	109	12	379	14
23	9	127	12	401	14
29	9	137	12	449	14
31	10	149	12	499	14
37	10	167	13	607	15
41	10	191	13	1021	15
47	10	211	13	2039	16
59	11	233	13		

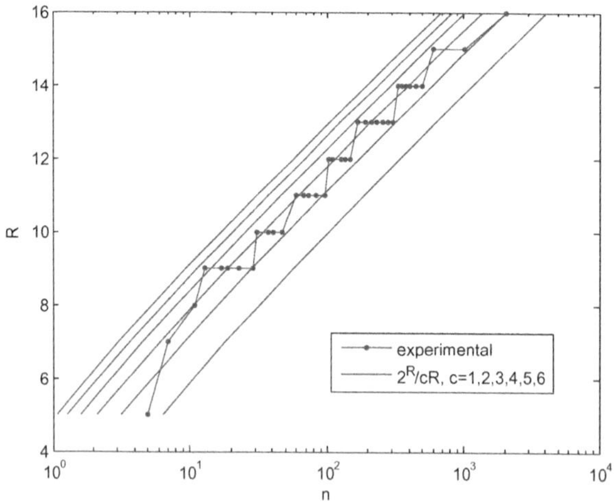

Fig. 1. Minimal value R for different values n and the "shortest" polynomials of degree n. The points on the staircase-like curve are experimental results. The other curves are $n = \frac{2^R}{cR}$ for $c = 1, 2, 3, 4, 5, 6$.

The algorithm always succeeded with a value R satisfying

$$\frac{2^R}{R} \geq 5n,$$

that is slightly larger than predicted by Equation 5 but still consistent with the expected $R = O(\log n)$. When $n \geq 17$, it always succeeded as long as $\frac{2^R}{R} \geq 4n$. The last points of Figure 1 for $n = 1021$ and $n = 2039$ are very close to the bound of Equation 5. The results confirm the analysis performed in this section and in the previous one. In Appendix B, we describe additional experiments performed on randomly chosen polynomials. All the results obtained are also consistent with our analysis.

6 Second Precomputing Algorithm

Our first precomputing algorithm is very efficient both in theory and in practice, but its correctness must likely rely on some *ad hoc* hypothesis. In this section, we provide an alternative algorithm precomputing messages of length bounded by n^2, resulting in preimages of length $O(n^3)$ after applying Lemma 4 and Proposition 3. On the one hand this second algorithm is worse than the first one since it produces larger preimages, but on the other hand it is deterministic and it runs in time $O(n^3)$, much faster than the first one. More importantly from a theoretical point of view, we provide a proof that it always succeeds when n is prime, and strong evidence that it has a very large probability of success when n is reasonably large and the polynomial p is chosen at random.

The Mesirov and Sweet's algorithm applied to p is guaranteed to succeed since p is irreducible. It provides a polynomial q of degree $n-1$ such that p and q are the first terms of a maximal length Euclidean sequence. By Equation 1, we have $\begin{pmatrix} p & q \end{pmatrix} = \begin{pmatrix} 1 & 0 \end{pmatrix} h'(\tilde{m}_1)$ for some $\tilde{m}_1 \in \{0,1\}^n$ that can be recovered with the Euclidean algorithm. For $i > 1$, let

$$\tilde{m}_i := \tilde{m}_{i-1} 0 \tilde{m}_1. \tag{6}$$

We first show that the messages $\tilde{m}_i$ satisfy the requirements of Lemma 4.

Lemma 6. *For any $i \geq 0$, $\begin{pmatrix} 1 & 0 \end{pmatrix} H'(\tilde{m}_i) \equiv \begin{pmatrix} 0 & q^i \end{pmatrix}$.*

Proof: For $i = 1$ the result is trivial. Moreover, assuming the property is satisfied for some i, it is also satisfied for $i+1$ since

$$\begin{aligned} \begin{pmatrix} 1 & 0 \end{pmatrix} H'(\tilde{m}_{i+1}) &= \begin{pmatrix} 1 & 0 \end{pmatrix} H'(\tilde{m}_i) A'_0 H'(\tilde{m}_1) \\ &\equiv \begin{pmatrix} 0 & q^i \end{pmatrix} \begin{pmatrix} X & 1 \\ 1 & 0 \end{pmatrix} \begin{pmatrix} 0 & q \\ \dots & \dots \end{pmatrix} \equiv \begin{pmatrix} q^i & 0 \end{pmatrix} \begin{pmatrix} 0 & q \\ \dots & \dots \end{pmatrix} \equiv \begin{pmatrix} 0 & q^{i+1} \end{pmatrix}. \end{aligned}$$ □

To apply Lemma 4 and Proposition 3, we must find a subset of $\{q^{2i} + X \bmod p, i \geq 1\}$ that is a basis of K. We start by studying the sets $S_j := \{q^{2(j+i)} \bmod p, i = 1, ..., n\}$.

Lemma 7. *If n is prime, then for any $j \geq 0$, the set $S_j := \{q^{2(j+i)} \bmod p, i = 1, ..., n\}$ is a basis of K over $\mathbb{F}_2$.*

PROOF: It suffices to show that each S_j is a free set of K. Let us assume by contradiction that there exists $(b_1, ..., b_n) \in \mathbb{F}_2^n \setminus \{(0, ..., 0)\}$ such that $0 = \sum_{i=1}^{n} b_i q^{2(j+i)}$. Since q is a polynomial of degree $n-1$, $q \neq 0, 1$ hence $q^2 \neq 0, 1$. The degree of the minimal polynomial of q^2 must divide n, hence if n is prime it is either 1 or n. Since $q^2 \neq 0, 1$ the minimal polynomial degree has degree larger than 1 and hence it has degree n. Now, let us define the polynomial $f : y \to f(y) = \sum_{i=0}^{n-1} b_{i-1} y^i$. We have $\deg(f) < n$. We also have $q^{2(j+1)} f(q^2) = 0$ hence $f(q^2) = 0$. Therefore f must be a multiple of the minimal polynomial of q^2, which brings us to a contradiction. □

The proof of Lemma 7 does not work if n is not prime since the degree of the minimal polynomial of q^2 may then be a nontrivial divisor of n. However, even if n is not prime, S_j is a basis for all j if and only if S_j is a basis for some j. If n_1 is a divisor of n, the probability that a random element of K has a minimal polynomial with degree dividing n_1 is $2^{n_1 - n}$, that is very small for reasonably large values of n (Tillich and Zémor suggested $n > 130$). Of course, q^2 is not a random element of K since q is one of the two polynomials making p and q the first terms of a maximal length Euclidean sequence. However, the best link known today between p and q is the Mesirov and Sweet's algorithm, and when p is chosen at random this algorithm does not seem to influence the degree of the minimal polynomial of q. We have confirmed this intuition experimentally: for large n and random p, S_0 was always a basis, while for very small values of n like $n = 4$ it was not always (although most often) the case[1].

Let $T_j := \{q^{2(i+j)} + X \bmod p, i \geq 1\}$. We now show that if S_0 is a basis over K, then there exists $j \leq n$ such that T_j is a basis of K. To this aim we first need the following lemma.

Lemma 8. *Let $\{\beta_i, i = 1, ..., n\}$ be a basis of K over $\mathbb{F}_2$ and let $e_i \in \mathbb{F}_2, i = 1, ..., n$ be such that $X = \sum_i e_i \beta_i$. Then $\{\alpha_i := \beta_i + X, i = 1, ..., n\}$ is a basis of K over $\mathbb{F}_2$ if and only if $\sum_i e_i = 0$.*

PROOF: We can write $X = \sum_i e_i \alpha_i + (\sum_i e_i)X$. If $\sum_i e_i = 1$, then $0 = \sum_i e_i \alpha_i$ hence $\{\alpha_i, i = 1, ..., n\}$ is not a free set of elements. On the other hand, if $\sum_i e_i = 0$ then $X = \sum_i e_i \alpha_i$. Let $\alpha \in K$ and let $b_i \in \mathbb{F}_2, i = 1, ..., n$ be such that $\alpha = \sum_i b_i \beta_i$. Let $a_i := b_i + (\sum_i b_i) e_i$. We have $\alpha = \sum_i b_i \alpha_i + (\sum_i b_i)X = \sum_i a_i \alpha_i$ hence $\{\alpha_i, i = 1, ..., n\}$ is a generating set. □

We are now ready to prove the following result.

Proposition 9. *If S_0 is a basis of K over $\mathbb{F}_2$ (in particular, if n is prime), then there exists $j < n$ such that T_j is a basis of K over $\mathbb{F}_2$.*

PROOF: We give a constructive proof of the result. Since S_0 is a basis of K over $\mathbb{F}_2$, we know that S_j is a basis of K over $\mathbb{F}_2$ for all $j \geq 0$. Let $e_i \in \mathbb{F}_2, i = 1, ..., n$

[1] The Tillich-Zémor hash function is *a priori* even weaker when n is not prime, due to the subgroup structure of $SL(2, K)$ [11].

such that $X = \sum_{i=1}^{n} e_i q^{2i}$. If $\sum_i e_i = 0$, then according to Lemma 8 we are done with $j = 0$. Otherwise, let j be the smallest index i such that $e_i = 1$. Since $q^2 \mod p$ belongs to K, the degree n' of its minimal polynomial p' divides n. (This polynomial can be easily computed, but it is not needed by the algorithm.) By definition, we have $p'_0 + p'_1 q^2 + ... + p'_{n-1} q^{2(n'-1)} + q^{2n'} = 0 \mod p$. Since p' is irreducible, we have $p'_0 = 1$ (otherwise $X|p'$) and $\sum_{i=0}^{n'} p'_i = 1$ (otherwise $X+1|p'$). Let us define $e_i := 0$ for $i > n$ and $p'_i := 0$ for $i > n'$. We have

$$X \equiv \sum_{i=1}^{n} e_i q^{2i} \equiv \sum_{i=1}^{n} e_i q^{2i} + q^{2j}\left(1 + p'_1 q^2 + ... + p'_{n'-1} q^{2(n'-1)} + q^{2n'}\right) \equiv \sum_{i=j+1}^{j+n} (e_i + p'_{i-j}) q^{2i}.$$

Moreover, $\sum_{i=j+1}^{j+n} (e_i + p'_{i-j}) = (1 + \sum_{i=1}^{n} e_i) + \left(1 + \sum_{i=0}^{n'} p'_i\right) = 0$. Together with Lemma 8, this shows that T_j is a basis of K over $\mathbb{F}_2$. □

In short, our second algorithm is as follows

1. Apply Mesirov and Sweet's algorithm to p; get q and $\tilde{m}_1$.
2. If n is not prime, check whether $S_0 = \{q^2, q^4, ..., q^{2n}\}$ is a basis of K over $\mathbb{F}_2$. If it is not, abort.
3. Decompose X in the basis S_0.
4. Determine j as in the proof of Proposition 9.
5. Compute $\tilde{m}_{j+1}, ..., \tilde{m}_{j+n}$ using Equation 6 and apply Lemma 4.

Step 1 and Step 3 both require solving a linear system of size $n \times n$ over $\mathbb{F}_2$ which can be done in time $O(n^3)$; the remaining steps are comparatively fast. The length of $\tilde{m}_i$ is $i(n+1)-1$ and we have $i \leq j+n$ and $j < n$. After application of the mappings μ_L and μ_U, we may apply Proposition 3 with $L = 4n^2+2n+1$, resulting in preimages of length $O(n^3)$ for any matrix. The algorithm is guaranteed to succeed if n is prime, and as argued above when n is composite but reasonably large it will likely succeed with a very large probability.

7 Discussion

In this paper, we presented very efficient algorithms computing preimages for the Tillich-Zémor hash function. We first gave a second preimage algorithm. Then we reduced the problem of finding preimages for the Tillich-Zémor hash function to the problem of precomputing a few preimages with certain properties. Subsequently, we gave two algorithms for the precomputing part:

1. The first algorithm produces messages of length $O(n)$, resulting in generic preimages of length $O(n^2)$. We provided theoretical and experimental evidence that it runs in probabilistic time $O(n^4)$ and succeeds with a very large probability on the function parameters.
2. The second algorithm produces messages of length $O(n^2)$, resulting in generic preimages of length $O(n^3)$. We gave a proof that it always succeeds when n is prime, and arguments that it succeeds for most polynomials p when n is not necessarily prime but is reasonably large. The algorithm runs in deterministic time $O(n^3)$.

Since the size of $SL(2,\mathbb{F}_{2^n})$ is about 2^{3n}, it seems reasonable to conjecture that preimages of length $3n$ exist for any matrix. However, even if this conjecture is true, it is not clear whether there exists an efficient algorithm computing preimages of this length. We leave that question as an interesting open problem. From a practical point of view, our first algorithm is the most interesting one since it produces shorter messages. On the other hand, the second algorithm is more appealing from a theoretical point of view. In particular, it provides a constructive proof that the Cayley graphs corresponding to the Tillich-Zémor hash function satisfy Babai's conjecture (that is, that they have a polylogarithmic diameter [7]), at least when we restrict n to the prime values. Besides those important results, in the argumentation for our first algorithm we provided an extension of Mesirov and Sweet's result [8] and a connection to some arithmetic sequence of polynomials, both of which are of independent interest.

Grassl et al.'s attack found collisions for the Tillich-Zémor hash function. In this paper, we showed that the function is not even one-way. The attacks also break its vectorial and projective variants [10]. Our work puts a final end to the story of the Tillich-Zémor hash function, one of the oldest and most elegant hash functions in the literature. Similar hash functions that are using the same design (replacing the group $SL(2,K)$ and the generators A_0, A_1 by other groups and generators) have also been cryptanalyzed recently [14,13,9].

Nevertheless, we point out that these particular attacks do not invalidate the generic design. The key tool in the cryptanalysis of Tillich-Zémor hash function is Mesirov and Sweet's algorithm which is specific to quotients X and $X+1$ in the Euclidean algorithm. At the current state of knowledge, collision and preimage resistances are recovered if we replace the matrices A_0 and A_1 by $B_0 := \begin{pmatrix} X^2 & 1 \\ 1 & 0 \end{pmatrix}$ and $B_1 := \begin{pmatrix} X+1 & 1 \\ 1 & 0 \end{pmatrix}$. Moreover, since current attacks do not allow controlling the form of the collisions and preimages, security might also be recovered by introducing some simple redundancy in the messages. It might even be sufficient to replace A_0 by A_0^2 or A_0^3. More generally, similar hash functions can be constructed from other non-Abelian groups and generators.

The generic design of the Tillich-Zémor hash function has many advantages over traditional hash functions like SHA: it has inherent parallelism, potentially efficient implementations in a wide range of contexts and a security equivalent to some concise mathematical problems [4]. For these reasons, we do not recommend to give it up but on the contrary, we suggest the community to look for secure and insecure instances. In the same way as many RSA instances can be insecure, especially when they are optimized for efficiency, we believe that the particularly efficient Tillich-Zémor hash function may be an unfortunately insecure instance of a more generally sound design.

Acknowledgements. We are grateful to Gilles Zémor for pointing us an error in an early version of Proposition 5. We also thank Sylvie Baudine, Franéis Koeune and Franéis-Xavier Standaert for their help in improving this paper.

References

1. Abdukhalikov, K.S., Kim, C.: On the security of the hashing scheme based on SL2. In: Vaudenay, S. (ed.) FSE 1998. LNCS, vol. 1372, pp. 93–102. Springer, Heidelberg (1998)
2. Charles, D., Goren, E., Lauter, K.: Cryptographic hash functions from expander graphs. J. Cryptology 22(1), 93–113 (2009)
3. Charnes, C., Pieprzyk, J.: Attacking the SL2 hashing scheme. In: Safavi-Naini, R., Pieprzyk, J.P. (eds.) ASIACRYPT 1994. LNCS, vol. 917, pp. 322–330. Springer, Heidelberg (1995)
4. de Meulenaer, G., Petit, C., Quisquater, J.-J.: Hardware implementations of a variant of Zémor-Tillich hash function: Can a provably secure hash function be very efficient? (2009) (preprint)
5. Geiselmann, W.: A note on the hash function of Tillich and Zémor. In: Gollmann, D. (ed.) FSE 1996. LNCS, vol. 1039, pp. 51–52. Springer, Heidelberg (1996)
6. Grassl, M., Ilic, I., Magliveras, S., Steinwandt, R.: Cryptanalysis of the Tillich-Zémor hash function. Cryptology ePrint Archive, Report 2009/376 (2009), `http://eprint.iacr.org/`
7. Helfgott, H.A.: Growth and generation in $SL_2(Z/pZ)$ (2005)
8. Mesirov, J.P., Sweet, M.M.: Continued fraction expansions of rational expressions with irreducible denominators in characteristic 2. Journal of Number Theory 27, 144–148 (1987)
9. Petit, C., Lauter, K., Quisquater, J.-J.: Full cryptanalysis of LPS and morgenstern hash functions. In: Ostrovsky, R., De Prisco, R., Visconti, I. (eds.) SCN 2008. LNCS, vol. 5229, pp. 263–277. Springer, Heidelberg (2008)
10. Petit, C., Quisquater, J.-J., Tillich, J.-P., Zémor, G.: Hard and easy components of collision search in the Zémor-tillich hash function: New attacks and reduced variants with equivalent security. In: Fischlin, M. (ed.) CT-RSA 2009. LNCS, vol. 5473, pp. 182–194. Springer, Heidelberg (2009)
11. Steinwandt, R., Grassl, M., Geiselmann, W., Beth, T.: Weaknesses in the $\mathrm{SL}_2(\mathbb{F}_{2^n})$ hashing scheme. In: Bellare, M. (ed.) CRYPTO 2000. LNCS, vol. 1880, p. 287. Springer, Heidelberg (2000)
12. Tillich, J.-P., Zémor, G.: Hashing with SL_2. In: Desmedt, Y. (ed.) CRYPTO 1994. LNCS, vol. 839, pp. 40–49. Springer, Heidelberg (1994)
13. Tillich, J.-P., Zémor, G.: Collisions for the LPS expander graph hash function. In: Smart, N.P. (ed.) EUROCRYPT 2008. LNCS, vol. 4965, pp. 254–269. Springer, Heidelberg (2008)
14. Tillich, J.-P., Zémor, G.: Group-theoretic hash functions. In: Cohen, G., Lobstein, A., Zémor, G., Litsyn, S.N. (eds.) Algebraic Coding 1993. LNCS, vol. 781, pp. 90–110. Springer, Heidelberg (1994)
15. Zémor, G.: Hash functions and graphs with large girths. In: Davies, D.W. (ed.) EUROCRYPT 1991. LNCS, vol. 547, pp. 508–511. Springer, Heidelberg (1991)
16. Zémor, G.: Hash functions and Cayley graphs. Des. Codes Cryptography 4(4), 381–394 (1994)

A Can We Also Compute Preimages? A Toy Example

In this section, we provide toy examples of our algorithms. We use $n = 11$ and the "smallest" irreducible polynomial of degree 11 which is $p(X) = X^{11}+X^2+1$.

The representation of the sentence "*Grassl et al. have shown how to find collisions. But can we also compute preimages?*" in ASCII is 47 72 61 73 73 6c 20 65 74 20 61 6c 2e 20 68 61 76 65 20 73 68 6f 77 6e 20 68 6f 77 20 74 6f 20 66 69 6e 64 20 63 6f 6c 6c 69 73 69 6f 6e 73 2e 20 42 75 74 20 63 61 6e 20 77 65 20 61 6c 73 6f 20 63 6f 6d 70 75 74 65 20 70 72 65 69 6d 61 67 65 73 3f to which corresponds the message m_{text} =01000111 01110010 01100001 01110011 01110011 01101100 00100000 01100101 01110100 00100000 01100001 01101100 00101110 00100000 01101000 01100001 01110110 01100101 00100000 01110011 01101000 01101111 01110111 01101110 00100000 01101000 01101111 01110111 00100000 01110100 01101111 00100000 01100110 01101001 01101110 01100100 00100000 01100011 01101111 01101100 01101100 01101001 01110011 01101001 01101111 01101110 01110011 00101110 00100000 01000010 01110101 01110100 00100000 01100011 01100001 01101110 00100000 01110111 01100101 00100000 01100001 01101100 01110011 01101111 00100000 01100011 01101111 01101101 01110000 01110101 01110100 01100101 00100000 01110000 01110010 01100101 01101001 01101101 01100001 01100111 01100101 01110011 00111111. The Tillich-Zémor hash value of this message for polynomial $p(X)$ is

$$h = \begin{pmatrix} X^7+X^5+X^4+X^2+1 & X^8+X^2+X+1 \\ X^9+X^8+X^7+X^5+X^4+X^3+X & X^9+X^6+X^5+X^4+X^2+X \end{pmatrix}.$$

We compute other preimages of this matrix using the algorithms of this paper.

We start with the second preimage algorithm of Section 3. The Mesirov and Sweet algorithm applied to p gives $d(X) = X^{10}+X^8+X^7+X^6+X^5+X^2+X+1$ and the message $m = 01011000010$. The message

$$\tilde{m} = \mu_L(m)\mu_L(m) = [(101111001011)(11011000010)0][(101111001011)(11011000010)0]$$

is a preimage of the identity matrix, hence $H(m_{text}\tilde{m}) = H(m_{text}) = h$.

We now apply our preimage algorithms to h. We first change the generators and we look for a preimage of

$$h' = \begin{pmatrix} X^{10}+X^8+X & X^9+X^8+X^7+X^5+X^4+X^3+X \\ X^9+X^6+X^5+X^3+X^2 & X^{10}+Xy+X^8+X^7+X^6+1 \end{pmatrix}$$

for the modified Tillich-Zémor hash function. We first write

$$\begin{pmatrix} A & B \\ C & D \end{pmatrix} = \begin{pmatrix} 1 & 0 \\ \alpha & 1 \end{pmatrix} \begin{pmatrix} X & 1 \\ 1 & 0 \end{pmatrix} \begin{pmatrix} 1 & \beta \\ 0 & 1 \end{pmatrix} \begin{pmatrix} X & 1 \\ 1 & 0 \end{pmatrix}^3 \begin{pmatrix} 1 & 0 \\ \gamma & 1 \end{pmatrix}$$

with

$$\begin{cases} \alpha = X^{10} + X^9 + X^8 + X^7 + X^6 + X^5 + X^4 + 1 \\ \beta = X^{10} + X^7 + X^6 + X^5 + X^3 + X^2 + X \\ \gamma = X^8 + X^4 + 1 \end{cases}.$$

Now, we illustrate our first precomputing algorithm. We take $R = 10$ and generate random polynomials p' of degree R. We apply Mesirov and Sweet's algorithm to $a = pp'$. If successful, we obtain a d value and compute the corresponding α value. If this α value is linearly independent (over $\mathbb{F}_{2^n}/\mathbb{F}_2$) with the previous values, we keep it and compute m such that $\left(a \; d \right) = \left(1 \; 0 \right) H'(m)$. The following table summarizes the results obtained.

p'	d	α	$\perp$?	m
$X^{10}+X^9+X^8+X^7+X^6+X^5+X^4+X^3+1$	$X^{20}+X^{19}+X^{15}+X^{14}+X^{13}+X^{11}+X^{10}+X^9+X^5+X^4+X$	$X^8+X^7+X^6+X^5+X^4+X^3+X^2$	yes	m_1 =00110100100010010010O
$X^{10}+X^6+X^5+X^3+X^2+X+1$	-	-	-	-
$X^{10}+X^9+X^7+X^6+X^5+X^4+X^3+X^2+1$	$X^{20}+X^{18}+X^{16}+X^{15}+X^{14}+X^{12}+X^9+X^7+X^5+X^3+X$	$X^{10}+X^9+X^8+X^7+X^6+X^5+X^4+1$	yes	m_2 =10111110100101110110O
$X^{10}+X^9+X^5+X^4+X^2+X+1$	$X^{20}+X^{19}+X^{18}+X^{15}+X^6+X^5+X^3+X^2+X+1$	$X^{10}+X^9+X^8+X^7+X^6+X^3+X+1$	yes	m_3 =01001011111010111110O
$X^{10}+X^9+X^7+X^5+X^2+X+1$	-	-	-	-
$X^{10}+X^9+X^8+X^5+1$	$X^{20}+X^{19}+X^{17}+X^{16}+X^{14}+X^{13}+X^9+X^6+X^5+X^4+X^2+1$	$X^{10}+X^9+X^6+X^5+X^4+X^3+X^2+X+1$	yes	m_4 =00101001111011100100l
$X^{10}+X^9+X^5+X+1$	-	-	-	-
$X^{10}+X^9+X^8+X^6+X^4+X^3+1$	-	-	-	-
$X^{10}+X^7+X^5+X^3+X^2+X+1$	-	-	-	-
$X^{10}+X^8+X^4+X^3+1$	-	-	-	-
$X^{10}+X^9+X^8+X^4+1$	-	-	-	-
$X^{10}+X^8+X^3+X^2+1$	$X^{20}+X^{17}+X^{14}+X^{10}+X^8+X^7+X^3+X+1$	$X^{10}+X^7+X^5+X^4+1$	yes	m_5 =010111010111101011110
$X^{10}+X^9+X^7+X^5+X^2+X+1$	-	-	-	-
$X^{10}+X^4+X^3+X^2+1$	-	-	-	-
$X^{10}+X^9+X^8+X^6+X^5+X^4+X^3+X^2+1$	$X^{20}+X^{15}+X^{13}+X^{10}+X^9+X^8+X^7+X^5+X^3+X$	$X^{10}+X^9+X^7+X^6$	yes	m_6 =100101101001110010110
$X^{10}+X^7+X^6+X^2+1$	-	-	-	-
$X^{10}+X^8+X^4+X^3+1$	-	-	-	-
$X^{10}+X^7+1$	$X^{20}+X^{18}+X^{16}+X^{14}+X^{12}+X^{11}+X^{10}+X^7+X^3+X^2+1$	$X^9+X^6+X^5+X^4+X^3+X$	yes	m_7 =010010001011100010001
$X^{10}+X^9+X^7+X^5+X^4+X^3+X^2+X+1$	-	-	-	-
$X^{10}+X^8+X^3+X^2+1$	$X^{20}+X^{17}+X^{14}+X^{10}+X^8+X^7+X^3+X+1$	$X^{10}+X^7+X^5+X^4+1$	no	
$X^{10}+X^6+X^5+X^3+X^2+X+1$	-	-	-	-
$X^{10}+X^8+X^5+X+1$	$X^{20}+X^{19}+X^{18}+X^{17}+X^{16}+X^{14}+X^{11}+X^{10}+X^8+X^4+X$	$X^8+X^7+X^6+X^5+X^3+X^2$	yes	m_8 =111110110010101111001
$X^{10}+X^7+X^4+X^3+1$	-	-	-	-
$X^{10}+X^9+X^7+X^5+X^4+X^3+X^2+X+1$	-	-	-	-
$X^{10}+X^9+X^8+X^7+1$	$X^{20}+X^{17}+X^{15}+X^{14}+X^{13}+X^{12}+X^9+X^8+X^7+X^5+X^4+X^2+1$	$X^8+X^5+X^4+X^3+X^2+X$	yes	m_9 =100001010010010001001
$X^{10}+X^9+X^8+X^5+X^4+X^2+1$	-	-	-	-
$X^{10}+X^9+X^7+X^6+X^4+X+1$	$X^{20}+X^{18}+X^{16}+X^{11}+X^9+X^8+X^5+X^4+X+1$	$X^9+X^8+X^5+X^2+X+1$	yes	m_{10} =101000011111000001010
$X^{10}+X^9+X^8+X^6+X^5+X^4+X^3+X^2+1$	$X^{20}+X^{15}+X^{13}+X^{10}+X^9+X^8+X^7+X^5+X^3+X$	$X^{10}+X^9+X^7+X^6$	no	
$X^{10}+X^7+X^6+X^4+X^2+X+1$	-	-	-	-
$X^{10}+X^7+X^6+X^5+X^2+X+1$	-	-	-	-
$X^{10}+X^9+X^8+X^6+X^2+X+1$	-	-	-	-
$X^{10}+X^9+X^8+X^7+1$	$X^{20}+X^{17}+X^{15}+X^{14}+X^{13}+X^{12}+X^9+X^8+X^7+X^5+X^4+X^2+1$	$X^8+X^5+X^4+X^3+X^2+X$	no	
$X^{10}+X^7+X^6+X^5+X^2+X+1$	-	-	-	-
$X^{10}+X^9+X^8+X^7+X^6+X^2+1$	-	-	-	-
$X^{10}+X^8+X^7+X^3+X^2+X+1$	$X^{20}+X^{17}+X^{16}+X^{15}+X^{14}+X^{13}+X^{11}+X^{10}+X^9+X^7+X$	$X^9+X^7+X^6+X^5+X^4+X+1$	yes	m_{11} =000011011010111000101

Writing α, β, γ in the basis obtained, we get $\alpha = \alpha_2$, $\beta = \alpha_2 + \alpha_8 + \alpha_{11}$ and $\gamma = \alpha_1 + \alpha_2 + \alpha_3 + \alpha_4 + \alpha_5 + \alpha_9 + \alpha_{10}$. Finally we obtain one preimage of h as

$$m' = m_\alpha 0 m_\beta 000 m_\gamma$$

where

$$\begin{aligned} m_\alpha &= \mu_L(m_2), \\ m_\beta &= \mu_U(m_2)\mu_U(m_8)\mu_U(m_{11}), \\ m_\gamma &= \mu_L(m_1)\mu_L(m_2)\mu_L(m_3)\mu_L(m_4)\mu_L(m_5)\mu_L(m_9)\mu_L(m_{10}). \end{aligned}$$

(Note that the terms composing m_β and m_γ can be permuted arbitrarily.)

Finally, we use our second precomputing algorithm to find yet another preimage. Let $\tilde{m_1} = 01011000010$ be the message obtained by applying Mesirov and Sweet's algorithm to $a = p$. The corresponding q value is $q = d = X^{10} + X^8 + X^7 + X^6 + X^5 + X^2 + X + 1$. We recursively define

$$\tilde{m_i} := \tilde{m_{i-1}} 0 \tilde{m_1}.$$

Since n is prime, we know that $S_0 := \{q^2, q^4, \cdot, q^{1+n}\}$ is a basis of $\mathbb{F}_{2^n}/\mathbb{F}_2$. We have $X = q^2 + q^4 + q^6 + q^8 + q^{12} + q^{18} + q^{22}$ so $T_j := \{q^{2(i+j)} + X, i = 1, ..., n\}$ is a basis for $j = 1$. Let $\alpha_i = q^{2(j+1)} + X$ for $i = 1, ..., n$.

Writing α, β, γ in this basis, we get $\alpha = \alpha_1 + \alpha_4 + \alpha_6 + \alpha_8 + \alpha_9 + \alpha_{10} + \alpha_{11}$, $\beta = \alpha_1 + \alpha_2 + \alpha_4 + \alpha_6 + \alpha_7 + \alpha_8 + \alpha_9 + \alpha_{10} + \alpha_{11}$ and $\gamma = \alpha_1 + \alpha_2 + \alpha_3 + \alpha_4 + \alpha_7 + \alpha_9 + \alpha_{11}$. Finally we compute a preimage of h as

$$m' = m_\alpha 0 m_\beta 000 m_\gamma$$

where
$m_\alpha = \mu_L(m_1)\mu_L(m_4)\mu_L(m_6)\mu_L(m_8)\mu_L(m_9)\mu_L(m_{10})\mu_L(m_{11})$,
$m_\beta = \mu_U(m_1)\mu_U(m_2)\mu_U(m_4)\mu_U(m_6)\mu_U(m_7)\mu_U(m_8)\mu_U(m_9)\mu_U(m_{10})\mu_U(m_{11})$,
$m_\gamma = \mu_L(m_1)\mu_L(m_2)\mu_L(m_3)\mu_L(m_4)\mu_L(m_7)\mu_L(m_9)\mu_L(m_{11})$.

B Further Experimental Results on Our First Precomputing Algorithm

Since it is unlikely that we can give a better theoretical analysis of our first precomputing algorithm, we provide additional experimental results in this section.

The results shown in Figure 1 were obtained with each "shortest" polynomial of degree n. Figure 2 shows similar results for randomly chosen polynomials. The algorithm always succeeds with a value R satisfying $\frac{2^R}{R} \geq 6n$. For reasonably large n, it always succeeds when $\frac{2^R}{R} \geq 4n$. When n increases the points get closer to the bound $\frac{2^R}{R} \geq 2n$. Some of the points of Figure 1 and Figure 2 differ, but the differences are small and they only appear for small n.

n	R	n	R	n	R
5	7	67	11	257	13
7	7	73	11	277	13
11	9	83	11	307	13
13	9	97	12	331	14
17	9	103	12	353	14
19	9	109	12	379	14
23	9	127	12	401	14
29	10	137	12	449	14
31	9	149	12	499	14
37	10	167	12	607	15
41	10	191	13	1021	15
47	11	211	13	2039	16
59	11	233	13		

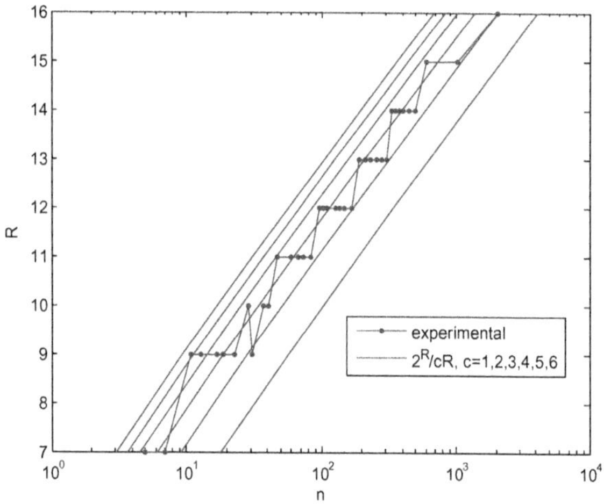

Fig. 2. Minimal value R for different values n and random polynomials. The points on the staircase-like curve are experimental results. The other curves are $n = \frac{2^R}{cR}$ for $c = 1, 2, 3, 4, 5, 6$.

To study these differences in more details, we generated twenty random polynomials of degrees $n = 11$, $n = 47$ and $n = 127$. For each polynomial, we recorded the shortest value of R for which the algorithm succeeded. (We started with short R values and increased R when 1000 α values linearly dependent with the previous ones were found). The results are presented in Table 1. The minimal value R for the success of the algorithm does not depend very much on the parameter p but only on its degree. Moreover, this dependence seems to

Table 1. Variability of the minimal R needed for the algorithm when the polynomial p is randomly chosen. For each degree n and each R value, the table indicates how many polynomials p among the 20 polynomials generated required at least a randomness R.

$n = 11$		$n = 47$		$n = 127$	
$R = 7$	3/20	$R = 10$	11/20	$R = 12$	20/20
$R = 8$	14/20	$R = 11$	9/20		
$R = 9$	3/20				

disappear for reasonably large degrees n. Therefore, the algorithm is likely to succeed for any p as long as $\frac{2^R}{R} \geq 4n$ (for reasonably large n values).

Choosing R close to the minimal value will improve the efficiency of the algorithm since it performs linear algebra on vectors of length $N + R$. On the other hand, if R is chosen too close to the minimum, the algorithm will have to generate more polynomials p' before getting n independent elements α_i. In Table 2, it seems more efficient to choose $R = 10$ instead of $R = 8$ for the polynomial $p(X) = X^{11} + X^2 + 1$, and $R = 12$ instead of $R = 10$ for the polynomial $p(X) = X^{47} + X^5 + 1$. The reason appears clearly in the toy example of the previous section, presented in Table 1: in this example, all the dependencies obtained between the α values do actually come from the fact that the same polynomials are generated various times.

To conclude this section, we observe that in the experiments of Table 2, the Mesirov and Sweet's system had solutions respectively 49, 21% and 51, 36% of times for the polynomials $p(X) = X^{11} + X^2 + 1$ and $p(X) = X^{47} + X^5 + 1$. This confirms the analysis of Section 5.1.

Table 2. Number of iterations needed to obtain a basis of K, for various R and the polynomials $p(X) = X^{11} + X^2 + 1$ and $p(X) = X^{47} + X^5 + 1$. The first row gives the total number of polynomials generated, the second row gives the number of times the Mesirov and Sweet's system had no solution, and the last row gives the number of times a new α value was linearly dependent on the previous ones. For each value R, we performed the experiment three times.

$p(X) = X^{11} + X^2 + 1$																		
	$R = 8$			$R = 9$			$R = 10$			$R = 15$			$R = 20$			$R = 50$		
# pol. generated	48	36	25	41	61	46	28	24	38	35	23	19	27	26	17	25	28	22
# no sol. MS	21	9	6	28	44	30	15	8	22	22	11	8	14	11	6	11	13	10
# dependencies	16	16	8	2	6	5	2	5	5	2	1	0	2	4	0	3	4	1

$p(X) = X^{47} + X^5 + 1$																		
	$R = 10$			$R = 11$			$R = 12$			$R = 15$			$R = 20$			$R = 50$		
# pol. generated	211	293	209	119	110	110	100	131	101	94	107	93	89	98	87	104	105	111
# no sol. MS	103	150	103	47	46	46	44	73	53	44	55	44	40	50	38	54	54	61
# dependencies	61	96	59	25	17	17	9	11	1	3	5	2	2	1	2	3	4	3

One-Time Signatures and Chameleon Hash Functions

Payman Mohassel

Computer Science Department, University of Calgary
pmohasse@cpsc.ucalgary.ca

Abstract. In this work we show a general construction for transforming any *chameleon hash function* to a *strongly unforgeable one-time signature* scheme. Combined with the result of [Bellare and Ristov, PKC 2007], this also implies a general construction of strongly unforgeable one-time signatures from Σ-protocols in the standard model.

Our results explain and unify several works in the literature which either use chameleon hash functions or one-time signatures, by showing that several of the constructions in the former category can be interpreted as efficient instantiations of those in the latter. They also imply that any "noticeable" improvement to the efficiency of constructions for chameleon hash functions leads to similar improvements for one-time signatures. This makes such improvements challenging since efficiency of one-time signatures has been studied extensively.

We further demonstrate the usefulness of our general construction by studying and optimizing specific instantiations based on the hardness of factoring, the discrete-log problem, and the worst-case lattice-based assumptions. Some of these signature schemes match or improve the efficiency of the best previous constructions or relax the underlying hardness assumptions. Two of the schemes have very fast signing (no exponentiations) which makes them attractive in scenarios where the signer has limited computational resources.

Keywords: One-time Signatures, Chameleon Hash Functions, Strong Unforgeability, Identification Schemes.

1 Introduction

One-time signature (OTS) schemes are digital signatures that can be used to sign a single message for each pair of verifiction/signing key. Despite their limited functionality, OTS schemes have found numerous applications. In fact, earlier constructions of standard signature schemes, use one-time signatures as their main component [21,22,28,30].

OTS schemes are used as building blocks in many cryptographic constructions such as the (i) design of online/offline signature schemes [18], (ii) design of CCA-secure public key encryption from identity-based encryption [8], (iii) transformation of standard signature schemes to those with *strong* unforgeability properties [26,5], and (iv) secure composition of multiple encryption schemes [17].

A. Biryukov, G. Gong, and D.R. Stinson (Eds.): SAC 2010, LNCS 6544, pp. 302–319, 2011.

Finally, OTS schemes are directly employed in networks protocols, for example to authenticate messages in sensor networks [16] or to provide source authentication in multicast and broadcast networks [35].

The earlier constructions of one-time signatures built such schemes from general assumptions such as the existence of one-way functions [28,6,18]. The main drawback of this family of constructions is that they produce very large signatures. In many cases, this has led researchers to search for alternative methods that avoid the use of OTS schemes. The following are just a few instances: IBE to IND-CCA PKE transformations [9,1], online/offline signatures [39], and transformations for strongly unforgeable signatures [40].

Chameleon hash functions (trapdoor hash functions), in particular, have proven to be an extremely useful tool in such scenarios. Several of the examples we gave above take advantage of chameleon hash functions in their constructions. Roughly speaking, chameleon hash functions [27] are randomized collision-resistant hash functions with the additional property that given a *trapdoor*, one can efficiently generate collisions. More specifically, each function in the family is associated with a pair of public and private (trapdoor) keys with the following properties (i) anyone who knows the public key can compute the associated hash function, (ii) for those who do not know the trapdoor the function is collision resistant in the usual sense, and (iii) the holder of the trapdoor information can easily find collisions for every input. As described in more detail in Section 4 several constructions of chameleon hash functions based on standard number theoretic assumptions are known [27,39,3]. Chameleon hash functions are also closely related to the notion of chameleon commitment schemes originally introduced by Brassard *et al.* [13].

1.1 Our Contribution

We design a black-box construction for transforming any chameleon hash function to a strongly unforgeable one-time signature scheme. Such a connection between one-time signatures and chameleon hash functions is not surprising. On the contrary, as alluded to earlier, the knowledge of a close relation between the two primitives seems to have been "in the air". For example, in [23] Groth shows how to design a DL-based one-time signature from the pedersen trapdoor commitment. However, it is not clear how to generalize his construction to work for arbitrary trapdoor commitments.

Our work appears to be the first to formally study this relation by designing a black-box transformation from one primitive to another, and exploring new and useful implications of this transformation. Next, we elaborate on these implications:

Unifying and explaining the previous work. Our general construction confirms that the usefulness of chameleon hash functions in replacing OTS schemes is not a coincidence. Particularly, in several instances, constructions in one work can be interpreted as efficient instantiations of those in another. Here is one example:

Starting with the work of Boneh *et al.* [10], several works in the literature studied constructions for transforming any standard unforgeable signature scheme to a *strongly* unforgeable scheme. While Boneh *et al.*'s construction only works for signature schemes with a special partitioning property, the later works of [26,40,5] develop techniques that work for any UF-CMA secure signature scheme. The work of [26] and [5] use strongly unforgeable one-time signatures while the work of [40] takes advantage of a chameleon hash function. Our results demonstrate that the construction of [40] can be interpreted as an efficient instantiation of the constructions of [26,5].

OTS schemes from identification protocols. It is well-known how to design standard signature schemes from identification schemes in the *random oracle model* via the fiat-shamir transform [19]. The only analogous result we know of in the standard model is the work of Bellare and Shoup [5] who show a construction of one-time signatures from ID schemes.

When we combine our general construction for OTS with the work of Bellare and Ristov [3] who design chameleon hash functions from three move ID schemes (Σ-protocols), we get a general construction of strongly unforgeable OTS schemes from any Σ-protocol that satisfies natural security requirements. Compared to the work of Bellare and Shoup [5], our security requirements appear to be more modest. Particularly, while there exist efficient Σ-protocols that satisfy our security requirements under assumptions such as the hardness of factoring or RSA inversion, the same is not known to be true about their work which requires the ID scheme to be secure against concurrent attacks.

When instantiated based on specific identification schemes, our transformation also leads to several constructions of one-time signatures.

New OTS schemes based on standard assumptions. We further study and optimize several instantiations of our general construction based on standard assumptions such as the hardness of factoring integers, the discrete-log problem and the worst-case lattice-based assumptions.

Our new factoring-based construction has a very fast signing algorithm that only involves a modular addition and multiplication. This is a useful property in scenarios where the signing entity is a low-powered device with limited computational resources, while the verification entity has more computational power. This is a common occurrence in sensor networks, MANETS and VANETs. As discussed in detail in Section 4, our construction appears to be the first scheme with such properties, based solely on the hardness of factoring RSA integers.

Our new discrete-log based construction (described in Appendix B also has a very fast signing. It improves the key size compared to the DL-based construction of Bellare and Shoup [5], and matches the efficiency of the DL-based fail-stop signature of Van Heyst and Pedersen [42], in almost all respects.

Our new lattice-based construction, has a signature size of $O(k \log k)$ where k is the security parameter. Compared to the signature scheme of Lyubashevsky and Micciancio [29] who design OTS schemes based on hard problems on *ideal lattices*, our signature scheme has the advantage of being based on a potentially weaker assumption, since we do not pose such restrictions on the structure of the lattice. On the other hand, their scheme provides smaller key sizes and a faster signing algorithm. Compared to the recent construction of [15] who design standard signature schemes based on worst-case lattice-based assumptions, our scheme has significantly shorter signatures. The work of Boyen [11], shows how to improve that by designing a standard signature scheme with signature size comparable to ours, but the verification key size is still significantly longer than that of ours.

Chameleon hash functions from CRHFs? An interesting open question is whether we can build chameleon hash functions from standard collision-resistant hash functions (CRHFs), and other symmetric-key primitives (e.g. can one use a hash function from the SHA family as the CRHF?). Such a construction has the potential of being significantly more efficient than the existing ones. Our results relate this question to the design of efficient and short OTS schemes based on the same primitives. More specifically, a new construction for chameleon hash functions based on CRHFs, would automatically lead to short (note that chameleon hash functions are compressing) OTS based on the same primitives. Unfortunately, the latter is a long standing open question.

2 Preliminaries

2.1 Collision and Target Collision Resistance

A hash function is a pair $\mathcal{H} = (K, H)$. The key generation algorithm K returns a key k, and the deterministic hash algorithm H takes k and an input x to return a hash value y. We say that $\mathcal{H}$ is collision-resistant (CR) if for every polynomial-time adversary A, the CR-advantage

$$\mathbf{Adv}^{cr}_{\mathcal{H}}(\mathsf{A}) = \Pr[H(k, x_1) = H(k, x_2) : k \stackrel{\$}{\leftarrow} K; (x_1, x_2) \stackrel{\$}{\leftarrow} \mathsf{A}(k)]$$

of A against $\mathcal{H}$ is negligible. Similarly, we say that $\mathcal{H}$ is target-collision resistant (TCR) if for every polynomial-time adversary A the TCR-advantage

$$\mathbf{Adv}^{tcr}_{\mathcal{H}}(\mathsf{A}) = \Pr[H(k, x_1) = H(k, x_2) : (x_1, st) \stackrel{\$}{\leftarrow} \mathsf{A}; k \stackrel{\$}{\leftarrow} K; x_2 \stackrel{\$}{\leftarrow} \mathsf{A}(k, st)]$$

of A against $\mathcal{H}$ is negilgible. This means that the TCR adversary has to commit to an element in the collision before seeing the hash key. As discussed in [4], TCR has some potential benefits over CR, such as being easier to achieve and allowing for shorter output lengths. In this paper, for the most part we need our hash functions to be target collision resistant. While formally such functions are keyed, for simplicity (and since in practice one often uses non-keyed constructions) we abuse the notation and drop the key for such functions in our constructions.

2.2 Chameleon Hash Functions

A family of chameleon hash functions [27] consists of a tuple of three algorithms $H = (Gen, h, h^{-1})$. The key generation algorithm $(ek, td) \xleftarrow{\$} Gen(1^k)$ outputs a pair of keys named the evaluation key and the trapdoor key, respectively. The evaluation algorithm h takes the evaluation key ek, a message $m \in \mathcal{M}_{ek}$ and randomness $r \in \mathcal{R}_{ek}$ and outputs $h(ek, m, r) \in \mathcal{Y}_{ek}$.

Chameleon property. The chameleon property requires that h^{-1} on inputs the trapdoor key td, messages $m, m' \in \mathcal{M}_{ek}$ and randomness $r \in \mathcal{R}_{ek}$, returns $r' \leftarrow h^{-1}(td, m, r, m')$ such that $h(ek, m, r) = h(ek, m', r')$.

Uniformity property. The uniformity property guarantees that there exists a distribution over $\mathcal{R}_{ek}$, which we denote by $D_{\mathcal{R}_{ek}}$, such that for all $m \in \mathcal{M}_{ek}$, the distributions $(ek; h(ek, m, r))$ and $(ek; y)$ are computationally indistinguishable, where $(ek, td) \xleftarrow{\$} Gen(1^k)$, $r \xleftarrow{\$} D_{\mathcal{R}_{ek}}$ and y is chosen uniformly from $\mathcal{Y}_{ek}$. We note that for all existing constructions of chameleon hash functions, the uniformity property actually holds *statistically*.

Collision resistance. Finally, we require that given H and the evaluation key ek, it is hard to compute $(m, r) \neq (m', r')$ such that $h(ek, m, r) = h(ek, m', r')$. More formally we have:

$$\Pr\left[\, (m,r) \neq (m',r') \wedge h(ek,m,r) = h(ek,m',r') \;:\; (ek,td) \xleftarrow{\$} Gen(1^k) \,;\, (m,r,m',r') \xleftarrow{\$} \mathsf{A}(ek,H) \,\right]$$

is negligible for any probabilistic polynomial time adversary A.

It is possible to weaken the collision resistance property by only requiring that $m \neq m'$. However, all the instantiations of chameleon hash functions we know of possess this stronger property. Furthermore, we need this version of collision resistance in order to achieve signature schemes that are *strongly* unforgeable.

2.3 Security Definitions for Signature Schemes

We introduce the necessary definitions for signatures schemes in Appendix A.

3 One-Time Signatures from Chameleon Hash Functions

In this section we show general constructions of one-time signatures from chameleon hash functions. First we design an efficient one-time signature scheme that is only secure against apriori message attacks. As we will discuss later, it turns out that this level of security is sufficient for a number of applications of one-time signatures in the literature. Then, we show how to enhance the construction to achieve security against adaptively chosen message attacks.

3.1 A suf-ama Signature Scheme

We start with a simple construction of a one-time SUF-AMA signature scheme from a chameleon hash function.

Construction 31. *Let $H = (Gen, h, h^{-1})$ be a family of chameleon hash functions. We construct a one-time* SUF-AMA *signature scheme OTS in the following way:*

- **Key Generation:**
  1. *Compute $(ek, td) \xleftarrow{\$} Gen(1^k)$.*
  2. *Choose a uniformly random $r_s \in \mathcal{R}_{ek}$.*
  3. *Output (vk, sk) where $vk = (ek, z = h(ek, m_f, r_s))$ and $sk = (td, m_f, r_s)$. Here m_f can be an arbitrary message from $\mathcal{M}_{ek}$. There is no need to keep m_f secret, but it is also not needed for verification.*
- **Signing:** *On input message m, compute and return the signature $\sigma = h^{-1}(td, m_f, r_s, m)$.*
- **Verification:** *On input (m, σ), accept if $h(ek, m, \sigma) = z$ and reject otherwise.*

Claim. If H is a family of chameleon hash functions, the OTS scheme described above is a one-time SUF-AMA signature scheme.

Proof. Let A be the adversary that breaks the OTS scheme in the SUF-AMA game. Then, we build an adversary B that breaks the collision resistance of the chameleon hash function H. B is given ek and H. B runs A. A chooses a message m for his signature query. B generates a random $r \in \mathcal{R}_{ek}$, computes $h(ek, m, r)$, and returns $vk = (ek, h(ek, m, r))$ and the signature $\sigma = r$ of message m to A. Note that the uniformity property of the chameleon hash function implies that for any two messages m, m_f the distribution of $h(ek, m, r)$ and $h(ek, m_f, r_s)$ are computationally indistinguishable (from uniform) when r and r_s are chosen uniformly at random from $\mathcal{R}_{ek}$. Hence B successfully simulates A's view in the SUF-AMA game.

Eventually, A returns $(m', \sigma') \neq (m, \sigma)$ as his forgery. B outputs (m, σ) and (m', σ') as his collision pair for the hash function (see the definition of collision resistance in Section 2.2). It is easy to verify that if A is successful in forging a signature for m', B outputs a valid collision.

Remarks on the proof. Note that since B in the above reduction does not know the trapdoor for the hash function, he can only respond to a signature query for an apriori chosen message (before the verification key is fixed). Also note that the reason we only afford one-time security is that given a collision pair for the hash function, all bets about its collision-resistance in the future are off. In fact, for all existing instantiations of chameleon hash functions, given a collision pair one can easily generate many more collisions. Finally, note that the *chameleon property* of the hash function did not play a role in the security proof. Instead, it was needed for the functionality it provides, as it is used in the signing algorithm.

Efficiency and optimizations. The signature consists of a single element in $\mathcal{R}_{ek}$. The signing involves one invocation of the h^{-1} function. As we will see shortly, for a number of instantiations of chameleon hash functions, this leads to very efficient signing that only includes modular addition and multiplications (no exponentiations). The verification requires one evaluation of the chameleon hash function.

The verification key for the above signature scheme consists of the tuple $(ek, h(ek, m_f, r_s))$. However, we can shorten the verification key via use of a *target collision resistant* hash function. In other words, given a function T from a family of TCR functions, we can let the verification key be $vk = (ek, T(h(ek, m_f, r_s)))$. It is easy to verify that the above proof of security still goes through without any difficulties. Since $h(ek, m_f, r_s)$ is often a group element this simple optimization can lead to a decent improvement in the key size.

Unifying the previous works. The above construction explains and unifies several previous works that use one-times signatures and/or chameleon hash functions. Here we consider two use cases for chameleon hash functions in the literature. The first application is the design of offline/online signature schemes. The earlier work of Even *et al.* [18] used a one-time signature scheme to design an offline/online signature scheme. It is not hard to show that the notion of security they need for their one-time signature scheme is UF-AMA security (not the UF-CMA security). The later work of Tauman and Shamir [39], proposed the use of chameleon hash functions in order to design offline/online signature schemes. Our construction implies that the latter construction can be interpreted as an efficient instantiation of the former.

Another common application of chameleon hash functions is for transforming UF-AMA secure signature schemes to UF-CMA secure signature schemes (e.g. see [25,12]). Again, it is easy to verify that a UF-AMA secure one-time signature can also be used for such a transformation, and that the transformations based on chameleon hash functions can be seen as efficient instantiations of the construction of [18].

3.2 A Strongly Unforgeable uf-cma Scheme

Security against apriori message attacks is not sufficient in all applications of one-time signatures. In several instances, such as the design of IND-CCA PKE from IBE schemes [14] or general transformation of UF-CMA signature schemes to strongly UF-CMA signature schemes [26], the *strong unforgeability* and security against *chosen message attacks* of the OTS scheme seem crucial. Next we show how to enhance the previous construction to design such a signature scheme from chameleon hash functions as well.

Construction 32. Let $H = (Gen, h, h^{-1})$ be a family of chameleon hash functions as defined in section 2 and $T_{ek,ek'} : \mathcal{Y}_{ek} \rightarrow \mathcal{M}' \subseteq \mathcal{M}_{ek'}$ be a target collision resistant hash function, where ek and ek' are two evaluation keys for the chameleon hash family. We construct a one-time SUF-CMA signature OTS in the following way:

- **Key Generation:**
  1. Compute $(ek_i, td_i) \xleftarrow{\$} Gen(1^k)$ for $i \in \{0,1\}$.
  2. Choose uniformly random strings $r_s^0 \in \mathcal{R}_{ek_0}, r_s^1 \in \mathcal{R}_{ek_1}$.
  3. Compute $z_0 = h(ek_0, m_f, r_s^0)$ and $z_1 = T_{ek_1,ek_0}(h(ek_1, m_f, r_s^1))$. Here m_f is an arbitrary message in $\mathcal{M}_{ek_1}$. m_f can potentially be different for different signers. As before, there is no need to keep m_f secret, but it is also not needed for verification.
  4. Output (vk, sk) where $vk = (ek_0, ek_1, z_0)$ and $sk = (td_0, td_1, r_s^0, r_s^1, z_1)$.
- **Signing:** On input message m, return the signature $\sigma = (h^{-1}(td_1, m_f, r_s^1, m), h^{-1}(td_0, m_f, r_s^0, z_1))$.
- **Verification:** On input $(m, \sigma = (r, r'))$, accept if $h(ek_0, T_{ek_1,ek_0}(h(ek_1, m, r)), r') = z_0$. Else, reject.

Claim. If H is a family of chameleon hash functions, and T_{ek_1,ek_0} is a TCR hash function, then the OTS scheme described above is a one-time SUF-CMA secure signature scheme.

Proof. Let A be the adversary that breaks the OTS scheme in the SUF-CMA game. Then we build an adversary B that breaks the collision resistance of the chameleon hash function H. Let A's signature query and answer be $(m, \sigma = (\sigma_0, \sigma_1))$, and denote the forgery made by A with $(m^*, \sigma^* = (\sigma_0^*, \sigma_1^*))$. We divide the proof into two separate parts for two different types of forgers. Note that the two types of forger we consider are complements of each other and therefore partition the space of all possible forgers. Hence, adversary A is a member of exactly one of these two sets. Our adversary B has to randomly guess which type of forger A is going to be. He will be correct with probability 1/2 which leads to a factor of two reduction in tightness of security.

– **Type I Forger.** In this type of forgery we have that either $(m, \sigma_0) = (m^*, \sigma_0^*)$ or $h(ek_1, m, \sigma_0) \neq h(ek_1, m^*, \sigma_0^*)$. In this case B finds a collision for H under the public key ek_0. B is given ek_0.

  He generates $(ek_1, td_1) \xleftarrow{\$} Gen(1^k)$ on his own, computes $z_1 = T(h(ek_1, m_f, r))$ and $z_0 = h(ek_0, z_1, r')$ for random $r \in \mathcal{R}_{ek_0}, r' \in \mathcal{R}_{ek_1}$ and sends $vk = (ek_0, ek_1, z_0)$ to A. Note that even though B computes z_1 before seeing the signature query, the *uniformity property* of the chameleon hash function guarantees that A's view is indistinguishable from the real scheme.

  A makes a signature query for a message m. B computes $\sigma_0 = h^{-1}(td_1, m_f, r, m)$ and $\sigma_1 = r'$ and returns the signature $\sigma = (\sigma_0, \sigma_1)$ to A. A eventually sends a forgery $m^*, \sigma_0^*, \sigma_1^*$ where either $(m, \sigma_0) = (m^*, \sigma_0^*)$ or $h(ek_1, m, \sigma_0) \neq h(ek_1, m^*, \sigma_0^*)$. If the latter is the case, due to the target collision resistance of T_{ek_1,ek_0}, with all but negligible probability we have that $z_1 \neq z_1^*$ where $z_1 = T_{ek_1,ek_0}(h(ek_1, m, \sigma_0))$ and $z_1^* = T_{ek_1,ek_0}(h(ek_1, m^*, \sigma_0^*))$.

  Hence, it is easy to see that for this type of forger $(z_1, \sigma_1) \neq (z_1^*, \sigma_1^*)$ which is exactly what B outputs as his collision for H under the public key ek_0. Given the way the verification algorithm is defined, it is easy to see that B outputs a collision iff A successfully forges a signature for m^*.

– **Type II Forger.** In this type of forgery we have that $(m, \sigma_0) \neq (m^*, \sigma_0^*)$ and $h(ek_1, m, \sigma_0) = h(ek_1, m^*, \sigma_0^*)$. In this case B finds a collision for H under the public key ek_1. B is given ek_1.

  He generates $(ek_0, td_0) \stackrel{\$}{\leftarrow} Gen(1^k)$ on his own, computes $z_0 = h(ek_0, m_f, r)$ for a random $r \in \mathcal{R}_{ek_0}$ and sends $vk = (ek_0, ek_1, z_0)$ to A. A makes a signature query for a message m. B computes $z_1 = h(ek_1, m, r')$, lets $\sigma_0 = r'$ and $\sigma_1 = h^{-1}(td_0, m_f, r, z_1)$ and returns the signature (σ_0, σ_1) to A. Eventually, A will output a forgery $(m^*, \sigma_0^*, \sigma_1^*)$. B outputs the pair $(m, \sigma_0) \neq (m^*, \sigma_0^*)$ as his collision for H under the public key ek_1. It is easy to see that based on the way this type of forgery is defined B can successfully find a collision as long as he simulates A's view (which we showed he can).

Efficiency. We will shortly look at specific instantiations of the above construction based on standard assumptions, but it is useful to evaluate the efficiency of the general construction as well. The signature consists of two elements in $\mathcal{R}_{ek}$. In most instantiations of chameleon hash functions this translates to two elements from the underlying group. The cost of signing a message is two invocations of h^{-1}. As mentioned earlier, in a number of constructions for chameleon has functions, this translates to simple arithmetic operations and does not include exponentiations. In these cases, signing a message becomes very fast. The verification requires two invocations of the function h. The verification key for the scheme includes two evaluation keys for the chameleon hash function and one element from the range of the chameleon hash. Similar to the construction of previous section, the last element can be shortened by applying a target collision resistant hash function.

Strong OTS from Σ-protocols. Bellare and Ristov [3] design chameleon hash functions based on Σ-protocols that satisfy certain security properties (in the standard model). Combined with our result, this leads to a general transformation of Σ-protocols to strongly unforgeable one-time signature schemes in the standard model:

Theorem 33. *There exists an efficient transformation for building* SUF-CMA *one-time signature schemes from any Σ-protocol that satisfies* strong special soundness *and* strong HVZK.

We refer the reader to [3] for formal definitions of the above security notions where the authors show that these two requirements are already satisfied by several existing constructions such as the Schnorr [38] and GQ [24] protocols. It is also shown that for Σ-protocols such as Fiat-Shamir [19], Micali-Shamir [31], and Okamoto's [32], one can modify the original constructions to satisfy these properties without affecting the underlying hardness assumption or the efficiency of the original scheme. The one-time signature schemes one derives from several of these protocols are new, and warrant further study. In this paper, however, we focus on constructions that are directly based on the existing chameleon hash functions.

We point out that Bellare and Shoup [5] also show a general transformation for designing strong one-time signature schemes from Σ-protocols, but the security properties they require from the starting protocol appear to be stronger than ours (security against *concurrent attacks*). Particularly, while one can efficiently instantiate our construction based on the RSA problem or even the hardness of factoring integers, the same is not known about their constructions.

Unifying the previous works. Starting with the work of Boneh *et al.* [10], several works in the literature studied constructions for transforming any UF-AMA signature scheme to a *strongly* UF-CMA signature scheme. While Boneh *et al.*'s construction only works for signature schemes with a special partitioning property (a property not possessed by most signature schemes), the later works of [26,40,5] develop techniques that work for any UF-AMA secure signature scheme. The works of [5] and [26] use a strongly unforgeable one-time signature in their construction while that of [40] takes advantage of a chameleon hash function. Without going into the details of their constructions, we observe that based on our results the latter construction based on a chameleon hash function can be interpreted as an efficient instantiation of the former.

4 Instantiations Based on Standard Assumptions

Our general construction leads to a wide range of new constructions for strongly unforgeable one-time signature schemes. Several of these constructions match or improve the efficiency of the previous constructions based on similar assumptions or relax the underlying hardness assumption. Here, we study the properties of three specific instantiations of our construction based on assumptions such as the discrete-log problem, the hardness of factoring, and lattice-based assumptions.

4.1 A Construction Based on the Factoring Assumption

Next we describe an instantiation of our general construction based on the hardness of factoring integers. There are multiple constructions of chameleon hash functions based on factoring but we focus on the hash function of Shamir and Tauman [39], since it leads to a signature scheme with very fast signing (though the verification still requires exponentiation).

- **Key Generation:**
  1. Generate two random safe primes $p, q \in \{0,1\}^{k/2}$ and compute $n = pq$.
  2. Choose at random an element $g \in \mathbb{Z}_n^*$ of order $\lambda(n)$ where $\lambda(n) = \phi(n)/2 = (p-1)(q-1)/2$.
  3. The public key is $ek = (n, g)$ and the trapdoor key is $td = (p, q)$. The evaluation and inversion for the hash function $h(ek, \cdot) : \mathbb{Z}_n \times \mathbb{Z}_{\lambda_n} \to \mathbb{Z}_n^*$ is defined as:
- **Evaluation:** On message $m \in \mathbb{Z}_n$ and randomness $r \in \mathbb{Z}_{\lambda(n)}$, compute and return $g^{m||r} \mod n \in Z_n^*$. The concatenation treats m and r as bitstrings

where we assume that each $r \in \mathbb{Z}_{\lambda(n)}$ is represented using exactly k bits, even if some of the leading bits are zero.

- **Inversion:** On input messages $m, m' \in \mathbb{Z}_n$ and randomness $r \in \mathbb{Z}_{\lambda(n)}$, return $r' = 2^k(m - m') + r \mod \lambda(n)$.

See [39] for a proof that the above construction is a chameleon hash function based on the factoring assumption. An important property of the above construction is that the inversion function only requires one modular addition and a multiplication. Given the above hash function, the strongly unforgeable one-time signature scheme is as follows:

Construction 41. Let T_0, T_1 be target collision resistant functions, where T_0 maps elements of $\mathbb{Z}^*_{n_0}$ to bitstrings, and T_1 maps elements of $\mathbb{Z}^*_{n_1}$ to a subset of $\mathbb{Z}_{n_0}$.

- **Key Generation:**
  1. Compute $n_0 = p_0q_0$ and $n_1 = p_1q_1$ where p_i, q_i are safe primes, for $i \in \{0, 1\}$.
  2. Choose at random elements $g_0 \in \mathbb{Z}^*_{n_0}$ and $g_1 \in \mathbb{Z}^*_{n_1}$ of orders $\lambda(n_0)$ and $\lambda(n_1)$ respectively.
  3. Compute $z_0 = T_0(g_0^{0||r_0} \mod n_0)$ and $z_1 = T_1(g_1^{0||r_1} \mod n_1)$.
  4. Return $vk = (n_0, n_1, g_0, g_1, z_0)$ and $sk = ((p_0, q_0), (p_1, q_1), r_0, r_1, z_1)$.
- **Signing:** On a message $m \in \mathbb{Z}_n$, return the signature $\sigma = (\sigma_0, \sigma_1)$ where $\sigma_0 = 2^k(0 - z_1) + r_0 \mod \lambda(n_0)$ and $\sigma_1 = 2^k(0 - m) + r_1 \mod \lambda(n_1)$.
- **Verification:** On a message m and the signature $\sigma = (\sigma_0, \sigma_1)$
  1. Compute $y = T_1(g_1^{m||\sigma_1} \mod n_1)$.
  2. Compute $y' = T_0(g_0^{y||\sigma_0} \mod n_0)$.
  3. accept if $y' = z_0$ and reject otherwise.

Efficiency Comparison. The verification key contains two integers, two group elements, and one hash output. The signature consists of two group elements. The signing algorithm consists of two modular additions and two modular multiplications. The verification algorithm includes two exponentiations. Hence, the scheme is desirable in situations where the signer has low computational power, but the verifier does not have such limits.

General constructions of OTS schemes lead to secure schemes based on the factoring assumption, however the resulting constructions are impractical. Goldwasser *et al.* [22] also design a signature scheme from claw-free trapdoor permutations with instantiations based on the factoring assumption. Their signature scheme leads to short signatures, but the signing algorithm requires one exponentiation per bit of the message, which makes the resulting scheme inefficient. A number of works in the literature have studied the design of fail-stop signature schemes based on factoring-related assumptions [7,33,36,41,37]. However, almost all such constructions rely on assumptions that are stronger than the standard factoring assumption. The only exception is the construction of [7,33] which is based on the intractability of factoring integers $n = pq$ for p, q with $p = q = 3 \mod 4$ (i.e. Blum integers) and $p \neq q \mod 8$. However, it is not known if factoring integers of this special form is as hard as factoring arbitrary RSA integers (see [37] for a more detailed discussion).

Hence, to the best of our knowledge, our construction is the first short OTS based solely on the standard factoring assumption, where the signing algorithm only requires simple arithmetic operations.

More constructions based on factoring-related Assumptions. [3] and [2] design multiple constructions of chameleon hash functions based on factoring and the RSA problem, respectively. When plugged into our general construction, each of these leads to a new strongly unforgeable one-time signature scheme. However, the cost of signing for these schemes is higher than the scheme we described as they involve exponentiation.

4.2 A Construction from Lattice-Based Assumptions

We briefly describe the lattice-based chameleon hash function of [20,34] based on preimage samplable (trapdoor) function (PSF). Each function in the family is represented by matrices $A \in \mathbb{Z}_q^{k\times m_1}$ and $B \in \mathbb{Z}_q^{k\times m_2}$ where k is the security parameter, $q = poly(k)$ is an odd prime and $m_1, m_2 = O(k \log q)$. The message space is $\mathcal{M} = \{x \in \mathbb{Z}_q^{m_1} : ||x||_2 \leq \beta_1\}$, and the randomness domain is $\mathcal{R} = \{r \in \mathbb{Z}_q^{m_2} : 0 < ||r||_2 \leq \beta_2\}$ where β_1 and β_2 are chosen appropriately. The randomness distribution is a discrete Gaussian over $\mathbb{Z}_q^{m_2}$, and the range of the function is $\mathcal{Y} = \mathbb{Z}_q^k$.

A function in the family is defined by $h_{A,B}(m, r) = Am + Br$ where $m \in \mathcal{M}$ and $r \in \mathcal{R}$. The hardness of collision follows from the *short integer solution* (SIS) assumption, that is related to worst-case lattice-based assumptions such as approximating the shortest vector problem. The trapdoor is a short basis for the lattice whose parity-check matrix is B. The inversion function $h_{A,B}^{-1}$ involves simple linear algebra operations. We do not explain the details here but refer the reader to [20,34] for more information.

The strongly unforgeable one-time signature scheme is then obtained by plugging in the above chameleon hash function in our general construction. Hence we directly move to the analysis of the efficiency for the resulting scheme.

Efficiency and Comparison. The verification key for the resulting scheme consists of matrices A and B which leads to a key size of $O(k^2 \log k)$. The signature contains two elements in $\mathcal{R}$, and hence the signature is of size $O(k \log k)$. The signing algorithm requires two invocations of the inversion for the preimage samplable function described above.

Lyubashevsky and Micciancio [29] also design an asymptotically efficient one-time signature based on lattice-based assumptions, but they need to work with lattices with special structure (i.e. ideal lattices). As pointed out by the authors, it is desirable to avoid such extra assumptions while achieving a similar level of efficiency. Our construction removes this extra assumption, while still providing a signature of size $O(k \log k)$. However, the verification key and the signing cost for our scheme are larger than theirs.

Recently, Cash *et al.* [15] designed digital signature schemes based on worst-case lattice-based assumptions in the standard model. However, the signature size in their constructions is in the order of $O(k^2 \log k)$. In [11] Boyen improved their result by building a signature scheme with signature size linear in k, while the verification key size is still significantly longer than ours (i.e. cubic in k).

Acknowledgement. I would like to thank Greg Zaverucha for helpful discussions and the anonymous reviewers for valuable comments.

References

1. Abe, M., Cui, Y., Imai, H., Kiltz, E.: Efficient hybrid encryption from ID-based encryption. Designs, Codes and Cryptography 54(3), 205–240 (2010)
2. Ateniese, G., de Medeiros, B.: Identity-based chameleon hash and applications. In: Juels, A. (ed.) FC 2004. LNCS, vol. 3110, pp. 164–180. Springer, Heidelberg (2004)
3. Bellare, M., Ristov, T.: Hash functions from sigma protocols and improvements to VSH. In: Pieprzyk, J. (ed.) ASIACRYPT 2008. LNCS, vol. 5350, pp. 125–142. Springer, Heidelberg (2008)
4. Bellare, M., Rogaway, P.: Collision-resistant hashing: Towards making UOWHFs practical. In: Kaliski Jr., B.S. (ed.) CRYPTO 1997. LNCS, vol. 1294, pp. 470–484. Springer, Heidelberg (1997)
5. Bellare, M., Shoup, S.: Two-tier signatures, strongly unforgeable signatures, and fiat-shamir without random oracles. In: Okamoto, T., Wang, X. (eds.) PKC 2007. LNCS, vol. 4450, pp. 201–216. Springer, Heidelberg (2007)
6. Bleichenbacher, D., Maurer, U.M.: On the efficiency of one-time digital signatures. In: Kim, K., Matsumoto, T. (eds.) ASIACRYPT 1996. LNCS, vol. 1163, pp. 145–158. Springer, Heidelberg (1996)
7. Bleumer, G., Pfitzmann, B., Waidner, M.: A Remark on Signature Scheme Where Forgery Can Be Proved. In: Damgård, I.B. (ed.) EUROCRYPT 1990. LNCS, vol. 473, pp. 441–445. Springer, Heidelberg (1991)
8. Boneh, D., Canetti, R., Halevi, S., Katz, J.: Chosen-ciphertext security from identity-based encryption. SIAM Journal on Computing 36(5), 915–942 (2006)
9. Boneh, D., Katz, J.: Improved efficiency for CCA-secure cryptosystems built using identity-based encryption. In: Menezes, A. (ed.) CT-RSA 2005. LNCS, vol. 3376, pp. 87–103. Springer, Heidelberg (2005)
10. Boneh, D., Shen, E., Waters, B.: Strongly unforgeable signatures based on computational diffie-hellman. In: Yung, M., Dodis, Y., Kiayias, A., Malkin, T. (eds.) PKC 2006. LNCS, vol. 3958, pp. 229–240. Springer, Heidelberg (2006)
11. Boyen, X.: Lattice Mixing and Vanishing Trapdoors: A Framework for Fully Secure Short Signatures and More. In: Nguyen, P.Q., Pointcheval, D. (eds.) PKC 2010. LNCS, vol. 6056, pp. 499–517. Springer, Heidelberg (2010)
12. Brakerski, Z., Kalai, Y.T.: A Framework for Efficient Signatures, Ring Signatures and Identity Based Encryption in the Standard Model, `http://eprint.iacr.org/2010/086.pdf`
13. Brassard, G., Chaum, D., Crépeau, C.C.: Minimum disclosure proofs of knowledge. Journal of Computer and System Sciences 37(2), 156–189 (1988)

14. Canetti, R., Halevi, S., Katz, J.: Chosen-ciphertext security from identity-based encryption. In: Cachin, C., Camenisch, J. (eds.) EUROCRYPT 2004. LNCS, vol. 3027, pp. 207–222. Springer, Heidelberg (2004)
15. Cash, D., Hofheinz, D., Kiltz, E., Peikert, C.: Bonsai Trees, or How to Delegate a Lattice Basis. In: Gilbert, H. (ed.) EUROCRYPT 2010. LNCS, vol. 6110, pp. 523–552. Springer, Heidelberg (2010)
16. Dahmen, E., Krauß, C.: Short hash-based signatures for wireless sensor networks. In: Garay, J.A., Miyaji, A., Otsuka, A. (eds.) CANS 2009. LNCS, vol. 5888, pp. 463–476. Springer, Heidelberg (2009)
17. Dodis, Y., Katz, J.: Chosen-ciphertext security of multiple encryption. In: Kilian, J. (ed.) TCC 2005. LNCS, vol. 3378, pp. 188–209. Springer, Heidelberg (2005)
18. Even, S., Goldreich, O., Micali, S.: Online/offline signatures. Journal of Cryptology (1996)
19. Fiat, A., Shamir, A.: How to prove yourself: Practical solutions to identification and signature problems. In: Odlyzko, A.M. (ed.) CRYPTO 1986. LNCS, vol. 263, pp. 186–194. Springer, Heidelberg (1987)
20. Gentry, C., Peikert, C., Vaikuntanathan, V.: Trapdoors for hard lattices and new cryptographic constructions. In: Ladner, R.E., Dwork, C. (eds.) 40th Annual ACM Symposium on Theory of Computing, pp. 197–206. ACM Press, New York (May 2008)
21. Goldreich, O.: Two remarks concerning the goldwasser-micali-rivest signature scheme. In: Odlyzko, A.M. (ed.) CRYPTO 1986. LNCS, vol. 263, pp. 104–110. Springer, Heidelberg (1987)
22. Goldwasser, S., Micali, S., Rivest, R.L.: A digital signature scheme secure against adaptive chosen-message attacks. SIAM Journal on Computing 17(2), 281–308 (1988)
23. Groth, J.: Simulation-sound NIZK proofs for a practical language and constant size group signatures. In: Lai, X., Chen, K. (eds.) ASIACRYPT 2006. LNCS, vol. 4284, pp. 444–459. Springer, Heidelberg (2006)
24. Guillou, L.C., Quisquater, J.-J.: A Practical Zero-Knowledge Protocol Fitted to Security Microprocessor Minimizing Both Transmission and Memory. In: Günther, C.G. (ed.) EUROCRYPT 1988. LNCS, vol. 330, pp. 123–128. Springer, Heidelberg (1988)
25. Hohenberger, S., Waters, B.: Short and stateless signatures from the RSA assumption. In: Halevi, S. (ed.) CRYPTO 2009. LNCS, vol. 5677, pp. 654–670. Springer, Heidelberg (2009)
26. Huang, Q., Wong, D.S., Zhao, Y.: Generic transformation to strongly unforgeable signatures. In: Katz, J., Yung, M. (eds.) ACNS 2007. LNCS, vol. 4521, pp. 1–17. Springer, Heidelberg (2007)
27. Krawczyk, H., Rabin, T.: Chameleon signatures. In: ISOC Network and Distributed System Security Symposium – NDSS 2000. The Internet Society, San Diego (February 2000)
28. Lamport, L.: Constructing digital signatures from a one-way function. Technical Report SRI-CSL-98, SRI International Computer Science Laboratory (October 1979)
29. Lyubashevsky, V., Micciancio, D.: Asymptotically efficient lattice-based digital signatures. In: Canetti, R. (ed.) TCC 2008. LNCS, vol. 4948, pp. 37–54. Springer, Heidelberg (2008)
30. Merkle, R.C.: A certified digital signature. In: Brassard, G. (ed.) CRYPTO 1989. LNCS, vol. 435, pp. 218–238. Springer, Heidelberg (1990)

31. Micali, S., Shamir, A.: An improvement of the fiat-shamir identification and signature scheme. In: Goldwasser, S. (ed.) CRYPTO 1988. LNCS, vol. 403, pp. 244–247. Springer, Heidelberg (1990)
32. Okamoto, T.: Provably secure and practical identification schemes and corresponding signature schemes. In: Brickell, E.F. (ed.) CRYPTO 1992. LNCS, vol. 740, pp. 31–53. Springer, Heidelberg (1993)
33. Pedersen, T.P., Pfitzmann, B.: Fail-stop signatures. SIAM Journal on Computing 26, 291–330 (1997)
34. Peikert, C.: Bonsai trees (or, arboriculture in lattice-based cryptography). Cryptology ePrint Archive, Report 2009/359 (2009), `http://eprint.iacr.org/`
35. Perrig, A.: The BiBa one-time signature and broadcast authentication protocol. In: ACM CCS 2001: 8th Conference on Computer and Communications Security, pp. 28–37. ACM Press, New York (November 2001)
36. Safavi-Naini, R., Susilo, W.: Threshold fail-stop signature schemes based on discrete logarithm and factorization. In: Pieprzyk, J., Okamoto, E., Seberry, J. (eds.) ISW 2000. LNCS, vol. 1975, pp. 292–307. Springer, Heidelberg (2000)
37. Schmidt-Samoa, K.: Factorization-based fail-stop signatures revisited. In: López, J., Qing, S., Okamoto, E. (eds.) ICICS 2004. LNCS, vol. 3269, pp. 118–131. Springer, Heidelberg (2004)
38. Schnorr, C.-P.: Efficient signature generation by smart cards. Journal of Cryptology 4(3), 161–174 (1991)
39. Shamir, A., Tauman, Y.: Improved online/Offline signature schemes. In: Kilian, J. (ed.) CRYPTO 2001. LNCS, vol. 2139, pp. 355–367. Springer, Heidelberg (2001)
40. Steinfeld, R., Pieprzyk, J., Wang, H.: How to strengthen any weakly unforgeable signature into a strongly unforgeable signature. In: Abe, M. (ed.) CT-RSA 2007. LNCS, vol. 4377, pp. 357–371. Springer, Heidelberg (2006)
41. Susilo, W., Safavi-Naini, R.: An efficient fail-stop signature scheme based on factorization. In: Lee, P.J., Lim, C.H. (eds.) ICISC 2002. LNCS, vol. 2587, pp. 62–74. Springer, Heidelberg (2003)
42. van Heyst, E., Pedersen, T.P.: How to make efficient fail-stop signatures. In: Rueppel, R.A. (ed.) EUROCRYPT 1992. LNCS, vol. 658, pp. 366–377. Springer, Heidelberg (1993)
43. Zaverucha, G.M., Stinson, D.R.: Short one-time signatures. Cryptology ePrint Archive, Report 2010/446 2010, `http://eprint.iacr.org/`

A Security Definitions for Signature Schemes

A signature scheme is a tuple of the following algorithms:

- $Gen(1^k)$: The key generation algorithm outputs a key pair (vk, sk).
- $Sign(sk, m)$: The signing algorithm takes in a secret key sk, and a message m, and produces a signature σ.
- $Ver(vk, m, \sigma)$: The verification algorithm takes in a verification key vk, a message m, and a purported signature σ, and returns 1 if the signature is valid and 0 otherwise.

Unforgeability against Chosen Message Attacks

The standard security notion for signatures is existential unforgeability with respect to adaptive chosen-message attacks (uf-cma) as formalized by Goldwasser,

Micali and Rivest [22]. It is defined using the following game between a challenger and an adversary A over a message space $\mathcal{M}$:

- **Setup:** The challenger runs the algorithm $Gen(1^k)$ to obtain the verification key vk and the secret key sk, and gives vk to the adversary.
- **Queries:** Proceeding adaptively, the adversary may request a signature on any message $m \in \mathcal{M}$ and the challenger will respond with $\sigma = Sign(sk, m)$. Let Q be the set of messages queried by the adversary.
- **Output:** Eventually, the adversary will output a pair (m, σ) and is said to win the game if $m \notin Q$ and $Ver(vk, m, \sigma) = 1$.

We define $\mathbf{Adv}_{\text{uf-cma},\mathsf{A}}$ to be the probability that adversary A wins in the above game.

Definition 1. *(UF-CMA [22]) A signature scheme $(Gen, Sign, Ver)$ is existentially unforgeable with respect to adaptive chosen message attacks if for all probabilistic polynomial time adversaries* A, $\mathbf{Adv}_{\mathsf{A}}$ *is negligible in the security parameter.*

Unforgeability against Apriori Message Attacks

Several works (e.g. [25]) have considered a weaker definition called existential unforgeability with respect to apriori chosen-message attacks (uf-ama). It is defined using the following game between a challenger and an adversary A over message space $\mathcal{M}$:

- **Queries:** The adversary sends the challenger a list Q of messages $m_1, \ldots, m_n \in \mathcal{M}$.
- **Response:** The challenger runs the algorithm $Gen(1^k)$ to obtain the verification key vk and the secret key sk. Next, the challenger signs each queried message as $\sigma_i = Sign(sk, m_i)$ for $i = 1$ to n. The challenger then sends $vk, \sigma_1, \ldots, \sigma_n$ to the adversary.
- **Output:** Eventually, the adversary will output a pair (m, σ) and is said to win the game if $m \notin Q$ and $Ver(vk, m, \sigma) = 1$.

We define $\mathbf{Adv}_{\text{uf-ama},\mathsf{A}}$ to be the probability that adversary A wins in the above game.

Definition 2. *(UF-AMA) A signature scheme $(Gen, Sign, Ver)$ is existentially unforgeable with respect to apriori chosen message attacks if for all probabilistic polynomial time adversaries* A, $\mathbf{Adv}_{\text{uf-ama},\mathsf{A}}$ *is negligible in the security parameter.*

Strongly Unforgeable One-time Signatures

A signature is called *one-time* if the adversary A in the above games is only allowed to make a single message query before creating a forgery.

A signature scheme is called *strongly* unforgeable if in the above security games, the adversary A wins even if in the output stage he forges a signature for a message $m \in Q$, by creating a different signature for it. We denote the corresponding notions of security with SUF-CMA and SUF-AMA .

B A Construction Based on the Discrete-Log Assumption

We use a well-known chameleon hash function based on the DL problem for our construction. The signature scheme we obtain is new and is as efficient as the best existing constructions based on the DLP (see [5] and [42]). Recently, Zaverucha and Stinson [43] designed a new OTS scheme based on the discrete-log assumption that is shorter than all previous schemes including ours. Further improvements in efficiency of the underlying chameleon hash function would lead to even more efficient constructions. The DL-based chameleon hash function we use is described next:

- **Key Generation:**
  1. Fix a generator g_1 for a prime-order group G, of size p.
  2. Generate a random x in $\mathbb{Z}_p$, and compute $g_2 = g_1^x$.
  3. The public key $ek = (p, g_1, g_2)$ and the trapdoor key is $td = x$.
- **Evaluation:** On message m and randomness r in $\mathbb{Z}_p$, return $g_1^m g_2^r$.
- **Inversion:** On inputs messages m, m' and randomness r, compute $r' = x^{-1}(m - m') + r \mod p$.

Given the above hash functions, the strongly unforgeable one-time signature scheme is as follows:

Construction B1. A SUF-CMA one-time signature based on the DL problem

- **Key Generation:**
  1. Fix a generator g_1 for a prime order group G of size p. Let T be target collision hash function that maps elements of G to a subset of $\mathbb{Z}_p$.
  2. Generate random $x, x' \in \mathbb{Z}_p$ and compute $g_2 = g_1^x$ and $g_3 = g_1^{x'}$.
  3. Compute $z_0 = T(g_1 g_2^r)$ and $z_1 = T(g_1 g_3^{r'})$ for random $r, r' \in \mathbb{Z}_p$.
  4. The verification key is $vk = (g_1, g_2, g_3, z_0)$ and the signing key is $sk = (y = x^{-1}, y' = x'^{-1}, r, r', z_1)$[1].
- **Signing:** To sign a message m, compute and return signature $\sigma = (\sigma_0, \sigma_1)$ where $\sigma_0 = y'(1 - m) + r' \mod p$ and $\sigma_1 = y(1 - z_1) + r \mod p$.
- **Verification:** On message m and the signature $\sigma = (\sigma_0, \sigma_1)$, accept if $T(g_1^{T(g_1^m g_3^{\sigma_0})} g_2^{\sigma_1}) = z_0$ and reject otherwise.

Efficiency Comparison. The verification key contains three group elements and one TCR hash output. The signature consists of two integers in $\mathbb{Z}_p$. Signing is very fast and only includes simple arithmetic operations. Verification requires exponentiations.

[1] Note that in this instantiation we let the fixed message $m_f = 1$.

Compared to the DL-based construction of [5] which is based on Okamoto's identification scheme, our construction has a shorter verification key (one less group element). The signature sizes are the same and the signing algorithm for both schemes only requires arithmetic operations[2].

Our construction matches the efficiency of the DL-based construction of Van Heyst and Pedersen [42] in many respects such as the key and signature sizes and the cost of signing a message.

[2] We note that [5] designs a more efficient OTS scheme based on a stronger assumption called *one-more DLP*.

On the Minimum Communication Effort for Secure Group Key Exchange

Frederik Armknecht[1] and Jun Furukawa[2]

[1] Universität Mannheim, Germany
armknecht@informatik.uni-mannheim.de
[2] NEC Corporation, Japan
j-furukawa@ay.jp.nec.com

Abstract. Group key exchange protocols (GKE) allow a set of parties to establish a common key over an insecure network. So far the research on GKE mainly focused on identifying and formalizing appropriate security definitions that has led to a variety of different security models. Besides reaching a high security level, another important aspect is to reduce the communication effort. In many practical scenarios it is preferable (or possibly even indispensable) to reduce the number of messages to a minimum, e.g., to save time and/or energy.

We prove that any n-party GKE that provides forward security (FS) and mutual authentication (MA) against insider attackers needs at least two communication rounds and in that case at least $\frac{1}{2}n^2 + \frac{1}{2}n - 3$ messages. Observe that FS and MA are today accepted as basic security recommendations. Hence these bounds hold automatically as well for more elaborate security definitions.

Then, we describe a 2-round-GKE that requires $n + 1$ messages more than the derived lower bound. We prove that the protocol achieves UC-security (in the model by Katz and Shin (CCS'05)) in the common reference string (CRS) model. To the best of our knowledge, this represents the most communication efficient (in terms of number of rounds and messages) UC-secure GKE so far.

Keywords: Group key exchange, communication effort, UC security.

1 Introduction

Many cryptographic mechanisms, especially for confidentiality and authenticity, require a common secret to be shared between the communication partners. Therefore, key exchange protocols (KE) belong to the most practically relevant cryptographic primitives. However, while several secure and efficient KEs are known and used nowadays for the case of $n = 2$ parties, the situation becomes more complicated in the case of group key exchange protocols (GKE), where a key needs to be established between $n > 2$ parties.

Obviously, an optimal GKE should achieve the highest security goal with the lowest possible communication effort. Here, the communication effort is usually represented in the number of communication rounds and the number of messages. However, only little is known about the *minimum* communication effort of GKEs. This question is not only of theoretical interest. In practice the exchange of messages between the parties can be more time consuming than the computations themselves. Thus, reducing the

A. Biryukov, G. Gong, and D.R. Stinson (Eds.): SAC 2010, LNCS 6544, pp. 320–337, 2011.

number of messages can help to reduce the time effort. Furthermore, the energy effort for sending messages (wireless) is usually by magnitudes higher than for performing computations. Therefore, GKEs with reduced communication effort[1] are beneficial for application scenarios where low-weight devices with restricted resources are involved.

Actually, the minimum communication effort depends on several factors. For example, although it is common to identify each protocol run by an individual session identity (SID), differences exist on how to set up the SID. In principle, one can distinguish between two fundamental approaches: *external-SID* GKEs, where a globally unique SID is provided by an external environment, and *internal-SID* GKEs, where a SID is determined by the group members themselves during the protocol execution. As we will see later this already impacts the minimum communication effort.

Other factors are the considered security model and security goals. Up to now, a variety of different security models for GKEs exist. Based on the two-party case [3,4,2], Bresson et al. [9,7,8] gave the first formal security model for GKEs. They formalized the notions of authenticated key exchange (AKE) and mutual authentication (MA). AKE means informally that a group key is computationally indistinguishable from a random string while MA guarantees that each party is assured of the participation of every other party in the protocol. Initially, these definitions considered outsider attackers only, that is, adversaries who do *not* take part in the protocol. Later on, Katz and Shin [20] introduced the notion of insider attacks: an attacker can corrupt several group members and can actively participate into the protocol. They presented a security model for GKEs within the Universal Composability (UC) framework [14] and showed that their model covers insider attackers. They also presented the construction of UC-secure GKE. A UC-secure protocol maintains its security properties even when composed concurrently with an unbounded number of instances of other UC-secure protocols. In [11], Bresson et al. revised the model from [9] so that (among other things) insider attackers are captured as well. Another important security notion is contributiveness that has been brought up by Bohli et al. [5] and strengthened by Bresson and Manulis [10]. A protocol satisfying this property ensures that a proper subset of insiders cannot predetermine the session key. Gorantla et al. [17] showed how to define UC-secure GKEs that provide contributiveness. Evidently, the search for a comprehensive security model for GKEs is still within the focus of current research, bringing up new security notions like key compromise impersonation (e.g., Gorantla et al. [16]) or the consideration of special approaches like password-authenticated GKEs (e.g., Abdalla et al. [1]).

Intuitively, one can expect that most additional security requirements on GKEs will not "come for free". Making a GKE stronger will probably increase the computational and/or communication effort. Previous works mostly investigated GKEs from a security perspective, asking the question: *When is a GKE secure?* Here, we approach GKEs more from complexity theory and ask: *How much does it cost (in terms of messages and rounds) to make a GKE secure?*

Actually, we are only aware of the work by Furukawa et al. [15] that addressed directly the question of the *minimum* communication effort of GKEs. More precisely

[1] Of course, the communication effort depends on the length of the messages as well. We do not investigate this question in this work.

they proved that any 2-round UC-secure[2] GKE with internal-SID generation between n parties requires at least $2n^2 - 2n$ messages. Observe that this bound relies on two rather strong assumptions: (i) UC-security (which requires straight-line simulatability) and (ii) internal-SID generation. Therefore, it is plausible to assume that both aspects impact the minimum communication effort but the question is to what extent.

Contribution. In this work we pick up the question investigated by Furukawa et al. [15]. First, we derive lower bounds on the communication effort of GKEs based on a selection of minimum security requirements only: *forward secrecy* (FS) (the corruption of a party has no impact on the security of past protocol runs) and *mutual authentication* (MA) (an honest participant outputs a key only if all other participants in this group agreed to participate in the GKE and all honest parties generate the same key) in the presence of *insider attackers* (attackers that actively participate in the protocol). To have a clear separation between the effort for SID generation and key establishment, we consider external-SID GKEs only. We show that under these conditions, GKEs require at least two communication rounds and in this case at least $\frac{1}{2}n^2 + \frac{1}{2}n - 3$ messages in total. Interestingly this bound is significantly smaller than the lower bound derived in [15]. This sheds some lights on the "costs" for fulfilling additional requirements (as UC-security and SID-generation in this case). To the best of our knowledge the notions of forward secrecy and mutual authentication against insider attackers are covered by any recent security models for GKEs. Thus, they can be seen as basic requirements and the lower bounds should be valid for any current or upcoming security model[3]. We note that the number of messages might be smaller for GKEs that comprise more than two rounds. However, from our point of view, minimizing the number of rounds will have a more significant impact in reducing the time effort for GKEs than reducing the number of messages. The reason is that in practice, we expect that more time is spend for waiting for all messages within one round, i.e., waiting that a round is completed, than for generating the messages themselves. Therefore, minimizing the number of rounds was our primary focus.

Our second contribution is a 2-round GKE that requires $\frac{1}{2}n^2 + \frac{3}{2}n - 2$ messages, being $n + 1$ messages more than the derived lower bound. We prove that the protocol is UC-secure (based on the UC-model given by Katz and Shin [20]) in the common reference string model under the decisional Diffie-Hellman assumption. As UC-security implies FS and MA, the protocol illustrates that GKEs with almost optimal communication effort are possible. Of independent interest might be our observation that although we aim for "symmetric" security properties like mutual authentication, our protocol is highly asymmetric regarding the roles of the different participants. A further interesting observation is that both in the work by Furukawa et al. [15] and in our work, it is shown that one can construct GKEs that are UC-secure and have an almost optimal number of messages. This seems to indicate that considering UC-security has a rather minor impact on the minimum number of messages.

To the best of our knowledge, the most efficient (in number of messages) GKEs so far have been given by Furukawa et al. [15] and Gorantla et al. [17]. Both require 2 rounds

[2] If not mentioned otherwise, UC-secure refers to the Katz-Shin-model [20].

[3] Of course, the incorporation of additional assumptions might increase these bounds. We leave this question for future research.

and $2n^2 - 2n$ messages, but possess stronger properties: internal SID-generation and contributiveness, respectively. This makes them rather incomparable but indicates again the higher communication effort for stronger requirements.

Organization. The paper is organized as follows: Sec. 2 informally repeats the common communication model and the security notions of internal attackers, forward secrecy (FS), and mutual authentication (MA). Sec. 3 presents some lower bounds on the communication effort of external-SID GKEs that provide forward secrecy and mutual authentication in the presence of insider attackers. Sec. 4 proposes a concrete GKE protocol that almost meets this lower bound and Sec. 5 proves that it achieves UC-security. Sec. 6 concludes the paper.

2 Preliminaries

In this section we repeat some common aspects of GKE models. We assume for simplicity a fixed group of parties $\mathcal{P}$ of potential participants. A GKE is executed between the members of subset $pid = \{\Pi_1, \ldots, \Pi_n\} \subseteq \mathcal{P}$ where Π_i is the *party ID* of the i-th participant in the GKE. Each protocol execution is labeled by its own session ID (SID) *sid* that has to be globally unique. If a message $(sid, pid, \textsf{new-session})$ is send to an honest party $\Pi \in pid$, a new *instance* (Π, sid, pid) of Π is invoked. An instance can be seen as a copy of Π that has its own *instance state* (which, for example, stores all ephemeral values). All instances (Π, sid, pid), $\Pi \in pid$, start a new execution of a GKE π where each instance uses its own instance state. During this session, every instance (Π, sid, pid) communicates only with other instances (Π', sid', pid') if $(sid, pid) = (sid', pid')$, i.e., both instances participate into the same session *sid* with the same participants *pid*, and if $\Pi' \in pid$. If an instance (Π, sid, pid) finishes its participation into π, it outputs (Π, sid, pid, κ) with κ being the session key. Afterward, the instance (Π, sid, pid) and its corresponding instance state is deleted.

As pointed out in Sec. 1, the definition of an appropriate security model for GKEs is still in the focus of current research. However, several requirements exist that are commonly agreed to be part of any meaningful security model. In the following, we single out some of these and explain them shortly. We refer to Appendix A for a formal treatment of the considered security notions. We emphasize that the following list of conditions does not represent a full security model than rather a set of necessary basic requirements. In Sec. 3 we will show that these already imply some lower bounds on the communication effort. In consequence, the derived bounds automatically hold as well for any more elaborate security model that comprises the mentioned aspects.

An adversary can invoke a GKE between any subset $pid \subseteq \mathcal{P}$. In addition, she can control the communication within the network, and corrupt any party. Corruption means that she literally takes over control of the corrupted party and learns all its secrets. If corrupted parties participate into the protocol one speaks of *insider attackers*. Obviously, the secrecy of the key cannot be longer achieved in such cases but other security properties can still be true. One security requirement that is usually put on a GKE in the context of corruption is *forward secrecy*: if an attacker corrupts a party Π at some point in time, this does not impact the security of past protocol runs which Π participated to. Another established security requirement is *mutual authentication*: an honest party

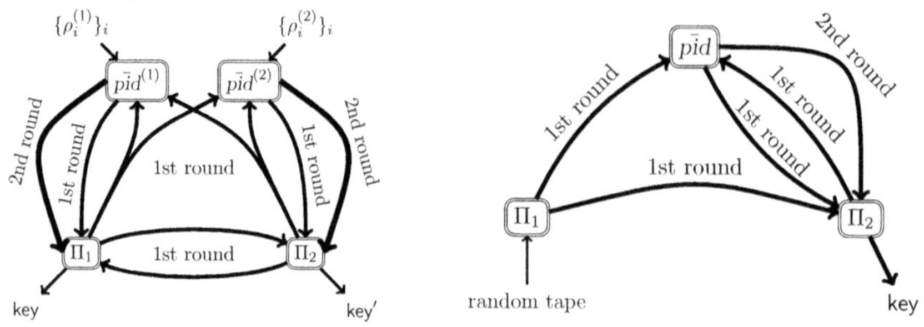

(a) Execution 1 (b) Execution 2

Fig. 1. The protocol executions discussed in the proof of Theorem 1

only outputs a key if all parties in the same group confirmed their participation and keys generated by honest parties are equal.

3 Lower Bounds on the Communication Effort

In this section, we derive lower bounds on the number of rounds and the number of exchanged messages in GKEs that provide forward secrecy and mutual authentication in the presence of insider attackers. We prove our lower bounds by contradiction. We show that if the communication effort is below the specified bounds, then there exists either an insider adversary who violates mutual authentication or an outsider adversary who breaks forward secrecy.

Theorem 1. *Consider a 2-round GKE between a group pid of parties that provides mutual authentication and forward secrecy in presence of insider attackers. For two different parties $\Pi, \Pi' \in$ pid and $r \in \{1,2\}$ denote by $m^r_{\Pi\to\Pi'}$ the message that Π sends toward*[4] *Π' in the r-th round. Furthermore, we define by $M^r_{\Pi,\Pi'} := \{m^r_{\Pi\to\Pi'}, m^r_{\Pi'\to\Pi}\}$ the set of messages exchanged between Π and Π' in the r-th round. It holds:*

1. *If $M^2_{\Pi_1,\Pi_2} = \emptyset$ for two different honest parties $\Pi_1, \Pi_2 \in$ pid, that is, Π_1 and Π_2 do not exchange any message in the second round, then the session key depends only on the random tapes of these two parties and some other public data, e.g., the session identity, the public keys of parties, etc.*
2. *There exists at most one pair (Π_1, Π_2) of honest parties such that $M^2_{\Pi_1,\Pi_2} = \emptyset$.*

Proof. The case of $n = 2$ parties is straightforward. There is only one possible pair of parties so that the claims are obviously true. Hence, we restrict to the case $n \geq 3$ in the following.

[4] Recall that it is not guaranteed that the message eventually reaches Π' as the attacker is assumed to have complete control over the network.

We describe for each claim a possible protocol execution (termed execution 1 and 2 and displayed in Fig. 1) where we show that if the claim is not fulfilled, the assumptions are violated. We start with the first claim and explain execution 1. Let $\Pi_1, \Pi_2 \in pid$ be two different honest parties in a 2-round GKE with $M^2_{\Pi_1,\Pi_2} = \emptyset$. We consider an adversary $\mathcal{A}$ who corrupts all parties in $\overline{pid} := pid \setminus \{\Pi_1, \Pi_2\}$. For each $\Pi_i \in \overline{pid}$, the adversary simulates two instances of Π_i, called $\Pi_i^{(1)}$ and $\Pi_i^{(2)}$. These use two independent random tapes, denoted by $\rho_i^{(1)}$ and $\rho_i^{(2)}$, respectively. Let $\overline{pid}^{(1)}$ denote the set of all instances $\Pi_i^{(1)}$ for $i \geq 3$, and define analogously $\overline{pid}^{(2)}$.

The core idea of the proof is to show that the adversary $\mathcal{A}$ who controls the communication within the network can execute the protocol such that Π_1 receives messages only from $\overline{pid}^{(1)} \cup \{\Pi_2\}$ while Π_2 receives messages only from $\overline{pid}^{(2)} \cup \{\Pi_1\}$. We explain now in more detail how each message is handled.

Each message from either Π_1 or Π_2 to any other party $\Pi_i \in \overline{pid}$ is forwarded to both instances $\Pi_i^{(1)}$ and $\Pi_i^{(2)}$. However, the other way around, only messages from $\overline{pid}^{(1)}$ to Π_1 and from $\overline{pid}^{(2)}$ to Π_2 are forwarded while both messages from $\overline{pid}^{(1)}$ to Π_2 and messages from $\overline{pid}^{(2)}$ to Π_1 are dropped. All messages between Π_1 and Π_2 are forwarded. All messages from $\overline{pid}^{(1)}$ to $\overline{pid}$ are only sent to the corresponding instance in $\overline{pid}^{(1)}$ and analogously for messages from $\overline{pid}^{(2)}$ to $\overline{pid}$. Any other messages are deleted. Execution 1 is displayed in Figure 1(a).

Observe that Π_1 communicates only with the instances in $\overline{pid}^{(1)} \cup \{\Pi_2\}$, and similarly Π_2 only with $\overline{pid}^{(2)} \cup \{\Pi_1\}$. Recall that all parties in $\overline{pid}$ are under the control of the adversary. Hence, he can force the instances $\Pi_i^{(1)}$, $\Pi_i^{(2)}$ to use the same session ID *sid* as Π_1 and Π_2. Furthermore note that Π_1 and Π_2 communicate with different party instances $\overline{pid}^{(1)}$ and $\overline{pid}^{(2)}$ which use different random tapes $\rho_i^{(1)}$ and $\rho_i^{(2)}$ respectively. As Π_1 and Π_2 exchange only messages in the first round, the communication between Π_1 and Π_2 does not depend on any message from $\overline{pid}$. Hence, they are not able to notice that each of them communicated with different instances from $\overline{pid}$.

Now, by assumption the protocol provides mutual authentication which implies that all (honest) parties generate the same session key. Hence, the key has to be independent of the random tapes of $\overline{pid}$ which shows the first claim.

Regarding the second claim, assume two different pairs of parties (Π_1, Π_2) and (Π_1', Π_2') who have no direct communication in the second round. Then it follows from claim 1 that either $\{\Pi_1, \Pi_2\} \cap \{\Pi_1', \Pi_2'\} \neq \emptyset$ or that the exchanged key is independent of the random tapes of all parties. The latter case contradicts the assumption that the protocol provides forward secrecy.

Hence, we can assume w.l.o.g. that $\{\Pi_1\} = \{\Pi_1, \Pi_2\} \cap \{\Pi_1', \Pi_2'\}$. This means in particular (with the same arguments as above) that the key depends only on the random tape of Π_1. Consider now execution 2 in which all messages are honestly forwarded by the adversary except of the following ones, which are discarded:

1. $\{m^1_{\Pi_i \to \Pi_1}\}_{i \geq 2}$ (all messages from $pid \setminus \{\Pi_1\}$ to Π_1 in the first round)
2. $M^2_{\Pi_i,\Pi_1}, i \geq 3$ (all messages between $pid \setminus \{\Pi_1, \Pi_2\}$ and Π_1 in the second round)
3. $\{m^2_{\Pi_2 \to \Pi_i}\}_{i \geq 3}$ (all messages from Π_2 to $pid \setminus \{\Pi_1, \Pi_2\}$ in the second round)

This execution is illustrated in Figure 1(b). In this execution, Π_2 cannot notice that some of messages are dropped since it receives only messages that are independent of the dropped messages. More precisely, Π_2 cannot notice that the messages $\{m^1_{\Pi_i \to \Pi_1}\}_{i \geq 2}$ are deleted as it has no communication with Π_1 in the second round by assumption. Furthermore, as none of the messages specified in 2. and 3. are addressed for Π_2 and as the protocol has in total two rounds, Π_2 cannot observe that these messages have been dropped. Concluding, from Π_2's point of view, the execution was correct and it outputs the correct session key at the end of the execution by assumption.

We also observe that Π_1 receives no messages from other parties and that all messages Π_1 sends in the second round are dropped. That means, an adversary can copy all the messages Π_1 sends in the first round of one session and later, even after the session is over (after the key is deleted), the adversary can corrupt $pid \setminus \Pi_1$ and recover the key exchanged in the session as Π_2 is able to compute the correct session key (as argued above). This contradicts forward secrecy, showing the claim. □

Theorem 2. *In the first round of a 2-round GKE π with n parties that achieves forward secrecy and mutual authentication in respect to insider attackers, at least $n-2$ messages are sent.*

Proof. In the case of $n = 2$ parties, this is obviously true as less than $n - 2 = 0$ messages are impossible. We consider the case of $n \geq 3$ parties in the following. We first borrow some vocabulary from graph theory (see [6] for a reference). A *path* is a sequence of vertices such that there is an edge between two consecutive vertices. Two vertices u and v in a graph are *connected* if the graph contains a path from u to v. Otherwise, they are *disconnected*. A *connected component* of a graph is a maximal subgraph in which any two vertices are connected to each other. Obviously each vertex belongs to exactly one connected component.

We consider parties of a GKE as vertices of a graph $\mathcal{G}$ and define an (undirected) edge between two parties Π_i and Π_j if Π_i sends a message directly to Π_j in the *first round* or vice versa. Then, there exists a unique (up to re-ordering) partition of the set of parties pid into disjunct subsets $pid_1, \ldots, pid_\ell$ such that each group pid_i a connected component of $\mathcal{G}$.

In case of $\ell = 3$, we construct an imaginary GKE $\bar{\pi}$ out of π as follows. We consider each group pid_1, pid_2, and pid_3 as a party in $\bar{\pi}$. For each i, the random tape of pid_i is the concatenation of the random tapes of all parties $\Pi \in pid_i$. If $\Pi \in pid_i$ sends a message to $\Pi' \in pid_i$, we consider it is an internal process of pid_i. When $\Pi \in pid_i$ sends a message to $\Pi' \in pid_j \neq pid_i$, we define that pid_i sends the message to pid_j. When some parties in pid_i output keys, we choose the first key that was given out and define it as being the key generated by pid_i. When $\Pi \in pid_i$ is corrupted, the whole set pid_i is corrupted as a party.

Since the parties pid_1, pid_2, and pid_3 are by definition different connected components, they are in particular pairwise disconnected. That is, no messages are exchanged in the first round of $\bar{\pi}$. Hence, we can ignore the first round of the original GKE and consider $\bar{\pi}$ as a 2-round GKE in which participants send no messages in the second round. In particular, pid_1 and pid_2 do not exchange any messages in the second round of $\bar{\pi}$. This implies that, as discussed in the proof of Theorem 1, the session key does not depend on the random tape of pid_3. By the same argument, the session key does not depend on the random tapes of pid_1 and pid_2 either. Therefore, there exists an attacker $\bar{\mathcal{A}}$ that violates the forward secrecy or mutual authentication of $\bar{\pi}$. Obviously, $\bar{\mathcal{A}}$ can be easily translated into an attacker $\mathcal{A}$ that successfully attacks π which contradicts the assumption.

Therefore, there are at most two connected components, w.l.o.g. pid_1 and pid_2. By the definition of connected components, at least $|pid_1| - 1$ messages are sent within pid_1 and likewise $|pid_2| - 1$ messages are sent within pid_2. This shows that at least $|pid_1| - 1 + |pid_2| - 1 = n - 2$ messages are sent. □

Corollary 1. *Let π denote any GKE with $n \geq 3$ that provides forward secrecy and mutual authentication against insider attackers. Then π requires at least two rounds. Furthermore, if π is composed of exactly two rounds, then at least $\frac{1}{2}n^2 + \frac{1}{2}n - 3$ messages are required.*

Proof. For the first claim, assume that π uses only one round. 1-round protocols can be considered as 2-round protocols, where no messages are sent in the first or second round. In the first case, Theorem 2 implies that the number n of parties is at most 2. In the second case, Theorem 1 implies that the number n of parties is at most 2 since there exists at most one pair of parties who does not exchange any messages in the second round. As we consider the case of $n \geq 3$ parties, this yields a contradiction. Hence, $n \geq 3$ implies that at least 2 rounds are required, showing the first claim.

Now consider a 2-round protocol. By Theorem 2, at least $n - 2$ messages are necessary in the first round. By Theorem 1, there exists at most one pair who does not exchange any message in the second round. As a consequence, the second round requires at least $\frac{n \cdot (n-1)}{2} - 1$ messages. Adding both together yields the second claim. □

4 The Proposed Protocol

In the following, we propose a 2-round group key exchange protocol which is an extension of the Burmester-Desmedt star-based protocol [12]. It requires $\frac{1}{2}n^2 + \frac{3}{2}n - 2$ messages which is exactly $n + 1$ more than the lower bound derived in the previous section. In that sense, our protocol is close to the lower bound and is asymptotically optimal. In Sec. 5 we prove that the protocol is UC-secure according to the model given by Katz and Shin [20].

Before we describe the protocol into details, we give an overview on the basic ideas and its structure. We index each party in *pid* by $i \in \{1, \ldots, n\}$, that is Π_i denotes the i-th party, and assume that the indices are uniquely determined from *pid*. Furthermore, we presume that one single party is fixed, w.l.o.g. Π_1. All parties can agree to the same single party without the need of additional communication, for example by choosing the party whose identifier is the first in lexicographical order in *pid*. Each party Π_i has its own pair of public/private keys (PK_i, SK_i) for signing messages and the public keys are known to all parties. Once a party Π_j receives a message $(sid, pid, \textsf{new-session})$, a party instance (Π_j, sid, pid) is created. For simplicity we identify the party instances (Π_j, sid, pid) with the parties Π_j.

The protocol is conceptually divided into 4 protocols $\pi_1, \ldots, \pi_4$, that run in parallel. These are briefly explained in Table 1. In protocols π_1 and π_2, all necessary information are distributed that allow for computing the group key κ. With protocol π_3 every party confirms to the others that it accepted to participate into a protocol identified by (sid, pid). This mechanism prevents an adversary from impersonating honest parties. Via protocol π_4, every party signs the commitment com and sends the signature to *some* other parties according to a *distribution schedule*. Here, in principle any schedule can be used as long as it guarantees that within each pair of parties, at least one of both receives a signature σ from the other. One possible realization is that Π_i sends the signatures to all Π_j with $i < j$. This allows the recipient to check if both share the same key. Observe that we do not require that every party gets a signature from every other party. We will show that this is still sufficient for guaranteeing mutual authentication. From our point of view, it is an interesting observation that an asymmetric condition is sufficient for ensuring a symmetric security property.

Table 1. High level description of the four sub-protocols

	Round 1
π_1	Π_1 exchanges a key x'_j with every other party Π_j.
π_2	Π_1 generates a group key κ and sends a commitment com on κ to every other party.
π_3	Every party Π_j for $j \neq i$ generates a signature σ'_j on (sid, pid) and sends it to Π_1.

	Round 2
π_2	Π_1 sends an encrypted opening of com to each $\Pi_{j \neq 1}$ (using the bilateral keys x'_j from π_1).
π_3	Π_1 distributes the set $\{\sigma'_\ell\}_\ell$ of signatures to all parties.
π_4	Every Π_j generates a signature σ_j on (sid, pid, com) and sends it to *some* other parties according to a predefined distribution schedule.

	Key generation (a party accepts the key κ if ...)
π_2	com is a commitment on κ.
π_3	Every σ'_ℓ is a valid signature of Π_ℓ on (sid, pid).
π_4	Π_j received all signatures σ_ℓ from Π_ℓ according to the distribution schedule.

We now present a concrete description. We use a 1-round 2-party key exchange protocol here, being essentially the Diffie-Hellman key-exchange protocol with authenticated channels where a universal hash function is applied to the result to generate a smooth key. To improve the efficiency of the protocol, Π_1 uses the same ephemeral state r_1 for all key exchange protocols.

Let (TGen, TCom, TVer, TOpen) be a trapdoor commitment scheme. Given a security parameter k', the probabilistic algorithm TGen outputs a pair of parameters and trapdoor (prm, τ). Given parameters prm and a message μ, the probabilistic algorithm TCom outputs a pair of commitment and decommitment $(\mathsf{com}, \mathsf{dec})$ on the message μ. Given $\mathsf{prm}, \mu, \mathsf{com}$, and dec, TVer accepts (and outputs (acc)) if com is a correct commitment on μ. Otherwise it rejects and outputs (rej). Given $\mathsf{prm}, \mu, \mathsf{dec}, \tau$, and another message μ', TOpen outputs another decommitment dec' such that TVer accepts $(\mathsf{prm}, \mu', \mathsf{com}, \mathsf{dec}')$. Although the following description of our protocol uses a trapdoor commitment scheme, our protocol also works with commitment schemes that do not provide a trapdoor. Actually, the trapdoor is only used to allow straight-line simulatability for the proof of UC-security (Sec. 5).

Let k, k', m, m', λ be security parameters, where k is the length of the group key and m is the minimum integer such that $\mathcal{D}$, defined as the space of decommitments dec, is a subset of $\{0,1\}^m$. Let p be a prime of size $k' + \lambda + 1$ and $\mathcal{G}$ be a cyclic group of prime orders p with a generator g. Let $\mathcal{UH}' : \{0,1\}^{k'} \times \{0,1\}^{m'} \to \{0,1\}^{k+m}$ be a universal hash function [18], $\phi : \mathcal{G} \to \{0,1\}^{k'}$ be a projection, and define $\mathcal{UH}(z,v) := \mathcal{UH}'(\phi(z), v)$. We assume k' and m' to be sufficiently large so that $(v, \mathcal{UH}(z,v))$ for randomly chosen $z \in \mathcal{G}$ and $v \in \{0,1\}^{m'}$ is indistinguishable from (v, x') when x' is randomly distributed in $\{0,1\}^{k+m}$. The necessary size of k' and m' are determined by the leftover hash lemma [18,19]. The system parameters are $k, k', m, m', \lambda, p, \mathcal{G}, g$, prm, and $\mathcal{UH}$.

We also require $\mathcal{G}, \phi$ to be chosen such that $\phi^{-1} : \{0,1\}^{k'} \to \mathcal{G}$ can be efficiently computed with overwhelming probability and that the size of $\phi^{-1}(y)$ for randomly chosen $y \in \{0,1\}^{k'}$ is sufficiently large. This is possible if $\mathcal{G}$ is an elliptic curve of a prime order p and ϕ extracts the least significant k' bits of the x-coordinate of given point in $\mathcal{G}$ with a large λ. Then, given a point in $\{0,1\}^{k'}$, there are 2^λ possible x-coordinates on average. For each candidate, there exists a y-coordinate with probability $1/2$ such that this pair is a point on the curve. Thus, if one tries 2^λ possible values in $\mathcal{G}$, an appropriate $z \in \mathcal{G}$ can be found with probability at least $1 - 1/2^{2^\lambda}$. Hence, choosing a sufficiently large λ, an appropriate $\mathcal{G}$ and ϕ can be found. This later allows the adversary to find $z \in \mathcal{G}$ such that $(\kappa, \mathsf{dec}) = \mathcal{UH}(z,v)$ for randomly given $\kappa \in \{0,1\}^k$, $\mathsf{dec} \in \mathcal{D}$, and $v \in \{0,1\}^{m'}$.

At the beginning of the protocol, a value prm is randomly chosen according to the distribution induced by TGen[5] and is given to all parties as a common reference string for the protocol. For the sake of readability, we implicitly assume that all participating parties received (presumably correct) messages according to the protocol and stores all necessary values that are required for a successful protocol run. For example, a party participates only into the protocol if it initially received a (*sid*, *pid*, new-session). If this does not happen in a certain time period, the party does not further take part into the protocol without some further actions (e.g., requesting the missing messages, aborting, etc.). The full description of the protocol is given in Fig. 2.

Communication effort. In the first round Π_1 sends $n-1$ messages and each of the other $n-1$ parties send exactly one message, thus $2(n-1)$ messages in total. In the second round, for each pair of parties, exactly one party sends one message to the other, giving $n(n-1)/2$ messages in the second round. Altogether, $2(n-1) + n(n-1)/2 = \frac{1}{2}n^2 + \frac{3}{2}n - 2$ messages are exchanged in the protocol.

5 Proof of Security

In this section we prove that the proposed protocol achieves UC-security according to the model given by Katz and Shin [20]. We suggest this work and [13] for a more detailed description of UC. Informally, a protocol π realizes a cryptographic task in an

[5] It is not necessary to execute TGen as long as prm can be sampled from the same distribution.

Round 1

Π_1, Computation: Π_1 randomly chooses a group key $\kappa \in \{0,1\}^k$ and generates a commitment on these values: $(\mathsf{com}, \mathsf{dec}) := \mathsf{TCom}(\kappa)$. Furthermore, it randomly picks $r_1 \in \mathbb{Z}/p\mathbb{Z}$ and computes $y_1 = g^{r_1}$. Finally, it samples random values $v_j \in \{0,1\}^{m'}$, $j = 2, \ldots, n$, and generates signatures $\sigma'_{1,j}$ on $(sid, pid, \mathsf{com}, y_1, v_j)$ for $j = 2, \ldots, n$.
Π_1, Storage: Π_1 stores $(sid, pid, \mathsf{dec}, \kappa, (v_j)_{j=2,\ldots,n}, r_1)$.
Π_1, Communication: Π_1 sends to each $\Pi_j \in pid \setminus \{\Pi_1\}$ the message $(\Pi_1; sid, pid, \mathsf{com}, y_1, v_j, \sigma'_{1,j})$

$\Pi_i \neq \Pi_1$, Computation: Π_i randomly chooses $r_i \in \mathbb{Z}/p\mathbb{Z}$ and computes $y_i = g^{r_i}$. Then Π_i generates a signature σ'_i on (sid, pid, y_i).
$\Pi_i \neq \Pi_1$, Storage: Π_i stores (sid, pid, r_i).
$\Pi_i \neq \Pi_1$, Communication: Π_i sends $(\Pi_i; sid, pid, y_i, \sigma'_i)$ to Π_1.

Round 2

Π_1, Computation: Π_1 verifies that each σ'_j is a valid signature on (sid, pid, y_j) by Π_j and generates $z_j = {y_j}^{r_1}, x_j = (\kappa, \mathsf{dec}) \oplus \mathcal{UH}(z_j, v_j)$. Π_1 also generates a signature σ_1 on (sid, pid, com).
Π_1, Storage: Π_1 updates its storage to $(sid, pid, \mathsf{com}, \kappa)$.
Π_1, Communication: Π_1 sends $(\Pi_1; sid, pid, \mathsf{com}, \sigma_1)$, x_j, and $(\sigma'_\ell, y_\ell)_{\ell>1}$ to each $\Pi_j \neq \Pi_1$.

$\Pi_i \neq \Pi_1$, Computation: Π_i verifies that $\sigma'_{1,i}$ is a valid signature on $(sid, pid, \mathsf{com}, y_1, v_i)$ by Π_1 and generates $z_i = {y_1}^{r_i}, x'_i = \mathcal{UH}(z_i, v_i)$ and a signature σ_i on (sid, pid, com).
$\Pi_i \neq \Pi_1$, Storage: Π_i updates its storage to $(sid, pid, \mathsf{com}, x'_i)$.
$\Pi_i \neq \Pi_1$, Communication: Π_i sends $(\Pi_i; sid, pid, \mathsf{com}, \sigma_i)$ to all $\Pi_j \in pid$ specified by the distribution schedule.

Key generation

Π_1, Computation: If every σ_j is a valid signature on (sid, pid, com) by Π_j, then Π_1 outputs (sid, pid, κ) and deletes its storage (instance state).
$\Pi_i \neq \Pi_1$, Computation: If all received signatures are correct, then it computes $(\kappa_i, \mathsf{dec}_i) = x'_i \oplus x_i$. If $acc = \mathsf{TVer}(\mathsf{prm}, \kappa_i, \mathsf{com}, \mathsf{dec}_i)$, then Π_i outputs (sid, pid, κ) and deletes its state.

Fig. 2. The protocol

UC-secure way if no pair of environment $\mathcal{Z}$ and real adversary $\mathcal{A}$, can distinguish the protocol execution in the real world, called *real execution*, from the execution of an ideal functionality $\mathcal{F}$ in an ideal world, called *ideal execution*. $\mathcal{F}$ can be seen as a kind of black box that ideally realizes the considered cryptographic task. We recall in Fig. 3 the definition of its ideal functionality for GKEs from Katz and Shin [20].

Ideal Functionality F_{GKE}

([20]) The ideal functionality $\mathcal{F}_{\mathrm{GKE}}$ interacts with parties $\Phi_1, \ldots, \Phi_n$ and an ideal adversary $\mathcal{S}$. $\mathcal{F}_{\mathrm{GKE}}$ runs on a security parameter k.
Initialization: Upon receiving $(sid, pid, \mathsf{new\text{-}session})$ from a party Φ_i for the first time (where $|pid| \geq 2$), $\mathcal{F}_{\mathrm{GKE}}$ records (sid, pid, Φ_i) and sends this to $\mathcal{S}$. Once the tuples (sid, pid, Φ_j) for all $\Phi_j \in pid$ are recorded, $\mathcal{F}_{\mathrm{GKE}}$ stores $(sid, pid, \mathsf{ready})$ and sends it to $\mathcal{S}$.
Key generation: Upon receiving a message (sid, pid, ok) from $\mathcal{S}$ where there is a recorded tuple $(sid, pid, \mathsf{ready})$, it checks if all $\Phi_j \in pid$ are uncorrupted. If this is the case, it chooses uniformly a key $\kappa \in \{0,1\}^k$ and stores (sid, pid, κ). If any of the parties $\Phi_j \in pid$ is corrupted, it waits for $\mathcal{S}$ to send a message $(sid, pid, \mathsf{key}, \kappa)$ and then stores (sid, pid, κ).
Key delivery: If $\mathcal{S}$ sends a message $(sid, pid, \mathsf{deliver}, \Phi_i)$ where there is a recorded tuple (sid, pid, κ) and $\Phi_i \in pid$, then $\mathcal{F}_{\mathrm{GKE}}$ sends (sid, pid, κ) to party Φ_i.
Player corruption: If $\mathcal{S}$ corrupts $\Phi_i \in pid$ where there is a recorded tuple (sid, pid, κ) but a message (sid, pid, κ) has not yet been sent to Φ_i, then $\mathcal{S}$ is given κ, otherwise nothing.

Fig. 3. The group key exchange functionality

Theorem 3. *The protocol described in Sec. 4 UC-realizes the ideal functionality of GKE if the used signature scheme is secure and if the decisional Diffie-Hellman assumption holds in the common reference string model.*

For the proof, we have to give an ideal adversary $\mathcal{S}$ such that no pair of environment $\mathcal{Z}$ and real adversary $\mathcal{A}$ can tell apart a real execution (i.e., real parties Π_i executing the protocol) and an ideal execution (i.e., $\mathcal{S}$ simulates parties $\Pi_i^{\mathcal{S}}$ compatibly to the outputs of the ideal functionality $\mathcal{F} := \mathcal{F}_{\mathrm{GKE}}$ that in turn communicates with ideal parties Φ_i).

We first define an ideal adversary $\mathcal{S}$ and show afterward in Lemmas 1 and 2 that it fulfills the condition from above. $\mathcal{S}$ has black box access to the real adversary $\mathcal{A}$. Messages from $\mathcal{Z}$ to $\mathcal{S}$ ($\mathcal{Z}$ believes it is sending to $\mathcal{A}$) are forwarded to $\mathcal{A}$ and vice versa. Additionally, $\mathcal{S}$ simulates the real parties Π_i on behalf of all uncorrupted ideal parties Φ_i. The simulated parties are denoted by $\Pi_i^{\mathcal{S}}$. As opposed to the ideal parties, the simulated parties participate in a protocol execution. At the beginning, $\mathcal{S}$ generates for every $\Pi_j^{\mathcal{S}}$ a public/private key pairs (PK_j, SK_j) for digital signatures and gives the public keys to $\mathcal{A}$. Any messages sent by $\mathcal{A}$ to Π_i are processed by $\Pi_i^{\mathcal{S}}$, and any messages output by $\Pi_i^{\mathcal{S}}$ are given to $\mathcal{A}$. $\mathcal{S}$ also runs $\mathsf{TGen}(k')$ for a security parameter k' to obtain (prm, τ). prm is the common reference string of the protocol.

In addition to the above, the ideal adversary $\mathcal{S}$ proceeds as follows:

Session Key Generation (SKG): If at any point in time a simulated party $\Pi_i^{\mathcal{S}}$ outputs a key (sid, pid, κ), $\mathcal{S}$ checks to see whether any of the parties in pid have been corrupted.

SKG.$\neg$cor.: If no parties in pid are corrupted, then:

SKG.$\neg$cor.$\neg$ok: If $\mathcal{S}$ has not yet sent (sid, pid, ok) to $\mathcal{F}$, then $\mathcal{S}$ checks that it has received the message $(sid, pid, \mathsf{ready})$ from $\mathcal{F}$. If not, $\mathcal{S}$ aborts. Otherwise, it sends to $\mathcal{F}$ the messages (sid, pid, ok) and $(sid, pid, \text{deliver}, \Phi_i)$.

SKG.¬cor.ok: If $\mathcal{S}$ has already sent the message (sid, pid, ok) to $\mathcal{F}$, then $\mathcal{S}$ sends the message $(sid, pid, \text{deliver}, \Phi_i)$ to $\mathcal{F}$.

SKG.cor.: Otherwise, say $C \subseteq pid \setminus \{\Phi_i\}$ are corrupted. Then:

SKG.cor.¬ok: If $\mathcal{S}$ has not yet sent (sid, pid, ok) to $\mathcal{F}$, then it sends on behalf of all $\Phi_j \in C$ the message $(sid, pid, \mathsf{new\text{-}session}, \Phi_j)$ to $\mathcal{F}$ who have not done so already, receives $(sid, pid, \mathsf{ready})$ from $\mathcal{F}$, and then sends (sid, pid, ok) to $\mathcal{F}$. (If $\mathcal{S}$ does not receive $(sid, pid, \mathsf{ready})$ after executing the above, it aborts.) Next, $\mathcal{S}$ sends $(sid, pid, \mathsf{key}, \kappa)$ and $(sid, pid, \mathsf{deliver}, \Phi_i)$ to $\mathcal{F}$.

SKG.cor.ok: If $\mathcal{S}$ has already sent (sid, pid, ok) to $\mathcal{F}$, then $\mathcal{S}$ checks that no parties in *pid* were corrupted at that point in time.

1. If this is the case, then $\mathcal{S}$ sends $(sid, pid, \mathsf{deliver}, \Phi_i)$ to $\mathcal{F}$.
2. Otherwise, $\mathcal{S}$ has already sent $(sid, pid, \mathsf{key}, \kappa')$ to $\mathcal{F}$ (i.e., a party in *pid* was corrupted at the time the "ok" message was sent). If $\kappa' \neq \kappa$ then $\mathcal{S}$ aborts. Otherwise, $\mathcal{S}$ sends the message $(sid, pid, \mathsf{deliver}, \Phi_i)$ to $\mathcal{F}$.

Corruption (COR): When $\mathcal{A}$ intends to corrupt a party Φ_i, $\mathcal{S}$ corrupts that party in the ideal world. $\mathcal{S}$ also provides $\mathcal{A}$ with the secret key SK_i and the current internal state of Φ_i as follows:

COR.¬ok: If $\mathcal{S}$ has not yet sent (sid, pid, ok) to $\mathcal{F}$, then $\mathcal{S}$ simply gives $\mathcal{A}$ the current instance state of $\Pi_i^{\mathcal{S}}$ if it exists.

COR.ok: Otherwise $\mathcal{S}$ has already sent (sid, pid, ok) to $\mathcal{F}$. Then:

COR.ok.¬del: If $\mathcal{S}$ has not yet sent $(sid, pid, \mathsf{deliver}, \Phi_i)$ to $\mathcal{F}$, then it checks if $\Pi_i^{\mathcal{S}}$ did finish the first round of the protocol. If this is not the case, then $\mathcal{S}$ aborts. Otherwise, $\mathcal{S}$ corrupts Φ_i to obtain a key κ from $\mathcal{F}$. This might either been provided by $\mathcal{S}$ before or been generated by $\mathcal{F}$. In the first case, $\mathcal{S}$ simply forwards the internal state of $\Pi_i^{\mathcal{S}}$ to $\mathcal{A}$. In the second case, we make use of the fact that $\mathcal{S}$ has already sent (sid, pid, ok). This implies either of the following:

¬Φ₁: When $i \neq 1$, at least Φ_1 in *pid* has already sent x_i to Φ_i. $\mathcal{S}$ uses the trapdoor τ to generate a fitting decommitment dec, that is $\mathsf{dec} = \mathsf{TOpen}(\mathsf{prm}, \kappa', \mathsf{dec}', \tau, \kappa)$. Here, (κ', dec') are the values generated by $\Pi_1^{\mathcal{S}}$, i.e., $(\mathsf{com}, \mathsf{dec}') = \mathsf{TCom}(\mathsf{prm}, \kappa')$. Then, $\mathcal{S}$ generates $x_i' = x_i \oplus (\kappa, \mathsf{dec})$ and hands to $\mathcal{A}$ the instance state $(sid, pid, \mathsf{com}, x_i')$. We note it is possible to find z_i such that $x_i' = \mathcal{UH}(z_i, v_i)$ with overwhelming probability if λ is long enough.

Φ₁: When $i = 1$, $\mathcal{S}$ hands to $\mathcal{A}$ the instance state $(sid, pid, \mathsf{com}, \kappa)$.

COR.ok.del: If $\mathcal{S}$ has already sent $(sid, pid, \mathsf{deliver}, \Phi_i)$ to $\mathcal{F}$, then $\mathcal{S}$ returns nothing (i.e., an empty instance state) to $\mathcal{A}$.

Next we show that the ideal adversary $\mathcal{S}$ aborts only with negligible probability (Lemma 1) and that the real and the ideal execution are indistinguishable (under the decisional Diffie-Hellman assumption) if $\mathcal{S}$ does not abort (Lemma 2). From these two Lemmas, Theorem 3 follows immediately.

Lemma 1. *The probability that the ideal adversary $\mathcal{S}$ defined above aborts is negligible.*

Proof. Suppose that there exists a real adversary $\mathcal{A}$ that can make the ideal adversary $\mathcal{S}$ abort. By the description of $\mathcal{S}$, there are exactly four situation when this might happen: SKG.¬cor.¬ok, SKG.cor.¬ok. COR.ok.¬del, and SKG.cor.ok.

Assume that the abort has happened in one of the two cases SKG.¬cor.¬ok or SKG.cor.¬ok. In both cases, a simulated party Π_i^S did output (sid, pid, κ) (session key generation) but $\mathcal{S}$ did not receive $(sid, pid, \mathsf{ready})$ from $\mathcal{F}$. This in turn means that there exists at least one uncorrupted simulated party $\Pi_j^S \in pid$ such that $\mathcal{Z}$ never sent $(sid, pid, \mathsf{new\text{-}session})$. Hence, Π_j^S has never signed any message. On the other hand, by the protocol specification Π_i^S only generates the key if it received a valid signature from all parties. Therefore, this case can only happen if $\mathcal{A}$ forged a signature.

Suppose now that the abort took place in the case of COR.ok.¬del. This means that on the one hand $\mathcal{S}$ has send before the message (sid, pid, ok) and hence there exists an uncorrupted simulated party $\Pi_j^S \in pid$ who has output (sid, pid, κ). On the other hand, the abort condition tells that there exists a simulated party Π_i^S that has not finished the first round at this point in time. In particular, Π_i^S had not send a signed message so far. With the same arguments as above, this can only happen if $\mathcal{A}$ forged a signature.

It remains to consider the final case: SKG.cor.ok. By definition $\mathcal{S}$ has to deal only with key generation if the key is generated by an uncorrupted party. The abort condition says in principle that two uncorrupted parties Π_i and Π_j have generated two different keys κ and κ', respectively. Recall that the key is reconstructed from a commitment distributed by Π_1. As the commitment has been signed by Π_1 and as at least one of the two parties can check if both received the same commitment, it must hold that Π_i and Π_j received the same commitment com (as none of them aborted) unless $\mathcal{A}$ has forged a signature. But then the binding property of the commitment schemes implies that $\kappa = \kappa'$ what contradicts the assumption[6]. Hence, this case can also only happen in the case of a signature forgery. □

Lemma 2. *Suppose that the ideal adversary does not abort. Then, for any environment and any real adversary, the ideal execution and the real execution are indistinguishable as long as the decisional Diffie-Hellman assumption holds in the standard model.*

Proof. Suppose that there exists an environment $\mathcal{Z}$ that can distinguish between the ideal execution and the real execution. We will first show that $\mathcal{Z}$ does not gain any useful information by corrupting parties. As a consequence we can restrict w.l.o.g. to an environment $\mathcal{Z}'$ that does no corruption at all. Finally, we will construct an algorithm $\mathcal{B}$ from $\mathcal{Z}'$ that allows for solving the decisional Diffie-Hellman problem.

Assume that $\mathcal{Z}$ corrupts a party before any key has been generated. By definition of $\mathcal{S}$, from this point on $\mathcal{Z}$ only communicates with the simulated parties (e.g., learns its states after corruption) and receives the results of the simulated protocol run. In other words, the ideal functionality $\mathcal{F}$ is no longer involved. Obviously, in this case the real and ideal executions are indistinguishable as the simulated parties behave exactly like real parties.

Now we turn our attention to the case that $\mathcal{Z}$ only corrupts after a key has been generated. By definition, this means that the key κ' of the simulated protocol run has

[6] Observe that the trapdoor τ is known only to $\mathcal{S}$ but not to any of the parties.

been replaced by a key κ that has been given by the ideal functionality. In particular all players have finished both rounds already (the information send around at the end of round 2 are a necessary pre-requisite for key generation). In the case that Π_1 gets corrupted, $\mathcal{Z}$ receives the values $(sid, pid, \mathsf{com}, \kappa)$ (where κ is the key generated by $\mathcal{F}$). This is obviously a perfect simulation. In the case that $\Pi_j \neq \Pi_1$ gets corrupted, the situation becomes a little bit more tricky: besides the values mentioned above, a real party would additionally store an encryption of a decommitment dec' that opens the distributed commitment com to the "real" key κ'. Here we make use of the trapdoor in the commitment scheme and replace dec' by another decommitment dec that opens com to κ (instead of κ'). By the definition of the commitment scheme, this yields a perfect simulation as well.

Concluding, an environment $\mathcal{Z}$ does not observe any differences between both executions via corruption. Thus, we can restrict to an environment $\mathcal{Z}'$ that does not corrupt at all. We construct from $\mathcal{Z}'$ an algorithm $\mathcal{B}$ that breaks the decisional Diffie-Hellman assumption. That is given a triple $(g, a, b, c) = (g, g^{\alpha}, g^{\beta}, g^{\gamma})$, we construct an algorithm $\mathcal{B}$ (based on $\mathcal{Z}'$) that decides whether $\alpha \cdot \beta = \gamma$ or not.

$\mathcal{B}$ behaves in principle like the ideal adversary $\mathcal{S}$ except of the following difference. $\mathcal{B}$ replaces the values occurring within the Diffie-Hellman key exchange by other parameters that are derived from the problem instance mentioned above as follows:

$$y_1 \leftarrow b, \quad y_j \leftarrow g^{\mu_j} a^{\nu_j} = g^{\mu_j + \alpha \cdot \nu_j}, \quad z_j \leftarrow b^{\mu_j} c^{\nu_j} = g^{\beta \cdot \mu_j + \gamma \cdot \nu_j}. \tag{1}$$

where $\{\mu_j, \nu_j \in \mathbb{Z}/p\mathbb{Z}\}_{j=1,\ldots,n}$ are randomly chosen. The fact that $\mathcal{B}$ does not know the discrete logarithms of these values (as opposed to the real execution) is not a problem as $\mathcal{Z}'$ does not corrupt by assumption. Observe that z_j is a Diffie-Hellman key derived from y_1 and y_j if and only if $\alpha \cdot \beta = \gamma$. Therefore, if $\alpha \cdot \beta = \gamma$, then $\mathcal{B}$ acts exactly like $\mathcal{S}$. By assumption $\mathcal{Z}'$ can distinguish between the ideal or real execution in this case. However, if $\alpha \cdot \beta \neq \gamma$ then the messages of the parties are independent of the key κ. Thus, $\mathcal{Z}'$ cannot have any advantage in this case. Now, $\mathcal{B}$ invokes $\mathcal{Z}'$ several times with different values of μ_j and ν_j and estimates the advantage of $\mathcal{Z}'$. If this is negligible, then $\mathcal{B}$ assumes that $\alpha \cdot \beta \neq \gamma$. Otherwise it guesses that $\alpha \cdot \beta = \gamma$. With the arguments above, this yields a distinguisher for the decisional Diffie-Hellman problem.

Concluding we have seen that (under the decisional Diffie-Hellman assumption) that for none of the three cases an environment can exist that efficiently distinguishes between both executions. □

6 Conclusion

We addressed the question of the communication complexity in group key exchange (GKE) protocols. We derived from basic security requirements, i.e., forward secrecy and mutual authentication, that any GKE needs at least two rounds and a lower bound on the number of messages for this case. Furthermore we presented a UC-secure protocol that almost achieves these bounds.

Still, several open questions remain. Some of them are: (1) Is it possible to either construct protocols that exactly meet these bounds or can it be proved that the minimum effort is actually higher? (2) Can we determine the effort for additional requirements, e.g., contributiveness, etc.? (3) Are UC-secure protocols possible with the same communication effort as our protocol but within the standard model? (4) Are less messages possible if one considers GKEs with more than 2 rounds?

References

1. Abdalla, M., Catalano, D., Chevalier, C., Pointcheval, D.: Password-authenticated group key agreement with adaptive security and contributiveness. In: Preneel, B. (ed.) AFRICACRYPT 2009. LNCS, vol. 5580, pp. 254–271. Springer, Heidelberg (2009)
2. Bellare, M., Pointcheval, D., Rogaway, P.: Authenticated key exchange secure against dictionary attacks. In: Preneel, B. (ed.) EUROCRYPT 2000. LNCS, vol. 1807, pp. 139–155. Springer, Heidelberg (2000)
3. Bellare, M., Rogaway, P.: Entity authentication and key distribution. In: Stinson, D.R. (ed.) CRYPTO 1993. LNCS, vol. 773, pp. 232–249. Springer, Heidelberg (1994)
4. Bellare, M., Rogaway, P.: Provably secure session key distribution: the three party case. In: STOC, pp. 57–66. ACM, New York (1995)
5. Bohli, J.-M., Vasco, M.I.G., Steinwandt, R.: Secure group key establishment revisited. Int. J. Inf. Sec. 6(4), 243–254 (2007)
6. Bondy, J.A., Murty, U.S.R.: Graph theory with applications. North-Holland, Amsterdam (1976)
7. Bresson, E., Chevassut, O., Pointcheval, D.: Provably authenticated group diffie-hellman key exchange - the dynamic case. In: Boyd, C. (ed.) ASIACRYPT 2001. LNCS, vol. 2248, pp. 290–309. Springer, Heidelberg (2001)
8. Bresson, E., Chevassut, O., Pointcheval, D.: Dynamic group diffie-hellman key exchange under standard assumptions. In: Knudsen, L.R. (ed.) EUROCRYPT 2002. LNCS, vol. 2332, pp. 321–336. Springer, Heidelberg (2002)
9. Bresson, E., Chevassut, O., Pointcheval, D., Quisquater, J.-J.: Provably authenticated group diffie-hellman key exchange. In: ACM Conference on Computer and Communications Security, pp. 255–264 (2001)
10. Bresson, E., Manulis, M.: Securing group key exchange against strong corruptions. In: ASIACCS, pp. 249–260 (2008)
11. Bresson, E., Manulis, M., Schwenk, J.: On security models and compilers for group key exchange protocols. In: Miyaji, A., Kikuchi, H., Rannenberg, K. (eds.) IWSEC 2007. LNCS, vol. 4752, pp. 292–307. Springer, Heidelberg (2007)
12. Burmester, M., Desmedt, Y.: A secure and efficient conference key distribution system. In: De Santis, A. (ed.) EUROCRYPT 1994. LNCS, vol. 950, pp. 275–286. Springer, Heidelberg (1995)
13. Canetti, R.: Universally composable security: A new paradigm for cryptographic protocols. Cryptology ePrint Archive, Report 2000/067 (2000), `http://eprint.iacr.org/` (revised in 2005)
14. Canetti, R.: Universally composable security: A new paradigm for cryptographic protocols. In: FOCS, pp. 136–145 (2001)
15. Furukawa, J., Armknecht, F., Kurosawa, K.: A universally composable group key exchange protocol with minimum communication effort. In: Ostrovsky, R., De Prisco, R., Visconti, I. (eds.) SCN 2008. LNCS, vol. 5229, pp. 392–408. Springer, Heidelberg (2008)
16. Gorantla, M.C., Boyd, C., González Nieto, J.M.: Modeling key compromise impersonation attacks on group key exchange protocols. In: Jarecki, S., Tsudik, G. (eds.) PKC 2009. LNCS, vol. 5443, pp. 105–123. Springer, Heidelberg (2009)

17. Gorantla, M.C., Boyd, C., Nieto, J.M.G.: Universally composable contributory group key exchange. In: ASIACCS, pp. 146–156 (2009)
18. Impagliazzo, R., Levin, L.A., Luby, M.: Pseudo-random generation from one-way functions (extended abstracts). In: STOC, pp. 12–24. ACM, New York (1989)
19. Impagliazzo, R., Zuckerman, D.: How to recycle random bits. In: FOCS, pp. 248–253. IEEE, Los Alamitos (1989)
20. Katz, J., Shin, J.S.: Modeling insider attacks on group key-exchange protocols. In: CCS 2005: Proceedings of the 12th ACM Conference on Computer and Communications Security, pp. 180–189. ACM Press, New York (2005)

A Forward Secrecy and MA Security

In this section, we formally define the security notions that are considered in this paper. The attacker's capabilities are modeled by a set of queries that she is allowed to do. These are defined in the following definition.

Definition 1 (Attacker Model). *An attacker $\mathcal{A}$ can make the following queries:*

Invoke$(\Pi, \mathsf{sid}, \mathsf{pid}, \textsf{new-session})$**:** *A new instance $(\Pi, \mathsf{sid}, \mathsf{pid})$ of Π is invoked by sending a message $(\mathsf{sid}, \mathsf{pid}, \textsf{new-session})$ to Π. $\mathcal{A}$ obtains the response of Π. We assume here that, if a party $\Pi \in \mathsf{pid}$ is uncorrupted, that is $\mathcal{A}$ has never queried Corrupt(Π) (see below), Π is never given the same triple $(\mathsf{sid}, \mathsf{pid}, \textsf{new-session})$ more than once.*

Send$(\Pi; M)$**:** *The message M is sent to Π and $\mathcal{A}$ receives the response.*

RevealKey$(\Pi, \mathsf{sid}, \mathsf{pid})$**:** *If Π has already generated an output $(\Pi, \mathsf{sid}, \mathsf{pid}, \kappa)$, $\mathcal{A}$ is given κ.*

Corrupt(Π)**:** *The long-term secret of Π is given to $\mathcal{A}$.*

Observe that the queries **Invoke** and **Send** model the attacker's capability of controlling the schedules of the parties and the communication in the network. We do not need to consider the strong corruption model where the adversaries are able to obtain instance states. The above weak adversaries are sufficient for our lower bounds.

For defining AKE-security, we introduce an additional query:

Definition 2. *The query* **Test**$(\Pi, \mathsf{sid}, \mathsf{pid})$ *is defined as follows. When Π has output $(\Pi, \mathsf{sid}, \mathsf{pid}, \kappa)$, $b \in \{0, 1\}$ is randomly chosen. Then, $\mathcal{A}$ is either given κ if $b = 1$, or a randomly chosen key if $b = 0$.*

We say that the query **Test**$(\Pi, \mathsf{sid}, \mathsf{pid})$ *is* fresh *if the following conditions hold for every $\Pi' \in \mathsf{pid}$:*

- *No query* **RevealKey**$(\Pi', \mathsf{sid}, \mathsf{pid})$ *is made after Π' outputs $(\Pi', \mathsf{sid}, \mathsf{pid}, \kappa')$ for some κ'.*
- *No query* **Corrupt**(Π') *is made before Π' outputs $(\Pi', \mathsf{sid}, \mathsf{pid}, \kappa')$ for some κ'.*

Definition 3. *We say that an external-SID GKE is AKE-secure if, for every poly-time adversary $\mathcal{A}$, the difference between the probability that $\mathcal{A}$ wins the following game and $1/2$ is negligible in some security parameter:*

AKE game:
After $\mathcal{A}$ and the parties are initialized by input of a security parameter, $\mathcal{A}$ interacts with the parties by making queries as specified in Definition 1. $\mathcal{A}$ is allowed to make one query **Test**$(\Pi, \text{sid}, \text{pid})$ *for some Π, sid, and pid such that Π has output $(\Pi, \text{sid}, \text{pid}, \kappa)$ once during the game under the condition that* **Test**$(\Pi, \text{sid}, \text{pid})$ *remains to be fresh until the end of the game. $\mathcal{A}$ outputs a bit $b' \in \{0, 1\}$ when the game ends. We say $\mathcal{A}$ wins the game if $b = b'$, where b is the bit that oracle generated when $\mathcal{A}$ queried* **Test**$(\Pi, \text{sid}, \text{pid})$.

Observe that the freshness requirements guarantees that $\mathcal{A}$ cannot simply obtained knowledge about the key by querying **RevealKey** or **Corrupt**. Although adversaries are allowed to corrupt parties after they output the target keys, the above AKE security requires that this faculty does not help adversary to guess the target key. This is the *Forward secrecy*.

Definition 4. *We say an external-SID GKE provides* mutual authentication in presence of insider attackers *if, for every poly-time adversary $\mathcal{A}$, the probability that $\mathcal{A}$ wins the following game is negligible:*

MA game:
After $\mathcal{A}$ and the parties are initialized by input of a security parameter, $\mathcal{A}$ interacts with the parties by making queries as defined in Definition 1. We say that $\mathcal{A}$ wins the game if two uncorrupted parties Π and Π' output $(\Pi, \text{sid}, \text{pid}, \kappa)$ and $(\Pi', \text{sid}, \text{pid}, \kappa')$, respectively, such that $\kappa \neq \kappa'$ before $\mathcal{A}$ stops.

Deterministic Differential Properties of the Compression Function of BMW

Jian Guo[1] and Søren S. Thomsen[2,⋆]

[1] Nanyang Technological University, Singapore
[2] DTU Mathematics, Technical University of Denmark

Abstract. In this paper, we give some determinstic differential properties for the compression function of SHA-3 candidate Blue Midnight Wish (tweaked version for round 2). The computational complexity is about 2^0 compression function calls. This applies to security parameters 0/16, 1/15, and 2/14. The efficient differentials can be used to find pseudo-preimages of the compression function with marginal gain over brute force. However, none of these attacks threaten the security of the BMW hash functions.

Keywords: Hash function cryptanalysis, Blue Midnight Wish, SHA-3, differential.

1 Introduction

Blue Midnight Wish [3] (BMW) is one of the 14 second round candidates of NIST's cryptographic hash algorithm competition [5]. It was tweaked after being selected for round 2, apparently in order to resist attacks by Thomsen [7]. Aumasson [1] and Nikolić et al. [6], independently of our work, found some distinguishers with data complexity 2^{19}, and for a modified variant of BMW-512 with probability $2^{-278.2}$, respectively. In this paper, we give explicit constructions of message pairs, by tracing the propagation of the differences, to show some interesting behaviour on certain bits of the output with probability 1.

The paper is organised as follows. Section 2 gives a brief description of BMW. Then, we introduce some general observations in Section 3, which are further extended to differentials for BMW variants with security parameters 0/16, 1/15, 2/14, in Sections 4, 5, 6, respectively. A pseudo-preimage attack on the compression function using such efficient differentials is discussed in Section 7. Section 8 concludes the paper.

2 Description of BMW

BMW is a family of hash functions, containing four major instances, BMW-n, with $n \in \{224, 256, 384, 512\}$, where n is the size of the hash output. It follows

⋆ Part of this work was carried out while the author was visiting Nanyang Technological University, by the support of the Singapore National Research Foundation under Research Grant NRF-CRP2-2007-03.

A. Biryukov, G. Gong, and D.R. Stinson (Eds.): SAC 2010, LNCS 6544, pp. 338–350, 2011.

a tweaked Merkle-Damgård structure with double-pipe design, i.e., the size of the chaining value is twice the output size. Since our differentials concentrate on the compression function only, we refer to (tweaked for round 2) submission documents [3] for the descriptions of padding, finalisation, etc.

The compression function bmw_n of BMW-n takes the chaining value H and a message block M as input, and produces the updated chaining value H^*. All H, M, and H^* are of 16 words, where the size of a word is 32 bits for BMW-224/256, and 64 bits for BMW-384/512. We use X_i ($i = 0, \ldots, 15$) to denote the i-th word of X. The compression function comprises three functions, called f_0, f_1, and f_2, in sequence. We introduce them here.

The f_0 function. A temporary W is introduced as

$$\begin{aligned} W_i \leftarrow & \pm(M_{i+5} \oplus H_{i+5}) \pm (M_{i+7} \oplus H_{i+7}) \pm (M_{i+10} \oplus H_{i+10}) \\ & \pm(M_{i+13} \oplus H_{i+13}) \pm (M_{i+14} \oplus H_{i+14}) \end{aligned} \qquad (1)$$

for $i = 0, \ldots, 15$. By '$\pm$' we mean '$+$' or '$-$'; which operator is used varies and does not seem to follow any simple pattern (see [3, Table 2.2] for details). Unless specified otherwise, all additions (and subtractions) are to be taken modulo 2^w (where w is the word size) and all indices for H and M are modulo 16 throughout this paper. The outputs of f_0 are Q_i, $i = 0, \ldots, 15$, which are computed as

$$Q_i \leftarrow s_{i \bmod 5}(W_i) + H_{i+1}, \qquad (2)$$

where s_i are predefined bijective functions with $i = 0, \ldots, 4$; see Appendix A for the definitions of these. Note that without the feed-forward of H_{i+1}, the output of f_0 would be a permutation of $H \oplus M$, since the computation of W corresponds to a multiplication by an invertible matrix.

The f_1 function. f_1 takes H, M, and $Q_0, \ldots, Q_{15}$ (the output from f_0) as input, and produces 16 new words Q_j, for $j = 16, \ldots, 31$. The output words are computed one at a time through 16 rounds. There are two types of rounds, $expand_1$ rounds and $expand_2$ rounds. We denote the number of $expand_1$ rounds by R, where R is a security parameter that can take any value between 0 and 16. There are $16 - R$ $expand_2$ rounds. For the sake of clarity, we shall denote a specific choice of security parameter by $R/(16 - R)$; the value of the security parameter suggested by the designers is 2/14 (in other words: 2 $expand_1$ rounds and 14 $expand_2$ rounds).

The 16 output words $Q_{16}, \ldots, Q_{31}$ are computed as follows. An $expand_1$ round computes

$$Q_{j+16} \leftarrow AddElement(j) + \sum_{i=0}^{15} s_{(i+1) \bmod 4}(Q_{i+j-16}). \qquad (3)$$

Here, $AddElement$ is defined as:

$$\begin{aligned} AddElement(j) \leftarrow & (M_j^{\lll (j \bmod 16)+1} + M_{j+3}^{\lll (j+3 \bmod 16)+1} \\ & - M_{j+10}^{\lll (j+10 \bmod 16)+1} + K_j) \oplus H_{j+7}, \end{aligned} \qquad (4)$$

where $X^{\lll n}$ denotes a left-rotation of register X by n positions (by left we mean towards the most significant bit). The words K_j are round constants equal to $(j+16)\cdot$ `0555555555555555`$_h$ for BMW-384/512 and $(j+16)\cdot$ `05555555`$_h$ for BMW-224/256. An $expand_2$ round computes

$$\begin{aligned}Q_{j+16} \leftarrow\ & Q_j + r_1(Q_{j+1}) + Q_{j+2} + r_2(Q_{j+3}) + Q_{j+4} + r_3(Q_{j+5}) + Q_{j+6}+ \\ & r_4(Q_{j+7}) + Q_{j+8} + r_5(Q_{j+9}) + Q_{j+10} + r_6(Q_{j+11})+ \\ & Q_{j+12} + r_7(Q_{j+13}) + s_4(Q_{j+14}) + s_5(Q_{j+15}) + AddElement(j).\end{aligned} \tag{5}$$

The functions r_i are rotation functions; see Appendix A for details.

The f_2 function. We list the description of H_0^*, since our result concerns this word only.

$$H_0^* \leftarrow (XH^{\lll 5} \oplus Q_{16}{}^{\ggg 5} \oplus M_0) + (XL \oplus Q_{24} \oplus Q_0), \tag{6}$$

where

$$\begin{aligned} XL &= Q_{16} \oplus \cdots \oplus Q_{23}, \\ XH &= Q_{16} \oplus \cdots \oplus Q_{31}. \end{aligned}$$

Some notations. The attacks described in this paper deal with input pairs for which there is a certain relation on the output pair. Hence, we shall be interested in how differences propagate through the BMW compression function. We use the following notation (apparently first introduced by De Cannière and Rechberger [2]) for the difference between two bits: '`-`' means there is no difference with probability 1, '`x`' means there is a difference with probability 1, and '`?`' means there may or may not be a difference (the probability of a difference is not 0 or 1, but also may be bounded away from 1/2). When we talk about a difference in a word, e.g., in a 32-bit word, we write (for instance)

`[?????????????????x--------------]`,

which means that the 14 least significant bits contain no difference, the 15th least significant bit contains a difference, and the 17 most significant bits may or may not contain a difference.

With the above descriptions, we are able to introduce our differentials starting with some important observations on the least significant bit (LSB) of H_0^*.

3 Observations

Let $X[n]$ denote the nth bit of the word X, where the least significant bit is the 0th bit. Since an addition takes no carry into the least significant bit, we can state the following expression for the LSB $H_0^*[0]$ of H_0^*:

$$H_0^*[0] = Q_{16}[5] \oplus M_0[0] \oplus XL[0] \oplus Q_{24}[0] \oplus Q_0[0].$$

Given the definition of XL, this expression can be restated as

$$H_0^*[0] = M_0[0] \oplus Q_0[0] \oplus Q_{16}[5] \oplus \bigoplus_{i=16}^{24} Q_i[0]. \tag{7}$$

Hence, $H_0^*[0]$ does not depend on $Q_{25}, \ldots, Q_{31}$. This means that if we can limit difference propagation through the first 9 rounds of f_1 (where $Q_{16}, \ldots, Q_{24}$ are computed), and if we can still keep the difference on $M_0[0]$ and $Q_0[0]$ under our control, then the bit $H_0^*[0]$ may be biased.

In the function f_1, differences may propagate only very slowly towards the LSB. Consider an *expand*$_2$ round:

$$\begin{aligned} Q_{j+16} \leftarrow Q_j &+ r_1(Q_{j+1}) + Q_{j+2} + r_2(Q_{j+3}) + Q_{j+4} + r_3(Q_{j+5}) + Q_{j+6} + \\ & r_4(Q_{j+7}) + Q_{j+8} + r_5(Q_{j+9}) + Q_{j+10} + r_6(Q_{j+11}) + \\ & Q_{j+12} + r_7(Q_{j+13}) + s_4(Q_{j+14}) + s_5(Q_{j+15}) + \mathit{AddElement}(j). \end{aligned} \tag{8}$$

The function s_5 is defined as

$$s_5(x) = x^{\gg 2} \oplus x.$$

Here $x^{\gg 2}$ means a right-shift by two bit positions. Hence, if Q_{j+15} contains a difference in an *expand*$_2$ round, then the function s_5 propagates this difference two positions down towards the LSB. For example, the difference

`[?????????????????x--------------]`

would become

`[???????????????????x------------]`.

4 The Security Parameter 0/16

Consider a variant of BMW with security parameter 0/16, meaning that all 16 rounds in f_1 are of the *expand*$_2$ type. Consider an input pair to the compression function such that there is a difference in Q_0 but in no word among $Q_1, \ldots, Q_{15}$, nor in M_0, M_3, M_{10}, and H_7. This difference on Q_0 will propagate to Q_{16}. Due to the additions, the difference may propagate towards the most significant bit (MSB), but never towards the LSB. Hence, if the t LSBs of Q_0 contain no difference, then these bits also contain no difference in Q_{16}. As an example, the difference `[----x----x---------x------------]` in Q_0 becomes `[???????????????????x------------]` in Q_{16}.

In the second round, Q_{16} will go through the function s_5, and the difference will be shifted two positions towards the least significant bit. In the example above, we would get `[?????????????????????x----------]`. Hence, there will be no difference in the $t-2$ least significant bits of $s_5(Q_{16})$. The word Q_0 no longer affects the function f_1, and if there is no difference in the $t-2$ least significant bits of *AddElement*(1), then Q_{17} will contain no difference in the $t-2$ LSBs. In the following round (under some conditions on M and H), the difference again propagates two positions towards the LSB, meaning that the $t-4$ LSBs contain no difference.

The condition that the only difference in the words $Q_0, \ldots, Q_{15}$ lies in Q_0 can be enforced by having the same difference in H_1 and in M_1, and no difference in all other words of H and M. This means that there is no difference in the permutation inside f_0, but the difference in H_1 will be fed forward to Q_0. Denote by Δ the difference on H_1 and M_1. If Δ has many trailing '0' bits, i.e., there is no difference in many LSBs of H_1 and M_1, then the behaviour described above occurs.

The word M_1 is involved in rounds 1, 7, and 14 of f_1, and H_1 is involved in round 10. In rounds 1 and 7, M_1 is rotated two positions left, and therefore, in order to keep differences out of the least significant bit positions, we need Δ to have '0' bits in the two MSB positions. In rounds 9–15, we do not worry about difference propagation, since this will affect only the words $Q_{25}, \ldots, Q_{31}$, which are not involved in the computation of $H_0^*[0]$.

The only remaining potential source of differences in the least significant bit positions are due to the rotation functions r_i. Looking closely at the effects of these functions one sees that they make no difference in the case of BMW-224/256, but they do have a significant effect in the case of BMW-384/512. On the other hand, in BMW-384/512, the "distance" to the LSB is greater, and therefore it is still possible to obtain interesting results as described now.

The difference Δ with the maximum value of t fulfilling the mentioned requirements is $\Delta = 2^{61}$ for BMW-384/512 (and $\Delta = 2^{29}$ for BMW-224/256). Hence, we have the difference

```
[--x-------------------------------------------------------------]
```

on H_1 and M_1, which becomes

```
[??x-------------------------------------------------------------]
```

in Q_0 due to the feed forward of H_1. The 16 words computed in f_1 will have the following differences:

$\Delta Q_{16} =$ `[??x-------------------------------------------------------------]`

$\Delta Q_{17} =$ `[????x-----------------------------------------------------------]`

$\Delta Q_{18} =$ `[??????x---------------------------------------------------------]`

$\Delta Q_{19} =$ `[?????????????x--------------------------------------------------]`

$\Delta Q_{20} =$ `[???????????????-------------------------------------------------]`

$\Delta Q_{21} =$ `[???????????????????????x----------------------------------------]`

$\Delta Q_{22} =$ `[?????????????????????????---------------------------------------]`

ΔQ_{23} = `[?????????????????????????????x----------------------------------]`
ΔQ_{24} = `[??????????????????????????????????------------------------------]`
ΔQ_{25} = `[????????????????????????????????????----------------------------]`
ΔQ_{26} = `[????????????????????????????????????????????x-------------------]`
ΔQ_{27} = `[??????????????????????????????????????????????x-----------------]`
ΔQ_{28} = `[??????????????????????????????????????????????????--------------]`
ΔQ_{29} = `[???????????????????????????????????????????????????????---------]`
ΔQ_{30} = `[?????????????????????????????????????????????????????????-------]`
ΔQ_{31} = `[????????????????????????????????????????????????????????????????]`

The end result in the output word H_0^* is the difference (one can verify this by substituting all above differences to Eqn. (6))

`[???????????????????????????????????????????????????????????-----]`.

Hence, there is no difference in the 5 LSBs with probability 1. In fact, there is also a strong bias in H_5^*, which has the difference `[??????????????????????????????????????????????????????????------]`.

For BMW-224/256 one gets a similar behaviour; the difference on H_0^* is

`[???????????????????????????-----]`,

and the difference on H_5^* is `[????????????????????????????x---]`.

5 The Security Parameter 1/15

When there is a single *expand*$_1$ round in the beginning of f_1, followed by 15 *expand*$_2$ rounds, we can get a similar behaviour as described in the previous section if we can find a difference Δ with many LSBs equal to 0, and such that $s_1(\Delta)$ also has many LSBs equal to 0. We shall investigate this in a moment.

Now, in order to keep the difference Δ from being changed by the feed-forward with H in f_0, we need a few more conditions on H and M compared to the security parameter 0/16. What we need is that $s_0(W_0)$ contains '0' bits in the positions where Δ contains '1' bits. An easy way to ensure this is by requiring that M_i and H_i are equal to zero for $i \in \{5, 7, 10, 13, 14\}$. Alternatively, without introducing any requirements, the condition is fulfilled with probability $2^{-||\Delta||}$, where $||\Delta||$ is the Hamming weight of Δ excluding the MSB.

5.1 Searching for Good Differences

In order to simplify the discussion we introduce the following function:

$$P(X) = \min\{i \mid \Delta X[i] \neq \text{`-'}\}.$$

In words, $P(X)$ is the number of consecutive least significant bits of X, which *certainly* contain no difference. It is clear that $P(X+Y) \geq \min(P(X), P(Y))$, and

$P(X^{\gg \ell}) = \max(P(X) - \ell, 0)$. In the case of rotations, we have that if $\ell \leq P(X)$, then $P(X^{\ggg \ell}) = P(X) - \ell$. For BMW-384/512, we have the following:

$$\begin{aligned}
P(s_5(X)) &= P(X) - 2, && \text{since } s_5(X) = X^{\gg 2} \oplus X \\
P(s_4(X)) &= P(X) - 1, && \text{since } s_4(X) = X^{\gg 1} \oplus X \\
P(r_7(X)) &= P(X) - 11, && \text{since } r_7(X) = X^{\lll 53} = X^{\ggg 11} \\
P(r_6(X)) &= P(X) - 21, && \text{since } r_6(X) = X^{\lll 43} = X^{\ggg 21} \\
P(r_5(X)) &= P(X) - 27, && \text{since } r_5(X) = X^{\lll 37} = X^{\ggg 27}.
\end{aligned}$$

The last three identities are on the condition that $\ell \leq P(X)$, where ℓ is the (right) rotation value.

As above, we assume that among $\{Q_0, \ldots, Q_{15}\}$, only Q_0 contains a difference, and among $\{H_i\} \cup \{M_i\}$, only H_1 and M_1 contain a difference. This happens if the differences in H_1 and M_1 are the same. Now we track the differences going into each of the first nine rounds of f_1. Below we have listed the (modified) input words that contain a difference in each round.

$$\begin{array}{ll}
Q_{16}: & s_1(Q_0) \\
Q_{17}: & s_5(Q_{16}),\ M_1^{\lll 2} \\
Q_{18}: & s_5(Q_{17}),\ s_4(Q_{16}) \\
Q_{19}: & s_5(Q_{18}),\ s_4(Q_{17}),\ r_7(Q_{16}) \\
Q_{20}: & s_5(Q_{19}),\ s_4(Q_{18}),\ r_7(Q_{17}),\ Q_{16} \\
Q_{21}: & s_5(Q_{20}),\ s_4(Q_{19}),\ r_7(Q_{18}),\ Q_{17},\ r_6(Q_{16}) \\
Q_{22}: & s_5(Q_{21}),\ s_4(Q_{20}),\ r_7(Q_{19}),\ Q_{18},\ r_6(Q_{17}),\ Q_{16} \\
Q_{23}: & s_5(Q_{22}),\ s_4(Q_{21}),\ r_7(Q_{20}),\ Q_{19},\ r_6(Q_{18}),\ Q_{17},\ r_5(Q_{16}),\ M_1^{\lll 2} \\
Q_{24}: & s_5(Q_{23}),\ s_4(Q_{22}),\ r_7(Q_{21}),\ Q_{20},\ r_6(Q_{19}),\ Q_{18},\ r_5(Q_{17}),\ Q_{16}
\end{array} \tag{9}$$

The goal is to find differences Δ in Q_0 such that the LSB of Q_i, for all i, $16 \leq i \leq 24$, contains a strong bias. This bias is preferably in the form of a difference or no difference with probability 1. We now identify the minimum requirements on Δ in order for this to happen. We assume the difference on H_1 and M_1 is also Δ, i.e., that there is no propagation of bit differences in the feed forward of H_1 in f_0.

We first find the bare requirements on Q_{16} in order to reach our goal. The round in which the P-value of Q_{16} drops the most is round 7 (computing Q_{23}), in which r_5 is computed on Q_{16}. This yields the requirement $P(Q_{16}) \geq 27$.

The requirements on Q_{17} are similarly found to be $P(Q_{17}) \geq 27$. This "updates" the requirement on Q_{16} due to the dependence of Q_{17} on Q_{16}, which means that we get $P(Q_{16}) \geq 29$.

If we continue like this, we find requirements on subsequent words of Q, which may iteratively require updates to requirements on previous words. The end result is that the requirement on Q_{16} becomes $P(Q_{16}) \geq 32$ and the requirement on M_1 is $P(M_1) \geq 25$ combined with the requirement that there is no difference in the two MSBs of M_1. Hence, we search for a difference Δ which has '0' bits in the two MSB positions, and such that Δ ends with 25 '0' bits and $s_1(\Delta)$ ends with 32 '0' bits.

The function s_1 can be described as a matrix multiplication over $\mathbb{F}_2$. The matrix S_1 has 64 rows and columns, and the input x is viewed as a 64-bit column vector. Then we have $s_1(x) = S_1 \cdot x$. Searching for a good difference Δ corresponds to finding the kernel of a submatrix $\hat{S}_1$ of S_1, in which rows $0, \ldots, 31$ and columns 0, 1, and $39, \ldots, 63$ are removed. Hence, we keep the columns corresponding to input bits that may contain a difference, and we keep the rows corresponding to output bits which must contain no difference. See Fig. 1.

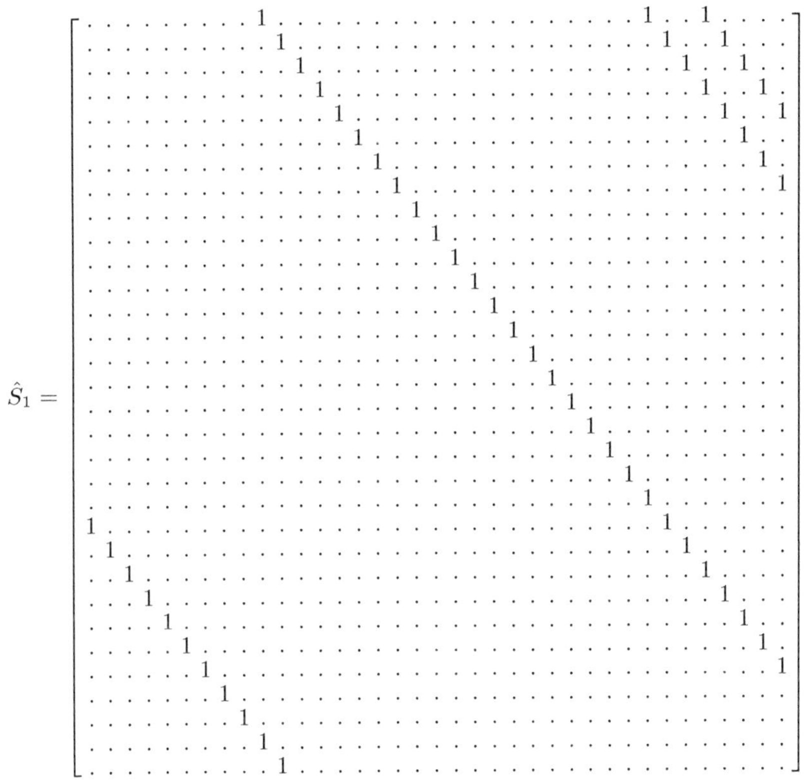

Fig. 1. The matrix $\hat{S}_1$ over $\mathbb{F}_2$ (a dot means '0')

The kernel of $\hat{S}_1$ has dimension 5 and hence contains $2^5 - 1 = 31$ non-zero vectors. Five basis vectors of the kernel correspond to the 64-bit words $\texttt{0204800008000000}_h$, $\texttt{0102400004000000}_h$, $\texttt{1004000040000000}_h$, $\texttt{0081200002000000}_h$, and $\texttt{2401000090000000}_h$, and so any linear combination of these (except 0) can be used as a value for Δ. As an example, if we choose $\Delta = \texttt{1004000040000000}_h$ (and assuming Δ is not changed by the feed-forward in f_0), we have the following differences with probability 1 (the words Q_i for $1 \leq i < 16$ contain no difference):

ΔQ_0 = [---x---------x-------------------x------------------------------]
ΔQ_{16} = [???????????????????????????????x--------------------------------]
ΔQ_{17} = [?????????????????????????????????x------------------------------]
ΔQ_{18} = [???????????????????????????????????x----------------------------]
ΔQ_{19} = [??x---------------------]
ΔQ_{20} = [??--------------------]
ΔQ_{21} = [??x-----------]
ΔQ_{22} = [??----------]
ΔQ_{23} = [??x-----]
ΔQ_{24} = [???-]

Hence, XL will be

[??x-----],

and from (7) we see that $H_0^*[0]$ will contain no difference with probability 1.

For BMW-224/256, a similar investigation results in a solution space for Δ of dimension 2, parametrised by the vectors 08901000_h and 20404000_h. As an example, with $\Delta = 20404000_h$ we have the following differences with probability 1:

ΔQ_0 = [--x------x-------x--------------]
ΔQ_{16} = [???????????????x----------------]
ΔQ_{17} = [?????????????????x--------------]
ΔQ_{18} = [???????????????????x------------]
ΔQ_{19} = [?????????????????????x----------]
ΔQ_{20} = [???????????????????????x--------]
ΔQ_{21} = [?????????????????????????x------]
ΔQ_{22} = [???????????????????????????x----]
ΔQ_{23} = [?????????????????????????????x--]
ΔQ_{24} = [???????????????????????????????x]

Hence, XL will be [?????????????????????????????x--], and $H_0^*[0]$ will contain a difference with probability 1. If we instead take Δ to be the xor of the two basis vectors, then $H_0^*[0]$ will contain *no* difference with probability 1.

6 The Security Parameter 2/14

The results described above cannot be directly extended to the security parameter 2/14. The reason is that the difference in Q_{16} goes through s_0 instead of s_5 in round 1. s_0 is much more effective in spreading differences than s_5.

However, we observe that it is still possible if we are lucky (as attacker) enough to get the differences in some LSBs cancelled. Note that when the security parameter is 2/14 instead of 1/15, we have the same dependencies (see (9)) except that Q_{17} depends on $s_0(Q_{16})$ instead of on $s_5(Q_{16})$. Hence, we may investigate whether the requirement $P(Q_{17}) \geq 27$ that we found above holds for some Δ among the 31 candidates mentioned above. Unfortunately, this is not the case.

Instead, we may allow differences in the 25 LSBs of Q_0 and hope that the modular addition cancels the differences in the 27 LSBs of $s_0(s_1(Q_0))$ and $M_1^{\lll 2}$, which are the only terms in the computation of Q_{17} that contain differences. We still need $s_1(Q_0)$ to contain no difference in the 32 LSBs, and we also need M_1 to have no difference in the two MSBs. So we search for Δ so that $s_0(s_1(\Delta))$ and $\Delta^{\lll 2}$ agree in the 27 LSBs, and so that $s_1(\Delta)$ has '0' bits in the 32 LSBs and Δ has '0' bits in the two MSBs.

Let S_0 and S_1 denote the bit matrices corresponding to the functions s_0 and s_1, and let R_2 denote the bit matrix corresponding to the operation $x^{\lll 2}$. Let $\Lambda = s_1(\Delta)$; this means that we are interested in Λ having 32 trailing '0' bits, and such that $S_0 \cdot \Lambda$ and $R_2 \cdot S_1^{-1} \cdot \Lambda$ agree in the 27 LSBs (where Λ in this case is viewed as a 64-bit column vector). Hence, similar to the situation above for the security parameter 1/15, we are in fact interested in the kernel of a submatrix of $S_0 - R_2 \cdot S_1^{-1}$. The submatrix is the 27×32 matrix where the last 32 columns and the first 37 columns are removed. Moreover, we need Λ to be such that $s_1^{-1}(\Lambda)$ has '0' bits in the two MSBs.

It turns out that the kernel of this submatrix has dimension 5 and is parametrised by the vectors that can be found in the table below, where also the corresponding Δs are listed.

Λ	$\Delta = s_1^{-1}(\Lambda)$
$\texttt{80D2227300000000}_h$	$\texttt{2B0D8FF05891139A}_h$
$\texttt{48002F6000000000}_h$	$\texttt{29A78CAE96017B01}_h$
$\texttt{22C4DC6100000000}_h$	$\texttt{89ABBD3D9226E308}_h$
$\texttt{10D27CB300000000}_h$	$\texttt{784296AD7493E598}_h$
$\texttt{01201CFD00000000}_h$	$\texttt{28E58FDD2900E7E8}_h$

Clearly, there are 7 (non-zero) linear combinations that contain only '0' bits in the two MSB positions and therefore admit a bias of the type '-' or 'x' in $H_0^*[0]$. One of these ($\Delta = \texttt{28E58FDD2900E7E8}_h$) also admits this type of bias in $H_0^*[1]$. Moreover, among the remaining 24 non-zero linear combinations, there are 16 which admit a weaker bias in the sense that $H_0^*[0]$ contains a difference with probability about 3/8 or 5/8 (i.e., a bias 1/8, estimated from many experiments). Note that a difference in the two MSBs of M_1 is no longer a problem in round 1, since we obtain the required difference in round 1 by having the differences in the 27 LSBs of $s_0(Q_{16})$ and $M_1^{\lll 2}$ cancel. This can be ensured through simple message modifications, as explained in the following.

First, we choose $H_1 = M_1 = 0$. Then we choose H_i and M_i at random, $i \in \{0, 2, 3, \ldots, 15\}$. We then correct M_5 such that $Q_0 = 0$. Hence, $Q_0 \oplus \Delta = \Delta$, and so all bit differences in Q_0 are of the form $0 \to 1$. We then correct Q_8 (through proper choice of H_9 and M_9, without affecting other words) such that $Q_{16} = 0$. This ensures that there is no carry propagation after adding the difference Λ on $s_1(Q_0)$. Hence, the difference on Q_{16} will be Λ as required. This, in turn, means that $s_0(Q_{16})$ will result in a difference that is the same as the difference on $M_1^{\lll 2}$ in the 27 LSB positions. All bit differences in $s_0(Q_{16})$ will be of the form $0 \to 1$. We can make the difference on $M_1^{\lll 2}$ cancel the difference on $s_0(Q_{16})$ (in the 27 LSBs) by making sure that all bit differences on $M_1^{\lll 2}$ are of the form $1 \to 0$. This is ensured by correcting M_{11} so that $AddElement(1) = 0$ and by choosing H_8 = FFFFFFFFFFFFFFFF$_h$. Note that this can be done in the very beginning, since these values do not depend on any values of Q. There are still many degrees of freedom left in the attack.

For BMW-224/256, we get the following three solutions:

Λ	$\Delta = s_1^{-1}(\Lambda)$
99108000$_h$	5CD58223$_h$
54E68000$_h$	6A2F79CC$_h$
245B0000$_h$	872008B6$_h$

Only the xor of the first two basis vectors fulfils the requirement that the two MSBs of Δ are '0' bits. Using this value of Δ (and with a similar message modification as above), one gets that the LSB of $H^*[0]$ is always '-'. Four out of the remaining six non-zero linear combinations yield a difference in the same bit with probability 3/8 or 5/8 (again an estimate based on experiments).

C program. The differential properties described in this section are demonstrated in a C program available for download [4].

7 Potential Applications

In this section, we show how to convert the efficient differentials into pseudo-preimages of the compression function. To describe the attack, we consider a small ideal case: assume we have a set of differences D_1, D_2, D_3 such that the differentials give [-x], [x-], and [xx] on two output bits, respectively. Given any target T, we perform the pseudo-preimage attack as follows.

1. Randomly choose (H, M) from the set of inputs that fulfil the requirements for the differentials. Compute $H^* = \mathsf{bmw}_n(H, M)$.
2. Compare H^* with T for the two bits.
3. If it gives [--], further compare others bits;
4. else if it gives [-x], compare $\mathsf{bmw}_n(H \oplus D_1, M \oplus D_1)$ with T;
5. else if it gives [x-], compare $\mathsf{bmw}_n(H \oplus D_2, M \oplus D_2)$ with T;
6. else if it gives [xx], compare $\mathsf{bmw}_n(H \oplus D_3, M \oplus D_3)$ with T.
7. Repeat steps 1-6 until a full match is found.

Note, steps 2-5 each gives a full match with probability $2^{2-n'}$ (with n' the size of the chaining value). Hence, the expected time complexity is $2^{n'-2} \times (1 + 3/4) \simeq 2^{n'-1.2}$, with negligible memory requirements. More generally, if there are $2^k - 1$ differences giving all possible $2^k - 1$ probability 1 differentials on k output bits of the compression function, then the pseudo-preimage takes time about $2^{n'-k} \cdot (2 - 2^{-k}) \simeq 2^{n'-k+1}$.

In the case of BMW-512, we only have differences giving differentials on the 2 LSBs of H_0^* with [x-], [?x], and [x?]. This can be converted into a pseudo-preimage of bmw_{512} in time $2^{1023.2}$.

An interesting problem here is to find more such differentials, such that the complexity could be further reduced. Moreover, if the differentials work on the lower half of the output bits (those to be taken as the output of the hash function), then the pseudo-preimage on the compression function can be further extended to a pseudo-preimage attack on the hash function.

8 Conclusion

We have described some determinstic differential properties for the BMW compression function with security parameters 0/16, 1/15 and 2/14: by choosing a certain xor difference in two input words to the compression function (and with conditions on absolute values of a few other words), a single (or a few) output bits of the compression function contain a difference with probability 0 or 1.

The differentials work for the compression function only, and do not affect the security of the hash function because of the additional blank invocation of the compression function before returning the hash output. Moreover, H_0^* is discarded in the final hash output, and only the least significant half (or less) bits of H^* of the final compression are taken.

Combining with more sophisticated message modification techniques, the differentials might be further extended to higher security parameters, hence increasing security parameter might not be enough to resist them. Tweaking the rotation values for the s_i and r_i functions may work, under the condition that the tweak does not affect other security properties.

Another interesting problem to consider is to devise differentials on other output words than merely H_0^*. In particular, a bias on one of the output words $H_8^*, \ldots, H_{15}^*$ would be interesting.

We note that tracing the propagation of differences, as done in this paper, might help to explain the distinguisher found by Aumasson [1].

Acknowledgements. Special thanks go to Nicky Mouha for presenting the paper on the conference for us. We would like to thank Jean-Philippe Aumasson and the anonymous reviewers of SAC 2010 for their helpful comments. The work in this paper is supported in part by the Singapore Ministry of Education under Research Grant T206B2204.

References

1. Aumasson, J.-P.: Practical distinguisher for the compression function of Blue Midnight Wish. Comment on the NIST Hash Competition (Feburary 2010), `http://131002.net/data/papers/Aum10.pdf`
2. De Cannière, C., Rechberger, C.: Finding SHA-1 Characteristics: General Results and Applications. In: Lai, X., Chen, K. (eds.) ASIACRYPT 2006. LNCS, vol. 4284, pp. 1–20. Springer, Heidelberg (2006)

3. Gligoroski, D., Klíma, V., Knapskog, S.J., El-Hadedy, M., Amundsen, J., Mjølsnes, S.F.: Cryptographic hash function BLUE MIDNIGHT WISH. Submission to NIST (Round 2) (September 2009), `http://people.item.ntnu.no/ danilog/Hash/BMW-SecondRound/Supporting_Documentation/BlueMidnightWishDocumentation.pdf` (March 22, 2010)
4. Guo, J., Thomsen, S.S.: C program that demonstrates the distinguisher, `http://www2.mat.dtu.dk/people/S.Thomsen/bmw/bmw-distinguisher.zip`
5. National Institute of Standards and Technology. Announcing Request for Candidate Algorithm Nominations for a New Cryptographic Hash Algorithm (SHA-3) Family. Federal Register 27(212), 62212–62220 (November 2007), `http://csrc.nist.gov/groups/ST/hash/documents/FR_Notice_Nov07.pdf` (April 7, 2009)
6. Nikolić, I., Pieprzyk, J., Sokołowski, P., Steinfeld, R.: Rotational Cryptanalysis of (Modified) Versions of BMW and SIMD. Comment on the NIST Hash Competition (March 2010), `https://cryptolux.org/mediawiki/uploads/0/07/Rotational_distinguishers_%28Nikolic%2C_Pieprzyk%2C_Sokolowski%2C_Steinfeld%29.pdf` (March 22, 2010)
7. Thomsen, S.S.: Pseudo-cryptanalysis of the Original Blue Midnight Wish. In: Hong, S., Iwata, T. (eds.) FSE 2010. LNCS, vol. 6147, pp. 304–317. Springer, Heidelberg (2010)

A Sub-functions Used in f_0 and f_1

The sub-functions s_i, $0 \leq i \leq 4$, and r_i, $1 \leq i \leq 7$, used in f_0 and f_1 are defined as follows.

BMW-224/256	BMW-384/512
$s_0(x) = x^{\gg 1} \oplus x^{\ll 3} \oplus x^{\lll 4} \oplus x^{\lll 19}$	$s_0(x) = x^{\gg 1} \oplus x^{\ll 3} \oplus x^{\lll 4} \oplus x^{\lll 37}$
$s_1(x) = x^{\gg 1} \oplus x^{\ll 2} \oplus x^{\lll 8} \oplus x^{\lll 23}$	$s_1(x) = x^{\gg 1} \oplus x^{\ll 2} \oplus x^{\lll 13} \oplus x^{\lll 43}$
$s_2(x) = x^{\gg 2} \oplus x^{\ll 1} \oplus x^{\lll 12} \oplus x^{\lll 25}$	$s_2(x) = x^{\gg 2} \oplus x^{\ll 1} \oplus x^{\lll 19} \oplus x^{\lll 53}$
$s_3(x) = x^{\gg 2} \oplus x^{\ll 2} \oplus x^{\lll 15} \oplus x^{\lll 29}$	$s_3(x) = x^{\gg 2} \oplus x^{\ll 2} \oplus x^{\lll 28} \oplus x^{\lll 59}$
$s_4(x) = x^{\gg 1} \oplus x$	$s_4(x) = x^{\gg 1} \oplus x$
$s_5(x) = x^{\gg 2} \oplus x$	$s_5(x) = x^{\gg 2} \oplus x$
$r_1(x) = x^{\lll 3}$	$r_1(x) = x^{\lll 5}$
$r_2(x) = x^{\lll 7}$	$r_2(x) = x^{\lll 11}$
$r_3(x) = x^{\lll 13}$	$r_3(x) = x^{\lll 27}$
$r_4(x) = x^{\lll 16}$	$r_4(x) = x^{\lll 32}$
$r_5(x) = x^{\lll 19}$	$r_5(x) = x^{\lll 37}$
$r_6(x) = x^{\lll 23}$	$r_6(x) = x^{\lll 43}$
$r_7(x) = x^{\lll 27}$	$r_7(x) = x^{\lll 53}$

Security Analysis of SIMD*

Charles Bouillaguet, Pierre-Alain Fouque, and Gaëtan Leurent

École Normale Supérieure – Département d'Informatique,
45 rue d'Ulm, 75230 Paris Cedex 05, France
{Charles.Bouillaguet,Gaetan.Leurent,Pierre-Alain.Fouque}@ens.fr

Abstract. This paper provides three important contributions to the security analysis of SIMD. First, we show a new free-start distinguisher based on symmetry relations. It allows to distinguish the compression function of SIMD from a random function with a single evaluation. Then, we show that a class of free-start distinguishers is not a threat to wide-pipe hash functions. In particular, this means that our distinguisher has a minimal impact on the security of the SIMD hash function. Intuitively, the reason why this distinguisher does not weaken the function is that getting into a symmetric state is about as hard as finding a preimage. Finally, we study differential path in SIMD, and give an upper bound on the probability of related key differential paths. Our bound is in the order of $2^{-n/2}$ using very weak assumptions.

Keywords: SIMD, SHA-3, hash function, distinguisher, security proof with distinguishers.

1 Introduction

SIMD is a SHA-3 candidate designed by Leurent, Fouque and Bouillaguet [11]. Its main feature is a strong message expansion whose aim is to thwart differential attacks. In this paper we study the security of SIMD, and we introduce three new results.

In Section 2 we study its resistance against self-similarity attacks [4]. This class of attack is inspired by the complementation property of DES and includes symmetry based attacks. In the case of SIMD, we show that it is possible to exploit the symmetry of the design using special messages. This shows that the constants included in the message expansion of SIMD are not sufficient to prevent symmetry relations, and non-symmetric constants should be added in the last steps of the message expansion. In-depth study of this symmetry property shows that it is much weaker than symmetry properties in CubeHash [1,9] or Lesamnta [4]. More precisely, most symmetry properties can be used to generate many symmetric states out of a single state, but this is not the case for SIMD.

In Section 3, we show a proof of security for the mode of operation used in SIMD, the truncated prefix-free Merkle-Damgård, in the presence of some efficient distinguishers on the compression function. The class of distinguisher we

* The full version of this paper appears as IACR ePrint report 2010/323 [5].

A. Biryukov, G. Gong, and D.R. Stinson (Eds.): SAC 2010, LNCS 6544, pp. 351–368, 2011.

consider includes the symmetry based distinguisher, and also includes differential paths with a non-zero chaining value difference. This shows that the properties of the compression function of SIMD found so far do not affect the security of the iterated hash function. This part is also of independent interest and applies to other wide-pipe hash functions.

In Section 4, we study differential attacks, and bound the probability of paths with a non-zero message difference, *i.e.*, related key attacks on the block cipher. We show an upper bound on such paths on the order of $2^{-n/2}$, and we argue that the best paths are probably much worse than this bound. We note that there are very few results known regarding resistance to related key attack for block ciphers. In particular, the differential properties of the AES have been extensively studied [13] but related key differential attacks have been shown recently [3]. In many hash function designs (in particular those based on the Davies-Meyer construction), related key attacks are a real concern and should be studied accordingly.

By combining the results of Section 3 and 4, we show that SIMD is resistant to differential cryptanalysis: a path with a non-zero difference in the chaining value input cannot be used to attack the hash function because it is wide-pipe, while a path a non-zero difference in the message can only have a low success probability.

1.1 Brief Description of SIMD

SIMD is built using a modified Davies-Meyer mode with a strong message expansion, as shown in Figure 1. The compression part is built from 4 parallel Feistel ladders (8 for SIMD-512) with 32-bit registers, and is shown in Figure 2. We can describe the step update function as:

$$D_j \leftarrow \left(D_j \boxplus W_j^{(i)} \boxplus \phi^{(i)}(A_j, B_j, C_j)\right)^{\lll s^{(i)}} \boxplus A_{p^{(i)}(j)}{}^{\lll r^{(i)}}$$

$$(A_j, B_j, C_j, D_j) \leftarrow (D_j, A_j^{\lll r^{(i)}}, B_j, C_j)$$

where j denotes the Feistel number, and i denotes the round number. A, B, C, and D are the four registers of the Feistel ladders, while $\phi^{(i)}$ is the Boolean function used at round i (which can be either IF or MAJ) and W is the expanded message. The parallel Feistels interact through the permutations $p^{(i)}$, which are built as $p^{(i)}(j) = j \oplus \alpha_i$, for some α_i. There are no explicit constants in the round function, but there are implicit constants in the message expansion.

The Message Expansion. The message expansion of SIMD is defined with the following operations:

1. Use a NTT transform (which is the same as a FFT over $\mathbb{F}_{257}$) to double the size of the message. The NTT is actually used as a Reed-Solomon code.
2. Make two copies of the NTT output.
3. The first copy is multiplied by 185, while the second copy is multiplied by 233. This step also doubles the size of the message, as the output are 16-bit words.
4. Permute the 16-bit words and pack them into 32-bit words.

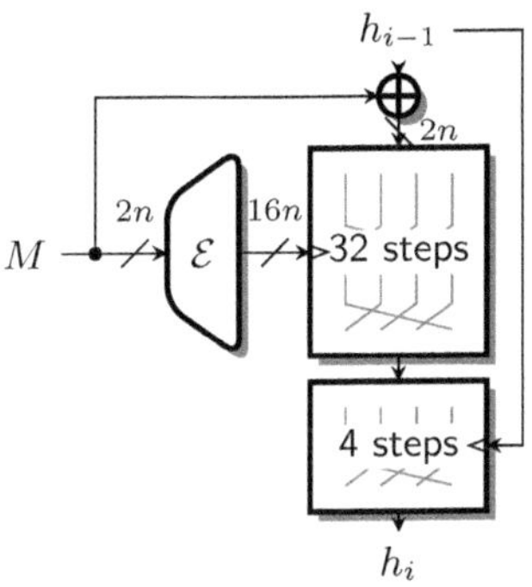

Fig. 1. SIMD modified Davies-Meyer mode

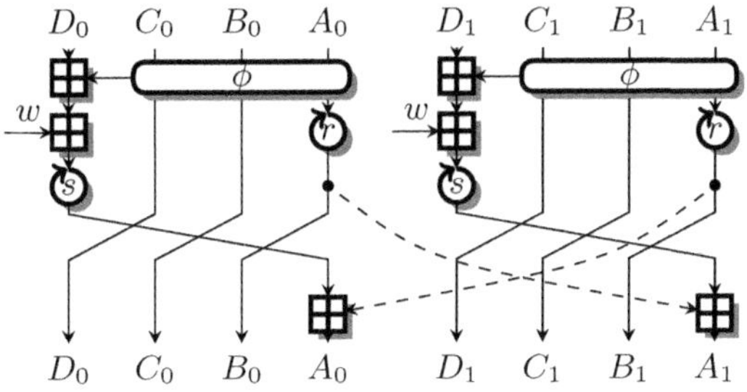

Fig. 2. SIMD compression rounds. There are 4 parallel Feistels in SIMD-256, and 8 parallel Feistels in SIMD-512.

Constants are added in the NTT layer, and make it an affine code instead of a linear one. They avoid special expanded messages such as the all-zero message. For more details, see the specification of SIMD [11].

2 A Distinguisher for the Compression Function of SIMD

Our distinguisher is based on symmetries in the design, and follows the ideas of [4]. Symmetry based properties have already been found in several hash function designs, such as CubeHash [1,9] or Lesamnta [4]. We describe the distinguisher in the case of SIMD-256, but it applies similarly to SIMD-512.

2.1 Building the Symmetric Messages

The basic idea is to build a message so that the expanded message is symmetric. Then, if the internal state is also symmetric, the compression rounds preserve the symmetry. This can also be used with a pair of symmetric messages, and a pair of symmetric states.

The NTT layer of the message expansion is an affine transformation, therefore it is easy to find inputs that satisfy some affine conditions on the output. Since it only doubles the size of the input, we have enough degrees of freedom to force equalities between pairs of output. The next expansion step is a multiplication by a constant, and it will preserve equality relations.

If we look at the permutations used in the message expansion, they have the following property[1]: the NTT words used to build the message words $W_0^{(i)}$, $W_1^{(i)}, W_2^{(i)}, W_3^{(i)}$ are always of the form $(y_{k_1}, y_{k_2}), (y_{k_1+2}, y_{k_2+2}), (y_{k_1+4}, y_{k_2+4}),$ (y_{k_1+6}, y_{k_2+6}) for some k_1 and k_2 (with $k_i = 0 \bmod 8$ or $k_i = 1 \bmod 8$). The full permutations are given in [11, Table 1.1]. Because of this property, if we have $y_i = y_{i\oplus 2}$ after the NTT, then we have $W_0^{(i)} = W_1^{(i)}$ and $W_2^{(i)} = W_3^{(i)}$. This allows us to build a symmetric message.

[1] This design choice was guided by implementation efficiency.

More precisely, let us use the notation $\overset{\leftrightarrow}{\bullet}$ to denote this symmetry relation, and $\underset{\leftrightarrow}{\bullet}$ and $\overset{\leftrightarrow}{\underset{\leftrightarrow}{\bullet}}$ to denote the other two possible symmetries:

$$\overleftrightarrow{(a,b,c,d)} = (b,a,d,c) \qquad \underleftrightarrow{(a,b,c,d)} = (c,d,a,b) \qquad \underleftrightarrow{\overleftrightarrow{(a,b,c,d)}} = (d,c,b,a)$$

We now consider two messages M and M'. We use y to denote the NTT output for M, and y' to denote the NTT output for M'. The equality constraints on the NTT output that are necessary to build a pair of symmetric expanded messages are (we use $\mathcal{E}$ to denote the message expansion):

$$y_i = y'_{i\oplus 2} \Leftrightarrow \mathcal{E}(M) = \overleftrightarrow{\mathcal{E}(M')} \qquad\qquad y_i = y'_{i\oplus 4} \Leftrightarrow \mathcal{E}(M) = \underleftrightarrow{\mathcal{E}(M')}$$

$$y_i = y'_{i\oplus 6} \Leftrightarrow \mathcal{E}(M) = \underleftrightarrow{\overleftrightarrow{\mathcal{E}(M')}}$$

By solving the corresponding linear systems, we can compute the sets of symmetric messages (the sets are described in the full version of this paper). We can count the symmetric messages M such that $\mathcal{E}(M) = \overleftrightarrow{\mathcal{E}(M)}$, and the pairs of messages M, M' such that $\mathcal{E}(M) = \overleftrightarrow{\mathcal{E}(M')}$:

Sym. class (SIMD-256)			msg	pairs
$\overset{\leftrightarrow}{\bullet}$	$y_i = y'_{i\oplus 2}$	$W_i = W'_{i\oplus 1}$	2^8	$256 \cdot 255$
$\underset{\leftrightarrow}{\bullet}$	$y_i = y'_{i\oplus 4}$	$W_i = W'_{i\oplus 2}$	2^{16}	$(256 \cdot 255)^2$
$\overset{\leftrightarrow}{\underset{\leftrightarrow}{\bullet}}$	$y_i = y'_{i\oplus 6}$	$W_i = W'_{i\oplus 3}$	2^8	$256 \cdot 255$

Sym. class (SIMD-512)		msg	pairs
$y_i = y'_{i\oplus 2}$	$W_i = W'_{i\oplus 1}$	2^8	$256 \cdot 255$
$y_i = y'_{i\oplus 4}$	$W_i = W'_{i\oplus 2}$	2^{16}	$(256 \cdot 255)^2$
$y_i = y'_{i\oplus 6}$	$W_i = W'_{i\oplus 3}$	2^8	$256 \cdot 255$
$y_i = y'_{i\oplus 8}$	$W_i = W'_{i\oplus 4}$	2^{32}	$(256 \cdot 255)^4$
$y_i = y'_{i\oplus 10}$	$W_i = W'_{i\oplus 5}$	2^8	$256 \cdot 255$
$y_i = y'_{i\oplus 12}$	$W_i = W'_{i\oplus 6}$	2^{16}	$(256 \cdot 255)^2$
$y_i = y'_{i\oplus 14}$	$W_i = W'_{i\oplus 7}$	2^8	$256 \cdot 255$

An important property of these message classes is that they are all disjoint: it is not possible to use the intersection of two symmetry classes.

2.2 Symmetry Property on the Compression Function

Let us consider a pair of symmetric messages for one of the symmetry relations (without loss of generality, we assume it's the $\overset{\leftrightarrow}{\bullet}$ symmetry): $\mathcal{E}(M') = \overleftrightarrow{\mathcal{E}(M)}$. We can take advantage of the symmetry of the Feistel part using those messages. If we have a pair of states $\mathcal{S}^{(i)}, \mathcal{S}'^{(i)}$ with $\mathcal{S}'^{(i)} = \overleftrightarrow{\mathcal{S}^{(i)}}$ and we compute one Feistel step with messages W and W' such that $W' = \overleftrightarrow{W}$, we obtain a new pair of states with $\mathcal{S}'^{(i+1)} = \overleftrightarrow{\mathcal{S}^{(i+1)}}$. The xor-based symmetry classes commute with the xor-based permutations $p^{(i)}$ used to mix the Feistels (and they are the only symmetry classes to do so).

Because the compression function is built using a modified Davies-Meyer mode (Figure 1), we need to start with H_{i-1} such that $H_{i-1} \oplus M$ is symmetric: $H'_{i-1} \oplus M' = \overleftrightarrow{H_{i-1} \oplus M}$. Then, in the feed-forward, H_{i-1} is used as the key to a few

Feistel rounds, and since H_{i-1} is not symmetric, those rounds will break the symmetry. However, it turns out the symmetric messages are very sparse, so H_i will be almost symmetric, and the feed-forward will mostly preserve the symmetry of the outputs.

This gives a distinguisher on the compression function: an almost symmetric chaining value is transformed into a somewhat symmetric chaining value. A concrete example of message and chaining value is given in the full version of this paper.

The distinguisher can be used either with a pair of messages and chaining values with $\mathcal{E}(M') = \overleftrightarrow{\mathcal{E}(M)}$ and $H'_{i-1} \oplus M' = \overleftrightarrow{H_{i-1} \oplus M}$, or with a single chaining value and message, with $\mathcal{E}(M) = \overleftrightarrow{\mathcal{E}(M)}$ and $H_{i-1} \oplus M = \overleftrightarrow{H_{i-1} \oplus M}$.

2.3 Non-ideality of the Compression Function

Here we define the bias of the compression function with the notations that will be used in Section 3. For each symmetric message M under a symmetry relation (denoted by $\overleftrightarrow{\bullet}$ without loss of generality), we have a first order relation between the inputs and output of the compression function:

$$\mathcal{R}_1^M(h, m, h') := \left(m = M \wedge h \oplus m = \overleftrightarrow{h \oplus m}\right) \Rightarrow P^{-1}(h', h) = \overleftrightarrow{P^{-1}(h', h)}$$

We use the feed-forward permutation P to define the relation, because it is tricky to describe exactly the somewhat symmetry of h' after the feed-forward. We have about 2^{16} such relations for SIMD-256 and about 2^{32} relations for SIMD-512. Similarly, for each symmetric message pair M, M', this gives a second order relation (there are about 2^{32} such relations for SIMD-256 and 2^{64} for SIMD-512):

$$\mathcal{R}_2^{M,M'}(h_1, m_1, h_2, m_2, h'_1, h'_2) :=$$
$$\left(m_1 = M \wedge m_2 = M' \wedge h_1 \oplus m_1 = \overleftrightarrow{h_2 \oplus m_2}\right) \Rightarrow P^{-1}(h'_1, h_1) = \overleftrightarrow{P^{-1}(h'_2, h_2)}$$

The corresponding weak states are:

$$\mathcal{W}_1^M := \{x \oplus M \mid x = \overleftrightarrow{x}\} \qquad \mathcal{W}_2^{M,M'} := \left\{(h, \overleftrightarrow{h} \oplus M' \oplus \overleftrightarrow{M})\right\}$$

The study of the symmetry classes of SIMD shows that:

$$|\mathcal{W}_1| \approx 2^{256} \cdot 2^{16} \qquad |\mathcal{W}_1| \approx 2^{512} \cdot 2^{32} \qquad \text{for SIMD-512}$$
$$|\mathcal{W}_2| < 2^{512} \cdot 2^{32} \qquad |\mathcal{W}_2| < 2^{1024} \cdot 2^{64} \qquad \text{for SIMD-512}$$

Each chaining value can be used with less than 2^{32} related chaining values (less than 2^{64} for SIMD-512) and each such pair can be used with a single message.

2.4 Impact of the Symmetry-Based Distinguisher

There are two main classes of attacks based on symmetric properties of the compression function. To attack the compression function, one can use the symmetry property to force the output of the compression function into a small subspace. This allows to find collisions in the compression function more efficiently than brute force, with the efficiency of this attack depending on the size of the symmetry classes. On the other hand, to attack the hash function, one can first try to reach a symmetric state using random messages, and then use symmetric messages to build a large set of symmetric states. To expand the set, the attacker will build a tree, starting with the symmetric state that was reached randomly. The degree and the depth of the tree can be limited depending on the symmetry property. In the case of SIMD, none of these attacks are effective for the following reasons:

- First, the modified Davies-Meyer mode of operation means that the compression function does not transform a symmetric state into a symmetric state, but it transforms an almost symmetric state into a somewhat symmetric state. We show in the full version of the paper that a "somewhat symmetric" output pair can only be used as an "almost symmetric" input pair with a very small probability. This prevents attacks based on building long chains of symmetric messages, like the attacks on CubeHash [1,9].
- Second, if a pair of almost symmetric states is reached, there is only a single message pair that can be used to reach a symmetric state in the Feistel rounds. This prevents attacks like the herding attack on Lesamnta [4], where one reaches a symmetric state and then uses a lot of different messages in order to explore the subset of symmetric outputs.
- Third, the final transformation of SIMD uses the message length as input. Therefore, the symmetry property can only be seen in the output of the hash function with messages of unrealistic length (almost 2^{512} bits for SIMD-256 and almost 2^{1024} bits for SIMD-512). Note that computing the hash of such a message is vastly more expensive than finding a preimage.
- Moreover the symmetry classes do not intersect. It is not possible to build a smaller symmetry classes in order to show collisions in the compression function, as was done for CubeHash [1,9]. Finding collisions in the compression function using the symmetry property costs $2^{n/2}$. It is more efficient than generic attacks on the compression function, but cannot be used to find collisions in the hash function faster than the birthday attack. We also note that the initial state of the SIMD hash function is not symmetric.

To summarize, reaching a symmetric state in SIMD is far less interesting than reaching a symmetric state in CubeHash or in Lesamnta. Table 1 gives a comparison of the symmetry properties found in these functions.

Another very important factor is that SIMD is a wide-pipe design. Therefore reaching a symmetric state is about as hard a finding a preimage for the hash function. In the next section, we provide a formal proof that this distinguisher has only a small effect on the security of SIMD. We can prove that the hash function behaves as a random oracle under the assumption that the compression function is a weak perfect function having this symmetry property.

Table 1. Comparison of symmetry properties in several hash functions

Function	Reach symm. state	Max. length	Max. degree	Free-start Collisions
Lesamnta-512	2^{256}	1	2^{256}	2^{128} (semi-free-start)
CubeHash (symm $C_1..C_7$)	2^{384}	∞	2^{128}	2^{32} (semi-free-start)
CubeHash (symm $C_8..C_{15}$)	2^{256}	∞	1	2^{64} (semi-free-start)
SIMD-512	2^{480}	1	1	2^{256}

3 Free-Start Distinguishers, Non-ideal Compression Functions and Wide-Pipe Designs

In this section, we discuss the security of the prefix-free iteration of non-ideal compression functions. While our primary objective is to show that the distinguisher for the compression function of SIMD presented in Section 2 does not void the security proof of SIMD, the reasoning and the proof presented here are pretty general and could very well be adapted to other functions.

Let $\mathcal{H} = \{0,1\}^p$ denote the set of chaining values, $\mathcal{M} = \{0,1\}^m$ denote the set of message blocks, and $\mathcal{F}$ be the set of all functions $\mathcal{H} \times \mathcal{M} \to \mathcal{H}$. Let $F \in \mathcal{F}$ be a compression function taking as input an p-bit chaining value and an m-bit message block. A mode of operation for a hash function $H^{\cdot}$ combined with a compression function F yields a full hash function H^F.

Following [12,8], we rely on the notion of indifferentiability of systems to reduce the security of SIMD to that of its compression function. The usual way of establishing the soundness of a mode of operation $H^{\cdot}$ is to show that it is indifferentiable from a random oracle. This is done by constructing a simulator $\mathcal{S}$ such that any distinguisher $\mathcal{D}$ cannot tell apart (H^F, F) and $(RO, \mathcal{S})$ without a considerable effort, where RO is a variable-input-length random oracle (VIL-RO, for short). When this is established, it is shown in [12] that any cryptosystem making use of a VIL-RO is not less secure when the random oracle is replaced by the hash function H^F, where F is an ideal compression function (*i.e.*, a fixed-input-length random oracle, FIL-RO for short). Informally, if F is ideal (*i.e.*, has no special property that a random function would not have), then H^F is secure up to the level offered by the indifferentiability proof. More precisely, if $H^{\cdot}$ is $(t_{\mathcal{D}}, t_{\mathcal{S}}, q_{\mathcal{S}}, q_0, \varepsilon)$-indifferentiable from a VIL-RO when the compression function is assumed to be a FIL-RO, then this means that there exists a simulator running in time $t_{\mathcal{S}}$, such that any distinguisher running in time $t_{\mathcal{D}}$ and issuing at most $q_{\mathcal{S}}$ (resp. q_0) queries to the FIL-RO (resp. VIL-RO) has success probability at most ε.

A property of this methodology is that as soon as the compression function used in a hash function turns out to be non-ideal, then the security argument offered by the indifferentiability proof becomes vacuous. For instance, distinguishers exhibiting a "non-random" behavior of the compression function are usually advertised by their authors to nullify the security proof of the full hash function.

This problematic situation was first tackled by the designers of Shabal, who provided a security proof taking into account the existence of an efficient distinguisher on the internal permutation of their proposal [6]. We will follow their track and demonstrate that the security of SIMD can be proved despite the existence of an efficient distinguisher on its compression function.

The mode of operation of SIMD can be "concisely" described as being the wide-pipe prefix-free[2] iteration of the compression function. Let H^F therefore denote the *prefix-free* Merkle-Damgård iteration of F. Formally, $g : \{0,1\}^* \to \mathcal{M}^*$ is a *prefix-free encoding* if for all x, x', $g(x)$ is not a prefix of $g(x')$. The mode of operation $H^{\cdot}$ simply applies the Merkle-Damgård iteration of F to the prefix-free encoding of the message.

The original security argument was that if the internal state and the hash are both p-bit wide, then prefix-free Merkle-Damgård is indifferentiable from a random oracle up to about $2^{p/2}$ queries [8]. Theorem 1 below gives a formal statement of this result.

Theorem 1. *Prefix-Free Merkle-Damgård is $(t_\mathcal{D}, t_\mathcal{S}, q_S, q_O, \varepsilon)$-indifferentiable from a VIL-RO when the compression function is modeled by a FIL-RO, for any running time $t_\mathcal{D}$ of the distinguisher, and $t_\mathcal{S} = \mathcal{O}\left((q_O + \kappa \cdot q_S)^2\right)$ where κ is an upper-bound on the size of the queries sent to the VIL-RO. If $q = q_S + \kappa \cdot q_O + 1$, then the success probability of the distinguisher is upper-bounded by:*

$$\varepsilon = 8 \cdot \frac{q^2}{2^p}$$

In SIMD where the internal state is $2n$ bits, this ensures the indifferentiability of the whole function up to roughly 2^n queries (if H is indifferentiable up to q queries, then the composition of a truncation that truncates half of the output and of H is also secure up to q queries).

To restore the security argument damaged by the distinguisher, we will show that the prefix-free iteration of a non-ideal compression function is to some extent still indifferentiable from a VIL-RO.

3.1 Deterministic Distinguishers for the Compression Function

Let us consider a non-ideal compression function F.

- For instance, it may have *weak states*, that are such that querying F thereon with a well-chosen message block produces a "special" output allowing to distinguish F from random in one query. Known examples include for instance the symmetry on the compression function of Lesamnta [4], CubeHash [1,9], and SIMD (described in Section 2).
- But F can also have *bad second-order properties*, meaning that the output of F on correlated input states (with well-chosen message blocks) produces

[2] this is not explicitly stated in the submission document, but SIMD has a different finalization function that effectively acts as a prefix-free encoding.

correlated outputs, allowing to distinguish F from random in two queries. A notable example of this property include the existence of differential paths with probability one in the compression function of Shabal [2]. Symmetry properties also give second order relations, which means that Lesamnta, CubeHash and SIMD have bad second-order properties as well.

Following the methodology introduced in [6], we model this situation by saying that there are two relations $\mathcal{R}_1$ and $\mathcal{R}_2$ such that:

$$\forall (h, m) \in \mathcal{H} \times \mathcal{M} : \quad \mathcal{R}_1(h, m, F(h, m)) = 1$$
$$\forall (h_1, h_2, m_1, m_2) \in \mathcal{H}^2 \times \mathcal{M}^2 : \quad \mathcal{R}_2(h_1, m_1, h_2, m_2, F(h_1, m_1), F(h_2, m_2)) = 1$$

We denote by $\mathcal{R}$ the relation formed by the union of $\mathcal{R}_1$ and $\mathcal{R}_2$, and we will denote by $\mathcal{F}[\mathcal{R}]$ the subset of $\mathcal{F}$ such that the above two equations hold. We require the relations to be efficiently checkable, *i.e.*, that given h, m and h', it is efficient to check whether $\mathcal{R}_1(h, m, h') = 1$. The relation can thus be used as an efficient distinguishing algorithm that tells $\mathcal{F}[\mathcal{R}]$ apart from $\mathcal{F}$.

A *weak state* is a state on which it is possible to falsify the relation $\mathcal{R}_1$. We formally define the set of weak states for $\mathcal{R}_1$ in the following way:

$$\mathcal{W} = \{h \in \mathcal{H} \mid \exists m, h' \in \mathcal{M} \times \mathcal{H} \text{ such that } \mathcal{R}_1(h, m, h') = 0\}$$

$\mathcal{W}$ should be a relatively small subset of $\mathcal{H}$ because the loss of security will be related to the size of $\mathcal{W}$. Moreover, we require that the IV is not in $\mathcal{W}$.

In the same vein, a *weak pair* is a pair of states on which it is possible to falsify the relation $\mathcal{R}_2$. We therefore define the set of *weak pairs* for $\mathcal{R}_2$ by an undirected graph $G_{\mathcal{R}_2} = (\mathcal{H}, \mathcal{WP})$, where $\mathcal{WP}$ is defined by:

$$\mathcal{WP} = \left\{h_1 \leftrightarrow h_2 \mid \exists m_1, m_2, h_1', h_2' \in \mathcal{M}^2 \times \mathcal{H}^2 \text{s.t.} \mathcal{R}_2(h_1, m_1, h_2, m_2, h_1', h_2') = 0\right\}$$

Similarly, $\mathcal{WP}$ should be a relatively small subset of $\mathcal{H}^2$ because the security loss will be related to the size of $\mathcal{WP}$. For the sake of expressing things conveniently, we define a variant of the same graph, $G'_{\mathcal{R}_2} = (\mathcal{H} \times \mathcal{M}, \mathcal{WP}')$, where $\mathcal{WP}'$ is defined by:

$$\mathcal{WP}' = \left\{(h_1, m_1) \leftrightarrow (h_2, m_2) \mid \exists h_1', h_2' \in \mathcal{H}^2 \text{s.t.} \mathcal{R}_2(h_1, m_1, h_2, m_2, h_1', h_2') = 0\right\}$$

To simplify the proof we also require that the connected component of $G'_{\mathcal{R}_2}$ have size at most two. This rules out some second-order relations, but it includes for instance the existence of a differential path with probability one with a non-zero difference in the input chaining value, as well as the symmetry in the compression function of SIMD or Lesamnta. We expect a similar result with larger connected components, but there will be a loss of security related to their size.

We also require the existence of *sampling algorithms* for $\mathcal{R}$, namely of two efficient algorithms $\mathbf{Sampler}_1$ and $\mathbf{Sampler}_2$ such that:

$\mathbf{Sampler}_1(h, m)$
  $h' \xleftarrow{\$} \{f(h, m) \mid f \in \mathcal{F}[\mathcal{R}]\}$; return h'

Sampler$_2(h_1, m_1, h_2, m_2, h'_1)$

$h'_2 \xleftarrow{\$} \{f(h_2, m_2) \mid f \in \mathcal{F}[\mathcal{R}] \text{ and } F(h_1, m_1) = h'_1\}$; return h'_2

Informally, the sampling algorithms should produce an output that looks as if it were produced by a random function constrained to conform to $\mathcal{R}$.

3.2 Adapting the Indifferentiability Proof to Non-ideal Compression Functions

We now assume that the compression function is a public function chosen uniformly at random in $\mathcal{F}[\mathcal{R}]$, and for the sake of convenience we will call it a "biased FIL-RO". We show that the prefix-free iteration of biased FIL-RO is indifferentiable from a VIL-RO. In fact, we extend Theorem 1 to the case where the compression function is biased.

Theorem 2. *Prefix-Free Merkle-Damgård is $(t_\mathcal{D}, t_\mathcal{S}, q_S, q_O, \varepsilon)$-indifferentiable from a VIL-RO, when the compression function is modeled by a biased FIL-RO conforming to the relation $\mathcal{R}$, for any running time $t_\mathcal{D}$ of the distinguisher, and $t_\mathcal{S} = \mathcal{O}\left((q_O + \kappa \cdot q_S)^2\right)$ where κ is an upper-bound on the size of the queries sent to the VIL-RO. If $q = q_S + \kappa \cdot q_o + 1$, then the probability of success of the distinguisher is upper-bounded by:*

$$\varepsilon = 16 \cdot \frac{q^2}{2^p} + 4 \cdot |\mathcal{W}| \cdot \frac{q}{2^p} + 4 \cdot |\mathcal{WP}| \cdot \frac{q^2}{(2^p - q)^2}$$

The first term of the expression of ε is similar to the result given in Theorem 1, when the compression function is ideal (up to a factor two that could be avoided by making the argument slightly more involved). The two other terms reflect the fact that the compression function is biased. The relation induces a security loss if $|\mathcal{W}|$ is at least of order $2^{p/2}$, or if $|\mathcal{WP}|$ is at least of order 2^p. Informally, it seems possible to iterate compression functions having a relatively high bias in a secure way.

Application to Free-start Differential Attacks. Let us assume that the compression function is weak because of the existence of a good differential path with a non-zero difference in the input chaining value. Even if the probability of the differential path is 1, this has a very limited effect on the security of the hash function: this leads to $\mathcal{W} = \emptyset$ and $|\mathcal{WP}| = 2^{p-1}$. The advantage of the distinguisher is at most twice as high, compared to the iteration of an ideal FIL-RO.

Application to SIMD. In SIMD-256 (resp. SIMD-512), the internal state has $p = 512$ bits (resp. $p = 1024$ bits), and the distinguisher of Section 2 yields $|\mathcal{W}| = 2^{p/2+16}$, $|\mathcal{WP}| = 2^{p+32}$ (resp. $|\mathcal{W}| = 2^{p/2+32}$, $|\mathcal{WP}| = 2^{p+64}$). Therefore the advantage of any distinguisher in telling apart SIMD-256 from a VIL-RO with q queries is upper-bounded by:

$$\varepsilon = 16 \cdot \frac{q^2}{2^p} + 4 \cdot \frac{2^{p/2+16} \cdot q}{2^p} + 4 \cdot 2^{p+32} \cdot \frac{q^2}{(2^p - q)^2}$$

SIMD-256 is then secure up to roughly 2^{256-16} queries (SIMD-512 is secure up to 2^{512-32} queries).

Application to Lesamnta. Lesamnta follows the prefix-free Merkle-Damgård mode of operation due to its special finalization function. An efficient distinguisher based on symmetries was shown in [4], with $|\mathcal{W}| = 2^{p/2}$ and $|\mathcal{WP}| = 2^{p-1}$. According to Theorem 2, the advantage of any distinguisher in telling apart Lesamnta-256 from a random oracle with q queries is upper-bounded by:

$$\varepsilon = 16 \cdot \frac{q^2}{2^p} + 4 \cdot \frac{2^{p/2} \cdot q}{2^p} + 4 \cdot 2^{p-1} \cdot \frac{q^2}{(2^p - q)^2} \approx 22 \cdot \frac{q}{2^{p/2}}$$

Note that since Lesamnta is a narrow-pipe design, we have $p = n$. Our result shows that Lesamnta remains secure against generic attacks up to the birthday bound. This is the best achievable proof for Lesamnta, since it does not behave as a good narrow-pipe hash function beyond that bound: a dedicated herding attack based on the symmetry property is shown in [4], with complexity $2^{n/2}$.

The proof is heavily based on the proof in the extended version of [8]. Due to space constraints, the proof is not included in this paper, but can be found in the full version.

4 On Differential Attacks against SIMD

In this section we will present our results concerning differential paths in SIMD. Using Integer Linear Programming, we show that if there is a difference in the message, then the probability of the path will be at most of the order of $2^{-n/2}$. We stress that this result is not tight, but the computational power needed to improve the bound using this technique grows exponentially.

Related Work. The first attempt to avoid differential attack in a SHA/MD-like hash function was proposed in [10], where Jutla and Patthak described a linear code similar to the message expansion of SHA-1, and proved that it has a much better minimal distance than the original SHA-1 message expansion. They proposed to use SHA-1 with this new message expansion and called the new design SHA-1-IME.

Our Results. The design of SIMD follows the same idea, using a strong message expansion with a high minimal distance. In this paper we show that we can prove the security of SIMD more rigorously than the security of SHA-1-IME. While the security of SHA-1-IME is based on the heuristic assumption that the path is built out of local collisions, our proof gives an upper bound on the probability of *any* differential characteristic with a non-zero difference in the message.

Our results prove the following: for any message pair with a non-zero difference, the probability of going from an input difference Δ_{in} to an output difference Δ_{out} is bounded by 2^{-132} for SIMD-256, and 2^{-253} for SIMD-512.

4.1 Modeling Differential Paths

To study differential attacks against SIMD, we assume that the attacker builds a differential path. The differential path specifies the message difference and the state difference at each step. For each step i, we study the probability $p(i)$ that the new step difference conforms to the differential path, assuming that the previous state difference and the message difference conforms to the path, but that the values themselves are random. Since SIMD heavily uses modular additions, our analysis is based on a signed differential, as used by Wang *et al.* [15]. A signed difference gives better differential paths than an XOR difference if two active bits cancel each other out: with an XOR difference this gives a probability 1/2, but with a signed difference we have a probability 1 if the signs are opposed.

To study differential paths, we will consider the inner state of SIMD, and the Boolean functions $\phi^{(i)}$. A state bit $A_j^{(i)}$ is called *active* if it takes two different values for a message pair following the differential path. Similarly, a Boolean function is called active if at least one of its inputs is *active*. A differential path consists of a set of active message bits, active state bits, active Boolean function, and the sign of each active element. We assume that the adversary first builds such a differential path, and then looks for a conforming pair of messages and chaining values. If we disregard the first and last rounds, each Boolean function has three inputs, and each state bit enters three Boolean functions. We use this simplification in Section 4.4.

4.2 The Message Expansion

The minimal distance of the message expansion of SIMD is at least 520. This distance counts the number of active bits, but we can also show that even if consecutive bits can collapse to give a single signed difference, we still have a minimal distance of 455 (respectively 903 for SIMD-512). The only case where adjacent differences can collapse to give a smaller signed difference is when the bits 15 and 16 are active in the two 16-bit words that are packed into a 32-bit word. In Section 4.4, we disregard this property and we just consider that the message introduces 520 differences through the message expansion, but the model used in Section 4.5 accounts precisely for that.

4.3 Structure of a Differential Path

The basic idea of our analysis is to use the lower bound on the number of active message bits to derive a lower bound on the number of active state bits. Each message difference must either introduce a new difference in the state, or cancel the propagation of a previous state difference. A single difference propagates to between 2 and 5 differences, depending on whether the Boolean functions absorb it or let it go through. This means that a collision corresponds to between 3 and 6 message differences.

For instance, if a difference is introduced in the state $A_1^{(5)}$ by $W_1^{(5)}$, it will appear in $A_1^{(5)}$, $B_1^{(6)}$, $C_1^{(7)}$, $D_1^{(8)}$. Each of the Boolean function $\phi_1^{(6)}, \phi_1^{(7)}, \phi_1^{(8)}$ can either absorb it or pass it. This difference will propagate to $A_0^{(6)}$, and to $A_1^{(9)}$. Moreover, it can propagate to $A_1^{(6)}$, $A_1^{(7)}$ and $A_1^{(8)}$ if the Boolean functions do not absorb it. Up to five active message bits can be used to cancel this propagation: $W_1^{(4)}$, $W_1^{(8)}$, $W_0^{(5)}$, and possibly $W_1^{(5)}$, $W_1^{(6)}$, $W_1^{(7)}$ if the corresponding Boolean functions are not absorbing.

We consider two parts of the compression function: the computation of ϕ, and the modular sum. In order to study the probabilities associated with these computations, we will count the conditions needed for a message pair to follow the characteristic.

ϕ-conditions. The Boolean functions MAJ and IF used in SIMD can either absorb or pass differences. When there is a single active input, the probability to absorb and to pass is 1/2. Each time a state difference enters a Boolean function, the differential characteristic specifies whether the difference should be passed or absorbed, and this gives one condition if the Boolean functions have a single active input. Thus, each isolated difference in the state will account for 3 ϕ-conditions: one for each Boolean function they enter.

$\boxplus$-conditions. When a difference is introduced in the state, it has to come from one of the inputs of the round function:

$$A_j^{(i)} = \left(D_j^{(i-1)} \boxplus W_j^{(i)} \boxplus \phi^{(i)}(A_j^{(i-1)}, B_j^{(i-1)}, C_j^{(i-1)})\right)^{\lll s^{(i)}} \boxplus \left(A_{p^{(i)}(j)}^{(i-1)}\right)^{\lll r^{(i)}}$$

The round function is essentially a sum of 4 terms, and the differential characteristic will specify which input bits and which output bits are active. Thus, the differential characteristic specifies how the carry should propagate, and this gives at least one condition per state difference.

In the end, a state difference accounts for 4 conditions.

4.4 Heuristics

We first give some results based on heuristics. We assume that the adversary can find message pairs that give a minimal distance in the expanded message, and we allow him to add some more constraints to the expanded message. Note that finding a message pair with a low difference in the expanded message is already quite difficult with the message expansion of SIMD.

Heuristic I. assumes that the adversary can find message pairs with minimal distance, but no other useful property. The adversary gets a message pair with minimal distance, and connects the dots to build a differential characteristic.

Heuristic II. assumes that the adversary can find message pairs with minimal distance and controls the relative positions of the message difference. He will use that ability to create local collisions.

Heuristic III. assumes that the adversary can find a message pair with any message difference, limited only by the minimal weight of the code. He will cluster local collisions to avoid many conditions.

Heuristic I. In this section, we assume that the adversary can find a message pair such that the expanded messages reach the minimal distance of the code, but we assume that the message pair has no further useful properties.

In this case, this adversary gets a message pair with a small difference and he has to connect the dots to build a differential path. This is somewhat similar to the attacks on MD4 [14]: the messages are chosen so as to make a local collision in the last round, and the attacker has to connect all the remaining differences into a path with a good probability.

It seems safe to assume that such a differential path will at least have as many active state bits as active message bits. Since an isolated difference in the state costs 4 conditions, we expect at least 2080 conditions (resp. 4128 for SIMD-512), which is very high.

Heuristic II. We now assume that the adversary can force some structure in the expanded message difference. Namely, he can choose the relative location of the differences in the expanded message. Since the probability of the path is essentially given by the number of active bits in the state, the path should minimize this. This is achieved with local collisions, and each local collision will use as many message differences as possible. Due to the structure of the round function of SIMD, a local collision can use between 3 and 6 message differences, depending on whether the Boolean functions absorb or pass the differences. In order to minimize the number of state differences, the path will make all the Boolean functions pass the differences, yielding six message differences per state difference. This is somewhat counter-intuitive because most attacks try to minimize the propagation of differences by absorbing them. However, in our case it is more efficient to let the differences go through the Boolean functions, and to use more message differences to cancel them, because we have a lower bound on the number of message differences.

Since the adversary only controls the relative position of the message differences, we assume that most local collisions will be isolated, so that each local collision gives 4 conditions. Thus, a differential is expected to have at least $520 \times 4/6 \approx 347$ conditions (688 for SIMD-512). This leaves a significant security margin, and even if the adversary can use message modifications in the first 16 rounds, it can only avoid half of those conditions.

This can be compared to the attacks on SHA-1 [7,15]. These attacks are based on local collisions, but we do not know how to find a message pair which would have both minimal distance and yield a series of local collisions in SHA-1. Instead, attacks on SHA-1 use the fact that the message expansion is *linear* and *circulant*: given a codeword, if we shift it by a few rounds we get another valid codeword and similarly if we rotate each word we get another valid codeword. Then we can combine a few rotated and/or shifted codewords so as to build local collisions. The attacks on SHA-1 start with a codeword of minimal distance, and combines 6 rotated versions. Thus the weight of the actual expanded message difference used in the attack is six times the minimal weight of the code.

Note that message expansion of SIMD is more complex than the one from SHA-1, and it seems very hard to find this kind of message pairs in SIMD. Moreover, the trick used in SHA-1 cannot be used here because the message expansion is neither linear nor circulant.

Heuristic III. We now remove all heuristic assumptions and we try to give a bound on *any* differential trail. However, to keep this analysis simple, we still disregard the specificities of the first round, and the fact that one can combine some of the message differences.

The adversary will still use local collisions to minimize the number of differences in the state, but he will also try to reduce the number of conditions for each local collision by clustering them. We have seen that an isolated state difference costs 4 conditions, but if two state differences are next to each other, the cost can be reduced when using a signed difference. For instance, if two inputs of the MAJ function are active, the adversary does not have to pay any probability: if both active inputs have the same sign, then the output is active with the same sign, but if the inputs have opposite signs then the output will be inactive. In this section we consider that a Boolean function with more than one active input does not cost any probability.

Thus, the best strategy for the adversary is to place the state differences so that each active Boolean function has two active inputs, in order to avoid any ϕ-conditions. Each state difference costs only one $\boxplus$-condition, and gets 4.5 message differences (these message differences corresponding to the Boolean functions are shared between two Boolean functions). This gives a lower bound of 116 conditions.

More rigorously, this can be described by a linear program, as shown in Linear Program 1. Equation (1) comes from counting the number of active inputs to the Boolean functions in two different ways, while Equation (2) counts the number of message differences that can be used. The objective value $S + \alpha - \beta$ counts the conditions: one for each state difference, plus one for each Boolean function with exactly one active input. The optimal solution to this program is $520/4.5 \approx 115.55$.

In the next section we will see how to improve this bound and get a bound on the probability of any differential path.

Comparison with SHA-1-IME. The security of SHA-1-IME is based on a heuristic that is quite similar to our Heuristic I. Jutla and Patthak assume that the adversary will use the same technique as the attacks on SHA-1, *i.e.* create local collisions using the fact that the code is linear and circulant. They deduce that the probability of a differential characteristic will be about $2^{75\times 2.5}$. They implicitly assume that the adversary cannot find minimal codewords that would already give local collisions. Our Heuristic II assumes that the attacker can find such codewords, and if we apply it to SHA-1-IME, it would only guarantee that we have at least 13 local collisions (each local collision accounts for 6 message differences). Since a local collision in SHA-1 has an average probability of $2^{-2.5}$, this would only prove that an attack has at least a complexity $2^{13\times 2.5} = 2^{32.5}$.

Program 1. Linear Program

Minimize $S + \alpha - \beta$ with the constraints:

$$3S = \alpha + \beta + \gamma \tag{1}$$

$$520 \leq 3S + \alpha \tag{2}$$

$$\gamma \leq \beta \leq \alpha \tag{3}$$

$\alpha \geq 0$ is the number of Boolean functions with at least one active input
$\beta \geq 0$ is the number of Boolean functions with at least two active inputs
$\gamma \geq 0$ is the number of Boolean functions with at least three active inputs
$S \geq 0$ is the number of active state bits

This shows that our Heuristic II and III are much weaker than the heuristic used in SHA-1-IME.

4.5 Upper Bounding the Probability of a Differential Path

The bound given by Heuristic III is slightly lower than $n/2$ so we would like to improve it. To find a better bound, we will follow the approach of Linear Program 1. Note that in the optimal solution, all the Boolean functions have either zero or two active inputs, but it is unlikely that such a path actually exists because of the way the Boolean functions share inputs. In order to remove some impossible solutions, we use a more detailed modeling of differential paths where each individual state bit is treated separately. This also allows us to express some extra constraints that will help to improve the lower bound.

Constraints related to the message expansion. We know that the message expansion gives at least 520 differences in the expanded message, but there are some constraints on the positions of these differences. Namely, we have at least 65 active words in each copy of the message, and each active word has at least 4 active bits. For instance, a difference pattern with 3 active bits in each word would have 768 bit differences, but it is not a valid pattern.

Better cost estimation. In Program 1, we only count a condition for the Boolean functions with a single active input. In fact, if we look at the truth table of the Boolean functions we see that the IF function still needs a condition when inputs 1 and 2, or 1 and 3 are active. Since we are using distinct variables for each of these inputs, we can include this in our description.

We can write all these constraints as a huge optimisation problem, but we need some tool to find the optimal solution of the system, or at least find a lower bound. We decided to write our problem as an Integer Linear Program.

Integer Linear Programming. Integer Linear Programming (ILP) is a generalisation of Linear Programming (LP) where some variables are restricted to integer values. While LP is solvable in polynomial time, ILP is NP-complete. ILP solvers usually use some variants of the branch-and-bound algorithm. In the case of minimization problem, the branch-and-bound algorithm computes a lower bound to the optimal solution and incrementally raises this lower bound. Meanwhile, non-optimal solutions give an upper bound, and when the two bounds meet, the search is over.

A simplified version of the ILP is given in the full version of this paper. The first equations and the objective value mirrors Program 1, but use many variables to allow for more precise extra constraints. The full program has 28,576 variables and 80,162 equations for SIMD-256. We used the solver SYMPHONY, an open-source solver for mixed-integer linear programs, available at `http://www.coin-or.org/SYMPHONY/`. The solver could not find an optimal solution to the program, but it reached an interesting lower bound after some time: a differential path for SIMD-256 has at least 132 conditions, while a differential path for SIMD-512 has at least 253. The computation for SIMD-512 took one month on a bi-quadcore machine.

Summary. The optimal strategy of the attacker is to use local collisions (avoiding any difference propagation) and to cluster the local collisions so as to avoid most conditions. Our modeling allows the adversary to do this because he can choose the message difference and the expanded message difference independently, and he can position the differences arbitrarily in the inner code. However, this is not possible in practice, and most solutions of the Integer Linear Program will require an expanded message difference that is not actually feasible.

Therefore, we expect that the best differential path in SIMD is much worse that our lower bound.

Acknowledgments

We would like to thank Praveen Gauravaram from Technical University of Denmark, Copenhagen for discussions on the proof of indifferentiability.

We would also like to thank Franck Landelle from CELLAR for insightful comments on the security of SIMD and limitations of our initial study of differential paths. Part of this work was supported by CELLAR.

Part of this work was supported by the European Commission through ECRYPT, and by the French government through the Saphir RNRT project.

References

1. Aumasson, J.P., Brier, E., Meier, W., Naya-Plasencia, M., Peyrin, T.: Inside the Hypercube. In: Boyd, C., González Nieto, J. (eds.) ACISP 2009. LNCS, vol. 5594, pp. 202–213. Springer, Heidelberg (2009)
2. Aumasson, J.P., Mashatan, A., Meier, W.: More on Shabal's permutation. Official Comment (2009)
3. Biryukov, A., Khovratovich, D.: Related-Key Cryptanalysis of the Full AES-192 and AES-256. In: Matsui, M. (ed.) ASIACRYPT 2009. LNCS, vol. 5912, pp. 1–18. Springer, Heidelberg (2009)
4. Bouillaguet, C., Dunkelman, O., Fouque, P.A., Leurent, G.: Another Look at Complementation Properties. In: Hong, S., Iwata, T. (eds.) FSE 2010. LNCS, vol. 6147, pp. 347–364. Springer, Heidelberg (2010)

5. Bouillaguet, C., Fouque, P.A., Leurent, G.: Security analysis of simd. Cryptology ePrint Archive, Report 2010/323 (2010), http://eprint.iacr.org/
6. Bresson, E., Canteaut, A., Chevallier-Mames, B., Clavier, C., Fuhr, T., Gouget, A., Icart, T., Misarsky, J.F., Naya-Plasencia, M., Paillier, P., Pornin, T., Reinhard, J.R., Thuillet, C., Videau, M.: Indifferentiability with Distinguishers: Why Shabal Does Not Require Ideal Ciphers. Cryptology ePrint Archive, Report 2009/199 (2009), http://eprint.iacr.org/
7. Chabaud, F., Joux, A.: Differential Collisions in SHA-0. In: Krawczyk, H. (ed.) CRYPTO 1998. LNCS, vol. 1462, pp. 56–71. Springer, Heidelberg (1998)
8. Coron, J.S., Dodis, Y., Malinaud, C., Puniya, P.: Merkle-Damgård Revisited: How to Construct a Hash Function. In: Shoup, V. (ed.) CRYPTO 2005. LNCS, vol. 3621, pp. 430–448. Springer, Heidelberg (2005)
9. Ferguson, N., Lucks, S., McKay, K.A.: Symmetric States and their Structure: Improved Analysis of CubeHash. Cryptology ePrint Archive, Report 2010/273 (2010), http://eprint.iacr.org/
10. Jutla, C.S., Patthak, A.C.: Provably Good Codes for Hash Function Design. In: Biham, E., Youssef, A.M. (eds.) SAC 2006. LNCS, vol. 4356, pp. 376–393. Springer, Heidelberg (2007)
11. Leurent, G., Bouillaguet, C., Fouque, P.A.: SIMD Is a Message Digest. Submission to NIST (2008)
12. Maurer, U.M., Renner, R., Holenstein, C.: Indifferentiability, Impossibility Results on Reductions, and Applications to the Random Oracle Methodology. In: Naor, M. (ed.) TCC 2004. LNCS, vol. 2951, pp. 21–39. Springer, Heidelberg (2004)
13. Park, S., Sung, S.H., Lee, S., Lim, J.: Improving the Upper Bound on the Maximum Differential and the Maximum Linear Hull Probability for SPN Structures and AES. In: Johansson, T. (ed.) FSE 2003. LNCS, vol. 2887, pp. 247–260. Springer, Heidelberg (2003)
14. Wang, X., Lai, X., Feng, D., Chen, H., Yu, X.: Cryptanalysis of the Hash Functions MD4 and RIPEMD. In: Cramer, R. (ed.) EUROCRYPT 2005. LNCS, vol. 3494, pp. 1–18. Springer, Heidelberg (2005)
15. Wang, X., Yin, Y.L., Yu, H.: Finding Collisions in the Full SHA-1. In: Shoup, V. (ed.) CRYPTO 2005. LNCS, vol. 3621, pp. 17–36. Springer, Heidelberg (2005)

Subspace Distinguisher for 5/8 Rounds of the ECHO-256 Hash Function*

Martin Schläffer

Institute for Applied Information Processing and Communications (IAIK)
Graz University of Technology, Inffeldgasse 16a, A-8010 Graz, Austria
martin.schlaeffer@iaik.tugraz.at

Abstract. In this work we present first results for the hash function of ECHO. We provide a subspace distinguisher for 5 rounds and collisions for 4 out of 8 rounds of the ECHO-256 hash function. The complexities are 2^{96} compression function calls for the distinguisher and 2^{64} for the collision attack. The memory requirements are 2^{64} for all attacks. To get these results, we consider new and sparse truncated differential paths through ECHO. We are able to construct these paths by analyzing the combined MixColumns and BigMixColumns transformation. Since in these sparse truncated differential paths at most one fourth of all bytes of each ECHO state are active, missing degrees of freedom are not a problem. Therefore, we are able to mount a rebound attack with multiple inbound phases to efficiently find according message pairs for ECHO.

Keywords: hash functions, SHA-3 competition, ECHO, cryptanalysis, truncated differential path, rebound attack, subspace distinguisher, near-collisions, collision attack.

1 Introduction

Many new and interesting hash function designs have been proposed in the NIST SHA-3 competition [17]. In this paper, we analyze the hash function ECHO [1], which is one of 14 Round 2 candidates of the competition. ECHO is a wide-pipe, AES based design which transforms 128-bit words similar as AES transforms bytes. Inside these 128-bit words, two standard AES rounds are used. So far, most cryptanalytic results of ECHO were limited to the internal permutation [13, 7]. Recently, reduced round attacks on the wide-pipe compression function of ECHO have been published in [18], which cover up to 4/8 rounds for ECHO-256 and 6/10 rounds of ECHO-512. However, a drawback of attacks on building blocks (such as compression functions or permutations) is that they cannot be used to compare SHA-3 candidates due to their great design variety and different requirements for building blocks.

Therefore, in this work we analyze the hash function of ECHO and present results for up to 5/8 rounds of ECHO-256. We use the subspace distinguisher [9, 10]

* Near-collisions for 4.5/8 rounds of the hash function and compression function results for 7/8 rounds without chosen salt are given in an extended version of this paper [19].

A. Biryukov, G. Gong, and D.R. Stinson (Eds.): SAC 2010, LNCS 6544, pp. 369–387, 2011.

to compare our distinguishing attacks with the generic complexity on ideal hash functions. Our results greatly improve upon previously results, which were attacks on a similar number of rounds of the compression function [18]. Furthermore, attacks on the compression function for up to 7/8 rounds of ECHO-256 and 7/10 rounds of ECHO-512 are given in an extended version of this paper [19]. The main improvement is to consider a new type of sparse truncated differential paths by placing only a single active byte in the ECHO state with 16 active AES states. In all previous paths, the full active ECHO states also had full active AES states. The construction of such paths is possible by combining the last MixColumns transformation of the second AES round with the BigMixColumns transformation of an ECHO round to a SuperMixColumns transformation.

The attack itself is a rebound attack [14] with multiple inbound phases. Similar attacks have been applied to the SHA-3 candidate LANE [12] and the hash function Whirlpool [9]. Since the truncated differential paths are very sparse, we have plenty degrees of freedom to merge the solutions of these multiple inbound phases. Note that using multiple inbound phases, we can control more distant parts of much longer truncated differential paths than in a start-from-the-middle attack [13] or simple Super-Sbox analysis [9,15,7] where the controlled rounds are limited to only the middle rounds. To merge independent solutions of multiple inbound phases, we use a technique based on the generalized birthday attack [20].

2 Description of ECHO

In this section we briefly describe the AES based SHA-3 candidate ECHO. For a detailed description of ECHO we refer to the specification [1]. Since ECHO heavily uses AES rounds, we describe the AES block cipher first.

2.1 The AES Block Cipher

The block cipher Rijndael was designed by Daemen and Rijmen and standardized by NIST in 2000 as the Advanced Encryption Standard (AES) [16]. The AES follows the wide-trail design strategy [4,5] and consists of a key schedule and state update transformation. Since ECHO does not use the AES key schedule, we just describe the state update here.

In the AES, a 4×4 state of 16 bytes is updated using the following 4 round transformations, with 10 rounds for AES-128. The non-linear layer SubBytes (SB) applies the AES S-Box to each byte of the state independently. The cyclical permutation ShiftRows (SR) rotates the bytes of row j to the left by j positions. The linear diffusion layer MixColumns (MC) multiplies each column of the state by a constant MDS matrix M_{MC}. AddRoundKey (AK) adds the 128-bit round key K_i to the AES state. Note that a round key is added prior to the first round and the MixColumns transformation is omitted in the last round of AES. For a detailed description of the AES we refer to [16].

2.2 The ECHO Hash Function

The ECHO hash function is a SHA-3 candidate submitted by Benadjila et al. [1]. It is a double-pipe, iterated hash function and uses the HAIFA [2] domain extension algorithm. More precisely, a padded t-block message M and a salt s are hashed using the compression function $f(H_{i-1}, M_i, c_i, s)$, where c_i is a bit counter, IV the initial value and $trunc(H_t)$ a truncation to the final output hash size of n bits:

$$\begin{aligned} H_0 &= IV \\ H_i &= f(H_{i-1}, M_i, c_i, s) \quad \text{for } 1 \leq i \leq t \\ h &= trunc_n(H_t). \end{aligned}$$

The message block size is 1536 bits for ECHO-256 and 1024 bits for ECHO-512, and the message is padded by adding a single 1 followed by zeros to fill up the block size. Note that the last 18 bytes of the last message block always contain the 2-byte hash output size, followed by the 16-byte message length.

The compression function of ECHO uses one internal 2048-bit permutation P which manipulates 128-bit words similar as AES manipulates bytes. The permutation consists of 8 rounds in the case of ECHO-256 and has 10 rounds for ECHO-512. The internal state of the permutation P can be modeled as a 4×4 matrix of 128-bit words. We denote one ECHO state by S_i and each 128-bit word or AES state is indexed by $[r, c]$, with rows $r \in \{0, ..., 3\}$ and columns $c \in \{0, ..., 3\}$ of the ECHO state.

The 2048-bit input of the permutation (which is also tweaked by the counter c_i and salt s) are the previous chaining variable H_{i-1} and the current message block M_i, concatenated to each other. After the last round of the permutation, a feed-forward (FF) is applied to get the preliminary output V:

$$V = P_{c_i,s}(H_{i-1}||M_i) \oplus (H_{i-1}||M_i). \tag{1}$$

To get the 512-bit chaining variable H_i for ECHO-256, all columns of the ECHO output state V are XORed. In the case of ECHO-512, the 1024 bit chaining variable H_i is the XOR of the two left and the two right columns of V. The feed-forward together with the compression of columns is called the BigFinal (BF) operation. To get the final output of the hash function, the lower half is truncated in the case of ECHO-256 and the right half is truncated for ECHO-512.

The round transformations of the ECHO permutation are very similar to AES rounds, except that 128-bit words are used instead of bytes. One round is the composition of the following three transformations in the given order: The non-linear layer BigSubWords (BSW) applies two AES rounds to each of the 16 128-bit words of the internal state. The first round key consists of a counter value initialized by c_i and increased for every AES state and round of ECHO. The second round key consists of the 128-bit salt s. The cyclical permutation BigShiftRows (BSR) rotates the 128-bit words of row j to the left by j words. The linear diffusion layer BigMixColumns (BMC) mixes the AES states of each ECHO column by the same MDS matrix M_{MC} but applied to those bytes with equal position inside the AES states.

3 Improved Truncated Differential Analysis of ECHO

In this section we describe the main concepts used to attack the ECHO hash function. We first describe the improved truncated differential paths which have a very low number of active S-boxes. These sparse truncated differential paths are the core of our attacks and for a better description of the attacks, we reorder the ECHO round transformations. This reordering gives two combined building blocks of ECHO, the SuperMixColumns and SuperBox transformations. We then show how to efficiently find both differences and values through these functions for a given truncated differential path.

3.1 Sparse Truncated Differential Paths for ECHO

In this section we construct truncated differential paths with a low number of active bytes. Since ECHO has the same properties for words as AES has for bytes, at least 25 AES states are active in each 4-round differential path of ECHO. However, we can reduce the number of active S-boxes in each AES state to get a sparse 4-round truncated differential path with only 245 active S-boxes. Note that the truncated differential path of the previously best known analysis of ECHO has already 320 active S-boxes in a single round [18]. A trivial lower bound [1] of active S-boxes for 4 rounds is 125.

The AES structure of ECHO ensures that the minimum number of active AES states (or words) for 4 rounds has the following sequence of active AES states:

$$1 \xrightarrow{r_1} 4 \xrightarrow{r_2} 16 \xrightarrow{r_3} 4 \xrightarrow{r_4} 1$$

Also, the same sequence of active bytes holds for 4 rounds of AES. In previous analysis of ECHO, truncated differential paths have been used with 16 active bytes in the AES states where the ECHO state has also 16 active words. In these attacks always one full active state with 256 active S-boxes was used. In the following, we show how to construct sparse truncated differential paths with a maximum of 64 active bytes in each single ECHO state.

The main idea is to place AES states with only one active S-box into those ECHO rounds with 16 active words. This way, the number of total active bytes (or S-boxes) can be greatly reduced. The resulting 4-round truncated differential path of ECHO is given in Fig. 1 and consists of only 245 active S-boxes. Since one round of ECHO consists of two AES rounds, it follows that the full active AES states result in those rounds of ECHO with 4 active words. The ECHO state with only one active word contains only one active byte in this AES state. Note that in the attacks on ECHO, we use this truncated differential path with small modifications to improve the overall complexity of the attacks.

3.2 An Equivalent ECHO Round Description

For an easier description of our attack, we use an equivalent description of one ECHO round. First, we swap the BigShiftRows transformation with the MixColumns transformation of the second AES round. Second, we swap SubBytes with ShiftRows of the first AES round. Swapping these operations does not change the computational result of ECHO and similar alternative descriptions have already been used in the analysis of AES. This way, we get two new super-round transformations separated just by byte shuffling operations: SuperMixColumns and SuperBox. These functions with adjacent byte shuffling operations are shown in Fig. 2. In the following subsections, we describe these transformations and show how to efficiently find differences and pairs according to a given truncated differential path for both transformations.

3.3 SuperMixColumns

The SuperMixColumns transformation combines the four MixColumns transformations of the second AES round with the 4 MixColumns transformations of BigMixColumns in the same 1×16 column slice of the ECHO state (see Fig. 2). We denote by column slice the 16 bytes of the same 1-byte wide column of the 16×16 ECHO state. Note that the BigMixColumns transformation consists of 16×4 parallel MixColumns transformations. Each of these MixColumns transformations mixes those four bytes of an ECHO column, which have the same position in the four AES states. Using the alternative description of ECHO (see Fig. 2), it is easy to see that four MixColumns operations of the second AES round work on the same column slice as four MixColumns operations of BigMixColumns. We combine these eight MixColumns transformations to get a SuperMixColumns transformation on a 1-byte wide column slice of ECHO.

We have determined the 16×16 matrix M_{SMC} of the SuperMixColumns transformation which is applied to the ECHO state instead of MixColumns and BigMixColumns. This matrix can be computed by the Kronecker product of two MixColumns MDS matrices M_{MC} and is given as follows:

$$M_{\mathsf{SMC}} = M_{\mathsf{MC}} \otimes M_{\mathsf{MC}} = \begin{bmatrix} 2&3&1&1\\ 1&2&3&1\\ 1&1&2&3\\ 3&1&1&2 \end{bmatrix} \otimes \begin{bmatrix} 2&3&1&1\\ 1&2&3&1\\ 1&1&2&3\\ 3&1&1&2 \end{bmatrix} = \begin{bmatrix} 4&6&2&2&6&5&3&3&2&3&1&1&2&3&1&1\\ 2&4&6&2&3&6&5&3&1&2&3&1&1&2&3&1\\ 2&2&4&6&3&3&6&5&1&1&2&3&1&1&2&3\\ 6&2&2&4&5&3&3&6&3&1&1&2&3&1&1&2\\ 2&3&1&1&4&6&2&2&6&5&3&3&2&3&1&1\\ 1&2&3&1&2&4&6&2&3&6&5&3&1&2&3&1\\ 1&1&2&3&2&2&4&6&3&3&6&5&1&1&2&3\\ 3&1&1&2&6&2&2&4&5&3&3&6&3&1&1&2\\ 2&3&1&1&2&3&1&1&4&6&2&2&6&5&3&3\\ 1&2&3&1&1&2&3&1&2&4&6&2&3&6&5&3\\ 1&1&2&3&1&1&2&3&2&2&4&6&3&3&6&5\\ 3&1&1&2&3&1&1&2&6&2&2&4&5&3&3&6\\ 6&5&3&3&2&3&1&1&2&3&1&1&4&6&2&2\\ 3&6&5&3&1&2&3&1&1&2&3&1&2&4&6&2\\ 3&3&6&5&1&1&2&3&1&1&2&3&2&2&4&6\\ 5&3&3&6&3&1&1&2&3&1&1&2&6&2&2&4 \end{bmatrix}$$

Note that the optimal branch number of a 16×16 matrix is 17, which could be achieved by an MDS matrix. Using Magma we have computed the branch number of SuperMixColumns which is 8. Hence, it is possible to find differential paths in SuperMixColumns such that the sum of active bytes at input and output is only 8. An according truncated differential path through MixColumns and BigMixColumns has the following sequence of active bytes:

$$4 \xrightarrow{\mathsf{MC}} 16 \xrightarrow{\mathsf{BMC}} 4$$

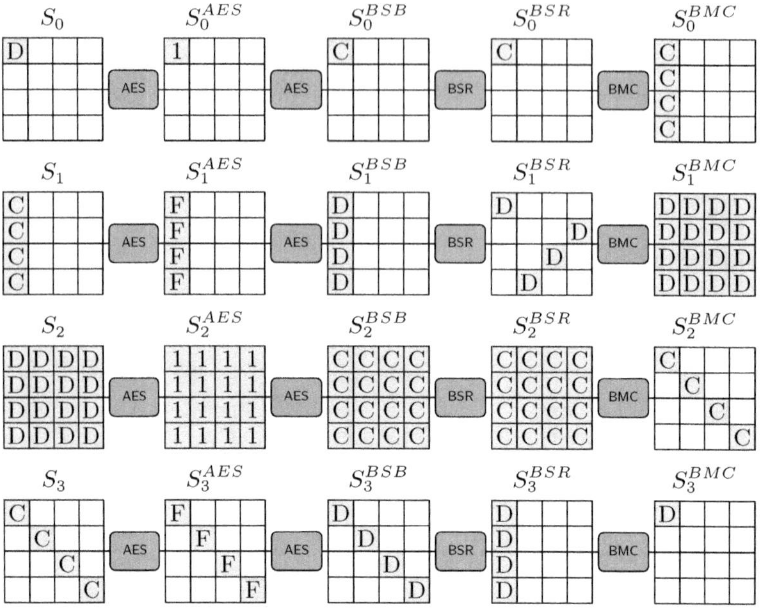

Fig. 1. The sparse truncated differential path for 4 rounds of ECHO. By 1, D, C, F we denote the pattern and number of active bytes in each AES state (also see [7]). A 1 denotes an AES state with only one active byte, a D an active diagonal (4 active bytes), a C an active column (4 active bytes) and an F denotes a full active state (16 active bytes). Note that a maximum of 64 bytes are active in each single ECHO state.

An example for a valid SuperMixColumns differential according to this truncated differential path is given as follows:

$$\text{SMC}([\text{E000 9000 D000 B000}]^{\text{T}}) = [\text{2113 0000 0000 0000}]^{\text{T}}$$

However, the probability for a truncated differential path from $4 \rightarrow 16 \rightarrow 4$ active bytes (with fixed position) through SuperMixColumns is 2^{-24}. Hence, only 2^8 (out of 2^{32}) such differentials for the given position of active bytes exist. In the sparse truncated differential path of Fig. 1, this $4 \rightarrow 16 \rightarrow 4$ transition through SuperMixColumns occurs in the second and forth round.

3.4 SuperBox

The SuperBox has first been used by the designers of AES in the differential analysis of two AES rounds [6]. Since one round of ECHO also consists of two consecutive AES rounds we use this concept in our analysis as well. Using SuperBoxes, we can represent two rounds of AES using a single non-linear layer and two adjacent linear layers. Since we can swap the SubBytes and ShiftRows operation

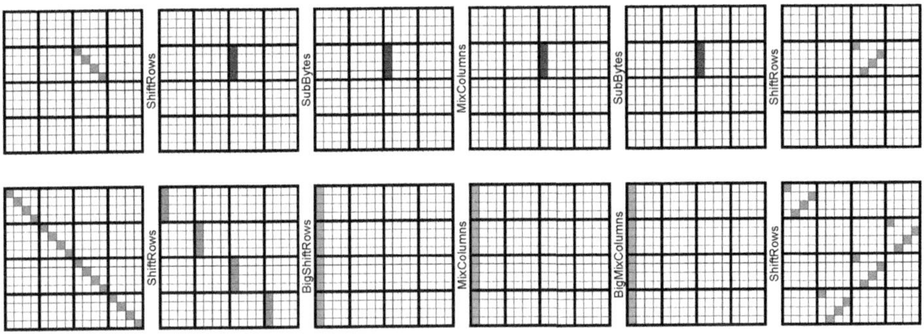

Fig. 2. The two super-round transformations of ECHO: SuperBox (top, red) and SuperMixColumns (bottom, green) with adjacent byte shuffling operations (ShiftRows and BigShiftRows)

of the first AES round, we get a sequence of SB-MC-SB transformations with independent columns in the middle. One such column is called a SuperBox and consists of 4 parallel S-boxes, one MixColumns operation and another 4 parallel S-boxes (see Fig. 2). Hence, a SuperBox is in fact a 32-bit non-linear S-box.

This separation of two AES rounds into parallel 32-bit SuperBoxes allows to efficiently find pairs for a given (truncated) differential. In a theoretical attack on ECHO or if we do not care about memory, we can simply pre-compute and store the whole differential distribution table (DDT) of the AES SuperBox with a time and memory complexity of 2^{64}. The DDT stores which input/output differentials of the SuperBox are possible and also stores all input values such that these differentials are fulfilled. Note that in ECHO, each SuperBox is keyed in the middle by the counter value. Hence, we need different DDTs for all SuperBoxes with different keys. To reduce the memory requirements and the maximum time to find values for given SuperBox differentials, a time-memory trade-off with average complexity one and memory requirements of 2^{32} can be used. This method has first been proposed in the analysis of the hash function Whirlpool [9, Appendix A] and applied to Grøstl in [15]. The same technique has been discovered independently in [7].

3.5 Expected Number of Pairs

At this point, we can already compute the expected number of pairs conforming to the 4-round truncated differential path given in Fig. 1. The resulting number of solutions determines the degrees of freedom we have in the attack. At the input of the path, we have a 2048-bit value and differences in 4 bytes. Therefore, the total number of possible inputs pairs (excluding the 128-bit salt) is about

$$2^{2048} \cdot 2^{8 \cdot 4} = 2^{8 \cdot 260} = 2^{2080}.$$

In general, the probability for a random pair to follow a truncated differential path from a to b active bytes (with $a+b \geq 5$) through MixColumns is $2^{-8 \cdot (4-b)}$. An exception is the propagation from $4 \rightarrow 16 \rightarrow 4$ bytes through SuperMixColumns, which has a probability of 2^{-24} (see Sect. 3.3). Multiplying all probabilities through MixColumns and SuperMixColumns gives the approximate probability for a random input pair to follow the whole truncate differential path. For the path given in Fig. 1, we get a probability significantly less than one for all MixColumns or SuperMixColumns transformation where a reduction in the number of active bytes occur. This happens in the 1st MC of round 1 (D – 1), the 2nd MC of round 2 ($4 \times$ F – D), the 1st MC ($16 \times$ D – 1) and SMC ($4 \times$ 1111 – FFFF – F000) of round 3, and the 2nd MC ($4 \times$ F – D) and BMC ($3 \times$ D – 0) of round 4. We then get for the total probability of the truncated differential path (in base 2 logarithm):

$$-8 \cdot (3 + 4 \cdot 12 + 16 \cdot 3 + 4 \cdot 3 + 4 \cdot 12 + 3 \cdot 4) = -8 \cdot 171$$

So in total, the expected number of solutions for this path is

$$2^{8 \cdot 260} \cdot 2^{-8 \cdot 171} = 2^{8 \cdot 89} = 2^{712}$$

and we have about 712 degrees of freedom in this 4-round truncated differential path.

4 Attacks on the ECHO-256 Hash Function

In this section we use the sparse truncated differential path and properties of SuperMixColumns to get attacks for up to 5 rounds of the ECHO-256 hash function. We first describe our main result, the subspace distinguisher for 5 rounds of ECHO-256 in detail. Then, we briefly show how to get near-collisions for 4.5 rounds and collisions for 4 rounds of ECHO-256.

4.1 Subspace Distinguisher for 5 Rounds

In this section we show that ECHO-256 reduced to 5 rounds can be distinguished from an ideal hash function. We are able to construct a large set of output differences which fall into a vector space of fixed dimension. But when does this result in a distinguisher on the hash function? An attacker could have chosen the vector space specifically to fit a previously computed set of differences. Also, finding up to x differences in subspace of dimension x is trivial, even for ideal functions. But once a subspace has been chosen, finding additional differences in this subspace should again have the generic complexity. We have a similar situation for preimage attacks: finding a preimage is trivial if the attacker can choose the hash value. Note that in most distinguishing attacks, the generic complexity also depends on the number of found solutions. To compare distinguishers with generic attacks, differential q-multicollisions have been used in the distinguishing attacks on AES [3]. More general, to analyze the complexity of finding differences in a vector space of fixed dimension, the subspace distinguisher has been introduced in the analysis of Whirlpool [9,10]. Before we describe the subspace distinguisher for 5 rounds of ECHO-256 in detail, we give an overview of the truncated differential path and provide a brief outline of the attack.

The Truncated Differential Path. For the attack we use two message blocks where the first block does not contain differences. For the second message block, we use the truncated differential path given in Fig. 3. We use colors (red, yellow, green, blue, cyan) to describe different phases of the attack and to denote their resulting solutions. Active bytes are denoted by black color and all AES states are active which contain at least one active byte. Hence, the sequence of active AES states for each round of ECHO is as follows:

$$5 \xrightarrow{r_1} 16 \xrightarrow{r_2} 4 \xrightarrow{r_3} 1 \xrightarrow{r_4} 4 \xrightarrow{r_5} 16$$

Note that in this path we keep the number of active bytes low as described in Sect. 3.1. Except for the beginning and end, at most one fourth of the ECHO state is active and therefore, we have enough freedom to find many solutions. Since the lower half of the state is truncated, we have most differences in the lower half of the message and there are no differences in the chaining input (blue). The padding of the second (and last) message block is denoted by cyan bytes. The last 16 bytes (one AES state) of the padding contain the message length, and the two bytes above contain the 2-byte value with the hash size. Note that the AES states containing the chaining values (blue) and padding (cyan) do not get mixed with other AES states until the first BigMixColumns transformation.

Attack Outline. To find input pairs according to this path we use the rebound attack [14] with multiple inbound phases [9,12]. The main advantage of multiple inbound phases is that we can first find pairs for each inbound phase independently and then, connect (or merge) the results. For the attack on 5 rounds of ECHO-256 we use an inbound phase in round 2 (red) and another inbound phase in round 3 (yellow). The 1st inbound phase finds values and differences for the red bytes which we connect with the chaining input (blue) and padding (cyan) by merging lists. Then, we compute the solutions of the 2nd inbound phase forwards in the outbound phase (green) to insure the propagation according to the truncated differential path until the end. Finally, we merge the solutions of the two inbound phases by determining the remaining (white) values using a generalized birthday attack on 4 independent columns of the state. Note that in some cases, the probability to find one solution is only close to one. However, for simplicity reasons of describing the attack we assume it is one, since we have enough freedom in the attack to repeat all phases with different starting points to get one solution on average.

1st Inbound. We start the 1st inbound phase with a random difference according to the truncated differential path through SuperMixColumns between state S_{14} and state S_{16} (see Sect. 3.3). We compute these differences backward to get the output differences of the SuperBoxes in state S_{12}. For each column in state S_7 we choose 2^{32} random differences for the given active bytes. We compute these differences forward through BigMixColumns to the input of the SuperBoxes. Note that for the

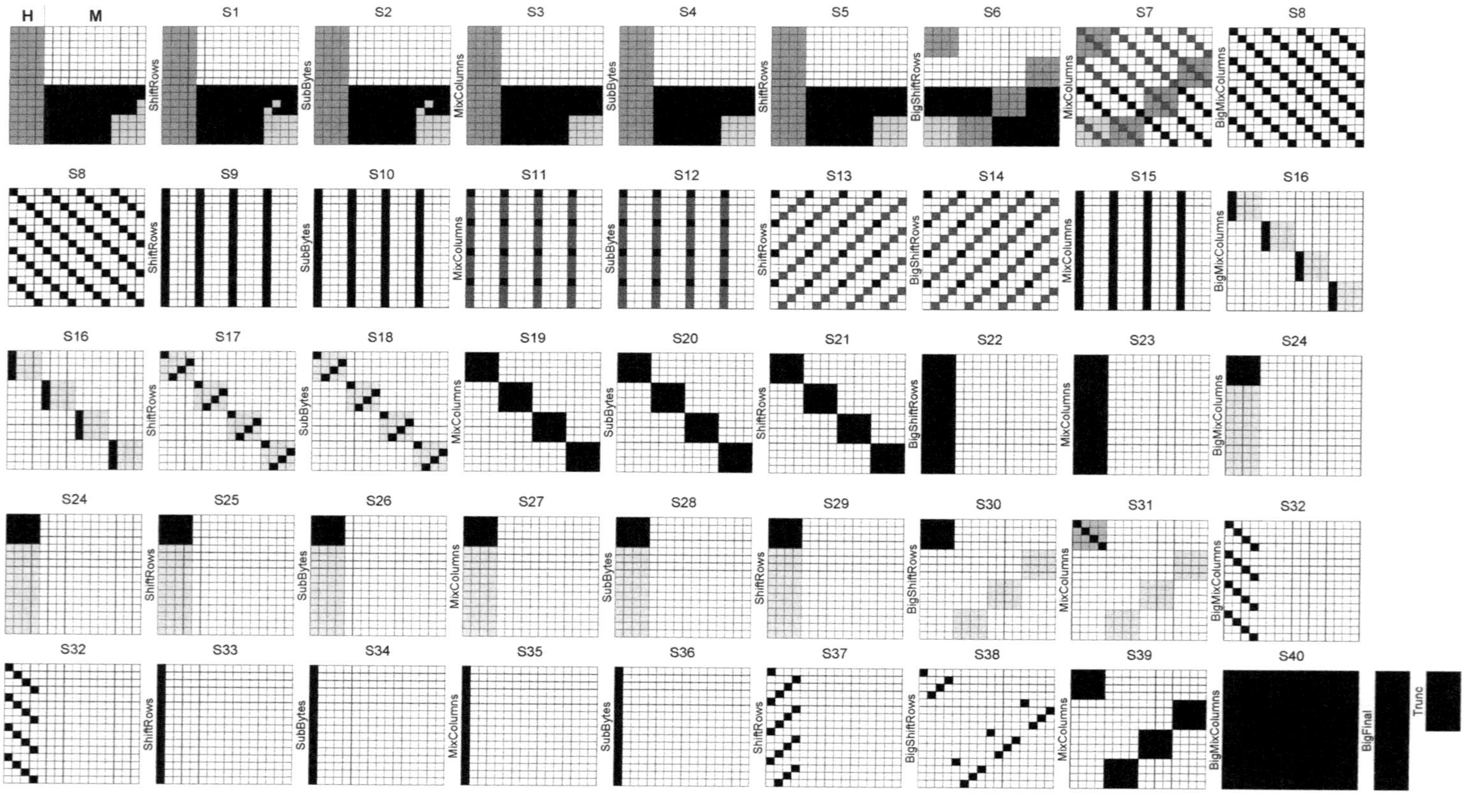

Fig. 3. The truncated differential path to get a subspace distinguisher for 5 rounds of ECHO-256. Black bytes are active, blue and cyan bytes are determined by the chaining input and padding, red bytes are values computed in the 1st inbound phase, yellow bytes in the 2nd inbound phase and green bytes in the outbound phase.

last column we could choose up to 2^{64} differences (8 active bytes), whereas in all other columns we have only 2^{32} possible differences (4 active bytes).

As described in Sect. 3.4, we find values according to the SuperBox differentials with an average complexity of 1 by using DDT lookups. Note that for some differentials no solutions exist, but for each possible differential we get more pairs which out-weight the non-existing ones (for more details we refer to [14]). In general, for each active AES S-box a differential is possible with a probability of about 2^{-1} and we get at least 2 pairs. Hence, for a full active AES state, one out of approximately 2^{16} differences gives a differential match and then, provides at least 2^{16} solutions. In the following attacks, it is reasonable to assume that for each differential we get one solution with average complexity one.

Since in the 1st inbound phase the columns of ECHO are independent, we get 2^{32} independent solutions for each of the four columns in state S_7 (red and black bytes) with complexity 2^{32} in time and memory. These solutions (or pairs) consist of differences and values for the black bytes, and values for the red bytes in S_7. Note that for each solution (and arbitrary choice of white bytes in S_7) the truncated differential path from state S_3 to state S_{23} is already fulfilled.

Merge Chaining Input. Next, we need to merge the solutions of the 1st inbound phase with the chaining input and bytes fixed by the padding. Therefore, we choose 2^{32} random first message blocks and compute the resulting chaining value after one compression function call of ECHO. Note that each AES state can be independently computed forward to state S_7 until the first BigMixColumns transformation. We do this for the chaining values (blue) and the AES state containing the message length (cyan). Note that we match the two remaining bytes and one bit of the padding at a later step.

We merge the 2^{32} chaining values with the solutions of the 1st inbound phase column by column. We start with column 0 where we need to match the padding state as well. Since we match 64 bits of overlapping red and blue/cyan bytes, the expected number of solutions is $2^{32} \times 2^{32} \times 2^{-64} = 1$. We compute this solution by merging the two lists of size 2^{32} and exploiting the birthday effect. For all other columns, we need to match only 4 red bytes in each blue AES state and we get $2^{32} \times 2^{-32} = 1$ solution as well. Since we only merge lists of size 2^{32} the complexity of this step is 2^{32} in time and memory.

After this step, we have found solutions where the values of all blue, cyan and red bytes, as well as the values of the black bytes between state S_7 and state S_{14} are determined. Furthermore, all differences (black bytes) from state S_4 up to state S_{17} can be computed.

2nd Inbound. In the 2nd inbound phase, we search for values and differences such that the truncated differential path in round 3 is fulfilled (yellow). Remember that the differences in state S_{17} have already been fixed due to the 1st inbound phase. We start with 2^{64} differences of state S_{24} and compute backwards to state S_{20}, the output of the SuperBoxes. Note that we have 16 independent SuperBoxes for the yellow AES states between state S_{17} and S_{20}. Again, we use the DDT of the SuperBoxes to find the according values for the given differentials. For 4 full active AES states, the probability of a differential is about $2^{-4 \cdot 16}$. Among the 2^{64} differentials, we expect to find one possible differential. Note that for a valid differential, the expected number of solutions for the 2nd inbound phase is 2^{64}. For each of these pairs, differences and values of all yellow and black bytes in round 3 are determined.

Outbound Phase. Next, we compute the 2^{64} differences and values of state S_{24} forward to S_{31}. With a probability of 2^{-96} we get 4 active bytes after MixColumns in state S_{31}. Hence, we have to repeat the 2nd inbound phase 2^{32} times to find one solution for the outbound phase as well and we get a total complexity of 2^{96}. After this step, the complete truncated differential path is fulfilled (except for two cyan bytes in the first states). Furthermore, all differences (black bytes) from state S_4 until state S_{33} are already determined. Also, the values of the yellow, red, blue, green and cyan bytes, and the values of the black bytes from state S_7 to S_{31} except for state S_{15} are determined. What remains is to find values for the white bytes such that the results of the two inbound phases (blue/cyan/red and yellow bytes) can be connected.

Merge Inbound. To merge the two inbound phases, we need to find according values for the white bytes. We first choose random values for all remaining bytes of the first two columns in state S_7 (gray and lightgray) and compute them forward to state S_{14}. Note that we need to try $2^{2 \cdot 8+1}$ values for AES state $S_7[2,1]$ to also match the 2-byte (cyan) and 1-bit padding at the input in AES state $S_0[2,3]$. To illustrate all further steps, we use only states and colors shown in Fig. 4. Note that all gray, lightgray and brows bytes have already been determined either by an inbound phase, chaining value, padding or just by choosing random values for the remaining free bytes of the first two columns of S_7. Also the cyan bytes are fixed already. However, all white, red, green, yellow and blue bytes are still free to choose.

By taking a look at the linear SuperMixColumns transformation, we observe that in each column slice, 14 out of 32 input/output values are already fixed. Hence, we expect to get 2^{16} solutions for this linear system of equations. Unfortunately, for the given position of already determined 14 bytes, the linear system of equations does not have a full rank. One can determine the resulting

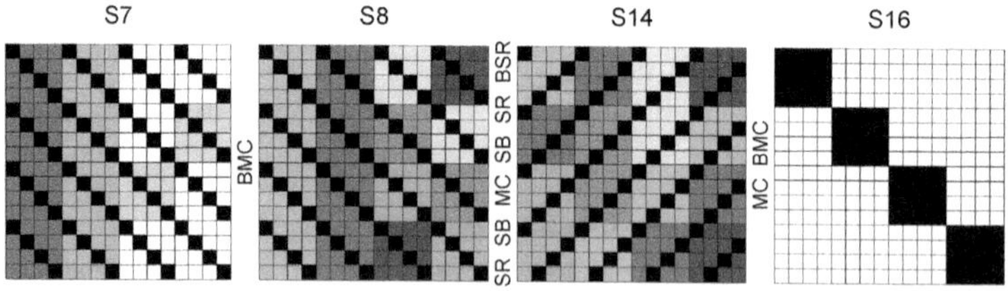

Fig. 4. States used to merge the two inbound phases with the chaining values. Gray, lightgray and brown bytes show values already determined. Green, blue, yellow and red bytes show independent values used in the generalized birthday attack and cyan bytes represent values with the target conditions.

system using the matrix M_{SMC} of SuperMixColumns. For the first column-slice the system is given as follows:

$$M_{\mathsf{SMC}} \cdot [a_0 L_0 L_1 L_2 a_1 L'_0 L'_1 L'_2 a_2 x_0 x_1 x_2 a_3 x_3 x_4 x_5]^T = [b_0 b_1 b_2 b_3 y_0 y_1 y_2 y_3 y_4 y_5 y_6 y_7 y_8 y_9 y_{10} y_{11}]$$

The free variables in this system are $x_0, \ldots, x_5$ (green). The values a_0, a_1, a_2, a_3, b_0, b_1, b_2, b_3 (brown) have been determined by the first or second inbound phase, and the values L_0, L_1, L_2 (lightgray) and L'_0, L'_1, L'_2 (gray) are determined by the choice of arbitrary values in state S_7. Since the values $y_0, \ldots, y_{11}$ (white) are free to choose we can remove their respective equations. We move terms which do not depend on x_i to the right side and get the following linear system with 4 equations and 6 variables:

$$\begin{bmatrix} 3&1&1&3&1&1 \\ 2&3&1&2&3&1 \\ 1&2&3&1&2&3 \\ 1&1&2&1&1&2 \end{bmatrix} \cdot \begin{bmatrix} x_0 \\ x_1 \\ x_2 \\ x_3 \\ x_4 \\ x_5 \end{bmatrix} = \begin{bmatrix} c_0 \\ c_1 \\ c_2 \\ c_3 \end{bmatrix} \tag{2}$$

On the right side, we have the constant values c_0, c_1, c_2, c_3 which are determined by a_0, a_1, a_2, a_3, b_0, b_1, b_2, b_3, L_0, L_1, L_2, L'_0, L'_1, L'_2 and we get for example:

$$c_0 = b_0 + 4a_0 + 6L_0 + 2L_1 + 2L_2 + 6a_1 + 5L'_0 + 3L'_1 + 3L'_2 + 2a_0 + 2a_1$$

The matrix of this linear system has rank 3 instead of 4 and therefore, we only get a solution with probability 2^{-8}. We can solve this system of equations by transforming the system into echelon form and get:

$$\begin{bmatrix} 1&0&0&1&0&0 \\ 0&1&0&0&1&0 \\ 0&0&1&0&0&1 \\ 0&0&0&0&0&0 \end{bmatrix} \cdot \begin{bmatrix} x_0 \\ x_1 \\ x_2 \\ x_3 \\ x_4 \\ x_5 \end{bmatrix} = \begin{bmatrix} c'_0 \\ c'_1 \\ c'_2 \\ c'_3 \end{bmatrix} \tag{3}$$

where the values c'_0, c'_1, c'_2, c'_3 are a linear combination of c_0, c_1, c_2, c_3. From the last equation, we get the 8-bit condition $c'_3 = 0$. Since also c'_3 depends linearly on L_i and L'_i, we can separate this linear equation into terms depending only on values of L_i and only on L'_i, and get $c'_3 = f_1(L_i) + f_2(L'_i) + f_3(a_i, b_i) = 0$. For all other 16 column-slices and fixed positions of gray bytes, we also get matrices of rank 3. In total, we get 16 8-bit conditions and the probability to find a solution for a given choice of gray and lightgray values in state S_{14} and S_{16} is 2^{-128}. However, we can also find a solution using the birthday effect with a complexity of 2^{64} in time and memory.

First, we start by choosing 2^{64} values for each of the first (gray) and second (lightgray) BigColumn in state S_7. We compute these values independently forward to state S_{14} and store them in two lists L and L'. We also separate all equations of the 128-bit condition into parts depending only on values of L and L'. We apply the resulting functions f_1, f_2, f_3 to the elements of lists L_i and L'_i, and search for matches between the two lists using the birthday effect. Now, by solving (3) we get 2^{24} solutions for the fist column-slice. By doing the same for all other slices, we get 2^{24} independent solutions for each column-slice. Hence, in total we can get up to $2^{16 \cdot 24} = 2^{384}$ solutions for the whole ECHO state.

We continue with a generalized birthday match to find values for all remaining bytes of the state. For each column in state S_{14}, we independently choose 2^{64} values for the green, blue, yellow and red columns, and compute them independently backward to S_8. We need to match the values of the cyan bytes of state S_7, which results in a condition on 24 bytes or 192 bits. Since we have 4 independent lists with 2^{64} values in state S_8, we can use the generalized birthday attack [20] to find one solution with a complexity of $2^{192/3} = 2^{64}$ in time and memory. In detail, we need to match values after the BigMixColumns transformation in backward direction. Hence, we first multiply each byte of the 4 independent lists by the 4 multipliers of the InvMixColumns transformation. Then, we get 24 equations containing only XOR conditions on bytes between the target value and elements of the 4 independent lists. This can be solved using a generalized birthday attack.

After this step, all values and differences are determined. We can compute the input message pair, as well as the output differences for ECHO-256 reduced to 5 rounds. By simply repeating the merge inbound phase 2^{32} times, we can find at least 2^{32} solutions for the whole truncated differential path. The total complexity is still 2^{96} compression function evaluations and memory requirements of 2^{64}.

Subspace Distinguisher. Note that one message pair resulting in one output differences does not give a distinguisher. We need to find many output differences in a subspace with a complexity less than in the generic case. To determine the generic complexity of finding output differences in a vector space and the resulting advantage of our attack we use the subspace distinguisher. In general, the size of the output vector space is define by the number of active bytes prior to the linear transformations in the last round (16 active bytes after the last SubBytes), combined with the number of active bytes at the input due to the feed-forward (0 active bytes in our case). This would results in a vector space dimension of $(16 + 0) \cdot 8 = 128$. However, a weakness in the combined transformations SuperMixColumns, BigFinal and output truncation reduces the vector space to a dimension of 64 at the output of the hash function (for the given truncated differential path).

Note that we can move the BigFinal function prior to SuperMixColumns, since BigFinal is a linear transformation and the same linear transformation M_{SMC} is applied to all columns in SuperMixColumns. Hence, we get 4 active bytes in each column slice at the same position in each AES state. To each (active) column slice C_{16}, we first apply the SuperMixColumns multiplication with M_{SMC} and then, a matrix multiplication with M_{trunc} which truncates the lower 8 rows. Since only 4 bytes are active in C_{16}, these transformations can be combined into a transformation using a reduced 4×8 matrix M_{comb} applied to the reduce input C_4, which contains only the 4 active bytes of C_{16}:

$$M_{trunc} \cdot M_{\mathsf{SMC}} \cdot C_{16} = M_{comb} \cdot C_4$$

The multiplication with zero differences of C_{16} removes 12 columns of M_{SMC} while the truncation removes 8 rows of M_{SMC}. An example for the first active column slice is given as follows:

$$\begin{bmatrix} 1&0&0&0&0&0&0&0&0&0&0&0&0&0&0&0 \\ 0&1&0&0&0&0&0&0&0&0&0&0&0&0&0&0 \\ 0&0&1&0&0&0&0&0&0&0&0&0&0&0&0&0 \\ 0&0&0&1&0&0&0&0&0&0&0&0&0&0&0&0 \\ 0&0&0&0&1&0&0&0&0&0&0&0&0&0&0&0 \\ 0&0&0&0&0&1&0&0&0&0&0&0&0&0&0&0 \\ 0&0&0&0&0&0&1&0&0&0&0&0&0&0&0&0 \\ 0&0&0&0&0&0&0&1&0&0&0&0&0&0&0&0 \end{bmatrix} \cdot \begin{bmatrix} 4&6&2&2&6&5&3&3&2&3&1&1&2&3&1&1 \\ 2&4&6&2&3&6&5&3&1&2&3&1&1&2&3&1 \\ 2&2&4&6&3&3&6&5&1&1&2&3&1&1&2&3 \\ 6&2&2&4&5&3&3&6&3&1&1&2&3&1&1&2 \\ 2&3&1&1&4&6&2&2&6&5&3&3&2&3&1&1 \\ 1&2&3&1&2&4&6&2&3&6&5&3&1&2&3&1 \\ 1&1&2&3&2&2&4&6&3&3&6&5&1&1&2&3 \\ 3&1&1&2&6&2&2&4&5&3&3&6&3&1&1&2 \\ 2&3&1&1&2&3&1&1&4&6&2&2&6&5&3&3 \\ 1&2&3&1&1&2&3&1&2&4&6&2&3&6&5&3 \\ 1&1&2&3&1&1&2&3&2&2&4&6&3&3&6&5 \\ 3&1&1&2&3&1&1&2&6&2&2&4&5&3&3&6 \\ 6&5&3&3&2&3&1&1&2&3&1&1&4&6&2&2 \\ 3&6&5&3&1&2&3&1&1&2&3&1&2&4&6&2 \\ 3&3&6&5&1&1&2&3&1&1&2&3&2&2&4&6 \\ 5&3&3&6&3&1&1&2&3&1&1&2&6&2&2&4 \end{bmatrix} \cdot \begin{bmatrix} a \\ 0 \\ 0 \\ 0 \\ b \\ 0 \\ 0 \\ 0 \\ c \\ 0 \\ 0 \\ 0 \\ d \\ 0 \\ 0 \\ 0 \end{bmatrix} = \begin{bmatrix} 4&6&2&2 \\ 2&3&1&1 \\ 2&3&1&1 \\ 6&5&3&3 \\ 2&4&6&2 \\ 1&2&3&1 \\ 1&2&3&1 \\ 3&6&5&3 \end{bmatrix} \cdot \begin{bmatrix} a \\ b \\ c \\ d \end{bmatrix}$$

Analyzing the resulting matrix M_{comb} for all 4 active column slices shows that in each case, the rank of M_{comb} is 2 instead of 4. This reduces the dimension of the vector space in each active column slice from 32 to 16. Since we have 4 active columns, the total dimension of the vector space at the output of the hash function is 64.

We use [9, Corollary 1] and [9, Equation (19)] to compute the complexity of a generic distinguishing attack on the ECHO-256 hash function. We get the parameters $N = 256$ (hash function output size), $n = 64$ (dimension of vector space) and $t = 2^{32}$ (number of outputs in vector space) for the subspace distinguisher. Then, the generic complexity to construct 2^{32} elements in a vector space of dimension 64 is about $2^{111.8}$ compression function evaluations. Remember that in our attack on ECHO we also get 2^{32} pairs in a vector space of the same dimension. Hence, the total complexity for our subspace distinguisher on 5 rounds of the ECHO-256 hash function is about 2^{96} compression function evaluations with memory requirements of 2^{64}.

4.2 Collisions for 4 Rounds

Finally, we are able to construct collisions for 4 rounds of the ECHO-256 hash function. The attack and truncated differential path is similar as for the subspace distinguisher on 5 rounds. We use a two-block message and the truncated differential path for the second block is given in Fig. 5. Again, we start with the 1st inbound phase, merge the chaining input and continue with the 2nd inbound and outbound phase. To get a collision at the output we use differences in the feed-forward and do a 3rd inbound phase in two AES states in round 1. Finally, we merge the solutions of the two inbound phases to determining the remaining values. In the following, we only describe parts of the attack which are new or have been changed.

1st Inbound. The 1st inbound phase is the same as for the subspace distinguisher, except that in state S_7 we choose 2^{64} random differences for the active bytes of column 0 and 1, and 2^{32} random differences for column 2 and 3. Hence, after the 1st

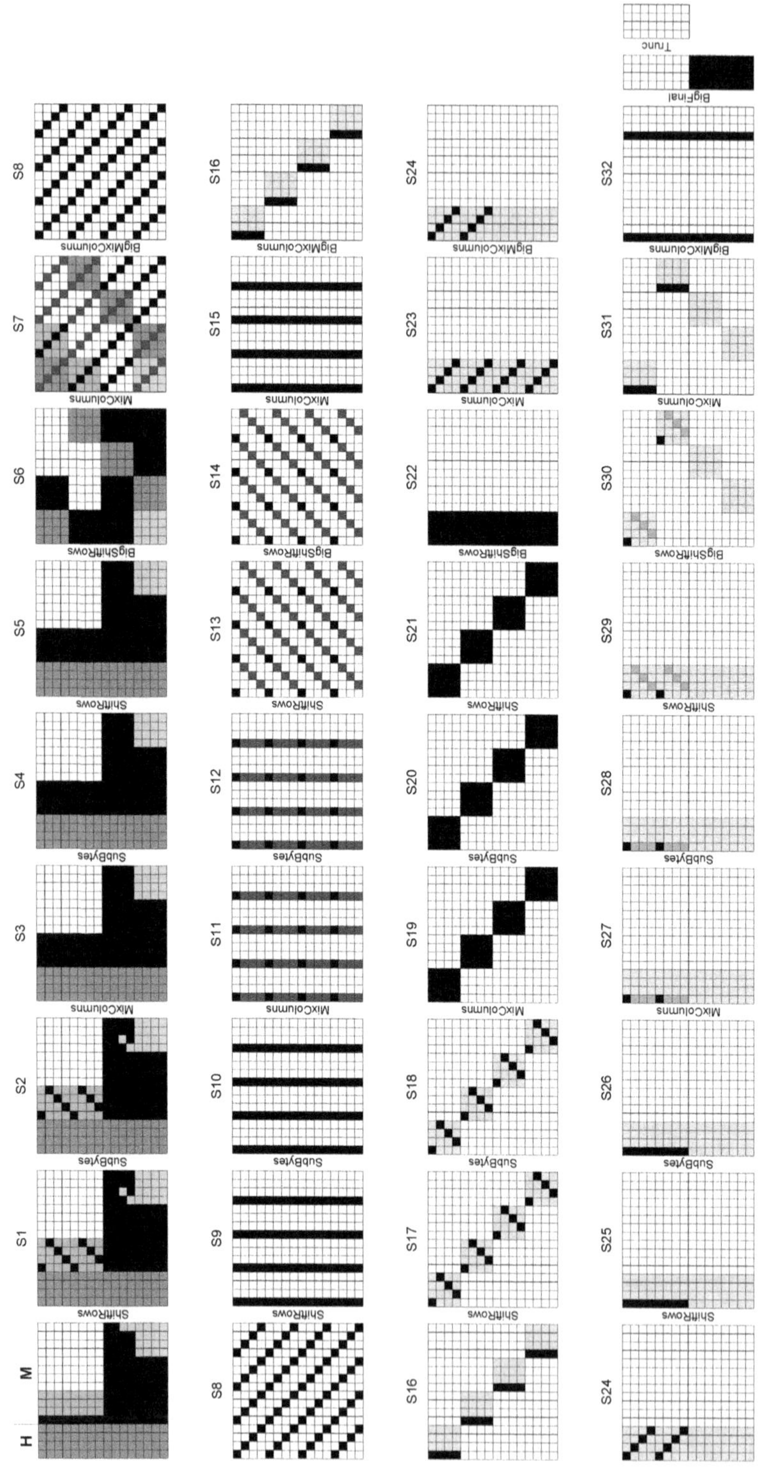

Fig. 5. The truncated differential path to get a collision on 4 rounds of ECHO-256. Black bytes are active, blue and cyan bytes are determined by the chaining input and padding, red bytes are values computed in the 1st inbound phase and yellow bytes in the 2nd inbound phase, green bytes in the outbound phase and gray bytes in the input inbound phase.

inbound phase we get 2^{64} independent solutions for each of the first two columns, and 2^{32} solutions for each of the last two columns in state S_7 (red and black bytes).

Merge Chaining Input. Again, we choose 2^{32} random first message blocks and merge them with the solutions of the 1st inbound phase column by column. We start with column 0 where we need to match the padding state as well. Since we match 64 bits of overlapping red and blue/cyan bytes, the expected number of solutions is $2^{32} \times 2^{64} \times 2^{-64} = 2^{32}$. For all other columns, we need to match only the 4 red bytes in each blue AES state with a probability of 2^{-32}. For column 1 we get 2^{32} solutions since we have computed 2^{64} results in the 1st inbound phase. For column 2 and 3, we have 2^{32} solutions from the 1st inbound phase and get one match on the overlapping 4 bytes.

2nd Inbound. To get the first solution for the 2nd inbound phase we need to try 2^{64} differences of state S_{24}, since the probability of a differential match in 4 full active AES states is only about $2^{-4 \cdot 16}$. Then, the expected number of solutions for the 2nd inbound phase is 2^{64} but we only need 2^{48} solutions to continue.

Outbound Phase. In the outbound phase we compute these 2^{48} differences and values of state S_{24} forward to S_{27}. With a probability of 2^{-48} we get one active byte after MixColumns in each active state of S_{27}. After this step, the complete truncated differential path (except for the three first states) is fulfilled. What remains is to determine differences in the first state to get a collision at the output and to find values for the white bytes.

3rd Inbound. To get a collision at the output, we use two additional active AES states in round 1. In $S_0[0,1]$ and $S_0[1,1]$, only the first column should be active such that the active bytes overlap with the active bytes at the output. For these active bytes at the input, we choose the differences to be $S_0[0,1] = S_{32}[0,0] \oplus S_{32}[0,3]$ and $S_0[1,1] = S_{32}[1,0] \oplus S_{32}[1,3]$. Then, these differences cancel each other by the feed-forward and we get a collision. In a 3rd inbound phase, we determine the remaining values of the gray and black bytes such that the given truncated differential for these two AES states in round 1 is satisfied. Again, we can find such values and differences with a complexity of about 1 using the DDT of the SuperBoxes, and compute 2^{32} solutions for each AES state. Since we still have 2^{32} solutions for each of column 0 and column 1 due to the 1st inbound phase, we expect to find a match for both differences and values of the overlapping 4 diagonal bytes of AES state $S_7[0,1]$ and $S_7[1,0]$.

Merge Inbound. Finally, we merge the 1st and 2nd inbound phases as in the previous attacks. Then, all values and differences are determined and we can compute the input message pair which results in a collision for ECHO-256 reduced to 4 rounds. The total complexity is 2^{64} in time and memory.

5 Conclusion

In this work we have presented the first analysis of the ECHO hash function. We give a subspace distinguisher for 5 rounds and collisions for 4 out of 8 rounds of the ECHO-256 hash function. Our results improve upon the previous results which are only on the (double-pipe) compression function of ECHO and for less rounds. Note that also near-collision resistance is a NIST requirement for a future SHA-3 [17]. In the extended version of this work [19] we provide near-collisions for 4.5/8 rounds of the hash function. Additionally we show distinguishers for 7 rounds and near-collisions for up to 6.5 rounds of the ECHO-256 and ECHO-512 without chosen salt.

In our improved attacks we combine the MixColumns transformation of the second AES round with the subsequent BigMixColumns transformation to a combined SuperMixColumns transformation. This allows us to construct very sparse truncated differential paths. In these paths, at most one fourth of the bytes are active throughout the whole computation of ECHO. This behavior is not known from the AES or AES based hash functions which strictly follow the wide-trail design strategy. Additionally, we are able to apply a rebound attack with multiple inbound phases to ECHO by using a generalized birthday technique to merge the inbound phases. Future work includes the search for even sparser truncated differential paths and the improvement of the given attacks by using the large degrees of available freedom. Also the separate search for differences and values as proposed in [13] and [8] may be used to improve the complexity of additional inbound phases.

Acknowledgements

We thank the members of the IAIK Krypto group, the designers of ECHO and especially Jérémy Jean and Florian Mendel for their comments and useful discussions. This work was supported in part by the Austrian Science Fund (FWF), project P21936, by the European Commission through the ICT programme under contract ICT-2007-216676 ECRYPT II, and by the IAP Programme P6/26 BCRYPT of the Belgian State (Belgian Science Policy).

References

1. Benadjila, R., Billet, O., Gilbert, H., Macario-Rat, G., Peyrin, T., Robshaw, M., Seurin, Y.: SHA-3 Proposal: ECHO. Submission to NIST (2008), http://crypto.rd.francetelecom.com/echo
2. Biham, E., Dunkelman, O.: A Framework for Iterative Hash Functions - HAIFA. Cryptology ePrint Archive, Report 2007/278 (2007), http://eprint.iacr.org/2007/278
3. Biryukov, A., Khovratovich, D., Nikolić, I.: Distinguisher and Related-Key Attack on the Full AES-256. In: Halevi, S. (ed.) CRYPTO 2009. LNCS, vol. 5677, pp. 231–249. Springer, Heidelberg (2009)
4. Daemen, J., Rijmen, V.: The Wide Trail Design Strategy. In: Honary, B. (ed.) Cryptography and Coding 2001. LNCS, vol. 2260, pp. 222–238. Springer, Heidelberg (2001)
5. Daemen, J., Rijmen, V.: The Design of Rijndael: AES - The Advanced Encryption Standard. Springer, Heidelberg (2002)

6. Daemen, J., Rijmen, V.: Understanding Two-Round Differentials in AES. In: De Prisco, R., Yung, M. (eds.) SCN 2006. LNCS, vol. 4116, pp. 78–94. Springer, Heidelberg (2006)
7. Gilbert, H., Peyrin, T.: Super-Sbox Cryptanalysis: Improved Attacks for AES-Like Permutations. In: Hong, S., Iwata, T. (eds.) FSE 2010. LNCS, vol. 6147, pp. 365–383. Springer, Heidelberg (2010)
8. Khovratovich, D., Naya-Plasencia, M., Röck, A., Schläffer, M.: Cryptanalysis of Luffa v2 Components. In: Biryukov, A., Gong, G., Stinson, D.R. (eds.) SAC 2010. LNCS, vol. 6544. Springer, Heidelberg (2011)
9. Lamberger, M., Mendel, F., Rechberger, C., Rijmen, V., Schläffer, M.: Rebound Distinguishers: Results on the Full Whirlpool Compression Function. In: Matsui [11], pp. 126–143
10. Lamberger, M., Mendel, F., Rechberger, C., Rijmen, V., Schläffer, M.: The Rebound Attack and Subspace Distinguishers: Application to Whirlpool. Cryptology ePrint Archive, Report 2010/198 (2010), `http://eprint.iacr.org/2010/198`
11. Matsui, M. (ed.): ASIACRYPT 2009. LNCS, vol. 5912. Springer, Heidelberg (2009)
12. Matusiewicz, K., Naya-Plasencia, M., Nikolic, I., Sasaki, Y., Schläffer, M.: Rebound Attack on the Full Lane Compression Function. In: Matsui [11], pp. 106–125
13. Mendel, F., Peyrin, T., Rechberger, C., Schläffer, M.: Improved Cryptanalysis of the Reduced Grøstl Compression Function, ECHO Permutation and AES Block Cipher. In: Jacobson Jr., M.J., Rijmen, V., Safavi-Naini, R. (eds.) SAC 2009. LNCS, vol. 5867, pp. 16–35. Springer, Heidelberg (2009)
14. Mendel, F., Rechberger, C., Schläffer, M., Thomsen, S.S.: The Rebound Attack: Cryptanalysis of Reduced Whirlpool and Grøstl. In: Dunkelman, O. (ed.) FSE 2009. LNCS, vol. 5665, pp. 260–276. Springer, Heidelberg (2009)
15. Mendel, F., Rechberger, C., Schläffer, M., Thomsen, S.S.: Rebound Attacks on the Reduced Grøstl Hash Function. In: Pieprzyk, J. (ed.) CT-RSA 2010. LNCS, vol. 5985, pp. 350–365. Springer, Heidelberg (2010)
16. National Institute of Standards and Technology (NIST). FIPS PUB 197: Advanced Encryption Standard. Federal Information Processing Standards Publication 197, U.S. Department of Commerce (November 2001), `http://www.itl.nist.gov/fipspubs`
17. National Institute of Standards and Technology (NIST). Announcing Request for Candidate Algorithm Nominations for a New Cryptographic Hash Algorithm (SHA-3) Family. Federal Register 27(212), 62212–62220 (November 2007), `http://csrc.nist.gov/groups/ST/hash/documents/FR_Notice_Nov07.pdf`
18. Peyrin, T.: Improved Differential Attacks for ECHO and Grøstl. Cryptology ePrint Archive, Report 2010/223 (2010), `http://eprint.iacr.org/2010/223`
19. Schläffer, M.: Subspace Distinguisher for 5/8 Rounds of the ECHO-256 Hash Function. Cryptology ePrint Archive, Report 2010/321 (2010), `http://eprint.iacr.org/2010/321`
20. Wagner, D.: A Generalized Birthday Problem. In: Yung, M. (ed.) CRYPTO 2002. LNCS, vol. 2442, pp. 288–303. Springer, Heidelberg (2002)

Cryptanalysis of *Luffa* v2 Components*

Dmitry Khovratovich[1], María Naya-Plasencia[2], Andrea Röck[3], and Martin Schläffer[4]

[1] University of Luxembourg, Luxembourg
[2] FHNW, Windisch, Switzerland
[3] Aalto University School of Science and Technology, Finland
[4] IAIK, Graz University of Technology, Austria

Abstract. We develop a number of techniques for the cryptanalysis of the SHA-3 candidate *Luffa*, and apply them to various *Luffa* components. These techniques include a new variant of the rebound approach taking into account the specifics of *Luffa*. The main improvements include the construction of good truncated differential paths, the search for differences using multiple inbound phases and a fast final solution search via linear systems. Using these techniques, we are able to construct non-trivial semi-free-start collisions for 7 (out of 8 rounds) of *Luffa*-256 with a complexity of 2^{104} in time and 2^{102} in memory. This is the first analysis of a *Luffa* component other that the permutation of *Luffa* v1. Additionally, we provide new and more efficient distinguishers also for the full permutation of *Luffa* v2. For this permutation distinguisher, we use a new model which applies first a short test on all samples and then a longer test on a smaller subset of the inputs. We demonstrate that a set of right pairs for the given differential path can be found significantly faster than for a random permutation.

Keywords: hash functions, SHA-3 competition, Luffa, cryptanalysis, rebound attack, semi-free-start collision, distinguisher.

1 Introduction

The hash function *Luffa* [5] is a Round 2 candidate of the NIST SHA-3 competition, and follows the wide-pipe design using a sponge-based mode of operation. *Luffa* shows its originality in the design of the compression function, which is based on the parallel call of 3, 4, or 5 permutations (depending on the output size). A similar design approach was used in the hash function LANE [8], but with different input and output transformations.

* The work described in this paper has been supported in part by the European Commission through the ICT program under contract ICT-2007-216676 ECRYPT II, by the French Agence Nationale de la Recherche under Contract ANR-06-SETI-013-RAPIDE, by the PRP "Security & Trust" grant of the University of Luxembourg, by the Academy of Finland under project 122736, and during the tenure of an ERCIM Alain Bensoussan Fellowship Programme.

A. Biryukov, G. Gong, and D.R. Stinson (Eds.): SAC 2010, LNCS 6544, pp. 388–409, 2011.

In this paper we present several results on various components of *Luffa*. First, we analyze the *Luffa* mode of operation and derive sufficient conditions for a differential path with low-weight input and output differences in the permutations. Then we proceed with the analysis of the *Luffa* permutations and construct a 7-round truncated differential path with using a meet-in-the-middle approach. We are able to exploit the rotational symmetry of *Luffa* to increase the number of differential paths and construct solutions for these paths with an advanced rebound attack [10].

Since the number of active S-boxes in the differential path is too large for a straightforward application of the rebound attack, we need to solve this issue with several refinements of the attack. We use *multiple inbound phases* and a *parallel matching technique* to find all possible differential paths for the truncated path first. We need a parallel matching technique to match large lists of differences through the S-box layer in the inbound phase. A gradual matching as in the attacks on AES is not possible for the not block-wise operating linear transformation of *Luffa*.

Using this advanced rebound attack we get a semi-free-start collision for 7 (out of 8) rounds of *Luffa*-256 v2 in Section 3, which can be extended to an 8-round semi-free-start distinguisher (see Section 4). We have also defined a new type of distinguisher which can be used to distinguish the full permutation of *Luffa* v2 in Section 5.

Note that the supporting document of *Luffa* provides a semi-free-start collision for *Luffa*-512 with complexity 2^{204} due to the properties of the message injection and using the generalized birthday problem [11]. For *Luffa*-256 this attack does not have a complexity lower than the birthday bound. Other previous results include the existence of a non-trivial differential path for 8 rounds of the internal permutation with probability 2^{-224}, and different variations of high-order differential distinguishers [1,4].

Table 1. Results. Note that the meaning and setting of "distinguisher" varies depending on the attack

building block	security parameter	time	memory	technique
		Distinguishers		
permutation v1	full (8)	2^{224}	-	differential [7]
compression v1	6	2^{84}	-	higher order diff. [4]
compression v1	7	2^{216}	-	higher order diff. [4]
permutation v1	full (8)	2^{82}	-	algebraic zero-sum [1]
permutation v2	full (8)	2^{116}	-	two-tier differential Sect. 5
compression *Luffa*-256 v2	full (8)	2^{104}	2^{102}	advanced rebound attack Sect. 4
		Semi-free-start collision		
compression *Luffa*-256 v2	7	2^{104}	2^{102}	advanced rebound attack Sect. 3

2 Description of *Luffa*

In this section we briefly describe the SHA-3 candidate *Luffa* [5]. For a more detailed description we refer to the submission document.

2.1 The Iteration

The hash function *Luffa* is a variant of a sponge function and consists of a linear message injection MI, w 256-bit permutations Q_j and a finalization function C''. The chaining value at instant i is represented by $(H_0^{(i)}, \ldots, H_{w-1}^{(i)})$. The size of each message block $M^{(i)}$, each value $H_j^{(i)}$ and starting variable V_j is 256 bits. In the iteration of the hash function *Luffa*, a padded t-block message M is hashed as follows:

$$
\begin{aligned}
(H_0^{(0)}, \ldots, H_{w-1}^{(0)}) &= (V_0, \ldots, V_{w-1}) \\
(X_0, \ldots, X_{w-1}) &= MI(H_0^{(i-1)}, \ldots, H_{w-1}^{(i-1)}, M^{(i)}) \quad \text{for } 1 \le i \le t \\
(H_0^{(i)}, \ldots, H_{w-1}^{(i)}) &= (Q_0(X_0), \ldots, Q_{w-1}(X_{w-1})) \quad \text{for } 1 \le i \le t \\
hash &= C''(H_0^{(t)}, \ldots, H_{w-1}^{(t)}).
\end{aligned}
$$

The parameter w depends on the hash output size and is specified to be $w = 3$ for *Luffa*-224 and *Luffa*-256, $w = 4$ for *Luffa*-384, and $w = 5$ for *Luffa*-512. Fig. 1 shows the iteration of the hash function *Luffa*-256 with $w = 3$. In the following, we describe the permutations Q_j and the message injection MI of *Luffa* in more detail.

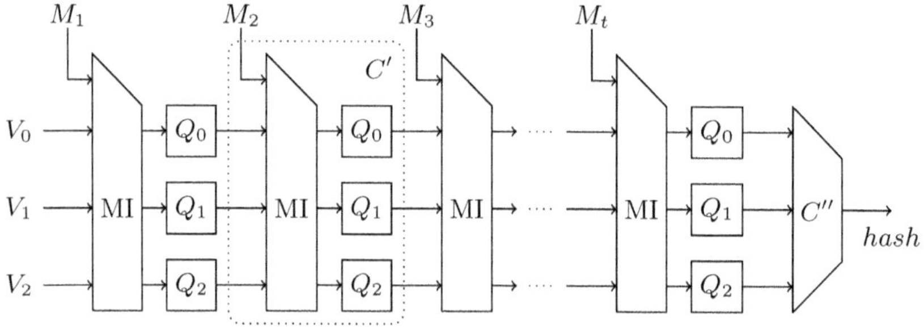

Fig. 1. The iteration of the hash function *Luffa*-256 ($w = 3$) with message injection MI, permutations Q_j and finalization function C''

2.2 The Permutations

The non-linear 256-bit permutations Q_j update a state of 8 32-bit words $a_0, a_1, \ldots, a_7$. Initially, an InputTweak is applied to the input of the permutations. Furthermore, each permutation consists of 3 round transformations SubCrumb,

MixWord, and AddConstant which are repeated for 8 rounds. The permutations Q_j differ only in the InputTweak and AddConstant transformation. In the following, we give a detailed description of the round transformations. We organize the state in 4×2 32-bit words with the LSB of each word at the right hand side (see Fig. 2). Furthermore, we call the 4 words a_0, a_1, a_2, a_3 left words (or left side) and the 4 words a_4, a_5, a_6, a_7 right words (or right side), and we call each 4-bit column of this state a nibble. In the following, we describe a specific difference in a nibble either by its bit pattern, e.g. 1011 (with the LSB on the right), or by its hexadecimal value, e.g. $0xB$, depending on which is more convenient for the understanding.

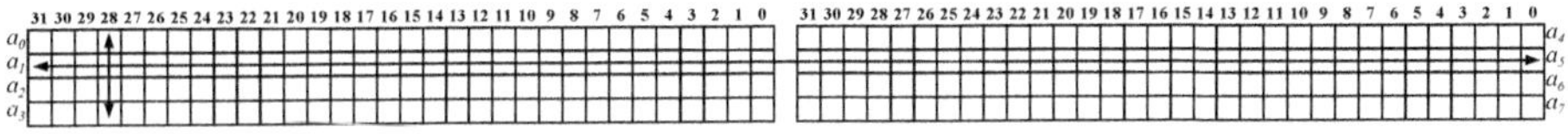

Fig. 2. The 256-bit state of each *Luffa* permutation Q_i is organized in 8 32-bit words. In this representation, SubCrumb is applied vertically to 4-bit columns (nibbles) and MixWord horizontally to 64-bit rows of the state.

In permutation Q_j, the InputTweak rotates the 4 right words a_4, a_5, a_6, a_7 to the left by j positions. This tweak has no influence on the four left words. In the non-linear SubCrumb layer, the same 4-bit S-box is applied to each nibble of the state. Hence, 64 independent S-boxes are applied to the columns of the state (see Fig. 2). Note that the wiring is different for the left and right side, which is equivalent to applying two different S-boxes S and S' on each side.

In MixWord, a linear mixing function is applied to two 32-bit words (a_k and a_{k+4} for $k = 0, \ldots, 3$) of the state. Hence, 4 independent linear functions are applied to each row of the state (see Fig. 2). We give here an alternative description of MixWord which is more suitable for our analysis. A detailed description of MixWord can be found in the specification of *Luffa* [6]. We denote by a_k^i and a_{k+4}^i the i-th bit of the words a_k and a_{k+4} with $k = 0, \ldots, 3$. Then, the output words b_k^i and b_{k+4}^i are computed as follows:

$$b_k^i = a_k^i \oplus a_k^{i+18} \oplus a_k^{i+20} \oplus a_k^{i+22} \oplus a_k^{i+30} \oplus a_{k+4}^i \oplus a_{k+4}^{i+18} \oplus a_{k+4}^{i+22}$$
$$b_{k+4}^i = a_k^{i+17} \oplus a_k^{i+29} \oplus a_k^{i+31} \oplus a_{k+4}^{i+17} \oplus a_{k+4}^{i+31},$$

with $0 \leq i \leq 31$, $k = 0, \ldots, 3$ and all indices modulo 32.

Note that each bit of the left output words b_k^i depends on 8 bits of the input and each bit of the right output words b_{k+4}^i depends on 5 bits of the input. For the backward direction the opposite holds: Each bit of the left input words a_k^i depends on 5 bits of the output and each bit of the right input words a_{k+4}^i depends on 8 bits of the output. In addition, we show in Fig. 3 the propagation of a 1-bit difference in forward and backward direction. Let us consider for example the case $k = 0$ in the figure. We have a difference in all the bits of b_0 and b_4

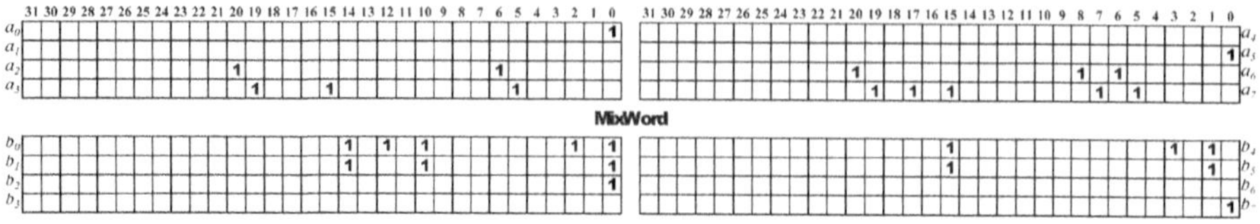

Fig. 3. Propagation of a single bit at the LSB of the left ($k = 0$) and right ($k = 1$) word in forward, and left ($k = 2$) and right ($k = 3$) word in backward direction. Empty bits are zero. Note that the 64-bit rows are independent in each MixWord transformation.

which depend on a_0^0, e.g.

$$b_0^0 = \underline{a_0^0} \oplus a_0^{18} \oplus a_0^{20} \oplus a_0^{22} \oplus a_0^{30} \oplus a_4^i \oplus a_4^{18} \oplus a_4^{22}.$$

2.3 The Message Injection

The message injection in *Luffa*-256 can be described by an operation in a ring of polynomials:

$$R = Z_2[x]/(x^8 + x^4 + x^3 + x + 1),$$

which is applied to those 8 bits of the state with equal bit position i in the 32-bit words a_k^i for $k = 0, \ldots, 7$. Hence, each bit of the message is mixed into two nibbles of the state. In the message injection, the chaining values H_j and the message block M are used to get the new intermediate chaining values X_i as follows:

$$\begin{pmatrix} X_0 \\ X_1 \\ X_2 \end{pmatrix} = \begin{pmatrix} x+1 & x & x & 1 \\ x & x+1 & x & x \\ x & x & x+1 & x^2 \end{pmatrix} \cdot \begin{pmatrix} H_0 \\ H_1 \\ H_2 \\ M \end{pmatrix}.$$

3 Semi-Free-Start Collision on *Luffa*-256 for 7 Rounds

In this section, we present a rebound technique to search for semi-free-start collisions in *Luffa*. With semi-free-start collision, we denote a collision on the internal state with no differences in the chaining value. Contrary to free-start collisions (with arbitrary differences in the chaining value), semi-free-start collisions are not trivial to find in sponge-like constructions. In our attack, we can find two distinct two-block messages M_1, M_2 and M_1^*, M_2^* such that

$$MI(M_2, P(MI(M_1, CV))) = MI(M_2^*, P(MI(M_1^*, CV))).$$

for some chaining value CV. In the following, we show that the complexity to find such a semi-free-start collision for 7 (out of 8) rounds of *Luffa*-256 is about 2^{104} in time and 2^{102} in memory.

3.1 Outline of the Attack

To search for semi-free-start collisions in reduced *Luffa*-256 we use an adapted and refined rebound attack. Since we do not allow differences in the chaining values, all 3 permutations need to be active. In the attack, we first search for truncated differential paths in Q_j which result in a semi-free-start collision for 7 rounds. Contrary to AES based designs, this step is already a non-trivial task. In the truncated differential path, we only consider active and non-active S-boxes (or nibbles) of the state. Hence, we will represent the truncated differential path using a line of 2x32 nibbles. We construct a path which has only one active S-boxes at the input and the end of the path. Furthermore, we also try to keep the number of active S-boxes in the middle rounds low. We use an improved rebound attack where we first filter for all possible differential paths and then solve for the values of the state to get corresponding input pairs for all three permutations. While filtering for differential paths, we also need to ensure that the input and output differences can be injected and erased by the message difference.

3.2 Matching the Message Injection

In the message injection, a difference in nibble i of M might affect two nibbles of the input of each permutations Q_j. Due to the InputTweak, these two nibbles are, at the left side the nibble at position i, and on the right side the nibble at position $i+j$. To get a sparse truncated differential path we aim for only one active S-box (one active nibble) in the first and the last round.

In the first message injection, the difference in all chaining values H_j is zero. Therefore, we get for the intermediate chaining variables X_j:

$$\begin{pmatrix} \Delta X_0 \\ \Delta X_1 \\ \Delta X_2 \end{pmatrix} = \begin{pmatrix} x+1 & x & x & 1 \\ x & x+1 & x & x \\ x & x & x+1 & x^2 \end{pmatrix} \cdot \begin{pmatrix} 0 \\ 0 \\ 0 \\ \Delta M \end{pmatrix} = \begin{pmatrix} \Delta M \\ x \cdot \Delta M \\ x^2 \cdot \Delta M \end{pmatrix}$$

In order to have only one active S-box at the input of each permutation, we require that $\Delta M, x \cdot \Delta M, x^2 \cdot \Delta M$ are polynomials either of degree < 4 or divisible by x^4. The most simple conditions which do not spread to the other nibble are

$$\Delta M = ax + b \text{ or } \Delta M = ax^5 + bx^4.$$

The first solution corresponds to a difference in a nibble on the left side and the second solution to a difference on the right side. The possible differences in these nibbles are 0001, 0010 or 0011.

In the second message injection, we need to erase all differences of the internal state. Hence, we get the following system of equations:

$$\begin{pmatrix} 0 \\ 0 \\ 0 \end{pmatrix} = \begin{pmatrix} x+1 & x & x & 1 \\ x & x+1 & x & x \\ x & x & x+1 & x^2 \end{pmatrix} \cdot \begin{pmatrix} \Delta H_0 \\ \Delta H_1 \\ \Delta H_2 \\ \Delta M \end{pmatrix}$$

Again, we consider only differences with only one active S-box, prior to the last (linear) MixWord transformation. This condition filters out most possible differences (we omit long calculations), and the only non-trivial solutions we have found are

$$\begin{pmatrix} \Delta H_0 \\ \Delta H_1 \\ \Delta H_2 \\ \Delta M \end{pmatrix} = \left\{ \begin{pmatrix} x^3 + x^2 + 1 \\ x^3 \\ x \\ x + 1 \end{pmatrix}, \begin{pmatrix} x^7 + x^6 + x^4 \\ x^7 \\ x^5 \\ x^5 + x^4 \end{pmatrix} \right\}.$$

The first solution corresponds to a difference in the left side and the second one to a difference in the right side. Thus, for each permutation we have one specific output difference for the single active S-box in the last round, for which we are sure that we can erase it by a difference in the message. Note that the output difference of the permutation is the same in each active nibble. The specific differences in the nibbles of H_0, H_1, H_2, and M are 1101, 1000, 0010, and 0011, respectively.

To summarize, we search for differential paths with only a single active S-box in the first and the last round. For an active S-box in a right nibble at position i of Q_0, only the two least significant bits of the input difference should be active. The possible differences are then 0001, 0010 or 0011. For permutation Q_j, the active S-box will be at position $i + j$ modulo 32 on the right side, due to the InputTweak and should have the same difference as in Q_0 but rotated j positions to the MSB. We get the differences 0010, 0100 or 0110 for Q_1, and 0100, 1000 or 1100 for Q_2. Note that we fix the output difference of the active S-box to only one possible difference depending on the permutation. The difference at the output of the single active S-box in round 7 has to be 1101 for Q_0, 1000 for Q_1 and 0010 for Q_2. Note that for these input and output differences of the three permutations, the differences of the injected message block have been computed deterministically.

3.3 Constructing Truncated Differential Paths

For the semi-free-start collision on 7 rounds of *Luffa*-256, we use many truncated differential paths for each permutation to get enough solutions for an attack. All paths have the same numbers of active S-boxes in each round which are given as follows:

$$1 - 5 - 27 - 52 - 26 - 5 - 1$$

We have one active S-box after the SubCrumb of round 7, and we have already determined which difference we must have in it's output for each lane. This one active nibble leads to differences in 8 nibbles after the MixWord. The differences will be the same in each nibble and can be eliminated by the method described in Section 3.2. In the following analysis we will omit this last step, since it has no influence on the differential path.

To get a truncated differential path with only 5 active S-boxes in the second and second last round, the single active S-box at the input has to be in the right side and the single active S-box at the output in the left side. Note that the position of the single active S-box in round 7 is identical in all permutations. However, the position of the active S-box in round 1 is rotated by j positions for permutation Q_j due to the InputTweak. However, for each permutation, we are able to find an equivalent truncated differential path with the same number of active S-boxes (see Appendix A). Therefore, in the following we only consider the path of the first permutation Q_0.

We have constructed the truncated differential path for Q_0 by first propagating forward and backward without constraints from a single active S-box in round 1 and round 7 (see Fig. 4). For each single active S-box, we have tried all 32 positions to get a good (sparse) truncated differential path for our attack. We have found a path with the following number of active nibbles after each SubCrumb and MixWord transformation in forward direction:

$$1 - \mathsf{SC} - 1 - \mathsf{MW} - 5 - \mathsf{SC} - 5 - \mathsf{MW} - 27 - \mathsf{SC} - 27 - \mathsf{MW} - 58$$

and in backward direction:

$$57 - \mathsf{MW} - 26 - \mathsf{SC} - 26 - \mathsf{MW} - 5 - \mathsf{SC} - 5 - \mathsf{MW} - 1 - \mathsf{SC} - 1$$

Since the 57 and 58 active nibbles have only 52 common active nibbles, we simply impose some constraints on the connecting MixWord transformation. This results in a $(58-52)\times 4 = 24$ bit condition for the forward part, and a $(57-52)\times 4 = 20$ bit condition for the backward part. These conditions are marked by red nibbles in Fig. 4 and are required to be zero. In this truncated differential path, the active S-box at the input is located in the right word in bit 0, and at the output in the left word in bit 14. Furthermore, in the *Luffa* permutations all XOR differential paths are rotation symmetric within 32-bit words. Hence, we actually get 32 truncated differential paths with active input the ith nibble of the right part and active output the nibble $i + 14$ modulo 32 of the left part for Q_0. In general, for Q_j we get for an active input at nibble $i + j$ of the right part, the same active output at nibble $i + 14$ of the left part (see Appendix A) due to the InputTweak.

3.4 Rebound Attack on *Luffa*

To find pairs conforming to the given truncated differential paths, we use the rebound attack [10]. Due to the different structure of *Luffa* compared to AES based hash functions, several improvements are needed. Since the truncated differential path consists of three rather active states in the middle a standard inbound phase cannot be used. Previous rebound attacks dealt with relatively short inbound phases to exploit the propagation of differences with probability one. Since this is not possible for longer inbound phases, a different strategy is needed to reduce the overall computational complexity of the attack.

The main idea is to first generate all possible differential paths which conform to the truncated paths. Note that we do not compute values or generate conditions in this step. We use 5 short inbound phases to filter for differential paths

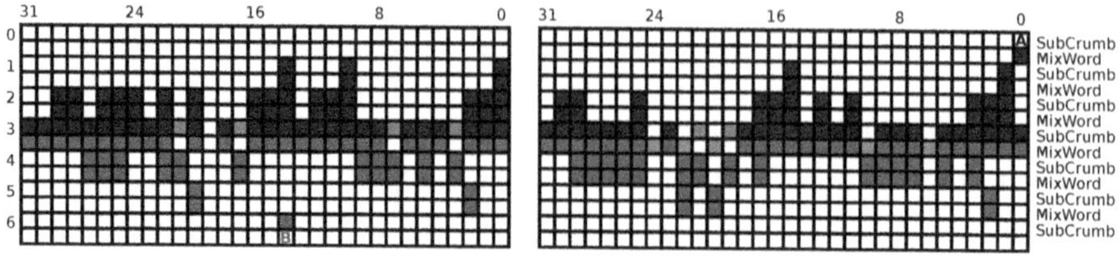

Fig. 4. An example for a truncated differential path followed in the first permutation for building the semi-free-start collisions. The difference in **A** can be one of 0001, 0010 or 0011, the difference in **B** has to be 1101 (see Section 3.2).

from both sides with a final filtering step in the middle (see Fig. 5). In each inbound phase, we first compute all possible differential paths independently and merge the results of two adjacent inbound phases. We have carefully estimated the number of possible differential paths. In each step, this number is significantly lower than 2^{128}. Note that we apply the inbound phase at every S-box layer and also need to merge the resulting solutions through the S-box layer. This is not trivial for very large lists and explained in detail in Section 3.6. Also note that in AES-based primitives, differences between input and output of S-boxes can be filtered gradually due to the column-wise operation of MixColumns. Since this is not the case for the MixWord transformation of *Luffa*, more complicated filtering steps are needed.

After determining all possible differential paths, the next step is to solve for conforming input pairs to the permutation. We start by computing values of SubCrumb in the middle rounds 2, 3, and 4 simultaneously using a linear approach, similar as in the linearized match-in-the-middle step of [9]. Also this step has to be adapted since some S-boxes are not active and therefore, do not behave linearly. For each solution of these three rounds, all values of the state are determined and we probabilistically compute the resulting pairs outwards in the outbound phase. Finally, those pairs which match the message injection will give a semi-free-start collision for *Luffa*-256.

3.5 The Inbound Phases

In this section, we filter the truncated path for all possible differential paths. In total, about $2^{68.7}$ differential paths are possible, given the constraints on the message injection. We determine these paths by applying 5 inbound phases in the 5 middle rounds. In these inbound phases, we only determine which differences are possible but do not choose actual values for the state. Note that each active S-box can have one out of $15 \sim 2^{3.9}$ differences at the input or at the output. However, only 96 out of these $15 \cdot 15$ differences are possible for the *Luffa* S-box (see the differential distribution table of this S-box). Hence, the probability of a differential match is about $96/225 \sim 2^{-1.23}$. Contrary to the AES S-box, we need to compute more exact probabilities to get correct results for *Luffa*.

The first inbound phase is applied to the truncated differential path $1-\mathsf{MW}-5-\mathsf{SC}-5-\mathsf{MW}-27$ in round 0 and 1. We can have $15 \sim 2^{3.9}$ non-zero differences

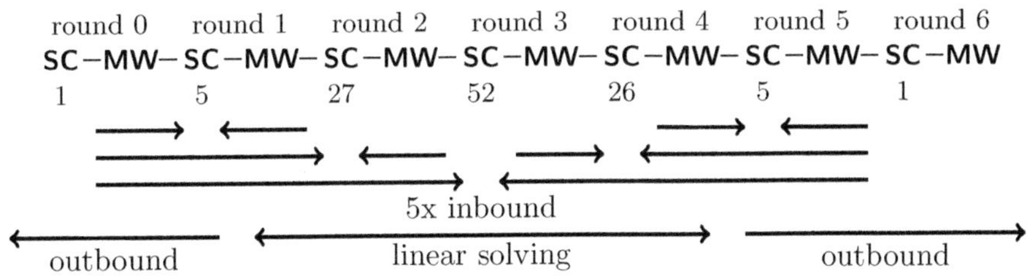

Fig. 5. A schematic view of the advanced rebound attack on *Luffa*. The attack consists of 5 small inbound phases to determine possible differential paths, a linear solving step to find the values and two outbound phases.

at the input of the S-box (one active nibble in the first MixWord) and $15^5 \sim 2^{19.5}$ non-zero differences at the output (5 active nibbles in the second MixWord). Since only a fraction of $2^{-1.23 \cdot 5} = 2^{-6.15}$ differentials are possible through the 5 active S-boxes, we get in total about

$$2^{3.9} \cdot 2^{19.5} \cdot 2^{-6.15} = 2^{17.3}$$

possible differential paths for the first inbound phase. To support this estimate, we have computed the exact number of differential paths conforming to this truncated path, which is $2^{17.49}$.

Next, we continue with a second inbound phase between rounds 0-2. In the forward direction, we take all solutions of the previous inbound phase and in backward direction, we determine all possible differences in $27 - \mathsf{MW} - 52$. Note that in general, 27 active nibbles would expand to 58 active nibbles through MixWord. Therefore, we get a 24-bit condition on these differences and consider only the valid $2^{3.9 \cdot 27 - 24} = 2^{81.5}$ differences in round 3. These differences match with the previously computed ones through the 27 active S-boxes with a probability of $2^{-1.23 \cdot 27} = 2^{-33.2}$. In total, we get

$$2^{17.3} \cdot 2^{81.5} \cdot 2^{-33.2} = 2^{65.6}$$

possible differential paths for the truncated differential path $1 - \mathsf{MW} - 5 - \mathsf{SC} - 5 - \mathsf{MW} - 27 - \mathsf{SC} - 27 - \mathsf{MW} - 52$.

Now, we repeat the same procedure in backward direction for the second half of the path. The third inbound phase deals with rounds 4-5 and the path $26 - \mathsf{MW} - 5 - \mathsf{SC} - 5 - \mathsf{MW} - 1$. Similarly to the first inbound phase, we get $2^{19.5}$ differences for MixWord in round 4 and $2^{3.9}$ in round 5, which results in $2^{17.3}$ differential paths for this inbound phase. We continue with the fourth inbound phase and combine these paths with all possible differences in round 3 for $52 - \mathsf{MW} - 26$. To get 52 active nibbles instead of 57, we need a 20-bit conditions and get $2^{3.9 \cdot 26 - 20} = 2^{81.6}$ differences. We match all differences in backward and forward direction at the 26 active S-boxes and get

$$2^{17.3} \cdot 2^{81.6} \cdot 2^{-31.9} = 2^{67}$$

possible differential paths for the truncated differential path 52 – MW – 26 – SC – 26 – MW – 5 – SC – 5 – MW – 1.

3.6 The Final Inbound Phase: Parallel Matching

Next, we need to match all $2^{65.6}$ paths of the first three rounds with the 2^{67} paths of the last three rounds at the middle S-box layer. Since we have 52 active S-boxes, only $2^{65.6+67-1.23 \cdot 52} = 2^{68.8}$ differential paths will survive. However, the complexity of a straight forward filtering step is $2^{65.6} \cdot 2^{67} = 2^{132.6}$, which exceeds the birthday bound for collisions in *Luffa*-256. Therefore, we use a *parallel matching* technique to independently match differences in sets of 13 S-boxes. This reduces the complexity of the final inbound phase to about 2^{102} table lookups.

We first generate two sorted lists $\mathcal{A}$ and $\mathcal{B}$ from the differential paths found in the previous two inbound phases: List $\mathcal{A}$ contains all $2^{65.6}$ paths of round 0-2, sorted by the 52 non-zero input differences $\{x_1, \ldots, x_{52}\}$ of the active S-boxes in round 3. Similarly, list $\mathcal{B}$ contains all 2^{67} paths of round 3-5, sorted by the 52 non-zero output differences $\{y_1, \ldots, y_{52}\}$ of the same S-boxes. Next, we separate these 52 S-boxes into sets of 13 S-boxes which we match independently. Note that for each set of 13 S-boxes only $15^{13} = 2^{50.8}$ non-zero input or output differences exist. It follows that we can associate $2^{65.6-50.8} = 2^{14.8}$ elements from list $\mathcal{A}$ or $2^{67-50.8} = 2^{16.2}$ elements from list $\mathcal{B}$ to each of these $2^{50.8}$ differences.

Using the two lists $\mathcal{A}$ and $\mathcal{B}$, we generate two new and sorted lists $\mathcal{C}$ and $\mathcal{D}$ with differential matches for the first 13 and second 13 active S-boxes. List $\mathcal{C}$ contains differential matches between $\{x_1, \ldots, x_{13}\}$ and $\{y_0, \ldots, y_{13}\}$, and list $\mathcal{D}$ between $\{x_{14}, \ldots, x_{26}\}$ and $\{y_{14}, \ldots, y_{26}\}$. The resulting size of each list is $2^{50.8+50.8-13 \cdot 1.23} = 2^{85.6}$. The complexity to match two times $2^{50.8}$ differences at 13 S-boxes is about 2^{102} table lookups.

Next, we associate the differences $\{x_{14}, \ldots, x_{52}\}$ of $\mathcal{A}$ to $\mathcal{C}$, and the differences $\{y_1, \ldots, y_{13}, y_{27}, \ldots, y_{52}\}$ of $\mathcal{B}$ to $\mathcal{D}$. The resulting list $\mathcal{C}'$ contains the differences $\{y_1, \ldots, y_{13}, x_1, \ldots, x_{52}\}$ sorted by $\{y_1, \ldots, y_{13}\}$, and list $\mathcal{D}'$ contains the differences $\{x_{14}, \ldots, x_{26}, y_1, \ldots, y_{52}\}$ sorted by $\{x_{14}, \ldots, x_{26}, y_1, \ldots, y_{13}\}$. The size of the resulting new list $\mathcal{C}'$ is the size of $\mathcal{C}$ multiplied by all elements of $\mathcal{A}$ which can be associated to each of $x_1, \ldots, x_{13}$. The same holds for $\mathcal{D}'$ with elements of $\mathcal{B}$. Hence, we get $2^{85.6+14.8} = 2^{100.4}$ entries in $\mathcal{C}'$ and $2^{85.6+16.2} = 2^{101.8}$ entries in $\mathcal{D}'$.

Finally, we merge the two lists $\mathcal{C}'$ and $\mathcal{D}'$ by their overlapping differences $\{y_1, \ldots, y_{13}, x_{14}, \ldots, x_{26}\}$. Since we need to match differences in 26 active nibbles, we get a 101.4-bit condition. This results in about $2^{100.4+101.8-101.4} = 2^{100.8}$ solutions with a complexity of about 2^{102} simple table lookups (we do not need to consider S-box differentials here anymore) and memory. Of these solutions, about $2^{-1.23 \cdot 26} = 2^{-32}$ differential paths give valid differentials also for the remaining 26 S-boxes. Hence, we get in total about $2^{100.8-32} = 2^{68.8}$ differential paths for round 0-6.

3.7 Linear Solving for Pairs

In the previous step, we have constructed all $2^{68.8}$ possible differential paths for the given truncated differential path of Section 3.3. However, to get conforming input pairs, we still need to determine the actual values. Note that we can only find values for a fraction of the differential paths. In the following, we show how to determine these paths and how to construct all values with a low average cost, by extending the linear approach published in [9].

We start by constructing solutions which satisfy the differential path in rounds 2-4 first. Since these rounds contain most active S-boxes, they are usually considered as the most expensive rounds. Note that each active S-box in *Luffa* restricts the number of possible values to either 2 or 4 elements, which can be described by an affine space: If there are two solutions, the input values can be described as $ax + b$, and the output values as $cx + d$. In this case x is a boolean variable common for input and output, and a, b, c, d are elements from Z_2^4. If there are four solutions, they are defined by two binary variables and two affine equations, one for the input and one for the output.

Hence, we can describe the set of all possible values in the active S-boxes of the three middle rounds using about $1.23 \cdot (26+52+27) = 129$ boolean variables. Note that this number is slightly different for each particular path, depending on the actual number of solutions for each S-box. These variables are linked by the equations of the linear MixWord transformation and the (affine) AddConstant in round 3 and 4. In total, we get at least $(26 + 27) \cdot 4 = 212$ equations which link the active S-boxes of the three middle rounds.

Unfortunately, these equations involve 12 inactive S-boxes in round 3, whose input and output values can not be described by affine spaces with common boolean variables. However, the input and output values can be described by a linear space separately. Note that there is also one inactive S-boxes which does not influence the active S-boxes of round 4. Thus, only those 4 variables describing its input are involved in the linear system. For the remaining 11 inactive S-boxes we get $11 \cdot 8 = 88$ additional variables. In total, we have to match the result over 11 S-boxes and get 212 equations in $129 + 4 + 88 = 221$ variables.

To summarize, we expect to get 2^9 solutions for each differential path with a complexity of 2^{23} simple bit operations. Most of these solutions are actually filtered out by the 44-bit filter of the 11 inactive S-boxes. In total, we therefore get $2^{68.8+9-44} = 2^{33.8}$ solutions for the three middle rounds. The complexity of this step does not exceed 2^{80} simple bit operations. Next, we compute these solutions forwards and backwards and check whether they also conform to the remaining differential path in the outbound phase.

3.8 The Outbound Phase

In the outbound phase, we simply propagate the solutions of the three middle rounds outwards and check whether the remaining path and the conditions on the message injection (see Section 3.2) are fulfilled. The probability that a solution of the previous step also fulfills the differential of the 5 active S-boxes in round 1 and 6 is $2^{-(4-1.23)\cdot 10} = 2^{-27.7}$. Therefore, we get in total about $2^{33.8} \cdot 2^{-27.7} \sim 2^6$ pairs for the whole 7-round truncated differential path:

$$1 - \mathsf{MW} - 5 - \mathsf{SC} - 5 - \mathsf{MW} - 27 - \mathsf{SC} - 27 - \mathsf{MW} - 52 - \mathsf{SC}- \\ 52 - \mathsf{MW} - 26 - \mathsf{SC} - 26 - \mathsf{MW} - 5 - \mathsf{SC} - 5 - \mathsf{MW} - 1.$$

To satisfy the required differences at the input, we need to get one out of three 2-bit difference at the input of the single active S-box in round 0. At the output of the single active S-box in round 7 we need to match one specific difference. Hence, the conditions at both input and output are satisfied with a probability of $\frac{3}{15} \cdot \frac{1}{15} = 2^{-6.2}$.

Next, we repeat all previous steps for each of the three permutations and check whether we can find a message according to the input and output differences of the permutations. Note that the input difference of one permutation can be corrected by choosing an appropriate message differences. Hence, we only need to ensure that the input differences in two permutations match. The probability that these three 2-bit differences match is $\frac{1}{3^2} = 2^{-3.2}$. Hence, the probability to get the right input and output differences in all three permutations is $2^{3\cdot(6-6.2)-3.2} = 2^{-3.8}$, which is actually not enough to get a semi-free-start collision for *Luffa*-256.

However, as already noted in Section 3.3, we can rotate the differential path 32 times. Since the values cannot be rotated due to the addition of the round constant we need to repeat the search for conforming pairs from Section 3.7, but not the expensive part of finding the differences that verify the path. To get a semi-free-start collision for *Luffa*-256, we have to repeat this about $2^{3.8} = 14$ times. To summarize, the most expensive part of the attack is the computation of all possible differential paths in the final inbound phase for each of the three permutations. Hence, the complexity to find a semi-free-start collision for *Luffa*-256, or equivalently a collision on the internal state of 768 bits, is about 2^{104} in time and 2^{102} memory.

4 Building an 8-Round Distinguisher from the 7-Round Semi-Free-Start Collision

If we consider the previous explained procedure for building the semi-free-start collision on 7 rounds, and we look at the differential path, it is easy to see that one round later, so after the eighth rounds, if the path is followed, only 8 nibbles will be active before the last MixWord and all the other ones inactive. By considering not the bits but the linear combination of bits, we get the same result after the last MixWord. We can then build a distinguisher on the compression function for 8 rounds, with the same complexity as before, where we will find $(64 - 8) \times 3$ combination of nibbles in the output without any difference, what means a collision on 672 bits with a complexity of about 2^{104}, which is much lower than the birthday paradox. If we would try to build such a collision exploiting a generic attack on the general mode, we could control one permutation with the message insertion, but this will mean colliding on 512 bits, and if we want to have some active nibbles in all the permutations, we couldn't do any better than the birthday paradox on 672 bits, so our distinguisher has clearly a lower complexity.

5 Distinguisher for 8 Rounds of the Permutation

We use a differential distinguisher which sends a certain number of queries to a black-box B and will decide in the end if the black-box is the permutation of *Luffa* or a random oracle. The innovative idea is that the distinguishing algorithm works in two parts. In the first part, we apply a first test $\mathcal{T}_1$ to N input quadruples, where one value is chosen randomly and the three others differ from the first one in some nibbles in a deterministic manner. The test $\mathcal{T}_1$ is passed if the quadruple fulfills a specific property $\mathcal{P}$. As we will see later, to test the property $\mathcal{P}$ of a quadruple we need on average $2(1+p)$ queries to the black-box, where $p << 1/2$ is a given probability. Thus, $\mathcal{T}_1$ involves $2(1+p)N \approx 2N$ queries to the black-box. Only a subset of the original quadruples will pass $\mathcal{T}_1$. To this subset we will apply a second test $\mathcal{T}_2$ which uses several calls to the black-box for each tested quadruple. However, since the number of quadruples we have to test for $\mathcal{T}_2$ is much lower, the overall complexity is determined by the one of $\mathcal{T}_1$. The probability of passing the two tests is much higher for the permutation of *Luffa* than for a random oracle.

The distinguisher is based on a differential path represented in Fig. 6. As we will see later, the path over the eight rounds is divided in four parts: one inverted first round, three rounds of differential path, three rounds of truncated differential path, and one last round which maintains a distinguishing linear property. Let a quadruple be defined by the four 256-bit states $z = (z_1, z_2, z_3, z_4)$. Our goal is to find quadruples such that the pairs (z_1, z_2) and (z_3, z_4) follow the path. Because of the first inverted round, a quadruple is constructed in the following way: We choose the first message z_1 randomly. Let $LS(z_j^i)$, $RS(z_j^i)$ denote the i'th nibble on the left and right side of z_j, respectively, which will enter the first S-box layer. Then, for the messages z_j, $2 \leq j \leq 4$, we keep $64 - k_j$ out of the 64 nibbles as in z_1, and replace k_j nibbles by $f^L(LS(z_1^i), \alpha) = S^{-1}(S(LS(z_1^i)) \oplus \alpha)$ and $f^R(RS(z_1^i), \alpha) = S'^{-1}(S'(RS(z_1^i)) \oplus \alpha)$, respectively. The numbers of changed nibbles are $k_2 = 32$, $k_3 = 11$ and $k_4 = 29$, where 28 nibbles are the same in all four states. The construction of a quadruple can be easily done by either computing f^L and f^R each time or by a lookup in two tables of 16×15 entries. We are able to perform this inversion of the first round (and not more) as it is going to determine a big structured subset of valid input quadruples with the previous equations, where there is no difference in 28 nibbles and all the $LS(z_1^i)$ and $RS(z_1^i)$ can be randomly chosen. For example, if more rounds were inverted, the validity of the distinguisher might become controversial as differences will spread over all the input and, for not having probability involved, some of those values should be fixed for having the wanted difference at the beginning of the differential path. So if there was no structure on the two pairs of inputs and the values were determined, this could be compared with just inverting the permutation from four outputs with the wanted property and obtaining four concrete inputs that have no structure at all, which for obvious reasons can not be considered a distinguisher. This is not the case when we just invert one round. In the following, we won't differentiate each time between the left and the right side if the general method stays the same, instead we use directly f and z_j. Because of the best probability of the differential transitions of the S-boxes, we choose the difference α to be either $0x2$ or $0x4$.

The differential path in Fig. 6 has no difference in 6 nibbles (24 bits) in round 7. The 8th round is formed by a SubCrumb and a MixWord phase. We consider first the SubCrumb phase, and we can notice that it is not going to modify the property of having 6 nibbles with no difference. Then the MixWord is applied. We recall here that this phase is linear. This will mean that, from the output after the 8th round, there are 24-bit linear relations which values collide when the differential path is verified. This is equivalent to finding the collision on the 6 nibbles before the MixWord linear phase, so for the sake of simplicity, we will look for collisions before the last MixWord phase.

A quadruple z fulfills the property $\mathcal{P}$ if and only if after applying the black-box B, we have a collision in the 24 bits of the pair $(\mathsf{MixWord}^{-1}(\mathsf{B}(z_1)), \mathsf{MixWord}^{-1}(\mathsf{B}(z_2)))$ *and* in the pair $(\mathsf{MixWord}^{-1}(\mathsf{B}(z_3)), \mathsf{MixWord}^{-1}(\mathsf{B}(z_4)))$. The probability of $\mathcal{P}$ is defined by the differential path (Section 5.1) and the property described in Section 5.2, which shows that for each pair following the path we can find another pair following the path with probability one.

Test $\mathcal{T}_2$ will use the non-trivial property that for a quadruple fulfilling $\mathcal{P}$ and thus passing $\mathcal{T}_1$, we can change some nibbles in the four states such that with high probability the new quadruple will again fulfill $\mathcal{P}$. This property is described in detail in Section 5.3. Thus from the subset of quadruples that pass $\mathcal{T}_1$, we will be able to find new quadruples passing $\mathcal{P}$ with a much lower complexity.

The distinguisher works on the permutation. However, it can be easily adapted to the compression function by choosing the message according to the chaining value and by considering only the output of one permutation. For a known CV and a random message, let us consider for example the first permutation. Let m_i, h_i be the nibbles of the message and the value determined by the CV, which are XORed as input of the permutation. Then, for the other three message of the corresponding to a quadruple we will change some nibbles from m_i to $f(m_i \oplus h_i, \alpha) \oplus h_i$.

Related Work. Our distinguisher is similar to some adaptive attacks on block ciphers. In these attacks a right pair for a differential provides information on the internal computations, which may speed up the search for the next pairs if it is required. In the attack on RC5 [3] the second and next right pairs could be obtained with significantly lower complexity. In the attack on AES a single right pair provides information on several key bytes, so the attacker partially controls the first round and gets right pairs for the next differential much faster [2].

5.1 The Differential Path

We use the differential path in Fig. 6 which consists of four parts. Note that the last round and thus, part 4 is not represented in this figure:

1. Precomputation (round 0): We can guarantee a given difference in round 1 by choosing the blue nibbles in round 0 accordingly.
2. Differential (round 1-4): We use a difference that has probability 2^{-2} of passing from the input of the S-box to the output (for S and S'), e.g. $\alpha = 0x2$ or $\alpha = 0x4$. This part is responsible for the final probability.
3. Considering unaffected bits (round 4-7): In the end of round 4 we have a difference in one nibble. We consider how many nibbles in round 7 are never "affected" by this difference.
4. Round 8: As mentioned above, the property of unaffected nibbles in round 7 can be checked by linear combination of bits after round 8. For simplicity reasons we will omit this part for the further discussion.

For the differential path we only consider a pair of states (either (z_1, z_2) or (z_3, z_4)) not a quadruple. We will denote by x the first state to which we will add some difference.

In round 0, at every place where there is no difference we choose a random nibble x_i. In the other places we use the pairs $(x_i, f(x_i, \alpha))$, where x_i is chosen randomly. Now we have guaranteed that we have the differences α after the S-box and the corresponding differences in the beginning of round 1.

In the next part, we have three S-boxes layers with a total of $23+23+8$ active S-boxes, before we arrive in round 4. This gives us a probability of $2^{-54\times 2}$ of following this part, as 2^{-2} is the probability of passing one active S-box for the chosen α.

At the beginning of round 4 we only have a one bit difference. From rounds 4-7, we are only interested in which bits are unaffected by the difference in round 4. Thus, from the one bit difference in round 4, with probability one we have no differences in 24 bits (6 nibbles) at the end of round 7.

5.2 Changing the Parity of Differences

We can change the parity of some differences in round 1 such that in the case of a pair following the differential path, the new pair will also follow the differential path with probability one. This property will be used in $\mathcal{T}_1$. The general concept of changing the parity of differences is mainly the following: we consider one nibble with a difference γ, that is a nibble taking the value y for message M_1 and the value $y \oplus \gamma$ for message M_2. If we change it's parity, it will take the value $y \oplus \gamma$ for message M_1 and the value y for message M_2. It is obvious to see that if this nibble is the only difference between M_1 and M_2, this parity change will have the effect of interchanging M_1 and M_2 and we will have gained nothing. However, if there is more than one difference, changing the parity of some of them will define two new input messages M_1' and M_2' with the same difference as the original ones and the same values in the nibbles without difference.

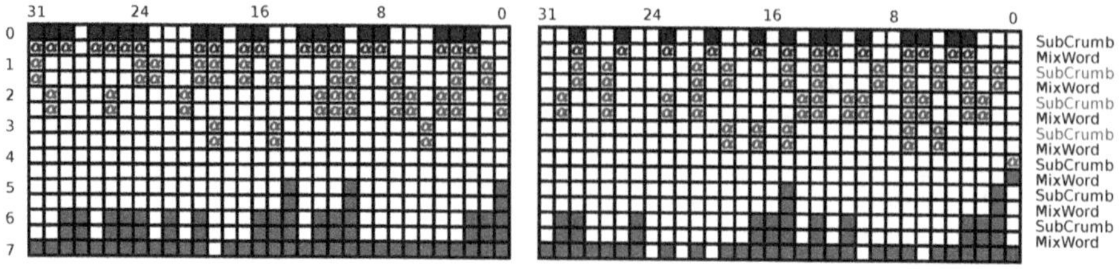

Fig. 6. Differential path used for the distinguisher over 8 rounds

Let us consider an example. Let $x_{i_1}, x_{i_2}, x_{i_3}$ be some nibbles in round 1. Let the pair with the corresponding difference be $x_{i_1} \oplus \alpha, x_{i_2}, x_{i_3} \oplus \alpha$. Then, changing the parity of the difference in x_{i_1} leads to the pair $x_{i_1} \oplus \alpha, x_{i_2}, x_{i_3}$ and $x_{i_1}, x_{i_2}, x_{i_3} \oplus \alpha$. This change is equivalent to adding α at the position of x_{i_1} in the two states.

We are going to see how changing the parity of some well chosen differences in a pair of states that satisfies the differential path will immediately give us another pair of states that also verifies the path with probability one. For this, we have to take into account the effect that changing the parity of some differences at round r might have some rounds later:

- SubCrumb Each active S-box that follows the path verifies $S(x \oplus \alpha) \oplus S(x) = \alpha$. This property still holds when we change the parity of the difference of the nibble. This means that through any SubCrumb phase where the only change is the parity of some differences, the path will still be verified.
- MixWord Every difference after the linear transformation that is affected by a parity change in the previous step will also have its parity changed. Thus, it does not introduce any problem for verifying the path in next round (we would be in the starting case). However, when two differences cancel out and one had it's parity changed but not the other, the value of the corresponding nibble (in both states) will change from x to $x \oplus \alpha$. This won't affect the verification of the differential path for this round, but might affect the round $(r+2)$: the values for the nibbles (that have no difference) obtained after the SubCrumb of round $(r+1)$ will change at these positions. This might affect the values associated to nibbles with differences after the MixWord phase of round $(r+1)$. Next, after the SubCrumb phase of round $(r+2)$ the active S-boxes might not output the same difference as for the original pair (as their values are changed).

We are going to use this, once we have obtained a pair of states that verify the differential path, to obtain another pair verifying the path with probability one. In the differential path we want to have the parity of some differences changed at the beginning of the first round. To achieve this, we have to add α after the first S-box to the corresponding positions, like in Fig. 7. We have chosen these three positions as they verify that they generate no changes of values one round later (no differences cancel out where an odd number of parity changes at the beginning of round 2), and this way they will only affect the S-box two

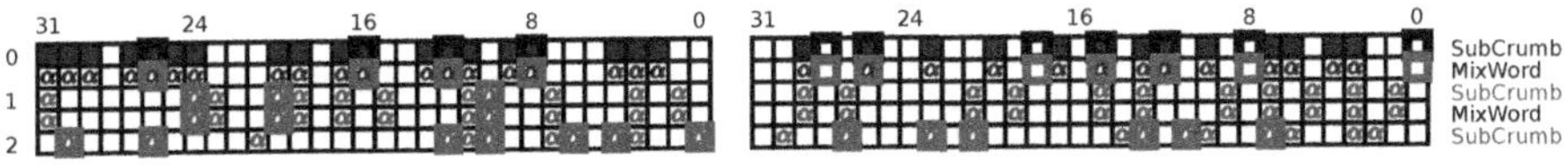

Fig. 7. Changing the parity of differences

rounds later (round 4), as we explained before. As the difference that the S-box of round 4 outputs is not important for the verification of the differential path. When changing the parities of the three difference, the remaining differential path from 1 to 8 will also be verified.

In Fig. 7, the red bordered rectangle means that we added α to the corresponding nibble. To see the effect that this has in the input pair, a thick black bordered rectangle in round 0 means that we have to change the value x_i to $f(x_i, \alpha)$. This can happen to positions with or without a difference in the original pair. With this, once we have found a pair of messages that verifies the path, if we generate a new pair from it by changing the nibbles associated to the positions of the black bordered rectangle in round 0 from the value x_i to the values $f(x_i, \alpha)$, we will have automatically generated a new pair that also verifies the path.

5.3 Changing Values without a Difference

If we change in round 1 the value of the nibble at the 14th position on the right side, this will have an effect on 4 S-boxes in round 3. The same happens when we change the nibble at position 17 on the right side. If we change the two at the same time, this has an effect on 7 S-boxes. This property will be used in $\mathcal{T}_2$. The influenced bits are shown in Fig. 8. A red, blue and violet squares mean that a nibble was influenced, respectively by the nibble 14, by the nibble 17 or by the two nibbles.

We have 15 possibilities to change only position 14, 15 possibilities to change only position 17 and $15 \times 15 = 225$ to change the two.

Getting all possible values of the nibble in position 14 is equivalent to adding the difference β to the nibble in round 1, for all $\beta \in \{0x1, \ldots, 0xF\}$. This can be done by changing 8 nibbles in round 0 from x_i to $f(x_i, \beta)$, which will add β to 8 nibbles after the first S-box layer. The position of the 8 nibbles are marked in Fig. 8. The same can be done for position 17. If we change the two nibbles at the same time we will have to change 8 nibbles to $f(x_i, \beta_{14})$ and 8 nibbles to $f(x_i, \beta_{17})$.

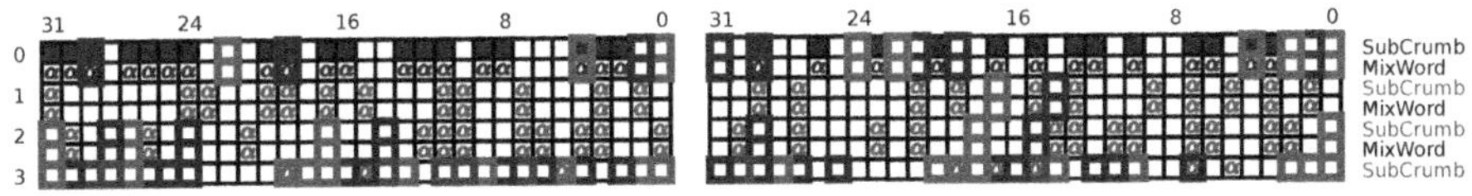

Fig. 8. Influence of the nibbles 14 and 17

Now for the original pair of messages we change the values of the nibbles at position 14 and 17 (on both messages) at round 1, send the corresponding values at round 0 to the black box and look if the result has again a collision in the 24 bits. For $i = 0, 1$, let p_i be the probability that when starting from a pair following the differential path and trying out all the 15 other values at round 0 that produce all the nibble values at position 14 (or 17), we obtain exactly i pairs with no differences in the 24 bits. Let q_i be the same probability when trying the 225 possibilities where the nibbles at position 14 and 17 are changed. Then we have

$$\begin{aligned} p_0 &= (1 - 2^{-8})^{15} \\ p_1 &= 15 \times 2^{-8}(1 - 2^{-8})^{14} \\ q_0 &= (1 - 2^{-14})^{225} \\ q_1 &= 225 \times 2^{-14}(1 - 2^{-14})^{224}. \end{aligned}$$

The total probability of having at least 2 new pairs out of 255 tried is

$$1 - \left(p_0^2 q_0 + 2p_0p_1q_0 + p_0^2 q_1\right) = 2^{-8.3}.$$

For a pair not following the differential path, this happens with a probability of

$$1 - (1 - 2^{-24})^{255} - 255 \times 2^{-24}(1 - 2^{-24})^{254} = 2^{-33}.$$

5.4 Complete Distinguisher

For a random state z_1 we define the quadruple z as following: The state z_2 is set such that together with z_1 it forms an input pair of the differential path. The states z_3, z_4 is obtained by changing the parity of difference of the pair (z_1, z_2).

Test $\mathcal{T}_1$. We try N different quadruples. For each quadruple z we first test if the pair (z_1, z_2) has a collision in the 24 bits. The probability of this property is 2^{-24} in the general case. The probability of following the differential path is 2^{-108}. Only if we find a collision, we will test the pair (z_3, z_4). For a pair following the path, this leads to a collision in the 24 bits with probability one, otherwise this will happen with probability 2^{-24}.

Thus in the case of the black-box being the permutation of *Luffa* we need $2N + 2^{-23}N + 2^{-107}N \approx 2N$ queries and find $N2^{-48} + N2^{-108}$ quadruples having the property $\mathcal{P}$ and, thus, passing $\mathcal{T}_2$.

In the case of a random function we will have $2N + 2^{-23}N \approx 2N$ queries and will find $N2^{-48}$ quadruples with property $\mathcal{P}$.

As this test is not enough for distinguishing *Luffa*'s permutation from a random one, we need to define test $\mathcal{T}_2$.

Test $\mathcal{T}_2$. This test is applied only on those pairs that passed $\mathcal{T}_1$. It exploits the property of Section 5.3. The test $\mathcal{T}_2$ on a quadruple z works as follows. For each of the 255 pair of differences $(\beta_{14}, \beta_{17}) \in \{0x0, 0x1, \ldots, 0xF\}^2 \backslash (0,0)$, we create a corresponding quadruple z' by an addition of this differences to the positions 14 and 17 in round 1 of z_1, z_2, z_3, z_4. The test $\mathcal{T}_2$ is passed if and only if, out of the 255 new quadruples, at least 2 have the property $\mathcal{P}$. For the test of $\mathcal{P}$ we check again first if (z'_1, z'_2) have a collision and only in this case we check (z'_3, z'_4).

For each quadruple z' it is still valid that the pair (z'_3, z'_4) is obtained from (z'_1, z'_2) by changing the parity of differences. Thus (z'_1, z'_2) follows the differential path if and only if (z'_3, z'_4) follows the differential path. In the case of a quadruple z following the differential path, we find at least 2 new quadruples z' following the differential path and thus having property $\mathcal{P}$ with probability $2^{-8.3}$.

In the random case, we find at least two z' such that (z'_1, z'_2) has a collision in the 24 bits with probability $2^{-33.1}$. The probability of each of these quadruples also having a collision for (z'_3, z'_4) is 2^{-24}. So the probability of passing $\mathcal{T}_2$ is $2^{-33.1-2\times 24} = 2^{-81.1}$. We get the same result by considering the probability

$$1 - (1 - 2^{-48})^{255} - 255 \times 2^{-48}(1 - 2^{-48})^{254} = 2^{-81}.$$

In the worst case we find a collision for all the 255 differences (β_{14}, β_{17}), which would mean that we have to send about 2^{10} queries to the black-box. However, the percentage of initial quadruples passing $\mathcal{T}_1$ is much less than 2^{-10}. This means that the dominant costs come from $\mathcal{T}_1$.

Combining the Two Tests. In the case of the permutation of *Luffa* the probability of finding a quadruple following the differential path and passing $\mathcal{T}_2$ is $2^{-108-8.3} = 2^{-116.3}$. For a random oracle, or in the general case, a quadruple build from a random value z_1 passes $\mathcal{T}_1$ and $\mathcal{T}_2$ with probability $2^{-48-81.1} = 2^{-129.1}$. Thus, for $N = 2^{116.3}$ we will be able to distinguish with high probability the permutation of *Luffa* from a random oracle. The time complexity of this distinguisher is $2N$ queries. The memory complexity is negligible, since we apply the two tests on the fly.

6 Conclusion

We developed a number of new differential techniques for the analysis of *Luffa*. Our results do not threaten the security of *Luffa* as they are on building blocks and not on the full hash function. Even though they do not contradict the designers' claims, our results improve upon previous work in several ways. When considering collision attacks on the hash function with limited access to internal variables, also less degrees of freedom are available for an attacker. Still, we argue that the new techniques in this paper will be very useful to analyze *Luffa* further in this setting. Also, the improvements to the rebound attack are likely to be useful in the attacks on non-AES-based designs.

Acknowledgements

We would like to thank Christian Rechberger for his many helpful comments and his contribution to this work.

References

1. Aumasson, J.P., Meier, W.: Zero-sum distinguishers for reduced Keccak-f and for the core functions of Luffa and Hamsi. NIST mailing list, http://www.131002.net/data/papers/AM09.pdf (2009)
2. Biryukov, A., Khovratovich, D., Nikolić, I.: Distinguisher and related-key attack on the full AES-256. In: Halevi, S. (ed.) CRYPTO 2009. LNCS, vol. 5677, pp. 231–249. Springer, Heidelberg (2009)
3. Biryukov, A., Kushilevitz, E.: Improved cryptanalysis of RC5. In: Nyberg, K. (ed.) EUROCRYPT 1998. LNCS, vol. 1403, pp. 85–99. Springer, Heidelberg (1998)
4. Watanabe, D., Hatano, Y., Yamada, T., Kaneko, T.: Higher Order Differential Attack on Step-Reduced Variants of Luffa v1. In: Hong, S., Iwata, T. (eds.) FSE 2010. LNCS, vol. 6147, pp. 270–285. Springer, Heidelberg (2010)
5. De Cannière, C., Sato, H., Watanabe, D.: Hash Function Luffa: Specification. Submission to NIST (Round 1) (2008), http://ehash.iaik.tugraz.at/uploads/e/ea/Luffa_Specification.pdf
6. De Cannière, C., Sato, H., Watanabe, D.: Hash Function Luffa: Specification. Submission to NIST (Round 2) (2009), http://www.sdl.hitachi.co.jp/crypto/luffa/Luffa_v2_Specification_20091002.pdf
7. De Cannière, C., Sato, H., Watanabe, D.: Hash Function Luffa: Supporting Document. Submission to NIST (Round 2) (2009), http://www.sdl.hitachi.co.jp/crypto/luffa/Luffa_v2_SupportingDocument_20090915.pdf
8. Indesteege, S.: The LANE hash function. Submission to NIST (2008), http://www.cosic.esat.kuleuven.be/publications/article-1181.pdf
9. Mendel, F., Peyrin, T., Rechberger, C., Schläffer, M.: Improved cryptanalysis of the reduced grøstl compression function, ECHO permutation and AES block cipher. In: Jacobson Jr., M.J., Rijmen, V., Safavi-Naini, R. (eds.) SAC 2009. LNCS, vol. 5867, pp. 16–35. Springer, Heidelberg (2009)
10. Mendel, F., Rechberger, C., Schläffer, M., Thomsen, S.S.: The Rebound Attack: Cryptanalysis of Reduced Whirlpool and Grøstl. In: Dunkelman, O. (ed.) FSE 2009. LNCS, vol. 5665, pp. 260–276. Springer, Heidelberg (2009)
11. Wagner, D.: A generalized birthday problem. In: Yung, M. (ed.) CRYPTO 2002. LNCS, vol. 2442, pp. 288–303. Springer, Heidelberg (2002)

A The Truncated Differential Path for Each Permutation

In the main article we showed only a differential path for the permutation Q_0. Here, we show also the remaining two paths for permutations Q_1 and Q_2 for the same position of the output difference as in Q_0. In all three examples, the output difference is in the 14th nibble of the left side.

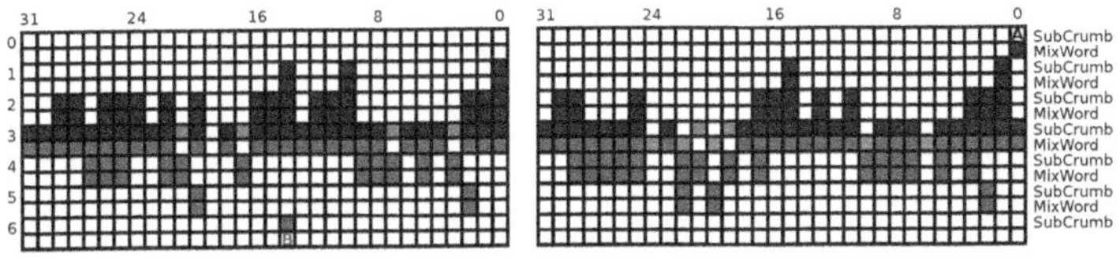

Fig. 9. Truncated differential path for Q_0. The value **A** corresponds to a difference of 0001, 0010 or 0011, the value **B** to 1101.

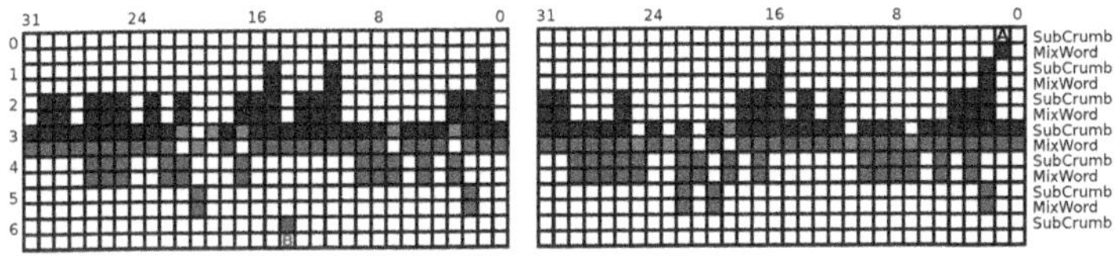

Fig. 10. Truncated differential path for Q_1. The value **A** corresponds to a difference of 0010, 0100 or 0110, the value **B** to 1000.

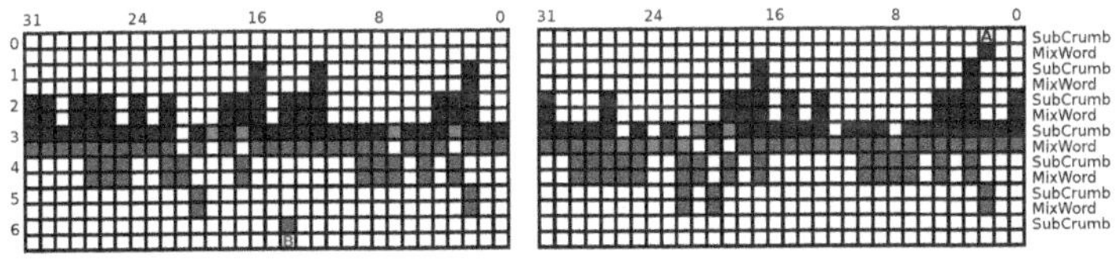

Fig. 11. Truncated differential path for Q_2. The value **A** corresponds to a difference of 0100, 1000 or 1100, the value **B** to 0010.

Author Index

GPSR Compliance

The European Union's (EU) General Product Safety Regulation (GPSR) is a set of rules that requires consumer products to be safe and our obligations to ensure this.

If you have any concerns about our products, you can contact us on ProductSafety@springernature.com

In case Publisher is established outside the EU, the EU authorized representative is:

Springer Nature Customer Service Center GmbH
Europaplatz 3
69115 Heidelberg, Germany

Batch number: 10844619

Printed by Printforce, the Netherlands